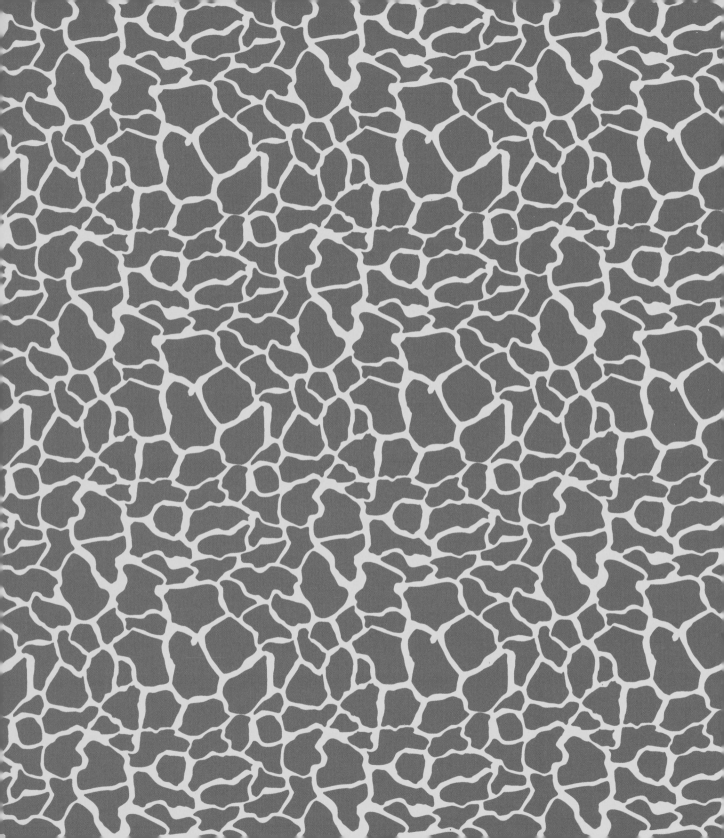

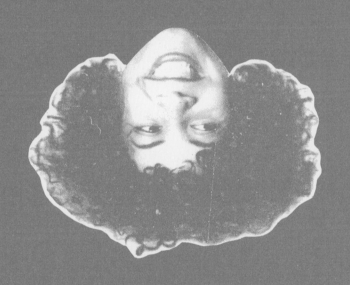

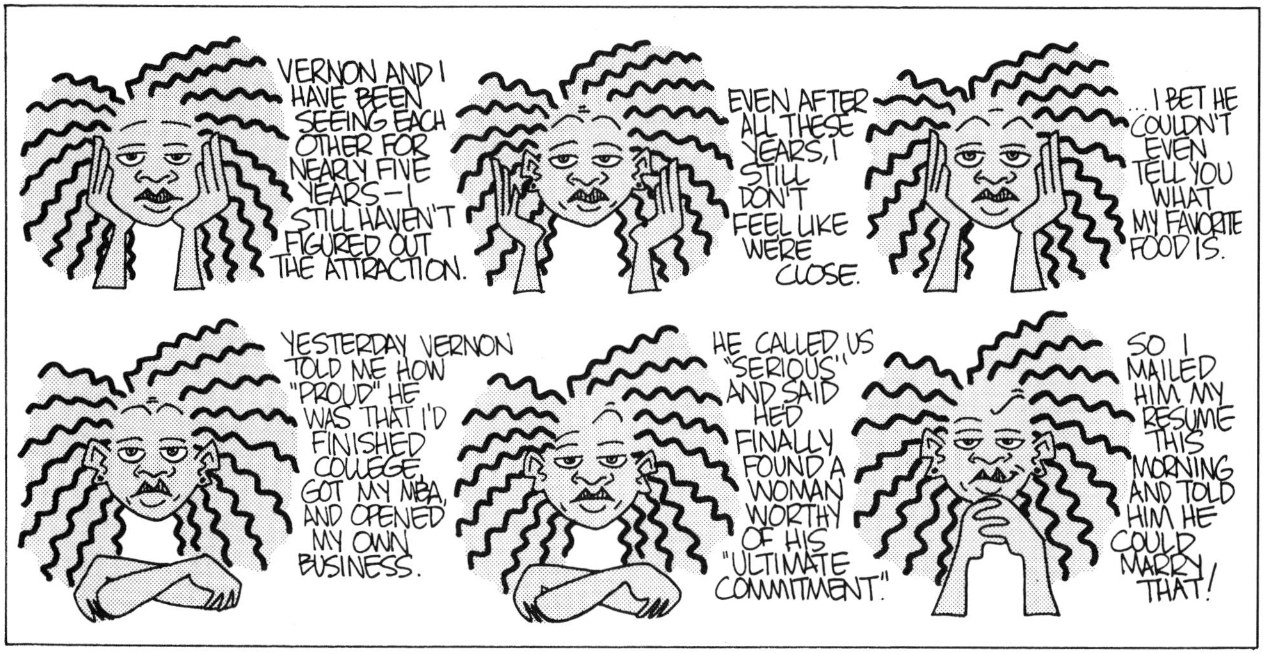
VERNON AND I HAVE BEEN SEEING EACH OTHER FOR NEARLY FIVE YEARS—I STILL HAVEN'T FIGURED OUT THE ATTRACTION.
EVEN AFTER ALL THESE YEARS, I STILL DON'T FEEL LIKE WERE CLOSE.
...I BET HE COULDN'T EVEN TELL YOU WHAT MY FAVORITE FOOD IS.
YESTERDAY VERNON TOLD ME HOW "PROUD" HE WAS THAT I'D FINISHED COLLEGE, GOT MY MBA, AND OPENED MY OWN BUSINESS.
HE CALLED US "SERIOUS" AND SAID HED FINALLY FOUND A WOMAN WORTHY OF HIS "ULTIMATE COMMITMENT".
SO I MAILED HIM MY RESUME THIS MORNING AND TOLD HIM HE COULD MARRY THAT!

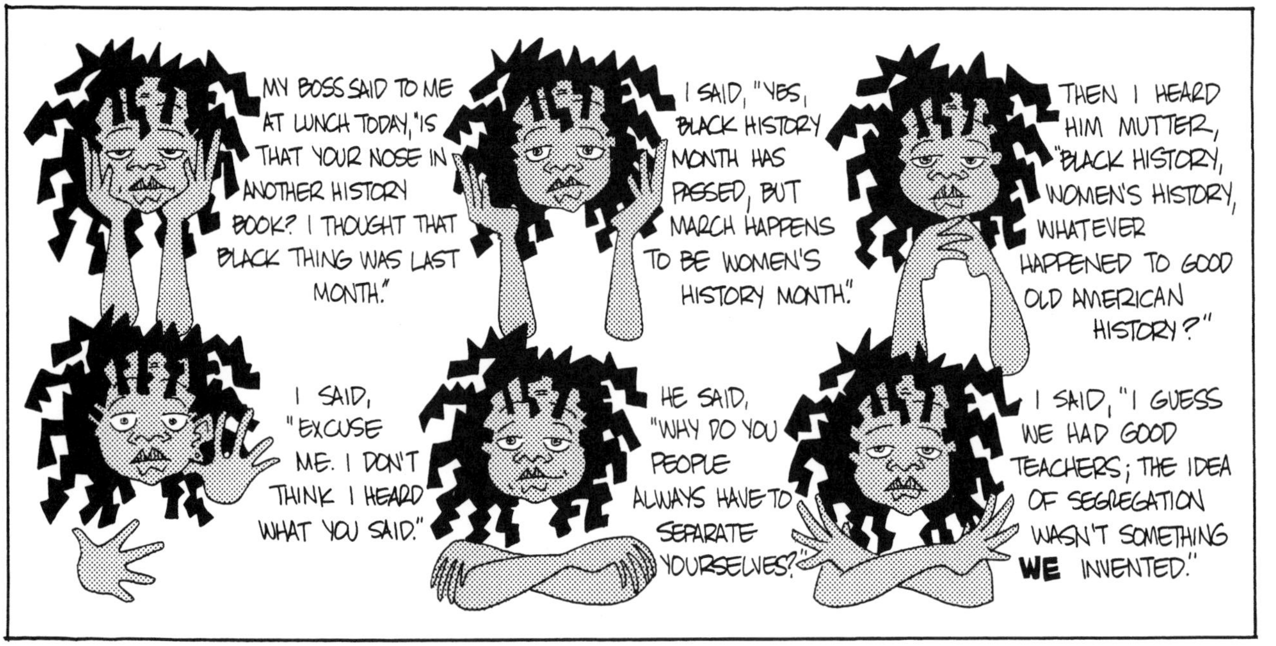
MY BOSS SAID TO ME AT LUNCH TODAY, "IS THAT YOUR NOSE IN ANOTHER HISTORY BOOK? I THOUGHT THAT BLACK THING WAS LAST MONTH."
I SAID, "YES, BLACK HISTORY MONTH HAS PASSED, BUT MARCH HAPPENS TO BE WOMEN'S HISTORY MONTH."
THEN I HEARD HIM MUTTER, "BLACK HISTORY, WOMEN'S HISTORY, WHATEVER HAPPENED TO GOOD OLD AMERICAN HISTORY?"
I SAID, "EXCUSE ME. I DON'T THINK I HEARD WHAT YOU SAID."
HE SAID, "WHY DO YOU PEOPLE ALWAYS HAVE TO SEPARATE YOURSELVES?"
I SAID, "I GUESS WE HAD GOOD TEACHERS; THE IDEA OF SEGREGATION WASN'T SOMETHING WE INVENTED."

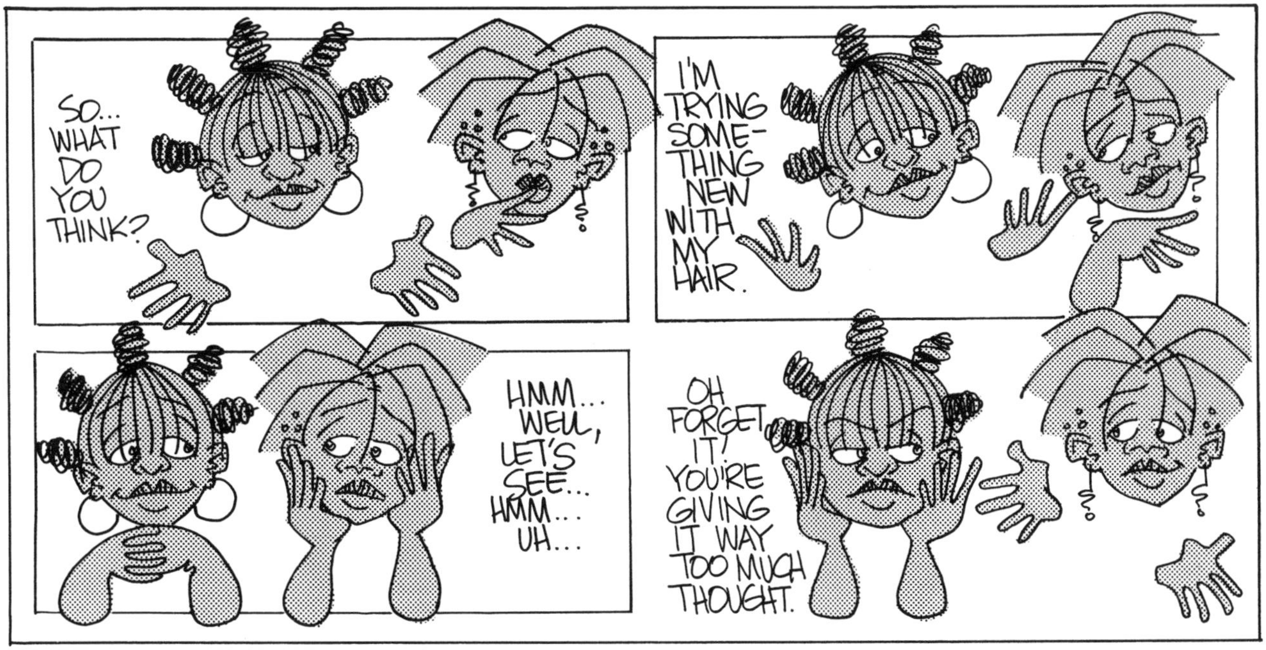
SO... WHAT DO YOU THINK?
I'M TRYING SOME-THING NEW WITH MY HAIR.
HMM... WELL, LET'S SEE... HMM... UH...
OH FORGET IT! YOU'RE GIVING IT WAY TOO MUCH THOUGHT.

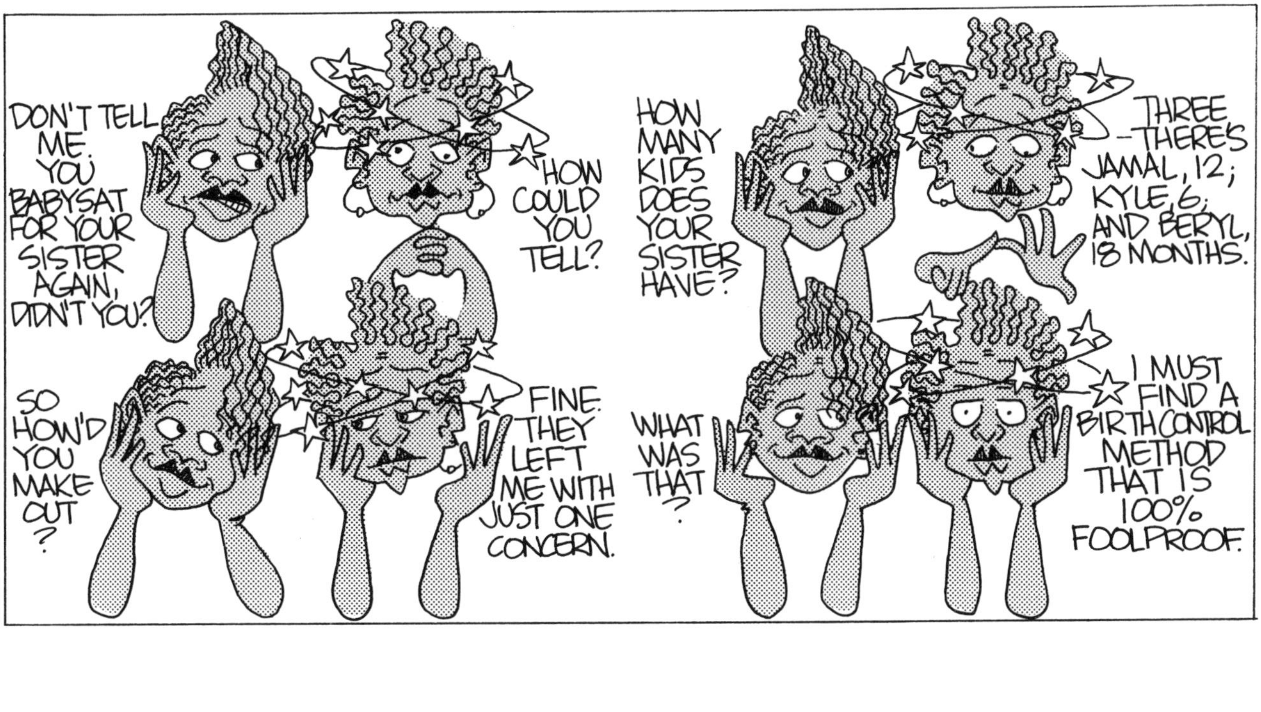
DON'T TELL ME. YOU BABYSAT FOR YOUR SISTER AGAIN, DIDN'T YOU?
HOW COULD YOU TELL?
SO HOW'D YOU MAKE OUT?
FINE. THEY LEFT ME WITH JUST ONE CONCERN.
HOW MANY KIDS DOES YOUR SISTER HAVE?
THREE -THERE'S JAMAL, 12; KYLE, 6; AND BERYL, 18 MONTHS.
WHAT WAS THAT?
I MUST FIND A BIRTH CONTROL METHOD THAT IS 100% FOOLPROOF.

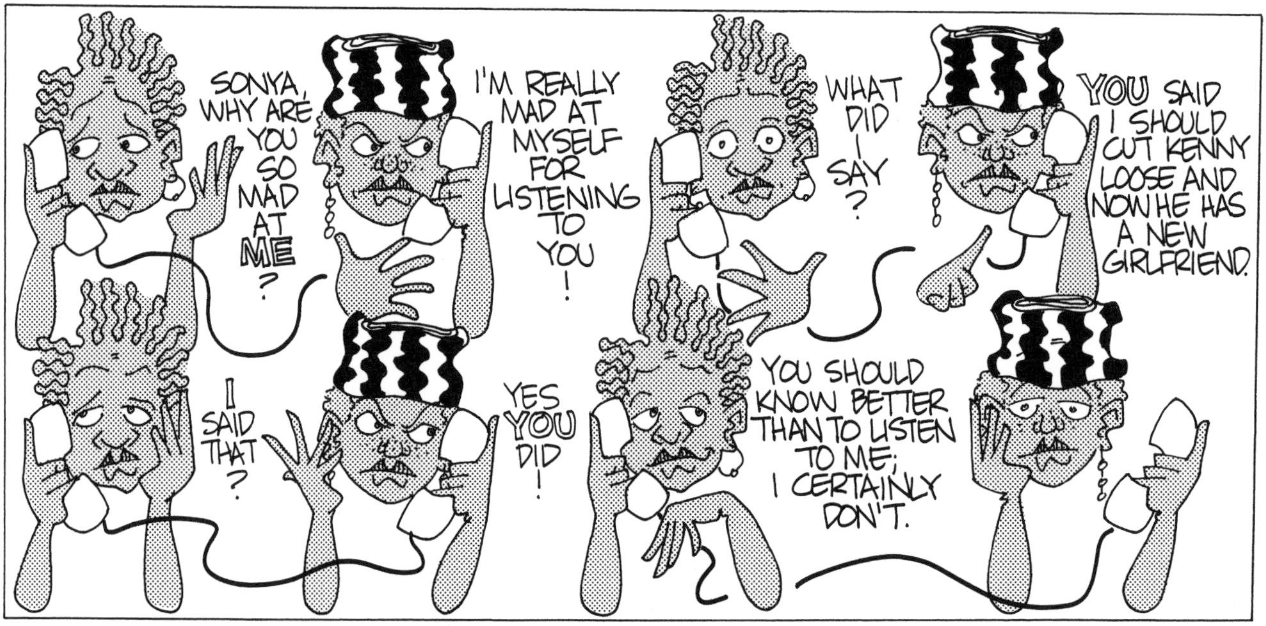
SONYA, WHY ARE YOU SO MAD AT ME ?
I'M REALLY MAD AT MYSELF FOR LISTENING TO YOU !
I SAID THAT ?
YES YOU DID !
WHAT DID I SAY ?
YOU SAID I SHOULD CUT KENNY LOOSE AND NOW HE HAS A NEW GIRLFRIEND.
YOU SHOULD KNOW BETTER THAN TO LISTEN TO ME; I CERTAINLY DON'T.

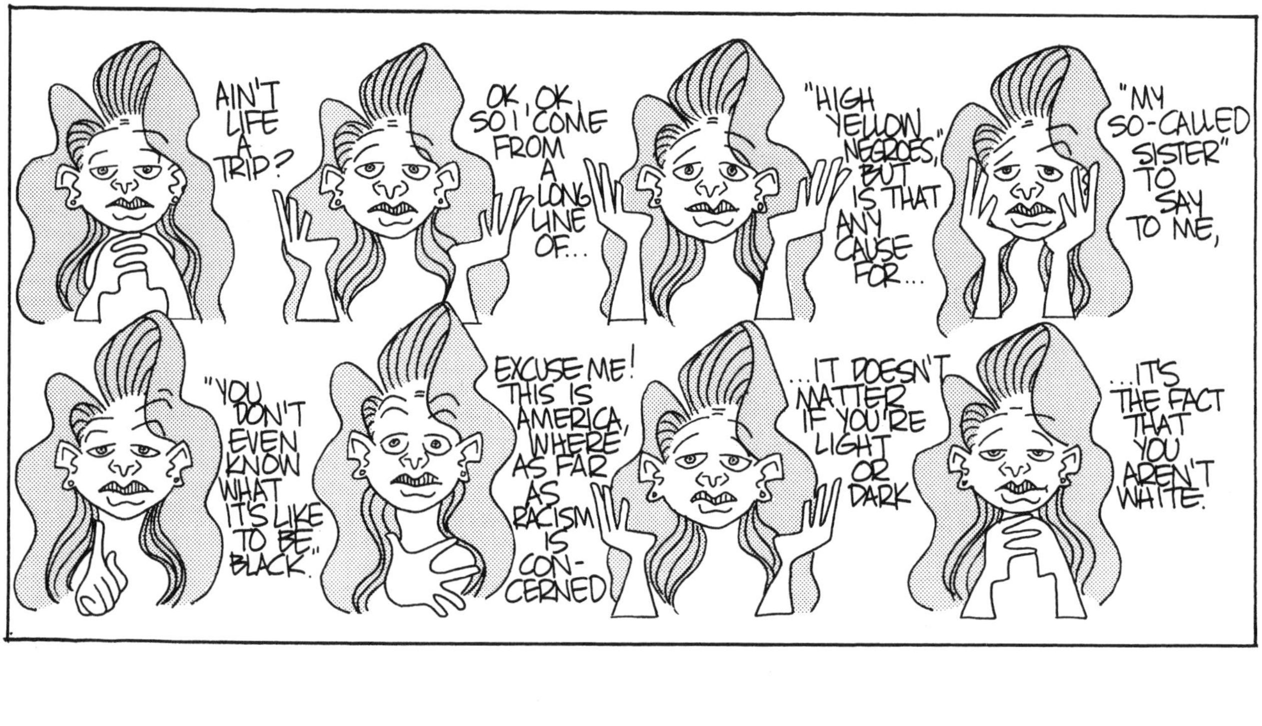
AIN'T LIFE A TRIP?
OK, OK, SO I COME FROM A LONG LINE OF...
"HIGH YELLOW NEGROES," BUT IS THAT ANY CAUSE FOR...
"MY SO-CALLED SISTER" TO SAY TO ME,
"YOU DON'T EVEN KNOW WHAT IT'S LIKE TO BE BLACK."
EXCUSE ME! THIS IS AMERICA, WHERE AS FAR AS RACISM IS CON-CERNED
...IT DOESN'T MATTER IF YOU'RE LIGHT OR DARK
...IT'S THE FACT THAT YOU AREN'T WHITE.

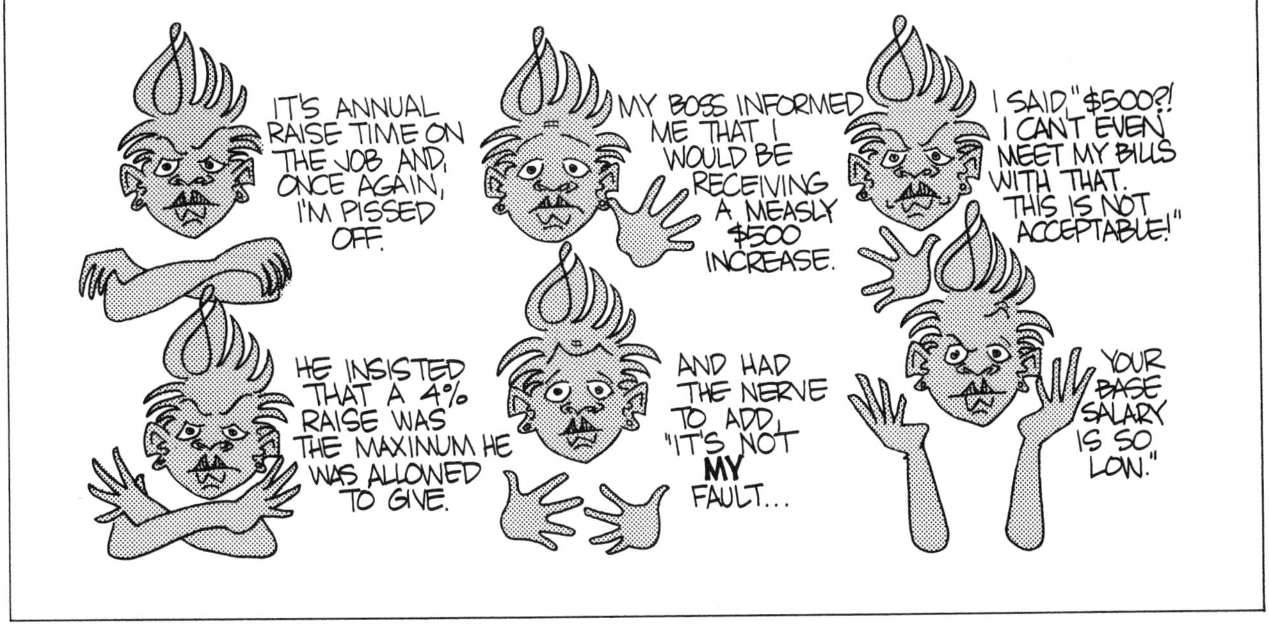
IT'S ANNUAL RAISE TIME ON THE JOB AND, ONCE AGAIN, I'M PISSED OFF.
MY BOSS INFORMED ME THAT I WOULD BE RECEIVING A MEASLY $500 INCREASE.
I SAID, "$500?! I CAN'T EVEN MEET MY BILLS WITH THAT. THIS IS NOT ACCEPTABLE!"
HE INSISTED THAT A 4% RAISE WAS THE MAXIMUM HE WAS ALLOWED TO GIVE.
AND HAD THE NERVE TO ADD, "IT'S NOT **MY** FAULT...
YOUR BASE SALARY IS SO LOW."

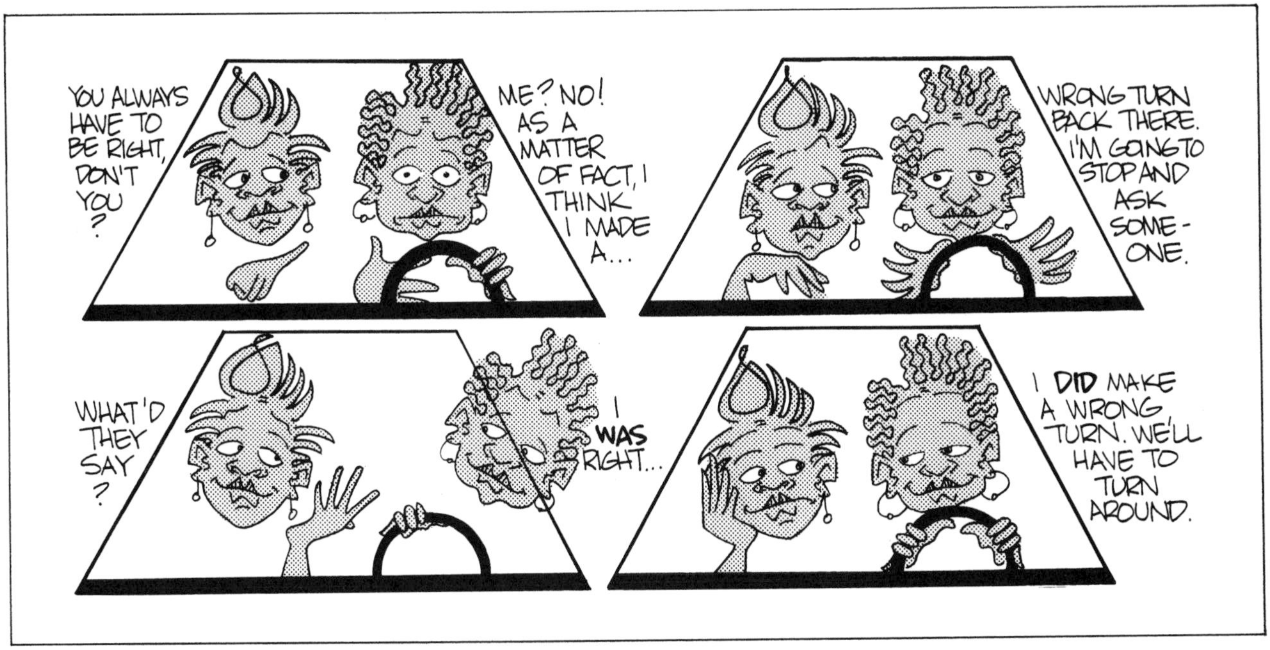
YOU ALWAYS HAVE TO BE RIGHT, DON'T YOU ?
ME? NO! AS A MATTER OF FACT, I THINK I MADE A...
WRONG TURN BACK THERE. I'M GOING TO STOP AND ASK SOME-ONE.
WHAT'D THEY SAY ?
I **WAS** RIGHT...
I **DID** MAKE A WRONG TURN. WE'LL HAVE TO TURN AROUND.

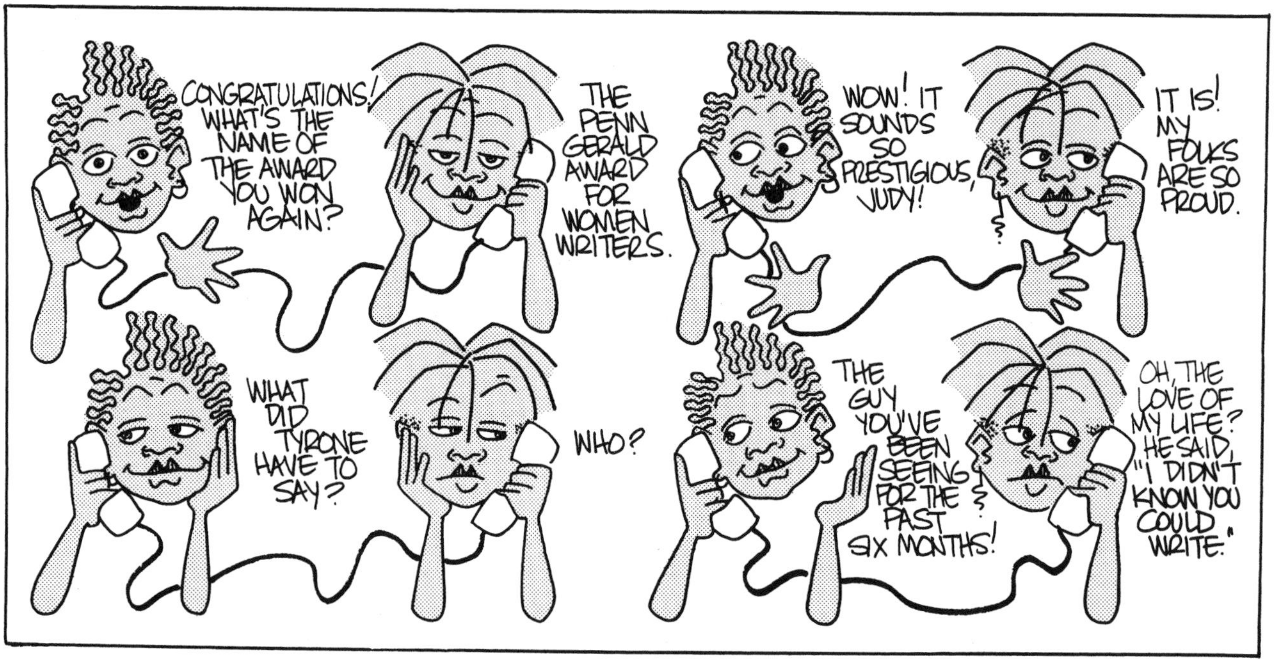
CONGRATULATIONS! WHAT'S THE NAME OF THE AWARD YOU WON AGAIN?
THE PENN GERALD AWARD FOR WOMEN WRITERS.
WOW! IT SOUNDS SO PRESTIGIOUS, JUDY!
IT IS! MY FOLKS ARE SO PROUD.
WHAT DID TYRONE HAVE TO SAY?
WHO?
THE GUY YOU'VE BEEN SEEING FOR THE PAST SIX MONTHS!
OH, THE LOVE OF MY LIFE? HE SAID, "I DIDN'T KNOW YOU COULD WRITE."

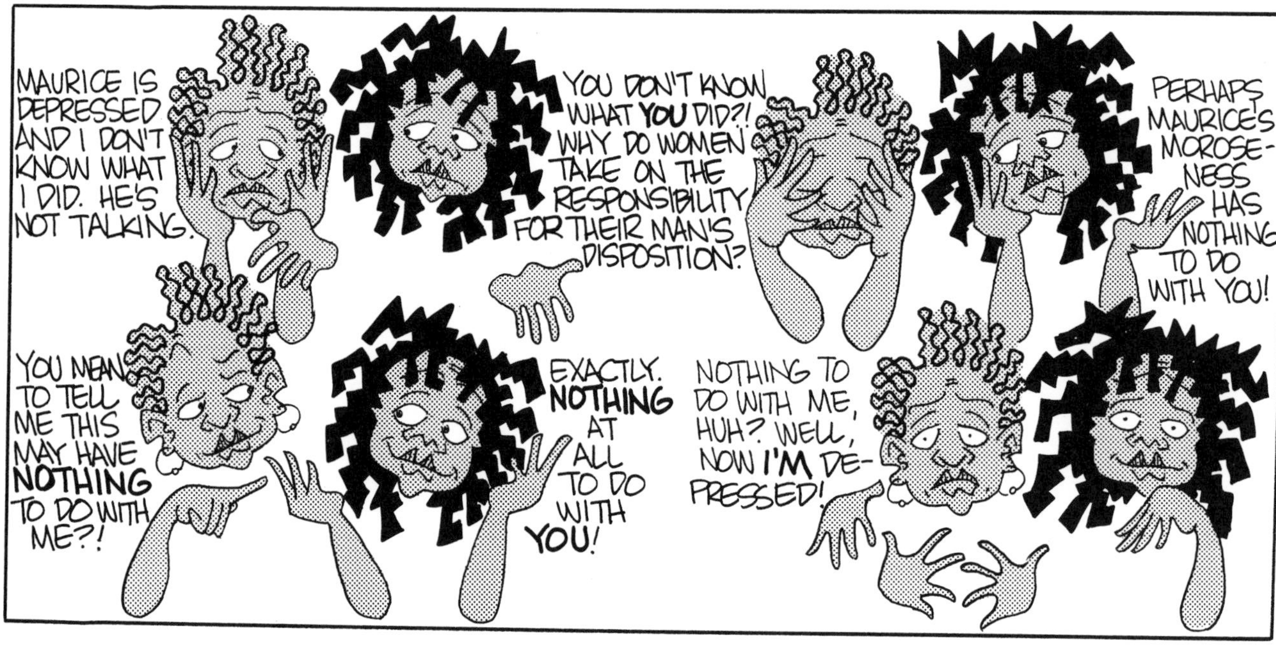
MAURICE IS DEPRESSED AND I DON'T KNOW WHAT I DID. HE'S NOT TALKING.
YOU DON'T KNOW WHAT **YOU** DID?! WHY DO WOMEN TAKE ON THE RESPONSIBILITY FOR THEIR MAN'S DISPOSITION?
PERHAPS MAURICE'S MOROSE-NESS HAS NOTHING TO DO WITH YOU!
YOU MEAN TO TELL ME THIS MAY HAVE **NOTHING** TO DO WITH ME?!
EXACTLY. **NOTHING** AT ALL TO DO WITH **YOU**!
NOTHING TO DO WITH ME, HUH? WELL, NOW **I'M** DE-PRESSED!

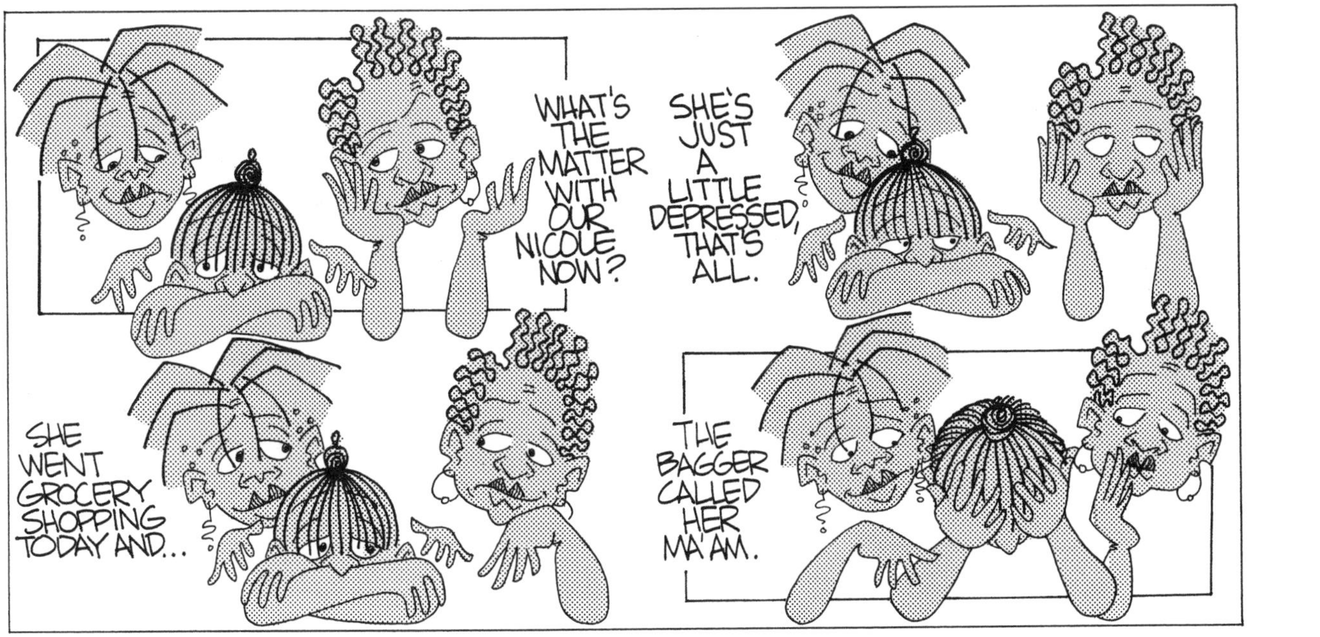
WHAT'S THE MATTER WITH OUR NICOLE NOW?
SHE'S JUST A LITTLE DEPRESSED, THAT'S ALL.
SHE WENT GROCERY SHOPPING TODAY AND...
THE BAGGER CALLED HER MA'AM.

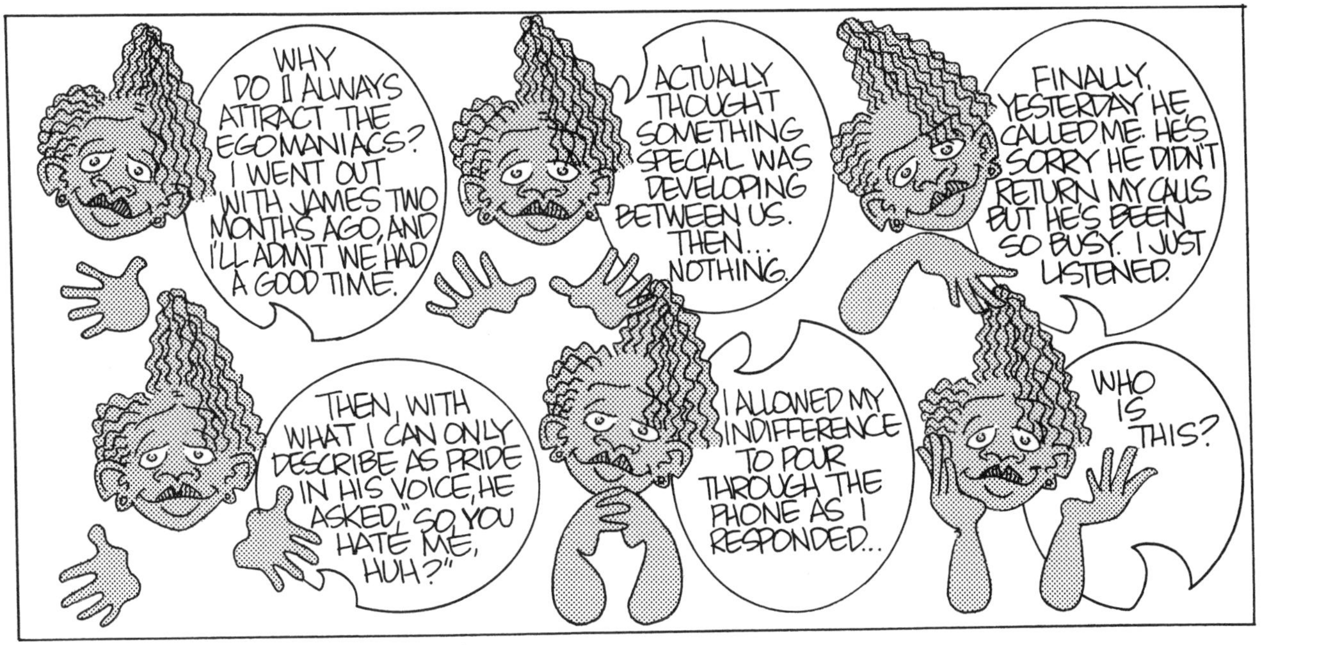
WHY DO I ALWAYS ATTRACT THE EGOMANIACS? I WENT OUT WITH JAMES TWO MONTHS AGO, AND I'LL ADMIT WE HAD A GOOD TIME.
I ACTUALLY THOUGHT SOMETHING SPECIAL WAS DEVELOPING BETWEEN US. THEN... NOTHING.
FINALLY, YESTERDAY HE CALLED ME. HE'S SORRY HE DIDN'T RETURN MY CALLS BUT HE'S BEEN SO BUSY. I JUST LISTENED.
THEN, WITH WHAT I CAN ONLY DESCRIBE AS PRIDE IN HIS VOICE, HE ASKED, "SO, YOU HATE ME, HUH?"
I ALLOWED MY INDIFFERENCE TO POUR THROUGH THE PHONE AS I RESPONDED...
WHO IS THIS?

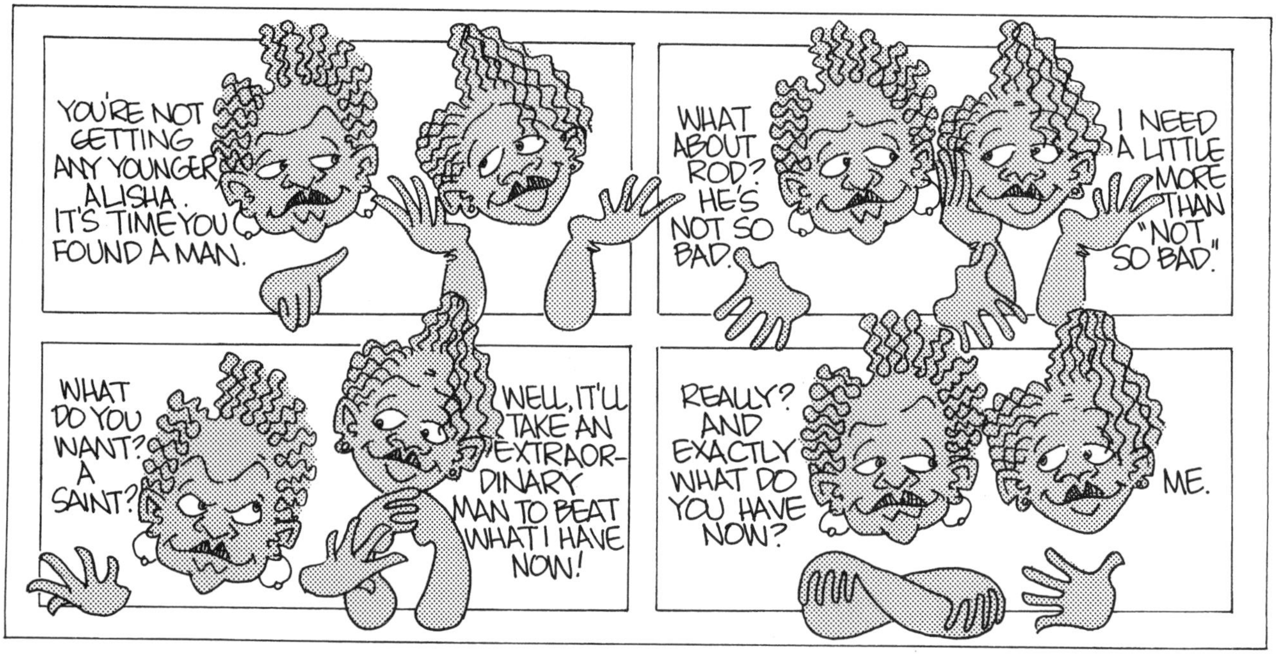
YOU'RE NOT GETTING ANY YOUNGER, ALISHA. IT'S TIME YOU FOUND A MAN.
WHAT DO YOU WANT? A SAINT?
WELL, IT'LL TAKE AN EXTRAORDINARY MAN TO BEAT WHAT I HAVE NOW!
WHAT ABOUT ROD? HE'S NOT SO BAD.
I NEED A LITTLE MORE THAN "NOT SO BAD."
REALLY? AND EXACTLY WHAT DO YOU HAVE NOW?
ME.

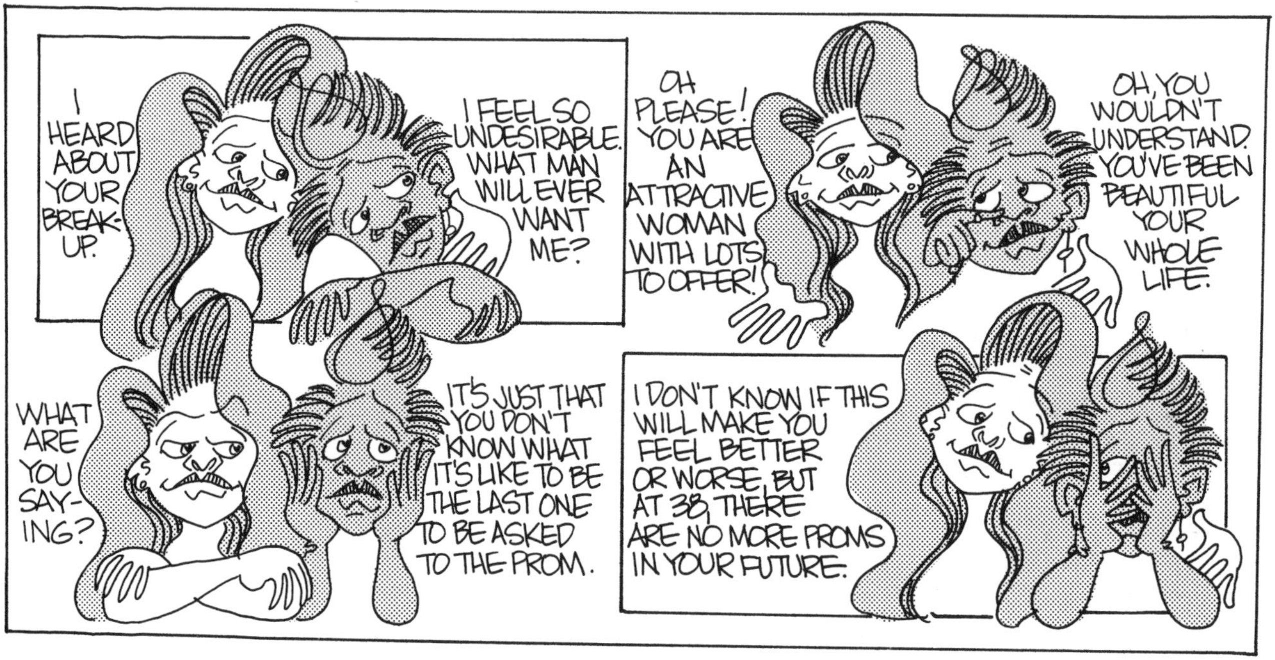
I HEARD ABOUT YOUR BREAK-UP.
I FEEL SO UNDESIRABLE. WHAT MAN WILL EVER WANT ME?
WHAT ARE YOU SAY-ING?
IT'S JUST THAT YOU DON'T KNOW WHAT IT'S LIKE TO BE THE LAST ONE TO BE ASKED TO THE PROM.
OH PLEASE! YOU ARE AN ATTRACTIVE WOMAN WITH LOTS TO OFFER!
OH, YOU WOULDN'T UNDERSTAND. YOU'VE BEEN BEAUTIFUL YOUR WHOLE LIFE.
I DON'T KNOW IF THIS WILL MAKE YOU FEEL BETTER OR WORSE, BUT AT 38, THERE ARE NO MORE PROMS IN YOUR FUTURE.

Comics and "Where I'm Coming From Now" copyright © 2023 Barbara Brandon-Croft. *Cartoonist Profiles* excerpt was originally published in 1992 and is used here, with permission. *Where I'm Coming From* was originally syndicated from 1991–2005. Post-syndication comics on pages 157–161 were drawn 2016–2022. "On Meeting Barbara" © 2023 Marty Claus. "That's Pretty Cool When You Think About It" © 2023 Sharon Pendana, and is reprinted from *THE TROVE* www.inthetrove.com. "Syndicated Sisterhood" © 2023 Rebecca Wanzo. Photo on page 154 © 2023 Theresa Dillon. Photo on page 167 by Jay LaPrete, courtesy of The Ohio State University Billy Ireland Cartoon Library & Museum. All rights reserved. No part of this book (except small portions for review purposes) may be reproduced in any form without written permission from Barbara Brandon-Croft or Drawn & Quarterly. Drawn & Quarterly would like to thank Charles Valauskas and Stu Reeves for their assistance on this project.

drawnandquarterly.com • ISBN 978-1-77046-568-8 • First edition: February 2023 • Printed in China • 10 9 8 7 6 5 4 3 2 1
Cataloguing data available from Library and Archives Canada

Published in the USA by Drawn & Quarterly, a client publisher of Farrar, Straus and Giroux • Published in Canada by Drawn & Quarterly, a client publisher of Raincoast Books • Published in the United Kingdom by Drawn & Quarterly, a client publisher of Publishers Group UK

WHERE I'M COMING FROM

BY BARBARA BRANDON-CROFT

Selected Strips 1991–2005

Drawn & Quarterly

"...I have a dream that one day this nation will rise up and live out the true meaning of its creed: 'we hold these truths to be self-evident — that all men are created equal.' I have a dream that..."

On Meeting Barbara   Marty Claus

In the 1980s, the *Detroit Free Press* began to take a serious look at why there was such a disconnect between the traditional newspaper and the diverse community we wanted to serve.

It didn't take a scientific survey to show that our staff was overwhelmingly white, and our daily pages reflected an overwhelmingly white world. We set out to do better, to reflect the diversity of our community.

It was also obvious that our comics pages, renowned for being among the best in the country, rarely reflected people of color.

Most comics in newspapers were—and are—provided by feature syndicates. We turned to the syndicates for help and made the point that diversity was essential. The syndicates' editors could help current cartoonists understand the need to reflect diversity in the characters they drew. The syndicates needed to work harder to find and develop cartoonists of color.

On our own, we sought to locate Black cartoonists and illustrators whose work was well known in minority publications. We wrote to ask for their help. One letter went to Brumsic Brandon, Jr., who was able to hand my letter to his talented daughter, an aspiring cartoonist.

Barbara Brandon-Croft's *Where I'm Coming From* landed on my desk in 1989—not just showcasing people of color but giving voice to women with opinions and humor

and personality. It wasn't an editorial cartoon, but it wasn't a simple panel or familiar comic strip, either. The format and the content were unique.

Barbara gave the *Free Press* something we didn't have. What we liked about *Where I'm Coming From* was its artistic style, its direct approach—Barbara's girls looked off the page directly at the reader—and Barbara's easy discussion of topics both thorny and humorous. Her girls said some things only a Black woman could say with authority, and other things that were universally true, about work and relationships and race.

We welcomed Barbara's creation to our lifestyle section, which was called "The Way We Live." Her work debuted in the Sunday *Free Press*, with a circulation of about 700,000.

We'd found a voice we were eager to share with our readers—and with newspapers and their readers all over the country. In 1991, Barbara would become the first syndicated Black female cartoonist in the nation.

Marty Claus, who was Managing Editor/Features & Business at the *Detroit Free Press*, was a charter inductee into the American Association of Sunday and Feature Editors Hall of Fame. She was a juror for the Pulitzer Prize for Editorial Cartooning in 1995. She became Vice President/News at Knight Ridder in 1993, and retired in 2003.

June 8, 1989

Dear Barbara,

My secretary is on vacation, so I'm more crippled than usual as a correspondent. Sorry this is late. As I said on the phone, we feel like we have a good 8-10 illustrations that need no more editing than punctuation we can do here. Take a look at the proposed order of those, and tell me if you'd change it.

Beyond that, you'll see editing suggestions from Mike Smith on the copies I'm sending back to you. I'm not sure I agree with him on the ''forefathers'' one .... Let me know what you think.

I do think the lifestyle section is the perfect place for Where I'm Coming From. We need to think about how to pace the first dozen or so; we need to appeal to the widest possible audience at first, readers need to feel like they're understanding the concept early. After that, I think we can take a few more chances with more unexpected themes.

You debut Sunday in about 700,000 papers. I hope we get good feedback. Our readers are usually pretty good about that.

Here is a note from Mike Smith, with his suggestions for you:

''We need to hit some universal touchstones in the first several weeks. We need to hit on some common themes, like dating and relationships and romance, that span age, racial, geographic and gender barriers. I've selected 10 that I think will draw a large audience. My goal for you is to be sassy and provocative without burning any bridges. For example, you don't want to come across as being anti-male.

''We need to develop a writing and punctuation style and then stick to it. I recommend every complete thought take a period.

''Do you plan to have your subjects comment on more than male-female relationships? You may want to consider parents, girlfriends, children, co-workers, bosses, etc.'' (All those would be appropriate for The Way We Live, obviously, as would the narrower concentration on male-female relationships. WE just need to be consistent.)

Sincerely,

Marty Claus

c: Mike Smith, Deb Withey, Heath Meriwether

Few Black Cartoonists have entered national syndication since the 1970's- None have been Black Women

Dear Editor,

I'd like to introduce my cartoon feature "Where I'm Coming From", a weekly comic strip featuring Black women and created by a Black woman.

I'm sure you'll agree, the integration of the comic pages was long in coming. Perhaps the belief was that there is nothing to be gained from the Black experience. Of course, nothing could be further from the truth. That kind of limited thinking is often characterized by an inability to see "Black themes" as universal. We all gain from the Black experience. Moreover, everyone's to gain from the Black female experience in particular.

In the '60s and '70s when the Black pioneer cartoonists entered syndication, their views were expressed through casts of children. I refer to strips like Morrie Turner's "Wee Pals", Ted Shearer's "Quincy" and "Luther," the feature my father, Brumsic Brandon, Jr., created. Out of the mouths of babes seemed the most palatable way to introduce Blacks to the funny pages.

I'm pleased to announce the <u>Detroit Free Press</u> has given me the opportunity to not only showcase adult African-American characters, but adult African-American women, who, like myself, speak their minds freely and candidly. "Where I'm Coming From" made its debut June 11, 1989. I'm proud to be the only Black female cartoonist published in a major newspaper in this country at this time.

It's the '90s and I'm optimistic. I'd like to see "Where I'm Coming From", now being self syndicated, distributed nationally. I only hope racial and sexual attitudes have matured to a point where those in key decision-making positions at newspapers and syndicates recognize the need for social commentary from the Black female perspective.

I am submitting several published comic strips along with samples that have yet to be published for your consideration.

I welcome your comments and I thank you for your time.

Sincerely,

Brandon-Croft's 1989 original pitch letter to syndicates

UNIVERSAL
PRESS
SYNDICATE

4900 Main Street • Kansas City, Missouri 64112 • 816/932-6600

October 26, 1989

Dear Ms. Brandon:

I received packages from both you and Marty Claus at the Free Press within a few days of each other. The Free Press is justifiably proud of discovering you; and you're rightfully proud to be in such a good newspaper.

The bite and tone of your humor are appealing. It's rare to have such a good ear for nuance and character.

I'm in the process of getting other reactions here, but thought I would at least pass along an idea in the interim: Have you thought about placing your cast of characters within the environment of a daily strip? There's a dearth of good material from your perspective, and a comic strip would have more impact -- and wider exposure -- than a weekly panel.

I'll get back to you soon.

Best regards.

Sincerely,

Lee Salem
Editorial Director

LS:bt

ups

Time & Life Building • Suite 3717 • 1271 Avenue of the Americas
New York, N.Y. 10020 • 212/582-0650

Detroit Free Press

321 W. LAFAYETTE
DETROIT, MICHIGAN 48231
(313) 222-5178

MARTY CLAUS
MANAGING EDITOR/FEATURES AND BUSINESS

August 30, 1991

Lee Salem, Vice President & Editorial Director
Universal Press Syndicate

Dear Lee:

I am so glad you've signed Barbara Brandon to a Universal contract. I've
been wanting a Barbara Brandon mug on my desk for so long!

"Where I'm Coming From" has brightened our lifestyle section on Sundays
for two years now, and I've long been convinced Barbara's "girls" would
be just as popular in other cities as they are in Motown.

Black women are so happy to see faces that reflect their own. Other women
enjoy the relationships commentary that hits home universally. And men
tune in to see what those girls are saying about them this week.

Other letters from fans include:

"Count me in as a member of 'the girls' fan club."

"Your Sunday comic is such a funny, on-target, and often truthful part of
the Free Press. Your work does not appear in my home paper, so I photo-
copy your comics to the top of stationery and use it to write letters to
friends at home."

"Every Sunday I can't wait to see what aspect of my life will be profiled
for all to see. It is also so nice to see African-American images regular-
ly instead of just during Black History Month."

"You really know what's going on with the mind of black women/men. My
friends say this comic was made just for me because I say a lot of the
things your character does. Keep up the great work."

"Thank you for making my Sunday morning! I don't know if you publish
your strip for any other publishers other than the Free Press, but it
would be a shame for only Detroit to enjoy such a funny and realistic
laugh at life."

Amen.

Barbara Brandon's "Where I'm Coming From" hits the hot buttons for the
'90s. It's popular with minority readers and with women; it's funny,
and it's a very fast read. It's a unique way to "write about" men and
women and friendships -- and life.

I hope you sell it everywhere.

Sincerely,

Marty Claus

CARTOONIST PROfiles

NO. 96, DEC. 1992

$8

See
Page
10!

Hair and makeup by Theresa Vuoso

BARBARA BRANDON

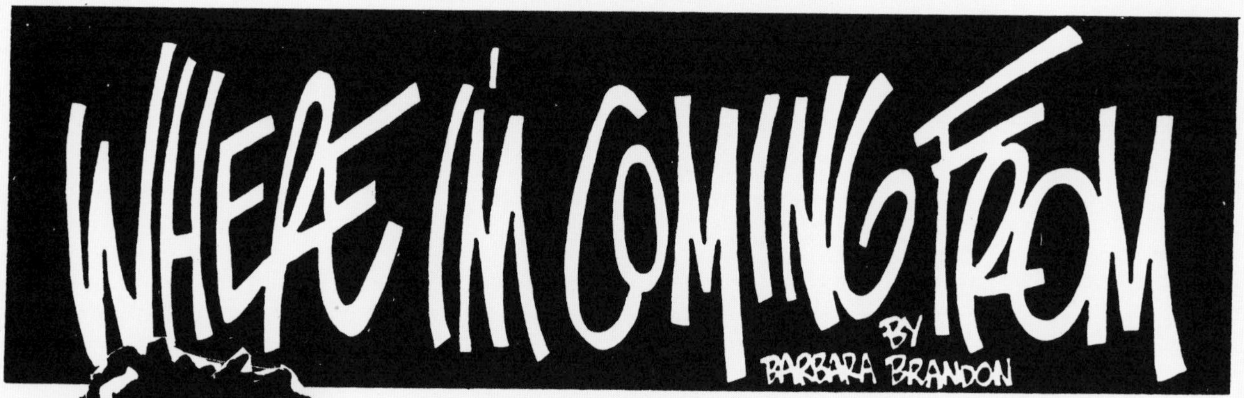
WHERE I'M COMING FROM
BY
BARBARA BRANDON

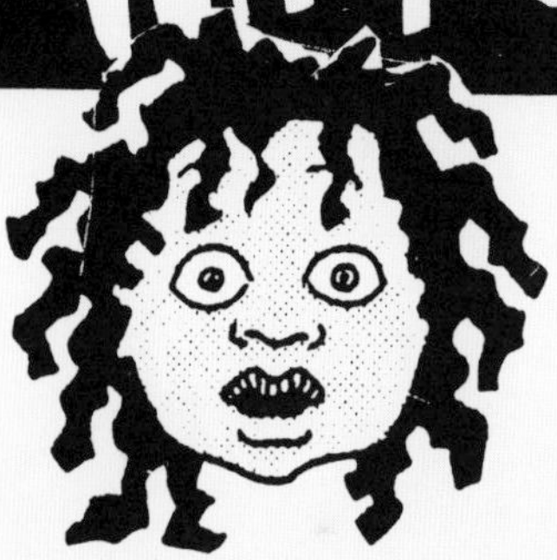

Barbara Brandon is a Black cartoonist whose comic strip, *Where I'm Coming From*, appears weekly in the *Detroit Free Press*. She recently signed a national syndication agreement with Universal Press Syndicate.

BY BARBARA BRANDON

Probably the most asked question I get is: Did you always know you wanted to be a cartoonist? Quite frankly, the answer is no. I had no idea what I wanted to be when I "grew up." And yet, somehow I knew I was destined for a career in the field of visual communications. Just how it would manifest itself, I had no clue.

Sure, as a teenager I worked as an apprentice under my father, Brumsic Brandon, Jr., helping him with his comic strip *Luther* (which was distributed nationally by The Los Angeles Times Syndicate for nearly eighteen years). I was responsible for applying the Zipatone, blacking in silhouettes, and on rare occasions, inking in the lettering. Only in hindsight is it clear that I'd been preparing all along for a career in cartooning. (As a teenager, it was just a means of earning an allowance.)

Not until 1981, a year after I left Syracuse University's School of Visual and Performing Arts (where I studied illustration), did my true ambition begin to reveal itself.

While interviewing for a job at *Elan*, a national magazine addressing the concerns of Black women, I expressed an interest in working in their art, editorial, or fashion department (I toted along my portfolio—just in case). The editor-in-chief/interviewer told me that she felt I had a sense of humor, and an ability to draw and wondered if I could create a cartoon feature for them.* I immediately replied, "Yes!" But to be honest, I wasn't sure I could at all.

I came home (yes, I was one of those post-college offspring who move back to the security of the nest) and my dad offered me his studio downstairs to try to work out my ideas. The sad part was, I didn't have any ideas.

After weeks of drawing blanks I came up with something that thought would work: Talking heads. Women. Black women. Nine opinionated Black women, some of a decidedly

*The editor who made this brilliant suggestion went on to have a long and acclaimed career as a literary agent—Marie Brown

feminist bent, wryly coping with life's everyday trials and tribulations. A strip that would explore the special relationships between women who are best friends. Real folks dealing with real life—speaking on friendships, careers, male-female relationships, single parenthood, racism, and women's rights. All right, so occasionally men find themselves at the butt of some jokes. Taking jabs for being irresponsible or unfaithful or just plain not being there when they're needed, but the women hold themselves up to equal scrutiny. They also "rag" each other for not standing their ground, for making excuses for situations they can control, for accepting less than they want from a relationship rather than face being alone. The humor is aimed squarely at adults, but not exclusively toward women or Blacks.

I called it *Where I'm Coming From*. What it offered (then and now) was a window through which a large segment of society can take a closer look at a smaller segment of society and discover that, when you get right down to it, we're all pretty much the same. I liked it. My dad liked it. And better yet, the magazine liked it.

I was asked to come up with more samples (I had presented them with three) so the editors and art director could decide how to pace my work in the magazine. So, it was back to my dad's studio. It wasn't long before I was prepared to show an additional nine strips. I made the call to *Elan* but was told that the editor-in-chief was no longer accepting appointments. I said, "There must be some mistake. I'm working on a project with her for the magazine. She's expecting to hear from me." The woman on the phone said to me calmly and gently, "You must not have heard yet, but as of yesterday, this magazine has folded." I was devastated.

Here I had this great idea for a cartoon feature and no place to publish it. All this time I didn't know I wanted to be a cartoonist and now—that it wasn't going to happen—I wanted to be nothing else.

I decided since I originally created it for a Black woman's magazine, I would send my work to the only other Black woman's magazine I knew—*Essence*. Initially, I received a favorable response. I was told the editors were taking *Where I'm Coming From* under "serious consideration" for publication. Bet.

I tried to be patient but my eagerness got the best of me. I found myself calling one poor editor once a week. I had been told that they had an editorial meeting every Monday morning where they discussed the possibility of adding new features to the magazine. So every Monday afternoon, I was calling to see if *Where I'm Coming From* was to be among the lucky newcomers. About six weeks into my Monday afternoon ritual I was informed that *Where I'm Coming From* "didn't fit their editorial format," but the editors were still interested in meeting me. (Apparently my work was impressive—even if they didn't want to publish it.)

Again, I dragged my portfolio in for an interview. Again, I was ready to accept a job on almost any level. When they found out I had been working as a fashion reporter and illustrator for a national trade publication, I saw light bulbs going off on top of their heads. As it turned out, their fashion and beauty writer was about to take off on maternity leave and they needed a replacement, quick. They asked if I would be willing to take an editorial test. I did. I passed. And I accepted the four-month-long gig as fashion and beauty writer. I ended up staying there in that capacity for five and a half years!

It wasn't that I had given up hope on the possibility of having *Where I'm Coming From* published. Every time I filed a story, I'd draw little characters on the copy pages, lest the editors forget where my true heart lay. Even still, *Where I'm Coming From* never made it to their printed page.

Okay, okay, so it's 1988. Enter the *Detroit Free Press*. The *DFP* sent my father a congratulatory letter after he received an award for being one of the pioneer Black cartoonists (my father is the third Black cartoonist to be nationally syndicated into the mainstream press—I make the eighth). In their letter they added a postscript asking if he knew of any other Black cartoonists. (How convenient for me!) They explained their ongoing search for Black cartoonists and their aim to have the funny pages better reflect their readership. (Talk about being in the right place at the right time!) My father promptly got ahold of me and asked, "Are you presentation ready?" I said, in all vigor, "YES!" Then meekly added, "What does 'presentation ready' mean?" He explained how I needed to have enough samples together to send to the *Free Press* so that they could get an idea of the consistency of my work. Like I had said, I was definitely presentation ready—and had been for some five and a half years now!

I mailed off *Where I'm Coming From* once again, but this time, not only did they like my work, they told me they were prepared to print it. June 11, 1989, *Where I'm Coming From* made its debut in the *Detroit Free Press*.

Feeling pumped, my next goal was to become nationally syndicated. I busily began putting together low-budget press kits* on *Where I'm Coming From*. (Since I had the advantage of having a nationally syndicated cartoonist in my home, I knew that syndicates produce press kits of the comic strips they represent to get the notice of newspapers, so I put together a press kit of my work to get the notice of the syndicates.)

It wasn't long before rejection letters began streaming in: "You can't do just heads." "You can't do just women." "Are you only going to do Black women?" "You can't do it that size." "It's too big." "It's too much like *Cathy*." "It's too much like Feiffer." "You can't do a weekly." "You must change your format." "You have to do a daily if you want to be published." "You must put your characters in environments." Blah blah blah!

I was rejected by some of the best.

However, there was one syndicate that gave me a ray of hope: Universal Press Syndicate. They told me that the bite and tone of my humor was appealing and that I had a good ear for nuance and character! They said they'd be in touch. I popped the champagne.

By 1990, Universal Press Syndicate offered me a development contract. Go on girl! I was on my way, and with a syndicate that clearly respected their artists. Not only did they not insist I change my approach (format or style), they encouraged me to do more of what I like doing most: writing more politically and socially stirring material. I couldn't ask for more. By 1991, I signed a full syndication deal!

With the support and encouragement of the *Detroit Free Press* and Universal Press Syndicate, I made it into the history books. I happen to be the first Black female cartoonist to become nationally syndicated into the mainstream press and I'm proud of it!

I was able to stick to what I believed. No, I wasn't going to put bodies on my characters. I'm tired of women being summed up by their body parts. (Why is it still necessary to show cleavage to sell beer?) I'm interested in giving my women a little more dignity. I want folks to understand that women—in addition to breasts—have ideas and opinions. Look us in the eye and hear what we're saying, please!

Where other syndicates feared newspapers wouldn't be interested in something so novel, my work can now be seen in more than sixty papers across the nation—and several spots around the world. Look for *Where I'm Coming From* in book form (Andrews McMeel Publishing, a Universal Press Syndicate company publisher) due out Spring 1993, which will be followed by a collection of greeting cards, t-shirts, and mugs. If your local newspaper isn't running *Where I'm Coming From*, write them and ask, why not?

*Elements of the original press kit are reprinted on page 1 & 22–25

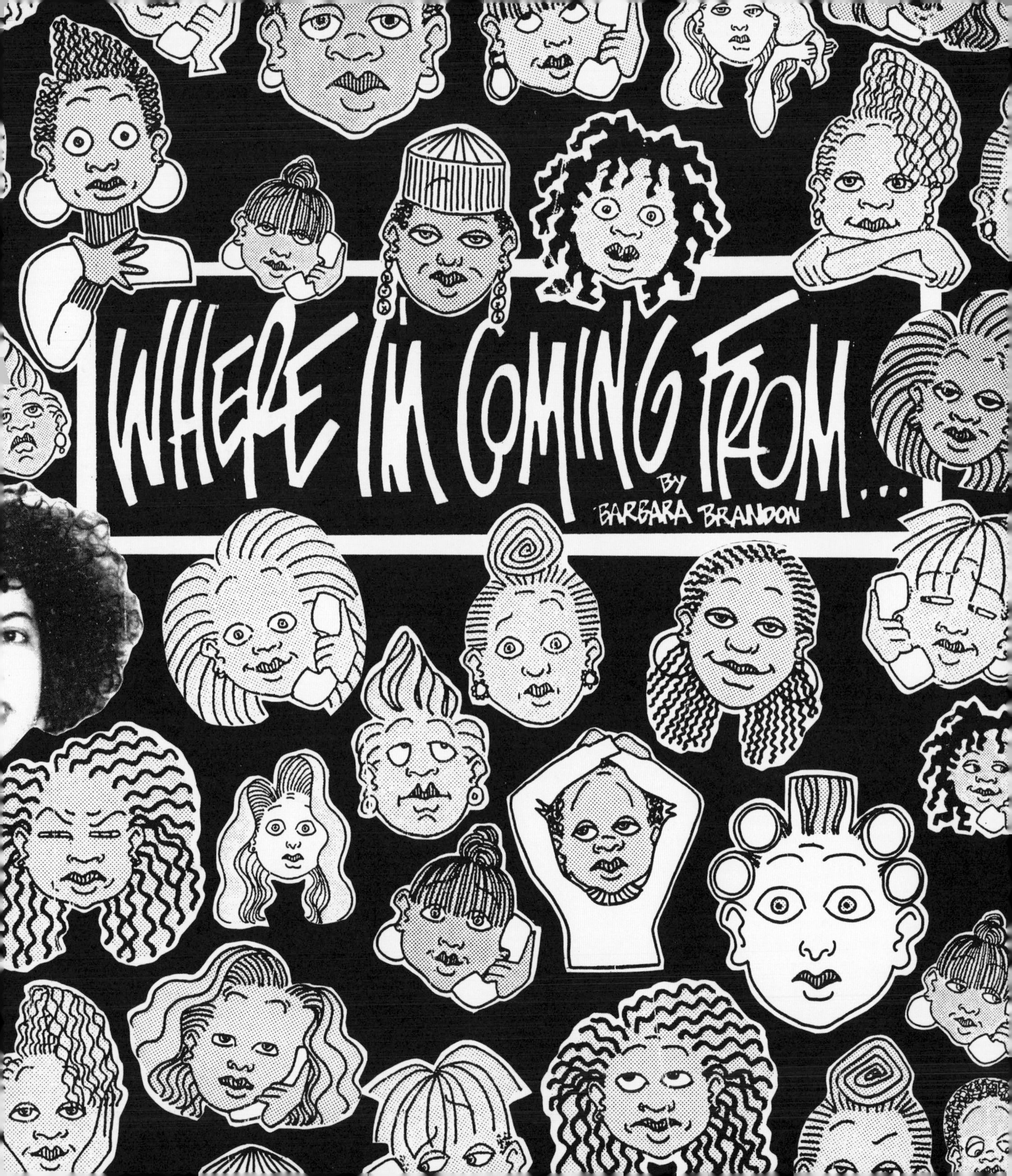
WHERE I'M COMING FROM...
BY BARBARA BRANDON

CHERYL

NICOLE

JACKIE

Loud-mouthed, sharp-tongued, cynical, wisecracking, sarcastic, and abrasive are all fair ways to describe Cheryl. Her caustic humor often puts her at odds with her friends, but usually not for very long. Her girlfriends accept her for who she is and appreciate her honesty.

The closest of all the characters to a "fly girl," she looks good, knows she looks good, and is not only proud of it—she flaunts it! Humility is not a word in her vocabulary. But looks aren't everything; common sense is her deficit.

The most high-strung of the crew, Jackie is on a constant emotional roller coaster. If it's not her on-again-off-again relationship with Victor, it's her obsession with her body's tendency to retain water. Her friends find her exasperating and lovable all at once.

ALISHA

"Pollyanna" is what her friends call her. She's a do-unto-others-as-you-would-have-them-do-unto-you kind of woman. Having a man isn't exactly a priority for Alisha—much to Cheryl's consternation. Her unshakable faith in divine destiny keeps her grounded.

JUDY

Judy takes on the role of an observer. She feels it gives her great insight into human relationships. Her friends love to talk to her because she's a good listener and they know they can come to her with their problems—especially Nicole.

LYDIA and ARETHA

The only mom in the bunch—and a single mom at that. Her daughter, Re-Re (short for Aretha), is a product of a past relationship. Along with a great deal of responsibility, motherhood has brought on something she didn't expect: a newfound social awareness.

A true stand-by-your-man kind of woman. Sonya is a firm believer in the concept that a woman doesn't exist unless she's with a man. In her case, his name is Kenny. She's a far cry from your traditional feminist, still and all, she don't take no mess from any man, including Kenny.

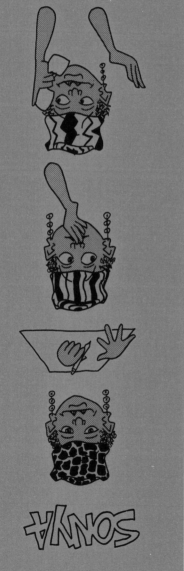

SONYA

Physically, Monica is a fair-skinned, hazel-eyed, sharp-featured woman who is sometimes mistaken for being white. That is, until she opens her mouth. It's a phenomenon she used to hate, but has grown to appreciate. She loves to point out the humor in the kind of irony her racially ambiguous looks provide.

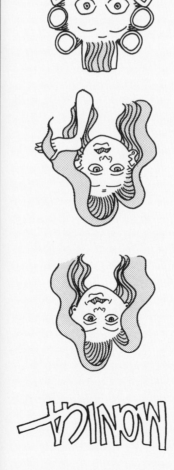

MONICA

Like Cheryl, Lekeisia is an unreserved say-what-you-mean-mean-what-you-say kind of woman. What sets them apart is Lekeisia's political consciousness. She is both pro-Black and pro-women and is well aware that some folks interpret this as anti-white and anti-men. With this, she can live.

LEKEESIA

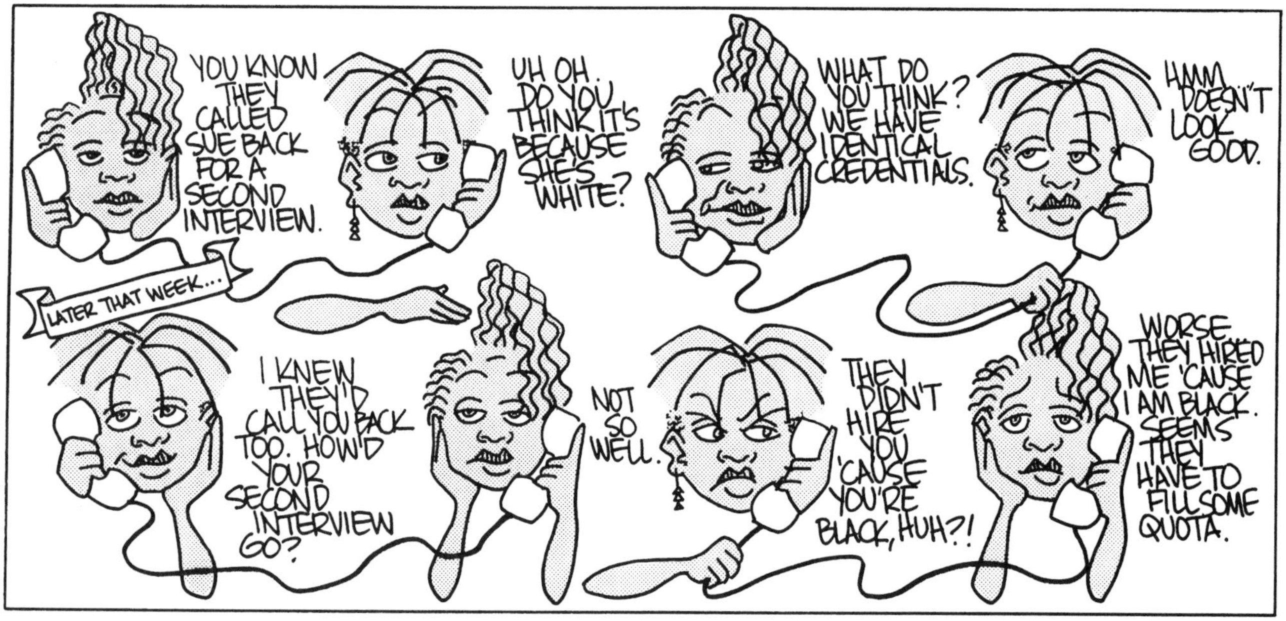
YOU KNOW THEY CALLED SUE BACK FOR A SECOND INTERVIEW.
UH OH. DO YOU THINK IT'S BECAUSE SHE'S WHITE?
WHAT DO YOU THINK? WE HAVE IDENTICAL CREDENTIALS.
HMM DOESN'T LOOK GOOD.
LATER THAT WEEK...
I KNEW THEY'D CALL YOU BACK TOO. HOW'D YOUR SECOND INTERVIEW GO?
NOT SO WELL.
THEY DIDN'T HIRE YOU 'CAUSE YOU'RE BLACK, HUH?!
WORSE. THEY HIRED ME 'CAUSE I AM BLACK. SEEMS THEY HAVE TO FILL SOME QUOTA.

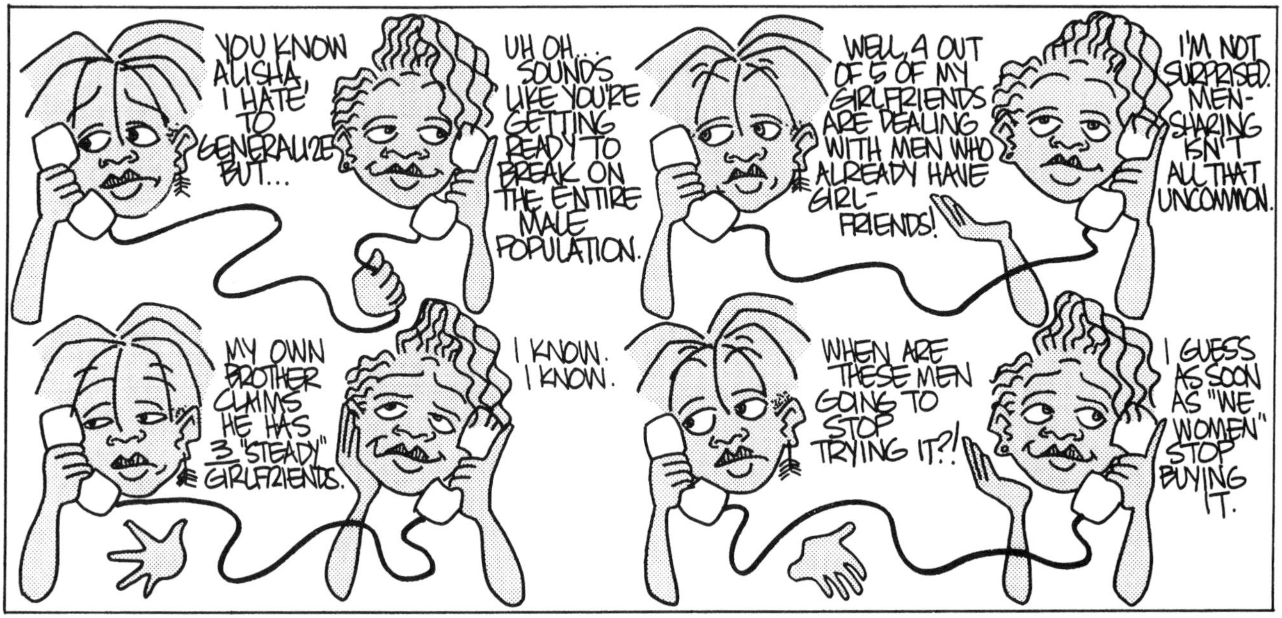
YOU KNOW ALISHA, I HATE TO GENERALIZE BUT...
UH OH... SOUNDS LIKE YOU'RE GETTING READY TO BREAK ON THE ENTIRE MALE POPULATION.
WELL, 4 OUT OF 5 OF MY GIRLFRIENDS ARE DEALING WITH MEN WHO ALREADY HAVE GIRL-FRIENDS!
I'M NOT SURPRISED. MEN-SHARING ISN'T ALL THAT UNCOMMON.
MY OWN BROTHER CLAIMS HE HAS 3 "STEADY" GIRLFRIENDS.
I KNOW. I KNOW.
WHEN ARE THESE MEN GOING TO STOP TRYING IT?!
I GUESS AS SOON AS "WE WOMEN" STOP BUYING IT.

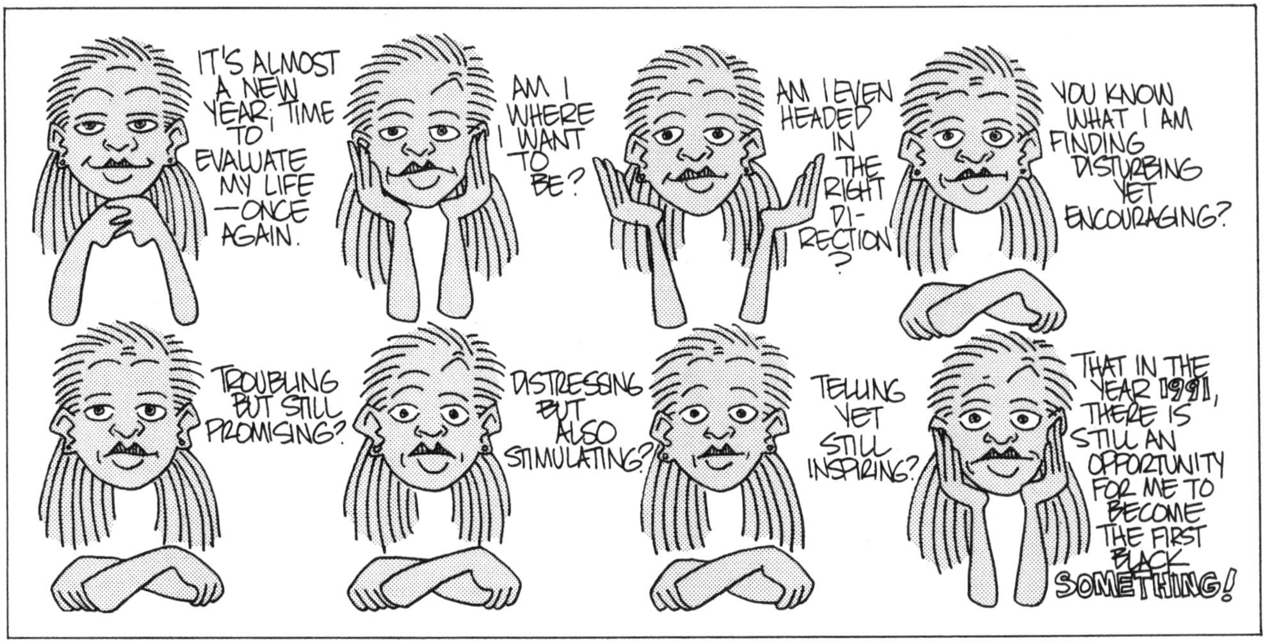

IT'S ALMOST A NEW YEAR; TIME TO EVALUATE MY LIFE —ONCE AGAIN.
AM I WHERE I WANT TO BE?
AM I EVEN HEADED IN THE RIGHT DI-RECTION?
YOU KNOW WHAT I AM FINDING DISTURBING YET ENCOURAGING?
TROUBLING BUT STILL PROMISING?
DISTRESSING BUT ALSO STIMULATING?
TELLING YET STILL INSPIRING?
THAT IN THE YEAR 1991, THERE IS STILL AN OPPORTUNITY FOR ME TO BECOME THE FIRST BLACK SOMETHING!

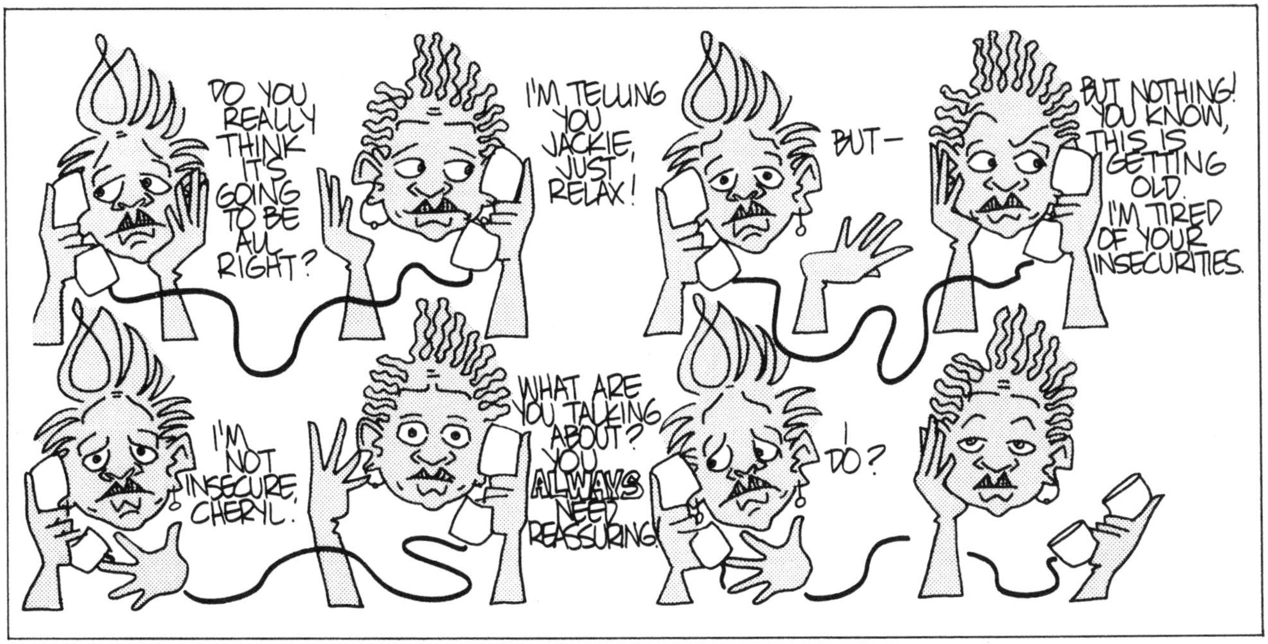

DO YOU REALLY THINK IT'S GOING TO BE ALL RIGHT?
I'M TELLING YOU JACKIE, JUST RELAX!
BUT—
BUT NOTHING! YOU KNOW, THIS IS GETTING OLD. I'M TIRED OF YOUR INSECURITIES.
I'M NOT INSECURE, CHERYL.
WHAT ARE YOU TALKING ABOUT? YOU ALWAYS NEED REASSURING!
I DO?

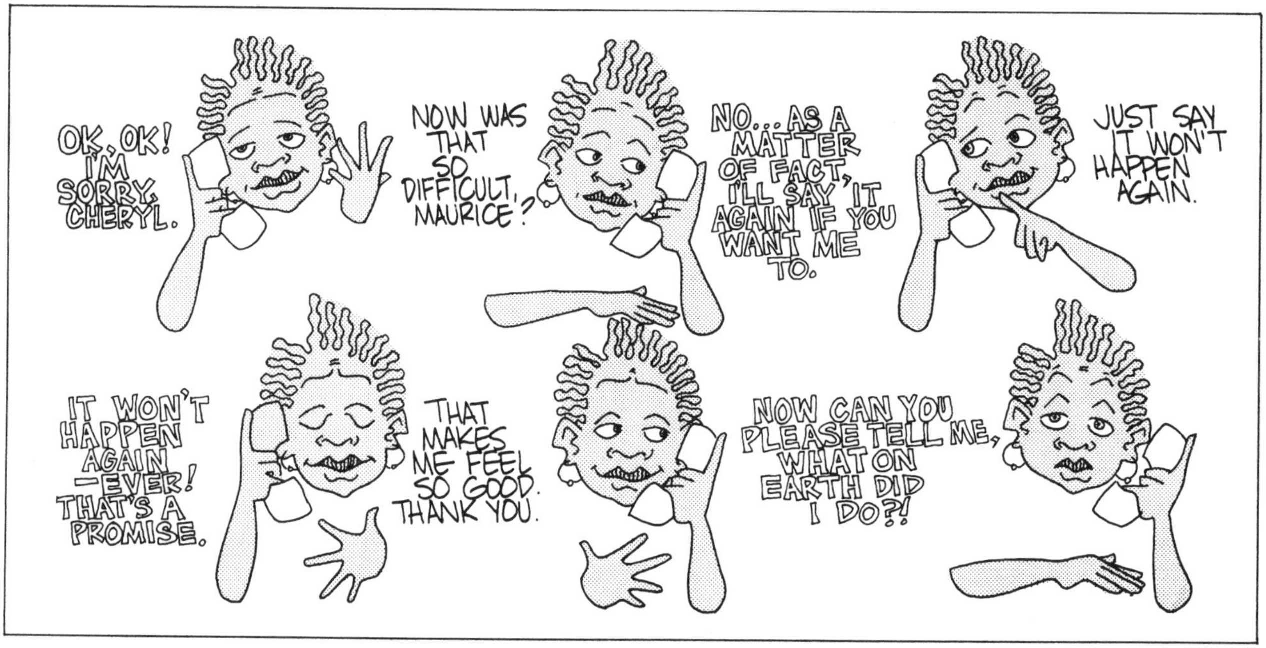
OK, OK! I'M SORRY, CHERYL.
NOW WAS THAT SO DIFFICULT, MAURICE?
NO... AS A MATTER OF FACT, I'LL SAY IT AGAIN IF YOU WANT ME TO.
JUST SAY IT WON'T HAPPEN AGAIN.
IT WON'T HAPPEN AGAIN —EVER! THAT'S A PROMISE.
THAT MAKES ME FEEL SO GOOD. THANK YOU.
NOW CAN YOU PLEASE TELL ME, WHAT ON EARTH DID I DO?!

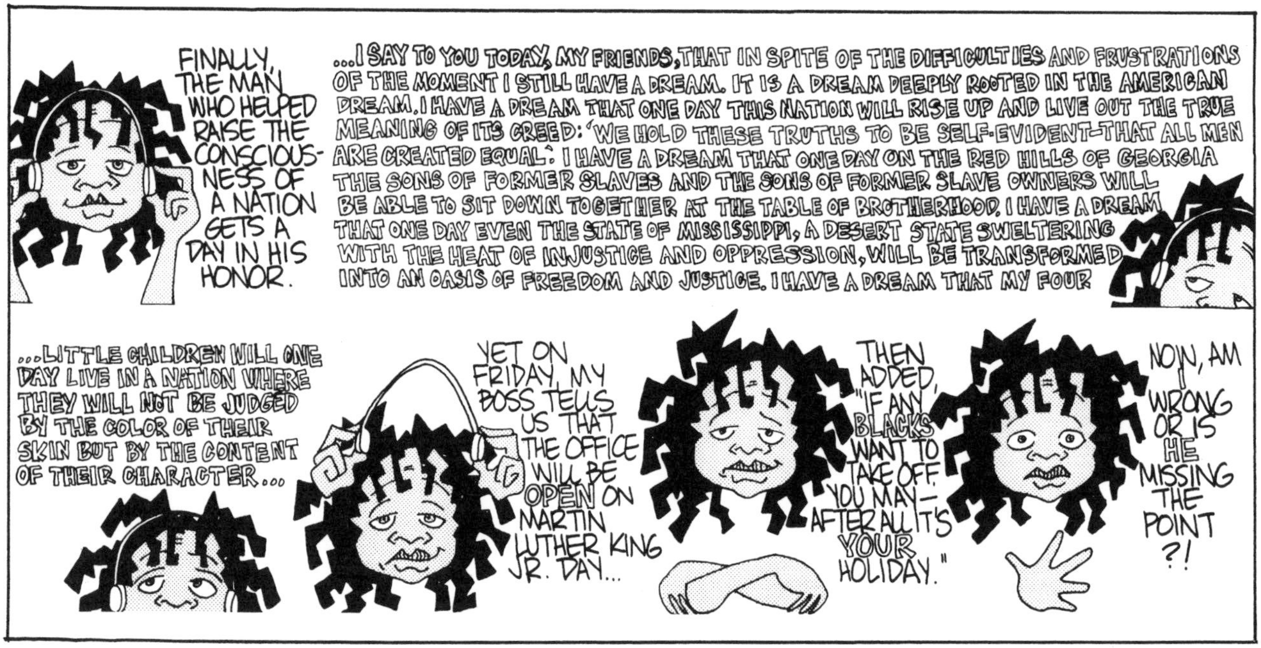
FINALLY, THE MAN WHO HELPED RAISE THE CONSCIOUSNESS OF A NATION GETS A DAY IN HIS HONOR.
...I SAY TO YOU TODAY, MY FRIENDS, THAT IN SPITE OF THE DIFFICULTIES AND FRUSTRATIONS OF THE MOMENT I STILL HAVE A DREAM. IT IS A DREAM DEEPLY ROOTED IN THE AMERICAN DREAM. I HAVE A DREAM THAT ONE DAY THIS NATION WILL RISE UP AND LIVE OUT THE TRUE MEANING OF ITS CREED: 'WE HOLD THESE TRUTHS TO BE SELF-EVIDENT—THAT ALL MEN ARE CREATED EQUAL.' I HAVE A DREAM THAT ONE DAY ON THE RED HILLS OF GEORGIA THE SONS OF FORMER SLAVES AND THE SONS OF FORMER SLAVE OWNERS WILL BE ABLE TO SIT DOWN TOGETHER AT THE TABLE OF BROTHERHOOD. I HAVE A DREAM THAT ONE DAY EVEN THE STATE OF MISSISSIPPI, A DESERT STATE SWELTERING WITH THE HEAT OF INJUSTICE AND OPPRESSION, WILL BE TRANSFORMED INTO AN OASIS OF FREEDOM AND JUSTICE. I HAVE A DREAM THAT MY FOUR
...LITTLE CHILDREN WILL ONE DAY LIVE IN A NATION WHERE THEY WILL NOT BE JUDGED BY THE COLOR OF THEIR SKIN BUT BY THE CONTENT OF THEIR CHARACTER...
YET ON FRIDAY, MY BOSS TELLS US THAT THE OFFICE WILL BE OPEN ON MARTIN LUTHER KING JR. DAY...
THEN ADDED, "IF ANY BLACKS WANT TO TAKE OFF, YOU MAY—AFTER ALL IT'S YOUR HOLIDAY."
NOW, AM I WRONG OR IS HE MISSING THE POINT ?!

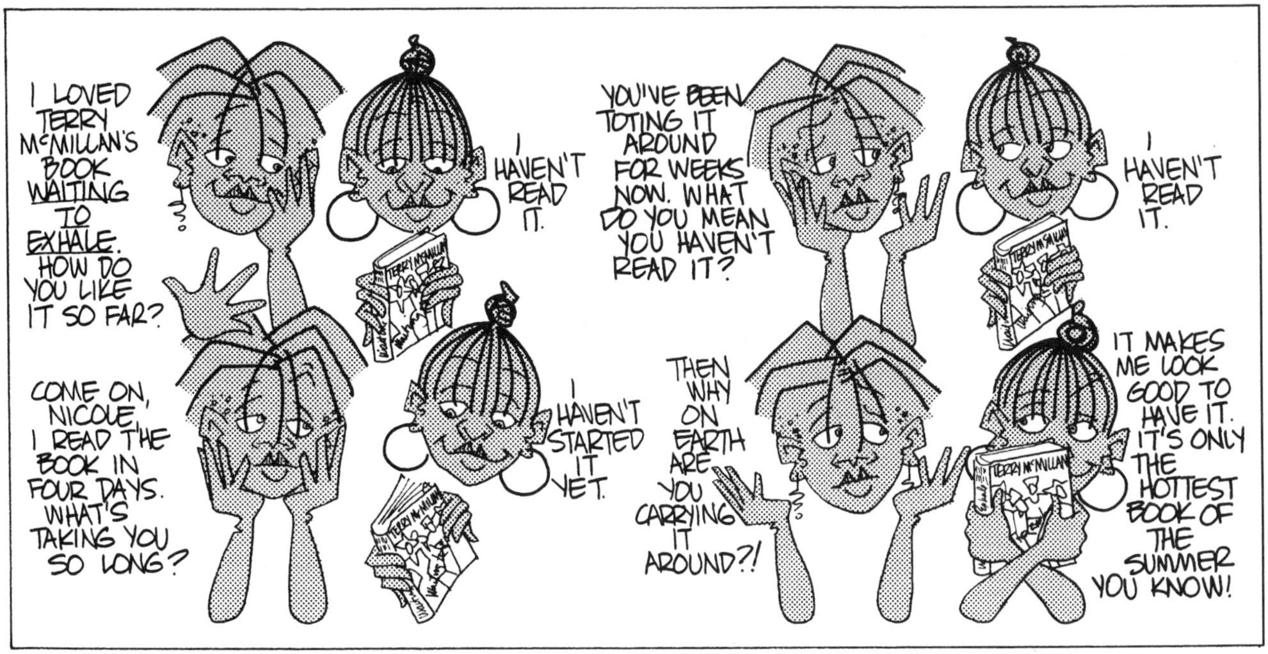
I LOVED TERRY McMILLAN'S BOOK WAITING TO EXHALE. HOW DO YOU LIKE IT SO FAR?
I HAVEN'T READ IT.
YOU'VE BEEN TOTING IT AROUND FOR WEEKS NOW. WHAT DO YOU MEAN YOU HAVEN'T READ IT?
I HAVEN'T READ IT.
COME ON, NICOLE, I READ THE BOOK IN FOUR DAYS. WHAT'S TAKING YOU SO LONG?
I HAVEN'T STARTED IT YET.
THEN WHY ON EARTH ARE YOU CARRYING IT AROUND?!
IT MAKES ME LOOK GOOD TO HAVE IT. IT'S ONLY THE HOTTEST BOOK OF THE SUMMER YOU KNOW!

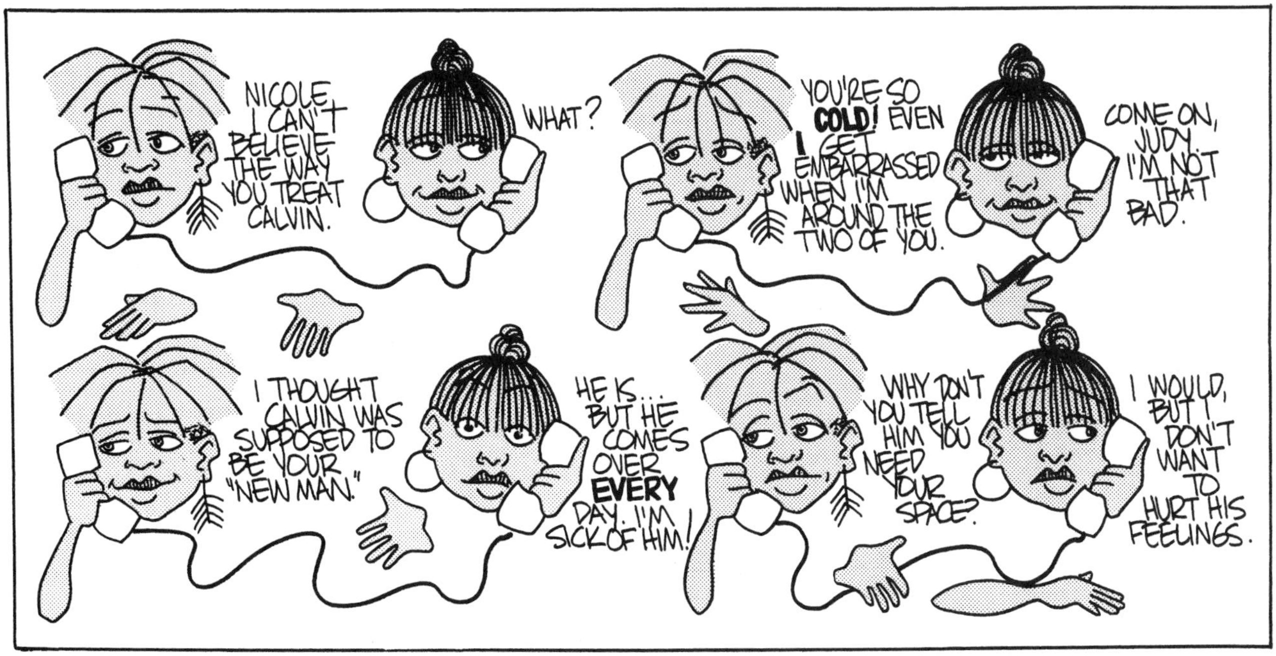
NICOLE, I CAN'T BELIEVE THE WAY YOU TREAT CALVIN.
WHAT?
YOU'RE SO COLD! EVEN I GET EMBARRASSED WHEN I'M AROUND THE TWO OF YOU.
COME ON, JUDY. I'M NOT THAT BAD.
I THOUGHT CALVIN WAS SUPPOSED TO BE YOUR "NEW MAN."
HE IS... BUT HE COMES OVER EVERY DAY. I'M SICK OF HIM!
WHY DON'T YOU TELL HIM YOU NEED YOUR SPACE?
I WOULD, BUT I DON'T WANT TO HURT HIS FEELINGS.

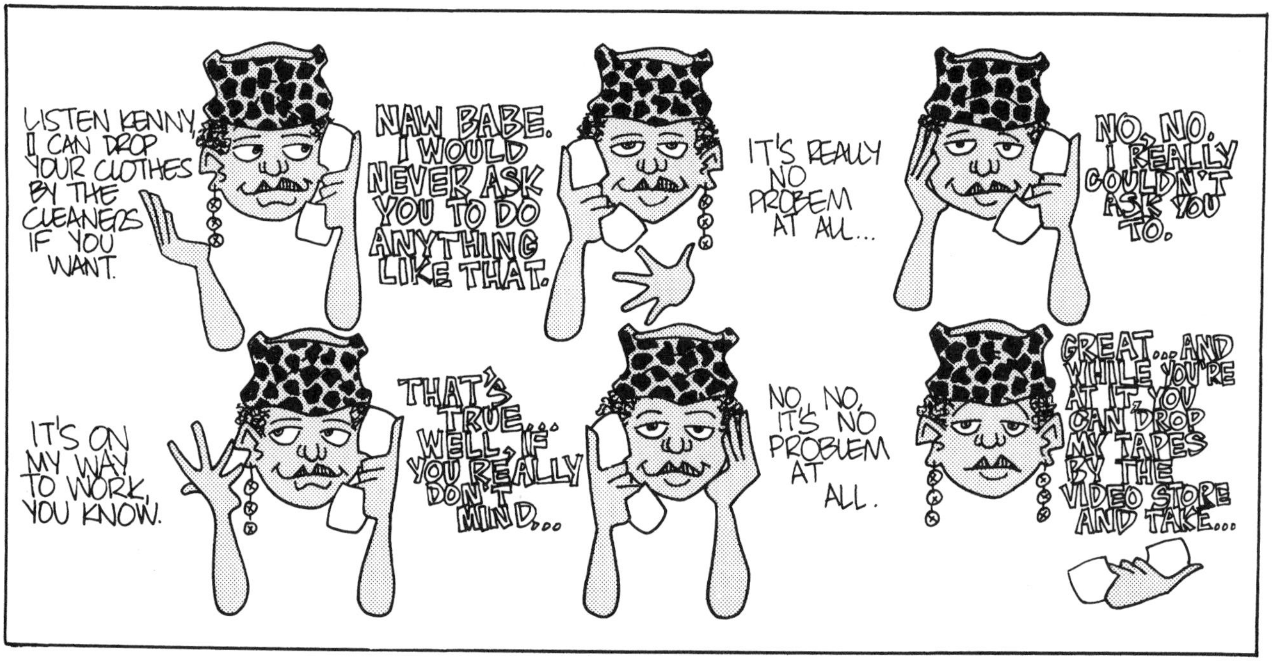
LISTEN KENNY, I CAN DROP YOUR CLOTHES BY THE CLEANERS IF YOU WANT.
NAW BABE. I WOULD NEVER ASK YOU TO DO ANYTHING LIKE THAT.
IT'S REALLY NO PROBEM AT ALL...
NO, NO. I REALLY COULDN'T ASK YOU TO.
IT'S ON MY WAY TO WORK, YOU KNOW.
THAT'S TRUE... WELL, IF YOU REALLY DON'T MIND...
NO, NO, IT'S NO PROBLEM AT ALL.
GREAT... AND WHILE YOU'RE AT IT, YOU CAN DROP MY TAPES BY THE VIDEO STORE AND TAKE...

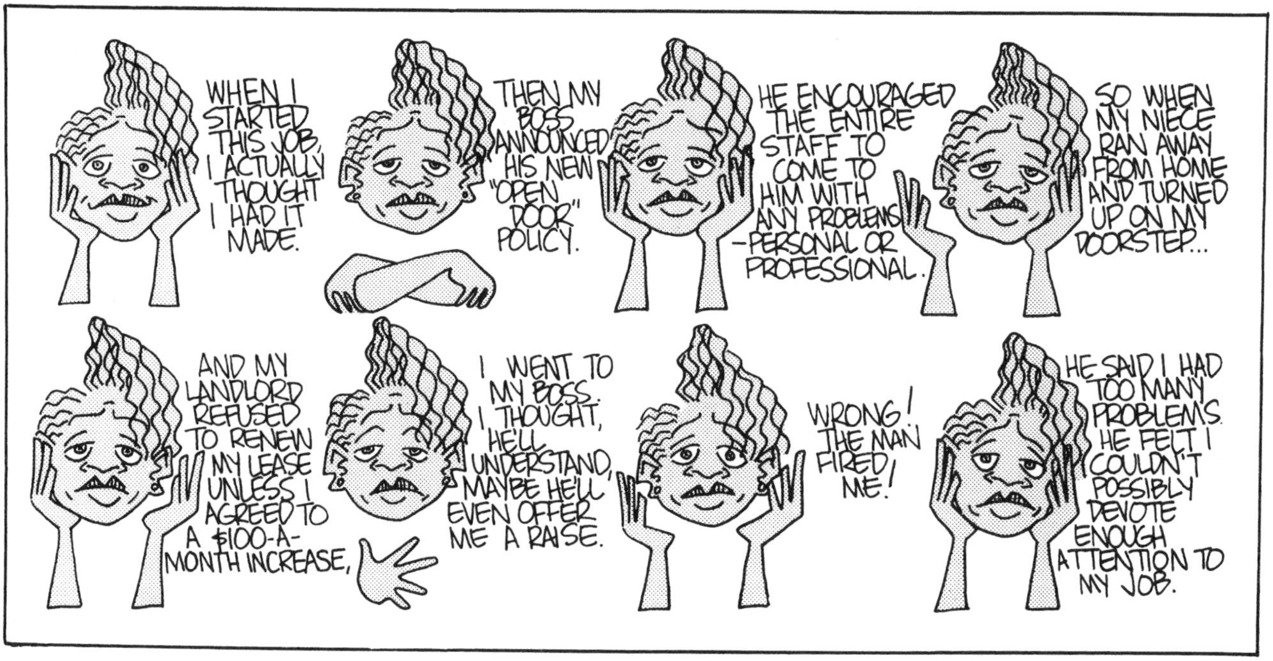
WHEN I STARTED THIS JOB, I ACTUALLY THOUGHT I HAD IT MADE.
THEN MY BOSS ANNOUNCED HIS NEW "OPEN DOOR" POLICY.
HE ENCOURAGED THE ENTIRE STAFF TO COME TO HIM WITH ANY PROBLEMS —PERSONAL OR PROFESSIONAL.
SO WHEN MY NIECE RAN AWAY FROM HOME AND TURNED UP ON MY DOORSTEP...
AND MY LANDLORD REFUSED TO RENEW MY LEASE UNLESS I AGREED TO A $100-A-MONTH INCREASE,
I WENT TO MY BOSS. I THOUGHT, HE'LL UNDERSTAND, MAYBE HE'LL EVEN OFFER ME A RAISE.
WRONG! THE MAN FIRED ME!
HE SAID I HAD TOO MANY PROBLEMS. HE FELT I COULDN'T POSSIBLY DEVOTE ENOUGH ATTENTION TO MY JOB.

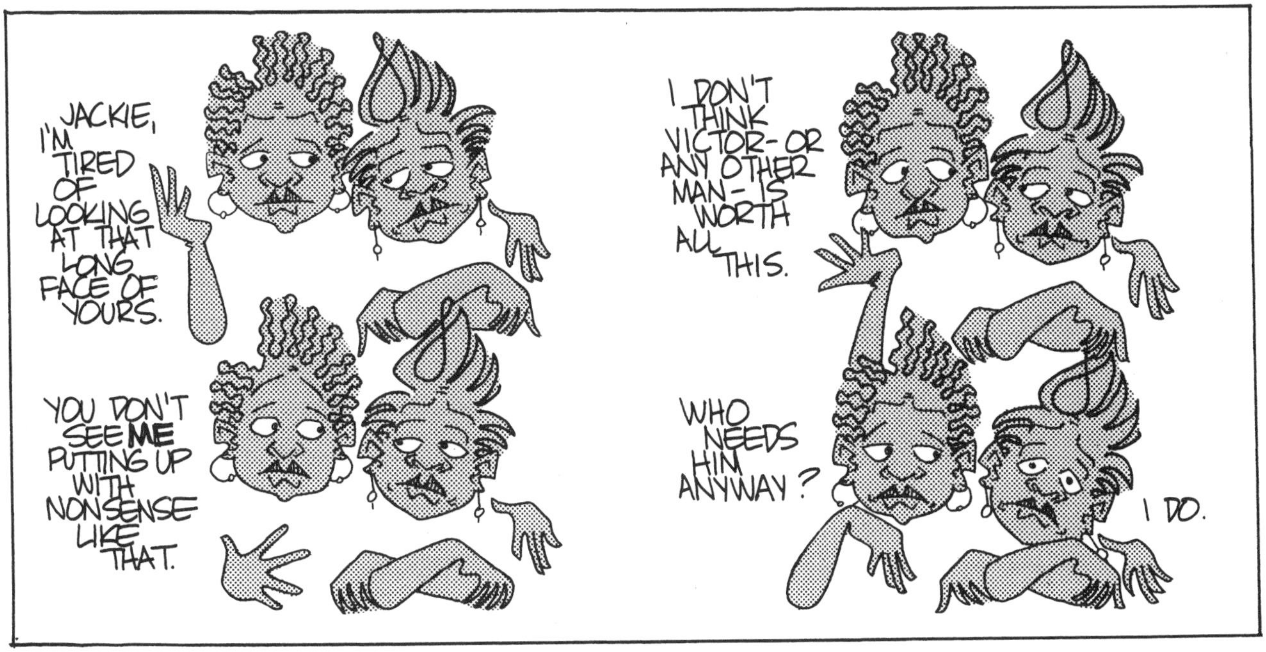
JACKIE, I'M TIRED OF LOOKING AT THAT LONG FACE OF YOURS.
YOU DON'T SEE **ME** PUTTING UP WITH NONSENSE LIKE THAT.
I DON'T THINK VICTOR- OR ANY OTHER MAN- IS WORTH ALL THIS.
WHO NEEDS HIM ANYWAY ?
I DO.

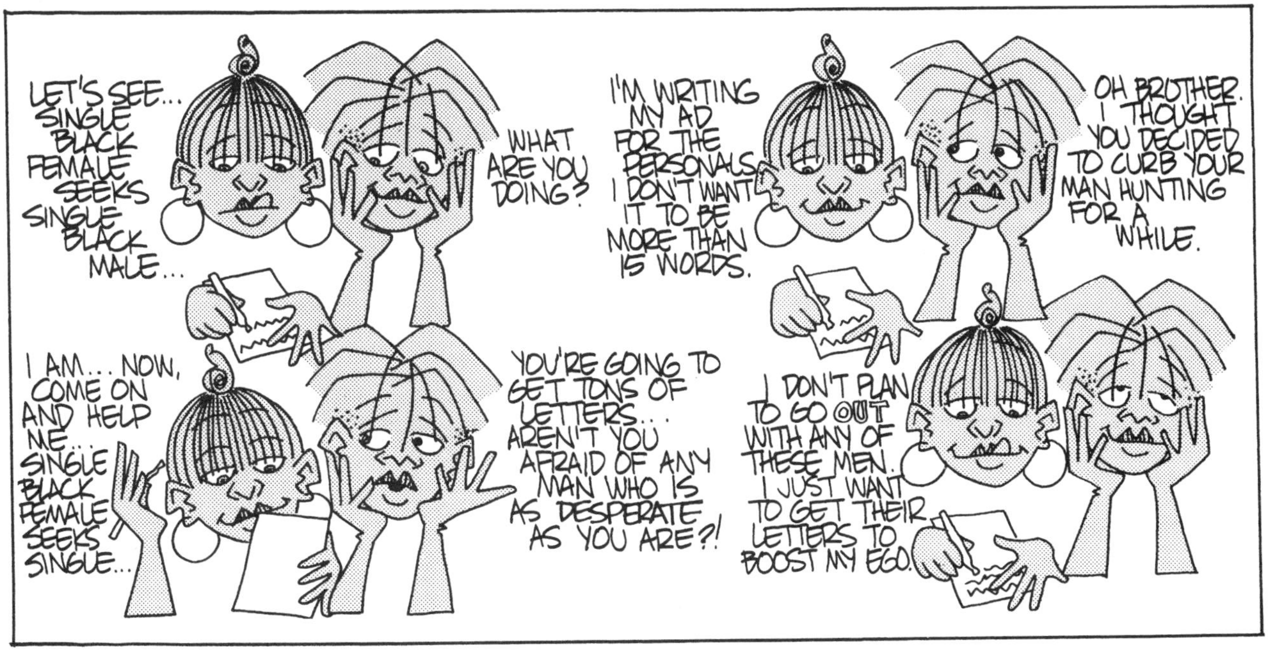
LET'S SEE... SINGLE BLACK FEMALE SEEKS SINGLE BLACK MALE...
WHAT ARE YOU DOING?
I AM... NOW, COME ON AND HELP ME... SINGLE BLACK FEMALE SEEKS SINGLE...
YOU'RE GOING TO GET TONS OF LETTERS... AREN'T YOU AFRAID OF ANY MAN WHO IS AS DESPERATE AS YOU ARE?!
I'M WRITING MY AD FOR THE PERSONALS. I DON'T WANT IT TO BE MORE THAN 15 WORDS.
OH BROTHER. I THOUGHT YOU DECIDED TO CURB YOUR MAN HUNTING FOR A WHILE.
I DON'T PLAN TO GO OUT WITH ANY OF THESE MEN. I JUST WANT TO GET THEIR LETTERS TO BOOST MY EGO.

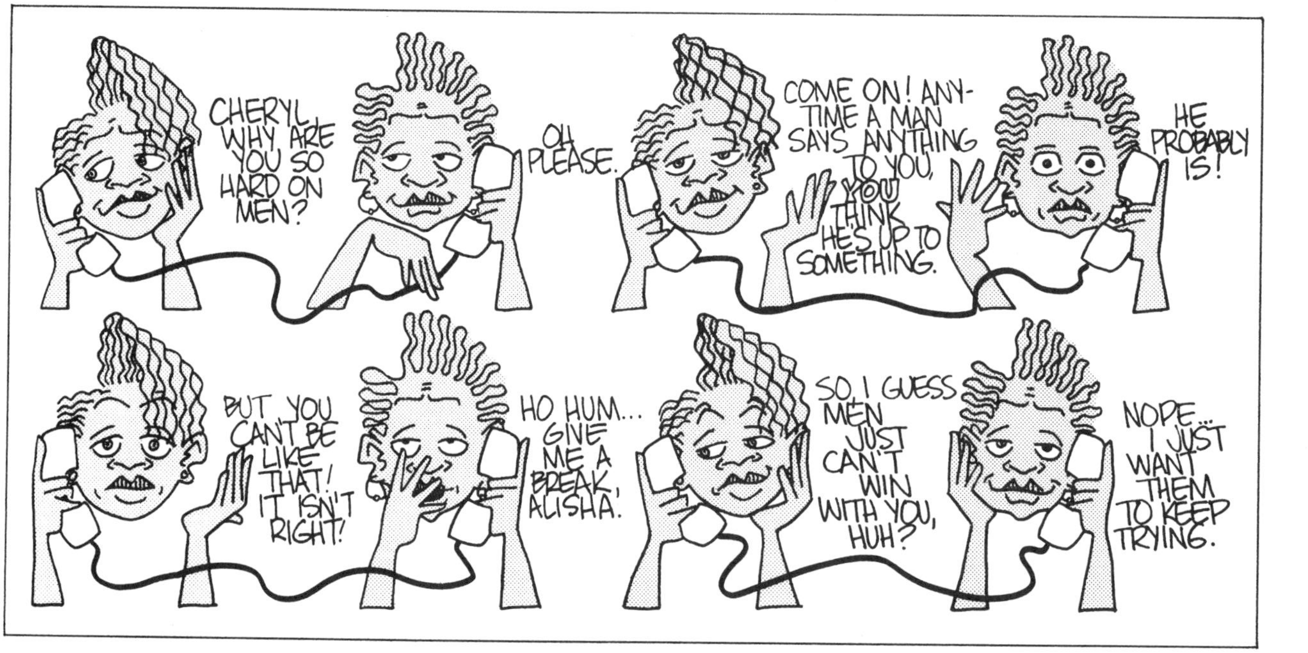
CHERYL, WHY ARE YOU SO HARD ON MEN?
OH PLEASE.
COME ON! ANYTIME A MAN SAYS ANYTHING TO YOU, YOU THINK HE'S UP TO SOMETHING.
HE PROBABLY IS!
BUT YOU CAN'T BE LIKE THAT! IT ISN'T RIGHT!
HO HUM... GIVE ME A BREAK, ALISHA.
SO I GUESS MEN JUST CAN'T WIN WITH YOU, HUH?
NOPE... I JUST WANT THEM TO KEEP TRYING.

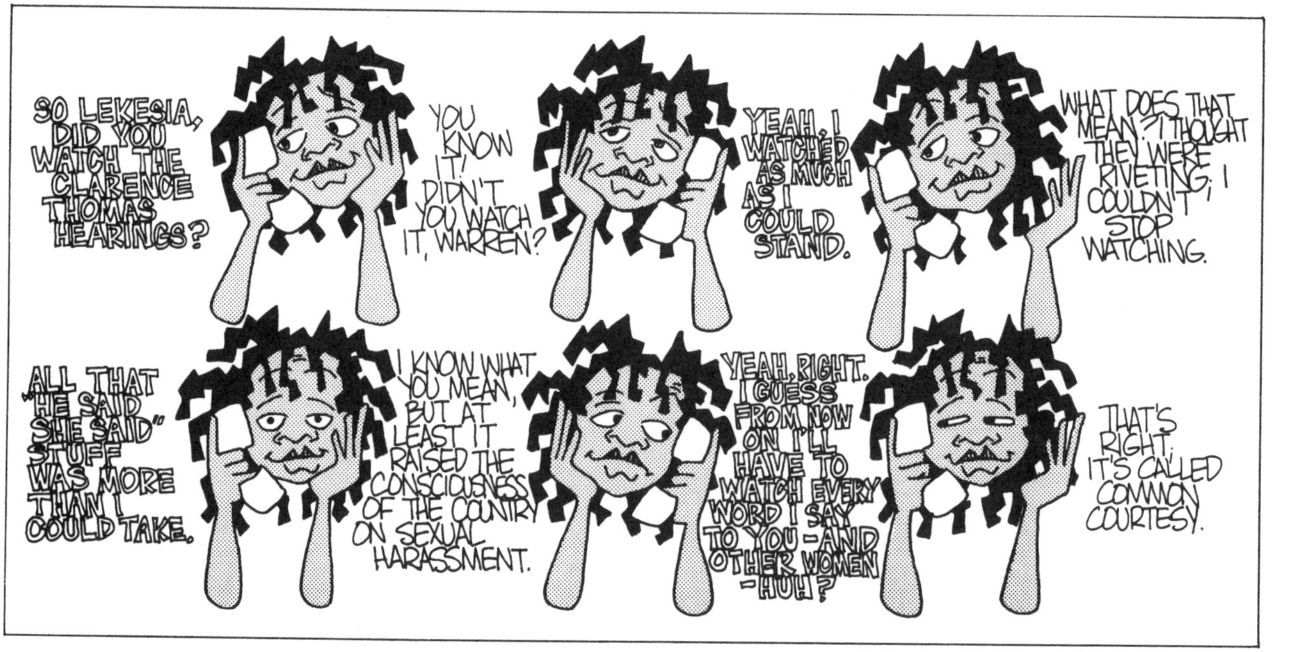
SO LEKESIA, DID YOU WATCH THE CLARENCE THOMAS HEARINGS?
YOU KNOW IT! DIDN'T YOU WATCH IT, WARREN?
YEAH, I WATCHED AS MUCH AS I COULD STAND.
WHAT DOES THAT MEAN? I THOUGHT THEY WERE RIVETING; I COULDN'T STOP WATCHING.
ALL THAT "HE SAID SHE SAID" STUFF WAS MORE THAN I COULD TAKE.
I KNOW WHAT YOU MEAN, BUT AT LEAST IT RAISED THE CONSCIOUSNESS OF THE COUNTRY ON SEXUAL HARASSMENT.
YEAH, RIGHT. I GUESS FROM NOW ON I'LL HAVE TO WATCH EVERY WORD I SAY TO YOU - AND OTHER WOMEN - HUH?
THAT'S RIGHT. IT'S CALLED COMMON COURTESY.

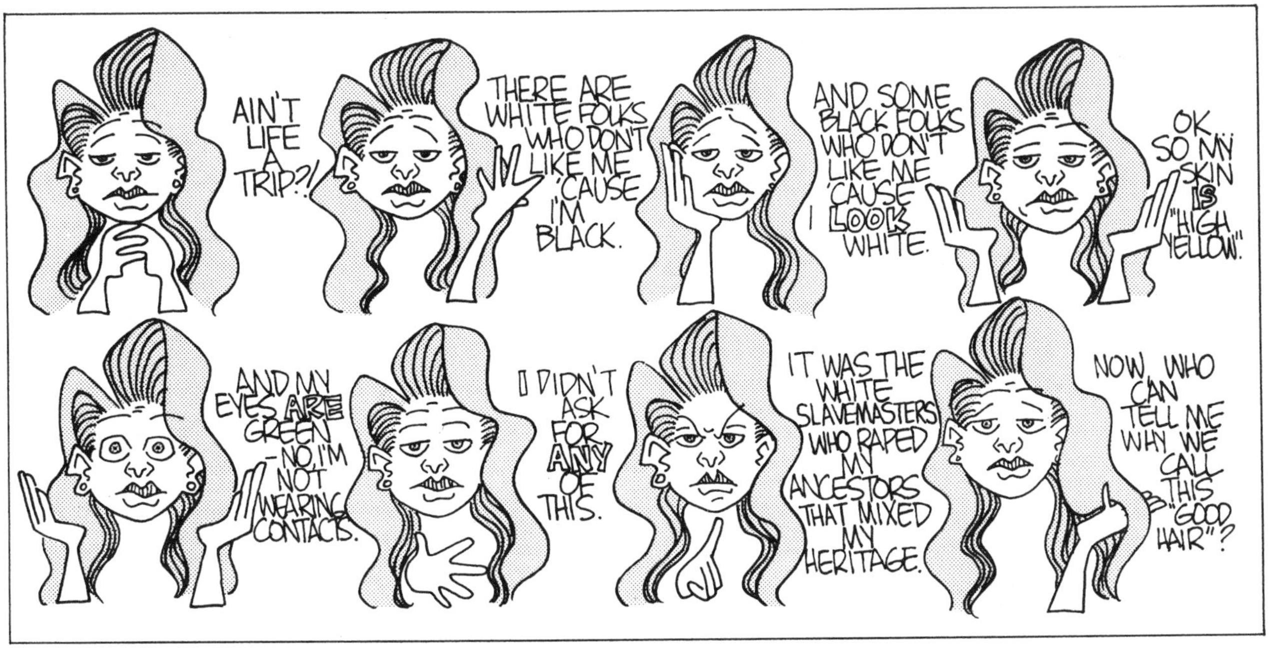

AIN'T LIFE A TRIP?!
THERE ARE WHITE FOLKS WHO DON'T LIKE ME 'CAUSE I'M BLACK.
AND SOME BLACK FOLKS WHO DON'T LIKE ME 'CAUSE I LOOK WHITE.
OK, SO MY SKIN IS "HIGH YELLOW".
AND MY EYES ARE GREEN — NO, I'M NOT WEARING CONTACTS.
I DIDN'T ASK FOR ANY OF THIS.
IT WAS THE WHITE SLAVEMASTERS WHO RAPED MY ANCESTORS THAT MIXED MY HERITAGE.
NOW, WHO CAN TELL ME WHY WE CALL THIS "GOOD HAIR"?

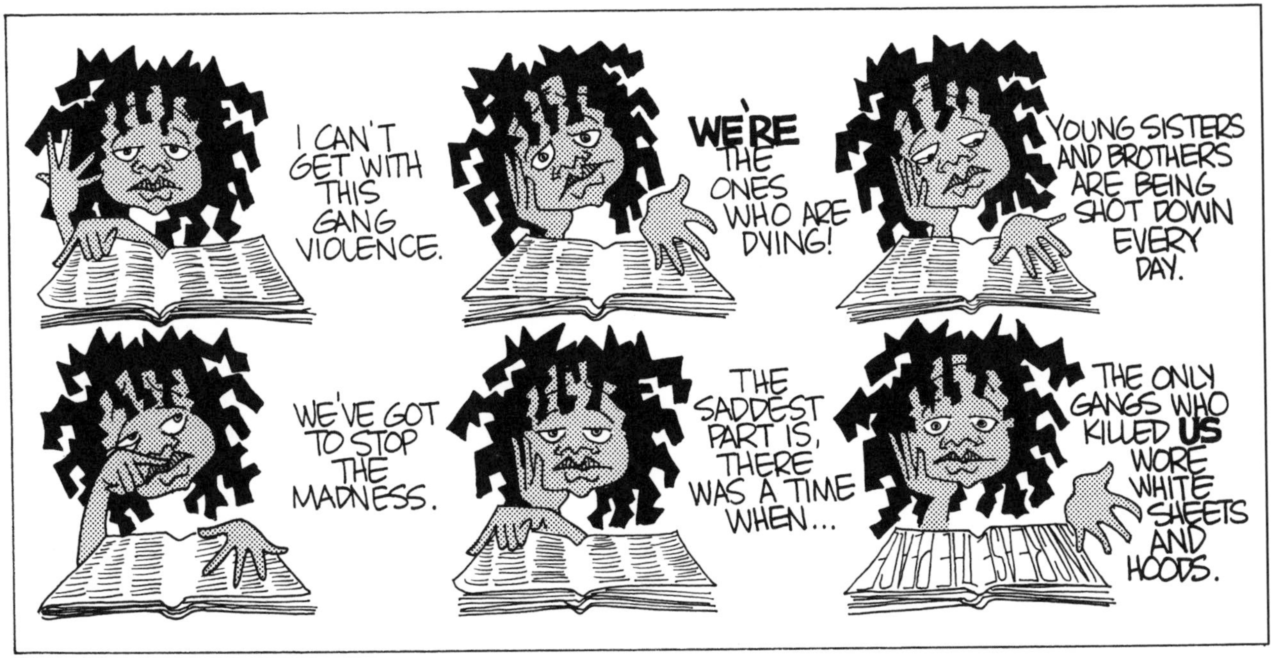

I CAN'T GET WITH THIS GANG VIOLENCE.
WE'RE THE ONES WHO ARE DYING!
YOUNG SISTERS AND BROTHERS ARE BEING SHOT DOWN EVERY DAY.
WE'VE GOT TO STOP THE MADNESS.
THE SADDEST PART IS, THERE WAS A TIME WHEN...
THE ONLY GANGS WHO KILLED US WORE WHITE SHEETS AND HOODS.

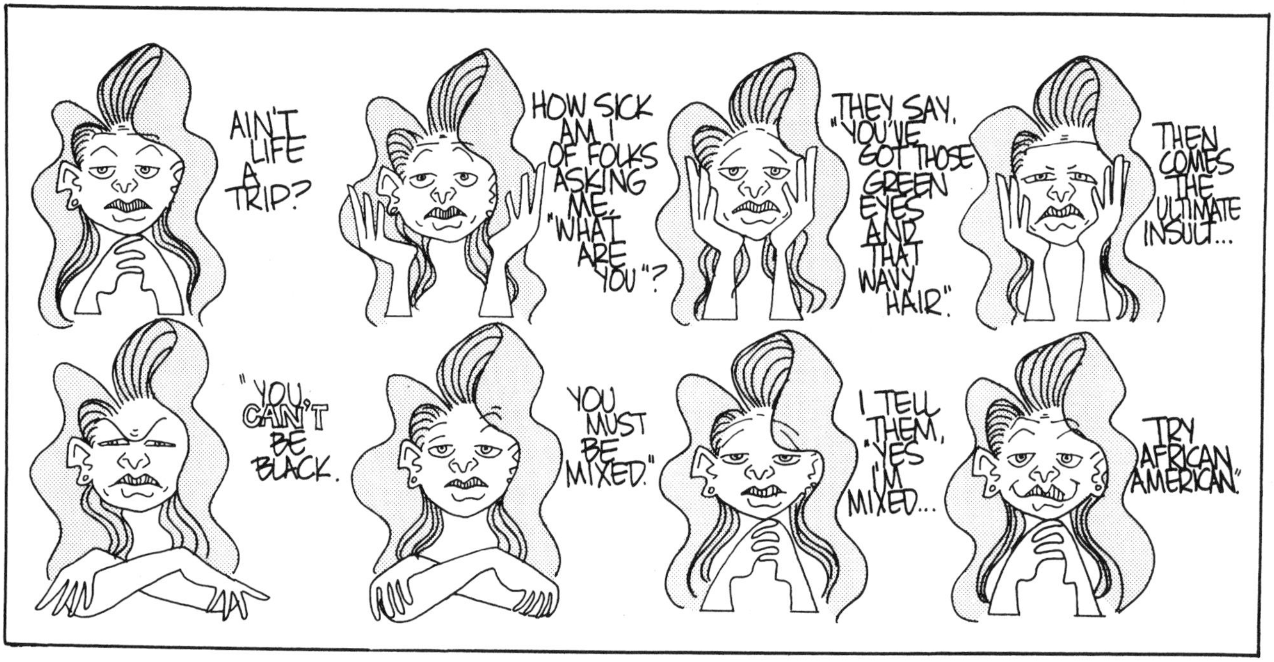
AIN'T LIFE A TRIP?
HOW SICK AM I OF FOLKS ASKING ME, "WHAT ARE YOU"?
THEY SAY, "YOU'VE GOT THOSE GREEN EYES AND THAT WAVY HAIR".
THEN COMES THE ULTIMATE INSULT...
"YOU CAN'T BE BLACK.
YOU MUST BE MIXED."
I TELL THEM, "YES I'M MIXED...
TRY AFRICAN AMERICAN."

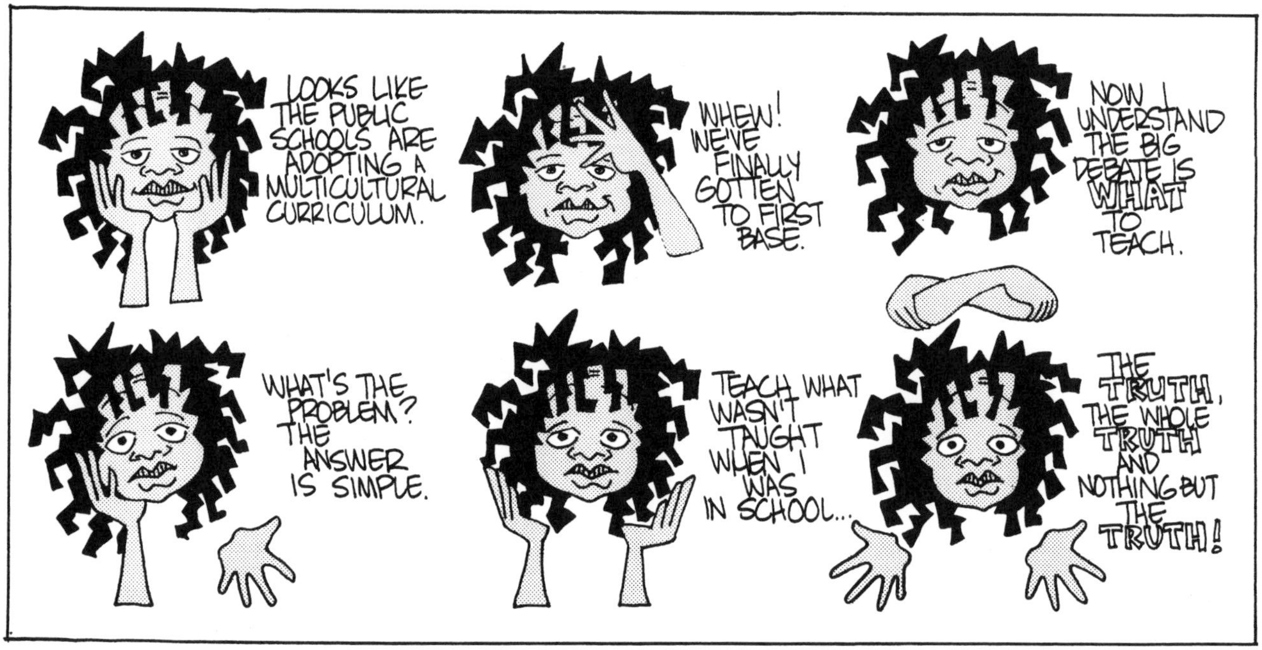
LOOKS LIKE THE PUBLIC SCHOOLS ARE ADOPTING A MULTICULTURAL CURRICULUM.
WHEW! WE'VE FINALLY GOTTEN TO FIRST BASE.
NOW I UNDERSTAND THE BIG DEBATE IS WHAT TO TEACH.
WHAT'S THE PROBLEM? THE ANSWER IS SIMPLE.
TEACH WHAT WASN'T TAUGHT WHEN I WAS IN SCHOOL...
THE TRUTH, THE WHOLE TRUTH AND NOTHING BUT THE TRUTH!

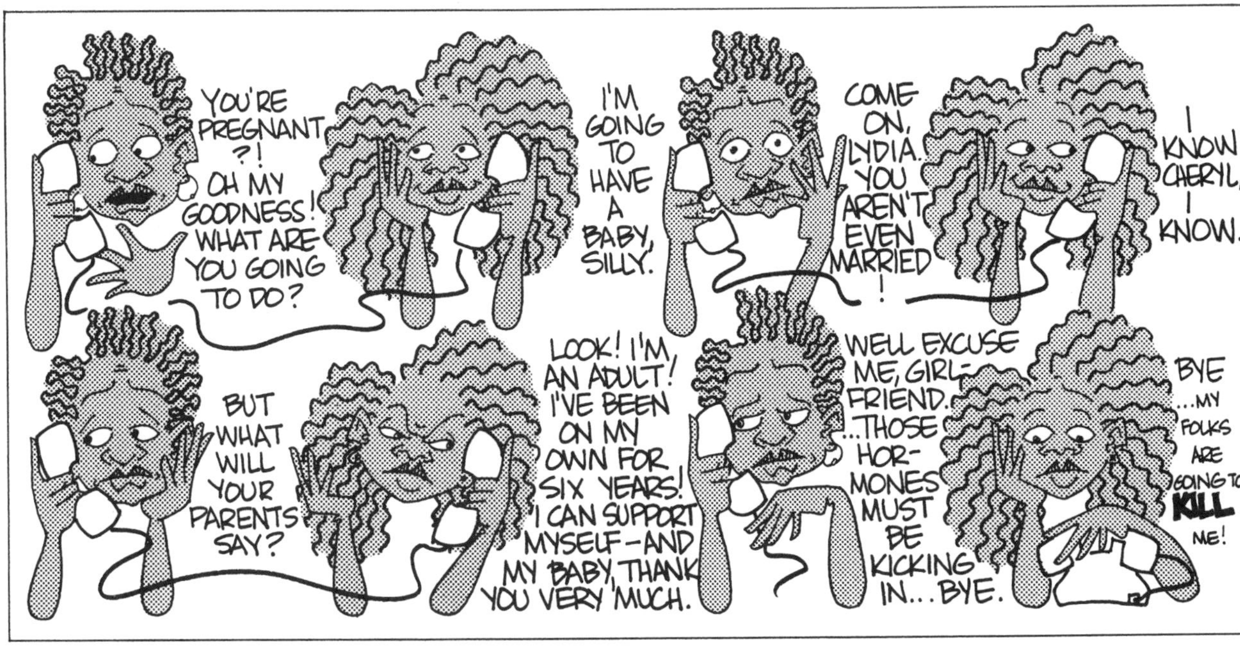
YOU'RE PREGNANT ?! OH MY GOODNESS! WHAT ARE YOU GOING TO DO?
I'M GOING TO HAVE A BABY, SILLY.
COME ON, LYDIA. YOU AREN'T EVEN MARRIED!
I KNOW CHERYL, I KNOW.
BUT WHAT WILL YOUR PARENTS SAY?
LOOK! I'M AN ADULT! I'VE BEEN ON MY OWN FOR SIX YEARS! I CAN SUPPORT MYSELF—AND MY BABY, THANK YOU VERY MUCH.
WELL EXCUSE ME, GIRLFRIEND. ...THOSE HORMONES MUST BE KICKING IN... BYE.
BYE ...MY FOLKS ARE GOING TO KILL ME!

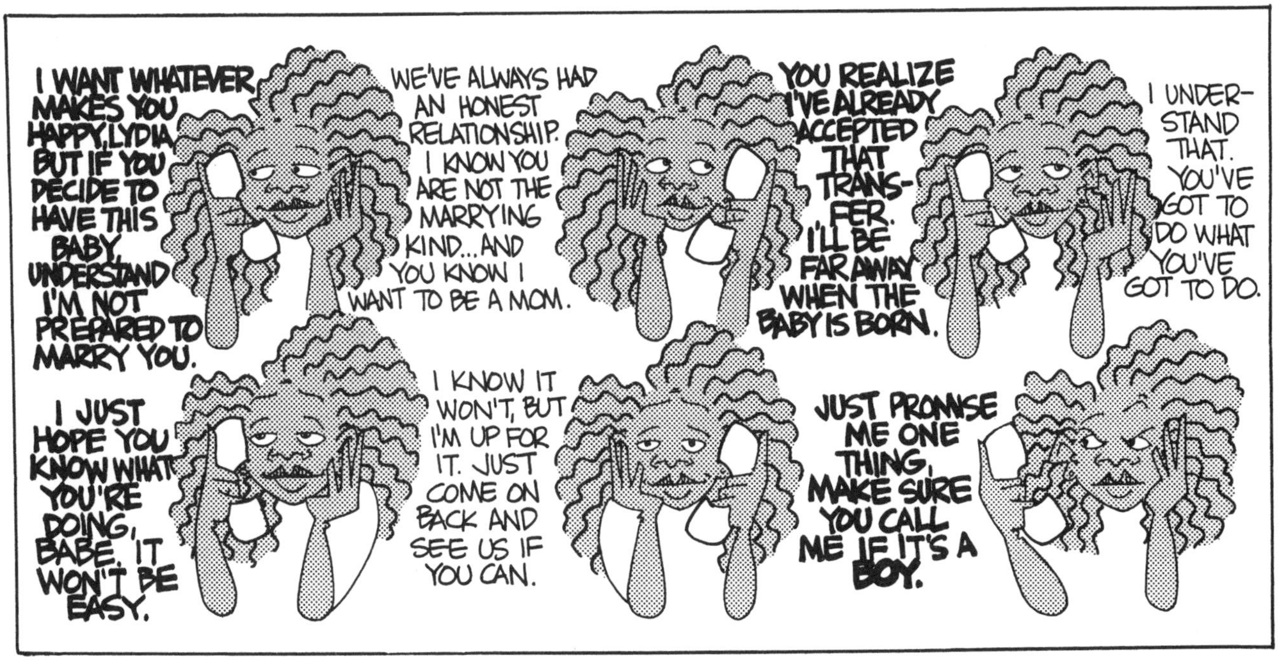
I WANT WHATEVER MAKES YOU HAPPY, LYDIA. BUT IF YOU DECIDE TO HAVE THIS BABY, UNDERSTAND I'M NOT PREPARED TO MARRY YOU.
WE'VE ALWAYS HAD AN HONEST RELATIONSHIP. I KNOW YOU ARE NOT THE MARRYING KIND... AND YOU KNOW I WANT TO BE A MOM.
YOU REALIZE I'VE ALREADY ACCEPTED THAT TRANSFER. I'LL BE FAR AWAY WHEN THE BABY IS BORN.
I UNDERSTAND THAT. YOU'VE GOT TO DO WHAT YOU'VE GOT TO DO.
I JUST HOPE YOU KNOW WHAT YOU'RE DOING, BABE. IT WON'T BE EASY.
I KNOW IT WON'T, BUT I'M UP FOR IT. JUST COME ON BACK AND SEE US IF YOU CAN.
JUST PROMISE ME ONE THING, MAKE SURE YOU CALL ME IF IT'S A BOY.

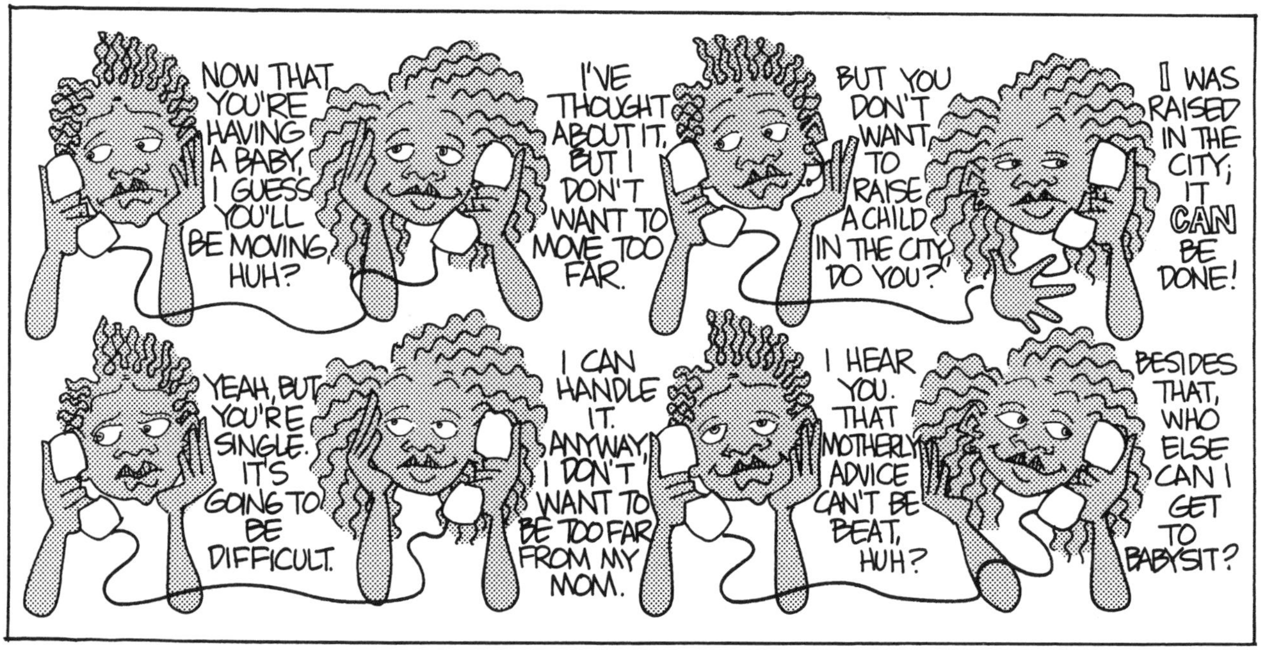
NOW THAT YOU'RE HAVING A BABY, I GUESS YOU'LL BE MOVING, HUH?
I'VE THOUGHT ABOUT IT, BUT I DON'T WANT TO MOVE TOO FAR.
BUT YOU DON'T WANT TO RAISE A CHILD IN THE CITY, DO YOU?
I WAS RAISED IN THE CITY; IT CAN BE DONE!
YEAH, BUT YOU'RE SINGLE. IT'S GOING TO BE DIFFICULT.
I CAN HANDLE IT. ANYWAY, I DON'T WANT TO BE TOO FAR FROM MY MOM.
I HEAR YOU. THAT MOTHERLY ADVICE CAN'T BE BEAT, HUH?
BESIDES THAT, WHO ELSE CAN I GET TO BABYSIT?

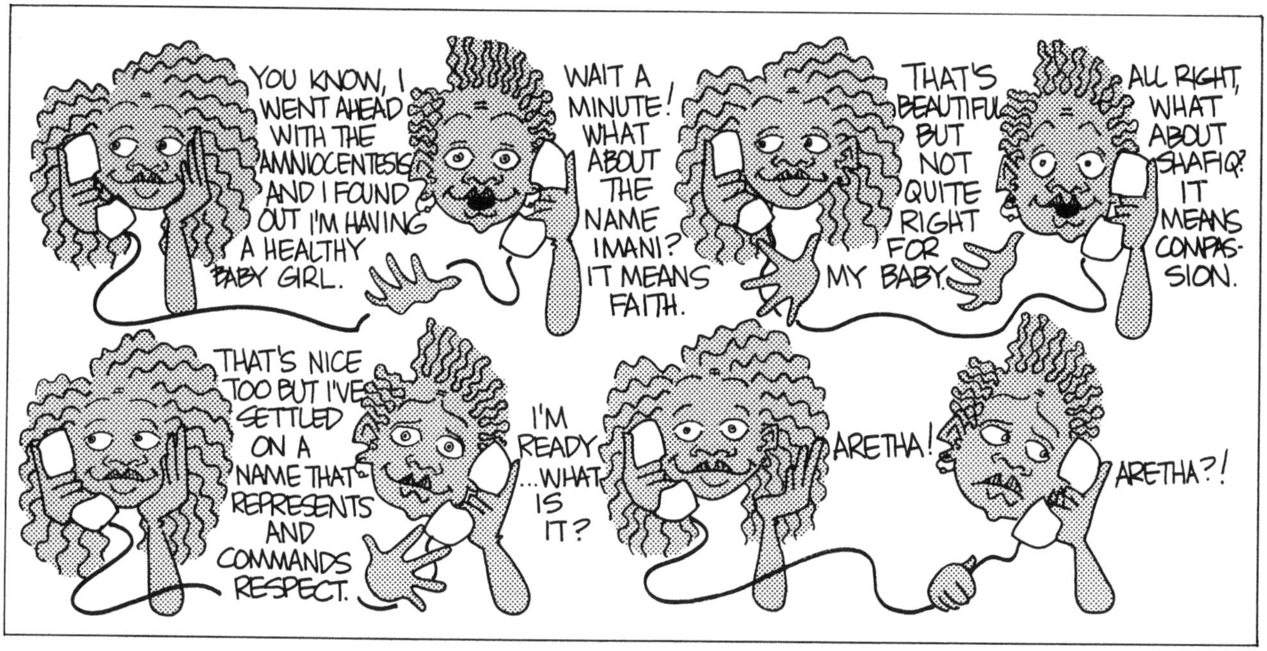
YOU KNOW, I WENT AHEAD WITH THE AMNIOCENTESIS AND I FOUND OUT I'M HAVING A HEALTHY BABY GIRL.
WAIT A MINUTE! WHAT ABOUT THE NAME IMANI? IT MEANS FAITH.
THAT'S BEAUTIFUL BUT NOT QUITE RIGHT FOR MY BABY.
ALL RIGHT, WHAT ABOUT SHAFIQ? IT MEANS COMPAS-SION.
THAT'S NICE TOO BUT I'VE SETTLED ON A NAME THAT REPRESENTS AND COMMANDS RESPECT.
I'M READY ...WHAT IS IT?
ARETHA!
ARETHA?!

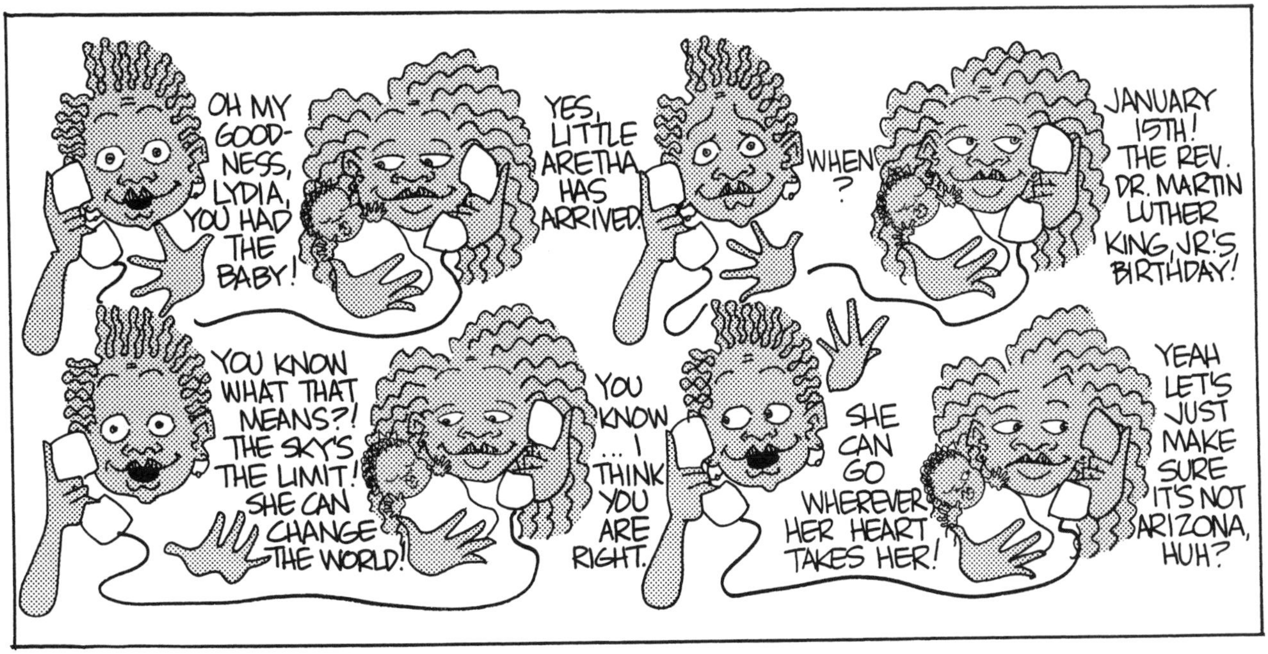
OH MY GOODNESS, LYDIA, YOU HAD THE BABY!
YES, LITTLE ARETHA HAS ARRIVED.
WHEN?
JANUARY 15TH! THE REV. DR. MARTIN LUTHER KING, JR.'S BIRTHDAY!
YOU KNOW WHAT THAT MEANS?! THE SKY'S THE LIMIT! SHE CAN CHANGE THE WORLD!
YOU KNOW ... I THINK YOU ARE RIGHT.
SHE CAN GO WHEREVER HER HEART TAKES HER!
YEAH LET'S JUST MAKE SURE IT'S NOT ARIZONA, HUH?

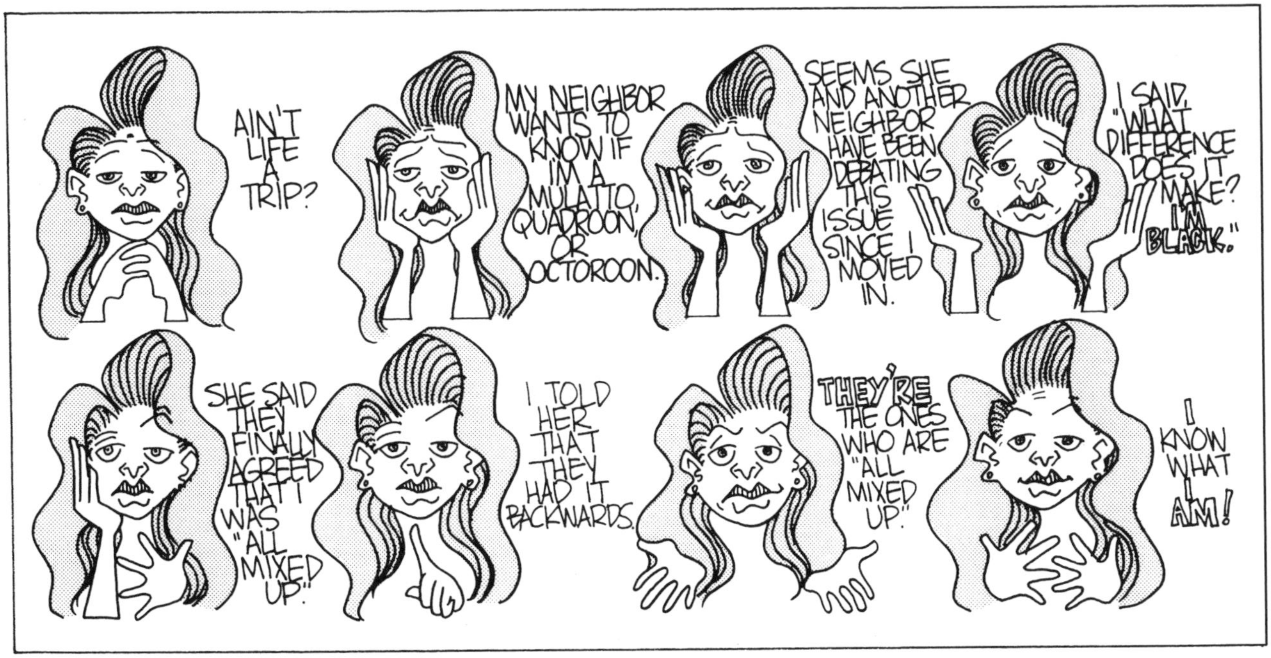
AIN'T LIFE A TRIP?
MY NEIGHBOR WANTS TO KNOW IF I'M A MULATTO, QUADROON, OR OCTOROON.
SEEMS SHE AND ANOTHER NEIGHBOR HAVE BEEN DEBATING THIS ISSUE SINCE I MOVED IN.
I SAID, "WHAT DIFFERENCE DOES IT MAKE? I'M BLACK."
SHE SAID THEY FINALLY AGREED THAT I WAS "ALL MIXED UP."
I TOLD HER THAT THEY HAD IT BACKWARDS.
THEY'RE THE ONES WHO ARE "ALL MIXED UP."
I KNOW WHAT I AM!

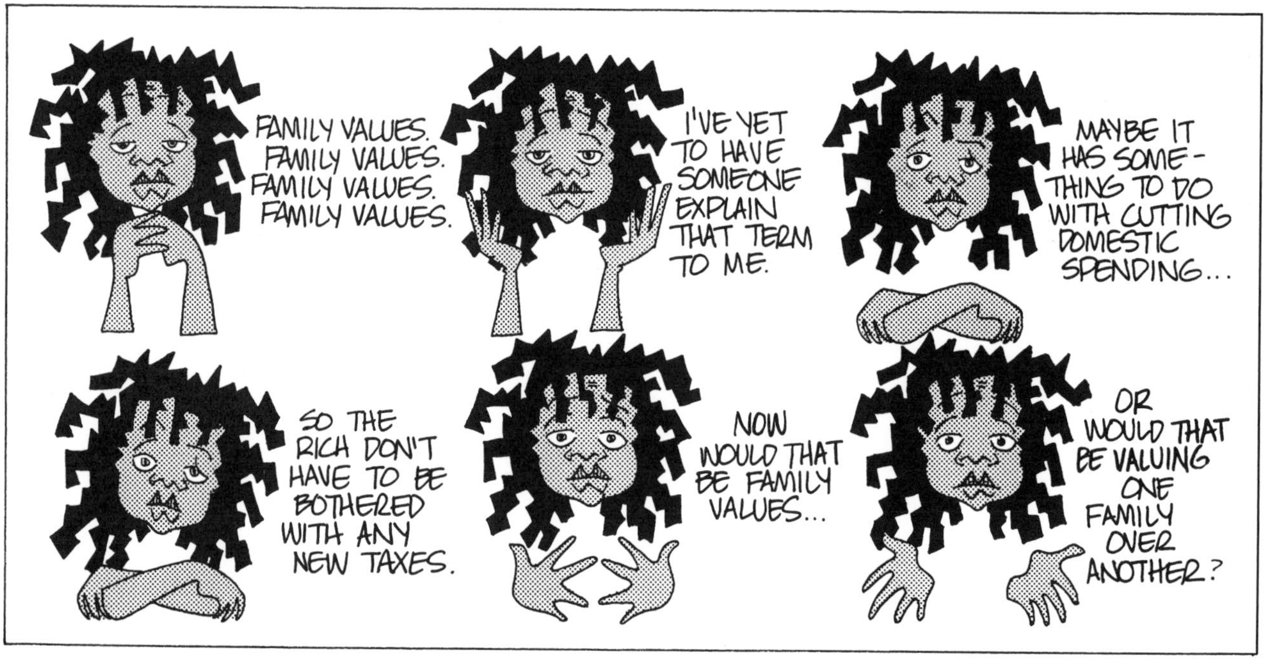
FAMILY VALUES. FAMILY VALUES. FAMILY VALUES. FAMILY VALUES.
I'VE YET TO HAVE SOMEONE EXPLAIN THAT TERM TO ME.
MAYBE IT HAS SOME-THING TO DO WITH CUTTING DOMESTIC SPENDING...
SO THE RICH DON'T HAVE TO BE BOTHERED WITH ANY NEW TAXES.
NOW WOULD THAT BE FAMILY VALUES...
OR WOULD THAT BE VALUING ONE FAMILY OVER ANOTHER?

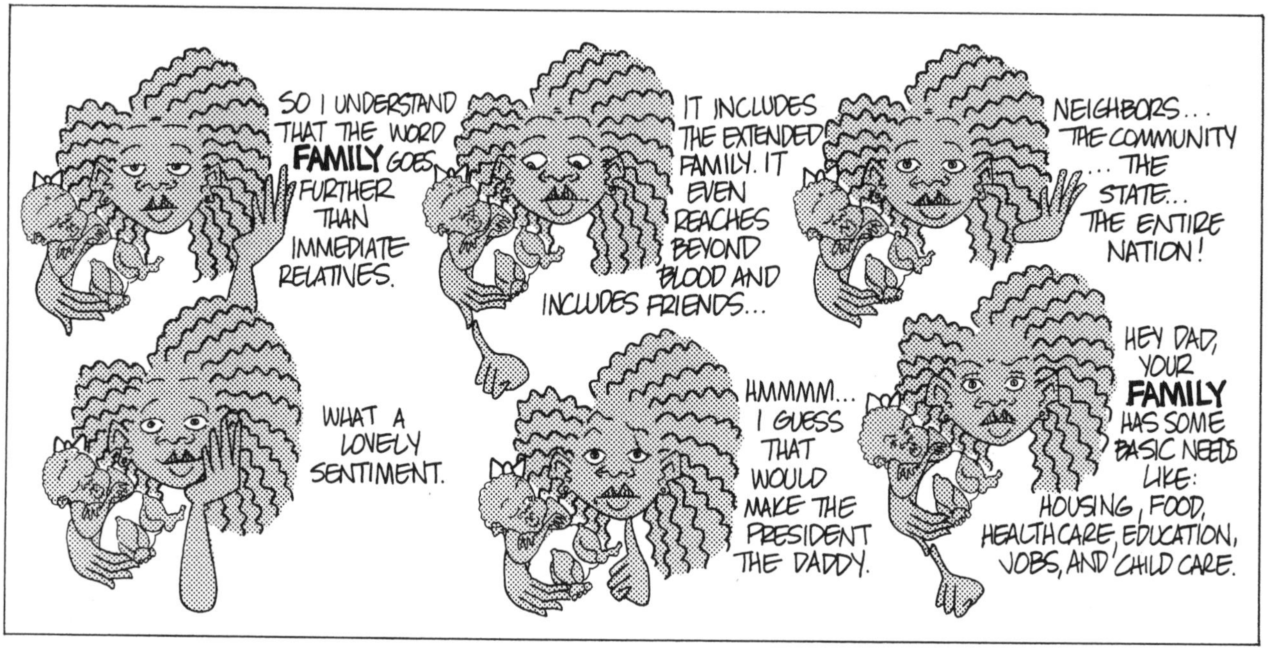
SO I UNDERSTAND THAT THE WORD FAMILY GOES FURTHER THAN IMMEDIATE RELATIVES.
IT INCLUDES THE EXTENDED FAMILY. IT EVEN REACHES BEYOND BLOOD AND INCLUDES FRIENDS...
NEIGHBORS... THE COMMUNITY ... THE STATE... THE ENTIRE NATION!
WHAT A LOVELY SENTIMENT.
HMMMM... I GUESS THAT WOULD MAKE THE PRESIDENT THE DADDY.
HEY DAD, YOUR FAMILY HAS SOME BASIC NEEDS LIKE: HOUSING, FOOD, HEALTHCARE, EDUCATION, JOBS, AND CHILD CARE.

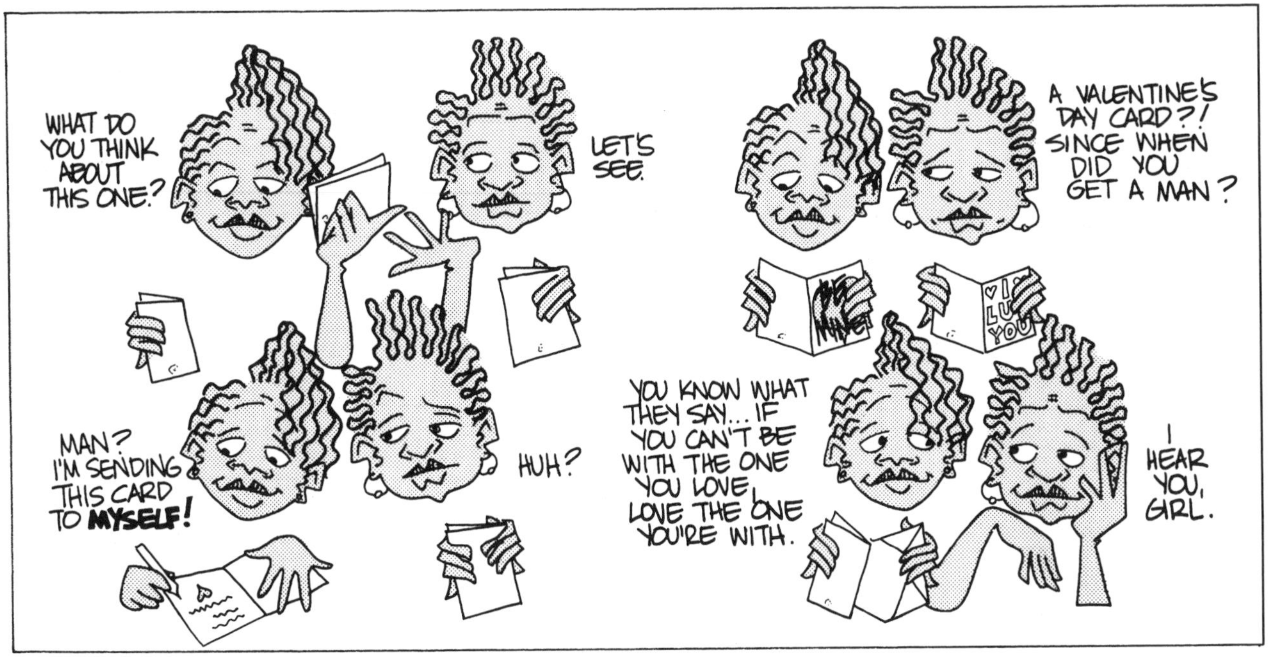
WHAT DO YOU THINK ABOUT THIS ONE?
LET'S SEE.
MAN? I'M SENDING THIS CARD TO **MYSELF!**
HUH?
A VALENTINE'S DAY CARD?! SINCE WHEN DID YOU GET A MAN?
YOU KNOW WHAT THEY SAY... IF YOU CAN'T BE WITH THE ONE YOU LOVE, LOVE THE ONE YOU'RE WITH.
I HEAR YOU, GIRL.

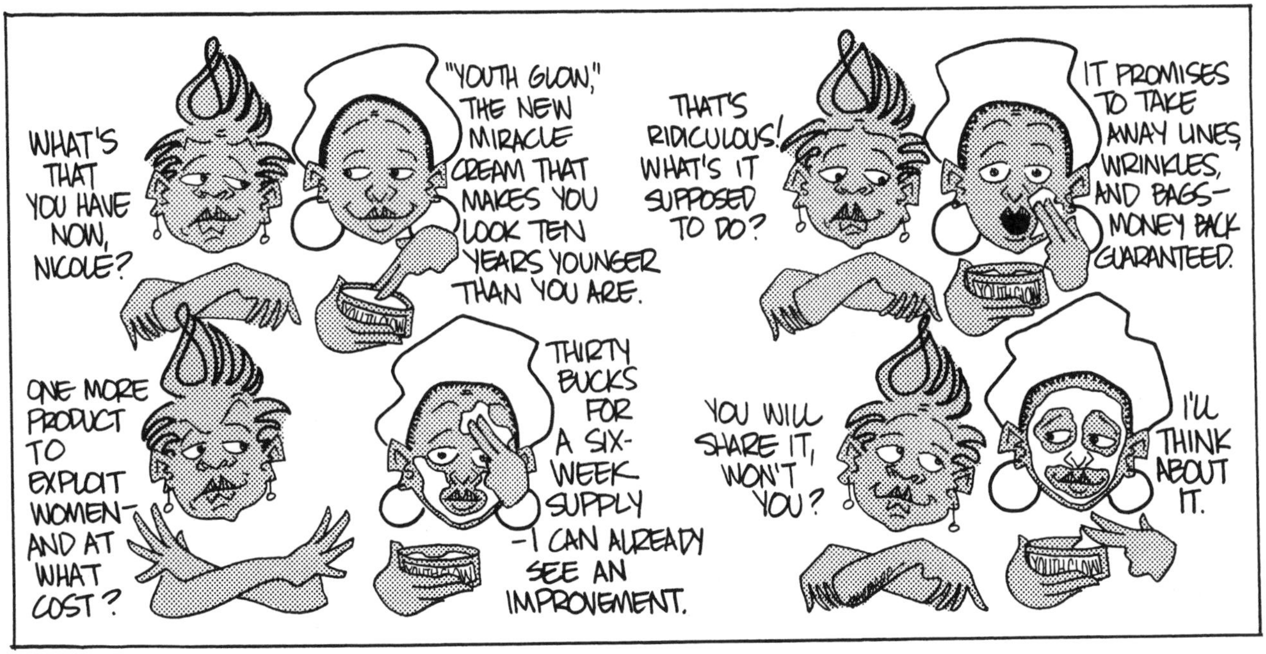
WHAT'S THAT YOU HAVE NOW, NICOLE?
"YOUTH GLOW," THE NEW MIRACLE CREAM THAT MAKES YOU LOOK TEN YEARS YOUNGER THAN YOU ARE.
THAT'S RIDICULOUS! WHAT'S IT SUPPOSED TO DO?
IT PROMISES TO TAKE AWAY LINES, WRINKLES, AND BAGS— MONEY BACK GUARANTEED.
ONE MORE PRODUCT TO EXPLOIT WOMEN— AND AT WHAT COST?
THIRTY BUCKS FOR A SIX-WEEK SUPPLY —I CAN ALREADY SEE AN IMPROVEMENT.
YOU WILL SHARE IT, WON'T YOU?
I'LL THINK ABOUT IT.

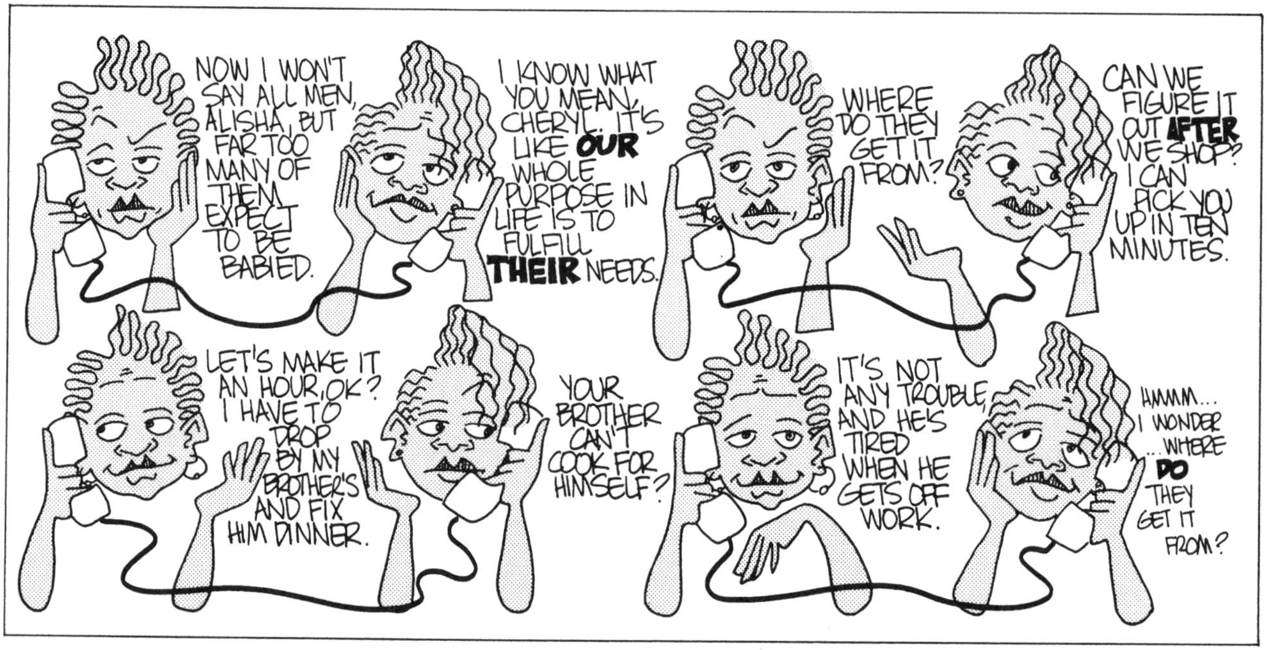
NOW I WON'T SAY ALL MEN, ALISHA, BUT FAR TOO MANY OF THEM EXPECT TO BE BABIED.
I KNOW WHAT YOU MEAN, CHERYL. IT'S LIKE **OUR** WHOLE PURPOSE IN LIFE IS TO FULFILL **THEIR** NEEDS.
WHERE DO THEY GET IT FROM?
CAN WE FIGURE IT OUT **AFTER** WE SHOP? I CAN PICK YOU UP IN TEN MINUTES.
LET'S MAKE IT AN HOUR, OK? I HAVE TO DROP BY MY BROTHER'S AND FIX HIM DINNER.
YOUR BROTHER CAN'T COOK FOR HIMSELF?
IT'S NOT ANY TROUBLE, AND HE'S TIRED WHEN HE GETS OFF WORK.
HMMM... I WONDER ...WHERE **DO** THEY GET IT FROM?

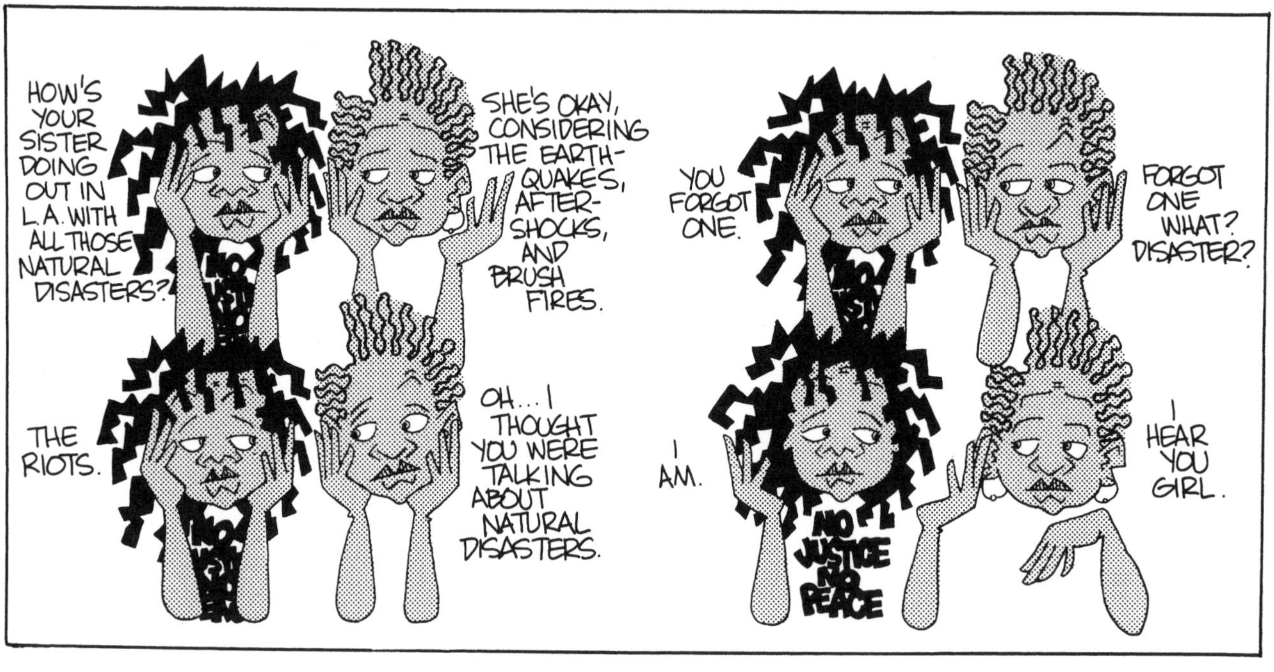
HOW'S YOUR SISTER DOING OUT IN L.A. WITH ALL THOSE NATURAL DISASTERS?
SHE'S OKAY, CONSIDERING THE EARTH-QUAKES, AFTER-SHOCKS, AND BRUSH FIRES.
THE RIOTS.
OH... I THOUGHT YOU WERE TALKING ABOUT NATURAL DISASTERS.
YOU FORGOT ONE.
FORGOT ONE WHAT? DISASTER?
I AM.
I HEAR YOU GIRL.
NO JUSTICE NO PEACE

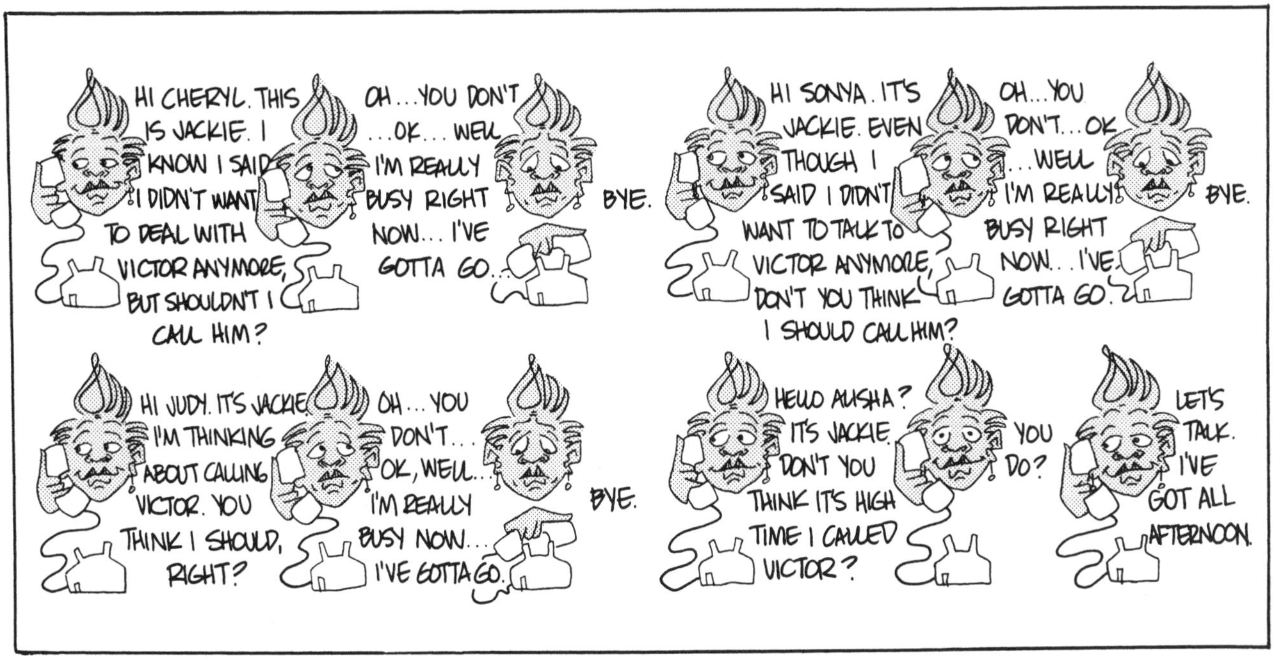
HI CHERYL. THIS IS JACKIE. I KNOW I SAID I DIDN'T WANT TO DEAL WITH VICTOR ANYMORE, BUT SHOULDN'T I CALL HIM?
OH... YOU DON'T ...OK... WELL I'M REALLY BUSY RIGHT NOW... I'VE GOTTA GO...
BYE.
HI SONYA. IT'S JACKIE. EVEN THOUGH I SAID I DIDN'T WANT TO TALK TO VICTOR ANYMORE, DON'T YOU THINK I SHOULD CALL HIM?
OH... YOU DON'T... OK ...WELL I'M REALLY BUSY RIGHT NOW... I'VE GOTTA GO.
BYE.
HI JUDY. IT'S JACKIE. I'M THINKING ABOUT CALLING VICTOR. YOU THINK I SHOULD, RIGHT?
OH... YOU DON'T... OK, WELL... I'M REALLY BUSY NOW... I'VE GOTTA GO.
BYE.
HELLO AUSHA? IT'S JACKIE. DON'T YOU THINK IT'S HIGH TIME I CALLED VICTOR?
YOU DO?
LET'S TALK. I'VE GOT ALL AFTERNOON.

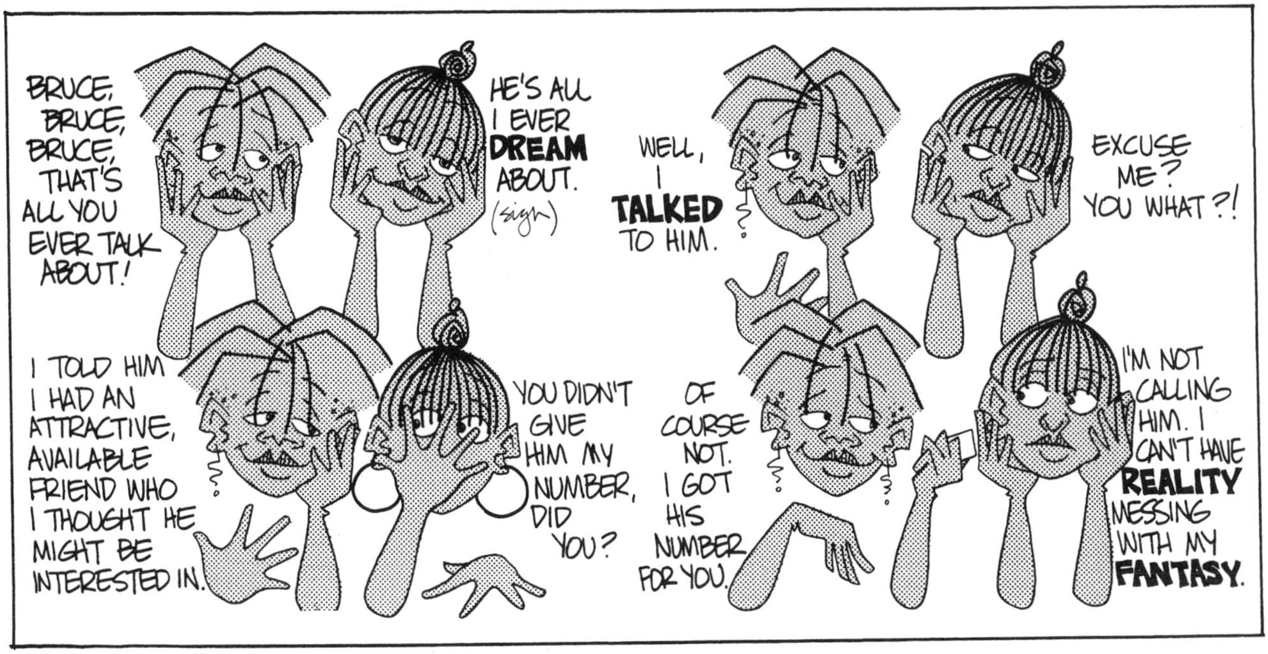
BRUCE, BRUCE, BRUCE, THAT'S ALL YOU EVER TALK ABOUT!
HE'S ALL I EVER DREAM ABOUT.
(sigh)
WELL, I TALKED TO HIM.
EXCUSE ME? YOU WHAT?!
I TOLD HIM I HAD AN ATTRACTIVE, AVAILABLE FRIEND WHO I THOUGHT HE MIGHT BE INTERESTED IN.
YOU DIDN'T GIVE HIM MY NUMBER, DID YOU?
OF COURSE NOT. I GOT HIS NUMBER FOR YOU.
I'M NOT CALLING HIM. I CAN'T HAVE REALITY MESSING WITH MY FANTASY.

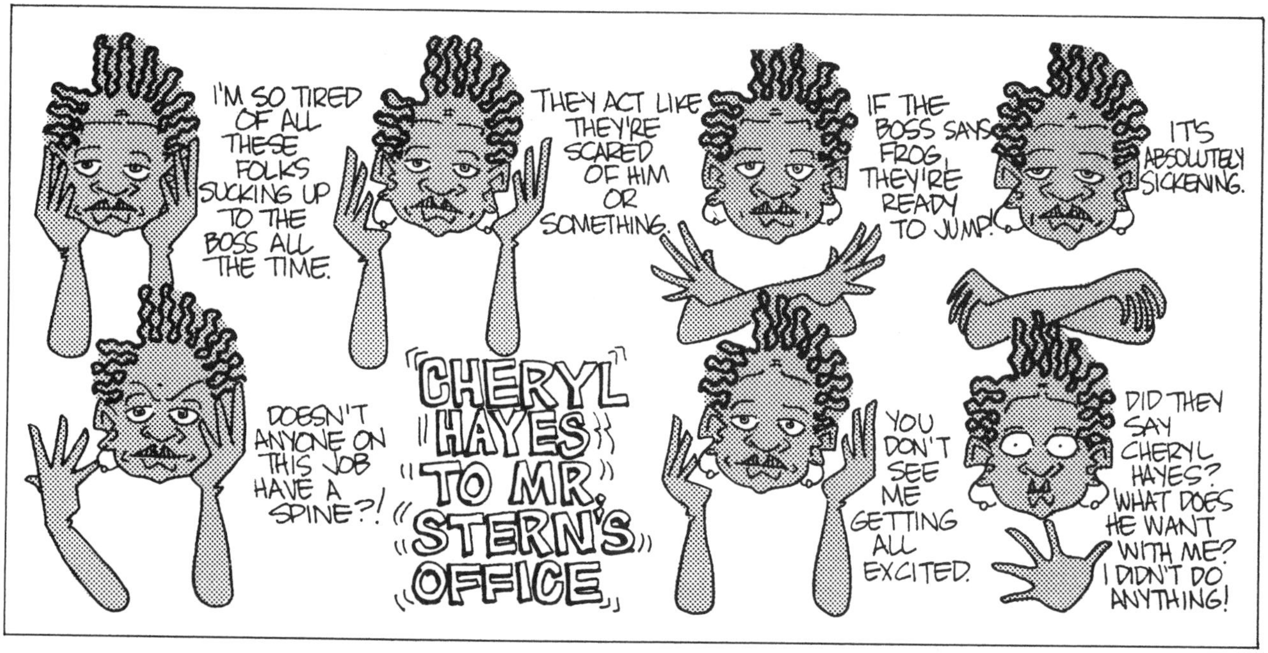
I'M SO TIRED OF ALL THESE FOLKS SUCKING UP TO THE BOSS ALL THE TIME.
THEY ACT LIKE THEY'RE SCARED OF HIM OR SOMETHING.
IF THE BOSS SAYS FROG, THEY'RE READY TO JUMP!
IT'S ABSOLUTELY SICKENING.
DOESN'T ANYONE ON THIS JOB HAVE A SPINE?!
"CHERYL HAYES TO MR. STERN'S OFFICE"
YOU DON'T SEE ME GETTING ALL EXCITED.
DID THEY SAY CHERYL HAYES? WHAT DOES HE WANT WITH ME? I DIDN'T DO ANYTHING!

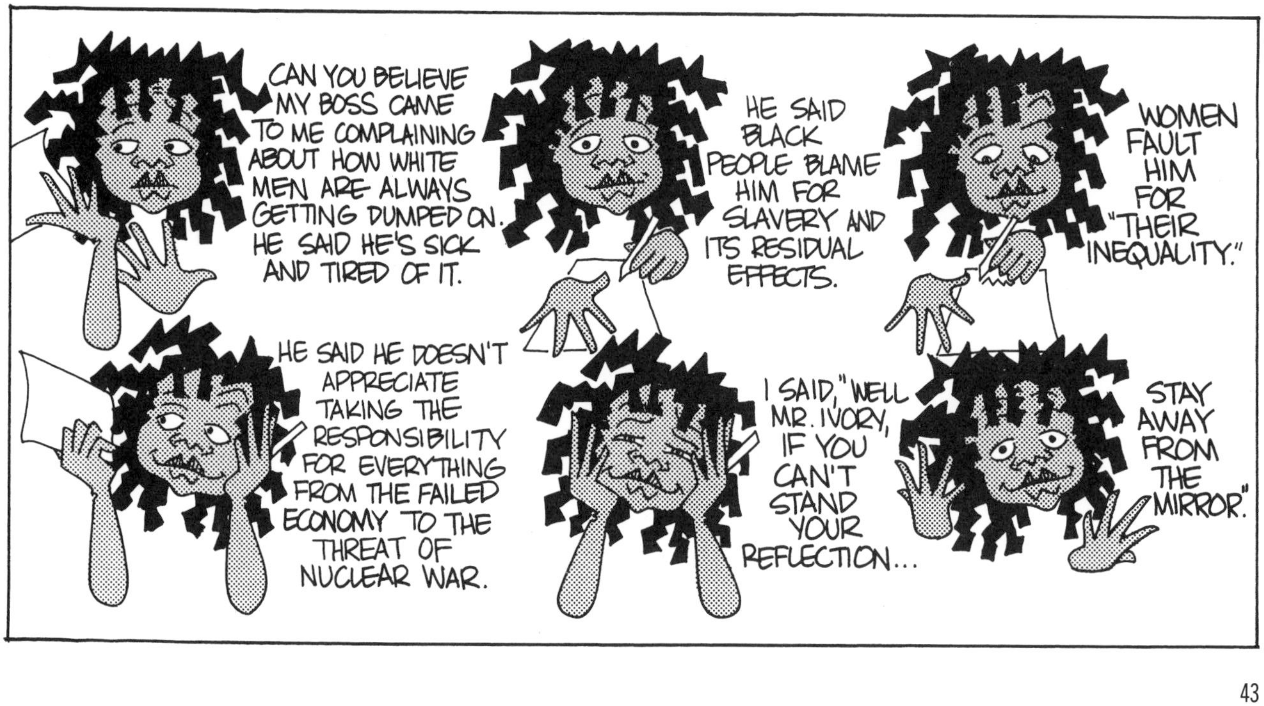
CAN YOU BELIEVE MY BOSS CAME TO ME COMPLAINING ABOUT HOW WHITE MEN ARE ALWAYS GETTING DUMPED ON. HE SAID HE'S SICK AND TIRED OF IT.
HE SAID BLACK PEOPLE BLAME HIM FOR SLAVERY AND ITS RESIDUAL EFFECTS.
WOMEN FAULT HIM FOR "THEIR INEQUALITY."
HE SAID HE DOESN'T APPRECIATE TAKING THE RESPONSIBILITY FOR EVERYTHING FROM THE FAILED ECONOMY TO THE THREAT OF NUCLEAR WAR.
I SAID, "WELL MR. IVORY, IF YOU CAN'T STAND YOUR REFLECTION...
STAY AWAY FROM THE MIRROR."

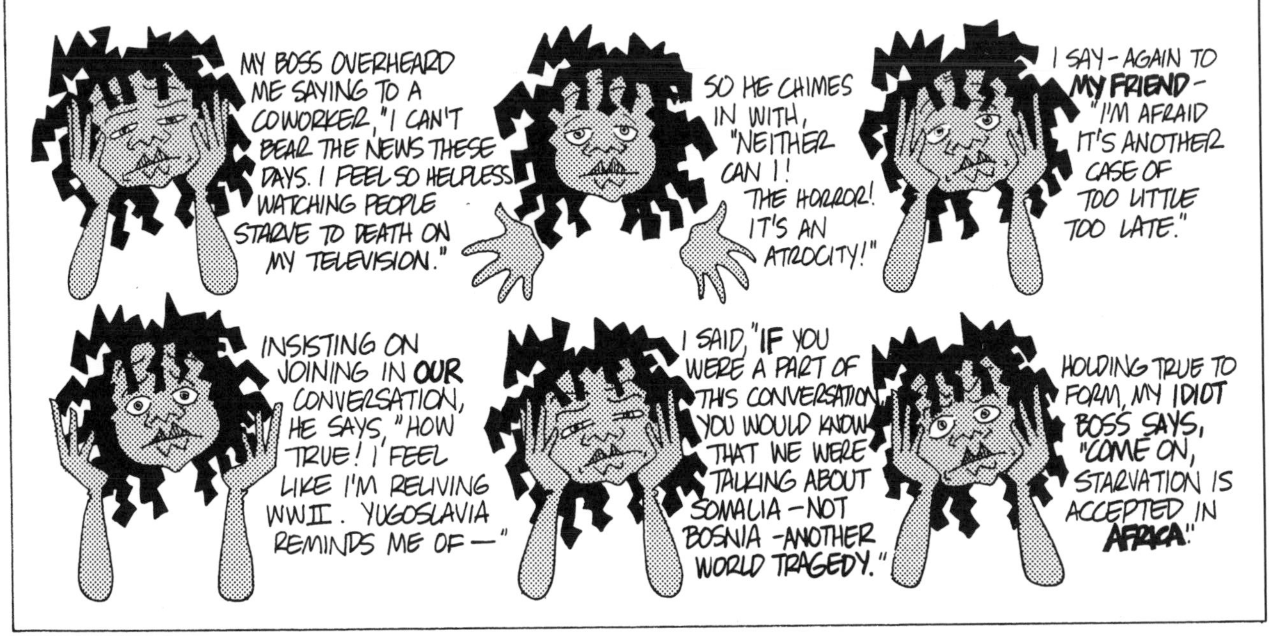
MY BOSS OVERHEARD ME SAYING TO A COWORKER, "I CAN'T BEAR THE NEWS THESE DAYS. I FEEL SO HELPLESS WATCHING PEOPLE STARVE TO DEATH ON MY TELEVISION."
SO HE CHIMES IN WITH, "NEITHER CAN I! THE HORROR! IT'S AN ATROCITY!"
I SAY - AGAIN TO MY FRIEND - "I'M AFRAID IT'S ANOTHER CASE OF TOO LITTLE TOO LATE."
INSISTING ON JOINING IN OUR CONVERSATION, HE SAYS, "HOW TRUE! I FEEL LIKE I'M RELIVING WWII. YUGOSLAVIA REMINDS ME OF —"
I SAID, "IF YOU WERE A PART OF THIS CONVERSATION YOU WOULD KNOW THAT WE WERE TALKING ABOUT SOMALIA - NOT BOSNIA - ANOTHER WORLD TRAGEDY."
HOLDING TRUE TO FORM, MY IDIOT BOSS SAYS, "COME ON, STARVATION IS ACCEPTED IN AFRICA."

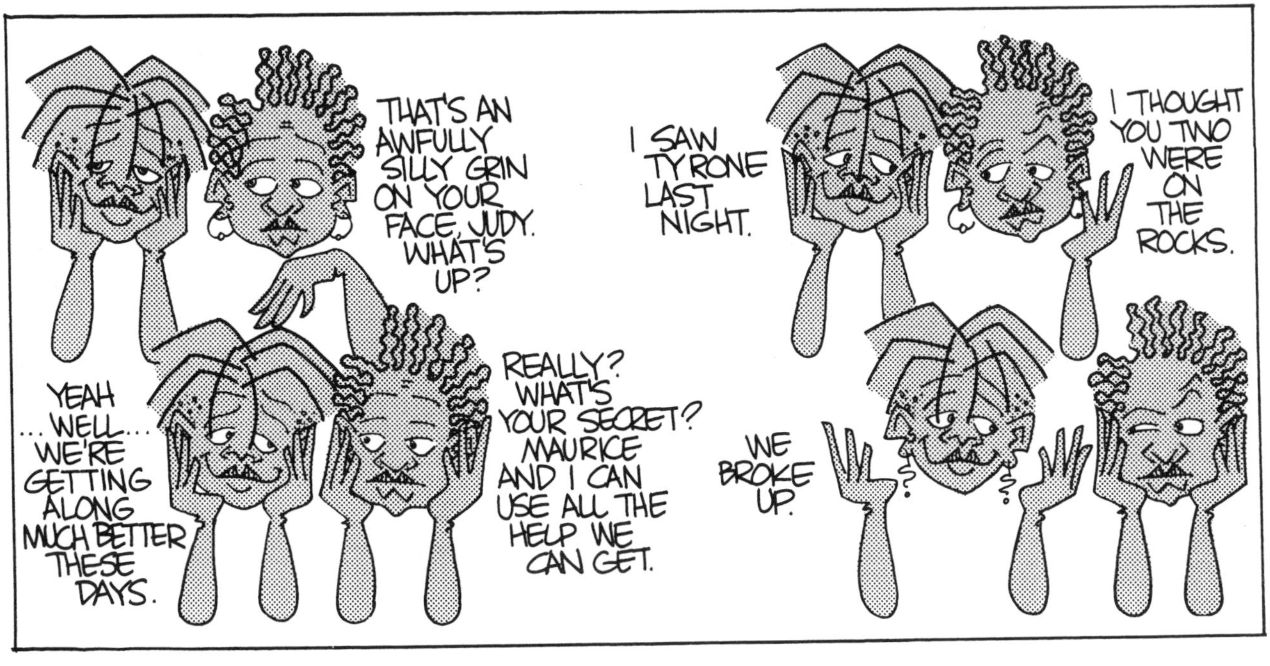
THAT'S AN AWFULLY SILLY GRIN ON YOUR FACE, JUDY. WHAT'S UP?
...YEAH WELL... WE'RE GETTING ALONG MUCH BETTER THESE DAYS.
REALLY? WHAT'S YOUR SECRET? MAURICE AND I CAN USE ALL THE HELP WE CAN GET.
I SAW TYRONE LAST NIGHT.
I THOUGHT YOU TWO WERE ON THE ROCKS.
WE BROKE UP.

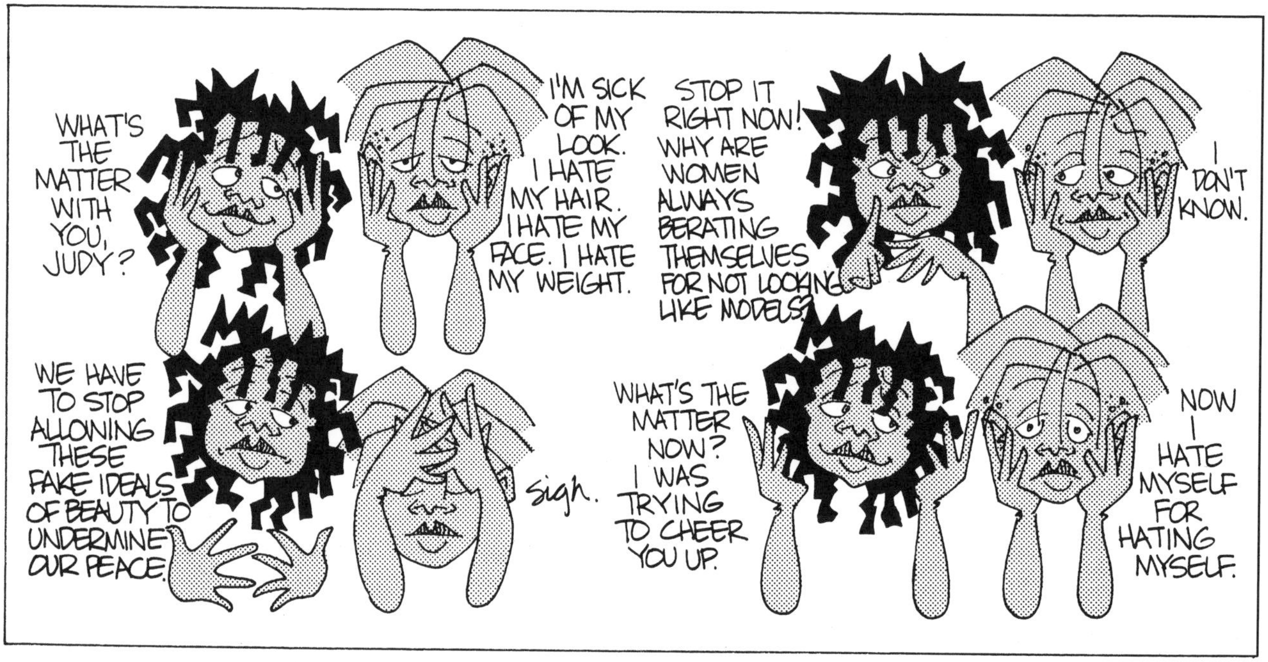
WHAT'S THE MATTER WITH YOU, JUDY?
I'M SICK OF MY LOOK. I HATE MY HAIR. I HATE MY FACE. I HATE MY WEIGHT.
STOP IT RIGHT NOW! WHY ARE WOMEN ALWAYS BERATING THEMSELVES FOR NOT LOOKING LIKE MODELS?
I DON'T KNOW.
WE HAVE TO STOP ALLOWING THESE FAKE IDEALS OF BEAUTY TO UNDERMINE OUR PEACE.
Sigh.
WHAT'S THE MATTER NOW? I WAS TRYING TO CHEER YOU UP.
NOW I HATE MYSELF FOR HATING MYSELF.

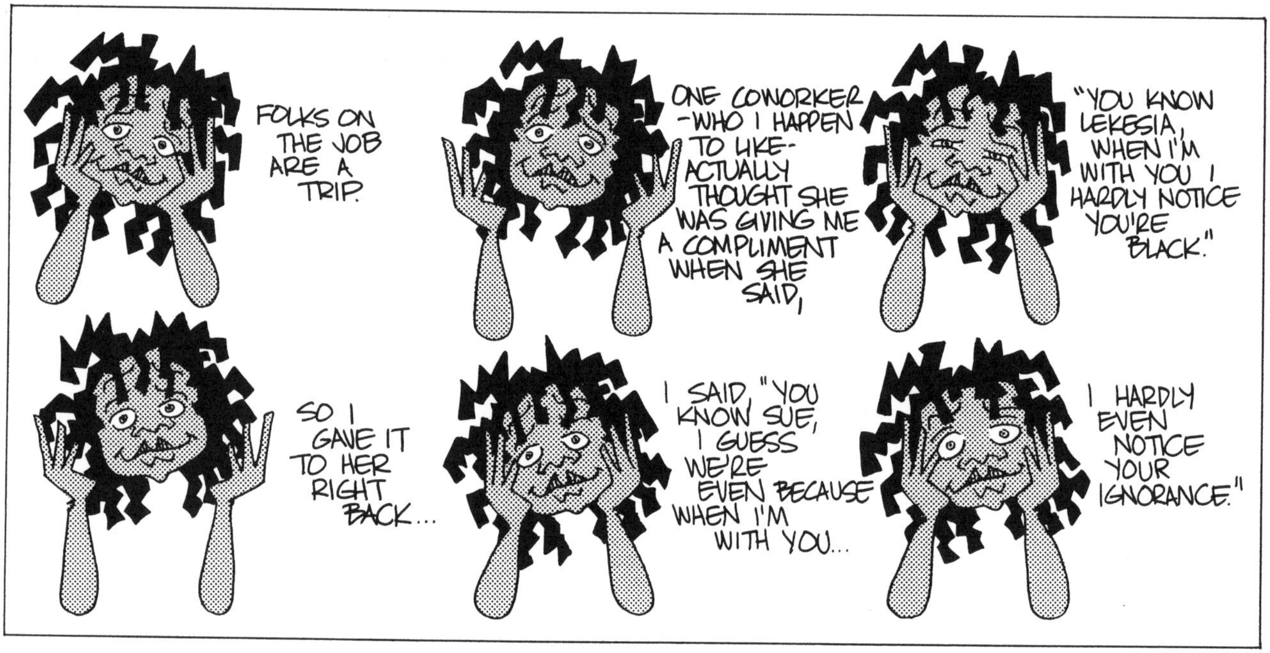
FOLKS ON THE JOB ARE A TRIP.
ONE COWORKER -WHO I HAPPEN TO LIKE- ACTUALLY THOUGHT SHE WAS GIVING ME A COMPLIMENT WHEN SHE SAID,
"YOU KNOW LEKESIA, WHEN I'M WITH YOU I HARDLY NOTICE YOU'RE BLACK."
SO I GAVE IT TO HER RIGHT BACK...
I SAID, "YOU KNOW SUE, I GUESS WE'RE EVEN BECAUSE WHEN I'M WITH YOU...
I HARDLY EVEN NOTICE YOUR IGNORANCE."

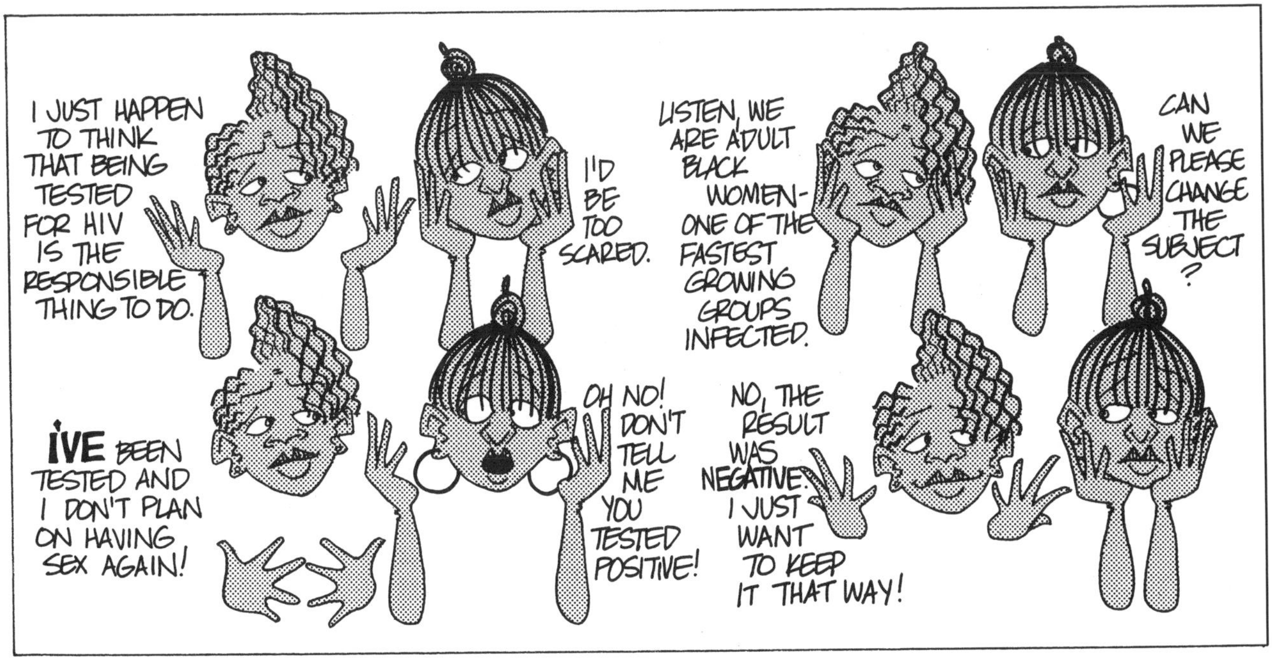
I JUST HAPPEN TO THINK THAT BEING TESTED FOR HIV IS THE RESPONSIBLE THING TO DO.
I'D BE TOO SCARED.
LISTEN, WE ARE ADULT BLACK WOMEN- ONE OF THE FASTEST GROWING GROUPS INFECTED.
CAN WE PLEASE CHANGE THE SUBJECT?
I'VE BEEN TESTED AND I DON'T PLAN ON HAVING SEX AGAIN!
OH NO! DON'T TELL ME YOU TESTED POSITIVE!
NO, THE RESULT WAS NEGATIVE. I JUST WANT TO KEEP IT THAT WAY!

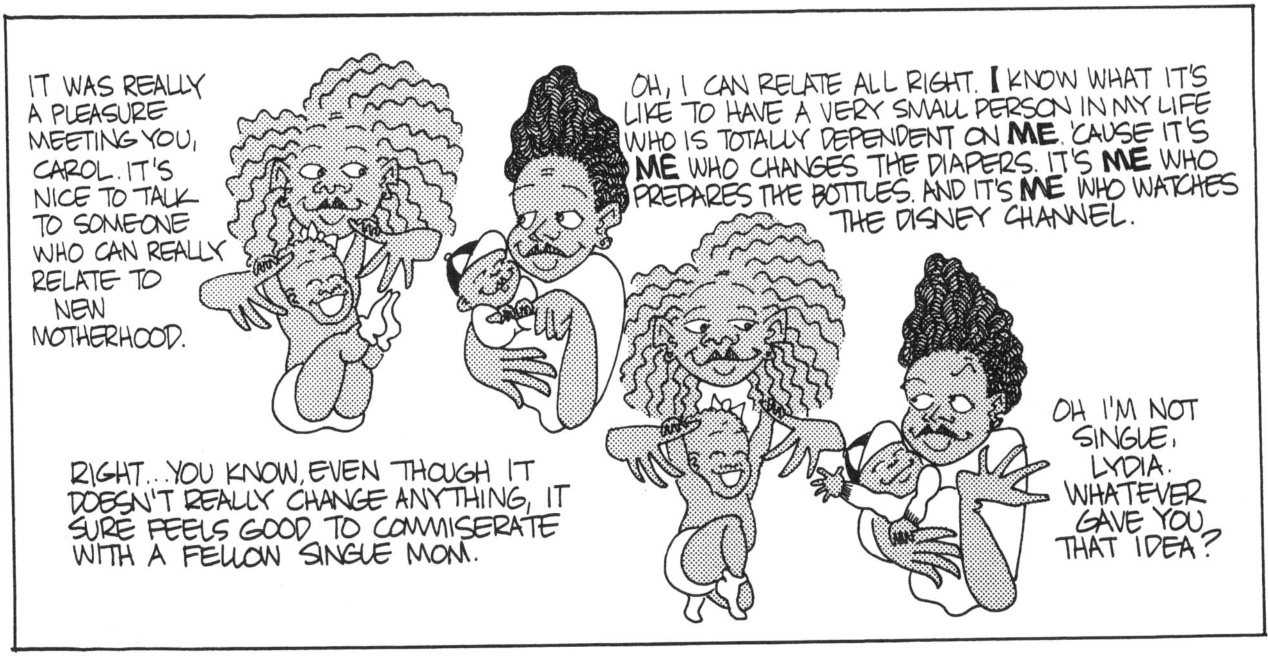
IT WAS REALLY A PLEASURE MEETING YOU, CAROL. IT'S NICE TO TALK TO SOMEONE WHO CAN REALLY RELATE TO NEW MOTHERHOOD.
OH, I CAN RELATE ALL RIGHT. I KNOW WHAT IT'S LIKE TO HAVE A VERY SMALL PERSON IN MY LIFE WHO IS TOTALLY DEPENDENT ON ME. 'CAUSE IT'S ME WHO CHANGES THE DIAPERS. IT'S ME WHO PREPARES THE BOTTLES. AND IT'S ME WHO WATCHES THE DISNEY CHANNEL.
RIGHT... YOU KNOW, EVEN THOUGH IT DOESN'T REALLY CHANGE ANYTHING, IT SURE FEELS GOOD TO COMMISERATE WITH A FELLOW SINGLE MOM.
OH I'M NOT SINGLE, LYDIA. WHATEVER GAVE YOU THAT IDEA?

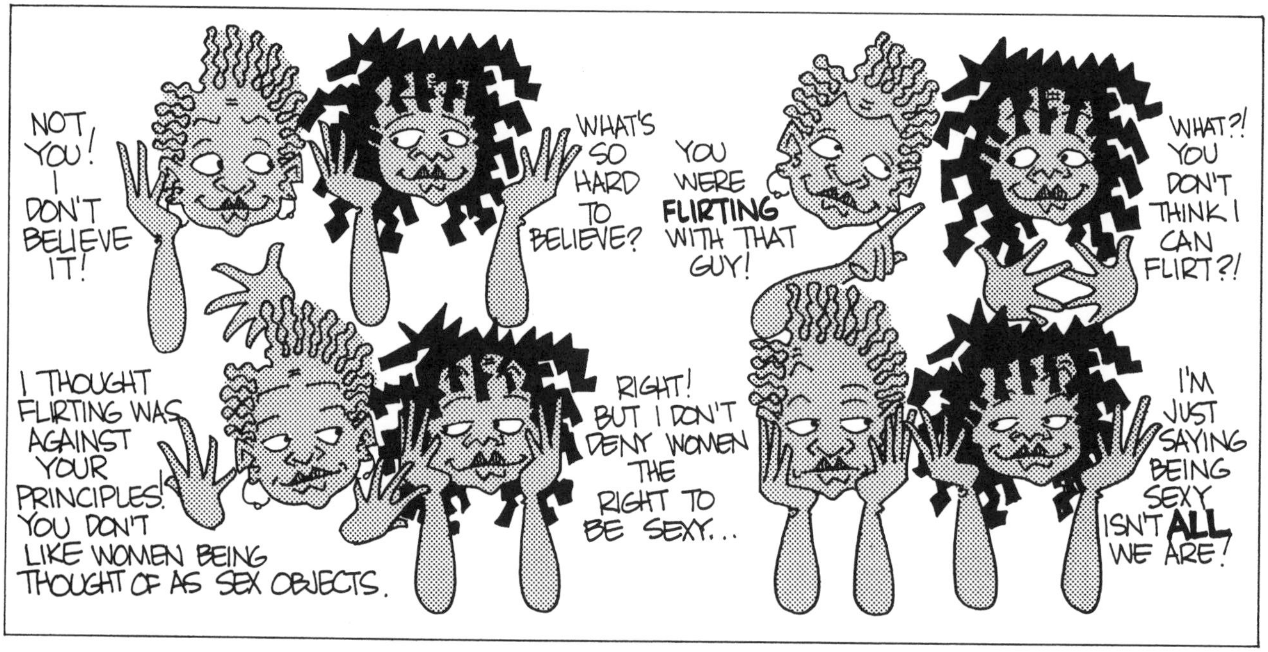
NOT YOU! I DON'T BELIEVE IT!
WHAT'S SO HARD TO BELIEVE?
I THOUGHT FLIRTING WAS AGAINST YOUR PRINCIPLES! YOU DON'T LIKE WOMEN BEING THOUGHT OF AS SEX OBJECTS.
RIGHT! BUT I DON'T DENY WOMEN THE RIGHT TO BE SEXY...
YOU WERE **FLIRTING** WITH THAT GUY!
WHAT?! YOU DON'T THINK I CAN FLIRT?!
I'M JUST SAYING BEING SEXY ISN'T **ALL** WE ARE!

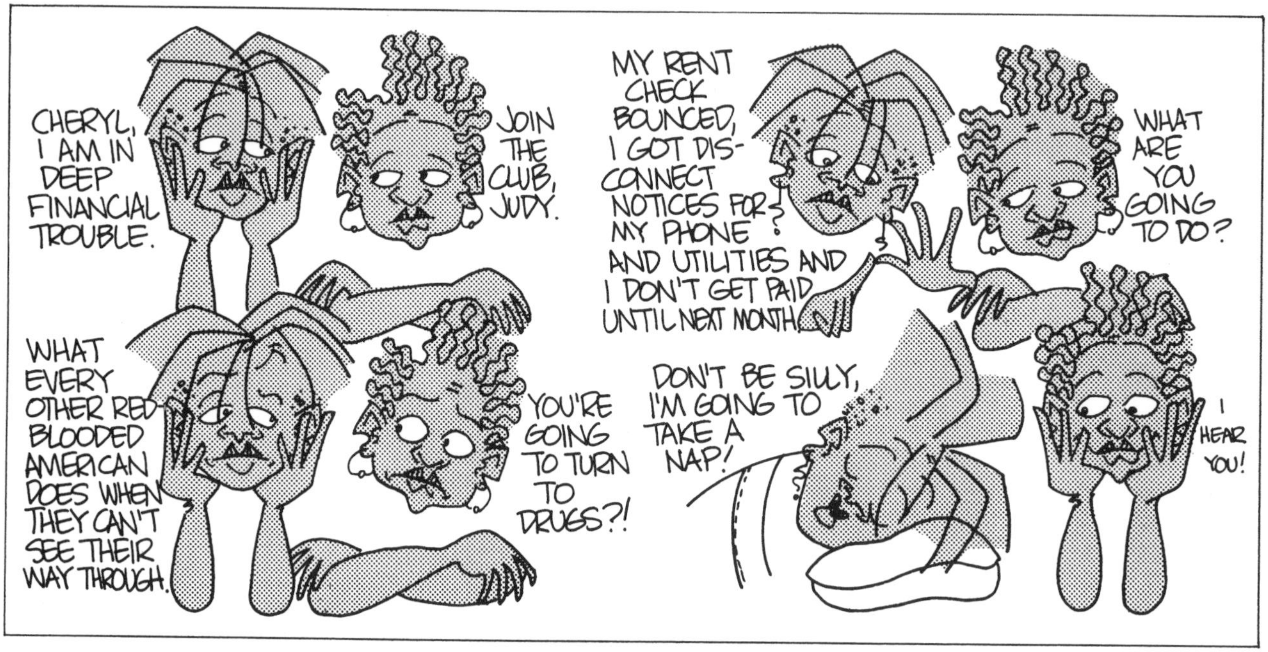
CHERYL, I AM IN DEEP FINANCIAL TROUBLE.
JOIN THE CLUB, JUDY.
WHAT EVERY OTHER RED-BLOODED AMERICAN DOES WHEN THEY CAN'T SEE THEIR WAY THROUGH.
YOU'RE GOING TO TURN TO DRUGS?!
MY RENT CHECK BOUNCED, I GOT DIS-CONNECT NOTICES FOR MY PHONE AND UTILITIES AND I DON'T GET PAID UNTIL NEXT MONTH.
WHAT ARE YOU GOING TO DO?
DON'T BE SILLY, I'M GOING TO TAKE A NAP!
I HEAR YOU!

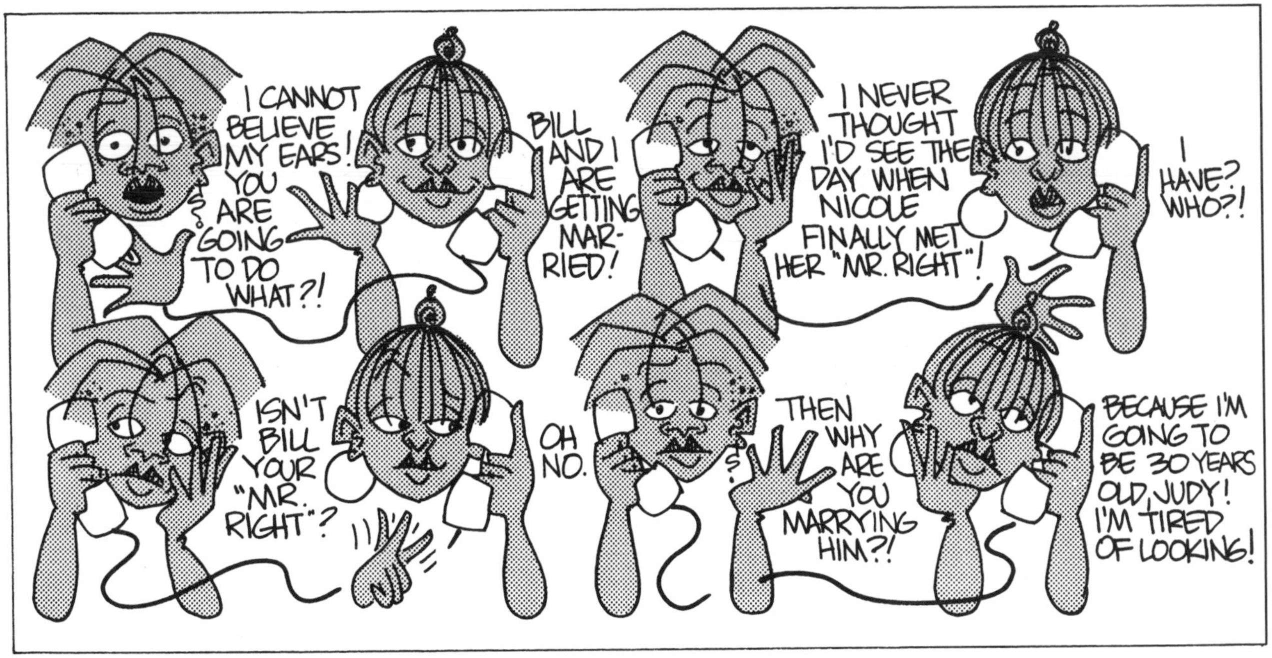
I CANNOT BELIEVE MY EARS! YOU ARE GOING TO DO WHAT?!
BILL AND I ARE GETTING MAR-RIED!
I NEVER THOUGHT I'D SEE THE DAY WHEN NICOLE FINALLY MET HER "MR. RIGHT"!
I HAVE? WHO?!
ISN'T BILL YOUR "MR. RIGHT"?
OH NO.
THEN WHY ARE YOU MARRYING HIM?!
BECAUSE I'M GOING TO BE 30 YEARS OLD, JUDY! I'M TIRED OF LOOKING!

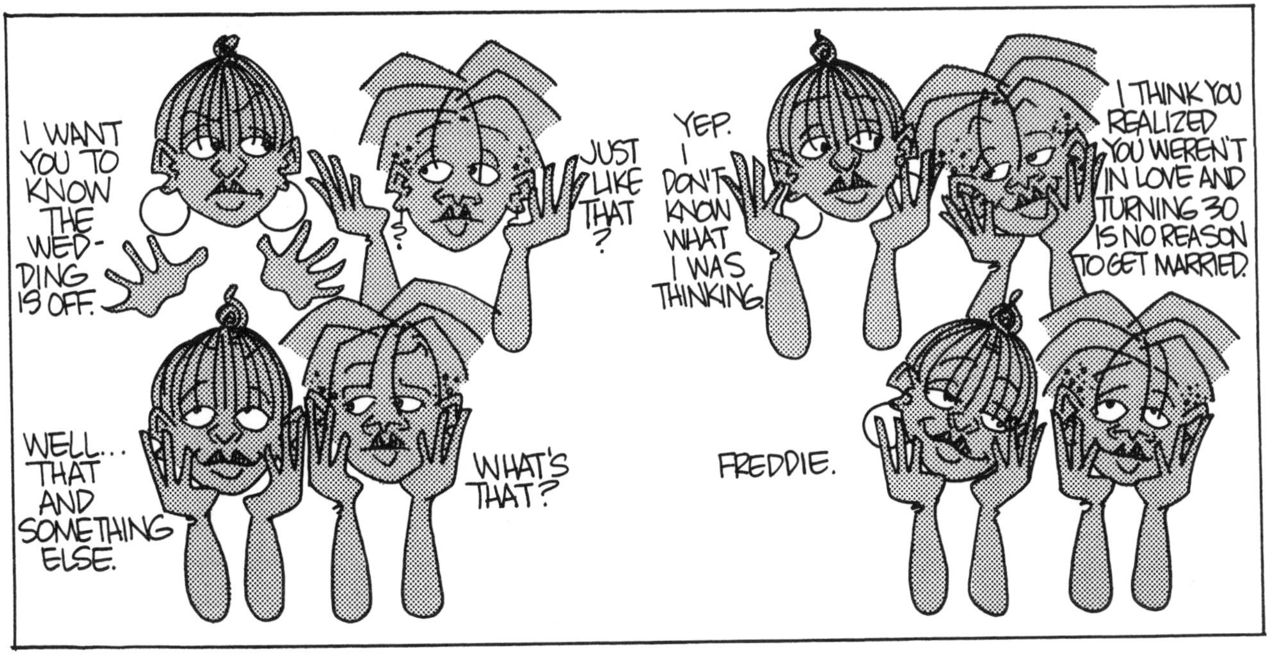
I WANT YOU TO KNOW THE WED-DING IS OFF.
JUST LIKE THAT?
YEP. I DON'T KNOW WHAT I WAS THINKING.
I THINK YOU REALIZED YOU WEREN'T IN LOVE AND TURNING 30 IS NO REASON TO GET MARRIED.
WELL... THAT AND SOMETHING ELSE.
WHAT'S THAT?
FREDDIE.

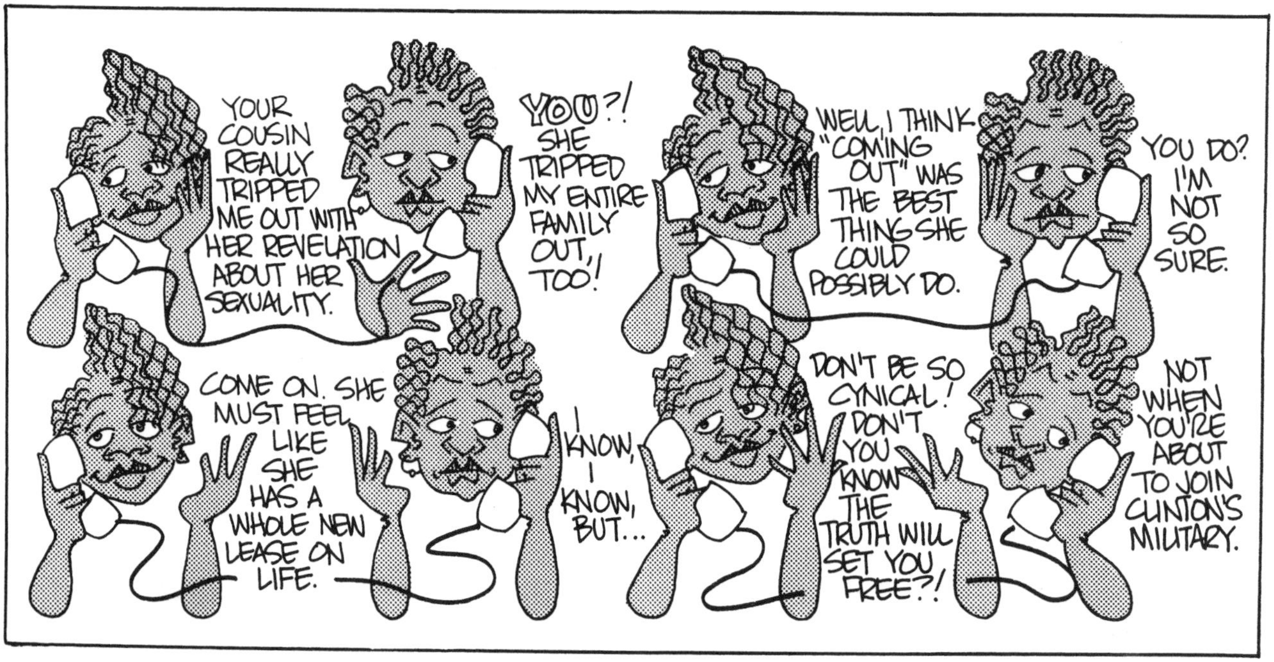
YOUR COUSIN REALLY TRIPPED ME OUT WITH HER REVELATION ABOUT HER SEXUALITY.
YOU?! SHE TRIPPED MY ENTIRE FAMILY OUT, TOO!
WELL, I THINK "COMING OUT" WAS THE BEST THING SHE COULD POSSIBLY DO.
YOU DO? I'M NOT SO SURE.
COME ON. SHE MUST FEEL LIKE SHE HAS A WHOLE NEW LEASE ON LIFE.
I KNOW, I KNOW, BUT...
DON'T BE SO CYNICAL! DON'T YOU KNOW THE TRUTH WILL SET YOU FREE?!
NOT WHEN YOU'RE ABOUT TO JOIN CLINTON'S MILITARY.

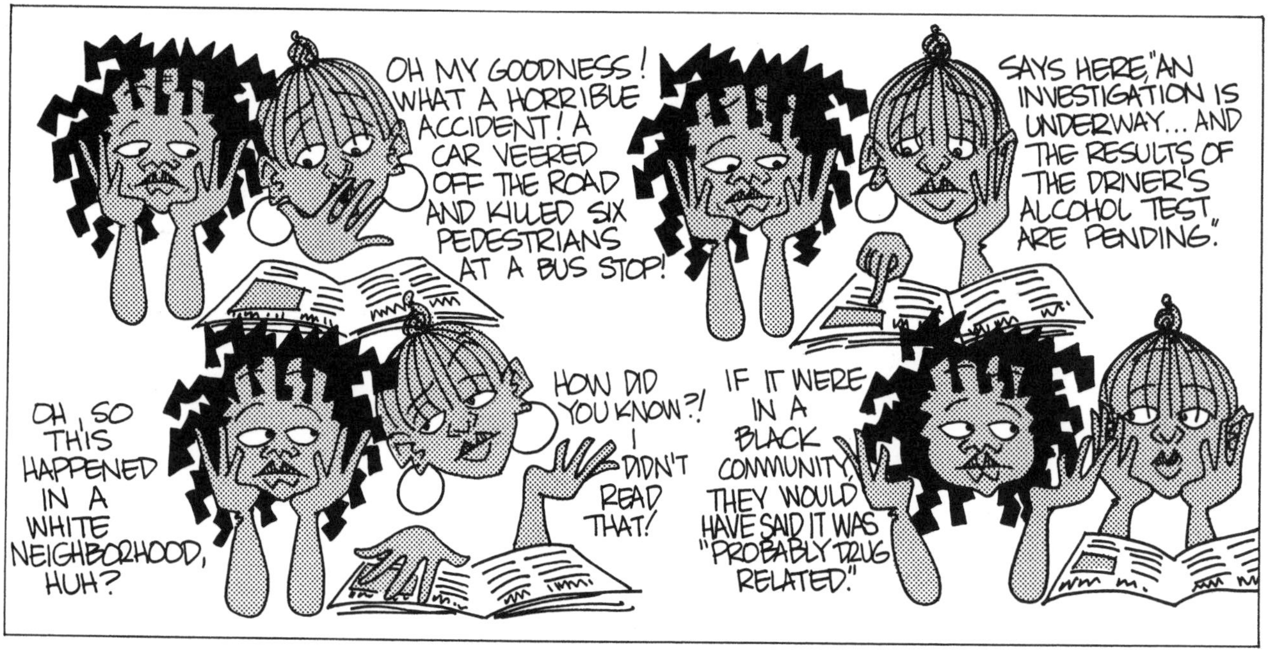
OH MY GOODNESS! WHAT A HORRIBLE ACCIDENT! A CAR VEERED OFF THE ROAD AND KILLED SIX PEDESTRIANS AT A BUS STOP!
SAYS HERE, "AN INVESTIGATION IS UNDERWAY... AND THE RESULTS OF THE DRIVER'S ALCOHOL TEST ARE PENDING."
OH, SO THIS HAPPENED IN A WHITE NEIGHBORHOOD, HUH?
HOW DID YOU KNOW?! I DIDN'T READ THAT!
IF IT WERE IN A BLACK COMMUNITY, THEY WOULD HAVE SAID IT WAS "PROBABLY DRUG RELATED."

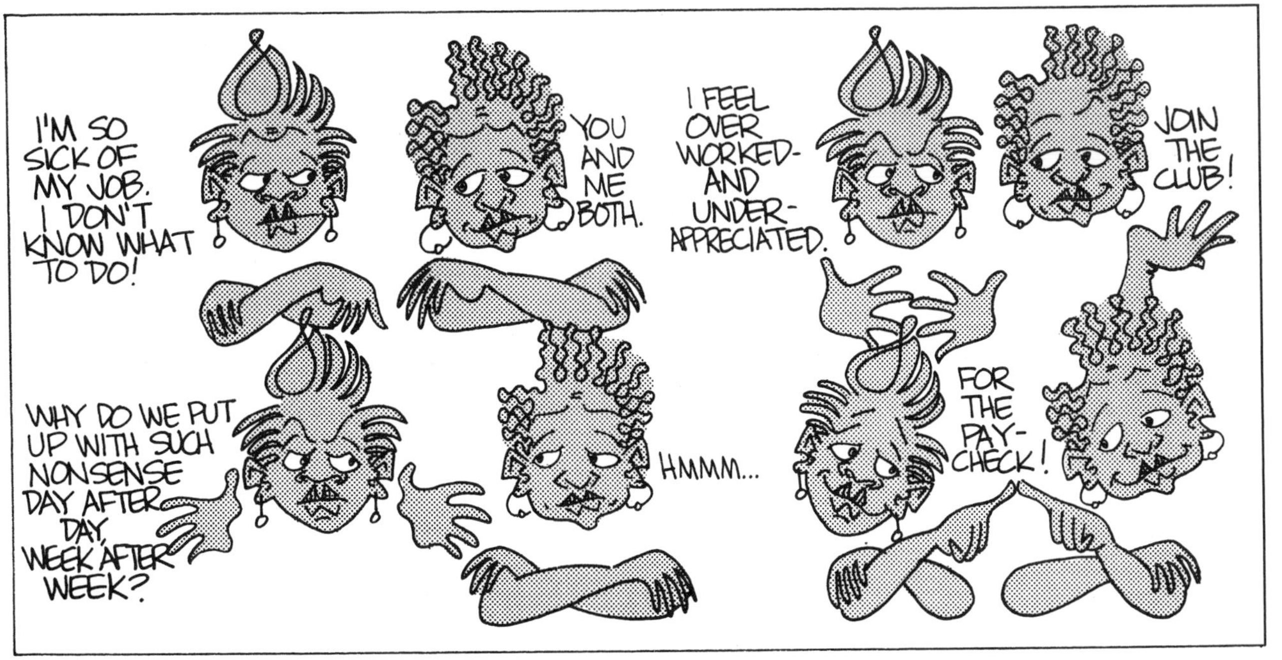
I'M SO SICK OF MY JOB. I DON'T KNOW WHAT TO DO!
YOU AND ME BOTH.
I FEEL OVER WORKED- AND UNDER-APPRECIATED.
JOIN THE CLUB!
WHY DO WE PUT UP WITH SUCH NONSENSE DAY AFTER DAY, WEEK AFTER WEEK?
HMMM...
FOR THE PAY-CHECK!

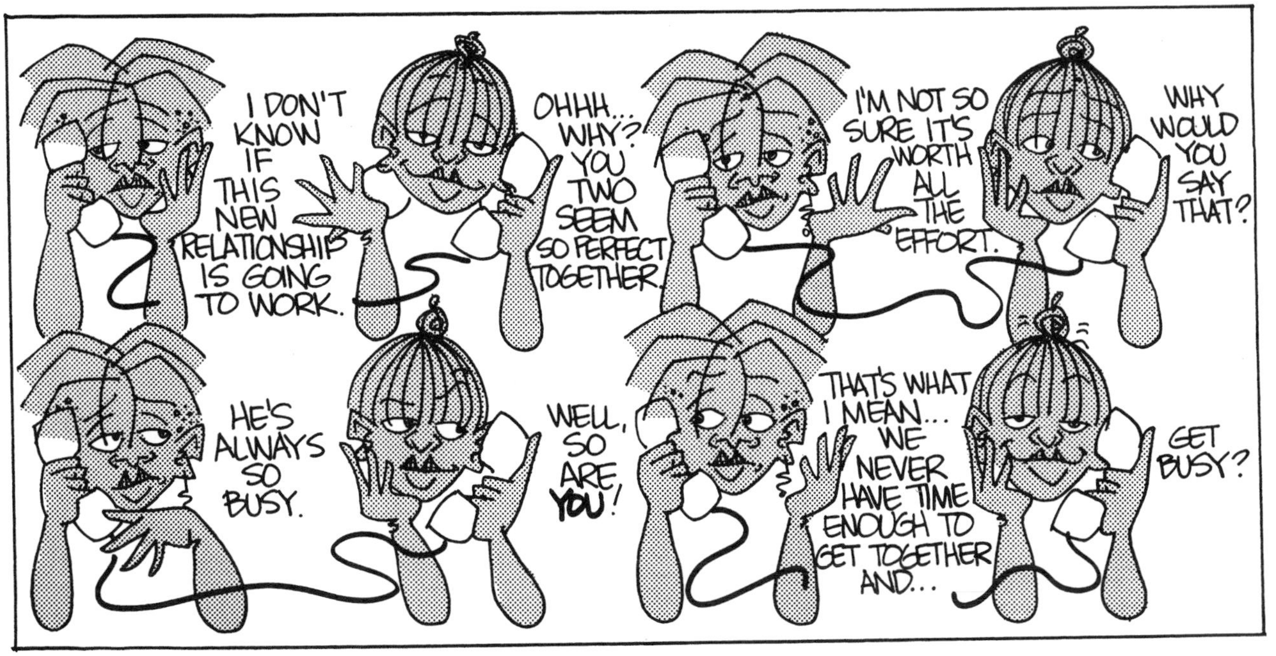
I DON'T KNOW IF THIS NEW RELATIONSHIP IS GOING TO WORK.
OHHH... WHY? YOU TWO SEEM SO PERFECT TOGETHER.
I'M NOT SO SURE IT'S WORTH ALL THE EFFORT.
WHY WOULD YOU SAY THAT?
HE'S ALWAYS SO BUSY.
WELL, SO ARE YOU!
THAT'S WHAT I MEAN... WE NEVER HAVE TIME ENOUGH TO GET TOGETHER AND...
GET BUSY?

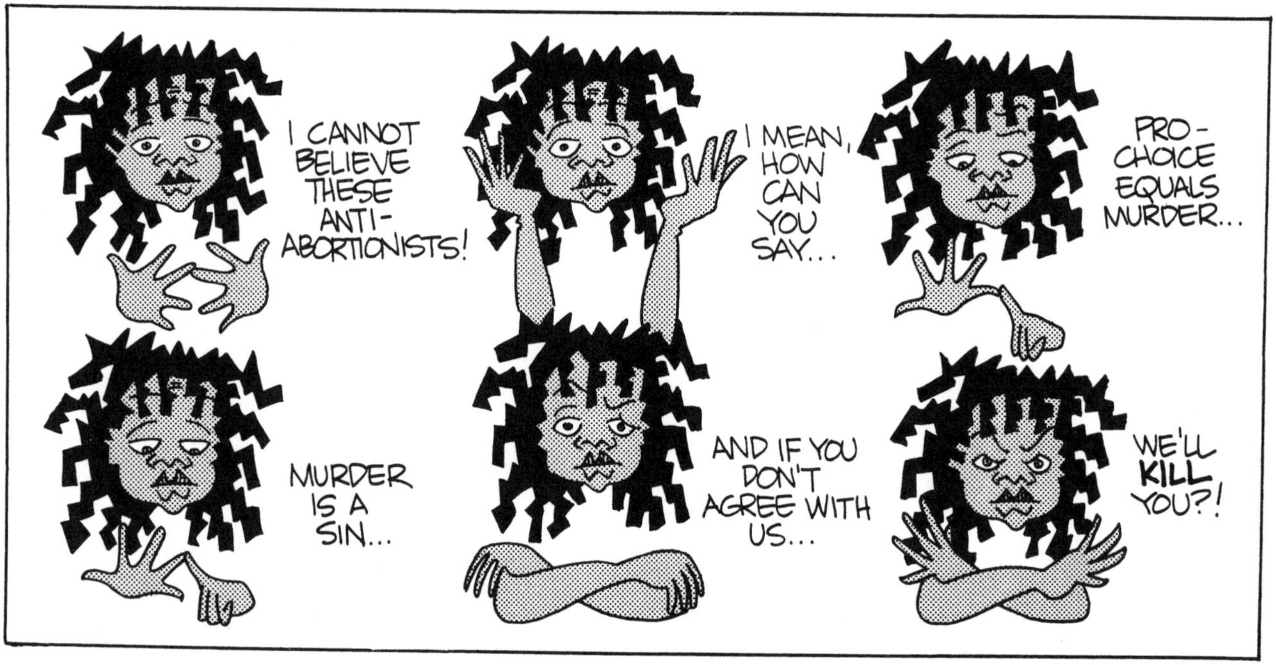
I CANNOT BELIEVE THESE ANTI-ABORTIONISTS!
I MEAN, HOW CAN YOU SAY...
PRO-CHOICE EQUALS MURDER...
MURDER IS A SIN...
AND IF YOU DON'T AGREE WITH US...
WE'LL **KILL** YOU?!

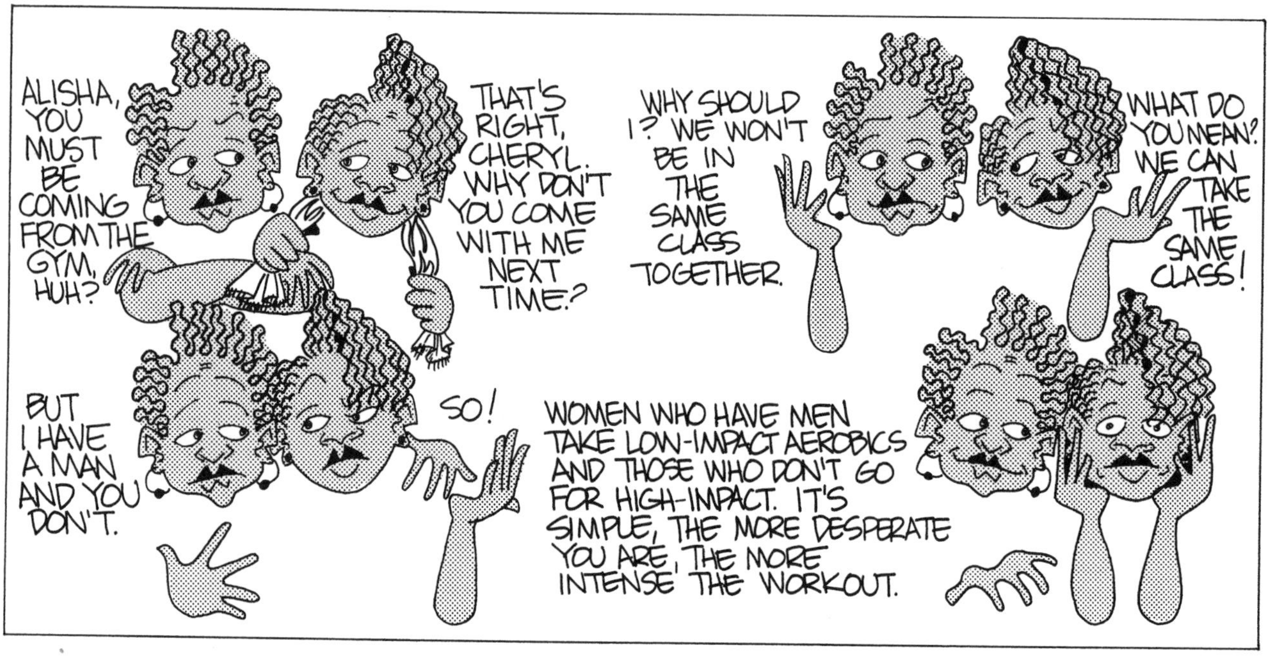
ALISHA, YOU MUST BE COMING FROM THE GYM, HUH?
THAT'S RIGHT, CHERYL. WHY DON'T YOU COME WITH ME NEXT TIME?
WHY SHOULD I? WE WON'T BE IN THE SAME CLASS TOGETHER.
WHAT DO YOU MEAN? WE CAN TAKE THE SAME CLASS!
BUT I HAVE A MAN AND YOU DON'T.
SO!
WOMEN WHO HAVE MEN TAKE LOW-IMPACT AEROBICS AND THOSE WHO DON'T GO FOR HIGH-IMPACT. IT'S SIMPLE, THE MORE DESPERATE YOU ARE, THE MORE INTENSE THE WORKOUT.

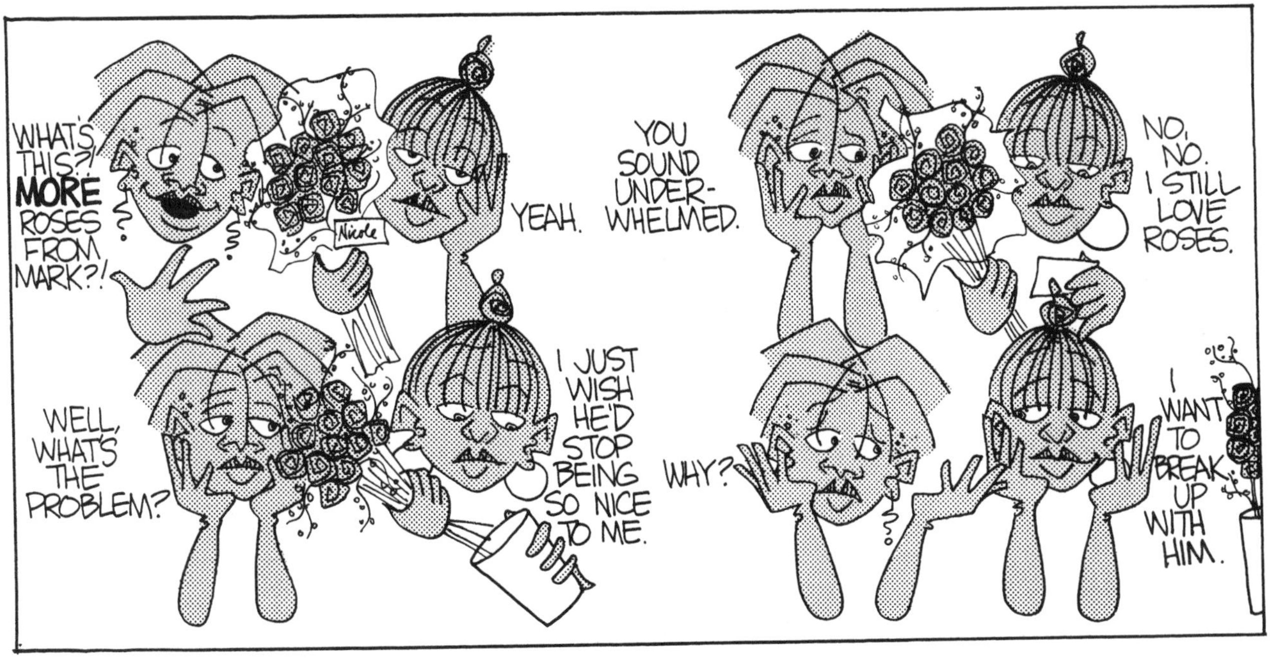
WHAT'S THIS?! MORE ROSES FROM MARK?!
YEAH.
WELL, WHAT'S THE PROBLEM?
I JUST WISH HE'D STOP BEING SO NICE TO ME.
Nicole
YOU SOUND UNDER-WHELMED.
NO, NO. I STILL LOVE ROSES.
WHY?
I WANT TO BREAK UP WITH HIM.

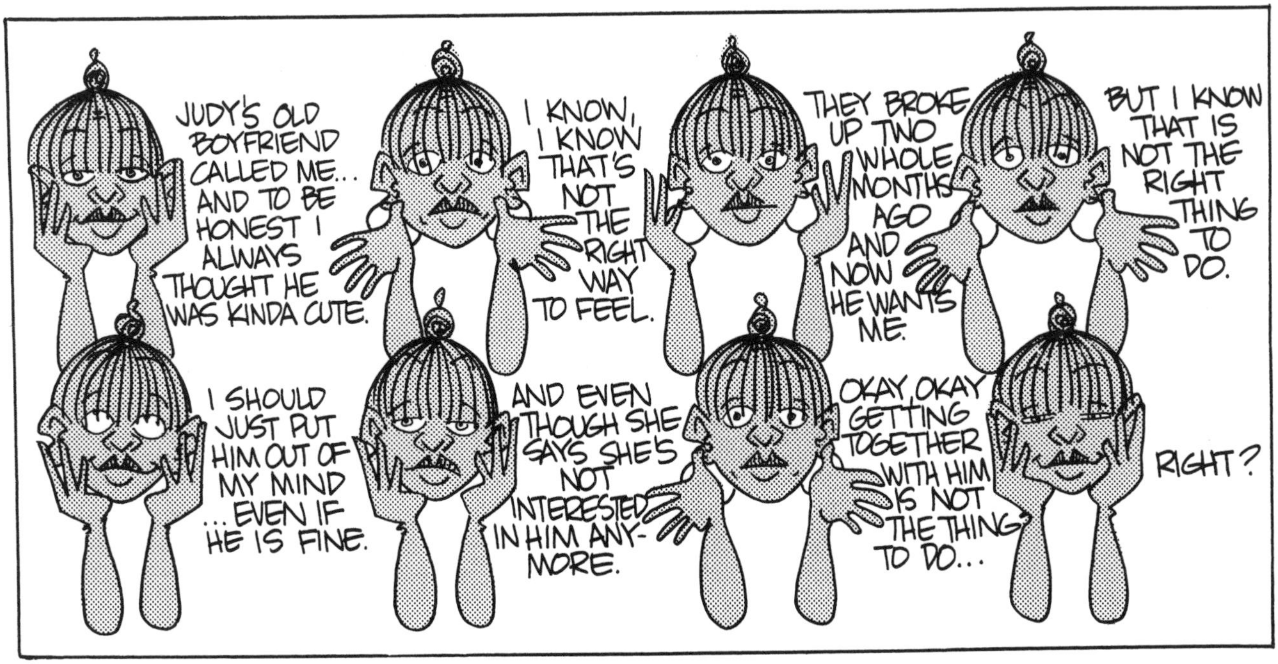
JUDY'S OLD BOYFRIEND CALLED ME... AND TO BE HONEST I ALWAYS THOUGHT HE WAS KINDA CUTE.
I SHOULD JUST PUT HIM OUT OF MY MIND ...EVEN IF HE IS FINE.
I KNOW, I KNOW THAT'S NOT THE RIGHT WAY TO FEEL.
AND EVEN THOUGH SHE SAYS SHE'S NOT INTERESTED IN HIM ANY-MORE.
THEY BROKE UP TWO WHOLE MONTHS AGO AND NOW HE WANTS ME.
OKAY, OKAY GETTING TOGETHER WITH HIM IS NOT THE THING TO DO...
BUT I KNOW THAT IS NOT THE RIGHT THING TO DO.
RIGHT?

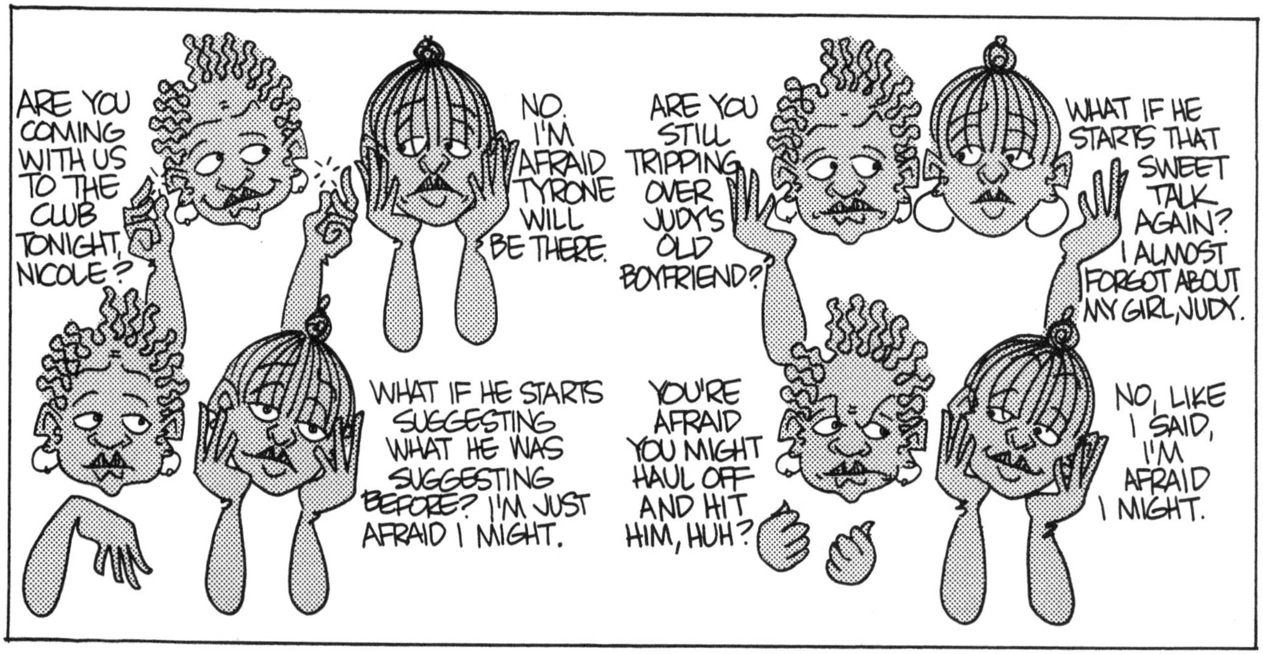
ARE YOU COMING WITH US TO THE CLUB TONIGHT, NICOLE?
NO. I'M AFRAID TYRONE WILL BE THERE.
WHAT IF HE STARTS SUGGESTING WHAT HE WAS SUGGESTING BEFORE? I'M JUST AFRAID I MIGHT.
ARE YOU STILL TRIPPING OVER JUDY'S OLD BOYFRIEND?
WHAT IF HE STARTS THAT SWEET TALK AGAIN? I ALMOST FORGOT ABOUT MY GIRL, JUDY.
YOU'RE AFRAID YOU MIGHT HAUL OFF AND HIT HIM, HUH?
NO, LIKE I SAID, I'M AFRAID I MIGHT.

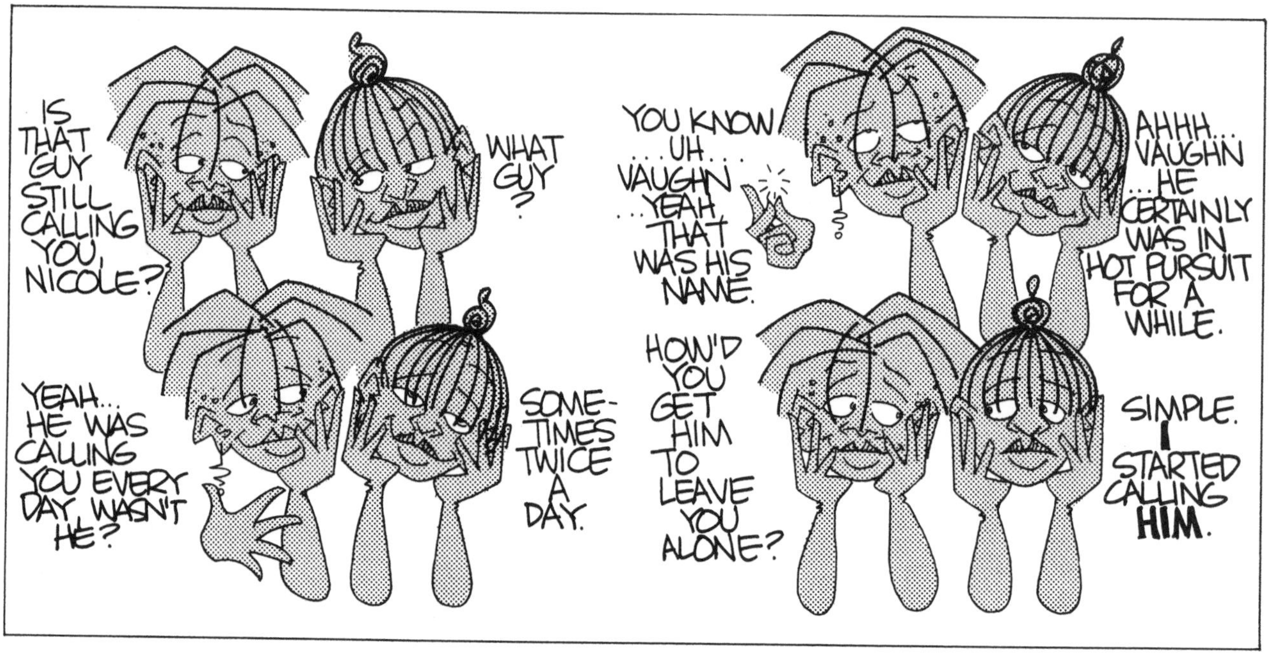
IS THAT GUY STILL CALLING YOU, NICOLE?
WHAT GUY?
YEAH... HE WAS CALLING YOU EVERY DAY, WASN'T HE?
SOME-TIMES TWICE A DAY.
YOU KNOW ...UH... VAUGHN ...YEAH THAT WAS HIS NAME.
AHHH... VAUGHN ...HE CERTAINLY WAS IN HOT PURSUIT FOR A WHILE.
HOW'D YOU GET HIM TO LEAVE YOU ALONE?
SIMPLE. I STARTED CALLING HIM.

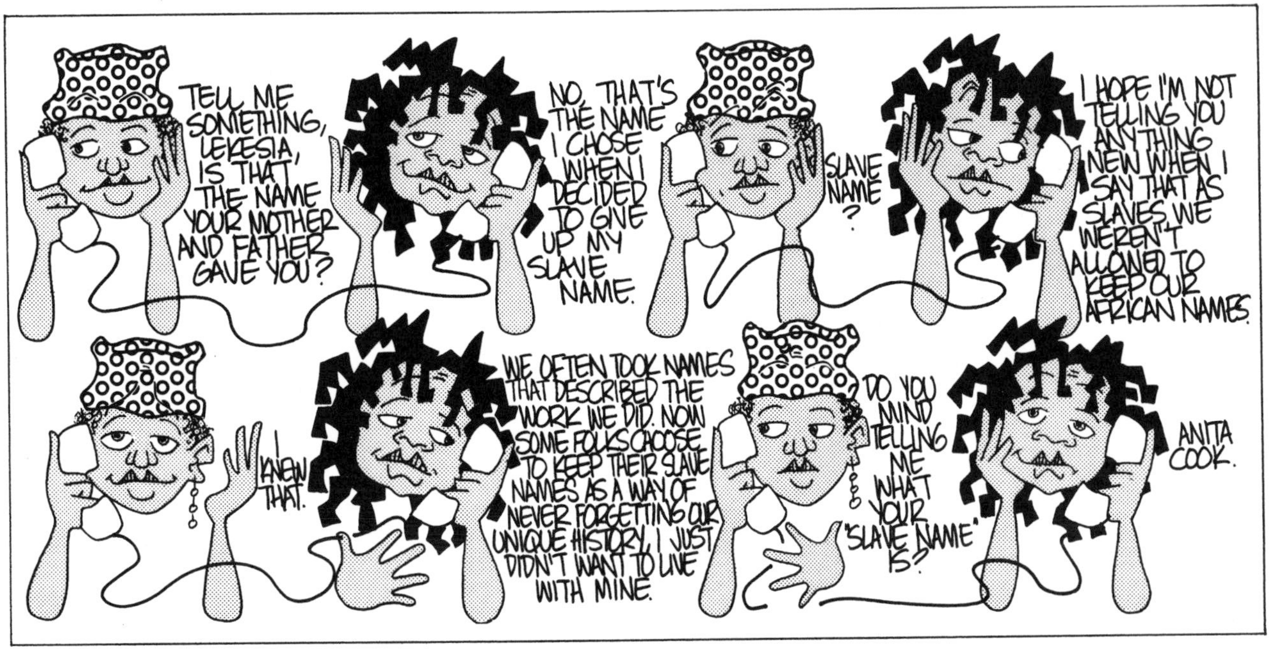
TELL ME SOMETHING, LEKESIA, IS THAT THE NAME YOUR MOTHER AND FATHER GAVE YOU?
NO, THAT'S THE NAME I CHOSE WHEN I DECIDED TO GIVE UP MY SLAVE NAME.
SLAVE NAME?
I HOPE I'M NOT TELLING YOU ANYTHING NEW WHEN I SAY THAT AS SLAVES WE WEREN'T ALLOWED TO KEEP OUR AFRICAN NAMES.
I KNEW THAT.
WE OFTEN TOOK NAMES THAT DESCRIBED THE WORK WE DID. NOW SOME FOLKS CHOOSE TO KEEP THEIR SLAVE NAMES AS A WAY OF NEVER FORGETTING OUR UNIQUE HISTORY. I JUST DIDN'T WANT TO LIVE WITH MINE.
DO YOU MIND TELLING ME WHAT YOUR "SLAVE NAME" IS?
ANITA COOK.

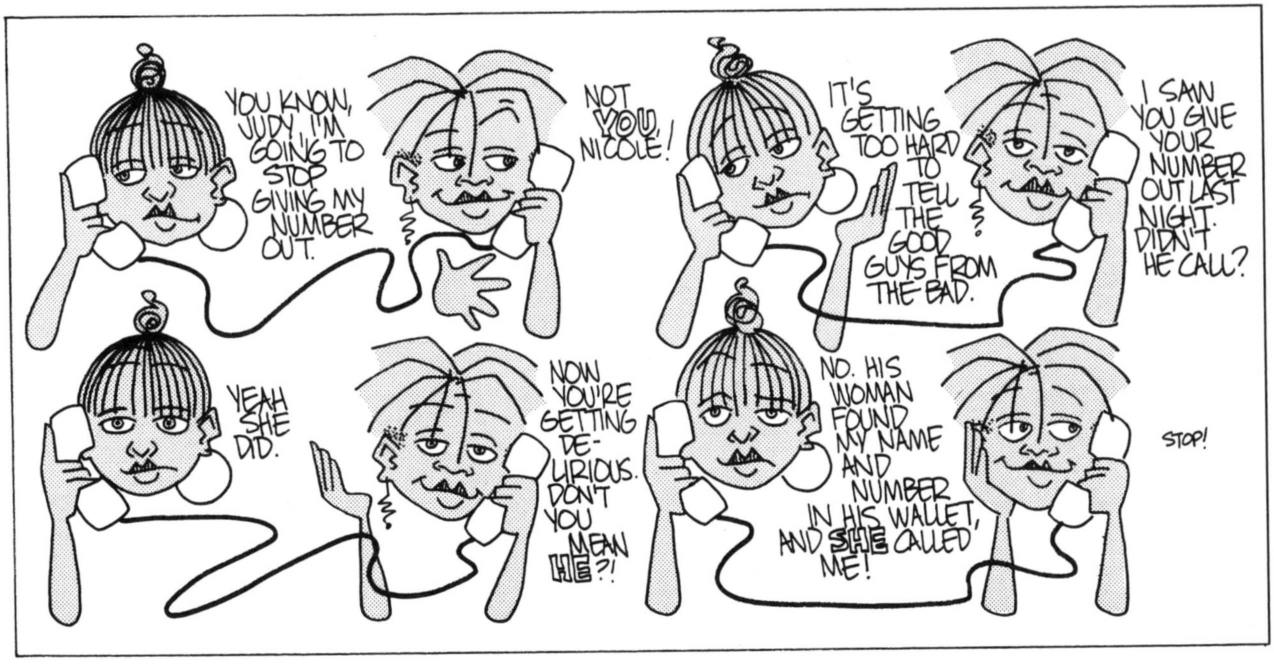
YOU KNOW, JUDY, I'M GOING TO STOP GIVING MY NUMBER OUT.
NOT YOU, NICOLE!
IT'S GETTING TOO HARD TO TELL THE GOOD GUYS FROM THE BAD.
I SAW YOU GIVE YOUR NUMBER OUT LAST NIGHT. DIDN'T HE CALL?
YEAH SHE DID.
NOW YOU'RE GETTING DE-LIRIOUS. DON'T YOU MEAN HE?!
NO. HIS WOMAN FOUND MY NAME AND NUMBER IN HIS WALLET, AND SHE CALLED ME!
STOP!

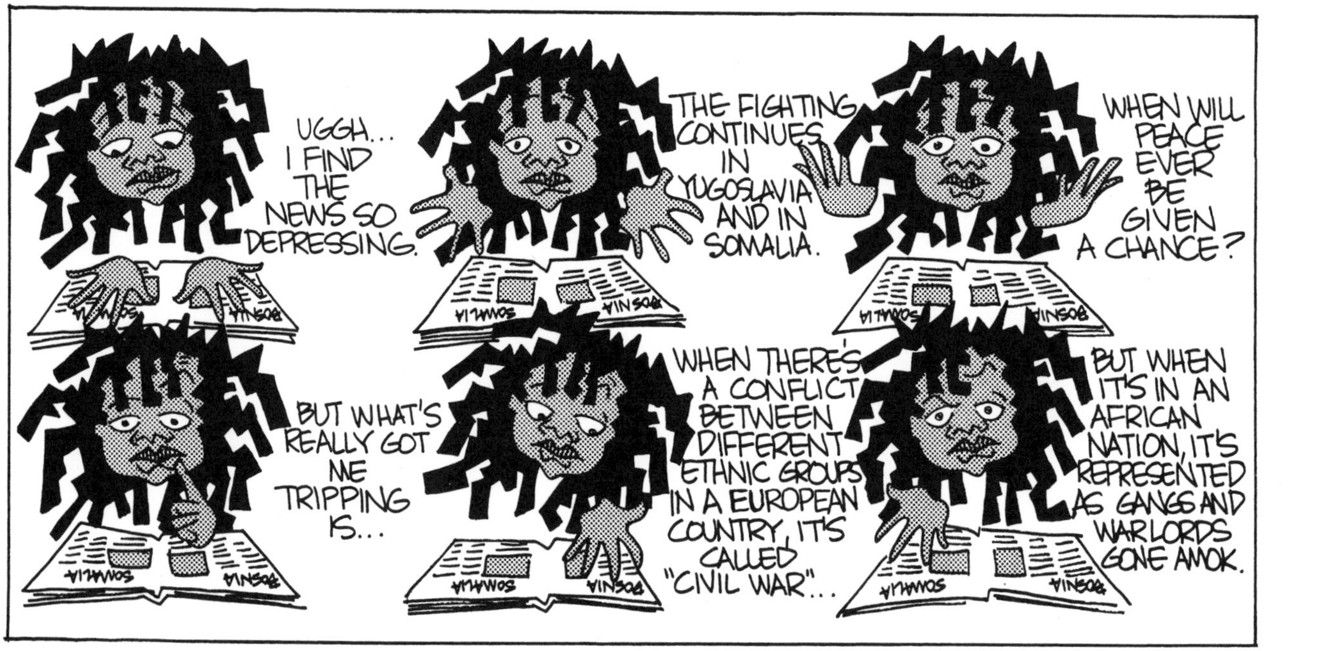
UGGH... I FIND THE NEWS SO DEPRESSING.
THE FIGHTING CONTINUES IN YUGOSLAVIA AND IN SOMALIA.
WHEN WILL PEACE EVER BE GIVEN A CHANCE?
BUT WHAT'S REALLY GOT ME TRIPPING IS...
WHEN THERE'S A CONFLICT BETWEEN DIFFERENT ETHNIC GROUPS IN A EUROPEAN COUNTRY, IT'S CALLED "CIVIL WAR"...
BUT WHEN IT'S IN AN AFRICAN NATION, IT'S REPRESENTED AS GANGS AND WARLORDS GONE AMOK.
BOSNIA
SOMALIA

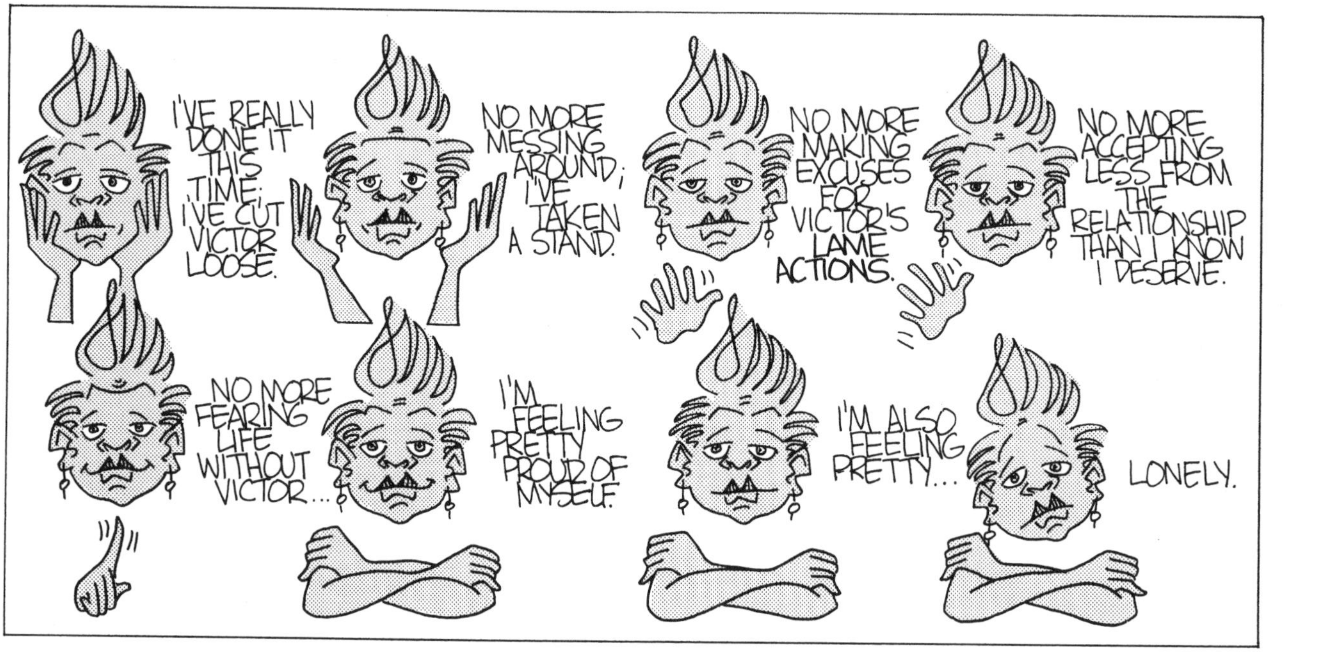
I'VE REALLY DONE IT THIS TIME. I'VE CUT VICTOR LOOSE.
NO MORE MESSING AROUND; I'VE TAKEN A STAND.
NO MORE MAKING EXCUSES FOR VICTOR'S LAME ACTIONS.
NO MORE ACCEPTING LESS FROM THE RELATIONSHIP THAN I KNOW I DESERVE.
NO MORE FEARING LIFE WITHOUT VICTOR...
I'M FEELING PRETTY PROUD OF MYSELF.
I'M ALSO FEELING PRETTY...
LONELY.

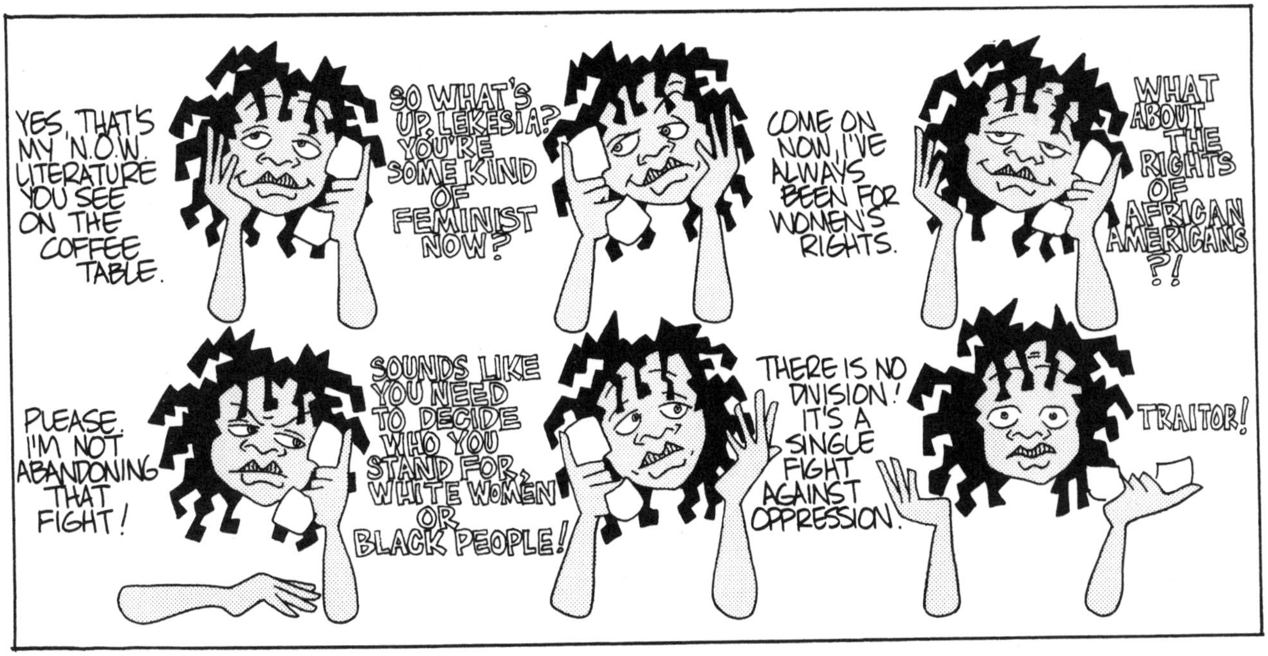
YES, THAT'S MY N.O.W. LITERATURE YOU SEE ON THE COFFEE TABLE.
SO WHAT'S UP, LEKESIA? YOU'RE SOME KIND OF FEMINIST NOW?
COME ON NOW, I'VE ALWAYS BEEN FOR WOMEN'S RIGHTS.
WHAT ABOUT THE RIGHTS OF AFRICAN AMERICANS ?!
PLEASE. I'M NOT ABANDONING THAT FIGHT!
SOUNDS LIKE YOU NEED TO DECIDE WHO YOU STAND FOR, WHITE WOMEN OR BLACK PEOPLE!
THERE IS NO DIVISION! IT'S A SINGLE FIGHT AGAINST OPPRESSION.
TRAITOR!

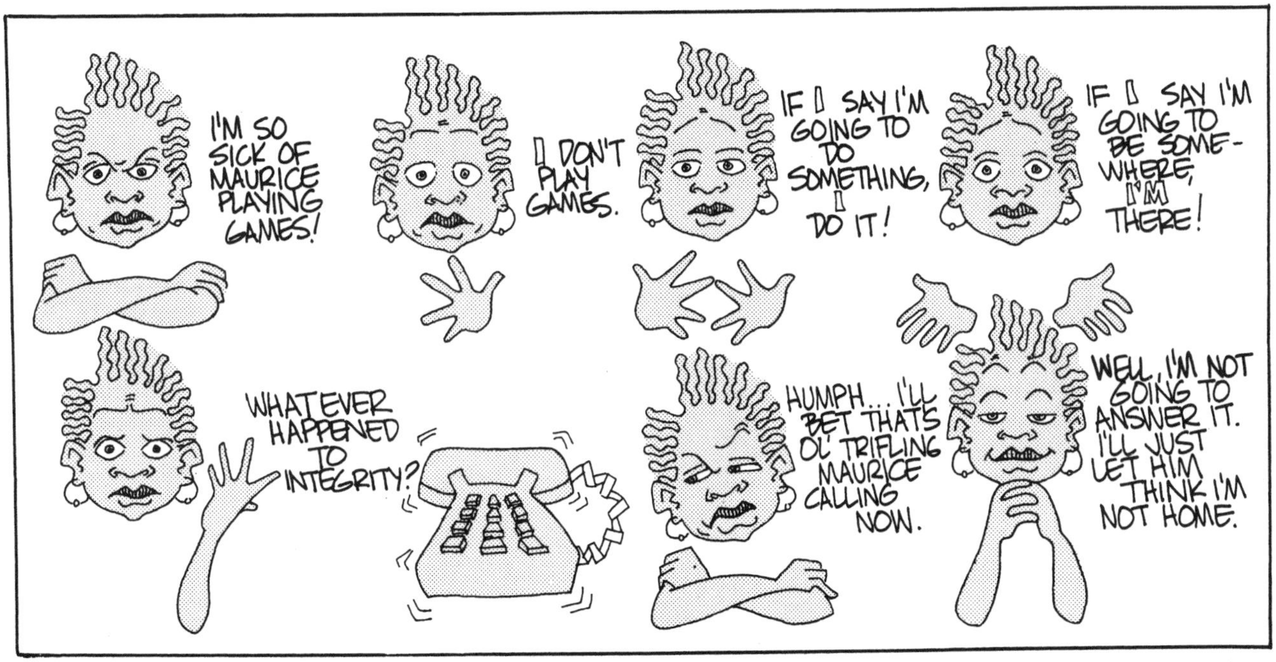
I'M SO SICK OF MAURICE PLAYING GAMES!
I DON'T PLAY GAMES.
IF I SAY I'M GOING TO DO SOMETHING, I DO IT!
IF I SAY I'M GOING TO BE SOME-WHERE, I'M THERE!
WHAT EVER HAPPENED TO INTEGRITY?
HUMPH... I'LL BET THAT'S OL' TRIFLING MAURICE CALLING NOW.
WELL, I'M NOT GOING TO ANSWER IT. I'LL JUST LET HIM THINK I'M NOT HOME.

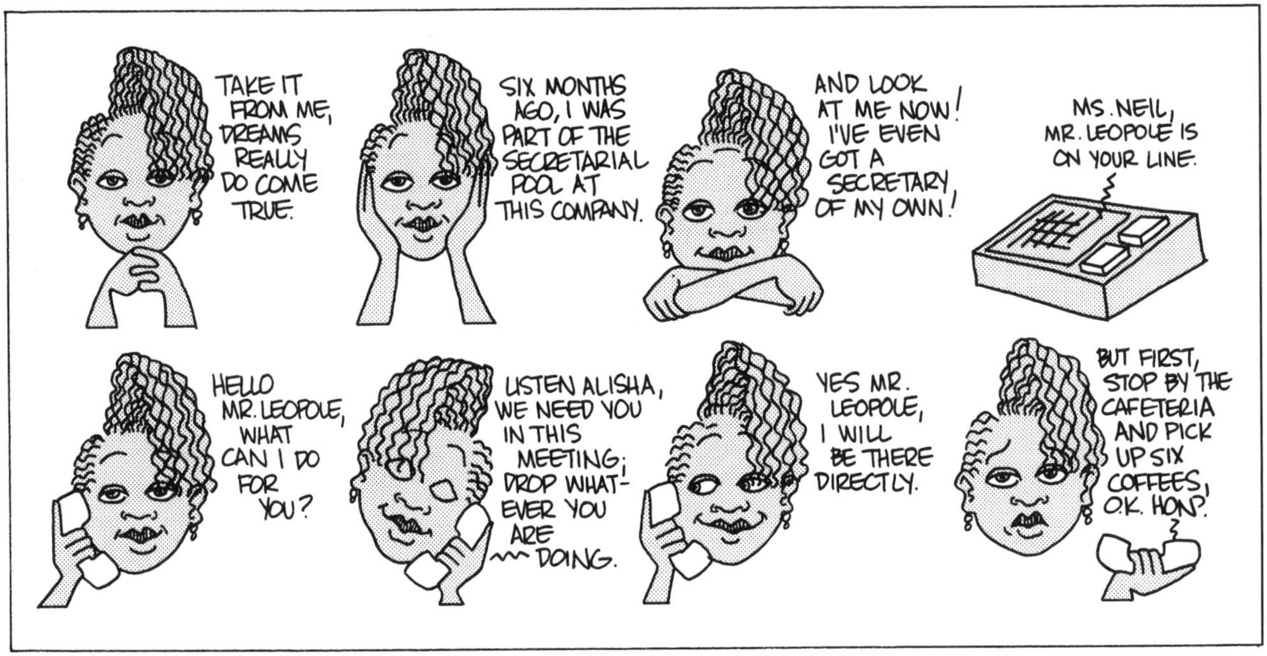
TAKE IT FROM ME, DREAMS REALLY DO COME TRUE.
SIX MONTHS AGO, I WAS PART OF THE SECRETARIAL POOL AT THIS COMPANY.
AND LOOK AT ME NOW! I'VE EVEN GOT A SECRETARY OF MY OWN!
MS. NEIL, MR. LEOPOLE IS ON YOUR LINE.
HELLO MR. LEOPOLE, WHAT CAN I DO FOR YOU?
LISTEN ALISHA, WE NEED YOU IN THIS MEETING; DROP WHAT-EVER YOU ARE DOING.
YES MR. LEOPOLE, I WILL BE THERE DIRECTLY.
BUT FIRST, STOP BY THE CAFETERIA AND PICK UP SIX COFFEES, O.K. HON?

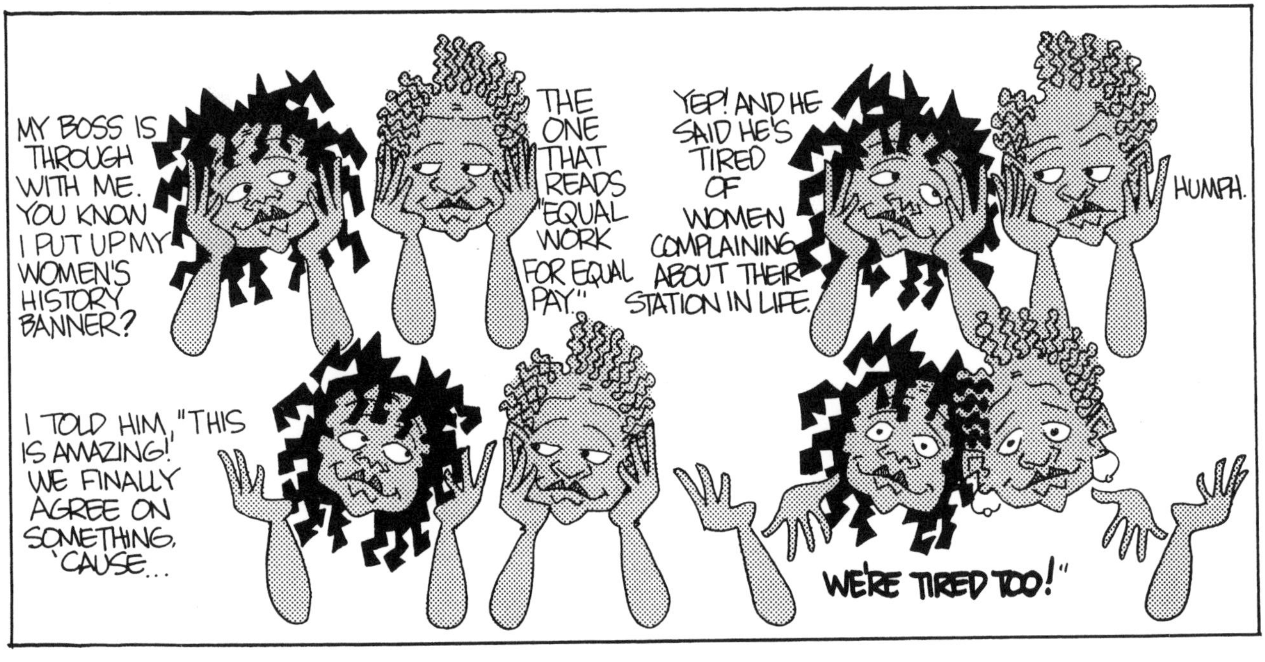
MY BOSS IS THROUGH WITH ME. YOU KNOW I PUT UP MY WOMEN'S HISTORY BANNER?
THE ONE THAT READS "EQUAL WORK FOR EQUAL PAY."
YEP! AND HE SAID HE'S TIRED OF WOMEN COMPLAINING ABOUT THEIR STATION IN LIFE.
HUMPH.
I TOLD HIM, "THIS IS AMAZING! WE FINALLY AGREE ON SOMETHING. 'CAUSE...
WE'RE TIRED TOO!"

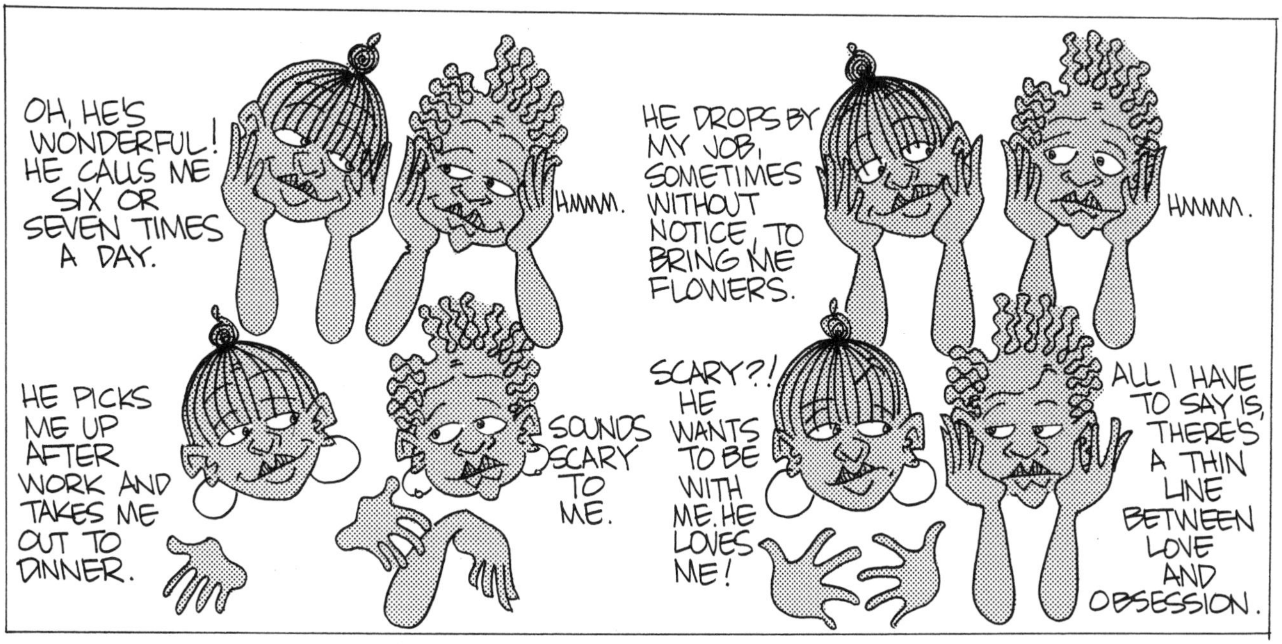
OH, HE'S WONDERFUL! HE CALLS ME SIX OR SEVEN TIMES A DAY.
HMMM.
HE PICKS ME UP AFTER WORK AND TAKES ME OUT TO DINNER.
SOUNDS SCARY TO ME.
HE DROPS BY MY JOB, SOMETIMES WITHOUT NOTICE, TO BRING ME FLOWERS.
HMMM.
SCARY?! HE WANTS TO BE WITH ME. HE LOVES ME!
ALL I HAVE TO SAY IS, THERE'S A THIN LINE BETWEEN LOVE AND OBSESSION.

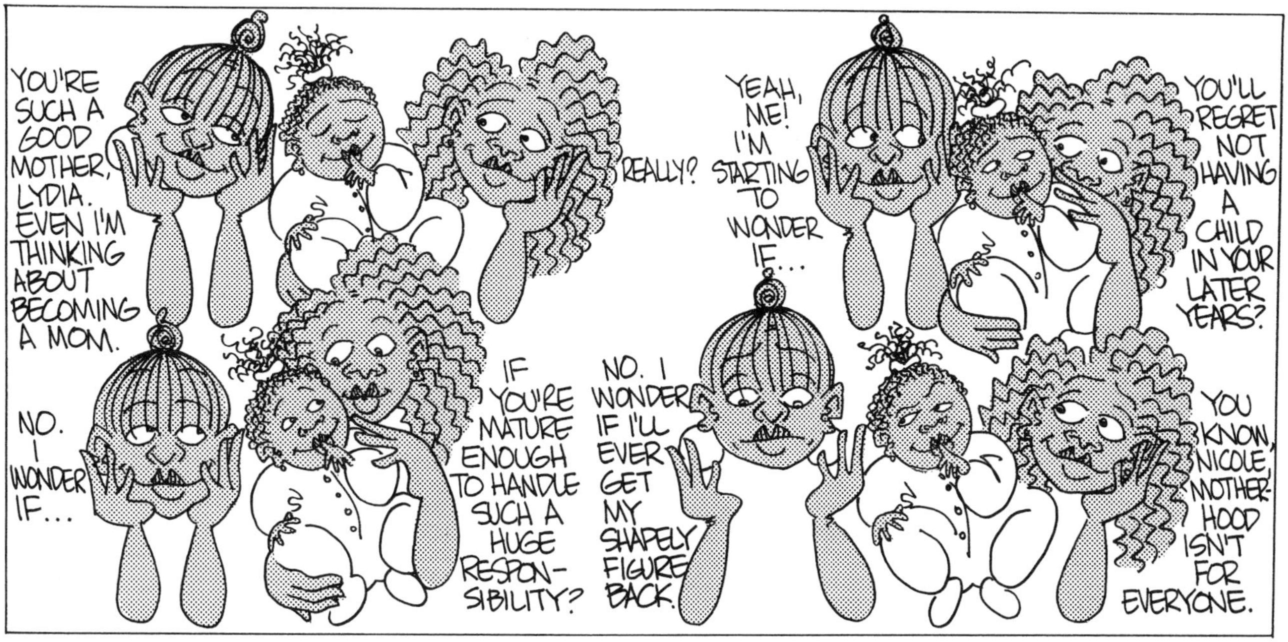
YOU'RE SUCH A GOOD MOTHER, LYDIA. EVEN I'M THINKING ABOUT BECOMING A MOM.
REALLY?
NO. I WONDER IF...
IF YOU'RE MATURE ENOUGH TO HANDLE SUCH A HUGE RESPON-SIBILITY?
YEAH, ME! I'M STARTING TO WONDER IF...
YOU'LL REGRET NOT HAVING A CHILD IN YOUR LATER YEARS?
NO. I WONDER IF I'LL EVER GET MY SHAPELY FIGURE BACK.
YOU KNOW, NICOLE, MOTHER-HOOD ISN'T FOR EVERYONE.

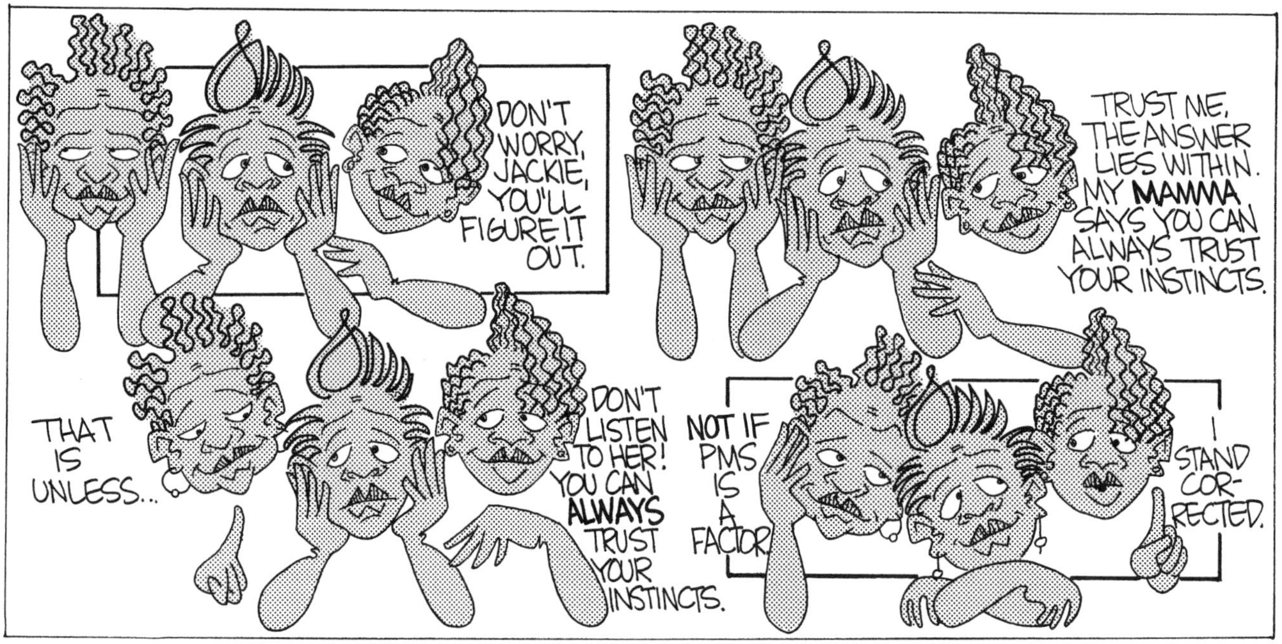
DON'T WORRY, JACKIE, YOU'LL FIGURE IT OUT.
TRUST ME, THE ANSWER LIES WITHIN. MY **MAMMA** SAYS YOU CAN ALWAYS TRUST YOUR INSTINCTS.
THAT IS UNLESS...
DON'T LISTEN TO HER! YOU CAN **ALWAYS** TRUST YOUR INSTINCTS.
NOT IF PMS IS A FACTOR.
I STAND COR-RECTED.

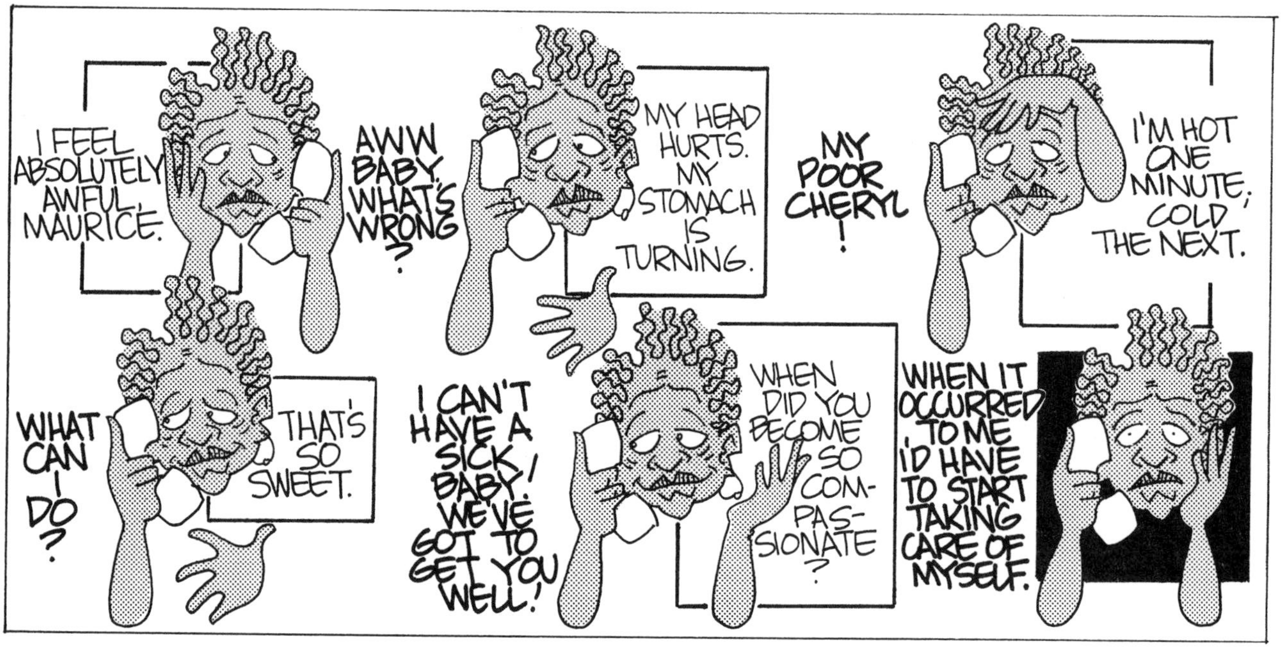
I FEEL ABSOLUTELY AWFUL, MAURICE.
AWW BABY, WHAT'S WRONG?
MY HEAD HURTS. MY STOMACH IS TURNING.
MY POOR CHERYL!
I'M HOT ONE MINUTE; COLD THE NEXT.
WHAT CAN I DO?
THAT'S SO SWEET.
I CAN'T HAVE A SICK BABY! WE'VE GOT TO GET YOU WELL!
WHEN DID YOU BECOME SO COM-PAS-SIONATE?
WHEN IT OCCURRED TO ME I'D HAVE TO START TAKING CARE OF MYSELF.

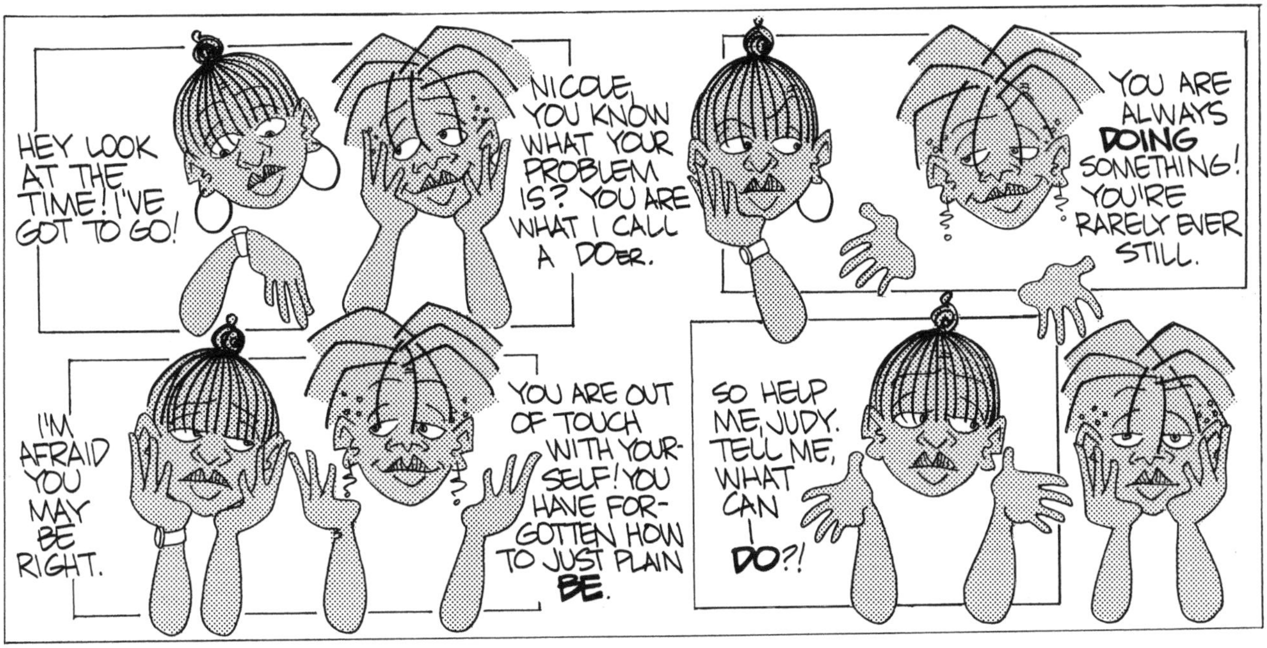
HEY LOOK AT THE TIME! I'VE GOT TO GO!
NICOLE, YOU KNOW WHAT YOUR PROBLEM IS? YOU ARE WHAT I CALL A DOer.
I'M AFRAID YOU MAY BE RIGHT.
YOU ARE OUT OF TOUCH WITH YOURSELF! YOU HAVE FORGOTTEN HOW TO JUST PLAIN BE.
YOU ARE ALWAYS DOING SOMETHING! YOU'RE RARELY EVER STILL.
SO HELP ME, JUDY. TELL ME, WHAT CAN I DO?!

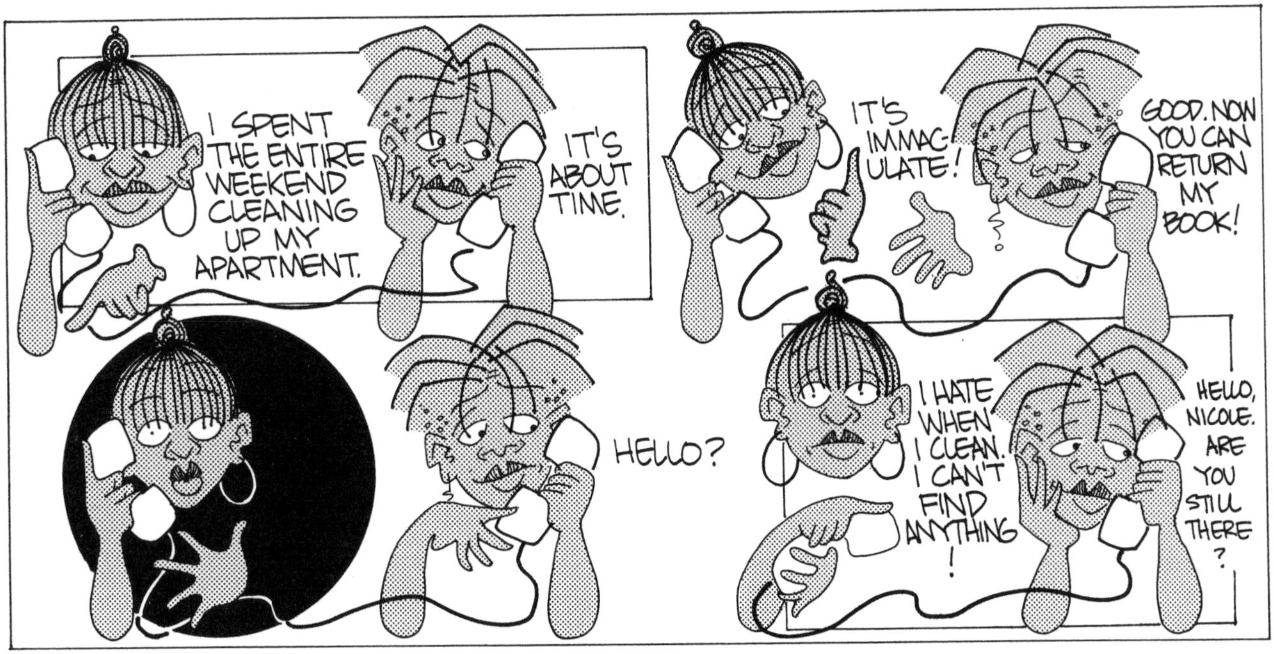
I SPENT THE ENTIRE WEEKEND CLEANING UP MY APARTMENT.
IT'S ABOUT TIME.
HELLO?
IT'S IMMACULATE!
GOOD. NOW YOU CAN RETURN MY BOOK!
I HATE WHEN I CLEAN. I CAN'T FIND ANYTHING!
HELLO, NICOLE. ARE YOU STILL THERE?

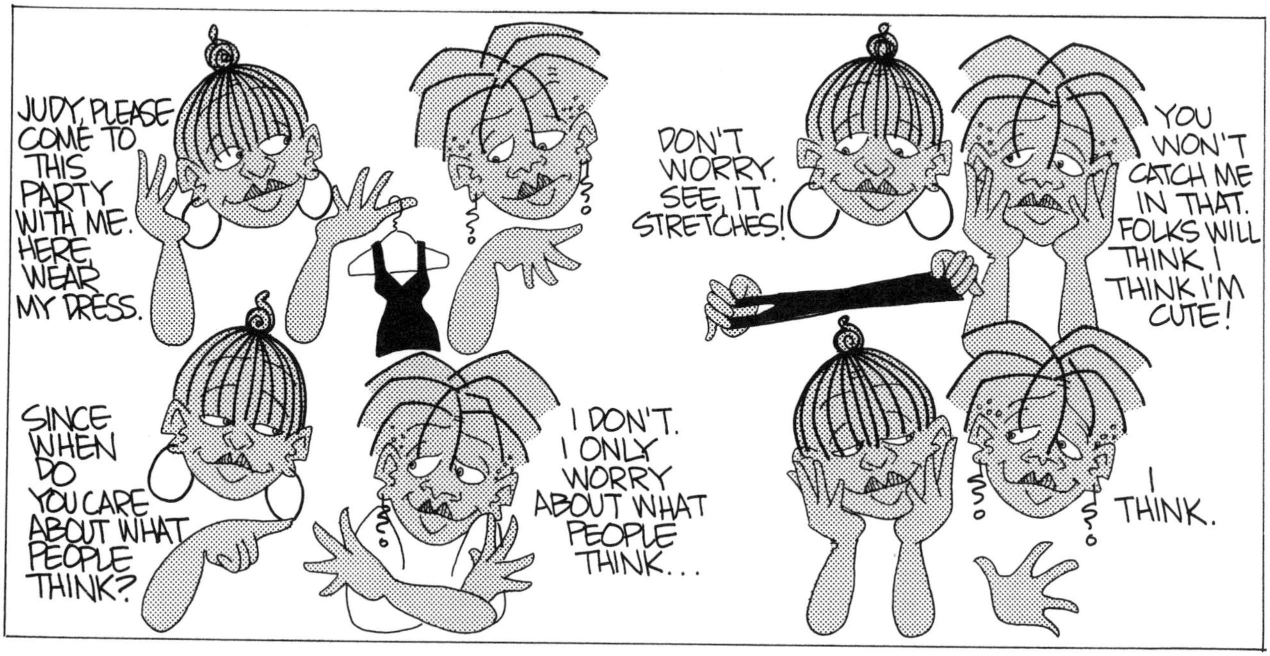
JUDY, PLEASE COME TO THIS PARTY WITH ME. HERE, WEAR MY DRESS.
SINCE WHEN DO YOU CARE ABOUT WHAT PEOPLE THINK?
I DON'T. I ONLY WORRY ABOUT WHAT PEOPLE THINK...
DON'T WORRY. SEE, IT STRETCHES!
YOU WON'T CATCH ME IN THAT. FOLKS WILL THINK I THINK I'M CUTE!
I THINK.

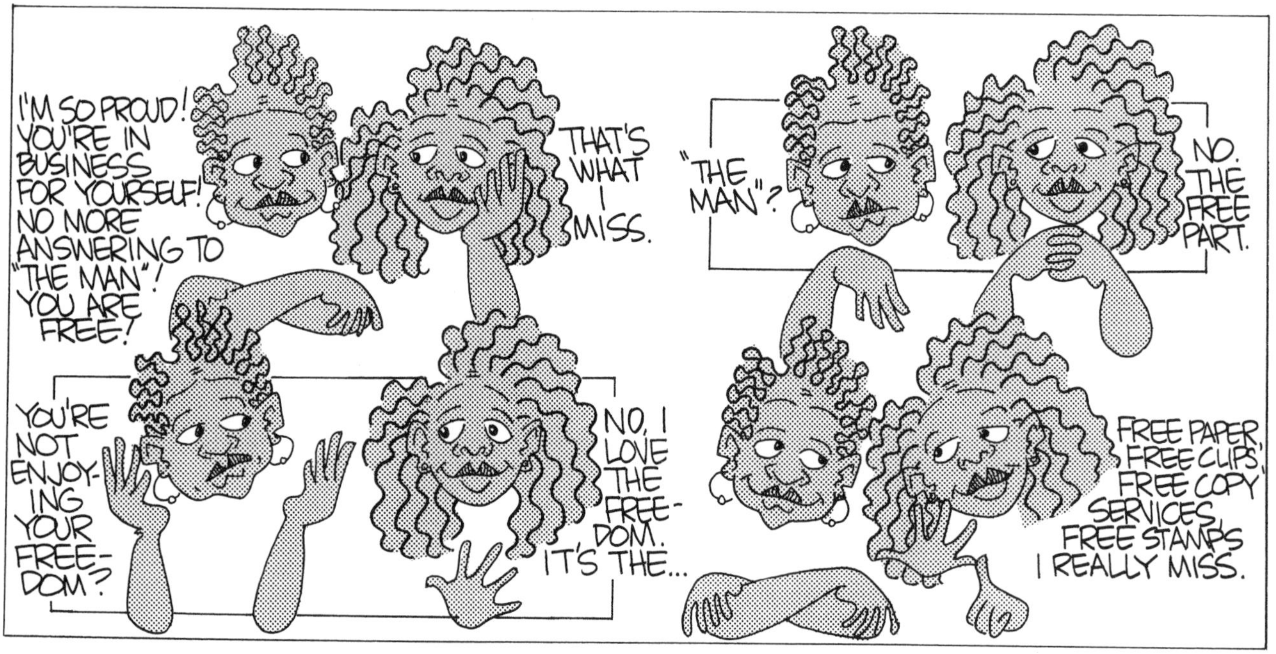
I'M SO PROUD! YOU'RE IN BUSINESS FOR YOURSELF! NO MORE ANSWERING TO "THE MAN"! YOU ARE FREE!
THAT'S WHAT I MISS.
YOU'RE NOT ENJOY-ING YOUR FREE-DOM?
NO, I LOVE THE FREE-DOM. IT'S THE...
"THE MAN"?
NO. THE FREE PART.
FREE PAPER, FREE CLIPS, FREE COPY SERVICES, FREE STAMPS I REALLY MISS.

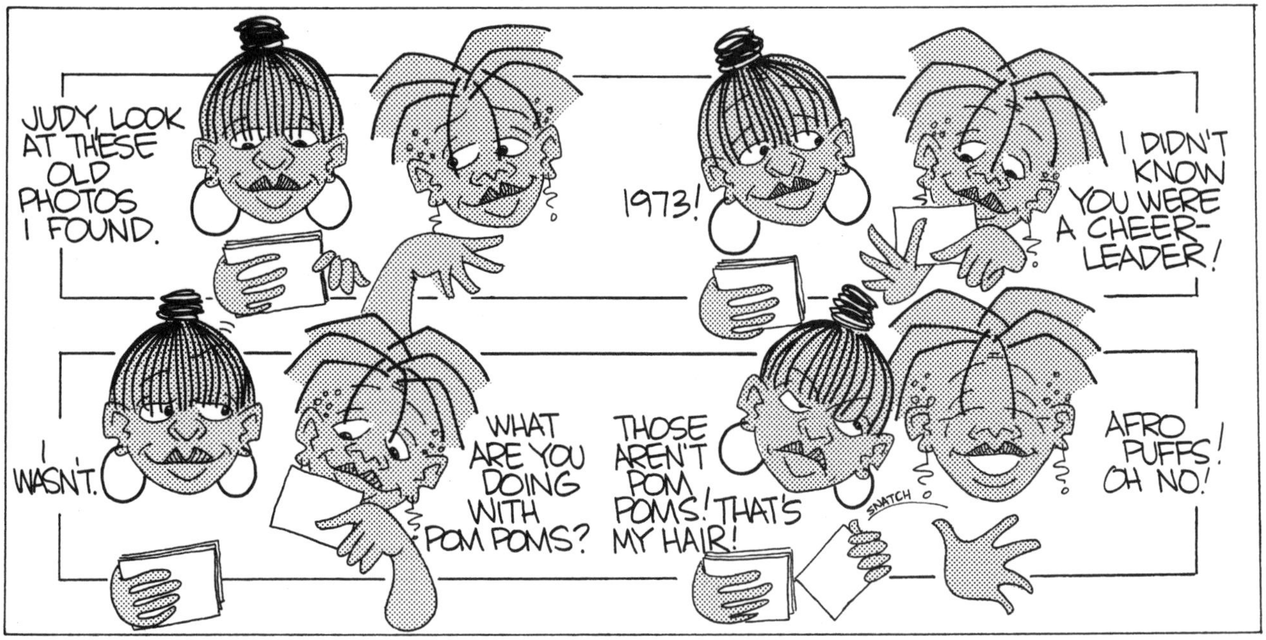
JUDY, LOOK AT THESE OLD PHOTOS I FOUND.
1973!
I DIDN'T KNOW YOU WERE A CHEER-LEADER!
I WASN'T.
WHAT ARE YOU DOING WITH POM POMS?
THOSE AREN'T POM POMS! THAT'S MY HAIR!
SNATCH
AFRO PUFFS! OH NO!

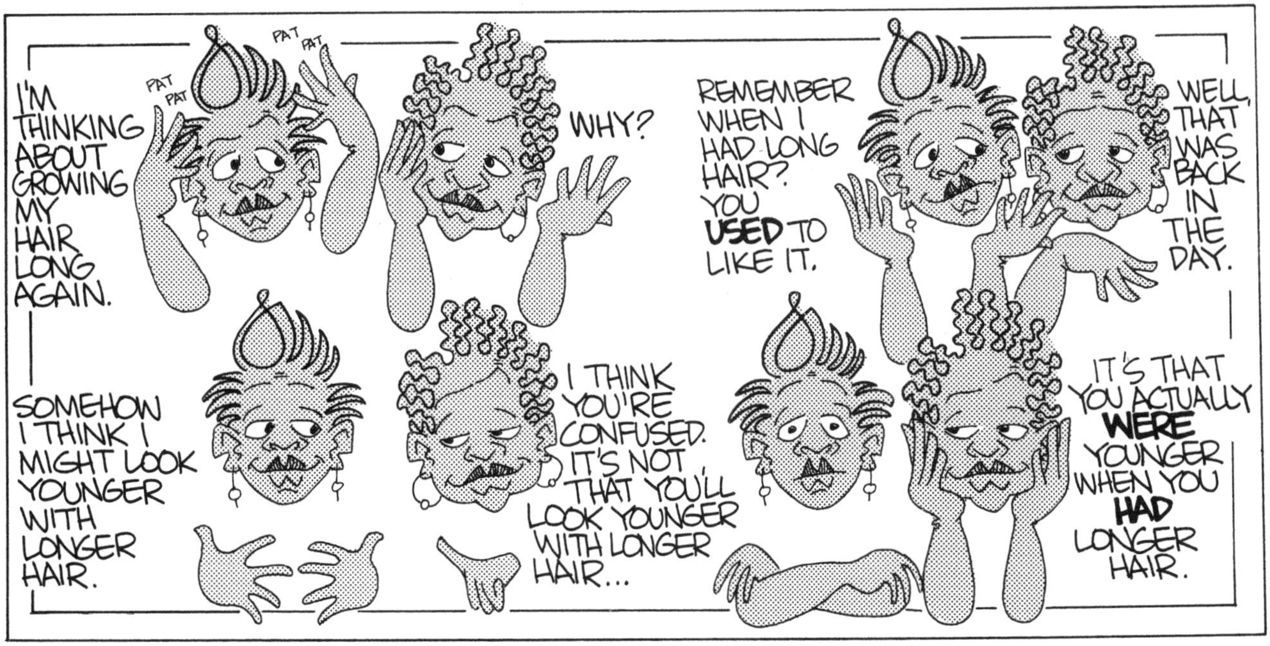
I'M THINKING ABOUT GROWING MY HAIR LONG AGAIN.
PAT PAT
PAT PAT
WHY?
REMEMBER WHEN I HAD LONG HAIR? YOU **USED** TO LIKE IT.
WELL, THAT WAS BACK IN THE DAY.
SOMEHOW I THINK I MIGHT LOOK YOUNGER WITH LONGER HAIR.
I THINK YOU'RE CONFUSED. IT'S NOT THAT YOU'LL LOOK YOUNGER WITH LONGER HAIR...
IT'S THAT YOU ACTUALLY **WERE** YOUNGER WHEN YOU **HAD** LONGER HAIR.

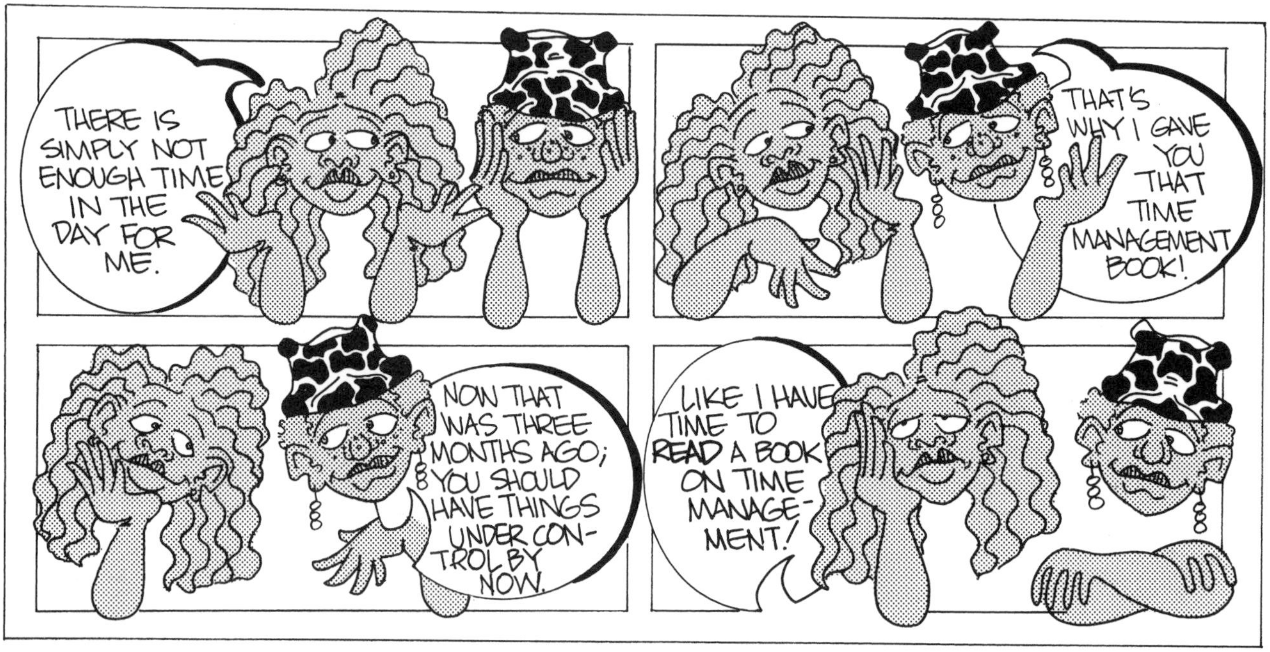
THERE IS SIMPLY NOT ENOUGH TIME IN THE DAY FOR ME.
THAT'S WHY I GAVE YOU THAT TIME MANAGEMENT BOOK!
NOW THAT WAS THREE MONTHS AGO; YOU SHOULD HAVE THINGS UNDER CON-TROL BY NOW.
LIKE I HAVE TIME TO READ A BOOK ON TIME MANAGE-MENT!

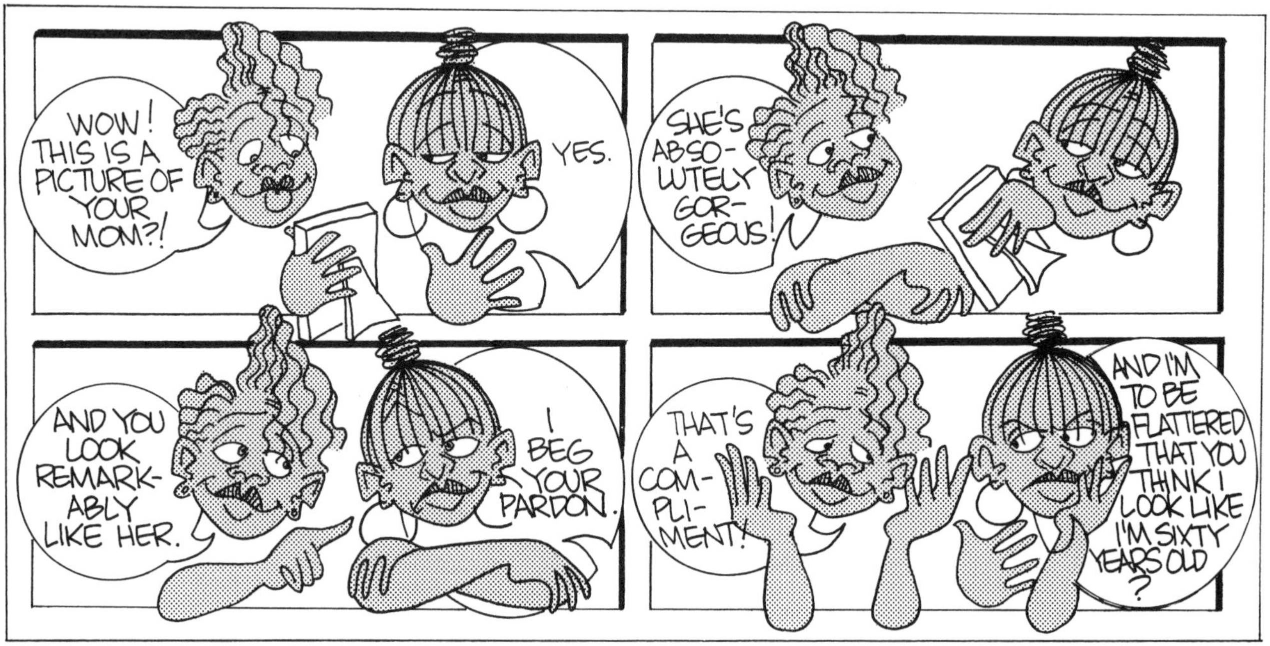
WOW! THIS IS A PICTURE OF YOUR MOM?!
YES.
SHE'S ABSO-LUTELY GOR-GEOUS!
AND YOU LOOK REMARK-ABLY LIKE HER.
I BEG YOUR PARDON.
THAT'S A COM-PLI-MENT!
AND I'M TO BE FLATTERED THAT YOU THINK I LOOK LIKE I'M SIXTY YEARS OLD?

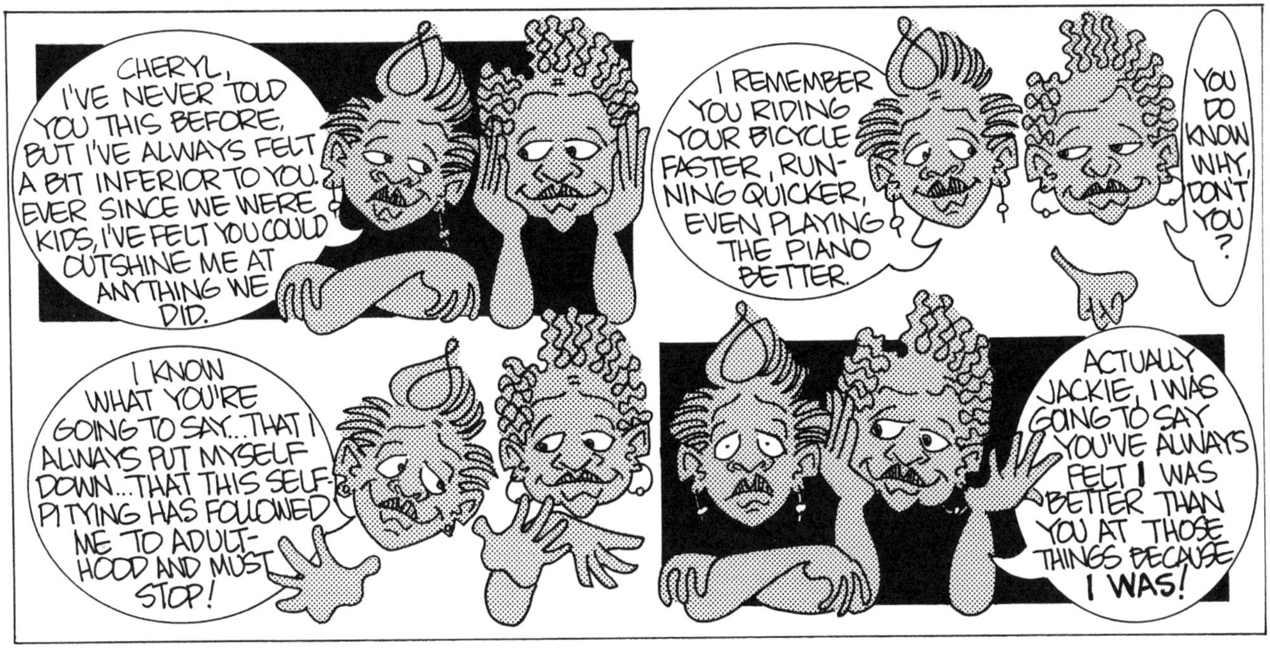
CHERYL, I'VE NEVER TOLD YOU THIS BEFORE, BUT I'VE ALWAYS FELT A BIT INFERIOR TO YOU. EVER SINCE WE WERE KIDS, I'VE FELT YOU COULD OUTSHINE ME AT ANYTHING WE DID.
I REMEMBER YOU RIDING YOUR BICYCLE FASTER, RUNNING QUICKER, EVEN PLAYING THE PIANO BETTER.
YOU DO KNOW WHY, DON'T YOU?
I KNOW WHAT YOU'RE GOING TO SAY...THAT I ALWAYS PUT MYSELF DOWN...THAT THIS SELF-PITYING HAS FOLLOWED ME TO ADULTHOOD AND MUST STOP!
ACTUALLY JACKIE, I WAS GOING TO SAY YOU'VE ALWAYS FELT I WAS BETTER THAN YOU AT THOSE THINGS BECAUSE I WAS!

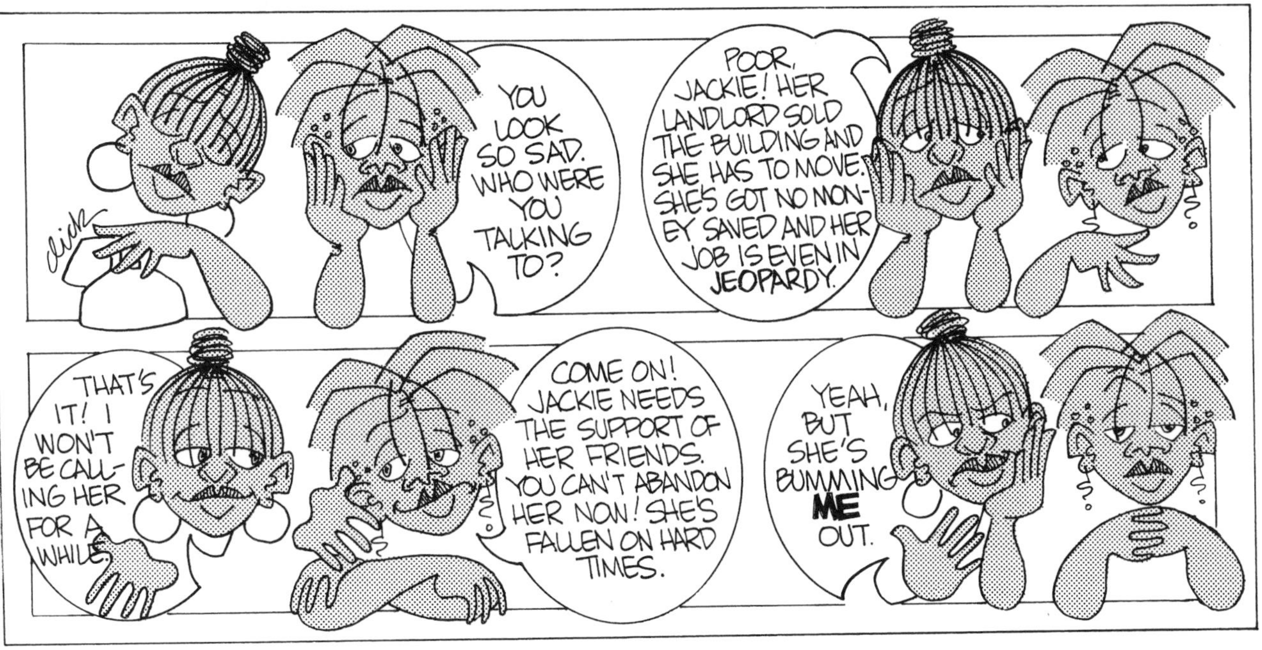
click
YOU LOOK SO SAD. WHO WERE YOU TALKING TO?
POOR, JACKIE! HER LANDLORD SOLD THE BUILDING AND SHE HAS TO MOVE. SHE'S GOT NO MONEY SAVED AND HER JOB IS EVEN IN JEOPARDY.
YEAH, BUT SHE'S BUMMING ME OUT.
COME ON! JACKIE NEEDS THE SUPPORT OF HER FRIENDS. YOU CAN'T ABANDON HER NOW! SHE'S FALLEN ON HARD TIMES.
THAT'S IT! I WON'T BE CALLING HER FOR A WHILE.

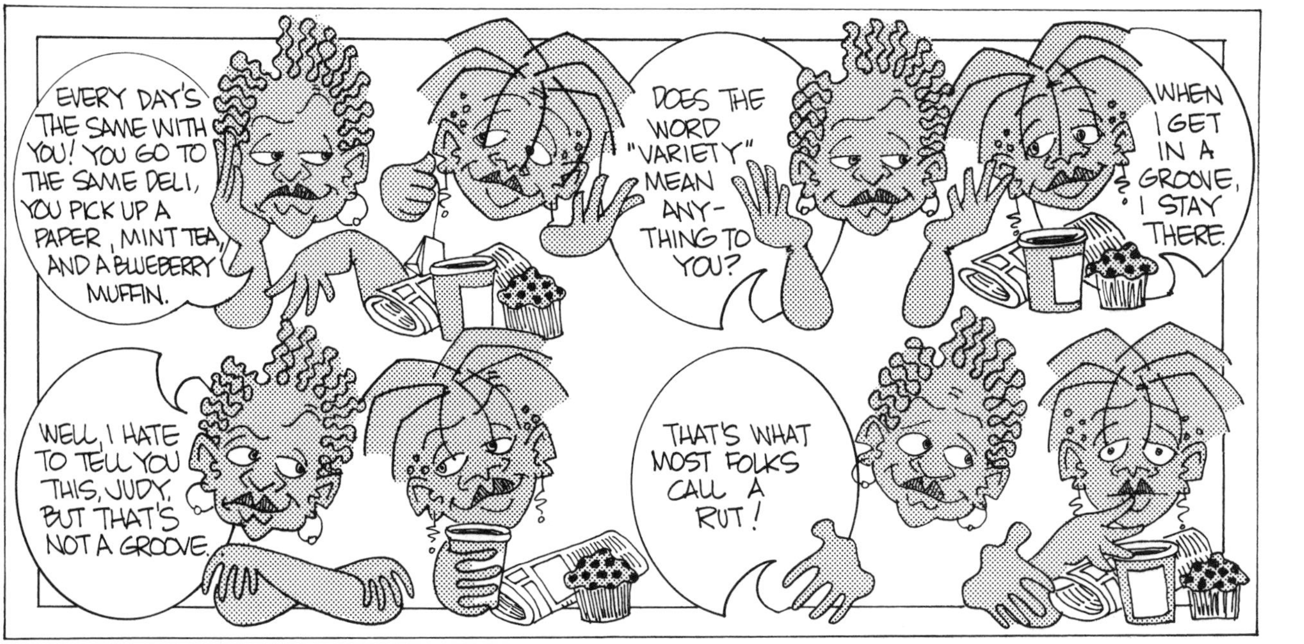
EVERY DAY'S THE SAME WITH YOU! YOU GO TO THE SAME DELI, YOU PICK UP A PAPER, MINT TEA, AND A BLUEBERRY MUFFIN.
DOES THE WORD "VARIETY" MEAN ANY-THING TO YOU?
WHEN I GET IN A GROOVE, I STAY THERE.
WELL, I HATE TO TELL YOU THIS, JUDY, BUT THAT'S NOT A GROOVE.
THAT'S WHAT MOST FOLKS CALL A RUT!

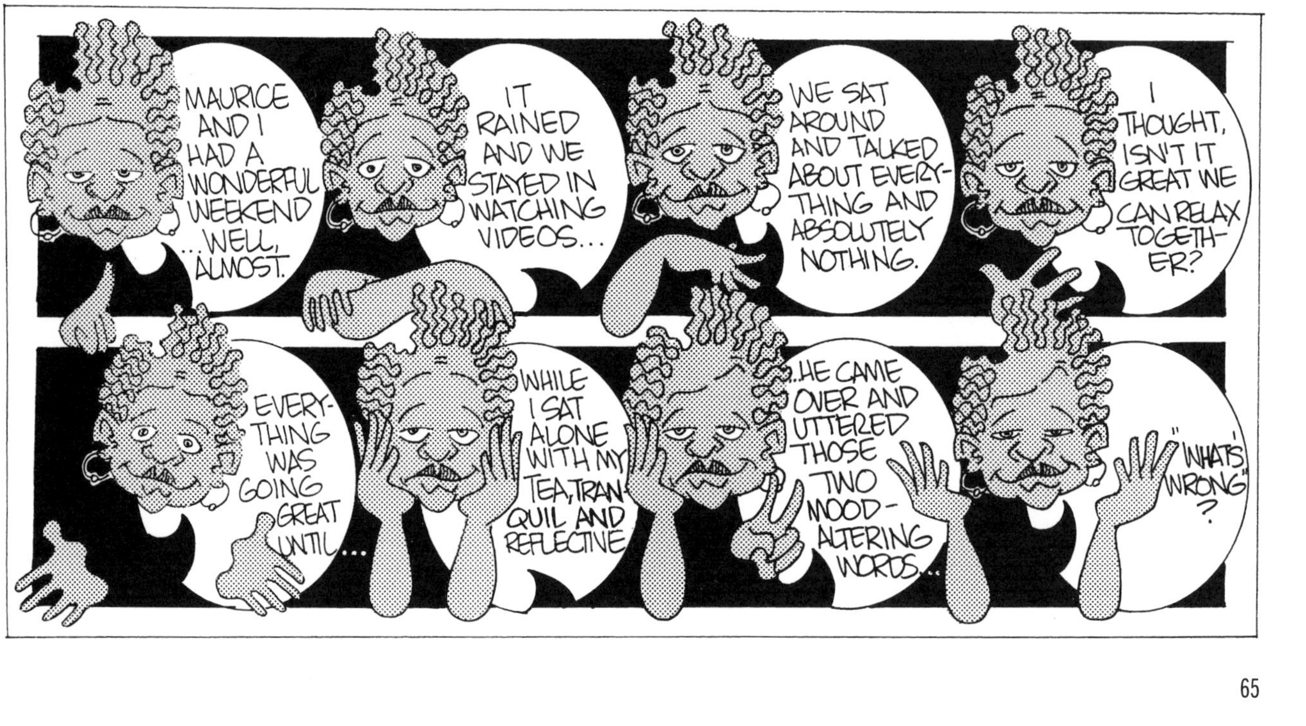
MAURICE AND I HAD A WONDERFUL WEEKEND ...WELL, ALMOST.
IT RAINED AND WE STAYED IN WATCHING VIDEOS...
WE SAT AROUND AND TALKED ABOUT EVERY-THING AND ABSOLUTELY NOTHING.
I THOUGHT, ISN'T IT GREAT WE CAN RELAX TOGETH-ER?
EVERY-THING WAS GOING GREAT UNTIL...
WHILE I SAT ALONE WITH MY TEA, TRAN QUIL AND REFLECTIVE
..HE CAME OVER AND UTTERED THOSE TWO MOOD-ALTERING WORDS...
"WHAT'S WRONG"?

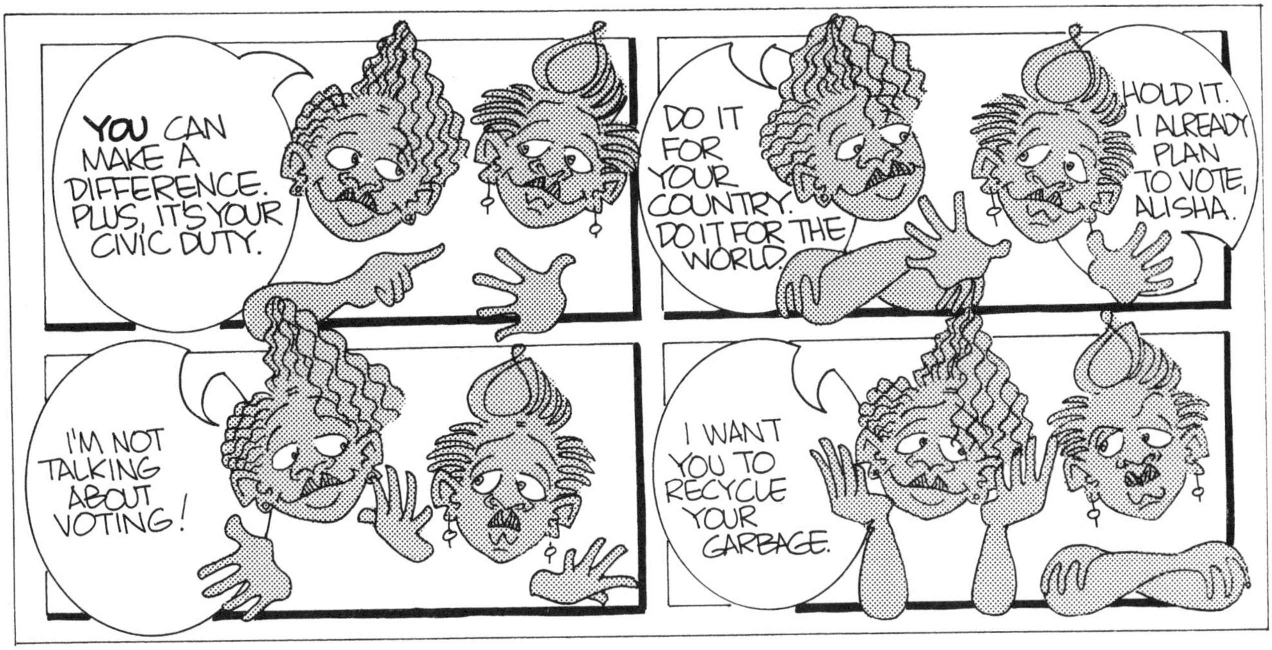
YOU CAN MAKE A DIFFERENCE. PLUS, IT'S YOUR CIVIC DUTY.
DO IT FOR YOUR COUNTRY. DO IT FOR THE WORLD.
HOLD IT. I ALREADY PLAN TO VOTE, ALISHA.
I'M NOT TALKING ABOUT VOTING!
I WANT YOU TO RECYCLE YOUR GARBAGE.

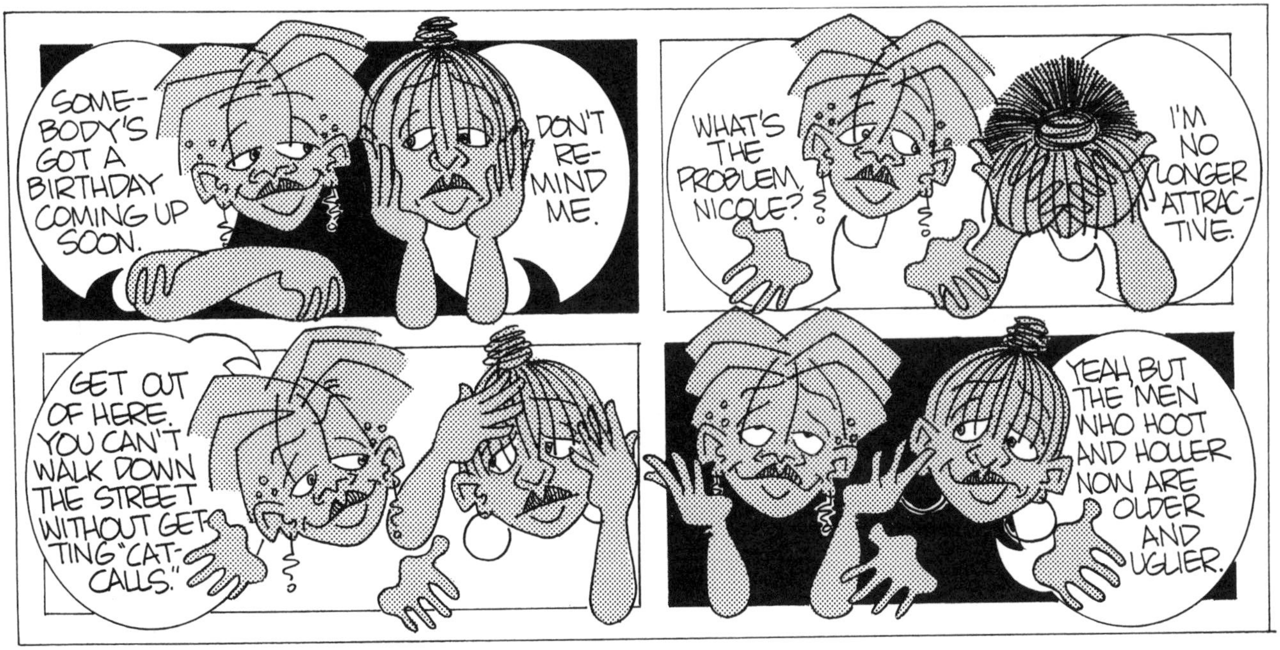
SOMEBODY'S GOT A BIRTHDAY COMING UP SOON.
DON'T RE-MIND ME.
WHAT'S THE PROBLEM, NICOLE?
I'M NO LONGER ATTRACTIVE.
GET OUT OF HERE. YOU CAN'T WALK DOWN THE STREET WITHOUT GETTING "CAT-CALLS."
YEAH, BUT THE MEN WHO HOOT AND HOLLER NOW ARE OLDER AND UGLIER.

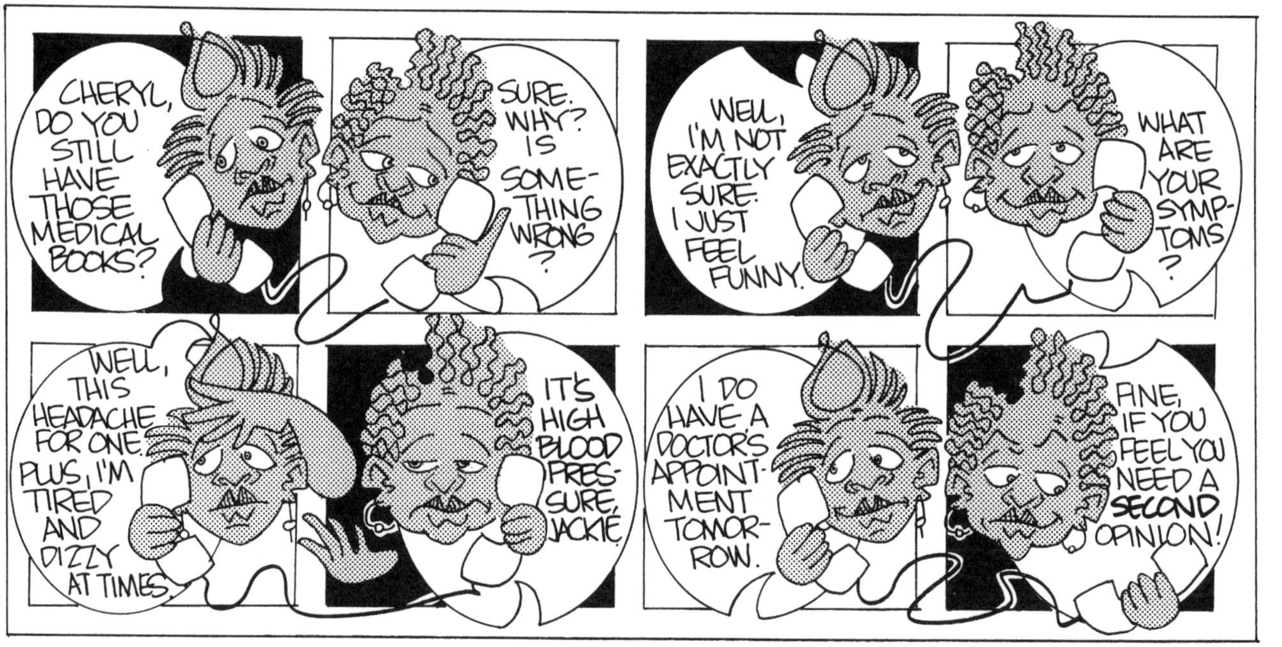
CHERYL, DO YOU STILL HAVE THOSE MEDICAL BOOKS?
SURE. WHY? IS SOME-THING WRONG?
WELL, I'M NOT EXACTLY SURE. I JUST FEEL FUNNY.
WHAT ARE YOUR SYMP-TOMS?
WELL, THIS HEADACHE FOR ONE. PLUS, I'M TIRED AND DIZZY AT TIMES.
IT'S HIGH BLOOD PRES-SURE, JACKIE.
I DO HAVE A DOCTOR'S APPOINT-MENT TOMOR-ROW.
FINE, IF YOU FEEL YOU NEED A SECOND OPINION!

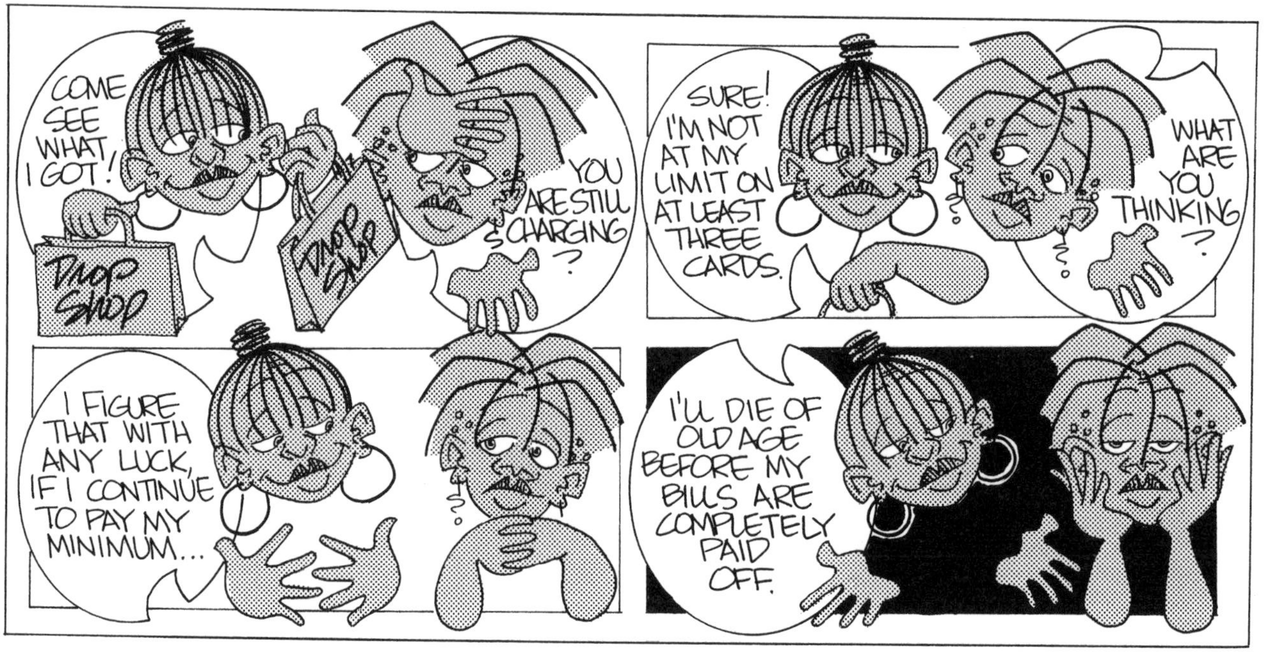
COME SEE WHAT I GOT!
YOU ARE STILL CHARGING?
SURE! I'M NOT AT MY LIMIT ON AT LEAST THREE CARDS.
WHAT ARE YOU THINKING?
I FIGURE THAT WITH ANY LUCK, IF I CONTINUE TO PAY MY MINIMUM...
I'LL DIE OF OLD AGE BEFORE MY BILLS ARE COMPLETELY PAID OFF.

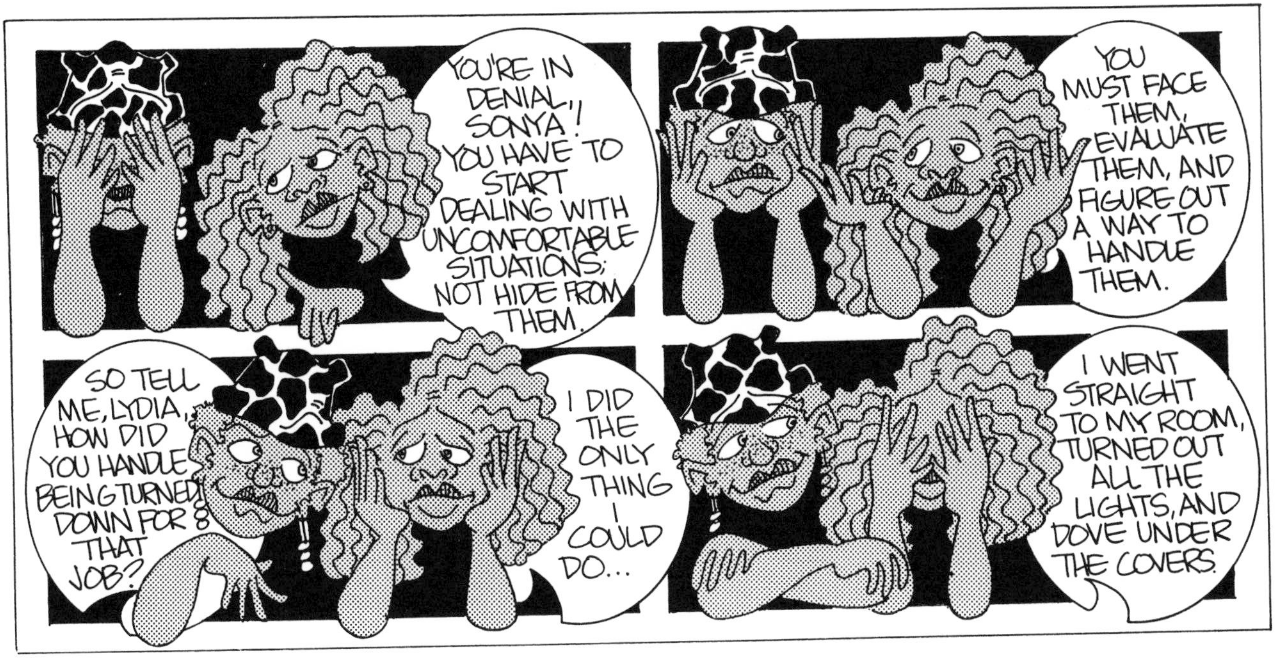
YOU'RE IN DENIAL, SONYA! YOU HAVE TO START DEALING WITH UNCOMFORTABLE SITUATIONS; NOT HIDE FROM THEM.
YOU MUST FACE THEM, EVALUATE THEM, AND FIGURE OUT A WAY TO HANDLE THEM.
SO TELL ME, LYDIA, HOW DID YOU HANDLE BEING TURNED DOWN FOR THAT JOB?
I DID THE ONLY THING I COULD DO...
I WENT STRAIGHT TO MY ROOM, TURNED OUT ALL THE LIGHTS, AND DOVE UNDER THE COVERS.

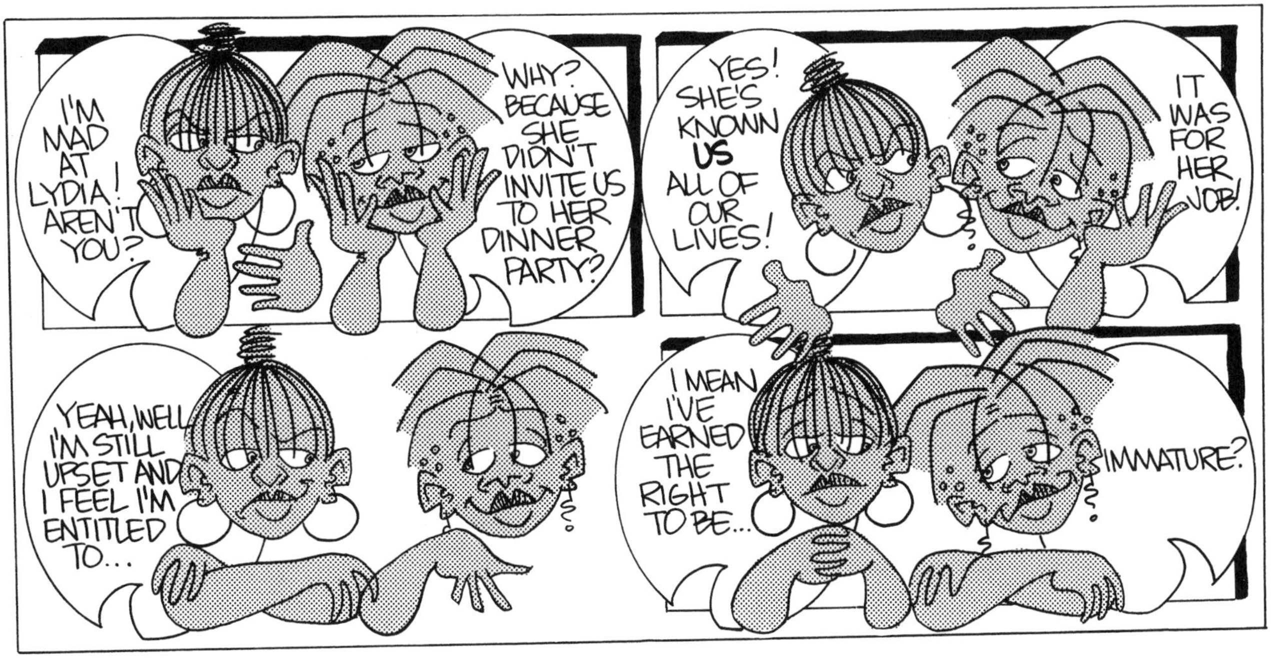
I'M MAD AT LYDIA! AREN'T YOU?
WHY? BECAUSE SHE DIDN'T INVITE US TO HER DINNER PARTY?
YES! SHE'S KNOWN US ALL OF OUR LIVES!
IT WAS FOR HER JOB!
YEAH, WELL I'M STILL UPSET AND I FEEL I'M ENTITLED TO...
I MEAN I'VE EARNED THE RIGHT TO BE...
IMMATURE?

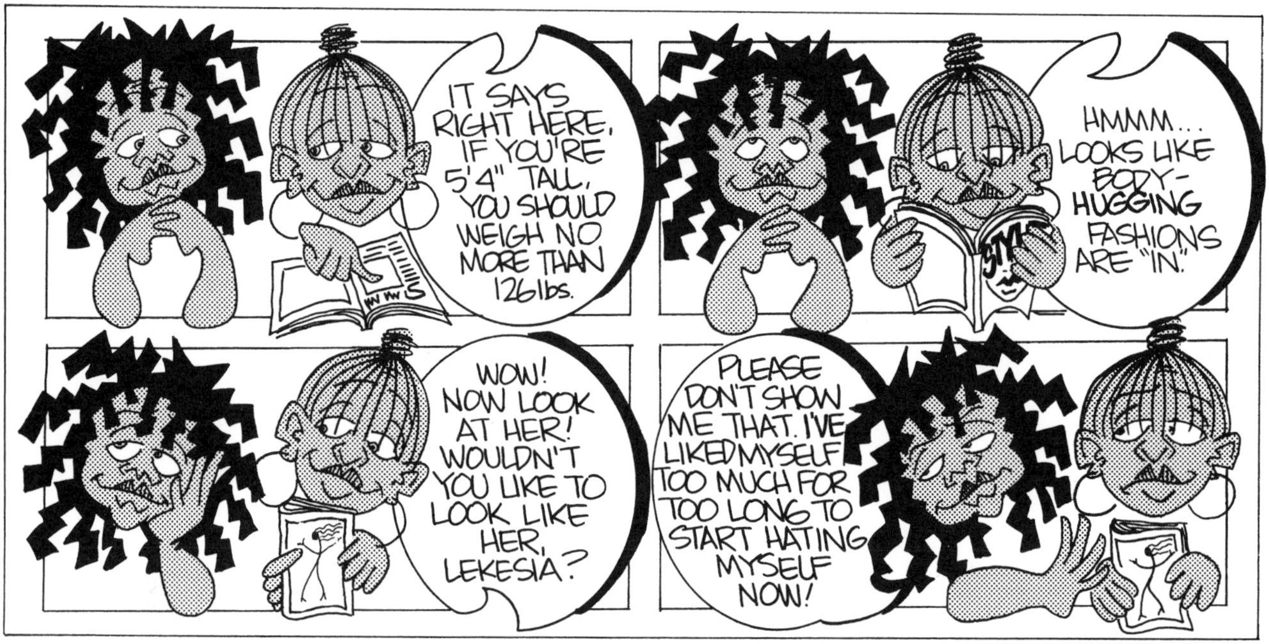
IT SAYS RIGHT HERE, IF YOU'RE 5'4" TALL, YOU SHOULD WEIGH NO MORE THAN 126lbs.
HMMM... LOOKS LIKE BODY-**HUGGING** FASHIONS ARE "IN."
WOW! NOW LOOK AT HER! WOULDN'T YOU LIKE TO LOOK LIKE HER, LEKESIA?
PLEASE DON'T SHOW ME THAT. I'VE LIKED MYSELF TOO MUCH FOR TOO LONG TO START HATING MYSELF NOW!

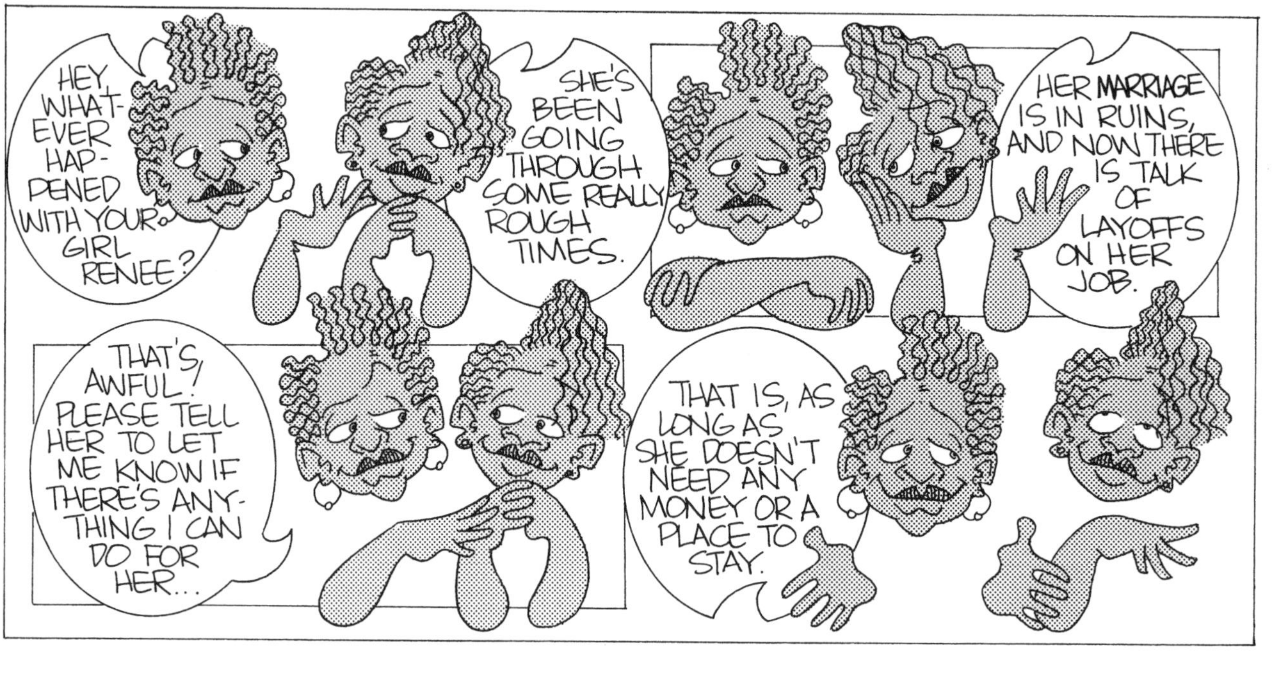
HEY, WHAT-EVER HAP-PENED WITH YOUR GIRL RENEE?
SHE'S BEEN GOING THROUGH SOME REALLY ROUGH TIMES.
HER **MARRIAGE** IS IN RUINS, AND NOW THERE IS TALK OF LAYOFFS ON HER JOB.
THAT'S AWFUL! PLEASE TELL HER TO LET ME KNOW IF THERE'S ANY-THING I CAN DO FOR HER...
THAT IS, AS LONG AS SHE DOESN'T NEED ANY MONEY OR A PLACE TO STAY.

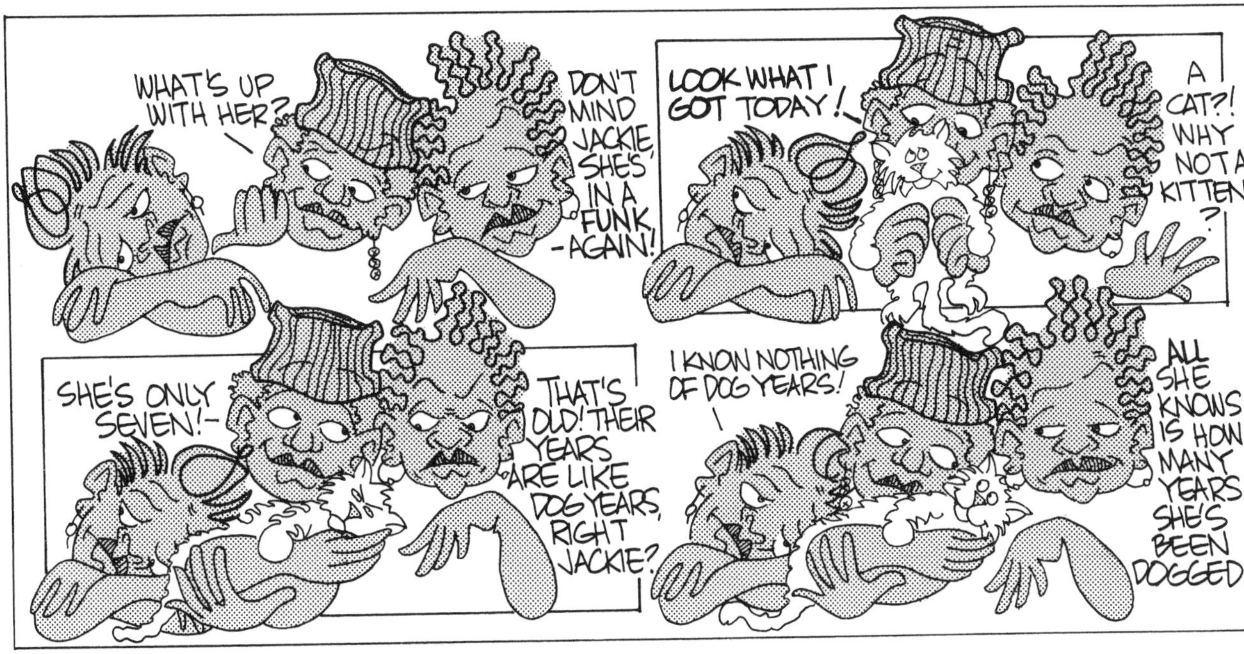
WHAT'S UP WITH HER?
DON'T MIND JACKIE, SHE'S IN A FUNK -AGAIN!
LOOK WHAT I GOT TODAY!
A CAT?! WHY NOT A KITTEN?
SHE'S ONLY SEVEN!
THAT'S OLD! THEIR YEARS ARE LIKE DOG YEARS, RIGHT JACKIE?
I KNOW NOTHING OF DOG YEARS!
ALL SHE KNOWS IS HOW MANY YEARS SHE'S BEEN DOGGED.

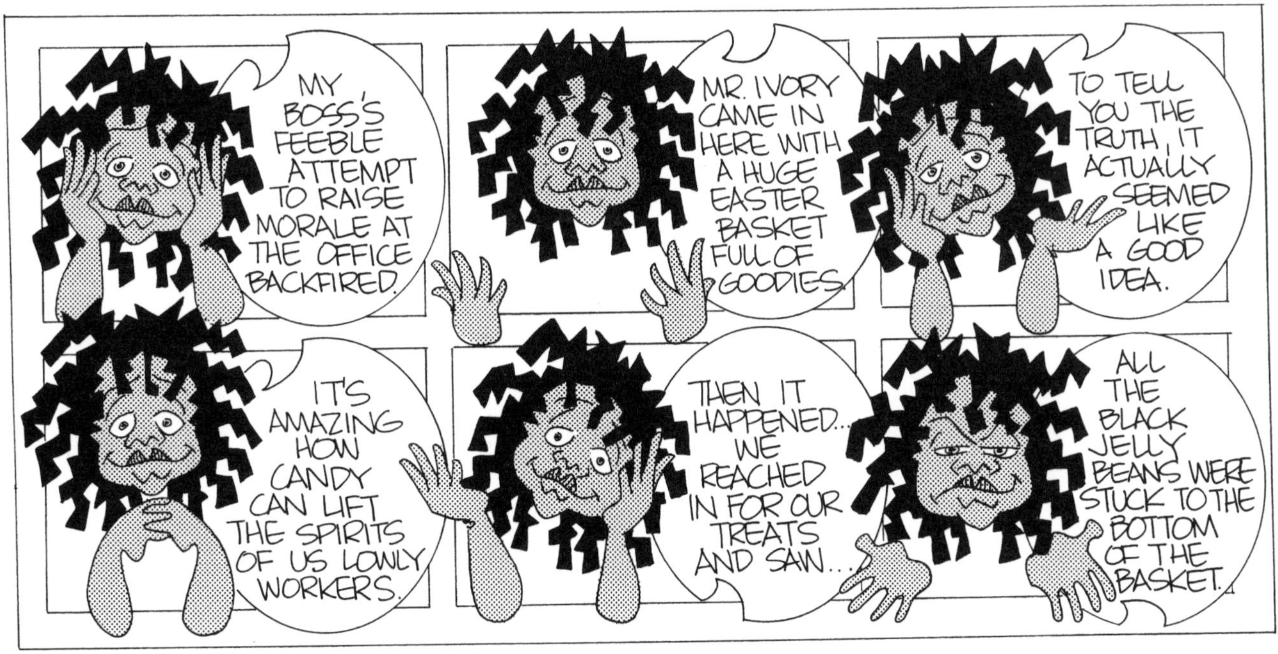
MY BOSS'S FEEBLE ATTEMPT TO RAISE MORALE AT THE OFFICE BACKFIRED.
MR. IVORY CAME IN HERE WITH A HUGE EASTER BASKET FULL OF GOODIES.
TO TELL YOU THE TRUTH, IT ACTUALLY SEEMED LIKE A GOOD IDEA.
IT'S AMAZING HOW CANDY CAN LIFT THE SPIRITS OF US LOWLY WORKERS.
THEN IT HAPPENED... WE REACHED IN FOR OUR TREATS AND SAW...
ALL THE BLACK JELLY BEANS WERE STUCK TO THE BOTTOM OF THE BASKET.

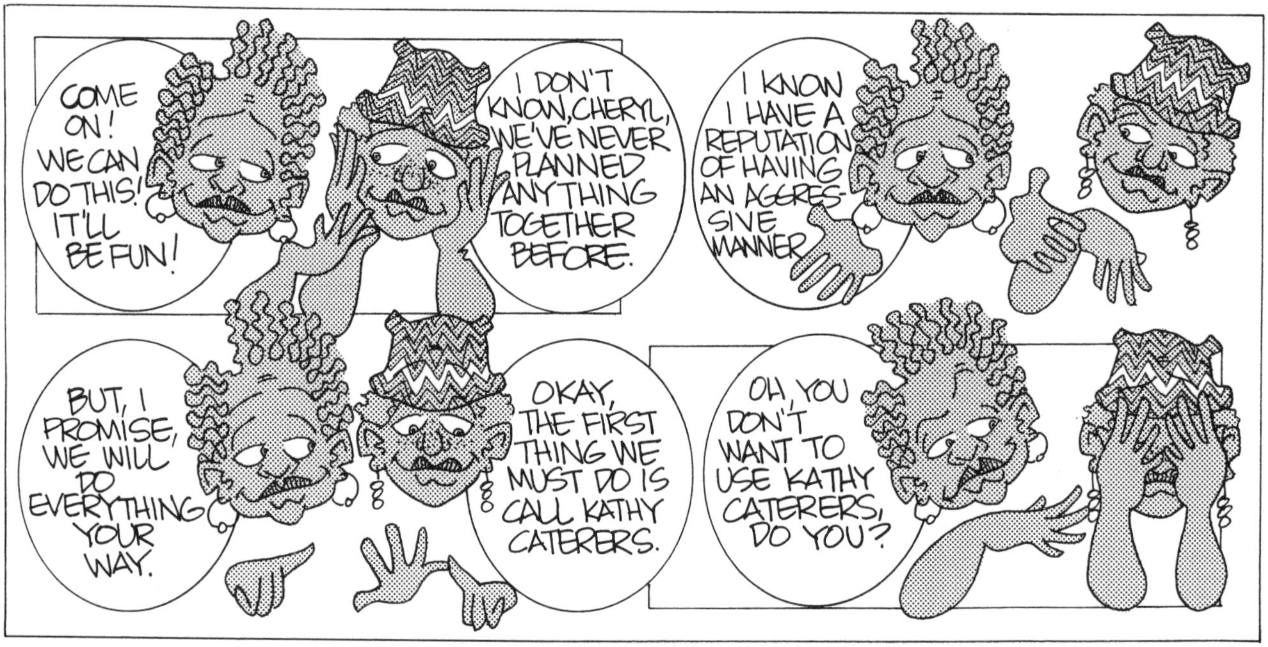
COME ON! WE CAN DO THIS! IT'LL BE FUN!
I DON'T KNOW, CHERYL, WE'VE NEVER PLANNED ANYTHING TOGETHER BEFORE.
I KNOW I HAVE A REPUTATION OF HAVING AN AGGRES-SIVE MANNER
BUT, I PROMISE, WE WILL DO EVERYTHING YOUR WAY.
OKAY, THE FIRST THING WE MUST DO IS CALL KATHY CATERERS.
OH, YOU DON'T WANT TO USE KATHY CATERERS, DO YOU?

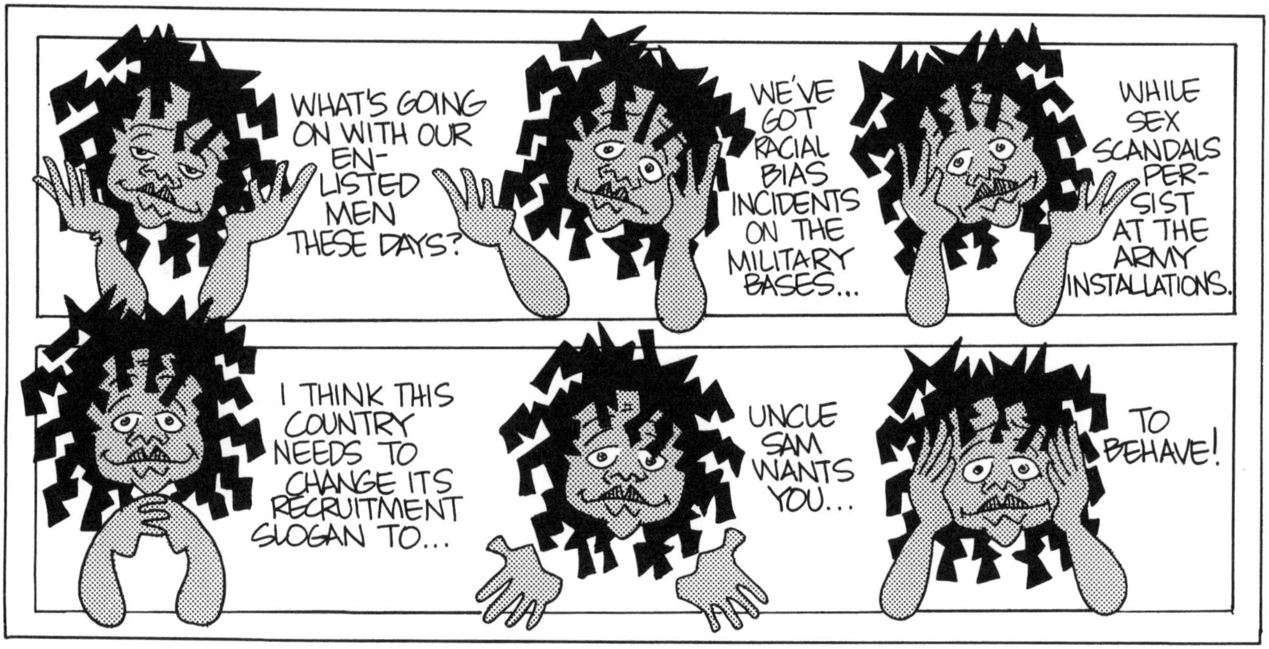
WHAT'S GOING ON WITH OUR EN-LISTED MEN THESE DAYS?
WE'VE GOT RACIAL BIAS INCIDENTS ON THE MILITARY BASES...
WHILE SEX SCANDALS PER-SIST AT THE ARMY INSTALLATIONS.
I THINK THIS COUNTRY NEEDS TO CHANGE ITS RECRUITMENT SLOGAN TO...
UNCLE SAM WANTS YOU...
TO BEHAVE!

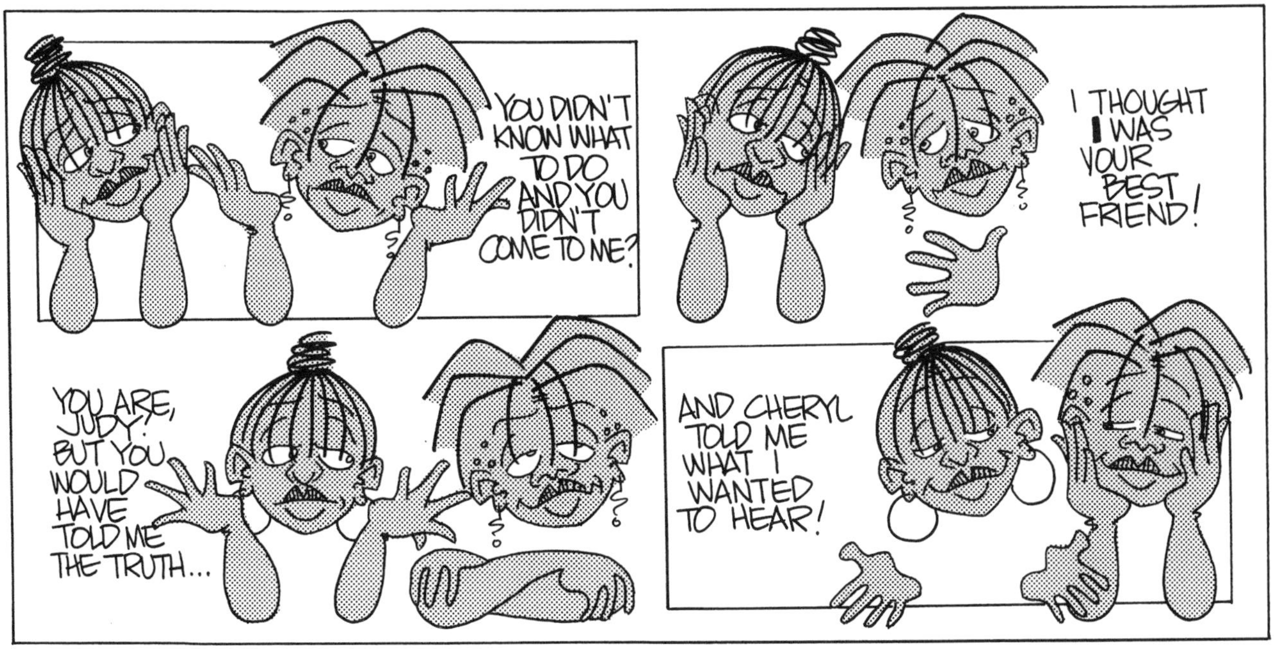
YOU DIDN'T KNOW WHAT TO DO AND YOU DIDN'T COME TO ME?
I THOUGHT I WAS YOUR BEST FRIEND!
YOU ARE, JUDY! BUT YOU WOULD HAVE TOLD ME THE TRUTH...
AND CHERYL TOLD ME WHAT I WANTED TO HEAR!

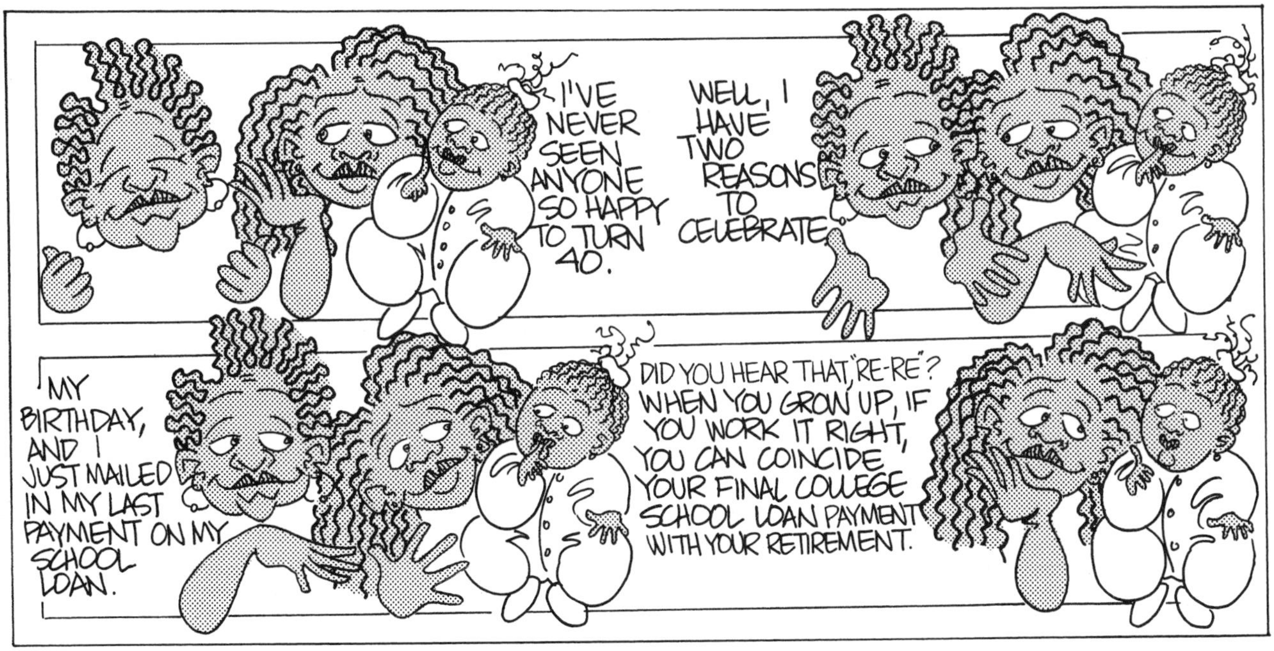
I'VE NEVER SEEN ANYONE SO HAPPY TO TURN 40.
WELL, I HAVE TWO REASONS TO CELEBRATE.
MY BIRTHDAY, AND I JUST MAILED IN MY LAST PAYMENT ON MY SCHOOL LOAN.
DID YOU HEAR THAT, "RE-RE"? WHEN YOU GROW UP, IF YOU WORK IT RIGHT, YOU CAN COINCIDE YOUR FINAL COLLEGE SCHOOL LOAN PAYMENT WITH YOUR RETIREMENT.

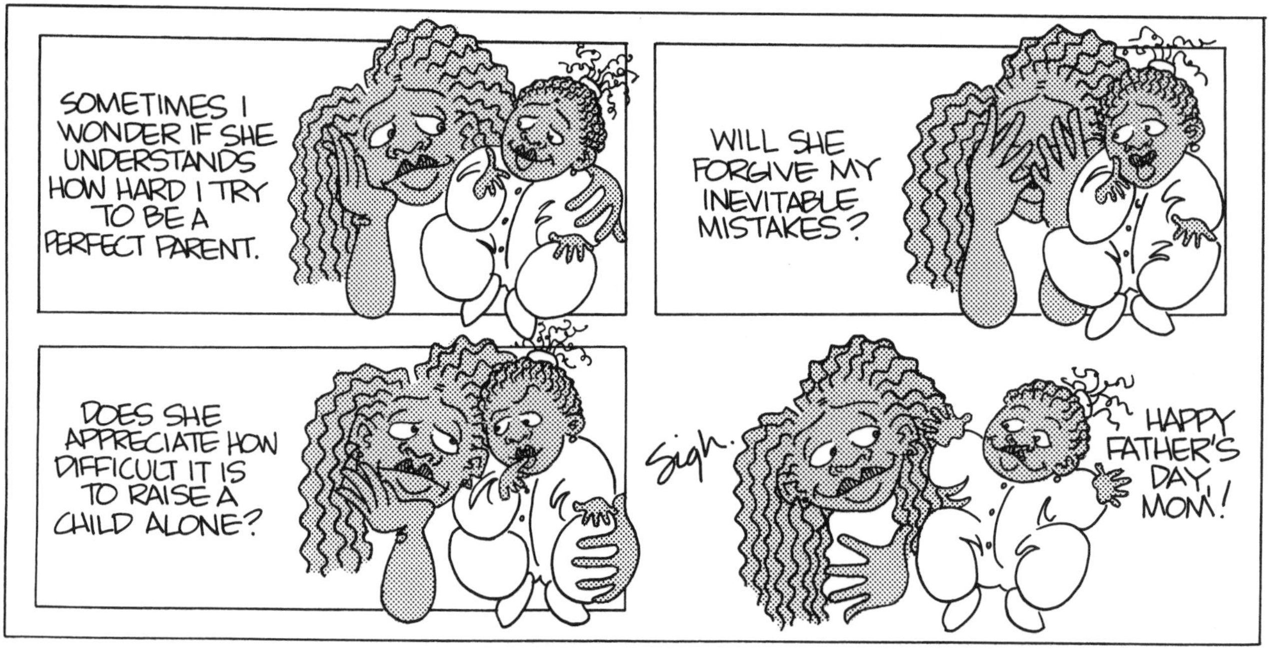
SOMETIMES I WONDER IF SHE UNDERSTANDS HOW HARD I TRY TO BE A PERFECT PARENT.
WILL SHE FORGIVE MY INEVITABLE MISTAKES?
DOES SHE APPRECIATE HOW DIFFICULT IT IS TO RAISE A CHILD ALONE?
Sigh...
HAPPY FATHER'S DAY, MOM!

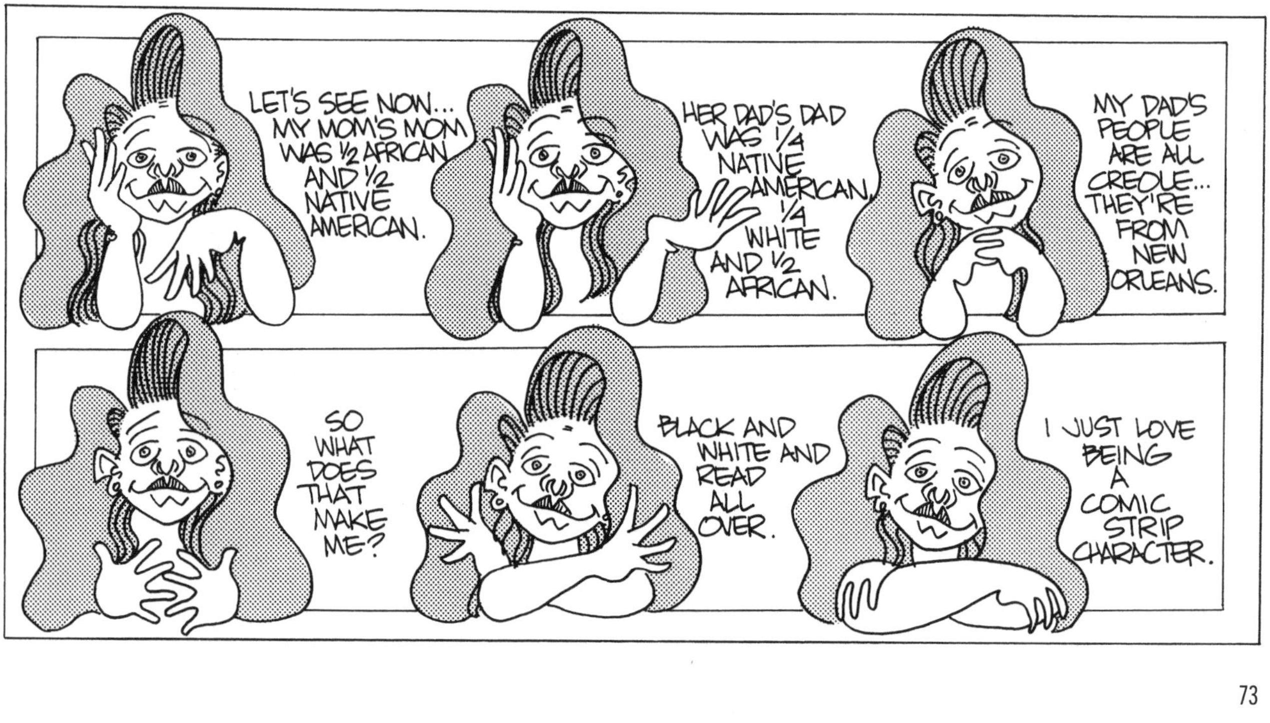
LET'S SEE NOW... MY MOM'S MOM WAS ½ AFRICAN AND ½ NATIVE AMERICAN.
HER DAD'S DAD WAS ¼ NATIVE AMERICAN, ¼ WHITE AND ½ AFRICAN.
MY DAD'S PEOPLE ARE ALL CREOLE... THEY'RE FROM NEW ORLEANS.
SO WHAT DOES THAT MAKE ME?
BLACK AND WHITE AND READ ALL OVER.
I JUST LOVE BEING A COMIC STRIP CHARACTER.

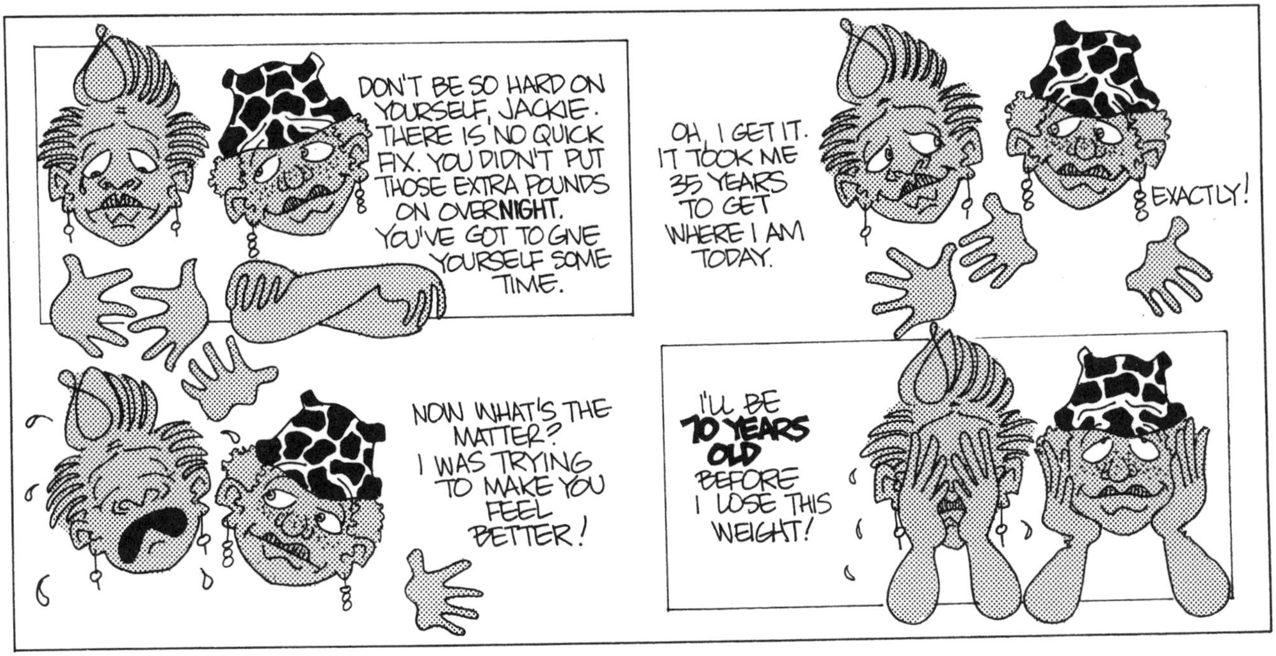
DON'T BE SO HARD ON YOURSELF, JACKIE. THERE IS NO QUICK FIX. YOU DIDN'T PUT THOSE EXTRA POUNDS ON OVERNIGHT. YOU'VE GOT TO GIVE YOURSELF SOME TIME.
OH, I GET IT. IT TOOK ME 35 YEARS TO GET WHERE I AM TODAY.
EXACTLY!
NOW WHAT'S THE MATTER? I WAS TRYING TO MAKE YOU FEEL BETTER!
I'LL BE 70 YEARS OLD BEFORE I LOSE THIS WEIGHT!

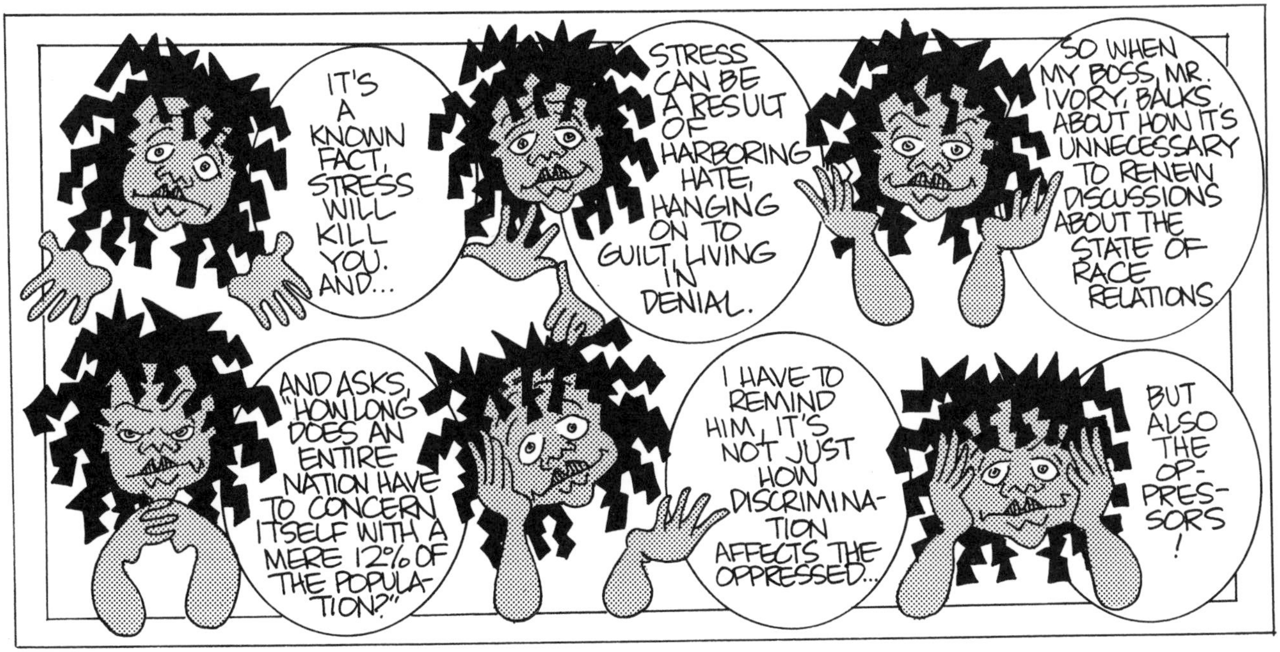
IT'S A KNOWN FACT, STRESS WILL KILL YOU. AND...
STRESS CAN BE A RESULT OF HARBORING HATE, HANGING ON TO GUILT, LIVING IN DENIAL.
SO WHEN MY BOSS, MR. IVORY, BALKS ABOUT HOW IT'S UNNECESSARY TO RENEW DISCUSSIONS ABOUT THE STATE OF RACE RELATIONS
AND ASKS, "HOW LONG DOES AN ENTIRE NATION HAVE TO CONCERN ITSELF WITH A MERE 12% OF THE POPULATION?"
I HAVE TO REMIND HIM, IT'S NOT JUST HOW DISCRIMINATION AFFECTS THE OPPRESSED...
BUT ALSO THE OPPRESSORS!

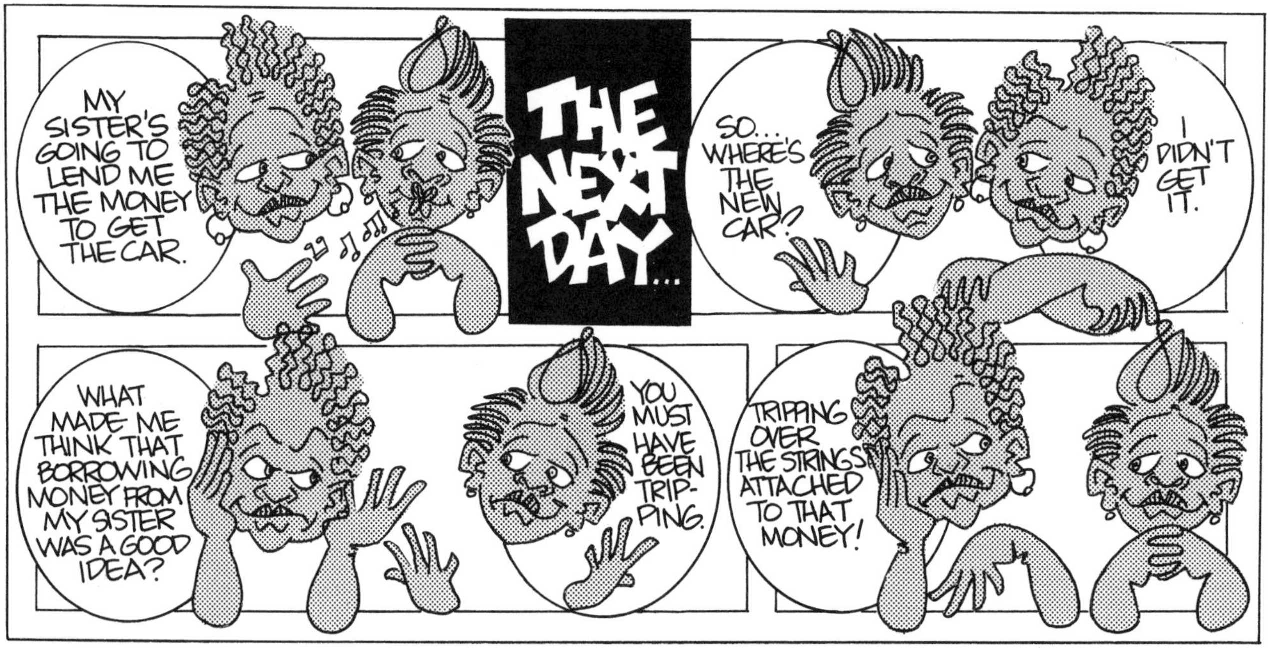
MY SISTER'S GOING TO LEND ME THE MONEY TO GET THE CAR.
THE NEXT DAY...
SO... WHERE'S THE NEW CAR?
I DIDN'T GET IT.
WHAT MADE ME THINK THAT BORROWING MONEY FROM MY SISTER WAS A GOOD IDEA?
YOU MUST HAVE BEEN TRIP-PING.
TRIPPING OVER THE STRINGS ATTACHED TO THAT MONEY!

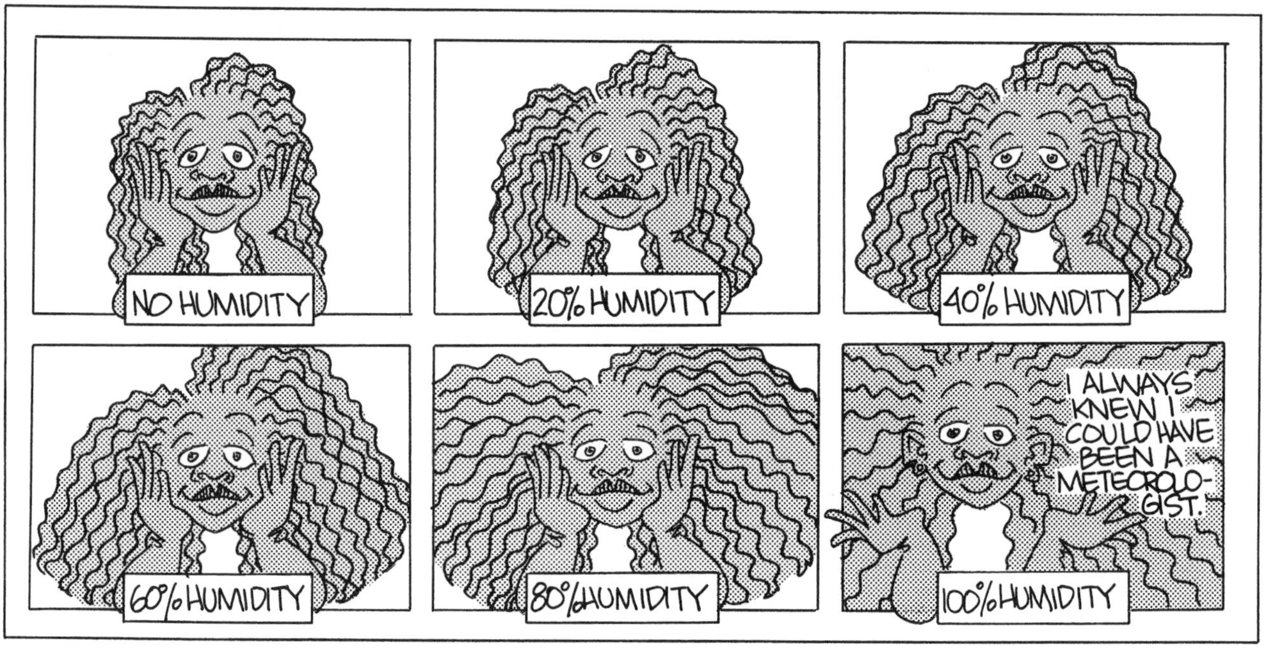
NO HUMIDITY
20% HUMIDITY
40% HUMIDITY
60% HUMIDITY
80% HUMIDITY
I ALWAYS KNEW I COULD HAVE BEEN A METEOROLO-GIST.
100% HUMIDITY

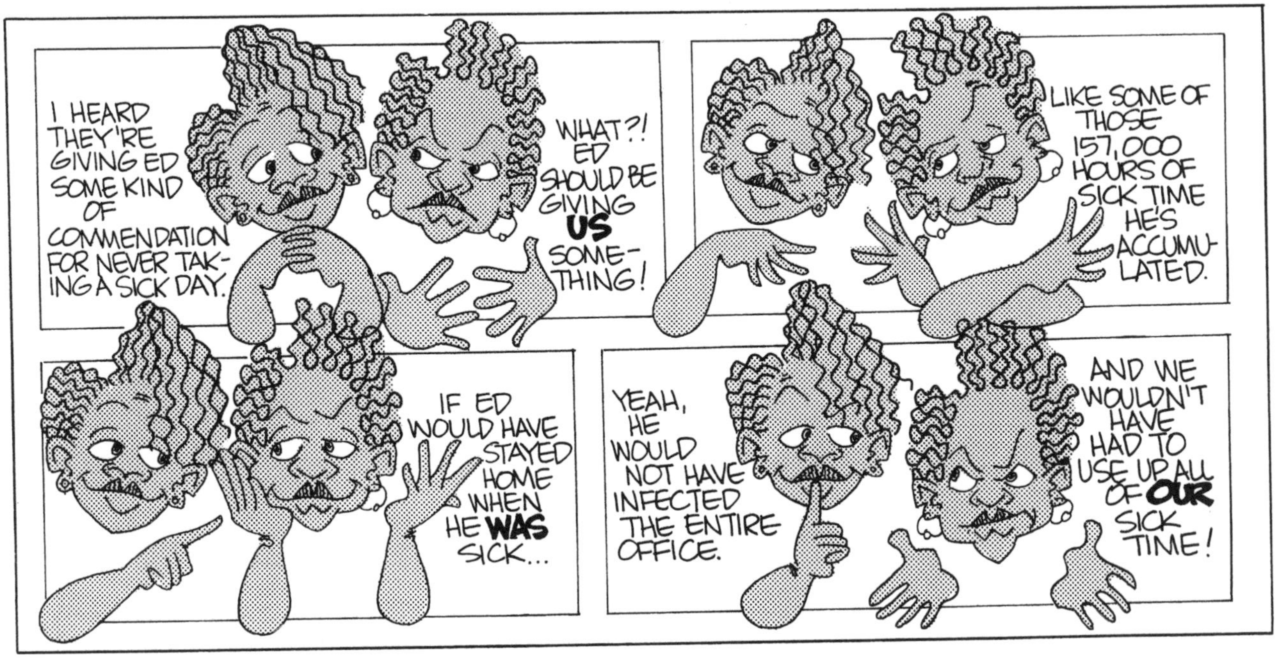
I HEARD THEY'RE GIVING ED SOME KIND OF COMMENDATION FOR NEVER TAKING A SICK DAY.
WHAT?! ED SHOULD BE GIVING **US** SOMETHING!
IF ED WOULD HAVE STAYED HOME WHEN HE **WAS** SICK...
YEAH, HE WOULD NOT HAVE INFECTED THE ENTIRE OFFICE.
LIKE SOME OF THOSE 157,000 HOURS OF SICK TIME HE'S ACCUMULATED.
AND WE WOULDN'T HAVE HAD TO USE UP ALL OF **OUR** SICK TIME!

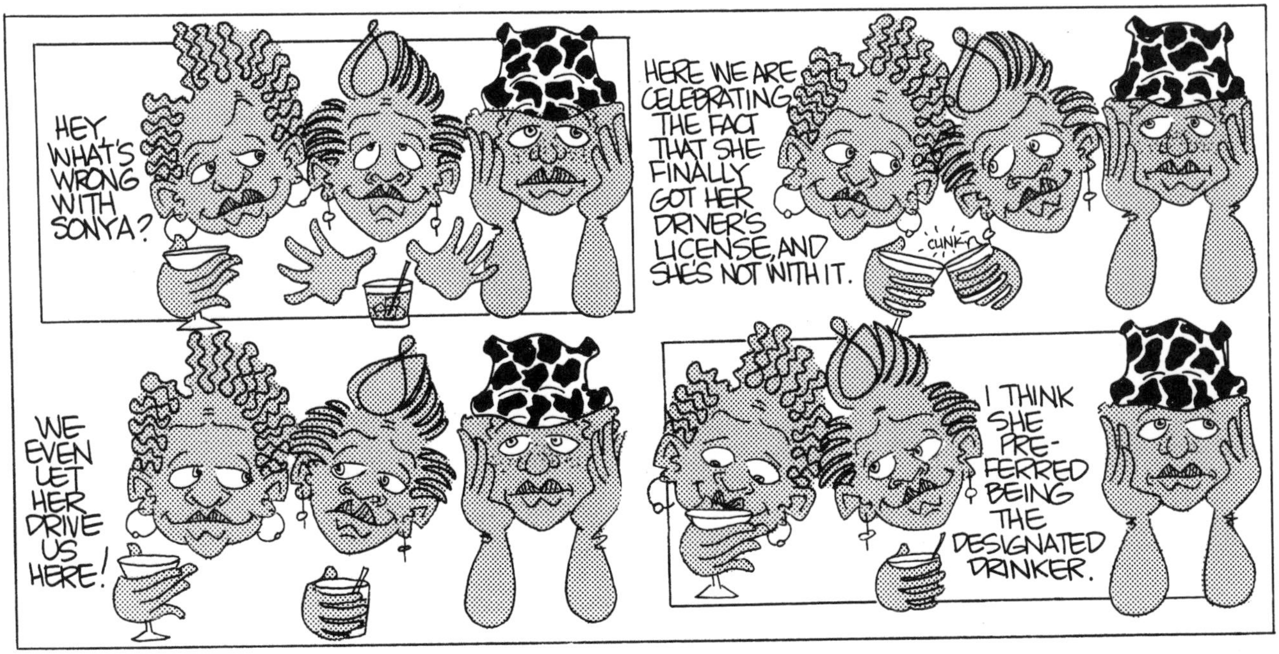
HEY, WHAT'S WRONG WITH SONYA?
HERE WE ARE CELEBRATING THE FACT THAT SHE FINALLY GOT HER DRIVER'S LICENSE, AND SHE'S NOT WITH IT.
CLINK
WE EVEN LET HER DRIVE US HERE!
I THINK SHE PREFERRED BEING THE DESIGNATED DRINKER.

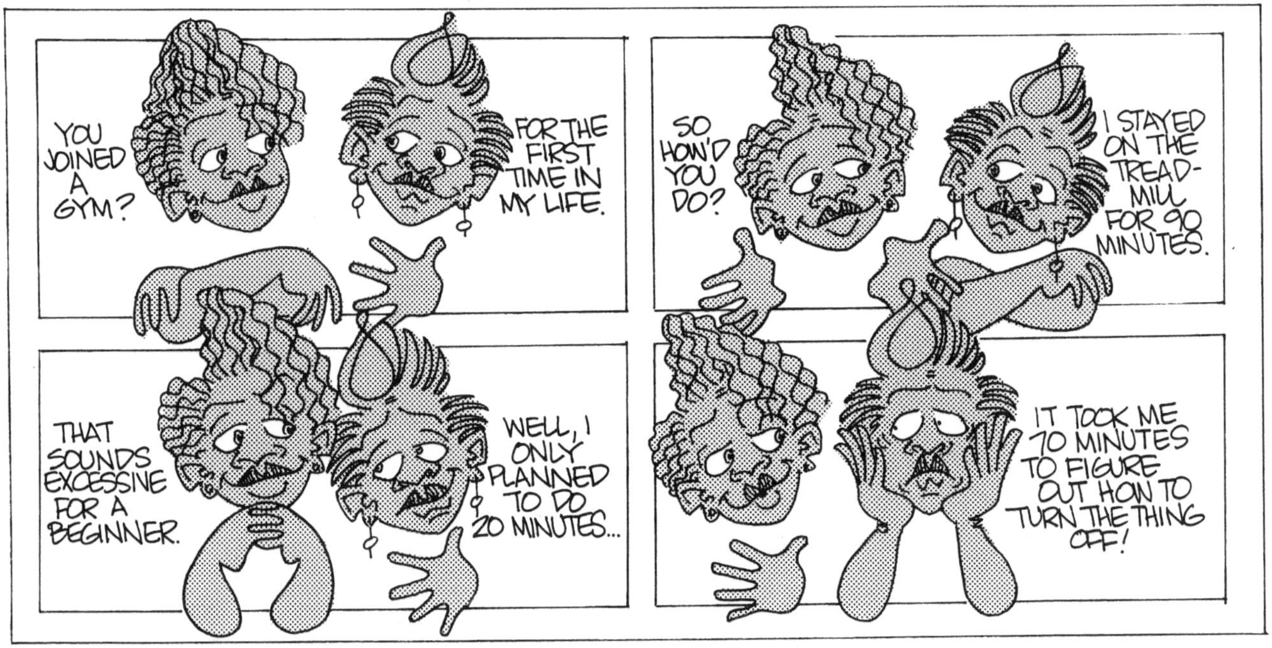
YOU JOINED A GYM?
FOR THE FIRST TIME IN MY LIFE.
THAT SOUNDS EXCESSIVE FOR A BEGINNER.
WELL, I ONLY PLANNED TO DO 20 MINUTES...
SO HOW'D YOU DO?
I STAYED ON THE TREAD-MILL FOR 90 MINUTES.
IT TOOK ME 70 MINUTES TO FIGURE OUT HOW TO TURN THE THING OFF!

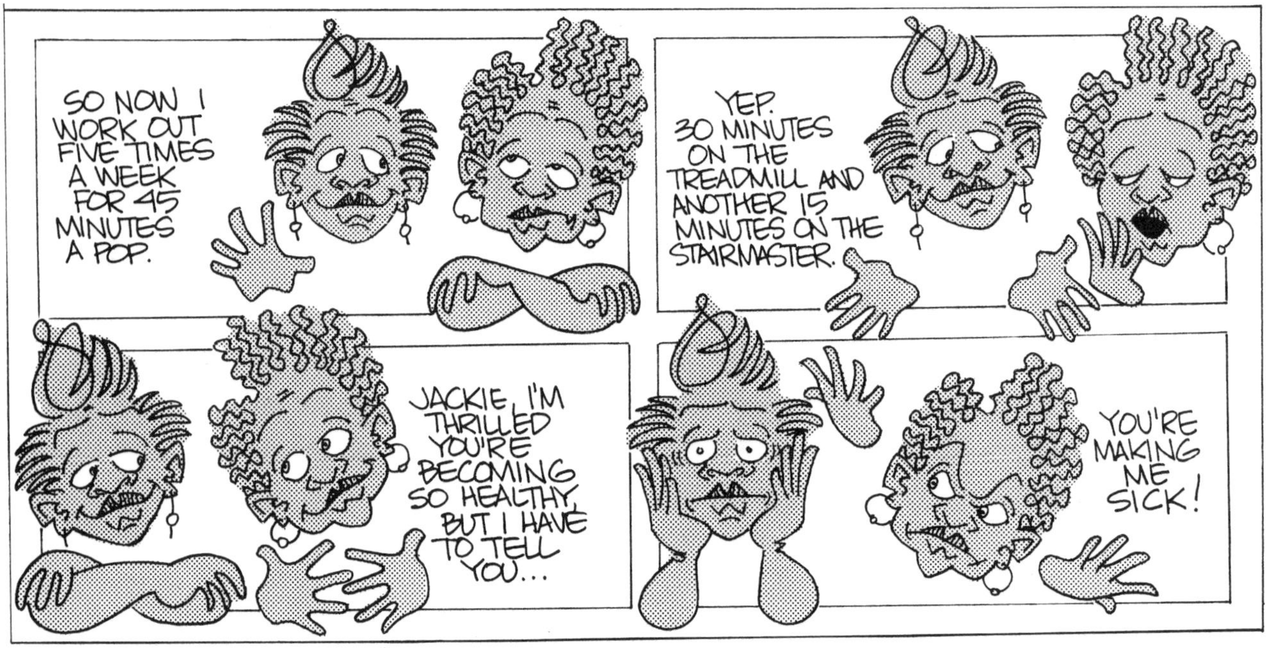
SO NOW I WORK OUT FIVE TIMES A WEEK FOR 45 MINUTES A POP.
JACKIE, I'M THRILLED YOU'RE BECOMING SO HEALTHY, BUT I HAVE TO TELL YOU...
YEP. 30 MINUTES ON THE TREADMILL AND ANOTHER 15 MINUTES ON THE STAIRMASTER.
YOU'RE MAKING ME SICK!

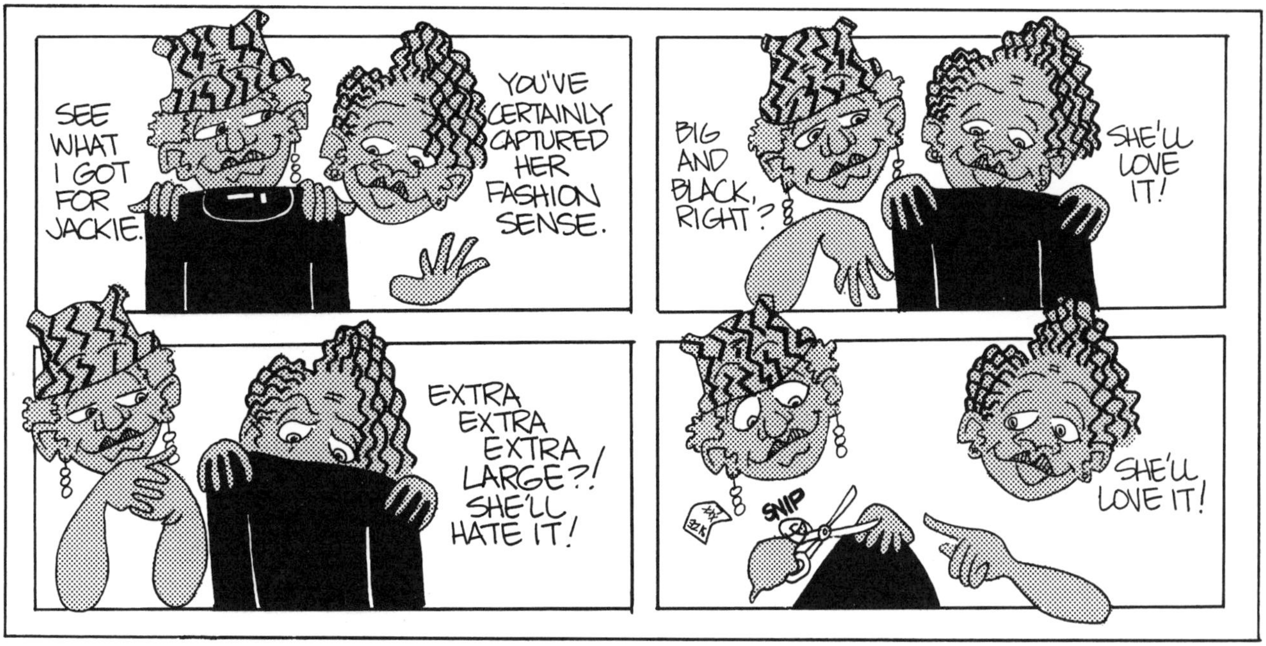
SEE WHAT I GOT FOR JACKIE.
YOU'VE CERTAINLY CAPTURED HER FASHION SENSE.
BIG AND BLACK, RIGHT?
SHE'LL LOVE IT!
EXTRA EXTRA EXTRA LARGE?! SHE'LL HATE IT!
SNIP
SHE'LL LOVE IT!

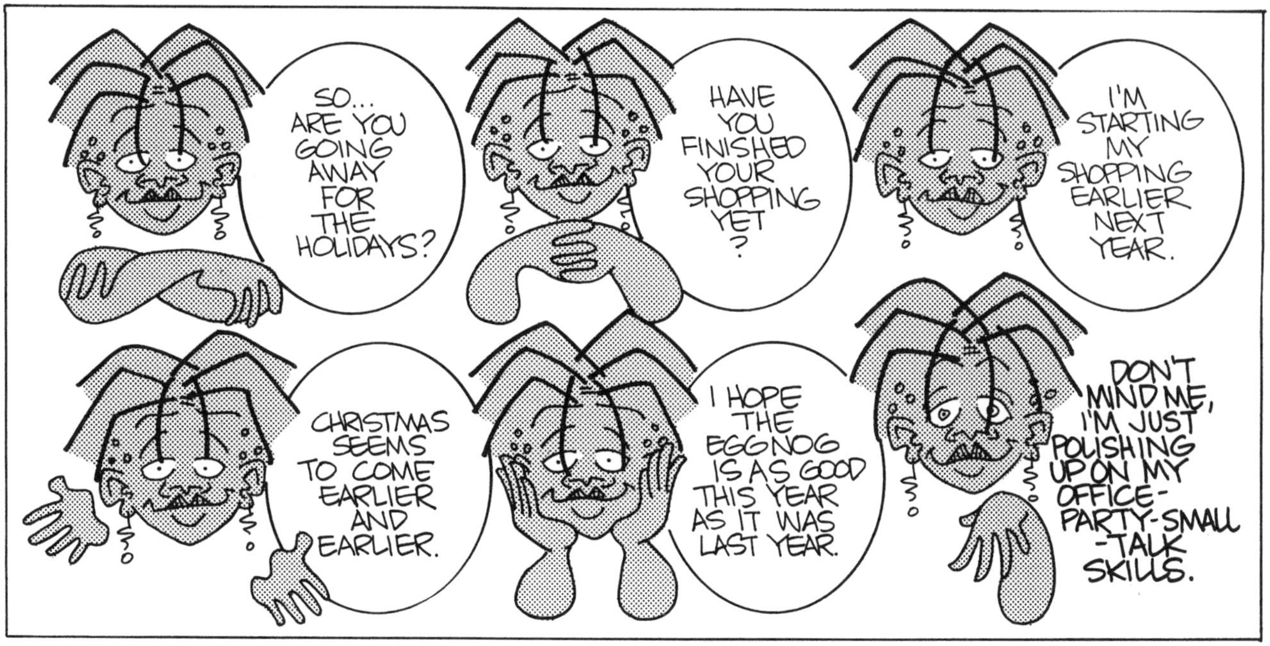
SO... ARE YOU GOING AWAY FOR THE HOLIDAYS?
HAVE YOU FINISHED YOUR SHOPPING YET?
I'M STARTING MY SHOPPING EARLIER NEXT YEAR.
CHRISTMAS SEEMS TO COME EARLIER AND EARLIER.
I HOPE THE EGGNOG IS AS GOOD THIS YEAR AS IT WAS LAST YEAR.
DON'T MIND ME, I'M JUST POLISHING UP ON MY OFFICE-PARTY-SMALL-TALK SKILLS.

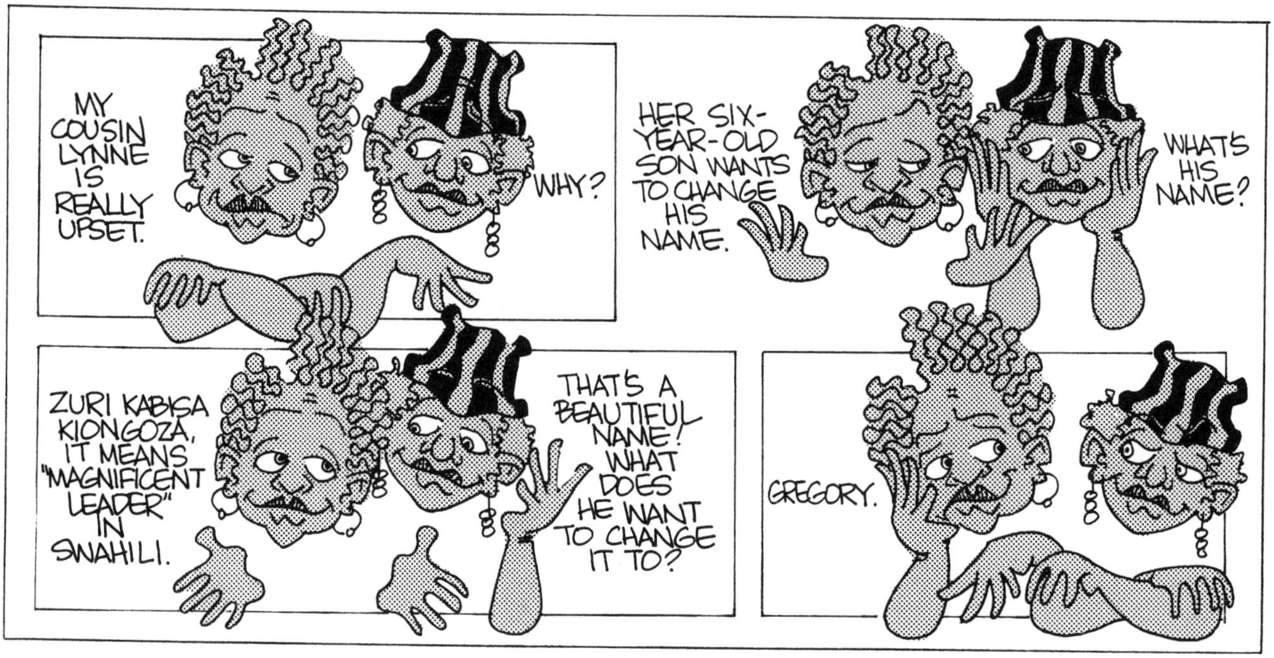
MY COUSIN LYNNE IS REALLY UPSET.
WHY?
HER SIX-YEAR-OLD SON WANTS TO CHANGE HIS NAME.
WHAT'S HIS NAME?
ZURI KABISA KIONGOZA, IT MEANS "MAGNIFICENT LEADER" IN SWAHILI.
THAT'S A BEAUTIFUL NAME! WHAT DOES HE WANT TO CHANGE IT TO?
GREGORY.

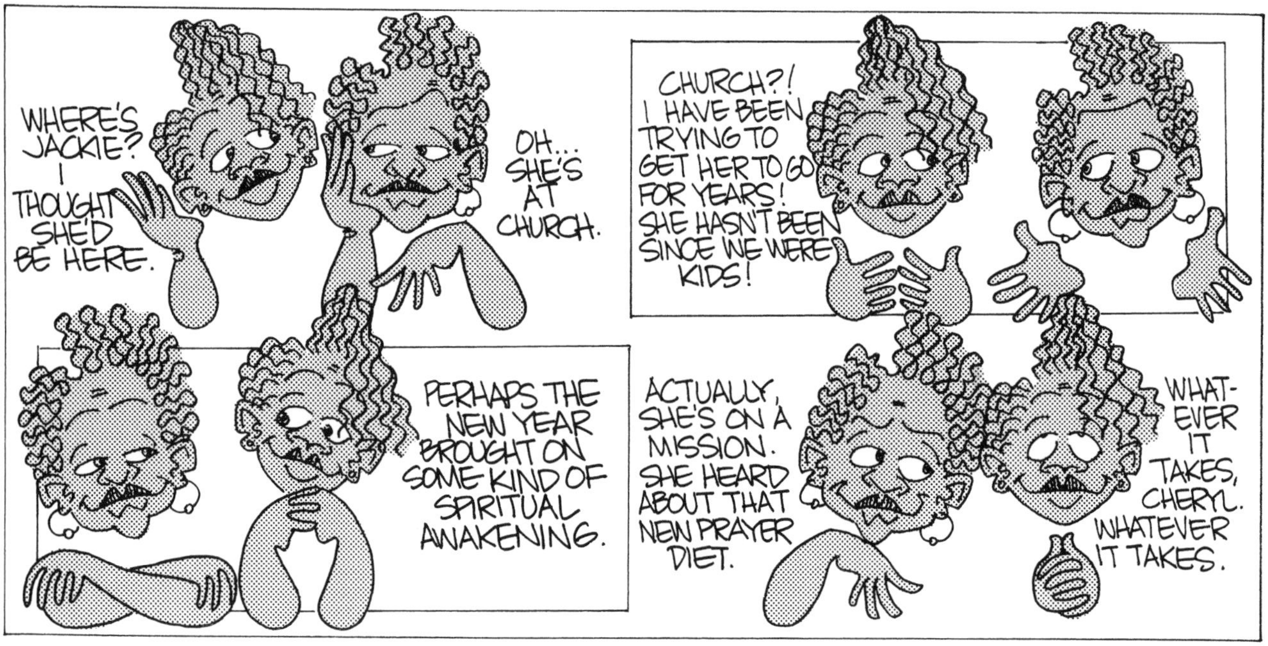
WHERE'S JACKIE? I THOUGHT SHE'D BE HERE.
OH... SHE'S AT CHURCH.
CHURCH?! I HAVE BEEN TRYING TO GET HER TO GO FOR YEARS! SHE HASN'T BEEN SINCE WE WERE KIDS!
PERHAPS THE NEW YEAR BROUGHT ON SOME KIND OF SPIRITUAL AWAKENING.
ACTUALLY, SHE'S ON A MISSION. SHE HEARD ABOUT THAT NEW PRAYER DIET.
WHAT-EVER IT TAKES, CHERYL. WHATEVER IT TAKES.

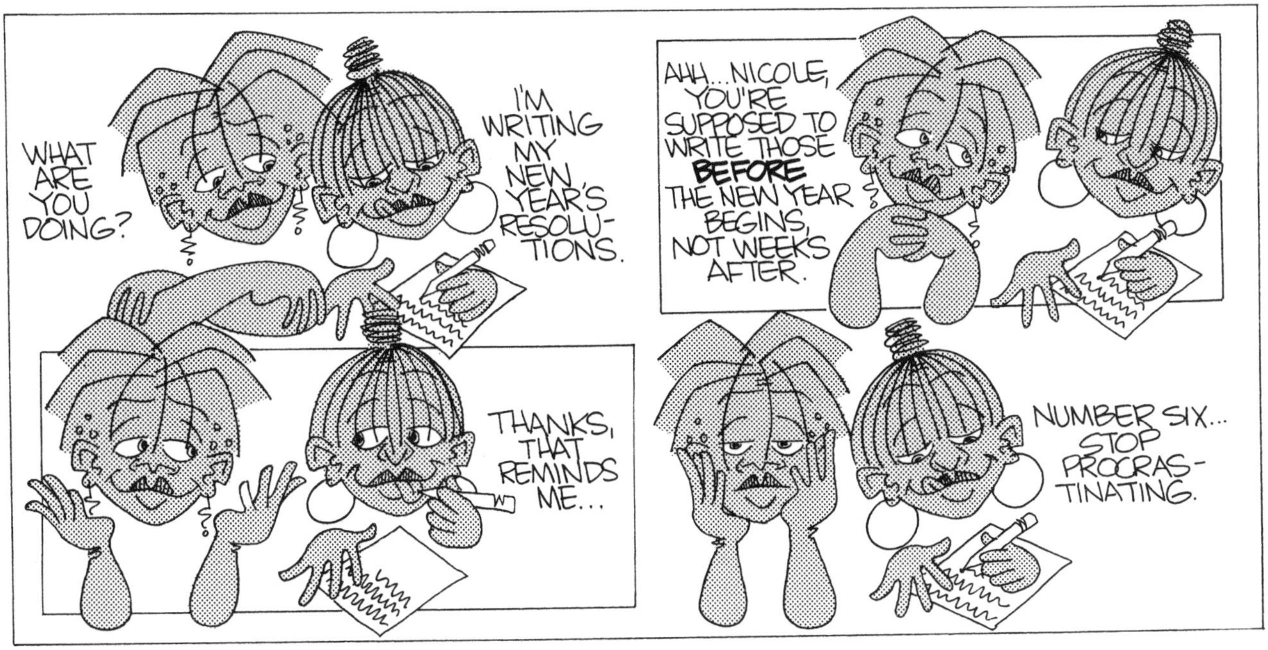
WHAT ARE YOU DOING?
I'M WRITING MY NEW YEAR'S RESOLU-TIONS.
THANKS, THAT REMINDS ME...
AHH...NICOLE, YOU'RE SUPPOSED TO WRITE THOSE **BEFORE** THE NEW YEAR BEGINS, NOT WEEKS AFTER.
NUMBER SIX... STOP PROCRAS-TINATING.

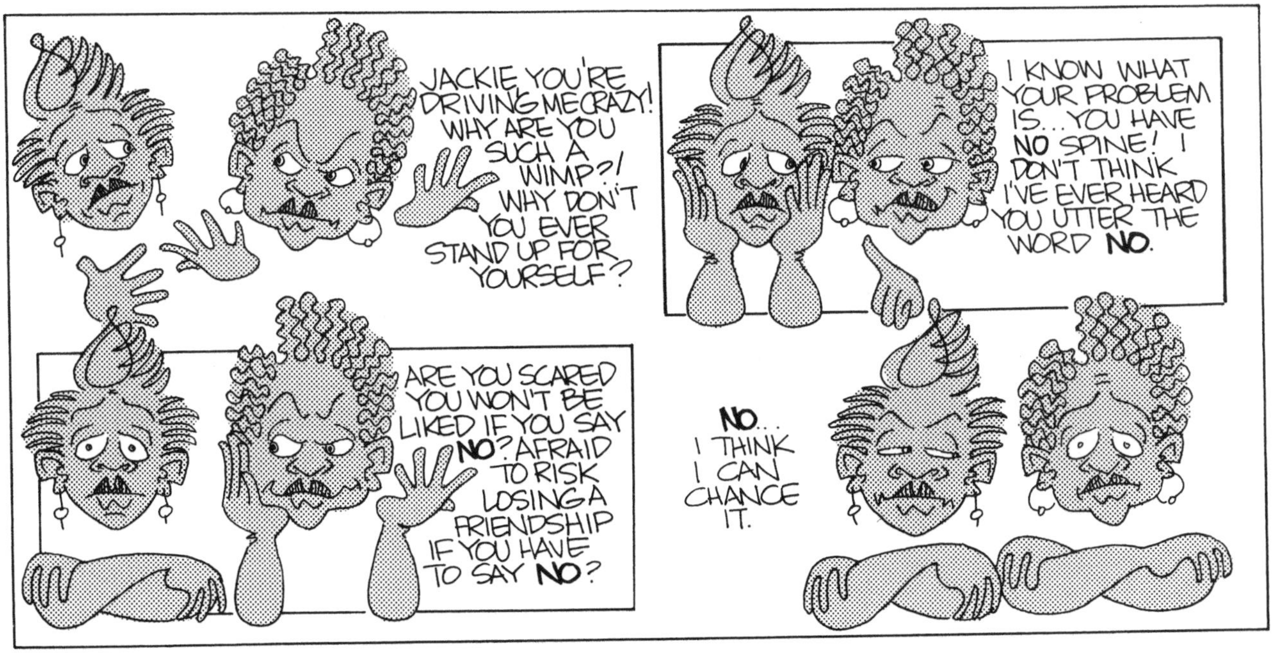
JACKIE YOU'RE DRIVING ME CRAZY! WHY ARE YOU SUCH A WIMP?! WHY DON'T YOU EVER STAND UP FOR YOURSELF?
ARE YOU SCARED YOU WON'T BE LIKED IF YOU SAY **NO**? AFRAID TO RISK LOSING A FRIENDSHIP IF YOU HAVE TO SAY **NO**?
I KNOW WHAT YOUR PROBLEM IS... YOU HAVE **NO** SPINE! I DON'T THINK I'VE EVER HEARD YOU UTTER THE WORD **NO**.
NO... I THINK I CAN CHANCE IT.

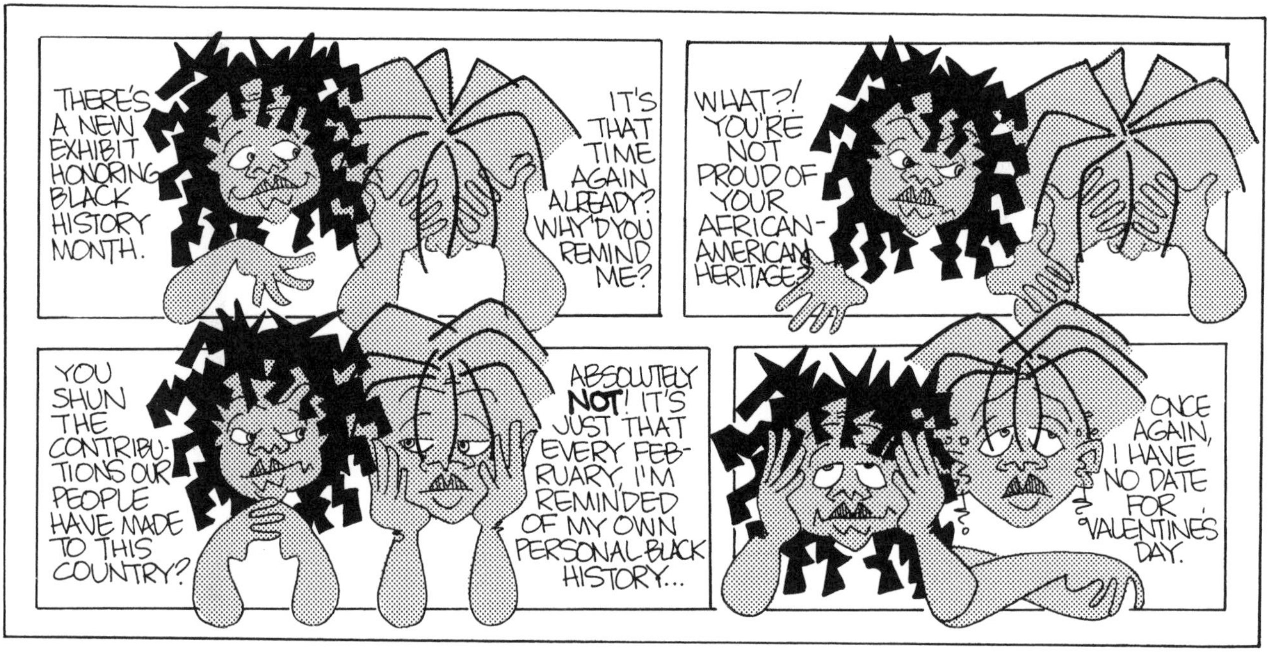
THERE'S A NEW EXHIBIT HONORING BLACK HISTORY MONTH.
IT'S THAT TIME AGAIN ALREADY? WHY'D YOU REMIND ME?
WHAT?! YOU'RE NOT PROUD OF YOUR AFRICAN-AMERICAN HERITAGE?
YOU SHUN THE CONTRIBUTIONS OUR PEOPLE HAVE MADE TO THIS COUNTRY?
ABSOLUTELY NOT! IT'S JUST THAT EVERY FEBRUARY, I'M REMINDED OF MY OWN PERSONAL BLACK HISTORY...
ONCE AGAIN, I HAVE NO DATE FOR VALENTINE'S DAY.

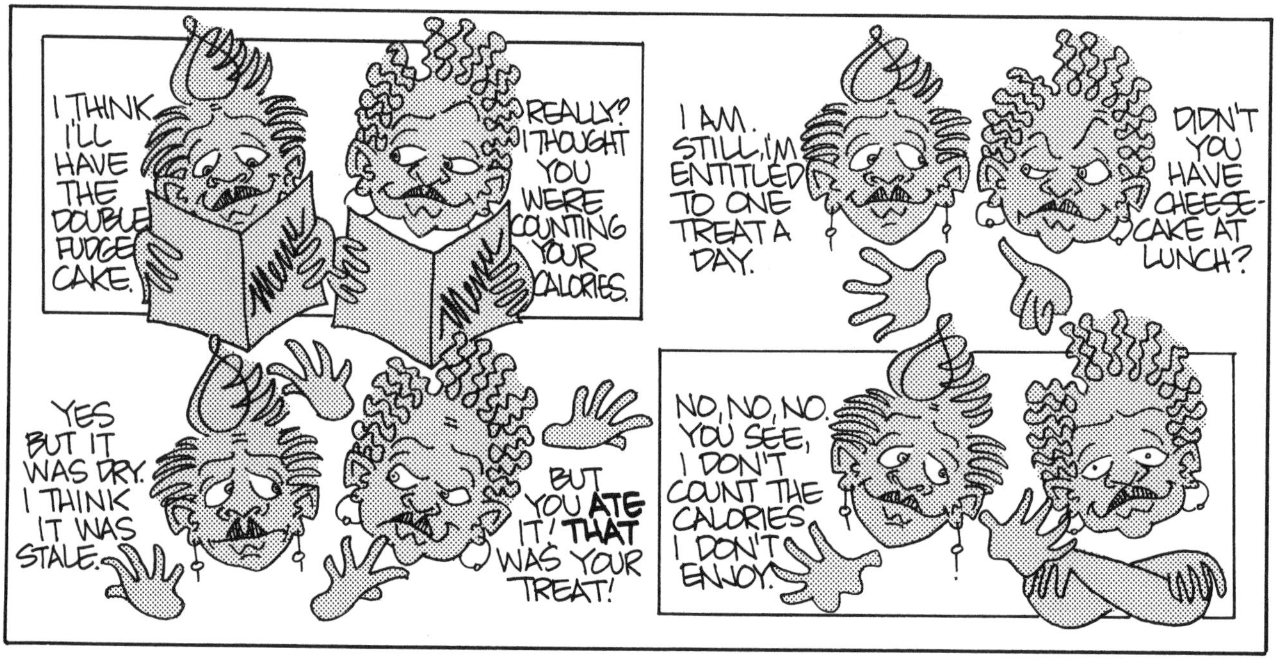
I THINK I'LL HAVE THE DOUBLE FUDGE CAKE.
REALLY? I THOUGHT YOU WERE COUNTING YOUR CALORIES.
I AM. STILL, I'M ENTITLED TO ONE TREAT A DAY.
DIDN'T YOU HAVE CHEESE-CAKE AT LUNCH?
YES BUT IT WAS DRY. I THINK IT WAS STALE.
BUT YOU ATE IT! THAT WAS YOUR TREAT!
NO, NO, NO. YOU SEE, I DON'T COUNT THE CALORIES I DON'T ENJOY.

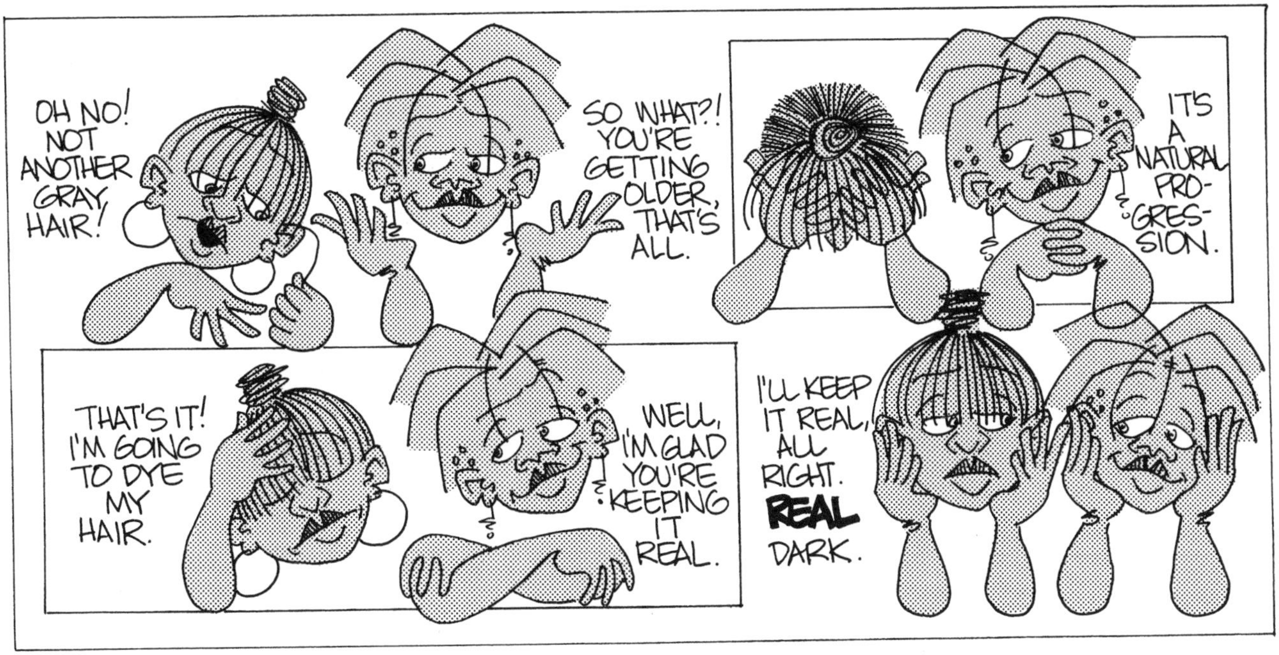
OH NO! NOT ANOTHER GRAY HAIR!
SO WHAT?! YOU'RE GETTING OLDER, THAT'S ALL.
IT'S A NATURAL PRO-GRES-SION.
THAT'S IT! I'M GOING TO DYE MY HAIR.
WELL, I'M GLAD YOU'RE KEEPING IT REAL.
I'LL KEEP IT REAL, ALL RIGHT. REAL DARK.

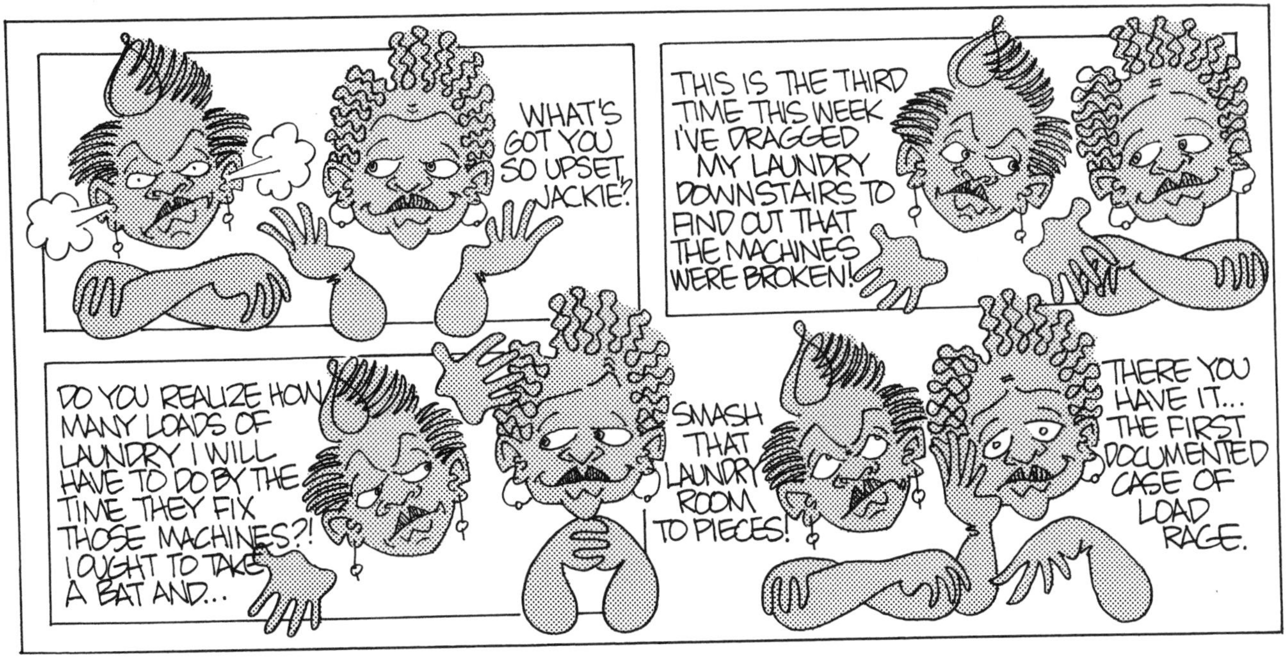
WHAT'S GOT YOU SO UPSET, JACKIE?
THIS IS THE THIRD TIME THIS WEEK I'VE DRAGGED MY LAUNDRY DOWNSTAIRS TO FIND OUT THAT THE MACHINES WERE BROKEN!
DO YOU REALIZE HOW MANY LOADS OF LAUNDRY I WILL HAVE TO DO BY THE TIME THEY FIX THOSE MACHINES?! I OUGHT TO TAKE A BAT AND...
SMASH THAT LAUNDRY ROOM TO PIECES!
THERE YOU HAVE IT... THE FIRST DOCUMENTED CASE OF LOAD RAGE.

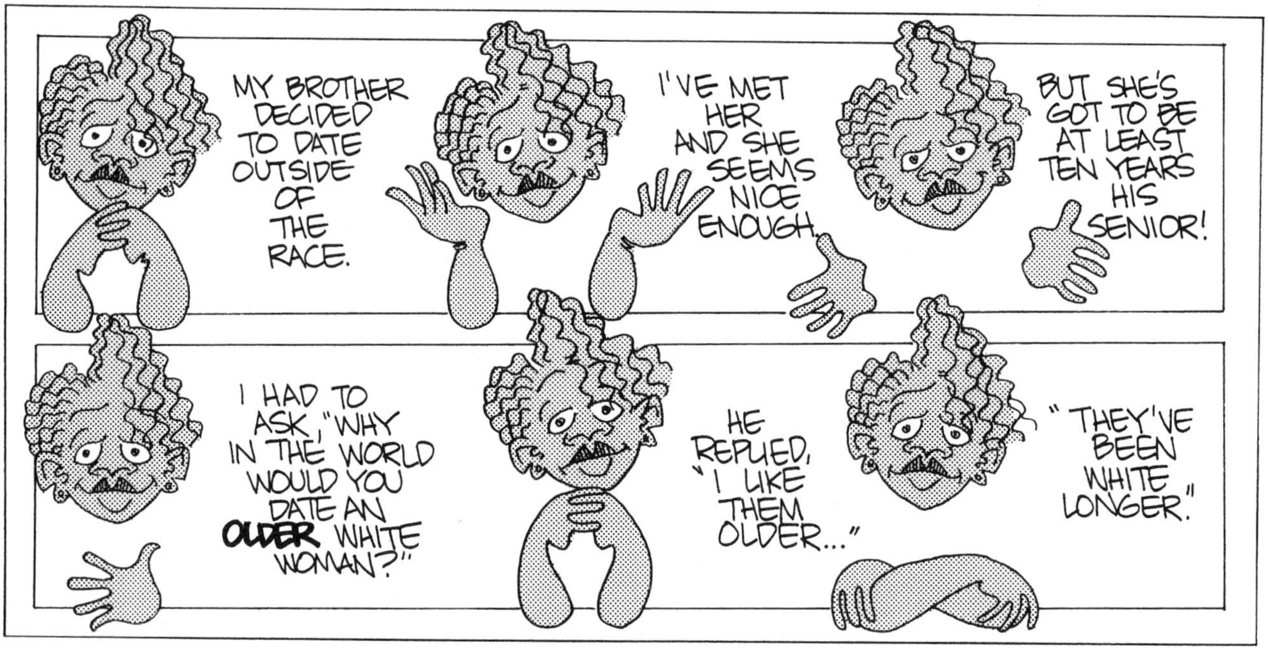
MY BROTHER DECIDED TO DATE OUTSIDE OF THE RACE.
I'VE MET HER AND SHE SEEMS NICE ENOUGH.
BUT SHE'S GOT TO BE AT LEAST TEN YEARS HIS SENIOR!
I HAD TO ASK, "WHY IN THE WORLD WOULD YOU DATE AN **OLDER** WHITE WOMAN?"
HE REPLIED, "I LIKE THEM OLDER..."
"THEY'VE BEEN WHITE LONGER."

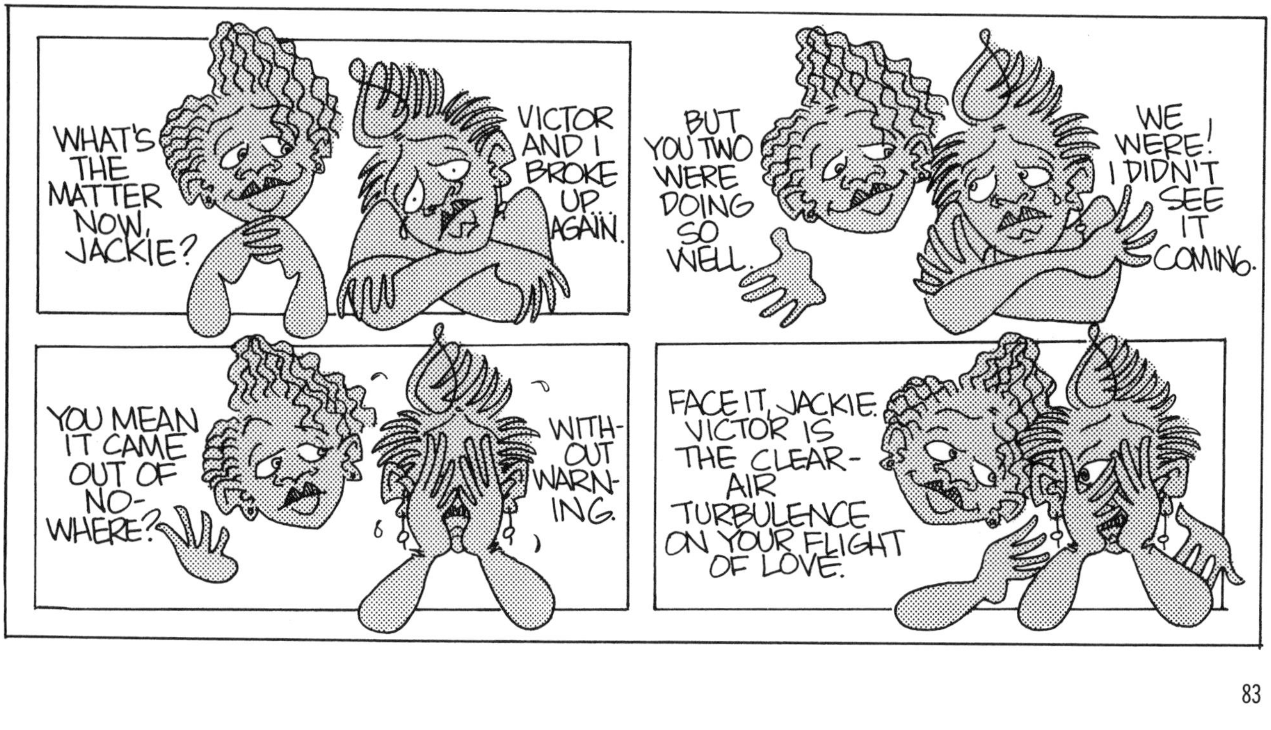
WHAT'S THE MATTER NOW, JACKIE?
VICTOR AND I BROKE UP AGAIN.
BUT YOU TWO WERE DOING SO WELL.
WE WERE! I DIDN'T SEE IT COMING.
YOU MEAN IT CAME OUT OF NO-WHERE?
WITH-OUT WARN-ING.
FACE IT, JACKIE. VICTOR IS THE CLEAR-AIR TURBULENCE ON YOUR FLIGHT OF LOVE.

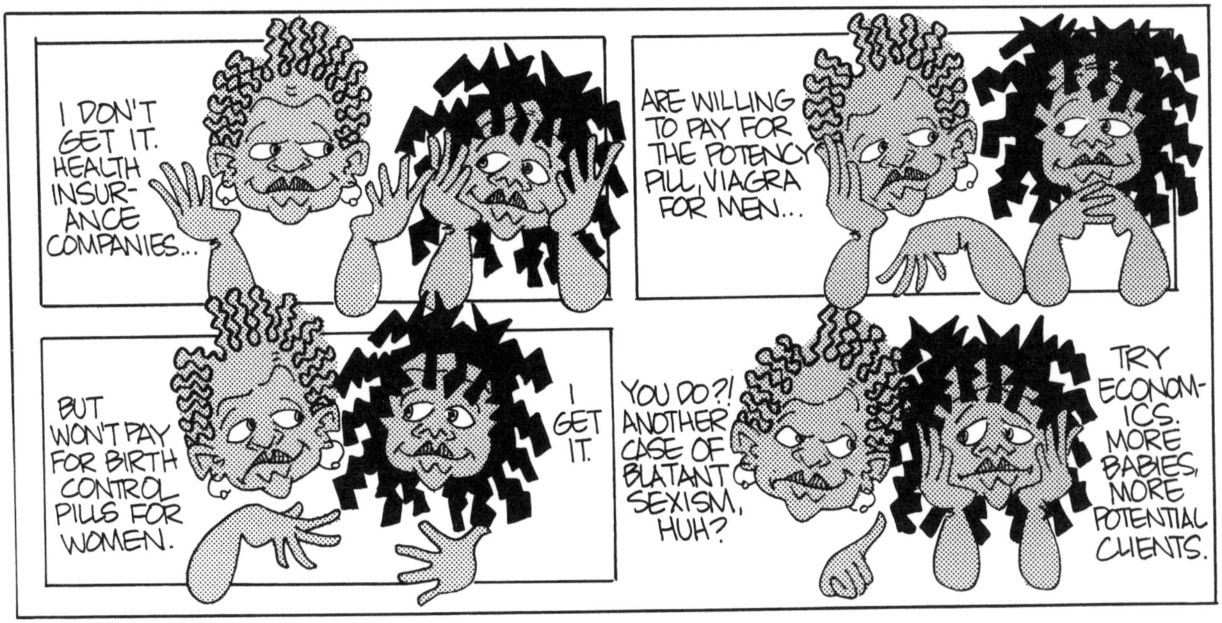
I DON'T GET IT. HEALTH INSURANCE COMPANIES...
ARE WILLING TO PAY FOR THE POTENCY PILL, VIAGRA FOR MEN...
BUT WON'T PAY FOR BIRTH CONTROL PILLS FOR WOMEN.
I GET IT.
YOU DO?! ANOTHER CASE OF BLATANT SEXISM, HUH?
TRY ECONOMICS. MORE BABIES, MORE POTENTIAL CLIENTS.

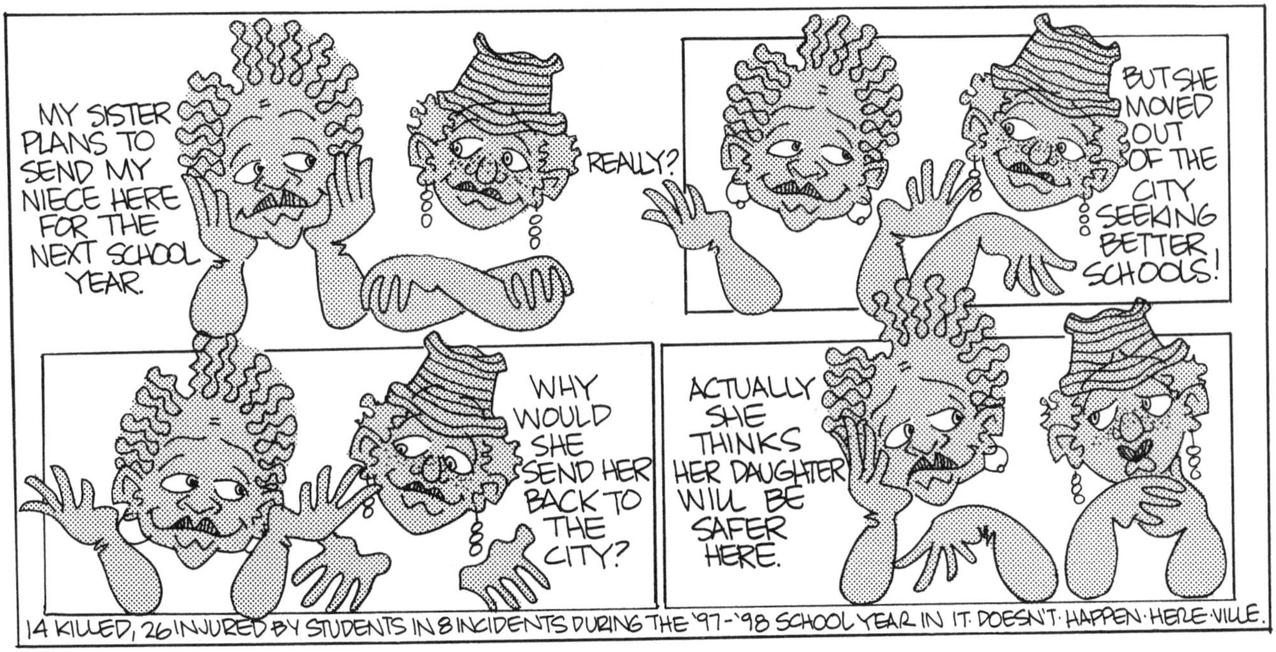
MY SISTER PLANS TO SEND MY NIECE HERE FOR THE NEXT SCHOOL YEAR.
REALLY?
BUT SHE MOVED OUT OF THE CITY SEEKING BETTER SCHOOLS!
WHY WOULD SHE SEND HER BACK TO THE CITY?
ACTUALLY SHE THINKS HER DAUGHTER WILL BE SAFER HERE.
14 KILLED, 26 INJURED BY STUDENTS IN 8 INCIDENTS DURING THE '97-'98 SCHOOL YEAR IN IT·DOESN'T·HAPPEN·HERE·VILLE.

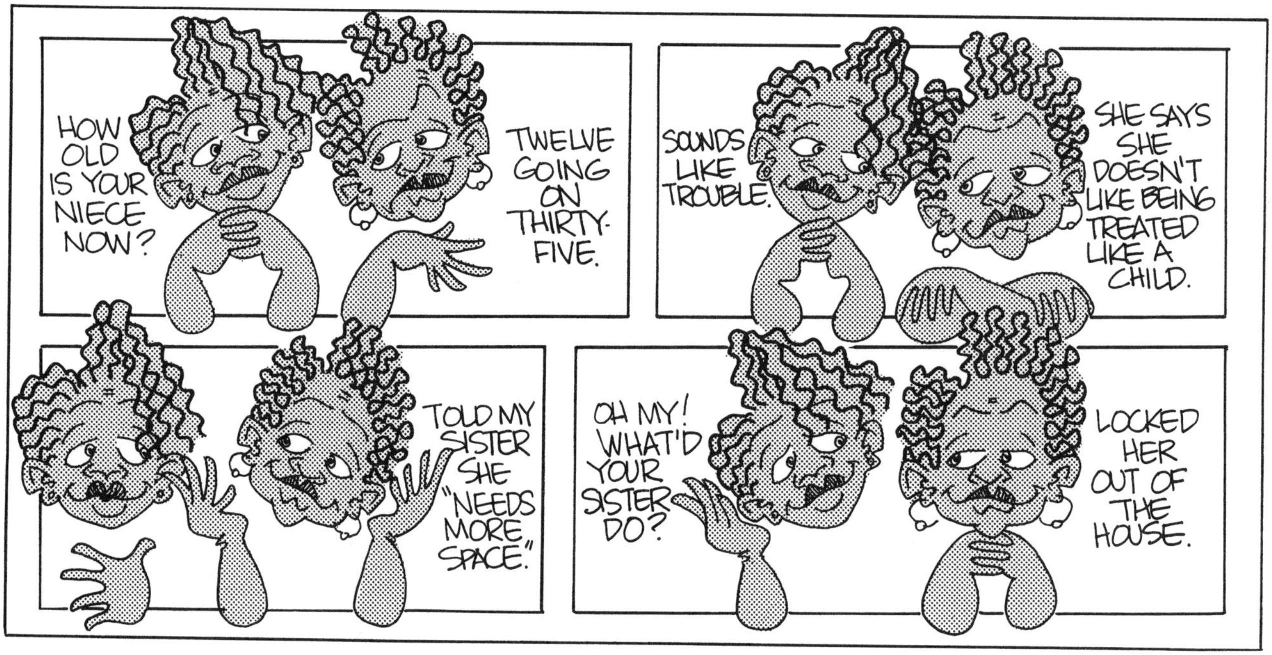
HOW OLD IS YOUR NIECE NOW?
TWELVE GOING ON THIRTY-FIVE.
SOUNDS LIKE TROUBLE.
SHE SAYS SHE DOESN'T LIKE BEING TREATED LIKE A CHILD.
TOLD MY SISTER SHE "NEEDS MORE SPACE."
OH MY! WHAT'D YOUR SISTER DO?
LOCKED HER OUT OF THE HOUSE.

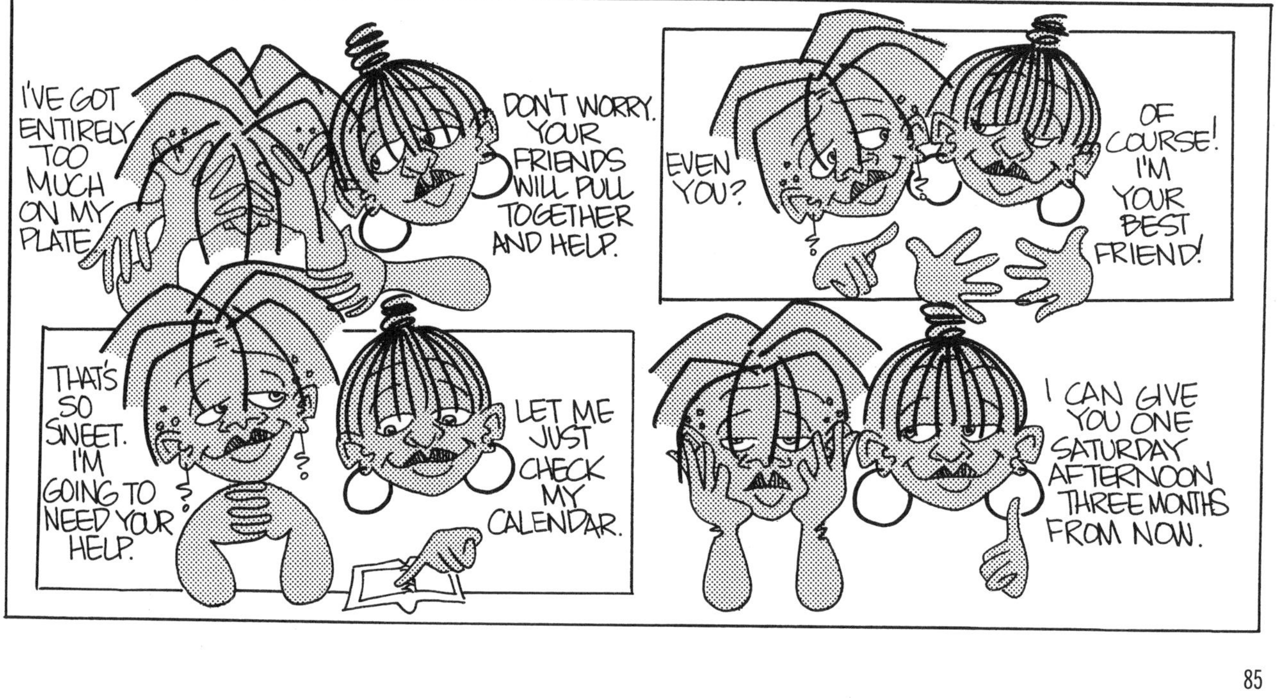
I'VE GOT ENTIRELY TOO MUCH ON MY PLATE.
DON'T WORRY. YOUR FRIENDS WILL PULL TOGETHER AND HELP.
EVEN YOU?
OF COURSE! I'M YOUR BEST FRIEND!
THAT'S SO SWEET. I'M GOING TO NEED YOUR HELP.
LET ME JUST CHECK MY CALENDAR.
I CAN GIVE YOU ONE SATURDAY AFTERNOON THREE MONTHS FROM NOW.

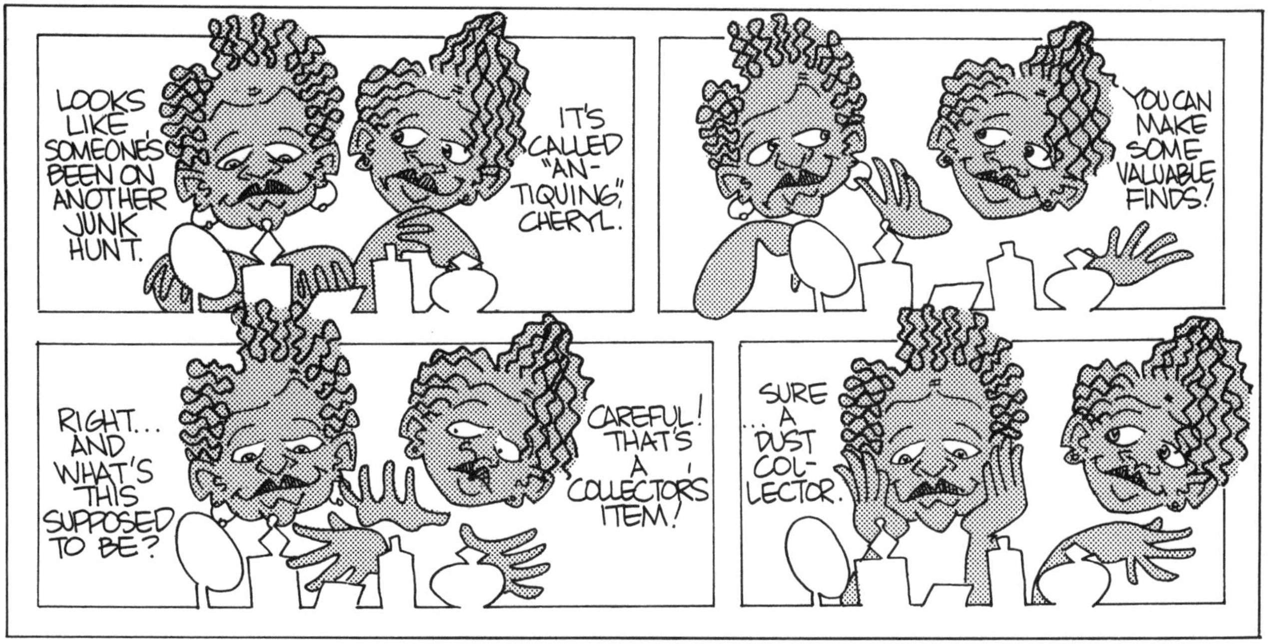

LOOKS LIKE SOMEONE'S BEEN ON ANOTHER JUNK HUNT.
IT'S CALLED "AN-TIQUING," CHERYL.
YOU CAN MAKE SOME VALUABLE FINDS!
RIGHT... AND WHAT'S THIS SUPPOSED TO BE?
CAREFUL! THAT'S A COLLECTOR'S ITEM!
SURE ...A DUST COL-LECTOR.

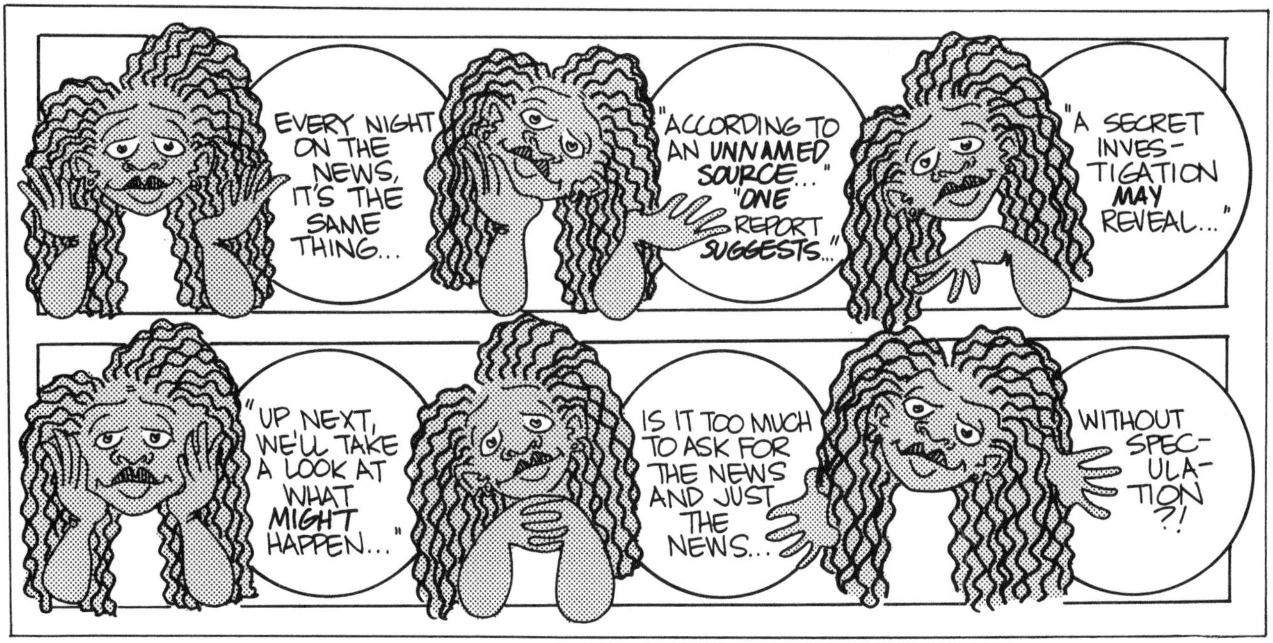

EVERY NIGHT ON THE NEWS, IT'S THE SAME THING...
"ACCORDING TO AN **UNNAMED SOURCE**..." "**ONE** REPORT **SUGGESTS**..."
"A SECRET INVES-TIGATION **MAY** REVEAL..."
"UP NEXT, WE'LL TAKE A LOOK AT WHAT **MIGHT** HAPPEN..."
IS IT TOO MUCH TO ASK FOR THE NEWS AND JUST THE NEWS...
WITHOUT SPEC-ULA-TION ?!

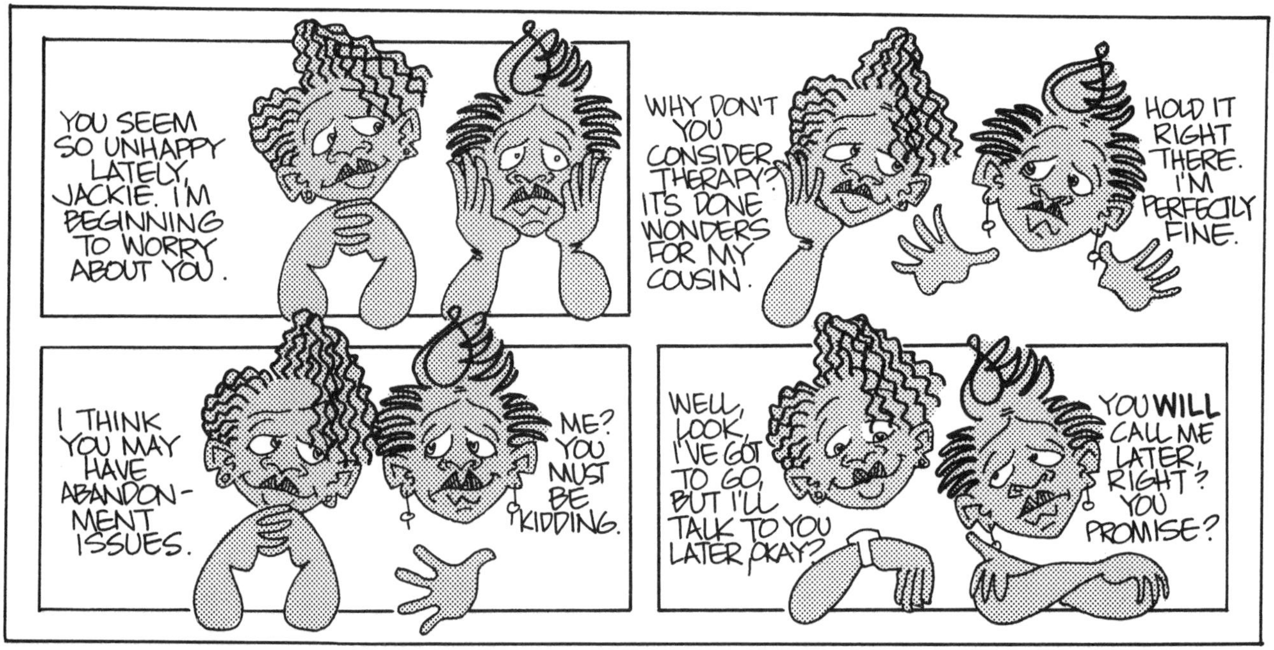
YOU SEEM SO UNHAPPY LATELY, JACKIE. I'M BEGINNING TO WORRY ABOUT YOU.
I THINK YOU MAY HAVE ABANDON-MENT ISSUES.
ME? YOU MUST BE KIDDING.
WHY DON'T YOU CONSIDER THERAPY? IT'S DONE WONDERS FOR MY COUSIN.
HOLD IT RIGHT THERE. I'M PERFECTLY FINE.
WELL, LOOK, I'VE GOT TO GO, BUT I'LL TALK TO YOU LATER OKAY?
YOU **WILL** CALL ME LATER, RIGHT? YOU PROMISE?

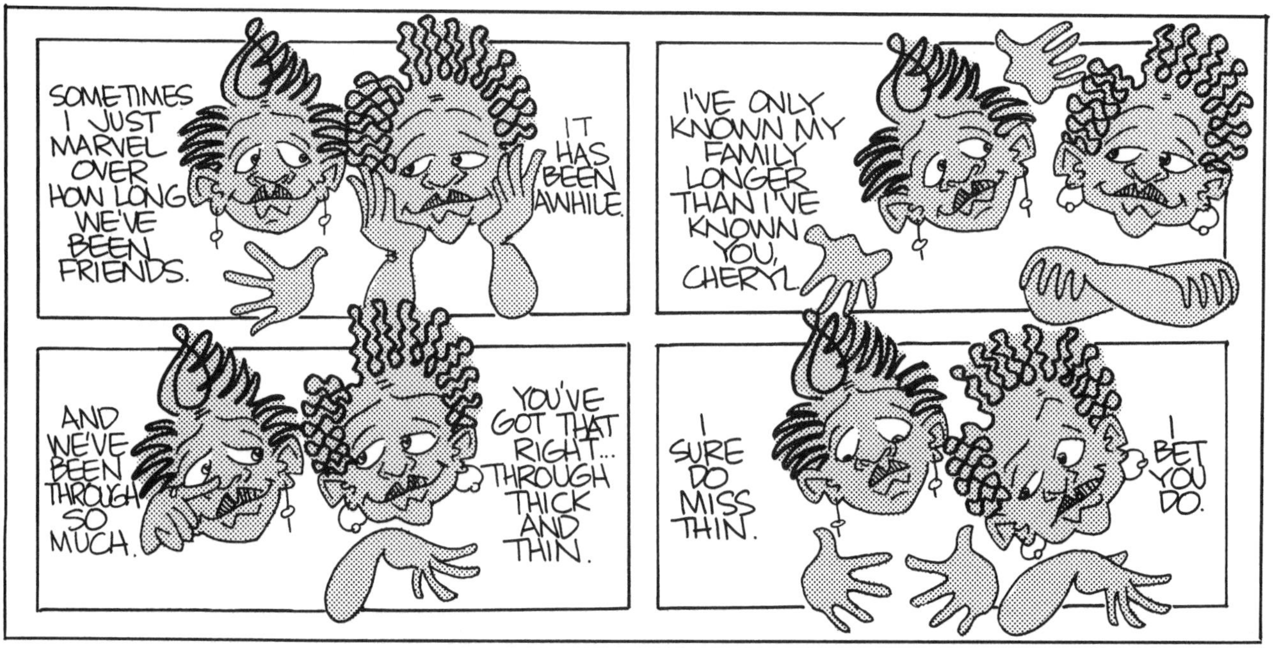
SOMETIMES I JUST MARVEL OVER HOW LONG WE'VE BEEN FRIENDS.
IT HAS BEEN AWHILE.
AND WE'VE BEEN THROUGH SO MUCH.
YOU'VE GOT THAT RIGHT... THROUGH THICK AND THIN.
I'VE ONLY KNOWN MY FAMILY LONGER THAN I'VE KNOWN YOU, CHERYL.
I SURE DO MISS THIN.
I BET YOU DO.

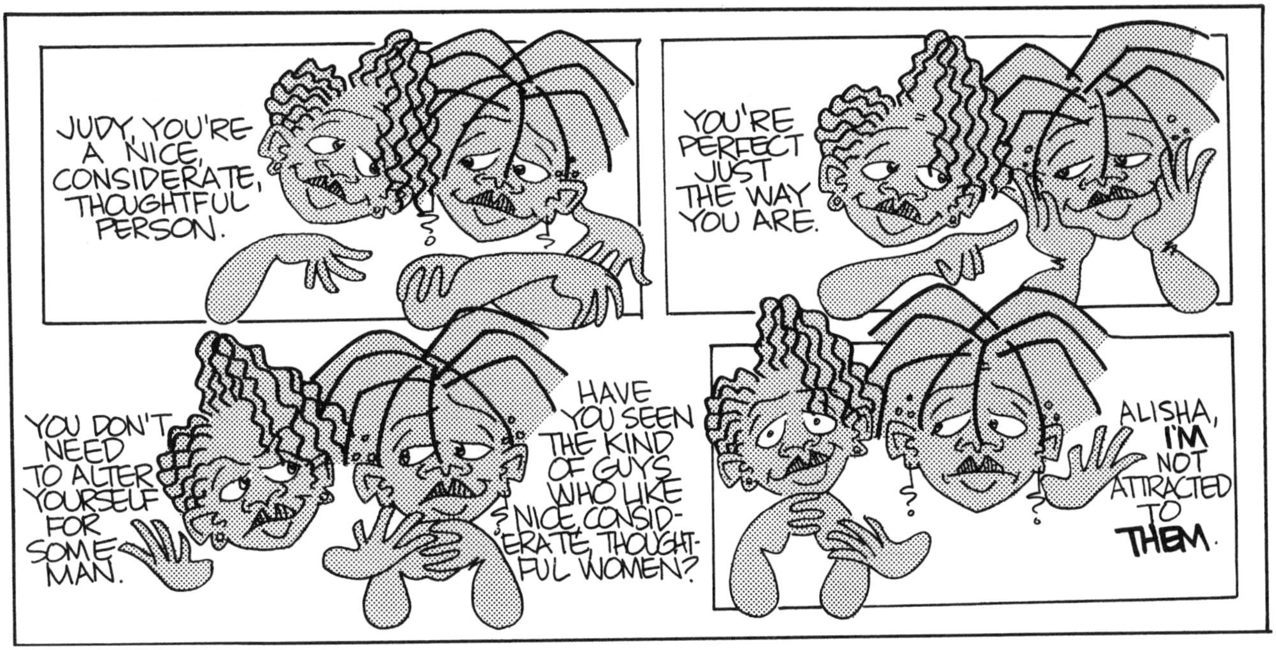
JUDY, YOU'RE A NICE, CONSIDERATE, THOUGHTFUL PERSON.
YOU'RE PERFECT JUST THE WAY YOU ARE.
YOU DON'T NEED TO ALTER YOURSELF FOR SOME MAN.
HAVE YOU SEEN THE KIND OF GUYS WHO LIKE NICE, CONSIDERATE, THOUGHTFUL WOMEN?
ALISHA, I'M NOT ATTRACTED TO THEM.

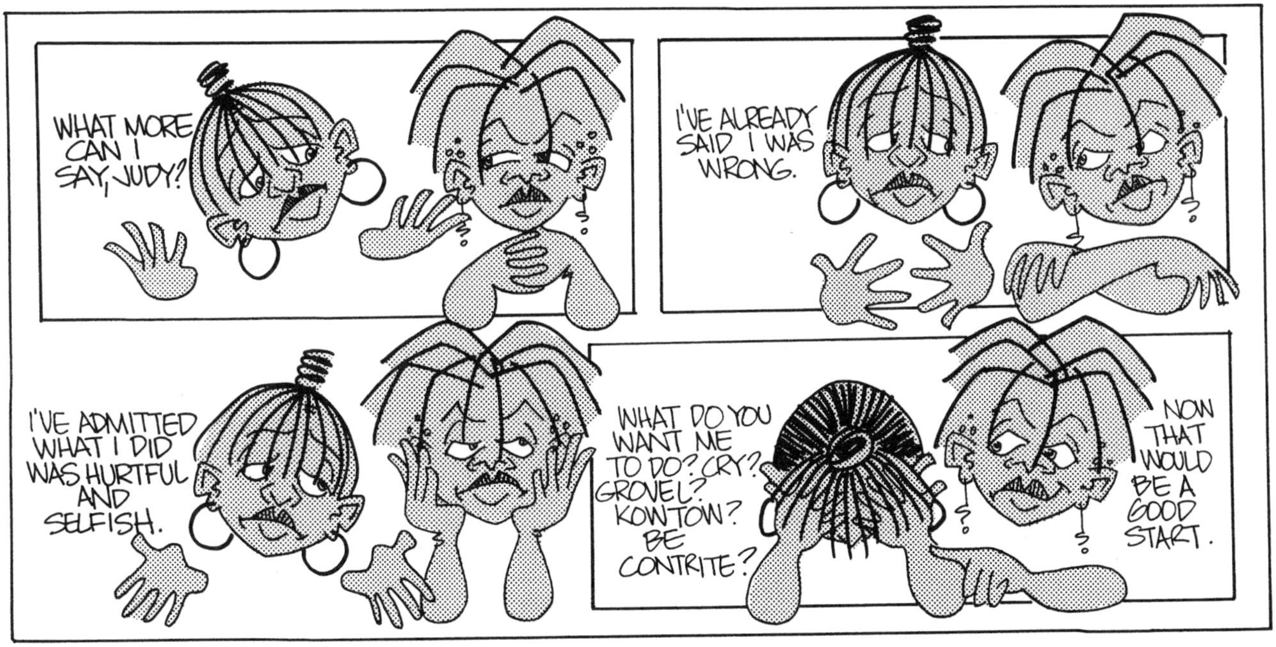
WHAT MORE CAN I SAY, JUDY?
I'VE ALREADY SAID I WAS WRONG.
I'VE ADMITTED WHAT I DID WAS HURTFUL AND SELFISH.
WHAT DO YOU WANT ME TO DO? CRY? GROVEL? KOWTOW? BE CONTRITE?
NOW THAT WOULD BE A GOOD START.

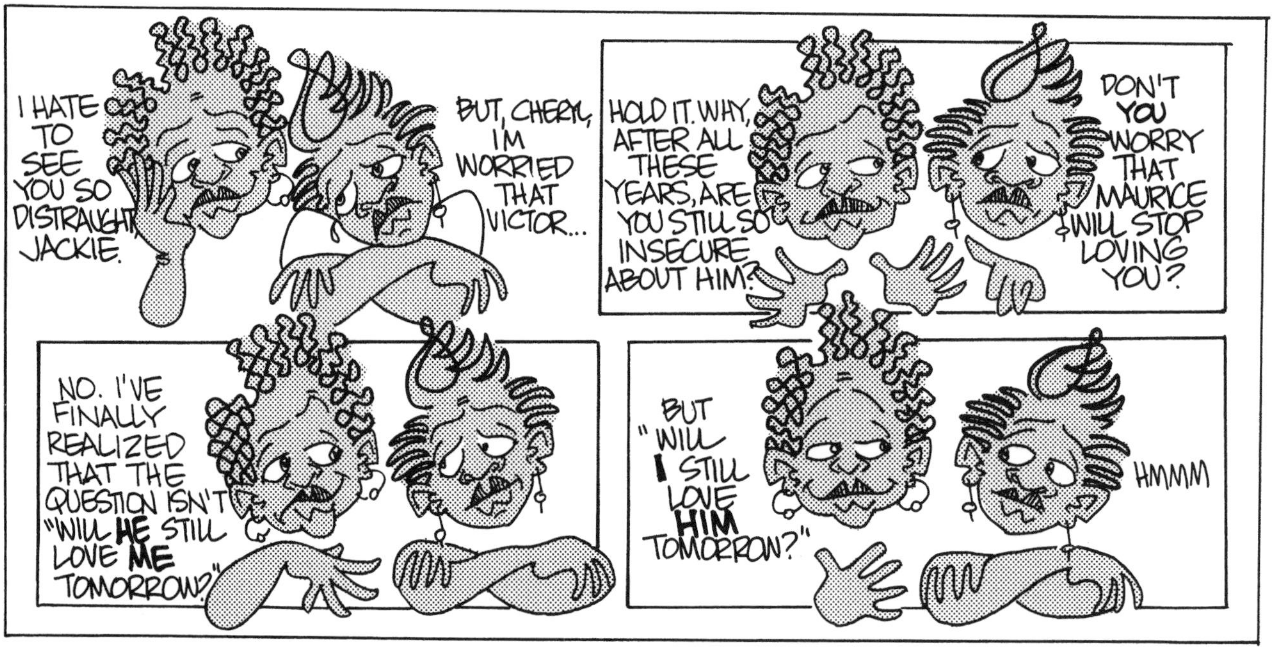
I HATE TO SEE YOU SO DISTRAUGHT, JACKIE.
BUT, CHERYL, I'M WORRIED THAT VICTOR...
HOLD IT. WHY, AFTER ALL THESE YEARS, ARE YOU STILL SO INSECURE ABOUT HIM?
DON'T YOU WORRY THAT MAURICE WILL STOP LOVING YOU?
NO. I'VE FINALLY REALIZED THAT THE QUESTION ISN'T "WILL HE STILL LOVE ME TOMORROW?"
BUT "WILL I STILL LOVE HIM TOMORROW?"
HMMM

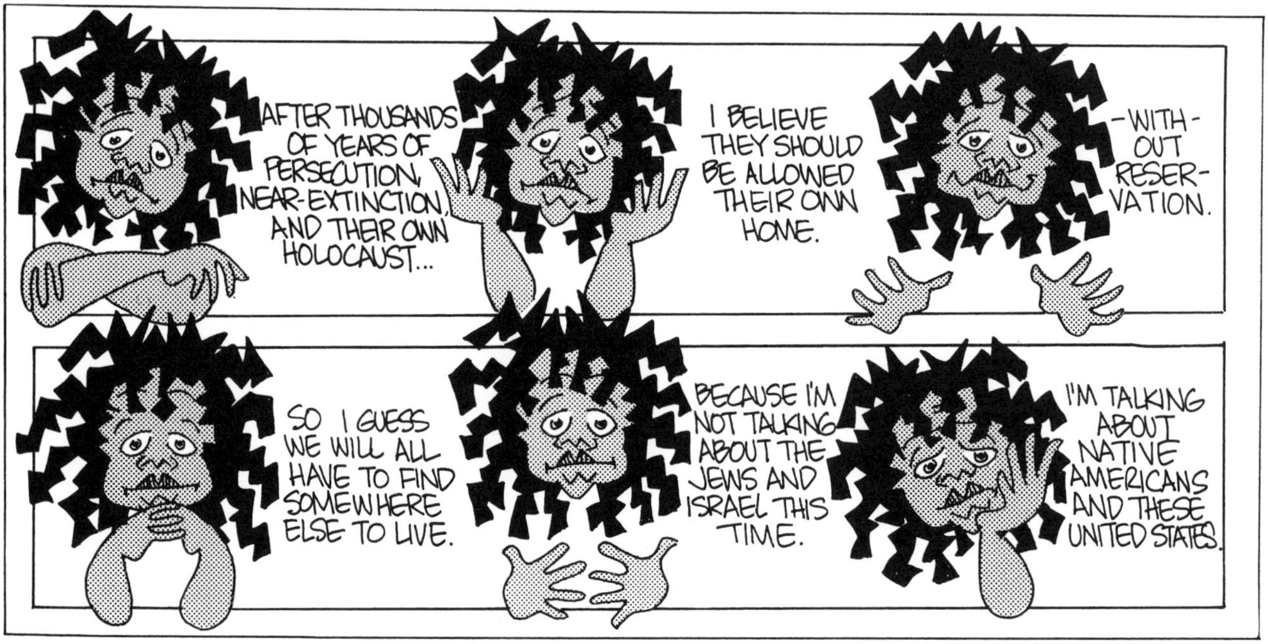
AFTER THOUSANDS OF YEARS OF PERSECUTION, NEAR-EXTINCTION, AND THEIR OWN HOLOCAUST...
I BELIEVE THEY SHOULD BE ALLOWED THEIR OWN HOME.
-WITH-OUT RESER-VATION.
SO I GUESS WE WILL ALL HAVE TO FIND SOMEWHERE ELSE TO LIVE.
BECAUSE I'M NOT TALKING ABOUT THE JEWS AND ISRAEL THIS TIME.
I'M TALKING ABOUT NATIVE AMERICANS AND THESE UNITED STATES.

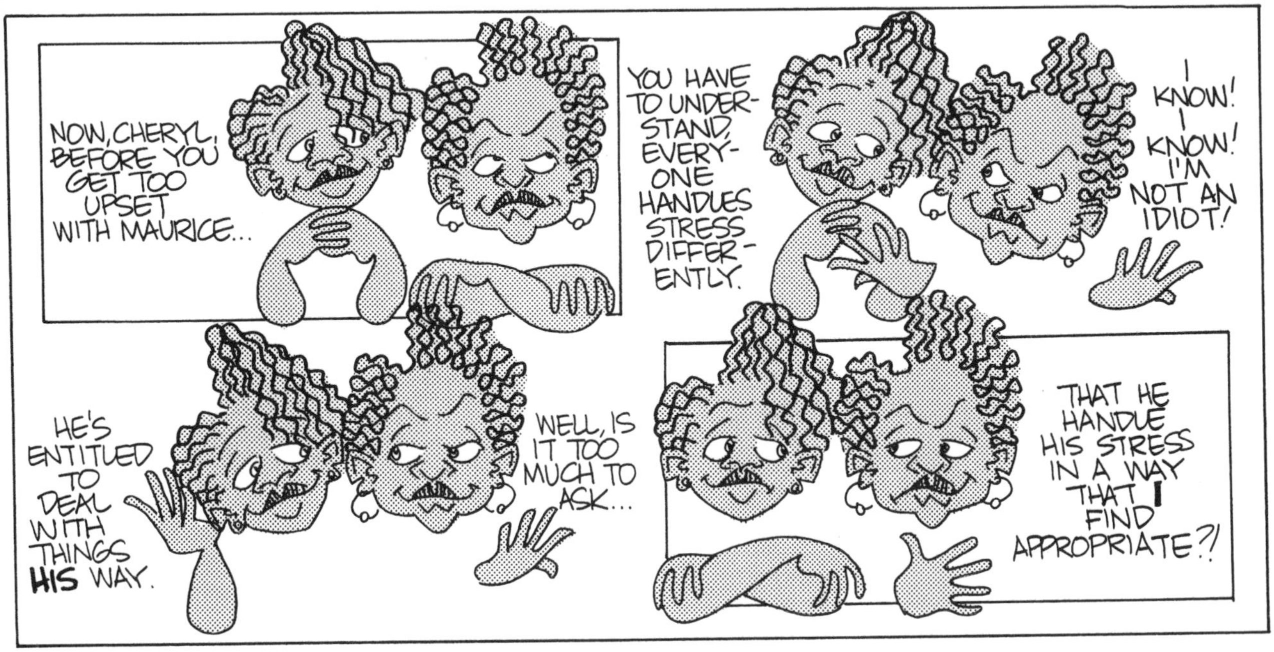
NOW, CHERYL, BEFORE YOU GET TOO UPSET WITH MAURICE...
YOU HAVE TO UNDERSTAND, EVERYONE HANDLES STRESS DIFFERENTLY.
I KNOW! I KNOW! I'M NOT AN IDIOT!
HE'S ENTITLED TO DEAL WITH THINGS **HIS** WAY.
WELL, IS IT TOO MUCH TO ASK...
THAT HE HANDLE HIS STRESS IN A WAY THAT **I** FIND APPROPRIATE?!

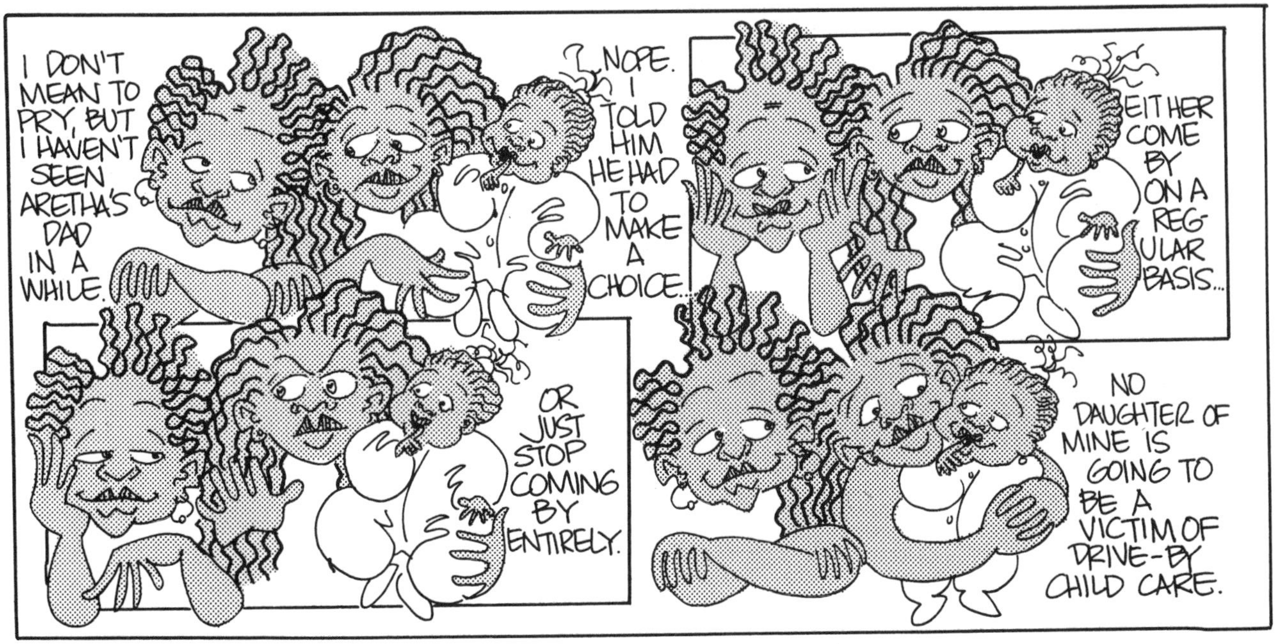
I DON'T MEAN TO PRY, BUT I HAVEN'T SEEN ARETHA'S DAD IN A WHILE.
NOPE. I TOLD HIM HE HAD TO MAKE A CHOICE...
EITHER COME BY ON A REGULAR BASIS...
OR JUST STOP COMING BY ENTIRELY.
NO DAUGHTER OF MINE IS GOING TO BE A VICTIM OF DRIVE-BY CHILD CARE.

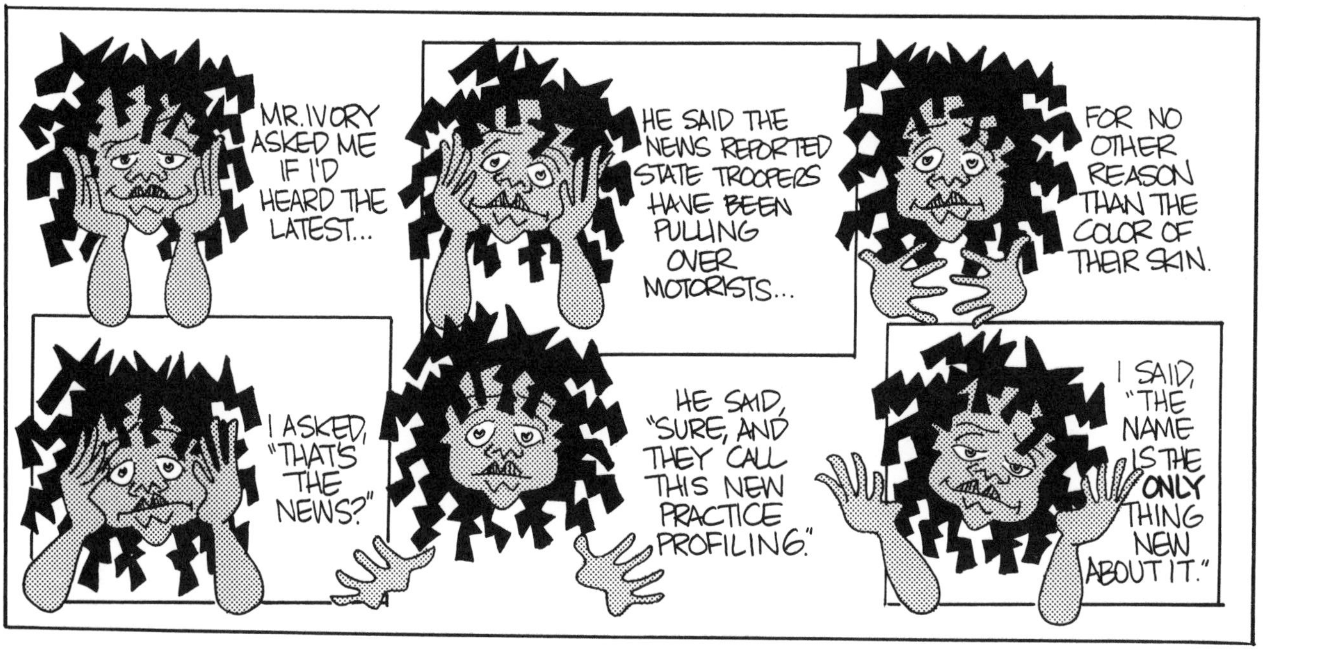
MR. IVORY ASKED ME IF I'D HEARD THE LATEST...
HE SAID THE NEWS REPORTED STATE TROOPERS HAVE BEEN PULLING OVER MOTORISTS...
FOR NO OTHER REASON THAN THE COLOR OF THEIR SKIN.
I ASKED, "THAT'S THE NEWS?"
HE SAID, "SURE, AND THEY CALL THIS NEW PRACTICE PROFILING."
I SAID, "THE NAME IS THE **ONLY** THING NEW ABOUT IT."

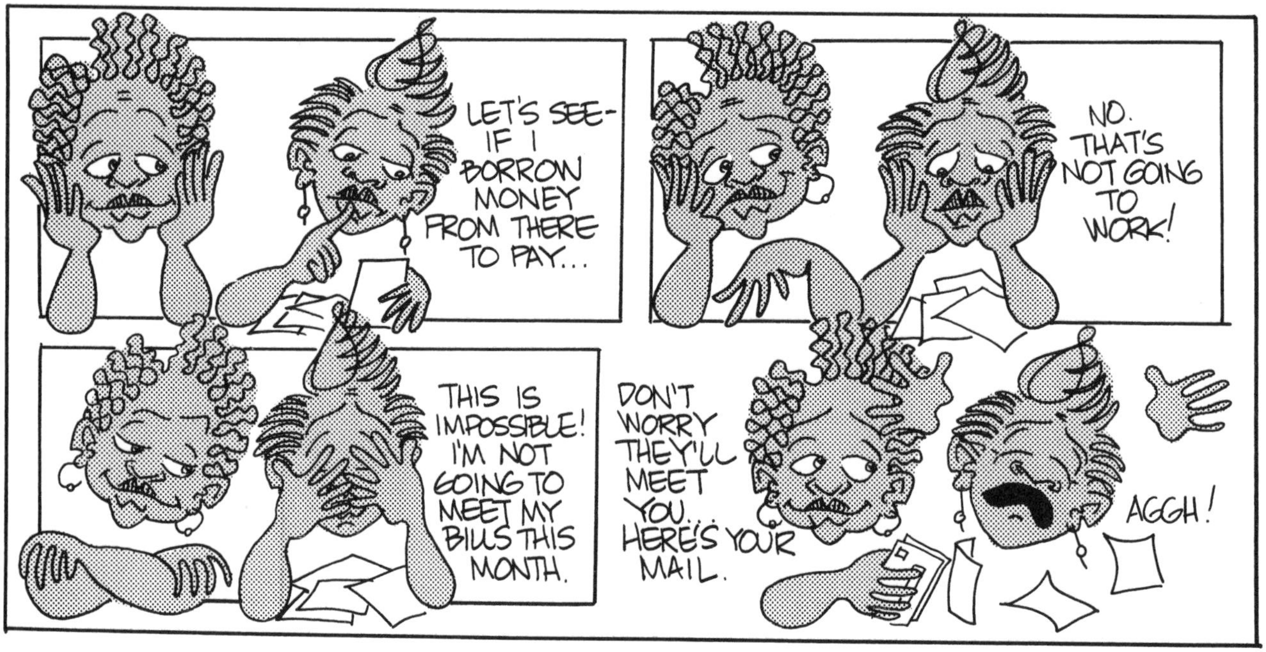
LET'S SEE- IF I BORROW MONEY FROM THERE TO PAY...
NO. THAT'S NOT GOING TO WORK!
THIS IS IMPOSSIBLE! I'M NOT GOING TO MEET MY BILLS THIS MONTH.
DON'T WORRY THEY'LL MEET YOU... HERE'S YOUR MAIL.
AGGH!

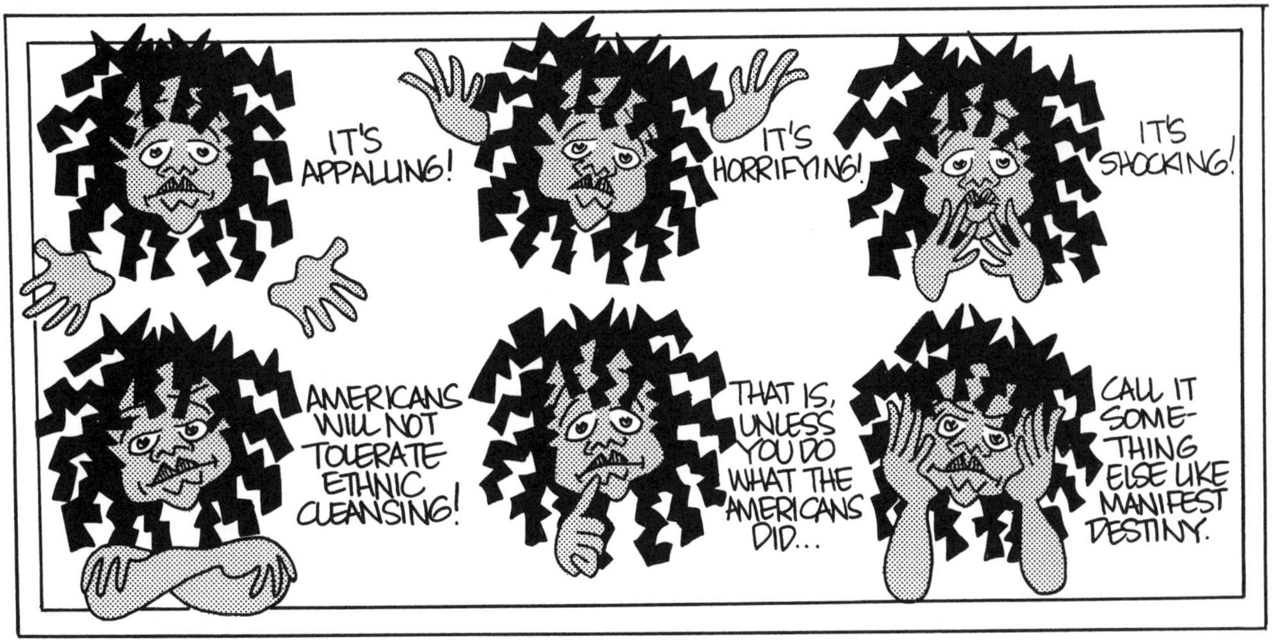
IT'S APPALLING!
IT'S HORRIFYING!
IT'S SHOCKING!
AMERICANS WILL NOT TOLERATE ETHNIC CLEANSING!
THAT IS, UNLESS YOU DO WHAT THE AMERICANS DID...
CALL IT SOME-THING ELSE LIKE MANIFEST DESTINY.

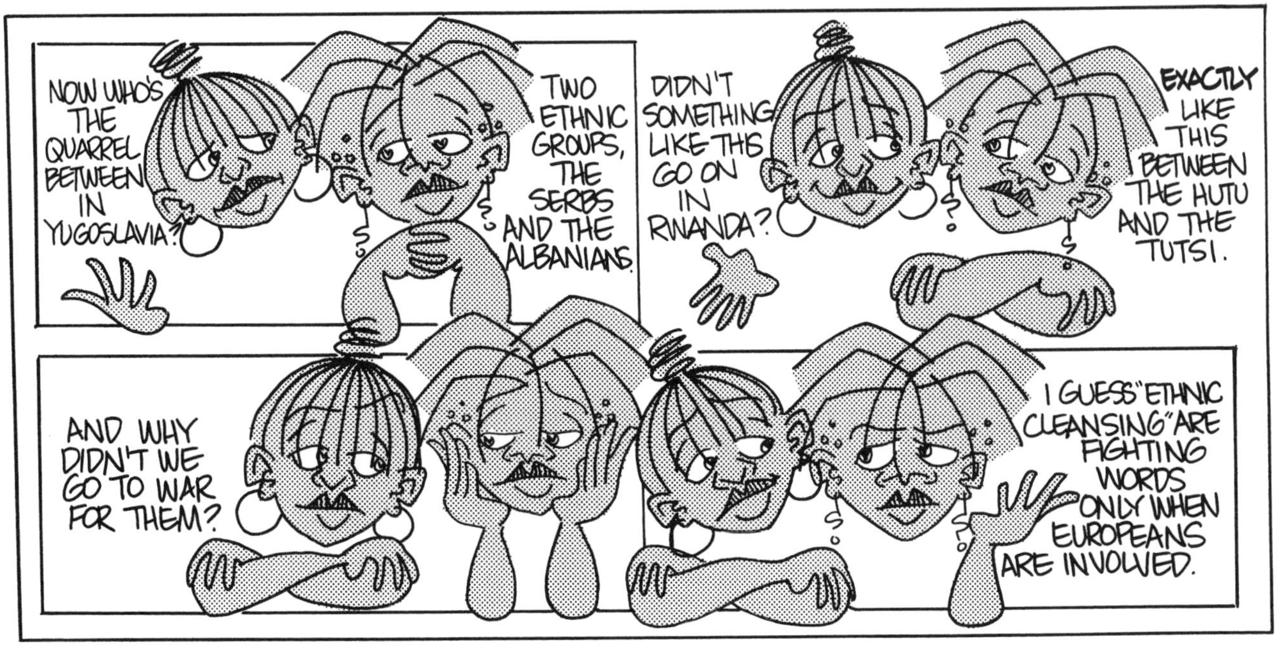
NOW WHO'S THE QUARREL BETWEEN IN YUGOSLAVIA?
TWO ETHNIC GROUPS, THE SERBS AND THE ALBANIANS.
DIDN'T SOMETHING LIKE THIS GO ON IN RWANDA?
EXACTLY LIKE THIS BETWEEN THE HUTU AND THE TUTSI.
AND WHY DIDN'T WE GO TO WAR FOR THEM?
I GUESS "ETHNIC CLEANSING" ARE FIGHTING WORDS ONLY WHEN EUROPEANS ARE INVOLVED.

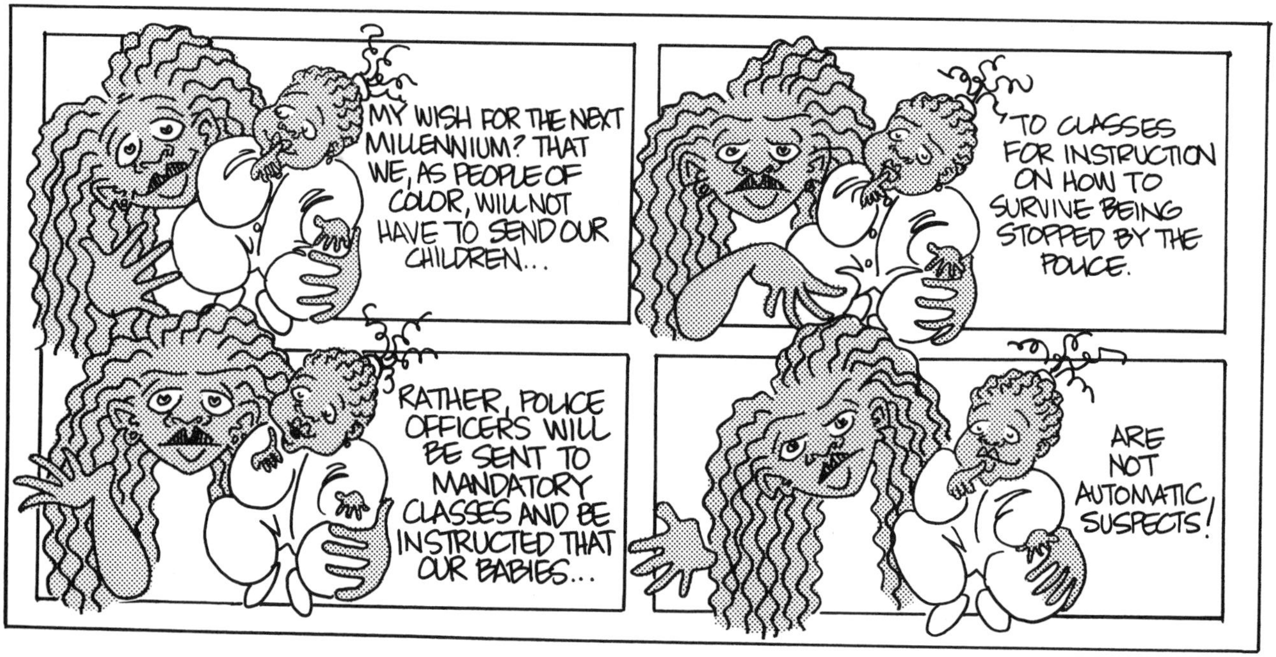
MY WISH FOR THE NEXT MILLENNIUM? THAT WE, AS PEOPLE OF COLOR, WILL NOT HAVE TO SEND OUR CHILDREN...
TO CLASSES FOR INSTRUCTION ON HOW TO SURVIVE BEING STOPPED BY THE POLICE.
RATHER, POLICE OFFICERS WILL BE SENT TO MANDATORY CLASSES AND BE INSTRUCTED THAT OUR BABIES...
ARE NOT AUTOMATIC SUSPECTS!

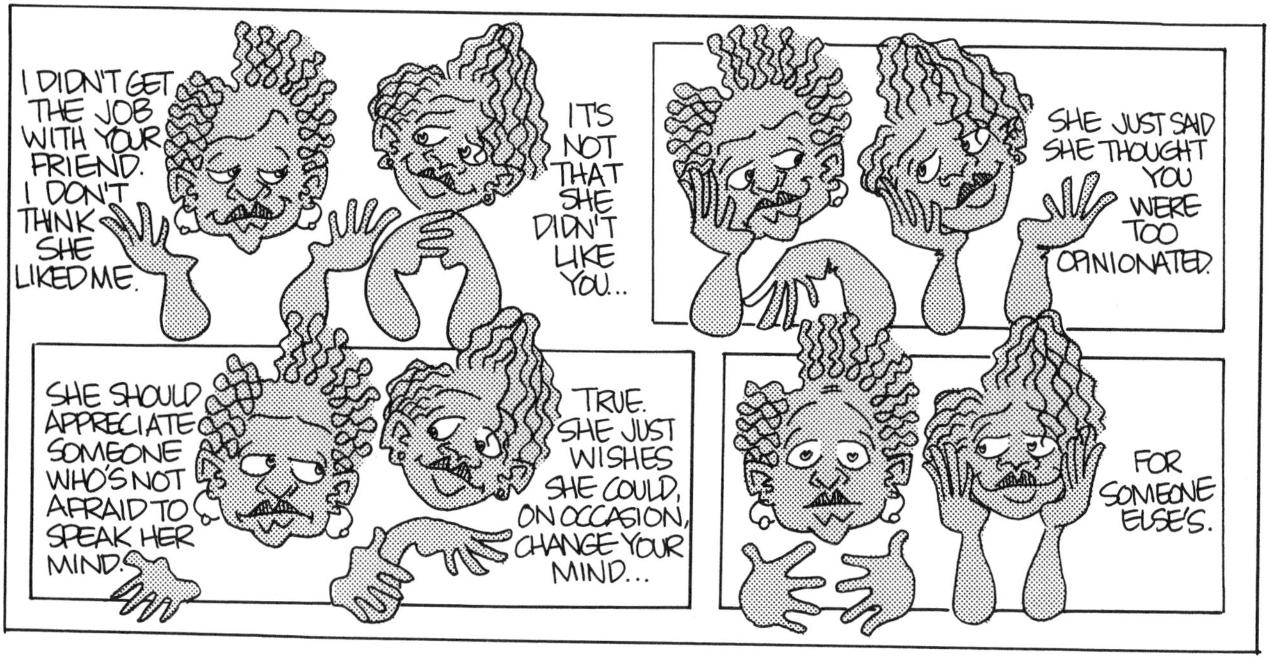
I DIDN'T GET THE JOB WITH YOUR FRIEND. I DON'T THINK SHE LIKED ME.
IT'S NOT THAT SHE DIDN'T LIKE YOU...
SHE JUST SAID SHE THOUGHT YOU WERE TOO OPINIONATED.
SHE SHOULD APPRECIATE SOMEONE WHO'S NOT AFRAID TO SPEAK HER MIND.
TRUE. SHE JUST WISHES SHE COULD, ON OCCASION, CHANGE YOUR MIND...
FOR SOMEONE ELSE'S.

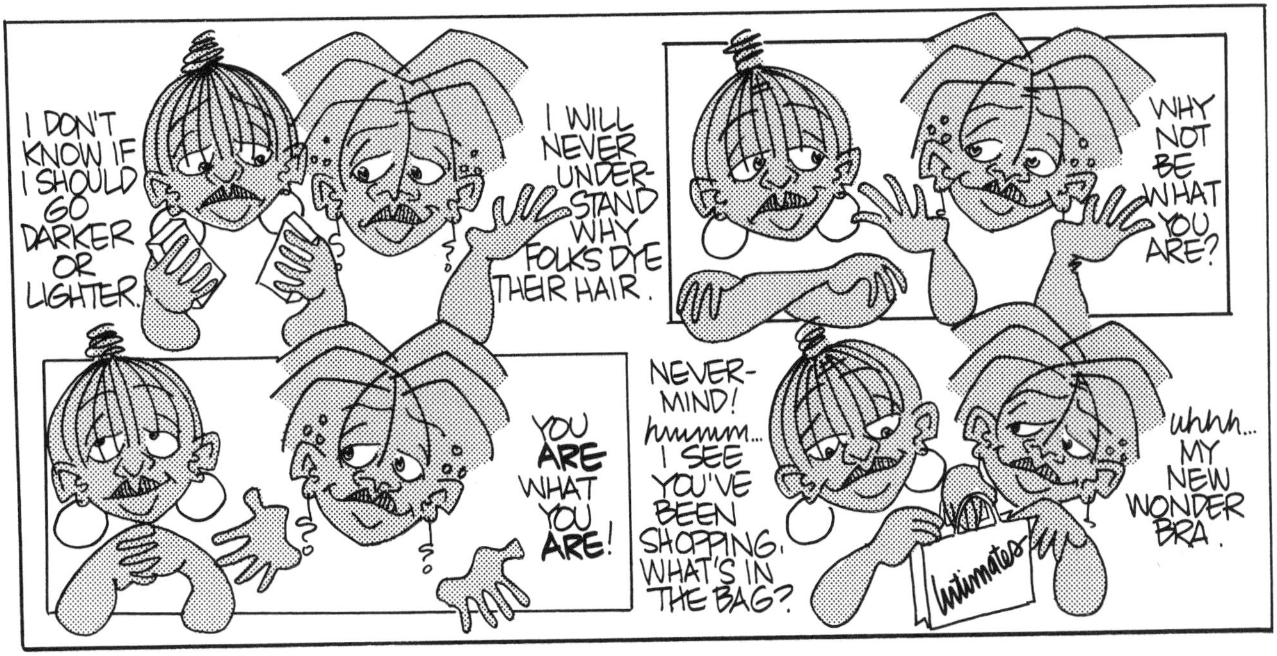
I DON'T KNOW IF I SHOULD GO DARKER OR LIGHTER.
I WILL NEVER UNDER-STAND WHY FOLKS DYE THEIR HAIR.
WHY NOT BE WHAT YOU ARE?
YOU ARE WHAT YOU ARE!
NEVER-MIND! hmmm... I SEE YOU'VE BEEN SHOPPING. WHAT'S IN THE BAG?
uhhh... MY NEW WONDER BRA.
Intimates

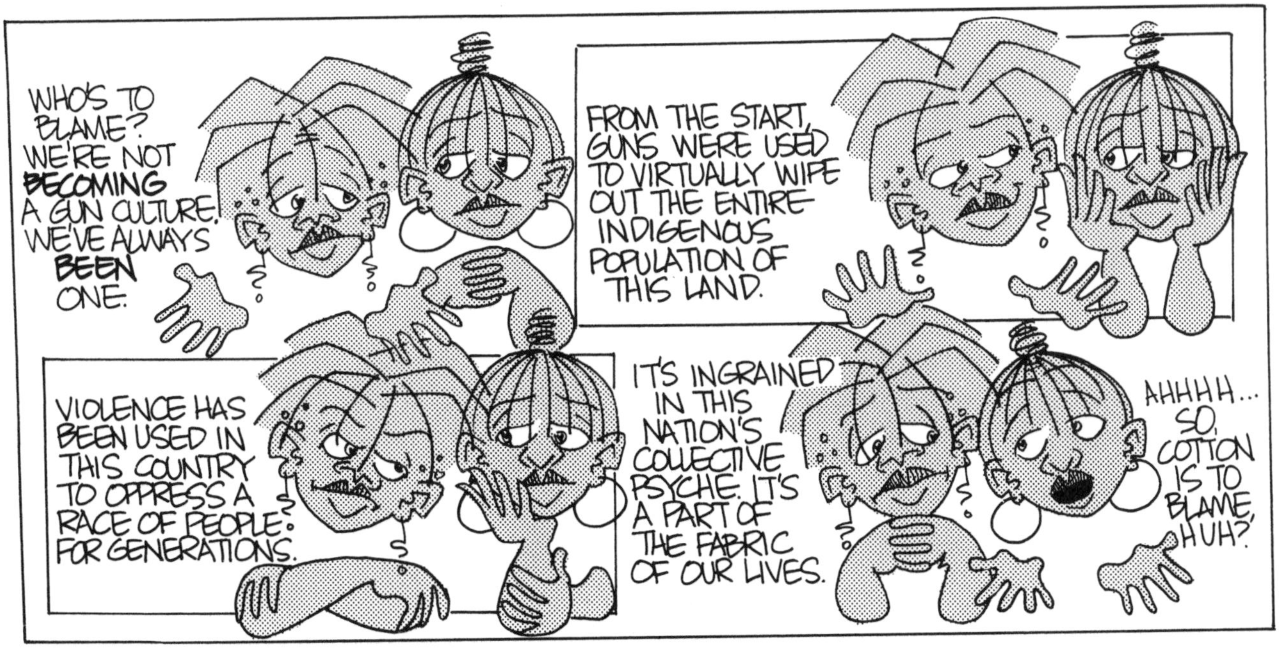
WHO'S TO BLAME? WE'RE NOT BECOMING A GUN CULTURE. WE'VE ALWAYS BEEN ONE.
FROM THE START, GUNS WERE USED TO VIRTUALLY WIPE OUT THE ENTIRE INDIGENOUS POPULATION OF THIS LAND.
VIOLENCE HAS BEEN USED IN THIS COUNTRY TO OPPRESS A RACE OF PEOPLE FOR GENERATIONS.
IT'S INGRAINED IN THIS NATION'S COLLECTIVE PSYCHE. IT'S A PART OF THE FABRIC OF OUR LIVES.
AHHHH... SO, COTTON IS TO BLAME, HUH?

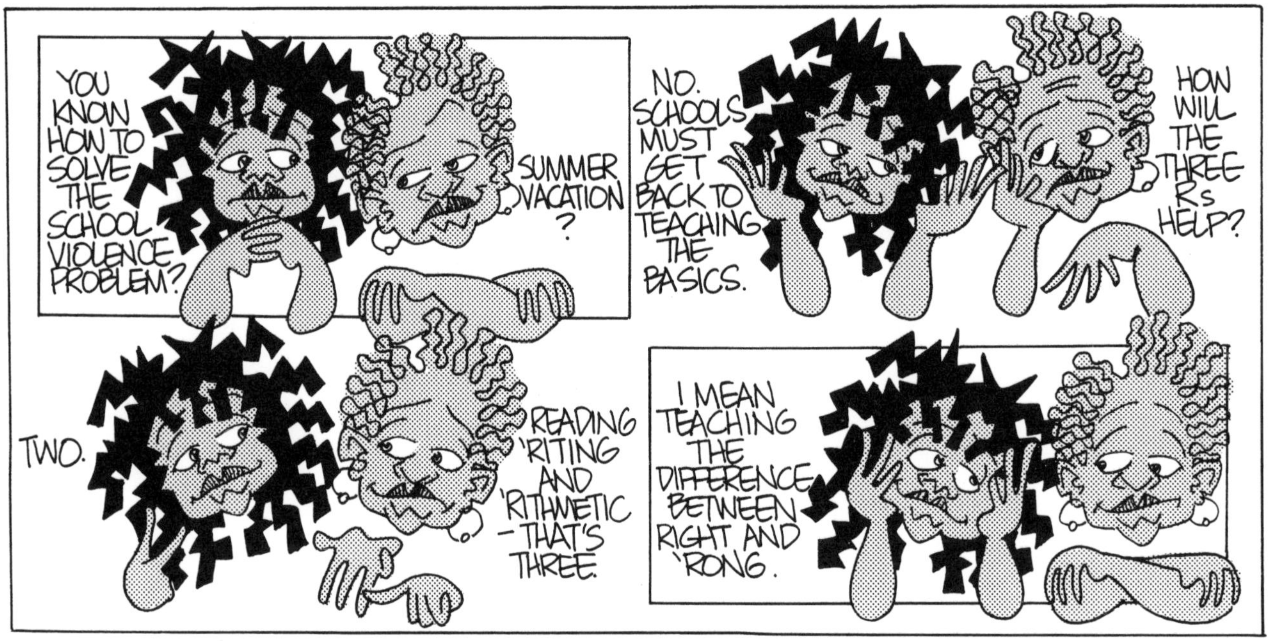
YOU KNOW HOW TO SOLVE THE SCHOOL VIOLENCE PROBLEM?
SUMMER VACATION?
NO. SCHOOLS MUST GET BACK TO TEACHING THE BASICS.
HOW WILL THE THREE Rs HELP?
TWO.
READING 'RITING AND 'RITHMETIC – THAT'S THREE.
I MEAN TEACHING THE DIFFERENCE BETWEEN RIGHT AND 'RONG.

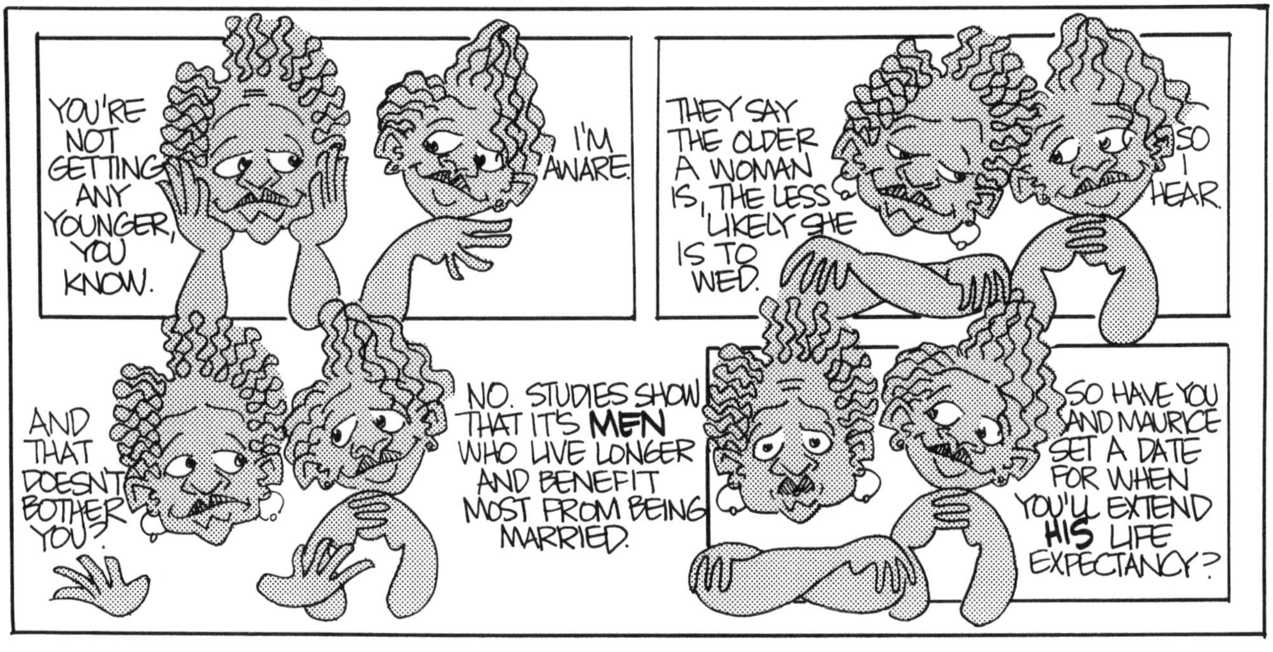
YOU'RE NOT GETTING ANY YOUNGER, YOU KNOW.
I'M AWARE.
THEY SAY THE OLDER A WOMAN IS, THE LESS LIKELY SHE IS TO WED.
SO I HEAR.
AND THAT DOESN'T BOTHER YOU?
NO. STUDIES SHOW THAT IT'S MEN WHO LIVE LONGER AND BENEFIT MOST FROM BEING MARRIED.
SO HAVE YOU AND MAURICE SET A DATE FOR WHEN YOU'LL EXTEND HIS LIFE EXPECTANCY?

Panel 1: IT'S ALL FINALLY COMING TOGETHER. NO MORE "EMOTIONAL JACKIE." I'VE TAKEN ON A NEW OUTLOOK.

Panel 2: IT'S PLEASURE IN, PRESSURE OUT. MY NEW MANTRA IS: RELEASE, RENEW, AND...

Panel 3: AHH... WHAT'S THAT LAST ONE? MAN! I CAN'T REMEMBER! THIS MAKES ME SO MAD! UGGH!

RELAX. YOU'LL RE-MEMBER.

Panel 4: THAT'S IT! RELEASE, RENEW, AND RELAX! THANKS.

Panel 5: MY AUNT BIRDIE WAS A SAINT. I WILL MISS HER.

Panel 6: SEEMS LIKE SHE WOULD CARRY THE WEIGHT OF THE WORLD ON HER SHOULDERS AND NOT ONCE COMPLAIN.

Panel 7: WOW. I WISH I COULD BE REMEMBERED THAT WAY ...BUT IT WON'T HAPPEN.

Panel 8: WHY NOT? YOU'RE TOTING QUITE A LOAD AS A SINGLE MOTHER AND ALL.

TRUE. BUT I **LOVE** TO COM-PLAIN.

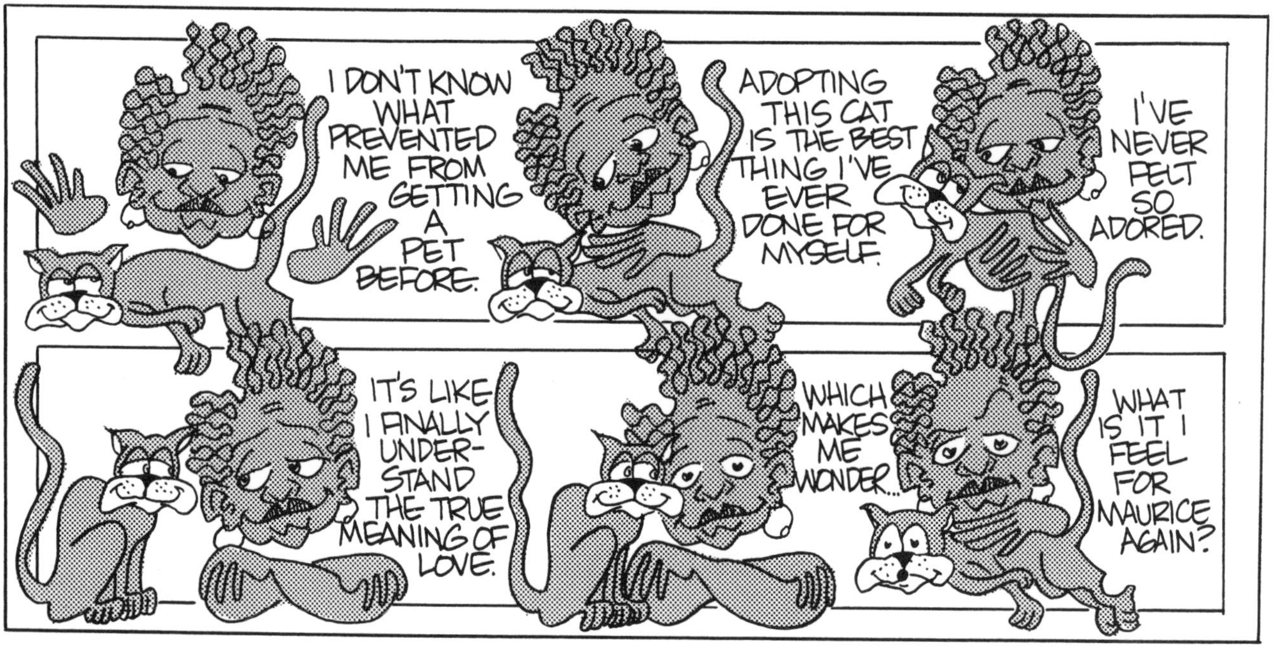
I DON'T KNOW WHAT PREVENTED ME FROM GETTING A PET BEFORE.
ADOPTING THIS CAT IS THE BEST THING I'VE EVER DONE FOR MYSELF.
I'VE NEVER FELT SO ADORED.
IT'S LIKE I FINALLY UNDER-STAND THE TRUE MEANING OF LOVE.
WHICH MAKES ME WONDER...
WHAT IS IT I FEEL FOR MAURICE AGAIN?

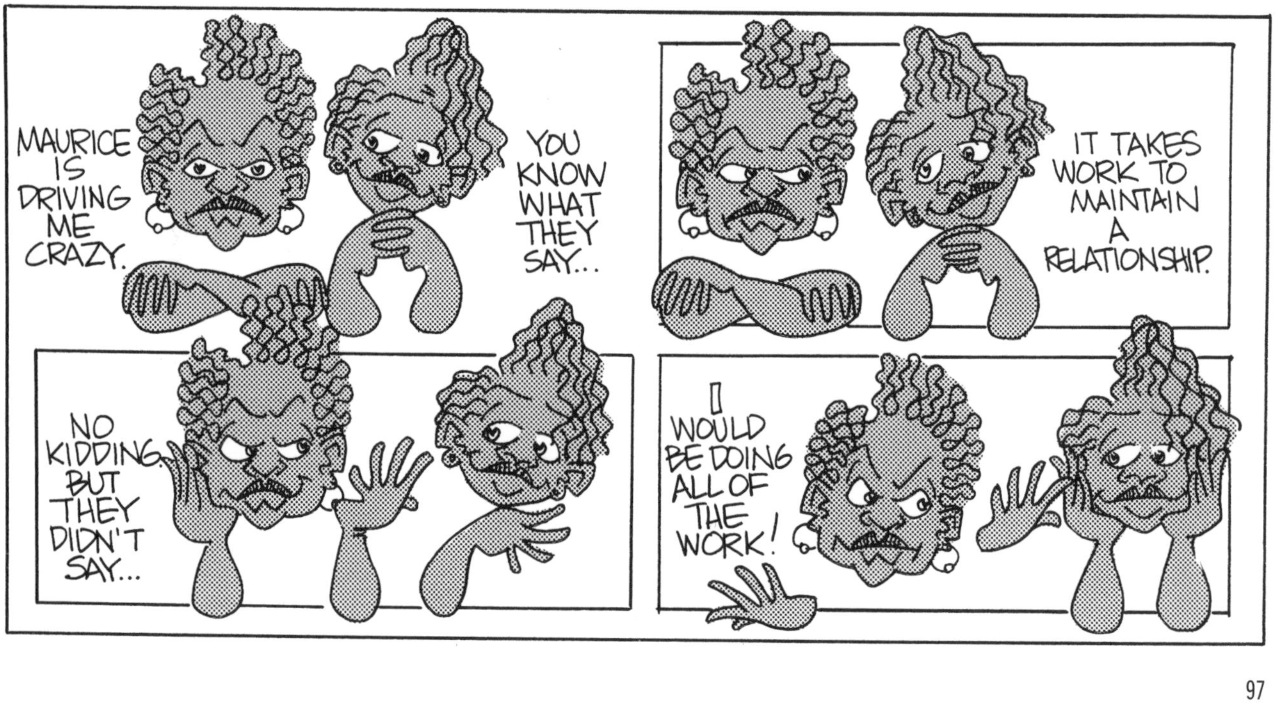
MAURICE IS DRIVING ME CRAZY.
YOU KNOW WHAT THEY SAY...
IT TAKES WORK TO MAINTAIN A RELATIONSHIP.
NO KIDDING. BUT THEY DIDN'T SAY...
I WOULD BE DOING ALL OF THE WORK!

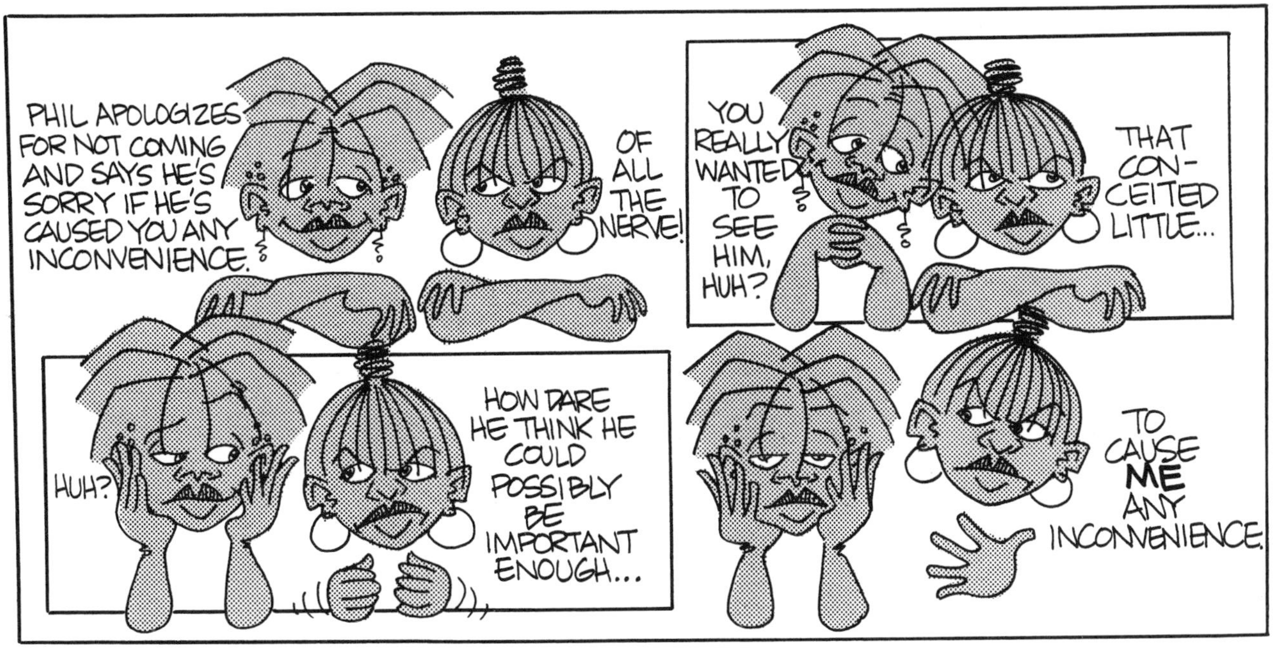
PHIL APOLOGIZES FOR NOT COMING AND SAYS HE'S SORRY IF HE'S CAUSED YOU ANY INCONVENIENCE.
OF ALL THE NERVE!
YOU REALLY WANTED TO SEE HIM, HUH?
THAT CON-CEITED LITTLE...
HUH?
HOW DARE HE THINK HE COULD POSSIBLY BE IMPORTANT ENOUGH...
TO CAUSE **ME** ANY INCONVENIENCE.

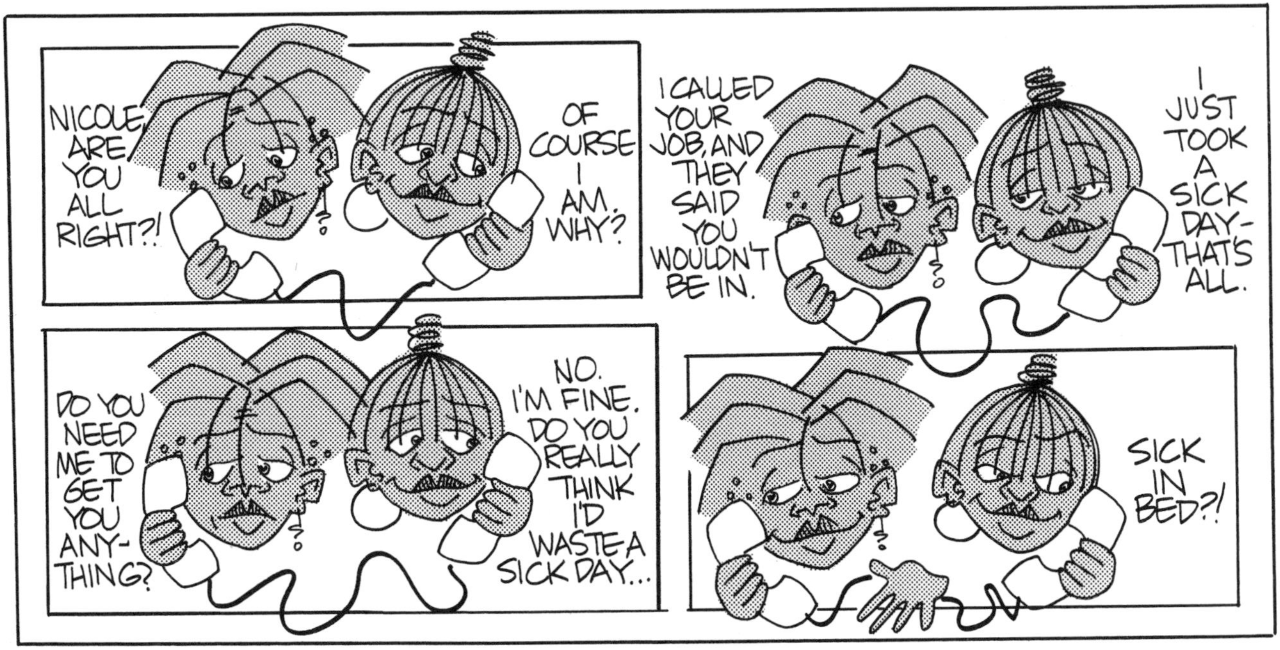
NICOLE, ARE YOU ALL RIGHT?!
OF COURSE I AM. WHY?
I CALLED YOUR JOB, AND THEY SAID YOU WOULDN'T BE IN.
I JUST TOOK A SICK DAY- THAT'S ALL.
DO YOU NEED ME TO GET YOU ANY-THING?
NO. I'M FINE. DO YOU REALLY THINK I'D WASTE A SICK DAY...
SICK IN BED?!

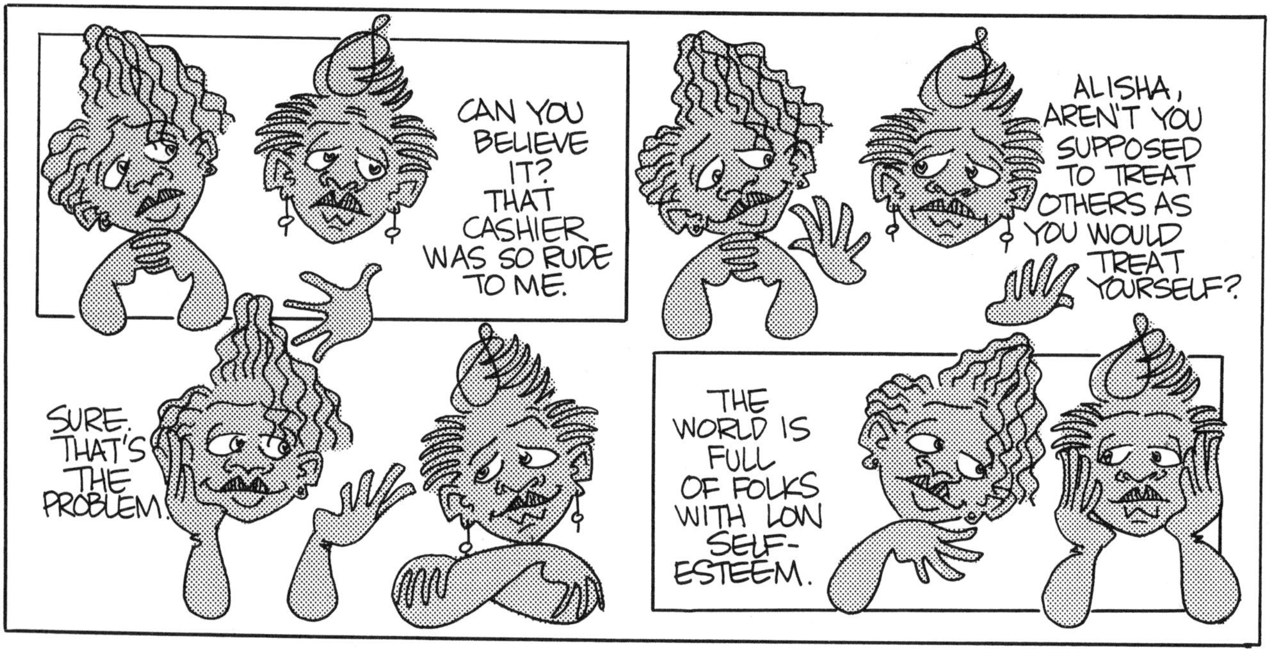
CAN YOU BELIEVE IT? THAT CASHIER WAS SO RUDE TO ME.
SURE. THAT'S THE PROBLEM.
ALISHA, AREN'T YOU SUPPOSED TO TREAT OTHERS AS YOU WOULD TREAT YOURSELF?
THE WORLD IS FULL OF FOLKS WITH LOW SELF-ESTEEM.

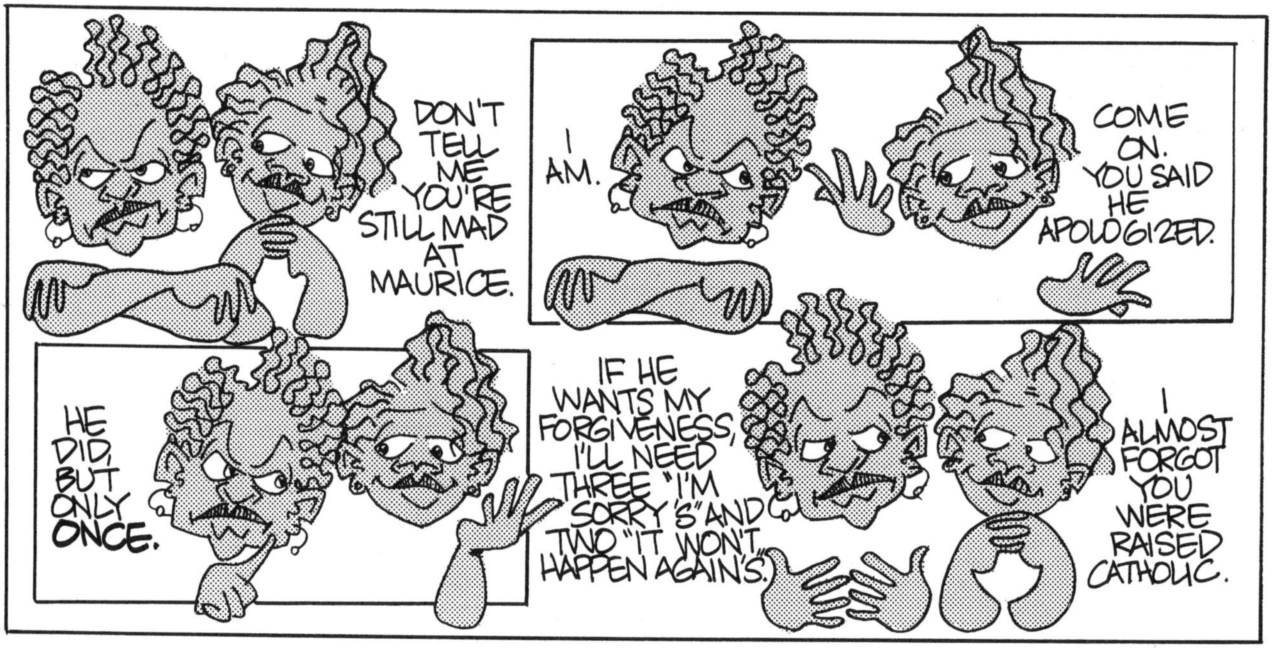
DON'T TELL ME YOU'RE STILL MAD AT MAURICE.
HE DID, BUT ONLY **ONCE.**
I AM.
COME ON. YOU SAID HE APOLOGIZED.
IF HE WANTS MY FORGIVENESS, I'LL NEED THREE "I'M SORRY'S" AND TWO "IT WON'T HAPPEN AGAIN'S."
I ALMOST FORGOT YOU WERE RAISED CATHOLIC.

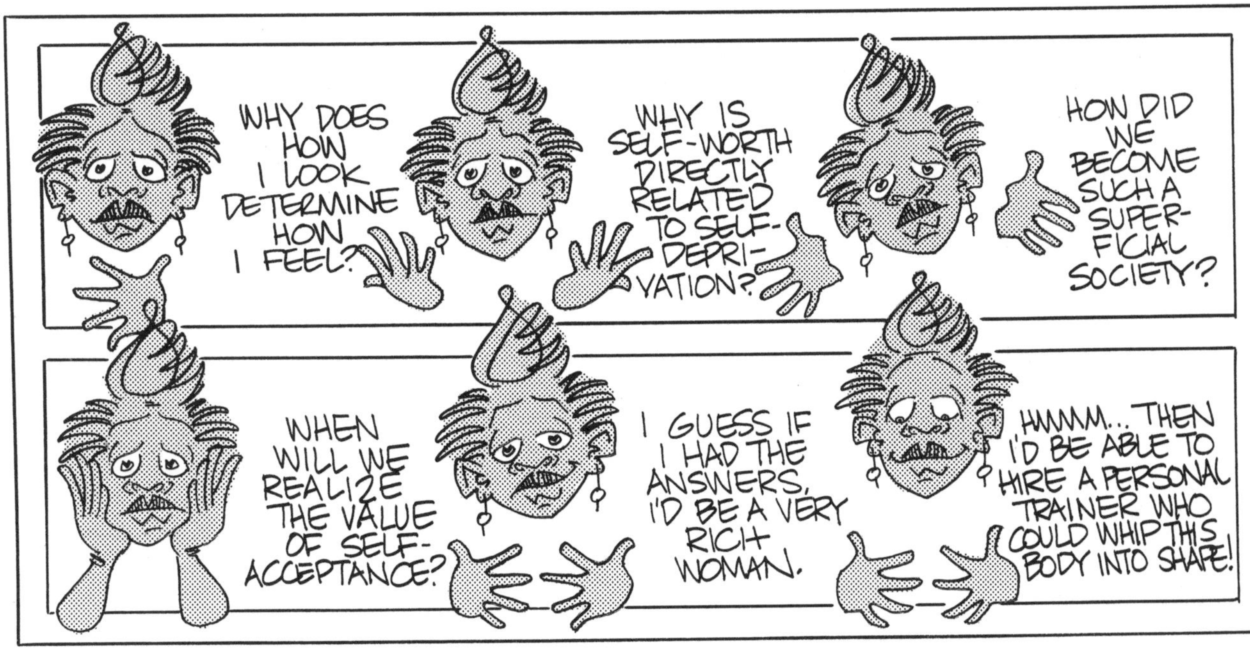
WHY DOES HOW I LOOK DETERMINE HOW I FEEL?
WHY IS SELF-WORTH DIRECTLY RELATED TO SELF-DEPRIVATION?
HOW DID WE BECOME SUCH A SUPERFICIAL SOCIETY?
WHEN WILL WE REALIZE THE VALUE OF SELF-ACCEPTANCE?
I GUESS IF I HAD THE ANSWERS, I'D BE A VERY RICH WOMAN.
HMMM... THEN I'D BE ABLE TO HIRE A PERSONAL TRAINER WHO COULD WHIP THIS BODY INTO SHAPE!

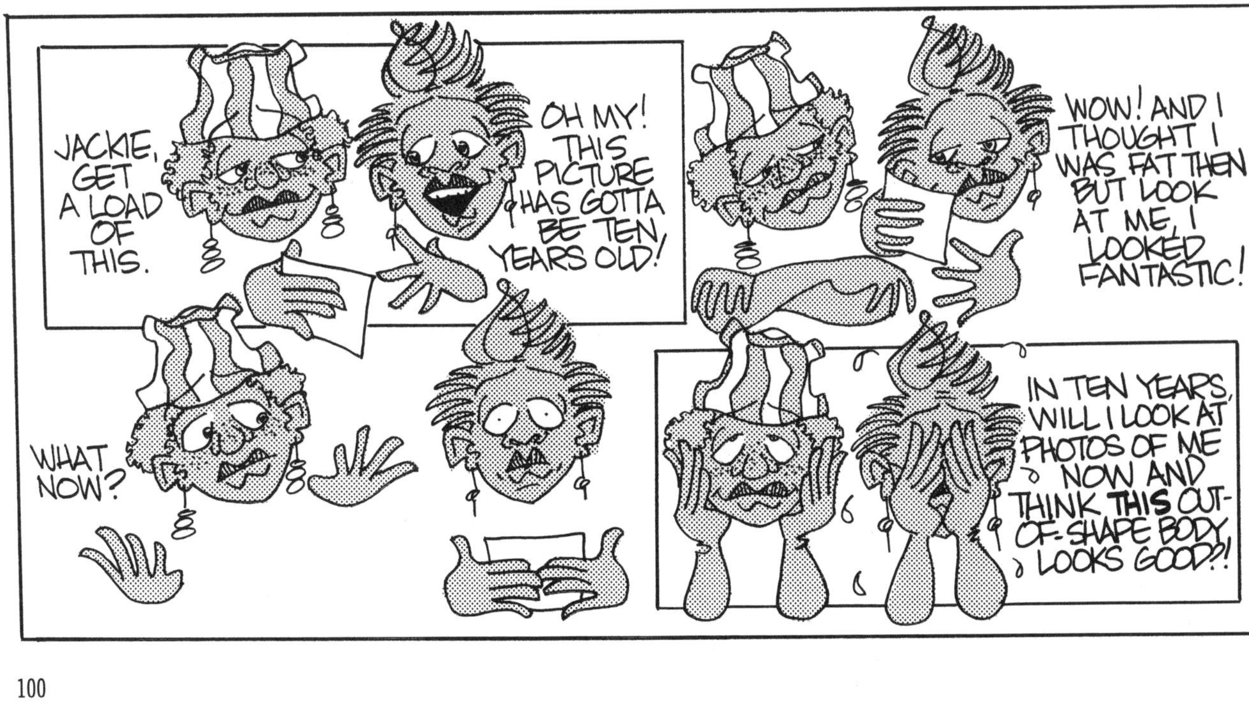
JACKIE, GET A LOAD OF THIS.
OH MY! THIS PICTURE HAS GOTTA BE TEN YEARS OLD!
WOW! AND I THOUGHT I WAS FAT THEN. BUT LOOK AT ME, I LOOKED FANTASTIC!
WHAT NOW?
IN TEN YEARS, WILL I LOOK AT PHOTOS OF ME NOW AND THINK **THIS** OUT-OF-SHAPE BODY LOOKS GOOD?!

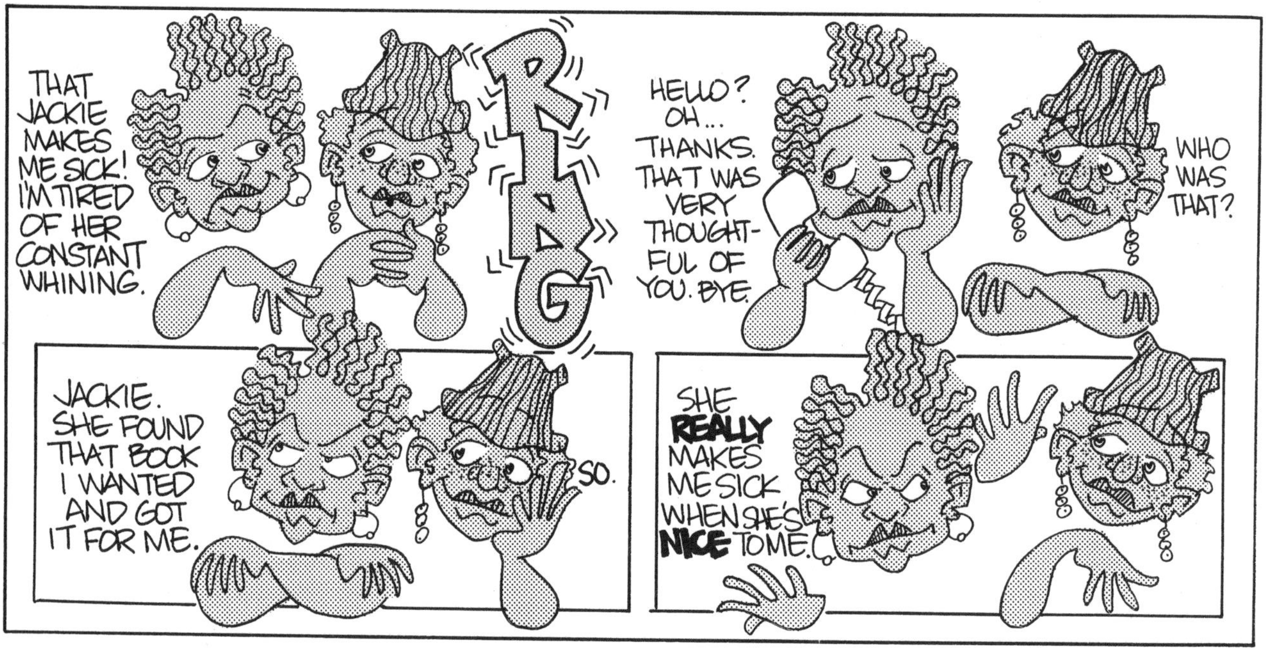
THAT JACKIE MAKES ME SICK! I'M TIRED OF HER CONSTANT WHINING.
RING
HELLO? OH... THANKS. THAT WAS VERY THOUGHT-FUL OF YOU. BYE.
WHO WAS THAT?
JACKIE. SHE FOUND THAT BOOK I WANTED AND GOT IT FOR ME.
SO.
SHE **REALLY** MAKES ME SICK WHEN SHE'S **NICE** TO ME.

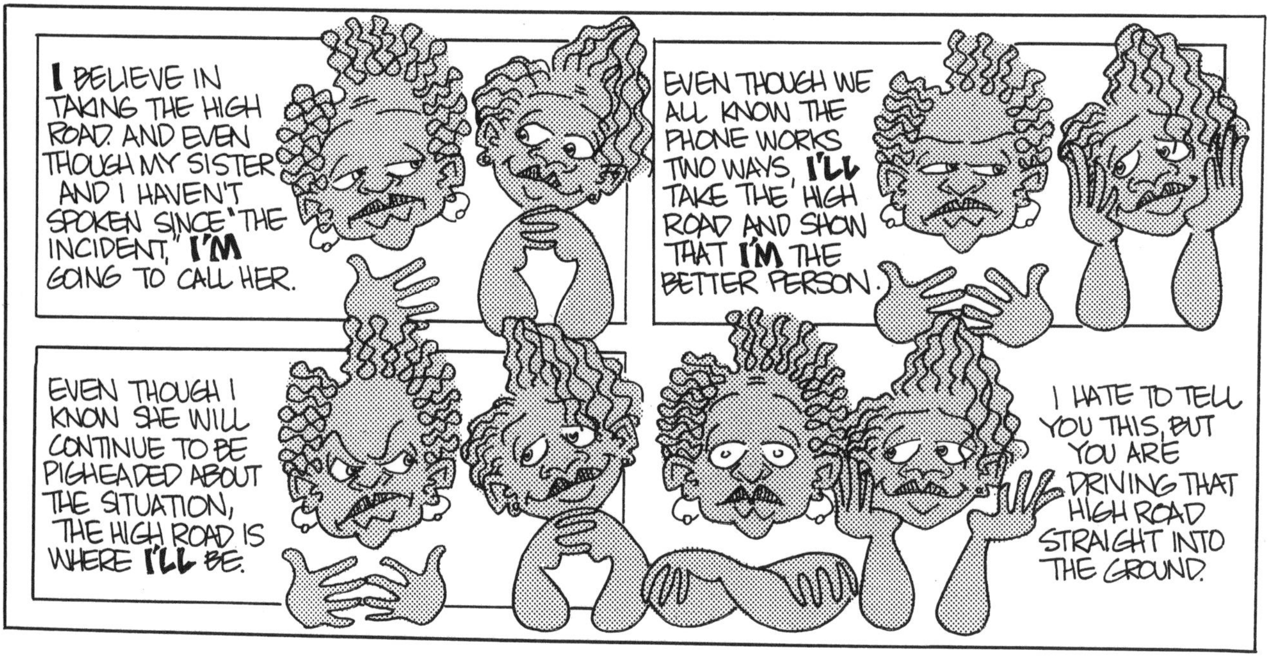
I BELIEVE IN TAKING THE HIGH ROAD. AND EVEN THOUGH MY SISTER AND I HAVEN'T SPOKEN SINCE "THE INCIDENT," **I'M** GOING TO CALL HER.
EVEN THOUGH WE ALL KNOW THE PHONE WORKS TWO WAYS, **I'LL** TAKE THE HIGH ROAD AND SHOW THAT **I'M** THE BETTER PERSON.
EVEN THOUGH I KNOW SHE WILL CONTINUE TO BE PIGHEADED ABOUT THE SITUATION, THE HIGH ROAD IS WHERE **I'LL** BE.
I HATE TO TELL YOU THIS, BUT YOU ARE DRIVING THAT HIGH ROAD STRAIGHT INTO THE GROUND.

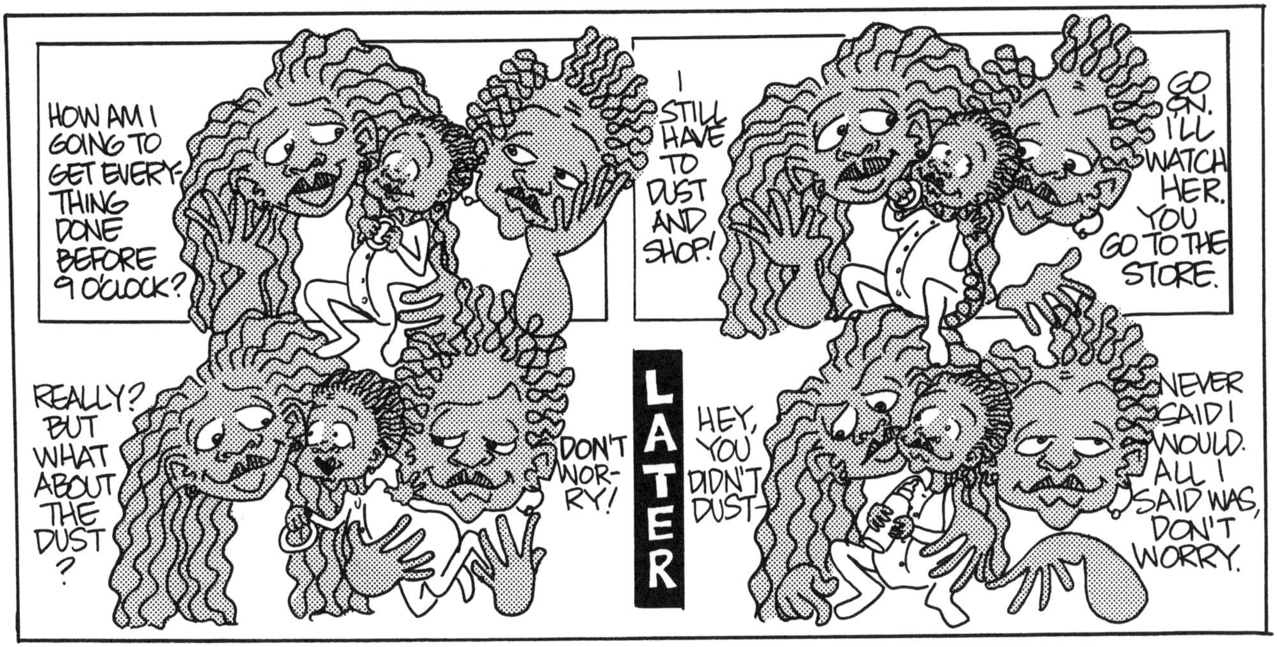
HOW AM I GOING TO GET EVERYTHING DONE BEFORE 9 O'CLOCK?
I STILL HAVE TO DUST AND SHOP!
GO ON. I'LL WATCH HER. YOU GO TO THE STORE.
REALLY? BUT WHAT ABOUT THE DUST?
DON'T WORRY!
LATER
HEY, YOU DIDN'T DUST-
NEVER SAID I WOULD. ALL I SAID WAS, DON'T WORRY.

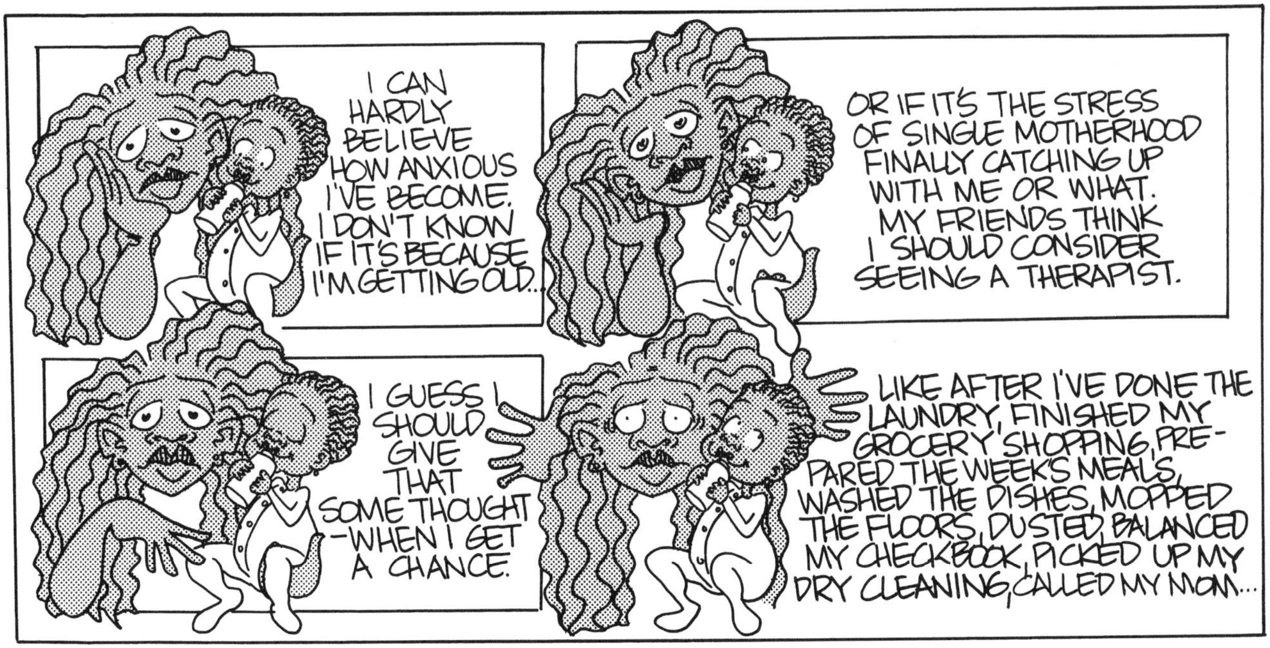
I CAN HARDLY BELIEVE HOW ANXIOUS I'VE BECOME. I DON'T KNOW IF IT'S BECAUSE I'M GETTING OLD...
OR IF IT'S THE STRESS OF SINGLE MOTHERHOOD FINALLY CATCHING UP WITH ME OR WHAT. MY FRIENDS THINK I SHOULD CONSIDER SEEING A THERAPIST.
I GUESS I SHOULD GIVE THAT SOME THOUGHT -WHEN I GET A CHANCE.
LIKE AFTER I'VE DONE THE LAUNDRY, FINISHED MY GROCERY SHOPPING, PREPARED THE WEEK'S MEALS, WASHED THE DISHES, MOPPED THE FLOORS, DUSTED, BALANCED MY CHECKBOOK, PICKED UP MY DRY CLEANING, CALLED MY MOM...

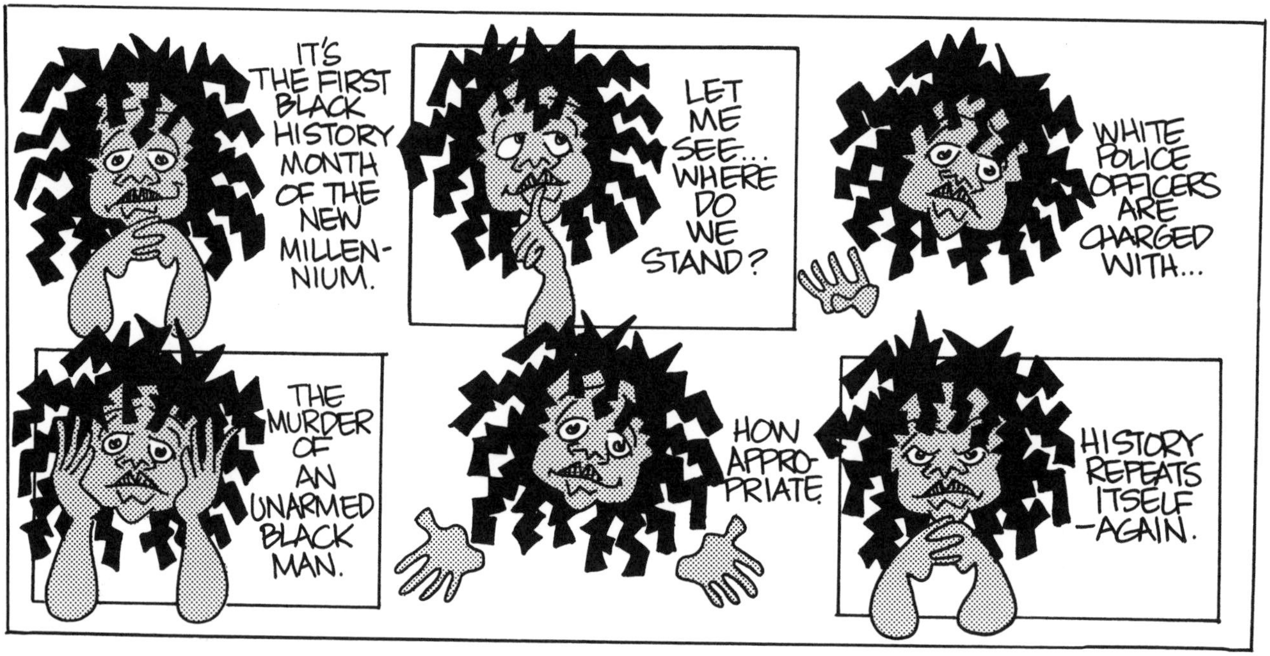
IT'S THE FIRST BLACK HISTORY MONTH OF THE NEW MILLEN-NIUM.
LET ME SEE... WHERE DO WE STAND?
WHITE POLICE OFFICERS ARE CHARGED WITH...
THE MURDER OF AN UNARMED BLACK MAN.
HOW APPROPRIATE.
HISTORY REPEATS ITSELF —AGAIN.

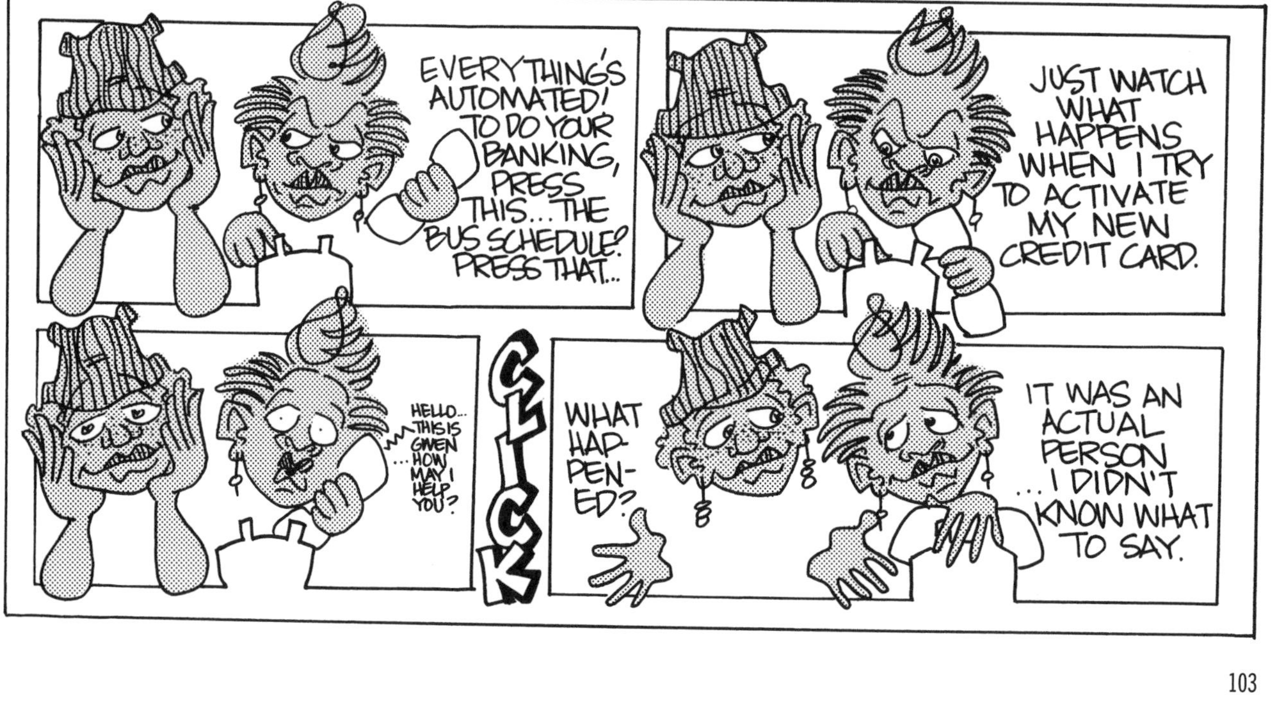
EVERYTHING'S AUTOMATED! TO DO YOUR BANKING, PRESS THIS... THE BUS SCHEDULE? PRESS THAT...
JUST WATCH WHAT HAPPENS WHEN I TRY TO ACTIVATE MY NEW CREDIT CARD.
HELLO... THIS IS GWEN ... HOW MAY I HELP YOU?
CLICK
WHAT HAP-PEN-ED?
IT WAS AN ACTUAL PERSON ... I DIDN'T KNOW WHAT TO SAY.

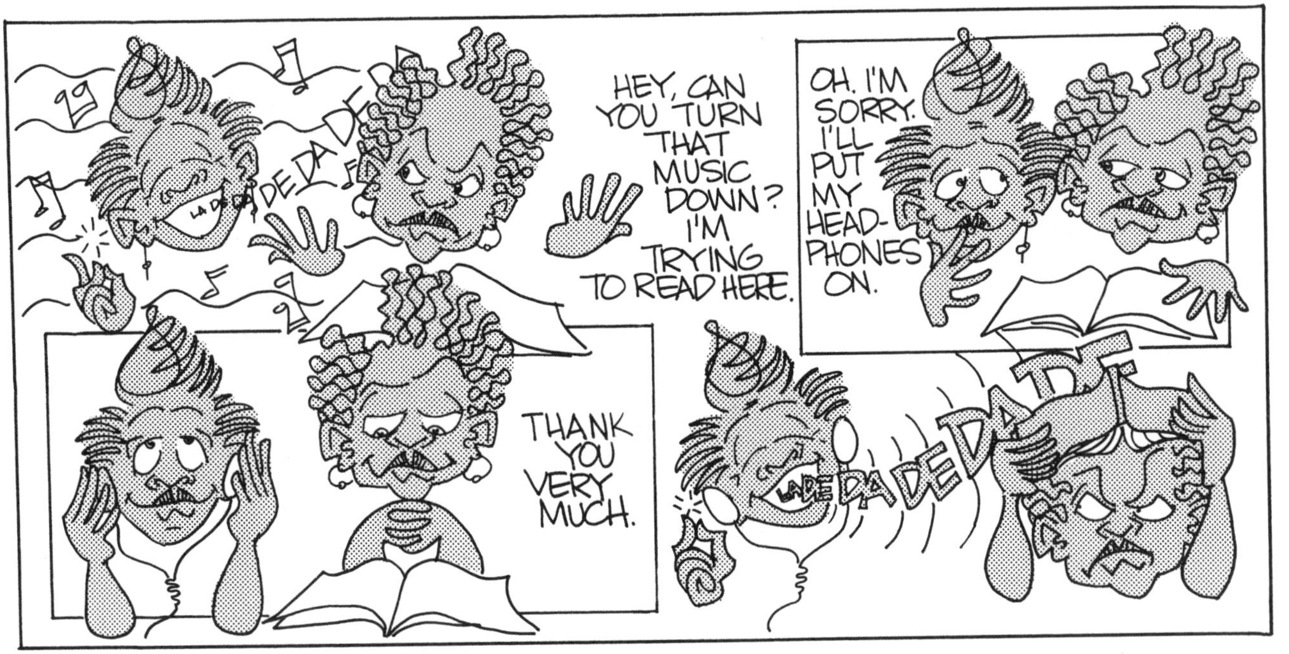
DE DA DE
HEY, CAN YOU TURN THAT MUSIC DOWN? I'M TRYING TO READ HERE.
OH. I'M SORRY. I'LL PUT MY HEADPHONES ON.
THANK YOU VERY MUCH.
DA DE DA DE

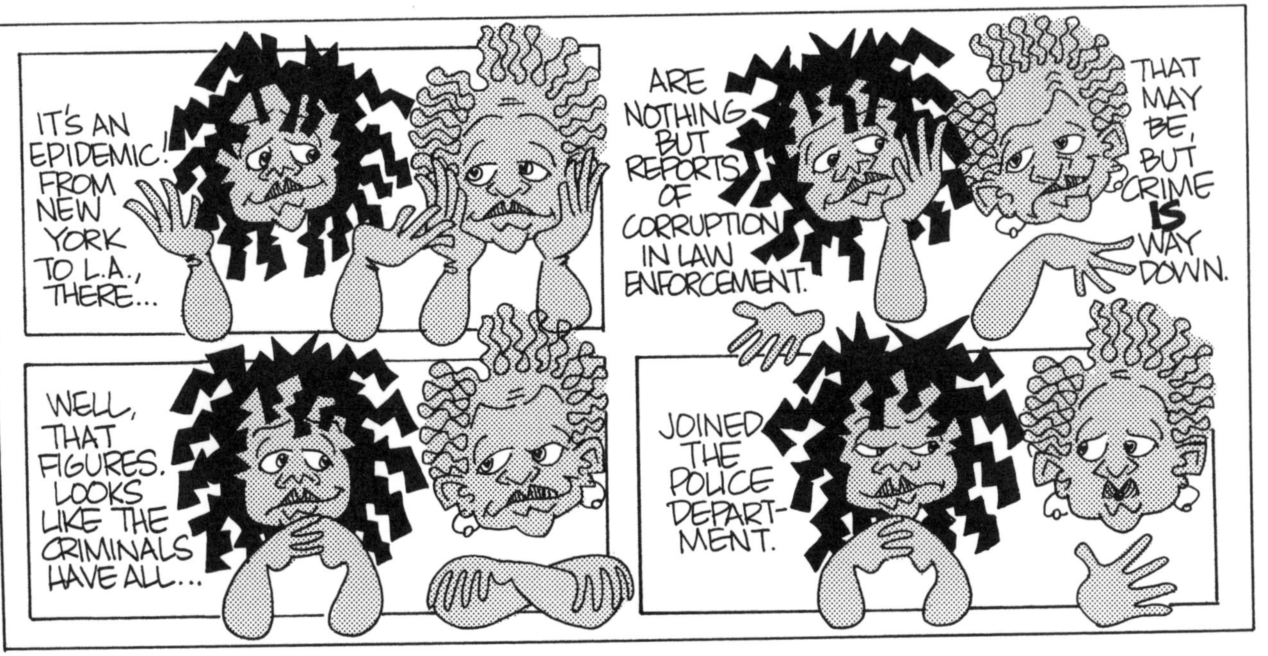
IT'S AN EPIDEMIC! FROM NEW YORK TO L.A., THERE...
ARE NOTHING BUT REPORTS OF CORRUPTION IN LAW ENFORCEMENT.
THAT MAY BE, BUT CRIME IS WAY DOWN.
WELL, THAT FIGURES. LOOKS LIKE THE CRIMINALS HAVE ALL...
JOINED THE POLICE DEPARTMENT.

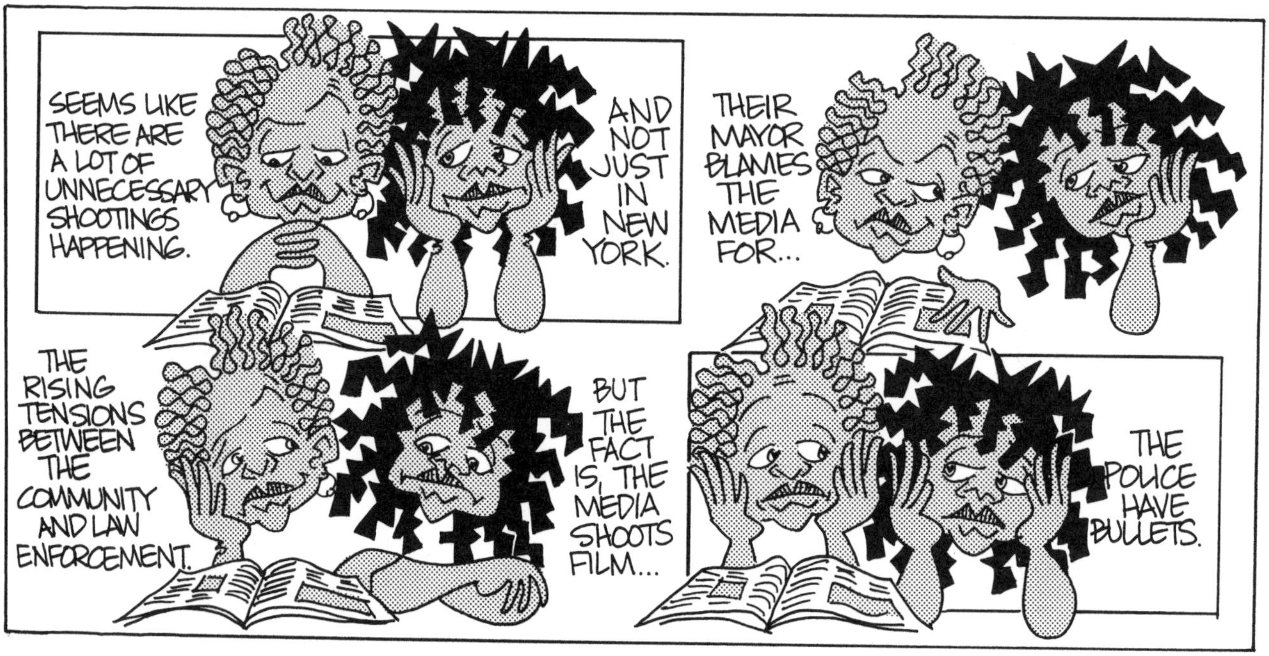
SEEMS LIKE THERE ARE A LOT OF UNNECESSARY SHOOTINGS HAPPENING.
AND NOT JUST IN NEW YORK.
THEIR MAYOR BLAMES THE MEDIA FOR...
THE RISING TENSIONS BETWEEN THE COMMUNITY AND LAW ENFORCEMENT.
BUT THE FACT IS, THE MEDIA SHOOTS FILM...
THE POLICE HAVE BULLETS.

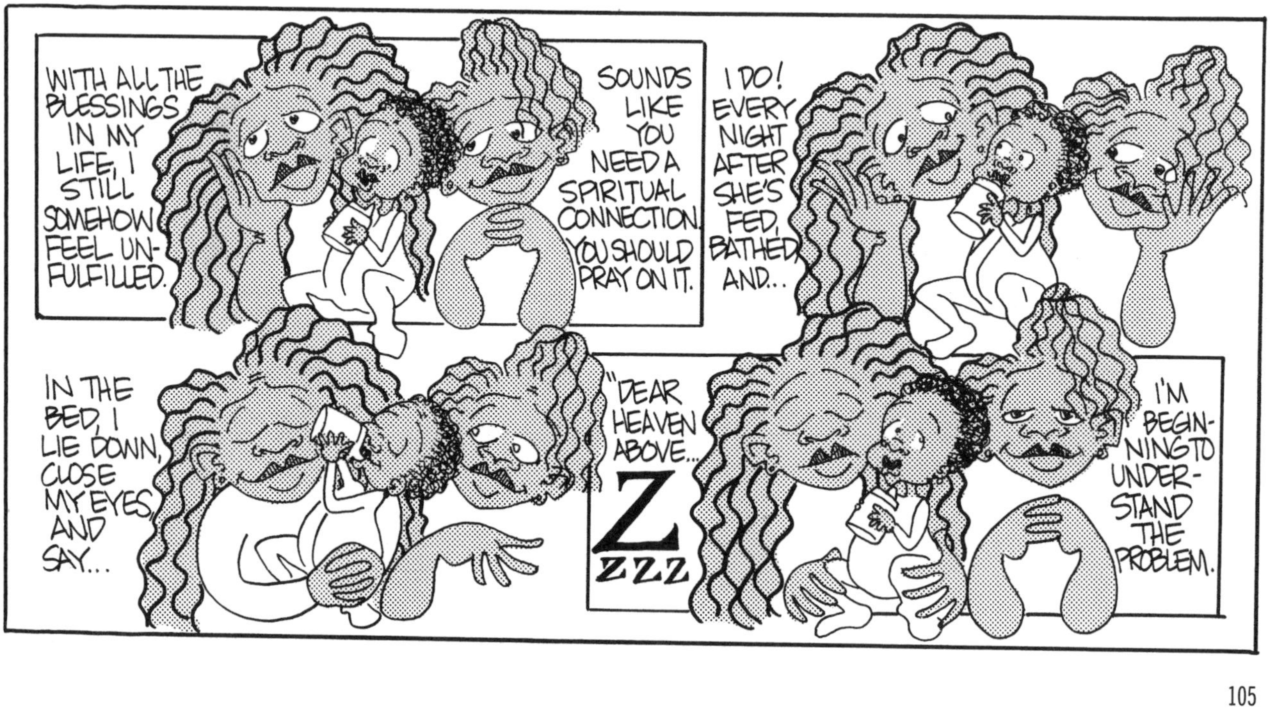
WITH ALL THE BLESSINGS IN MY LIFE, I STILL SOMEHOW FEEL UN-FULFILLED.
SOUNDS LIKE YOU NEED A SPIRITUAL CONNECTION. YOU SHOULD PRAY ON IT.
I DO! EVERY NIGHT AFTER SHE'S FED, BATHED, AND...
IN THE BED, I LIE DOWN, CLOSE MY EYES, AND SAY...
"DEAR HEAVEN ABOVE...
Z
ZZZ
I'M BEGIN-NING TO UNDER-STAND THE PROBLEM.

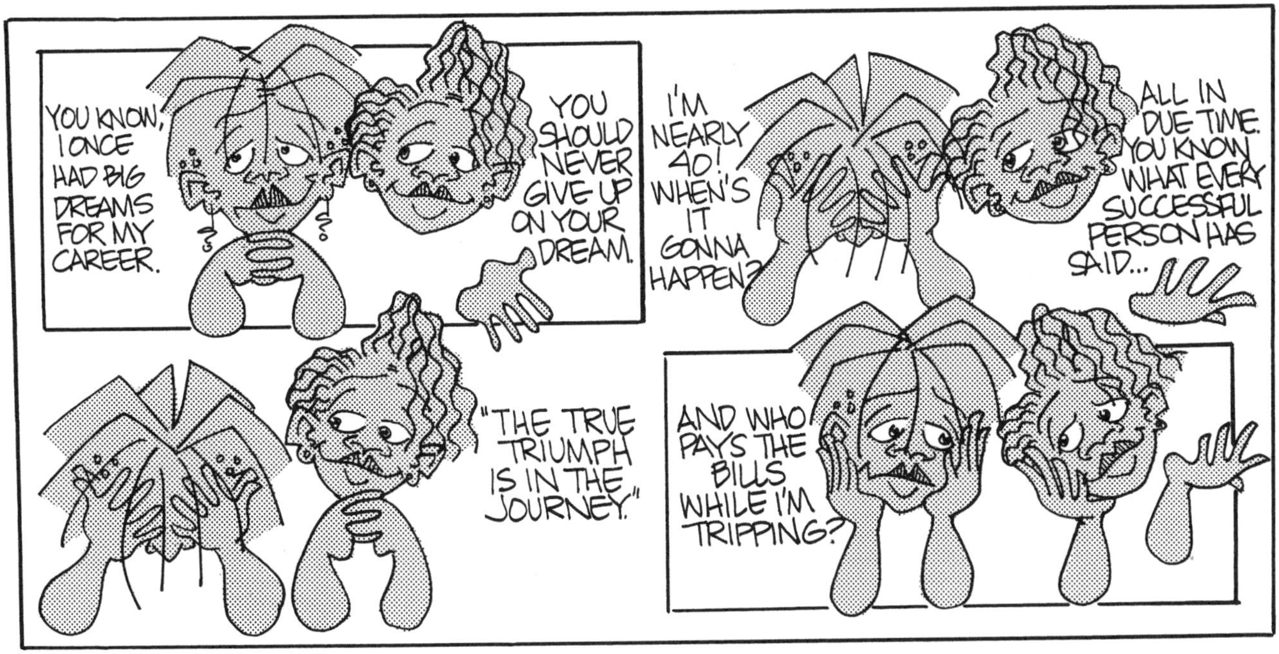
YOU KNOW, I ONCE HAD BIG DREAMS FOR MY CAREER.
YOU SHOULD NEVER GIVE UP ON YOUR DREAM.
I'M NEARLY 40! WHEN'S IT GONNA HAPPEN?
ALL IN DUE TIME. YOU KNOW WHAT EVERY SUCCESSFUL PERSON HAS SAID...
"THE TRUE TRIUMPH IS IN THE JOURNEY."
AND WHO PAYS THE BILLS WHILE I'M TRIPPING?

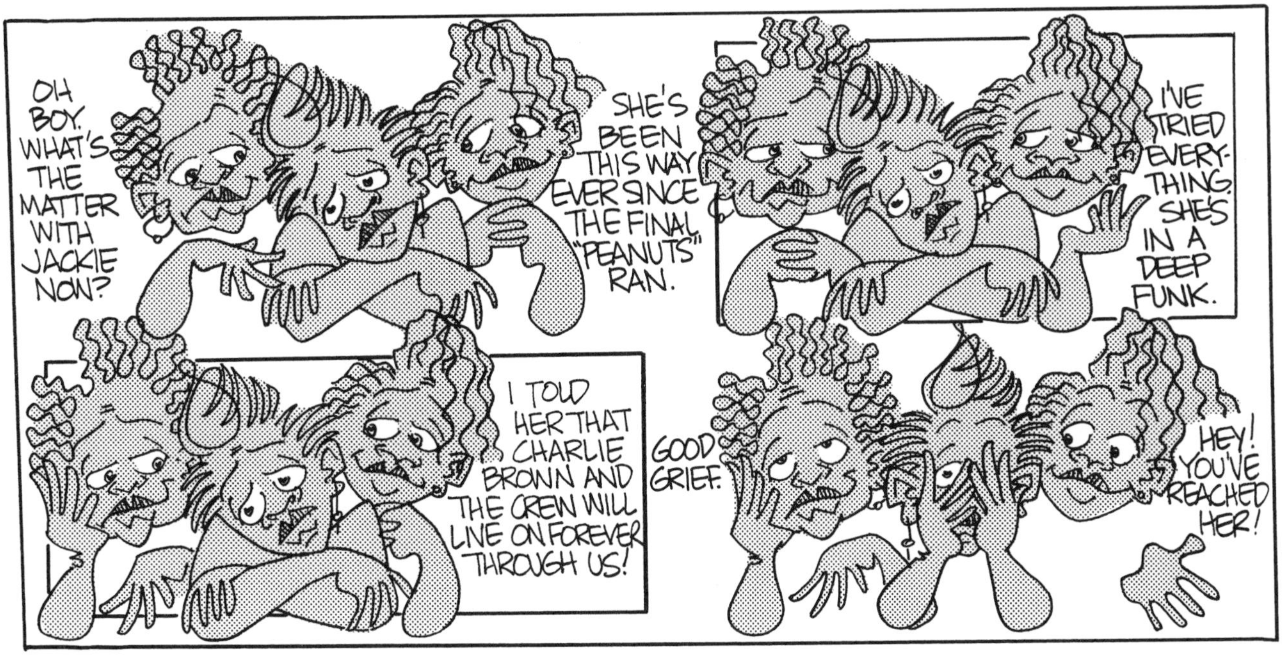
OH BOY. WHAT'S THE MATTER WITH JACKIE NOW?
SHE'S BEEN THIS WAY EVER SINCE THE FINAL "PEANUTS" RAN.
I'VE TRIED EVERYTHING. SHE'S IN A DEEP FUNK.
I TOLD HER THAT CHARLIE BROWN AND THE CREW WILL LIVE ON FOREVER THROUGH US!
GOOD GRIEF.
HEY! YOU'VE REACHED HER!

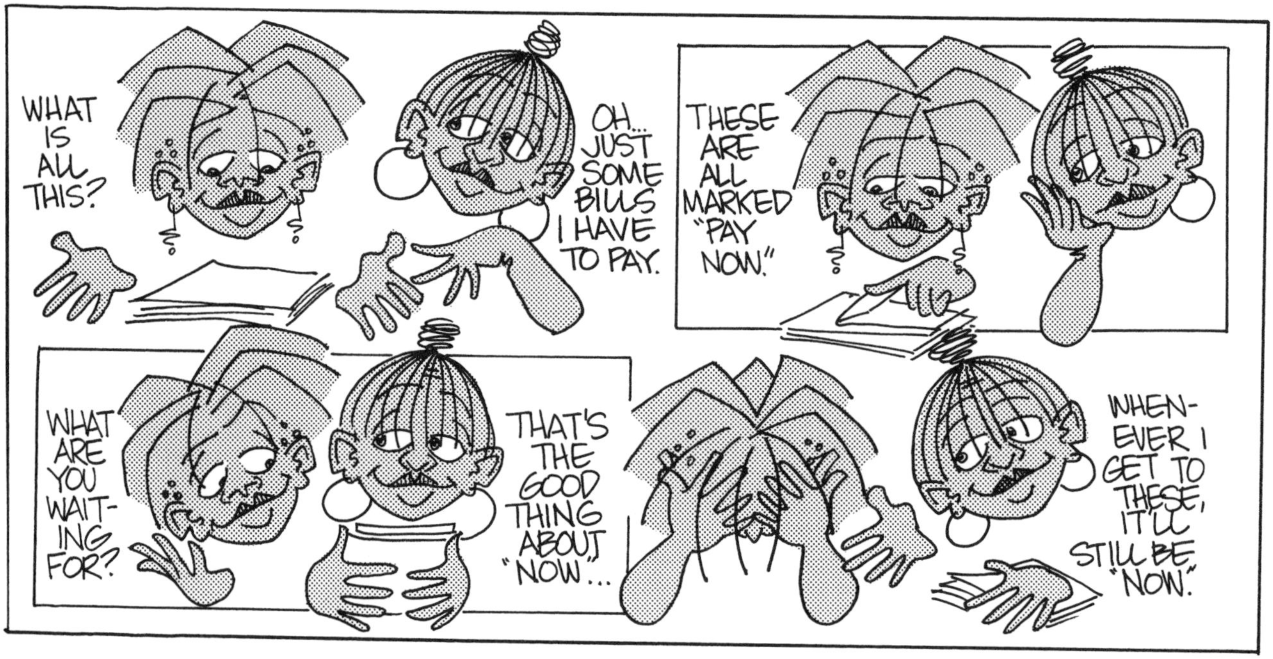
WHAT IS ALL THIS?
OH... JUST SOME BILLS I HAVE TO PAY.
THESE ARE ALL MARKED "PAY NOW."
WHAT ARE YOU WAIT-ING FOR?
THAT'S THE GOOD THING ABOUT "NOW"...
WHEN-EVER I GET TO THESE, IT'LL STILL BE "NOW."

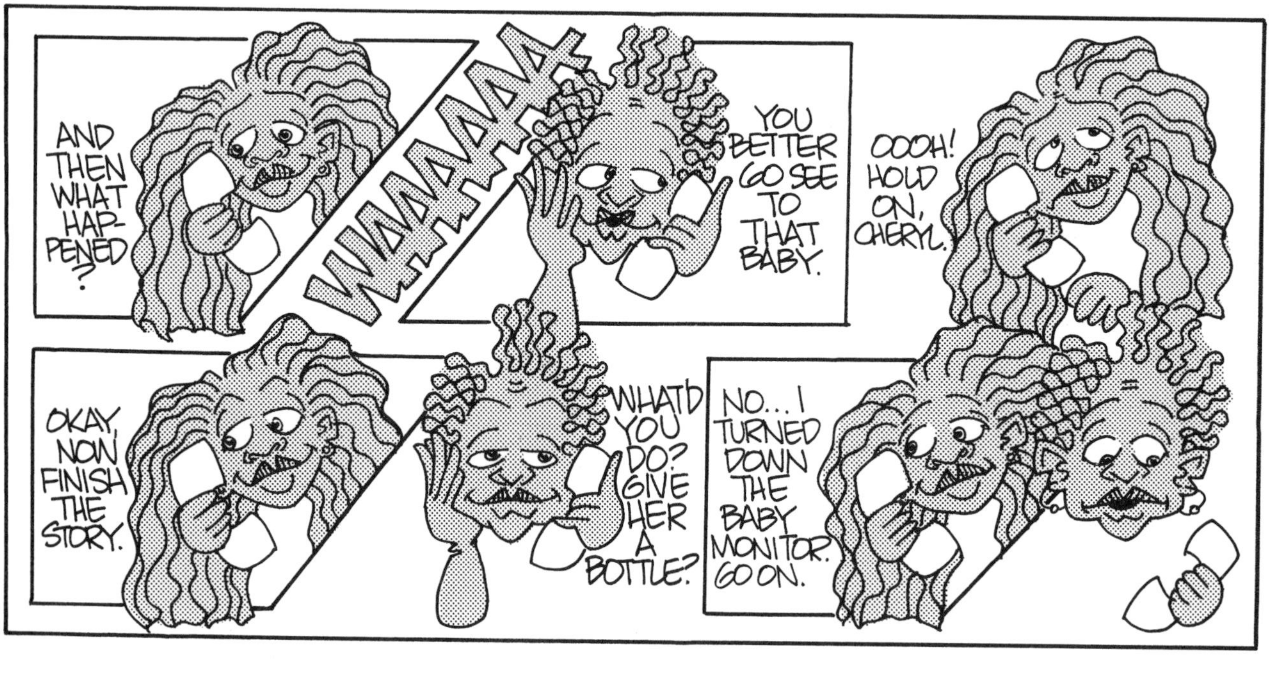
AND THEN WHAT HAP-PENED?
WAAAAAA!
YOU BETTER GO SEE TO THAT BABY.
OOOH! HOLD ON, CHERYL.
OKAY, NOW FINISH THE STORY.
WHAT'D YOU DO? GIVE HER A BOTTLE?
NO... I TURNED DOWN THE BABY MONITOR. GO ON.

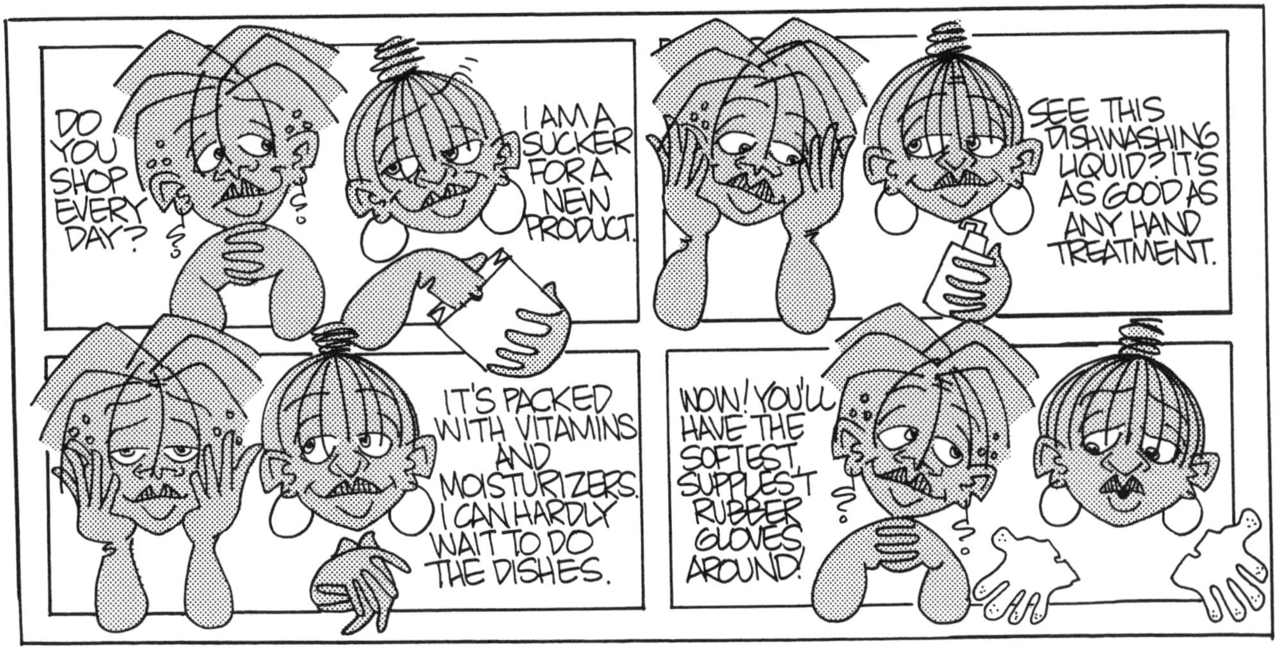
DO YOU SHOP EVERY DAY?
I AM A SUCKER FOR A NEW PRODUCT.
SEE THIS DISHWASHING LIQUID? IT'S AS GOOD AS ANY HAND TREATMENT.
IT'S PACKED WITH VITAMINS AND MOISTURIZERS. I CAN HARDLY WAIT TO DO THE DISHES.
WOW! YOU'LL HAVE THE SOFTEST, SUPPLEST RUBBER GLOVES AROUND!

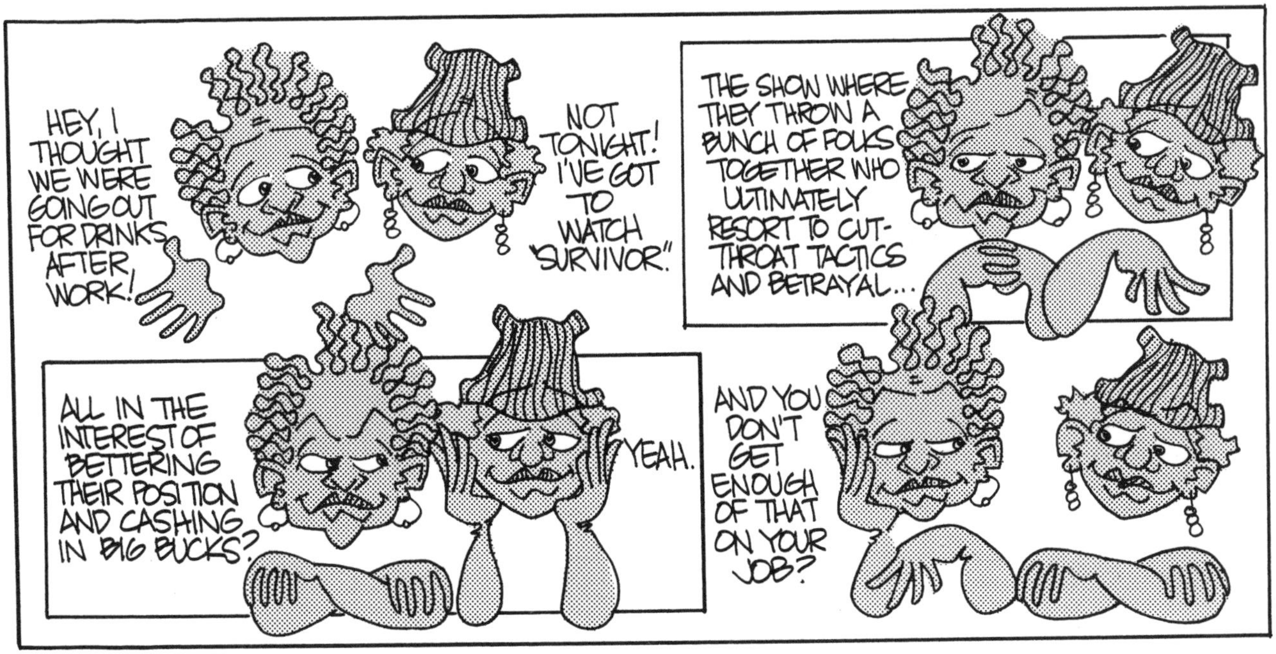
HEY, I THOUGHT WE WERE GOING OUT FOR DRINKS AFTER WORK!
NOT TONIGHT! I'VE GOT TO WATCH "SURVIVOR."
THE SHOW WHERE THEY THROW A BUNCH OF FOLKS TOGETHER WHO ULTIMATELY RESORT TO CUT-THROAT TACTICS AND BETRAYAL...
ALL IN THE INTEREST OF BETTERING THEIR POSITION AND CASHING IN BIG BUCKS?
YEAH.
AND YOU DON'T GET ENOUGH OF THAT ON YOUR JOB?

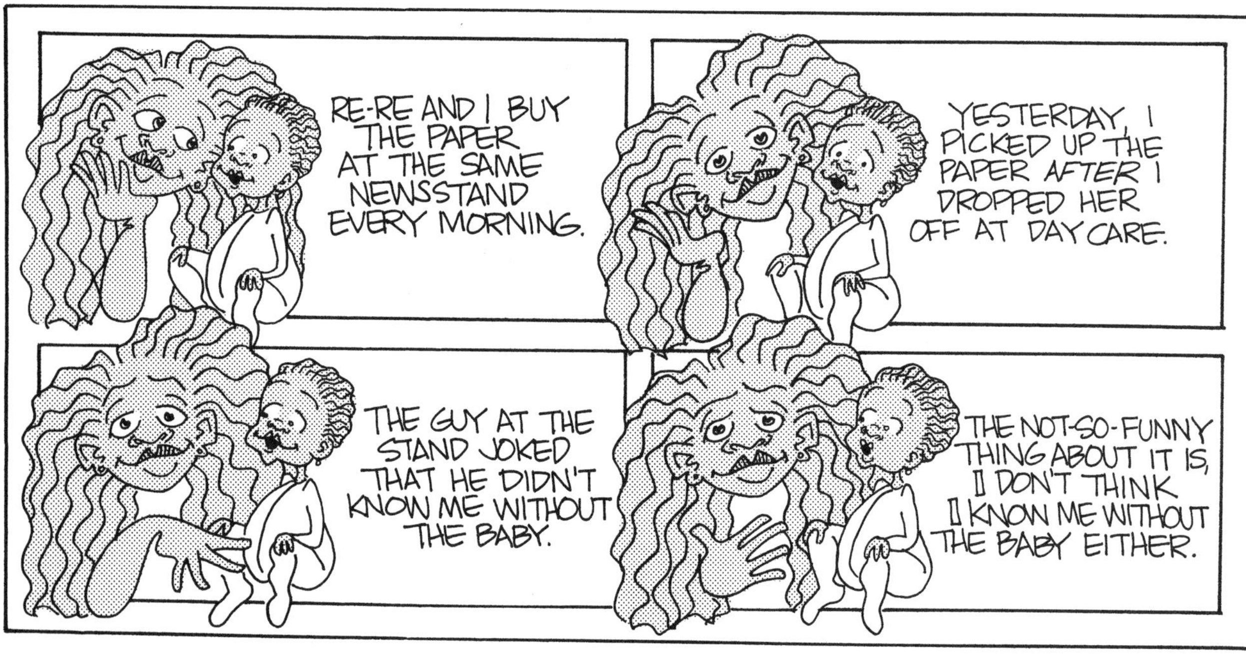
RE-RE AND I BUY THE PAPER AT THE SAME NEWSSTAND EVERY MORNING.
YESTERDAY, I PICKED UP THE PAPER AFTER I DROPPED HER OFF AT DAY CARE.
THE GUY AT THE STAND JOKED THAT HE DIDN'T KNOW ME WITHOUT THE BABY.
THE NOT-SO-FUNNY THING ABOUT IT IS, I DON'T THINK I KNOW ME WITHOUT THE BABY EITHER.

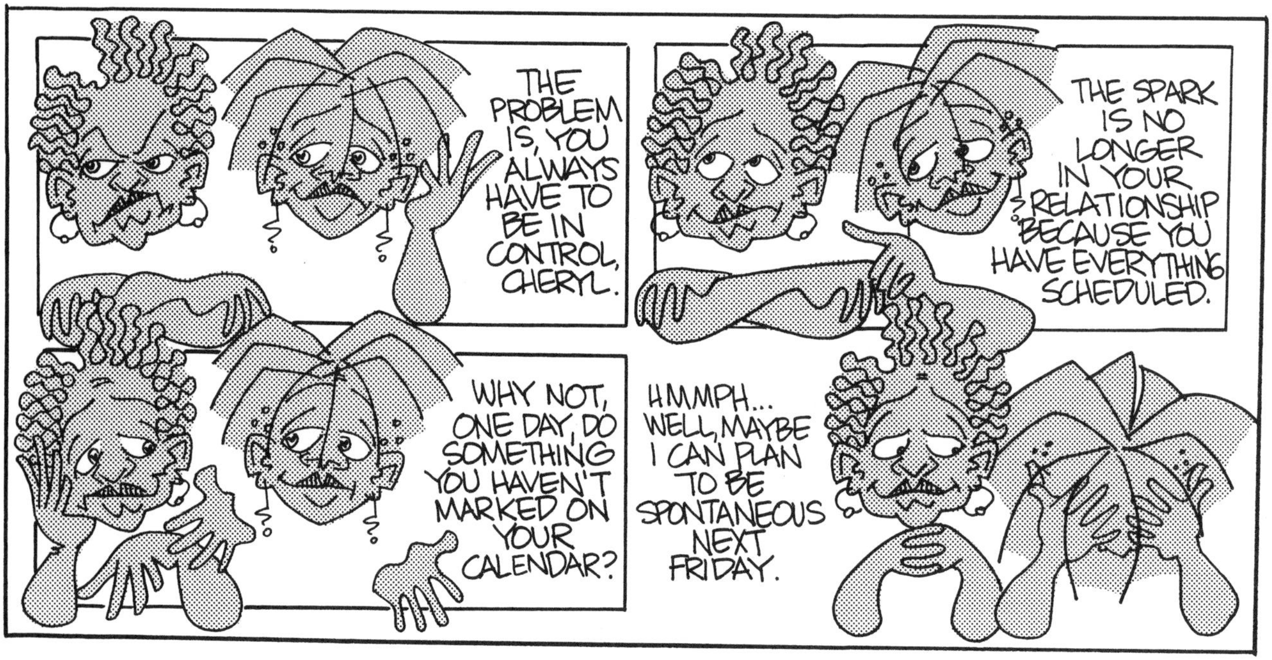
THE PROBLEM IS, YOU ALWAYS HAVE TO BE IN CONTROL, CHERYL.
THE SPARK IS NO LONGER IN YOUR RELATIONSHIP BECAUSE YOU HAVE EVERYTHING SCHEDULED.
WHY NOT, ONE DAY, DO SOMETHING YOU HAVEN'T MARKED ON YOUR CALENDAR?
HMMPH... WELL, MAYBE I CAN PLAN TO BE SPONTANEOUS NEXT FRIDAY.

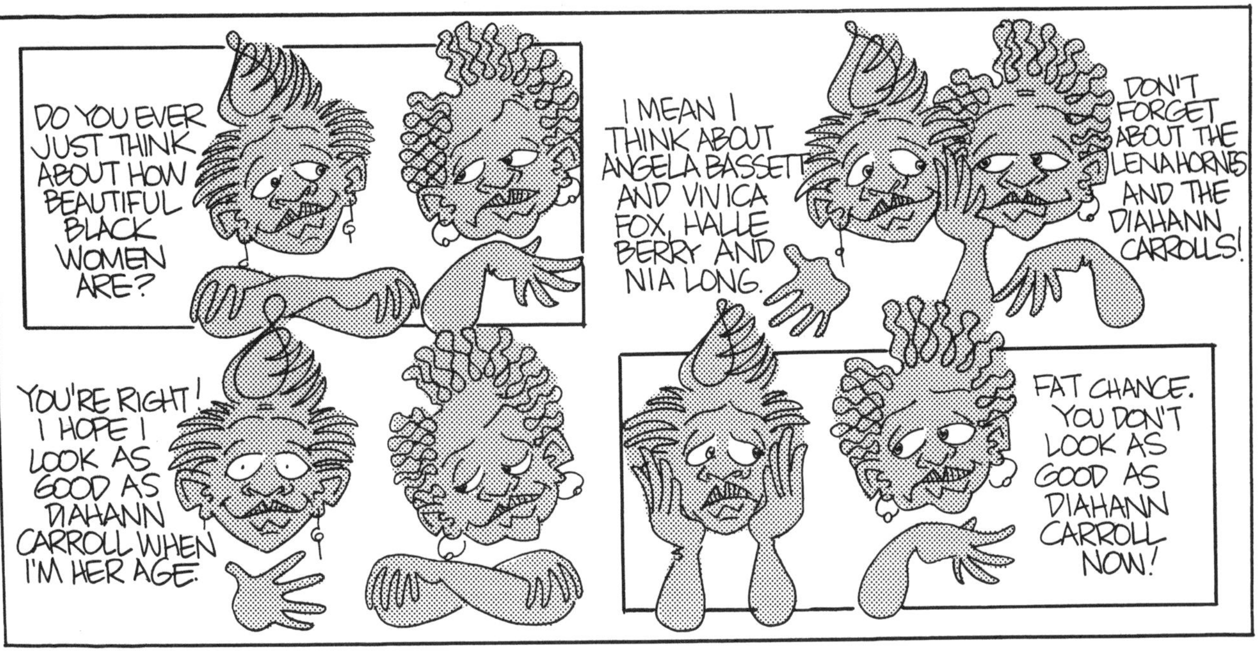
DO YOU EVER JUST THINK ABOUT HOW BEAUTIFUL BLACK WOMEN ARE?
I MEAN I THINK ABOUT ANGELA BASSETT AND VIVICA FOX, HALLE BERRY AND NIA LONG.
DON'T FORGET ABOUT THE LENA HORNES AND THE DIAHANN CARROLLS!
YOU'RE RIGHT! I HOPE I LOOK AS GOOD AS DIAHANN CARROLL WHEN I'M HER AGE.
FAT CHANCE. YOU DON'T LOOK AS GOOD AS DIAHANN CARROLL NOW!

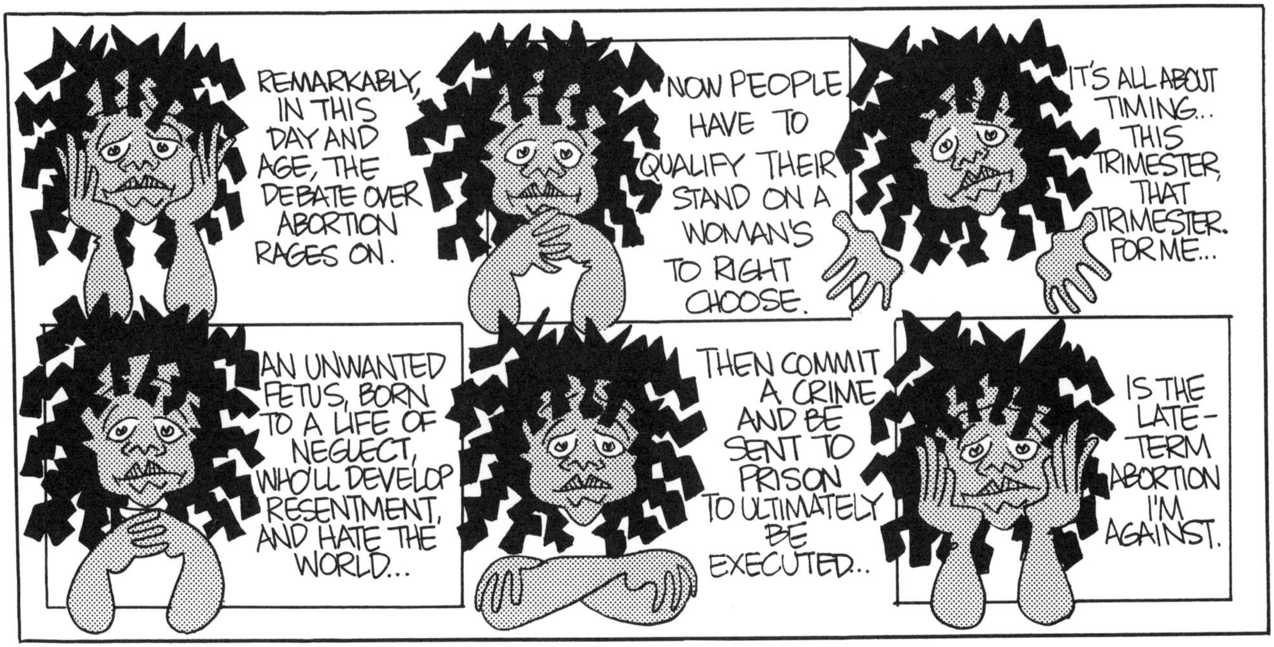
REMARKABLY, IN THIS DAY AND AGE, THE DEBATE OVER ABORTION RAGES ON.
NOW PEOPLE HAVE TO QUALIFY THEIR STAND ON A WOMAN'S TO RIGHT CHOOSE.
IT'S ALL ABOUT TIMING... THIS TRIMESTER, THAT TRIMESTER. FOR ME...
AN UNWANTED FETUS, BORN TO A LIFE OF NEGLECT, WHO'LL DEVELOP RESENTMENT, AND HATE THE WORLD...
THEN COMMIT A CRIME AND BE SENT TO PRISON TO ULTIMATELY BE EXECUTED...
IS THE LATE-TERM ABORTION I'M AGAINST.

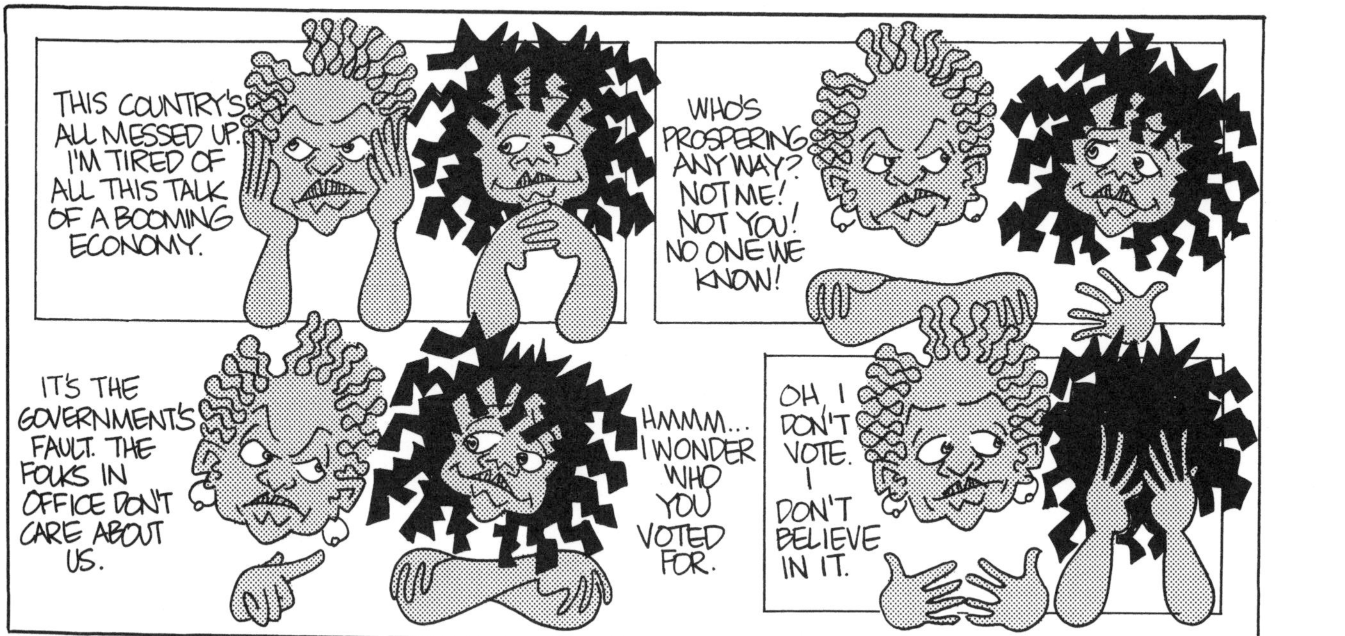
THIS COUNTRY'S ALL MESSED UP. I'M TIRED OF ALL THIS TALK OF A BOOMING ECONOMY.
WHO'S PROSPERING ANYWAY? NOT ME! NOT YOU! NO ONE WE KNOW!
IT'S THE GOVERNMENT'S FAULT. THE FOLKS IN OFFICE DON'T CARE ABOUT US.
HMMM... I WONDER WHO YOU VOTED FOR.
OH I DON'T VOTE. I DON'T BELIEVE IN IT.

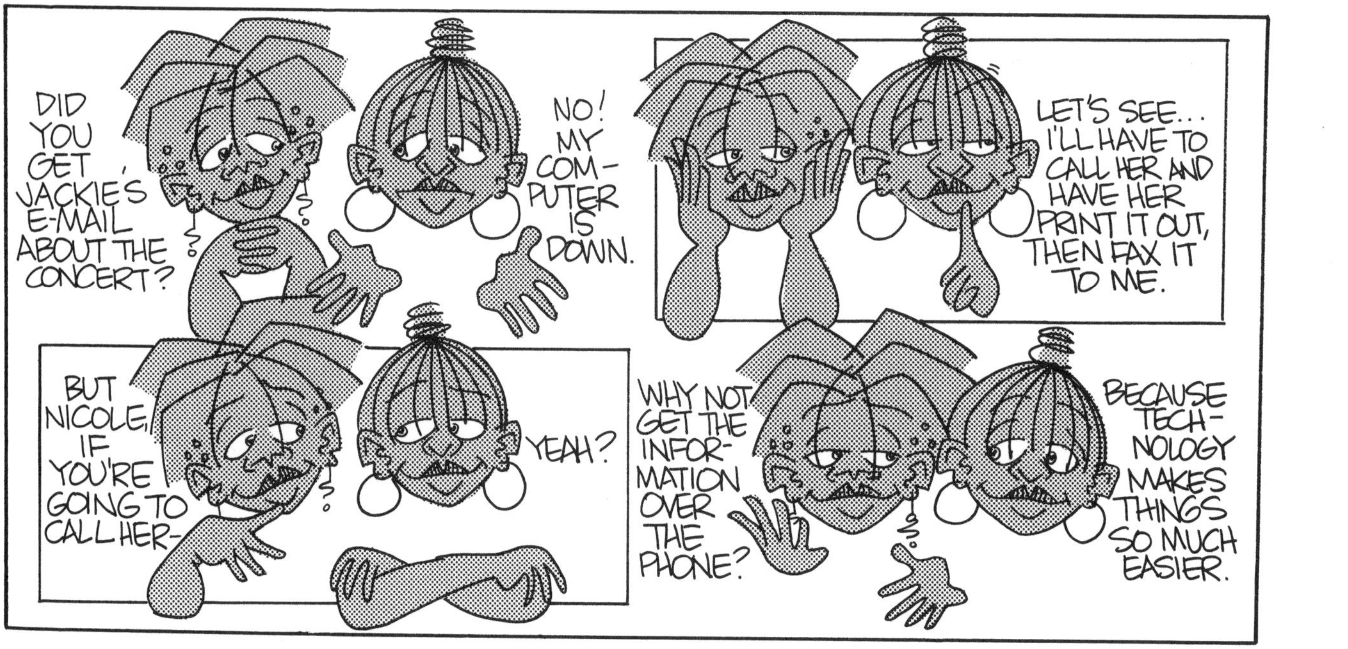
DID YOU GET JACKIE'S E-MAIL ABOUT THE CONCERT?
NO! MY COMPUTER IS DOWN.
LET'S SEE... I'LL HAVE TO CALL HER AND HAVE HER PRINT IT OUT, THEN FAX IT TO ME.
BUT NICOLE, IF YOU'RE GOING TO CALL HER-
YEAH?
WHY NOT GET THE INFORMATION OVER THE PHONE?
BECAUSE TECHNOLOGY MAKES THINGS SO MUCH EASIER.

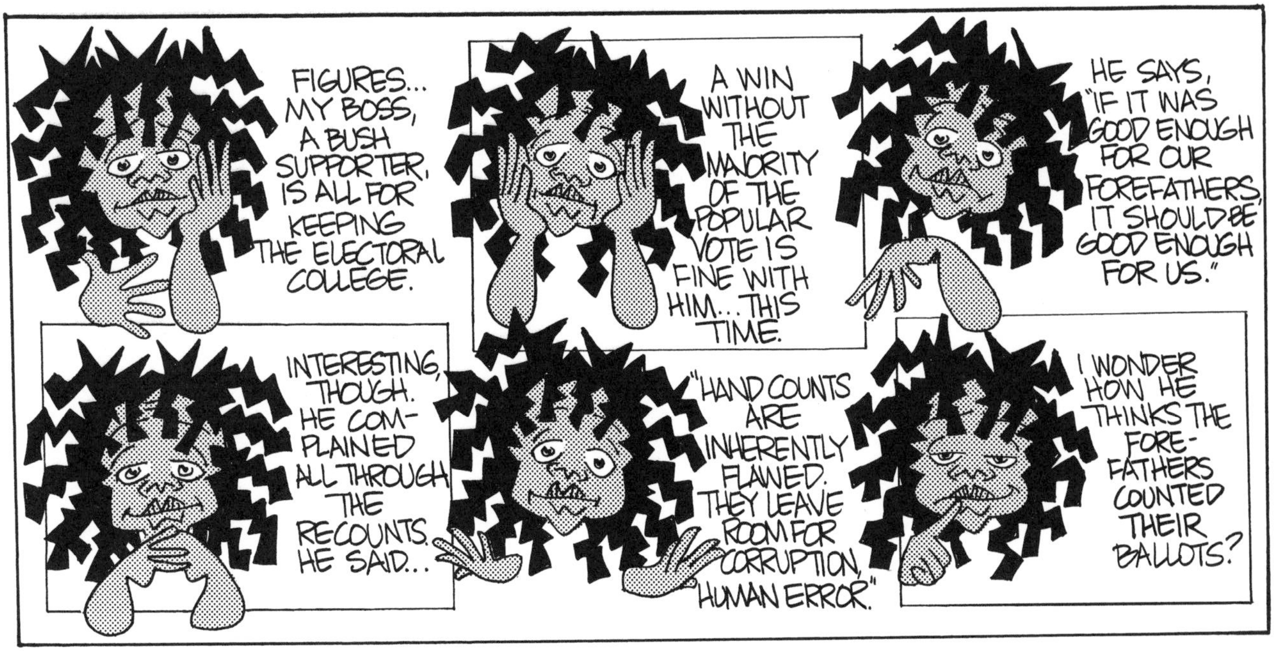
FIGURES... MY BOSS, A BUSH SUPPORTER, IS ALL FOR KEEPING THE ELECTORAL COLLEGE.
A WIN WITHOUT THE MAJORITY OF THE POPULAR VOTE IS FINE WITH HIM... THIS TIME.
HE SAYS, "IF IT WAS GOOD ENOUGH FOR OUR FOREFATHERS, IT SHOULD BE GOOD ENOUGH FOR US."
INTERESTING, THOUGH. HE COMPLAINED ALL THROUGH THE RECOUNTS. HE SAID...
"HAND COUNTS ARE INHERENTLY FLAWED. THEY LEAVE ROOM FOR CORRUPTION, HUMAN ERROR."
I WONDER HOW HE THINKS THE FOREFATHERS COUNTED THEIR BALLOTS?

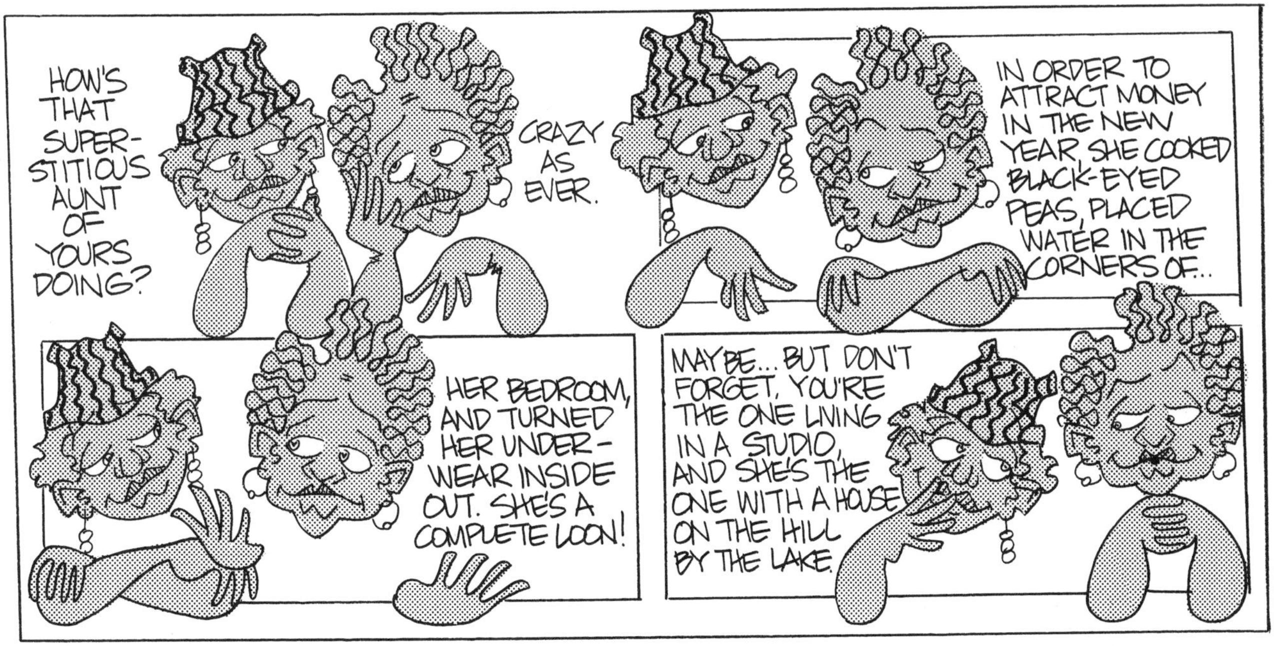
HOW'S THAT SUPERSTITIOUS AUNT OF YOURS DOING?
CRAZY AS EVER.
IN ORDER TO ATTRACT MONEY IN THE NEW YEAR, SHE COOKED BLACK-EYED PEAS, PLACED WATER IN THE CORNERS OF...
HER BEDROOM, AND TURNED HER UNDERWEAR INSIDE OUT. SHE'S A COMPLETE LOON!
MAYBE... BUT DON'T FORGET, YOU'RE THE ONE LIVING IN A STUDIO, AND SHE'S THE ONE WITH A HOUSE ON THE HILL BY THE LAKE.

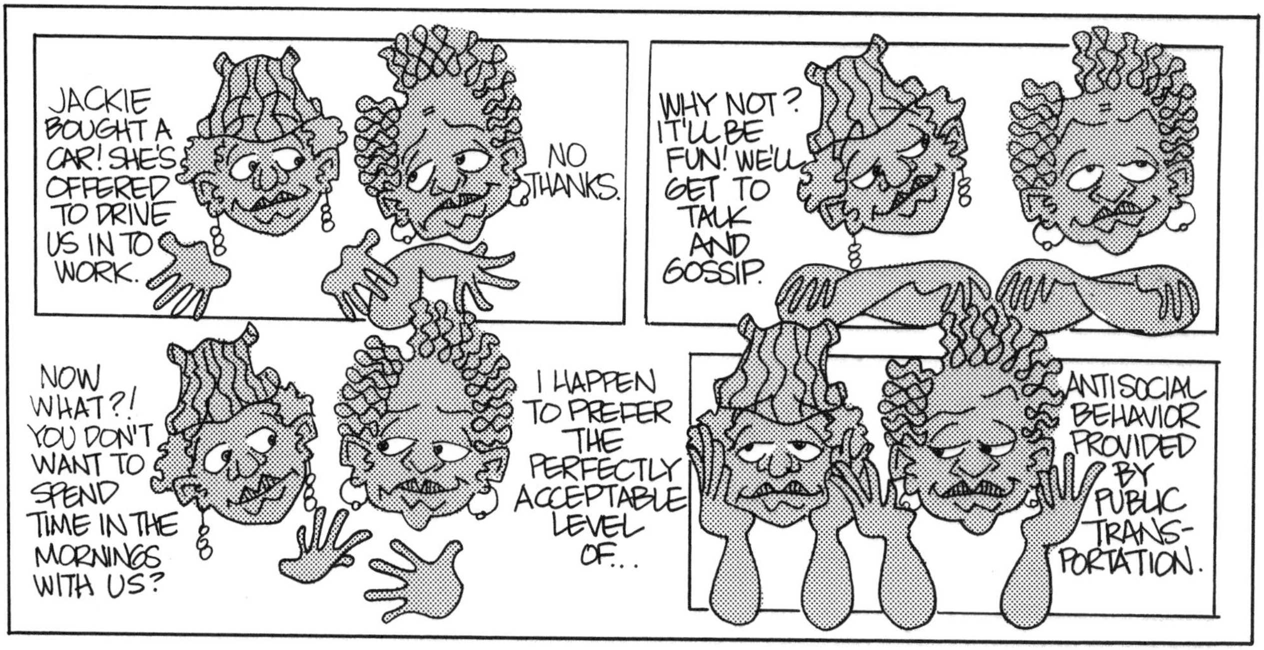
JACKIE BOUGHT A CAR! SHE'S OFFERED TO DRIVE US IN TO WORK.
NO THANKS.
NOW WHAT?! YOU DON'T WANT TO SPEND TIME IN THE MORNINGS WITH US?
I HAPPEN TO PREFER THE PERFECTLY ACCEPTABLE LEVEL OF...
WHY NOT? IT'LL BE FUN! WE'LL GET TO TALK AND GOSSIP.
ANTISOCIAL BEHAVIOR PROVIDED BY PUBLIC TRANS-PORTATION.

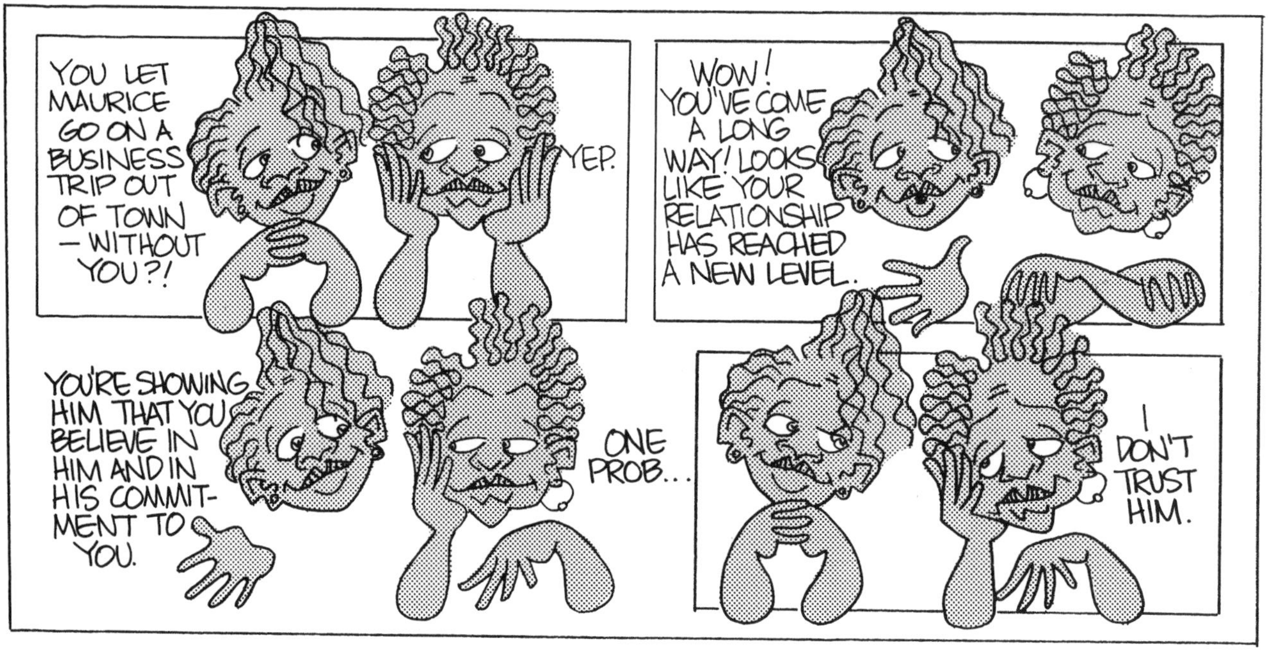
YOU LET MAURICE GO ON A BUSINESS TRIP OUT OF TOWN – WITHOUT YOU?!
YEP.
YOU'RE SHOWING HIM THAT YOU BELIEVE IN HIM AND IN HIS COMMIT-MENT TO YOU.
ONE PROB...
WOW! YOU'VE COME A LONG WAY! LOOKS LIKE YOUR RELATIONSHIP HAS REACHED A NEW LEVEL.
I DON'T TRUST HIM.

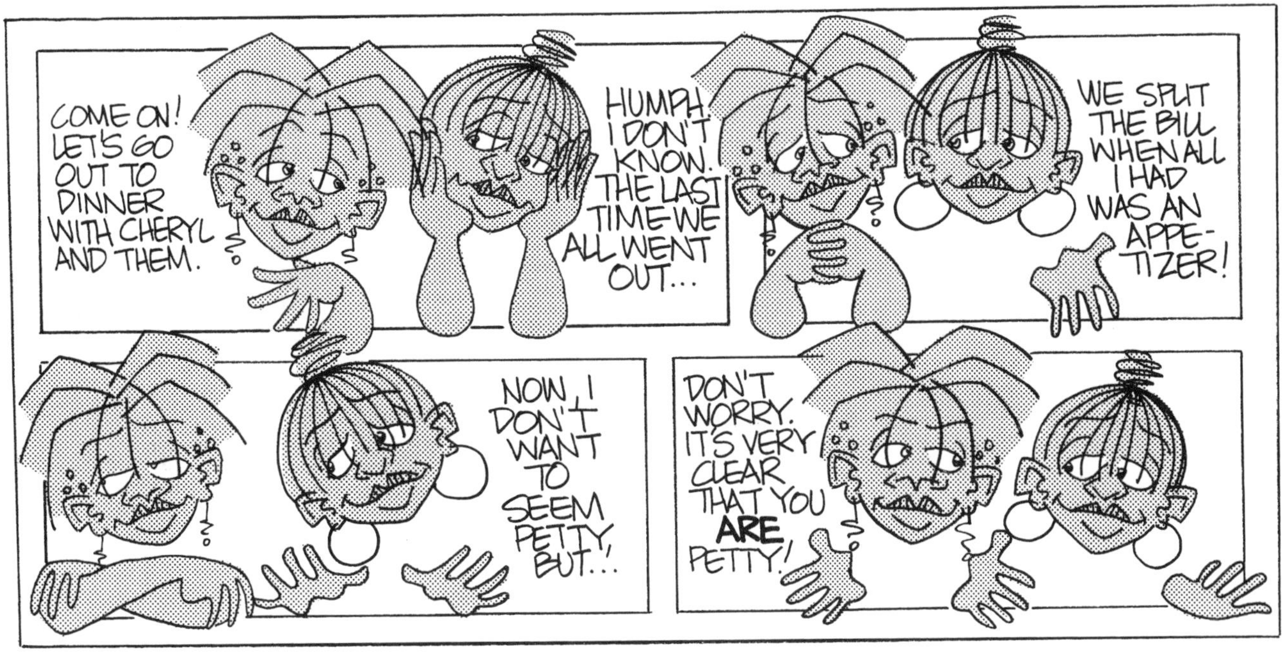
COME ON! LET'S GO OUT TO DINNER WITH CHERYL AND THEM.
HUMPH. I DON'T KNOW. THE LAST TIME WE ALL WENT OUT...
WE SPLIT THE BILL WHEN ALL I HAD WAS AN APPE-TIZER!
NOW, I DON'T WANT TO SEEM PETTY, BUT...!
DON'T WORRY. IT'S VERY CLEAR THAT YOU **ARE** PETTY!

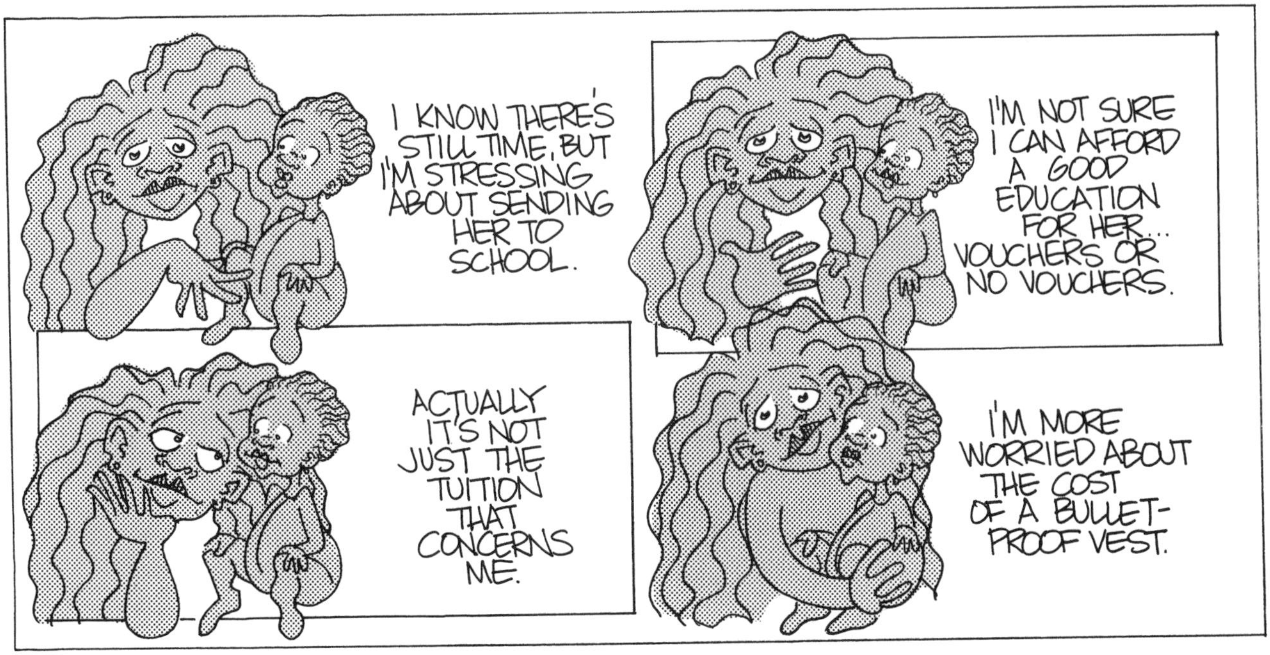
I KNOW THERE'S STILL TIME, BUT I'M STRESSING ABOUT SENDING HER TO SCHOOL.
I'M NOT SURE I CAN AFFORD A GOOD EDUCATION FOR HER... VOUCHERS OR NO VOUCHERS.
ACTUALLY IT'S NOT JUST THE TUITION THAT CONCERNS ME.
I'M MORE WORRIED ABOUT THE COST OF A BULLET-PROOF VEST.

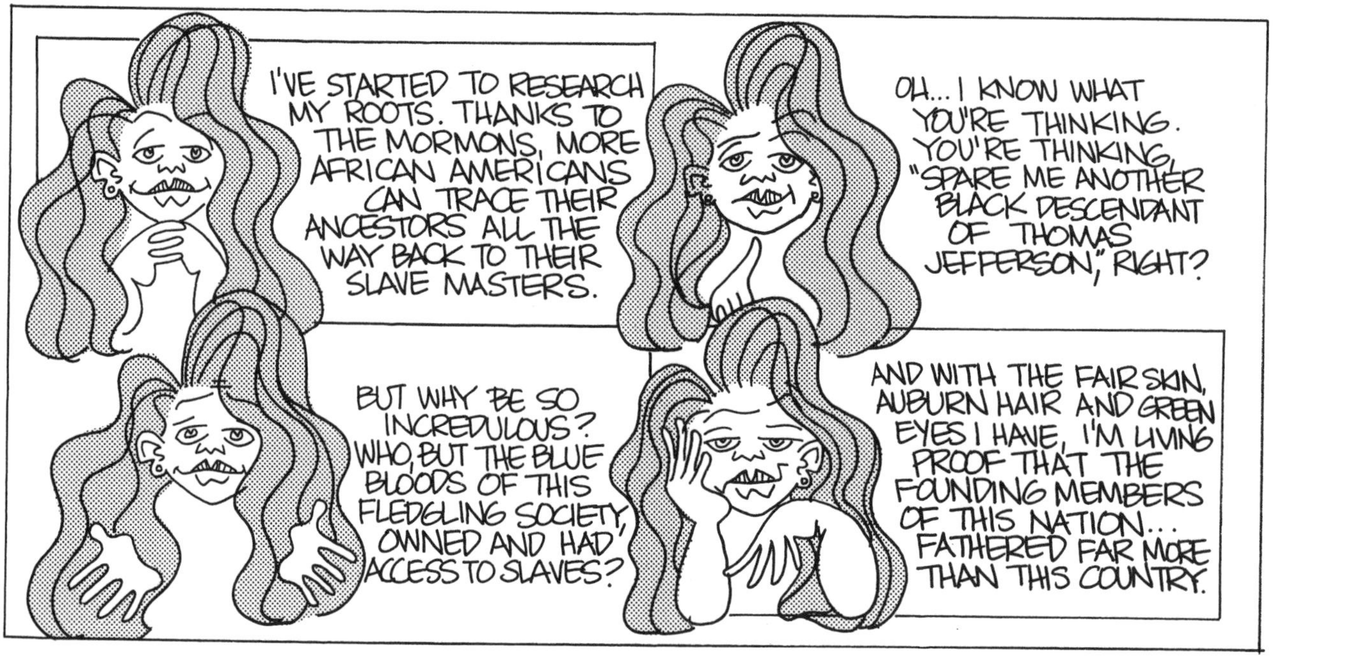
I'VE STARTED TO RESEARCH MY ROOTS. THANKS TO THE MORMONS, MORE AFRICAN AMERICANS CAN TRACE THEIR ANCESTORS ALL THE WAY BACK TO THEIR SLAVE MASTERS.
OH... I KNOW WHAT YOU'RE THINKING. YOU'RE THINKING, "SPARE ME ANOTHER BLACK DESCENDANT OF THOMAS JEFFERSON," RIGHT?
BUT WHY BE SO INCREDULOUS? WHO, BUT THE BLUE BLOODS OF THIS FLEDGLING SOCIETY, OWNED AND HAD ACCESS TO SLAVES?
AND WITH THE FAIR SKIN, AUBURN HAIR AND GREEN EYES I HAVE, I'M LIVING PROOF THAT THE FOUNDING MEMBERS OF THIS NATION... FATHERED FAR MORE THAN THIS COUNTRY.

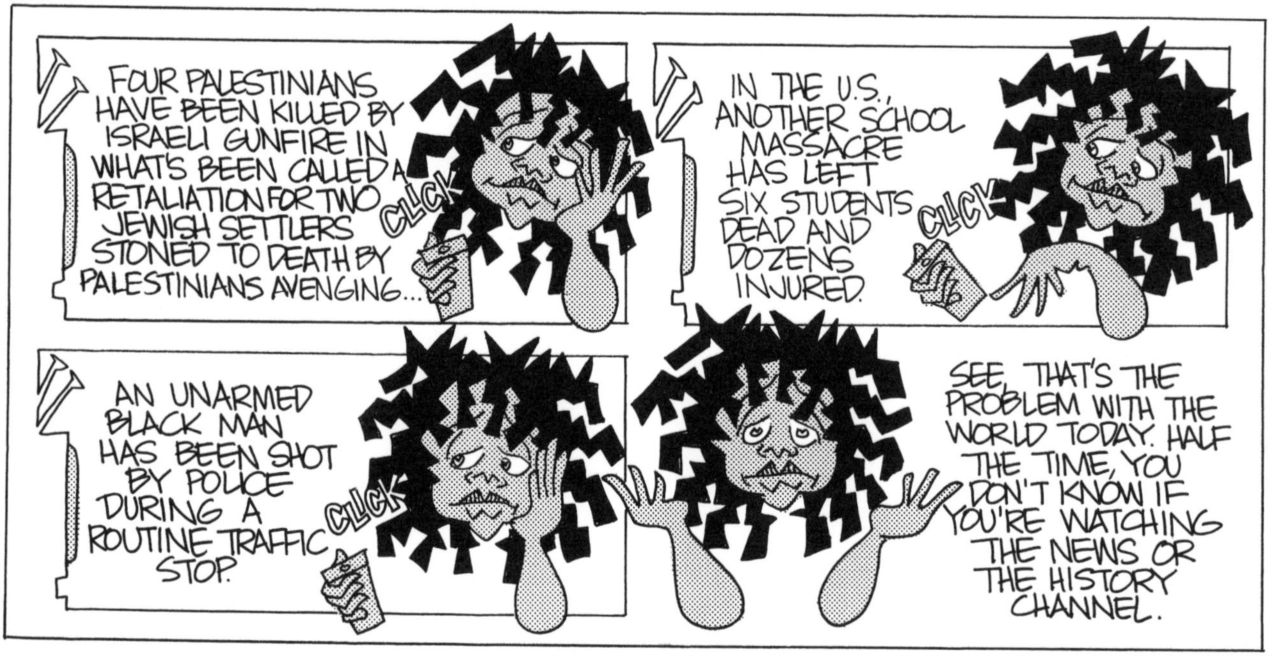
FOUR PALESTINIANS HAVE BEEN KILLED BY ISRAELI GUNFIRE IN WHAT'S BEEN CALLED A RETALIATION FOR TWO JEWISH SETTLERS STONED TO DEATH BY PALESTINIANS AVENGING...
CLICK
IN THE U.S., ANOTHER SCHOOL MASSACRE HAS LEFT SIX STUDENTS DEAD AND DOZENS INJURED.
CLICK
AN UNARMED BLACK MAN HAS BEEN SHOT BY POLICE DURING A ROUTINE TRAFFIC STOP.
CLICK
SEE, THAT'S THE PROBLEM WITH THE WORLD TODAY. HALF THE TIME, YOU DON'T KNOW IF YOU'RE WATCHING THE NEWS OR THE HISTORY CHANNEL.

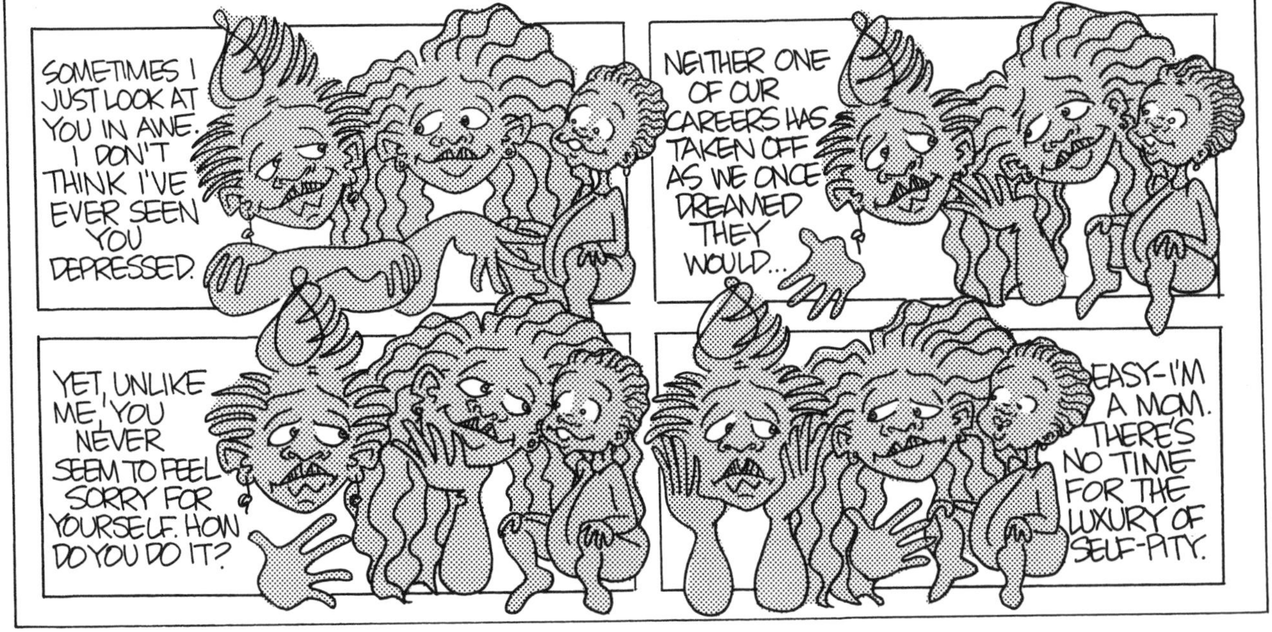
SOMETIMES I JUST LOOK AT YOU IN AWE. I DON'T THINK I'VE EVER SEEN YOU DEPRESSED.
NEITHER ONE OF OUR CAREERS HAS TAKEN OFF AS WE ONCE DREAMED THEY WOULD...
YET, UNLIKE ME, YOU NEVER SEEM TO FEEL SORRY FOR YOURSELF. HOW DO YOU DO IT?
EASY-I'M A MOM. THERE'S NO TIME FOR THE LUXURY OF SELF-PITY.

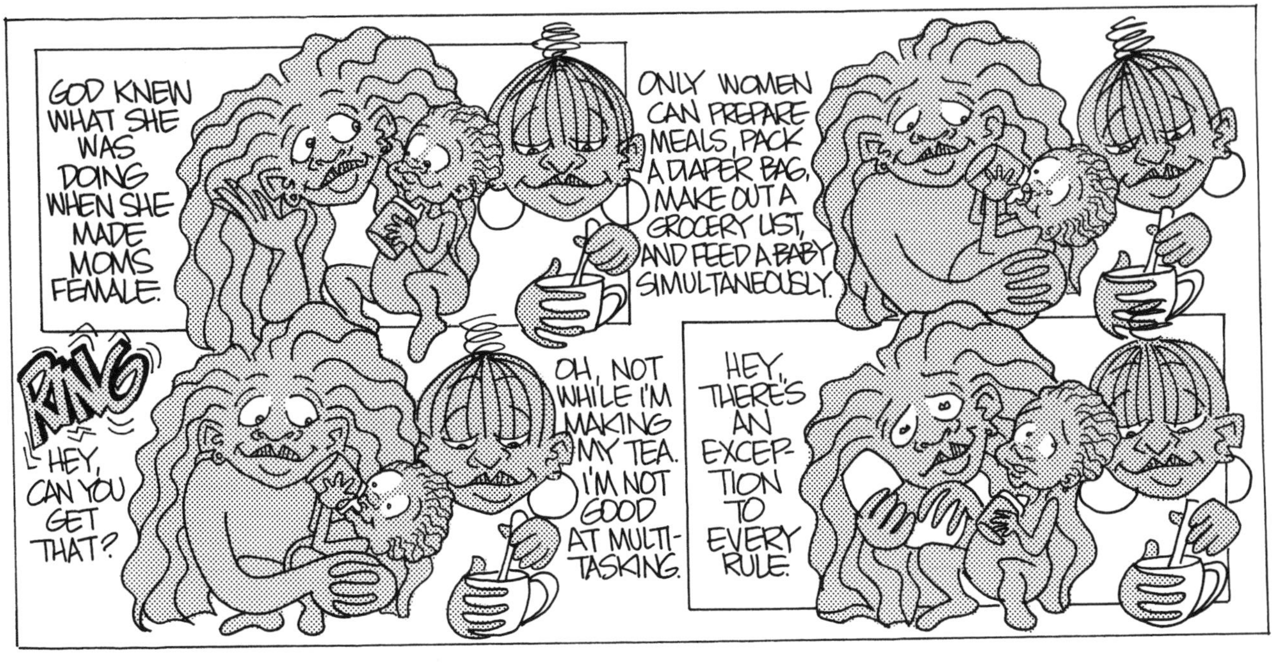
GOD KNEW WHAT SHE WAS DOING WHEN SHE MADE MOMS FEMALE.
ONLY WOMEN CAN PREPARE MEALS, PACK A DIAPER BAG, MAKE OUT A GROCERY LIST, AND FEED A BABY SIMULTANEOUSLY.
RING
HEY, CAN YOU GET THAT?
OH, NOT WHILE I'M MAKING MY TEA. I'M NOT GOOD AT MULTI-TASKING.
HEY, THERE'S AN EXCEPTION TO EVERY RULE.

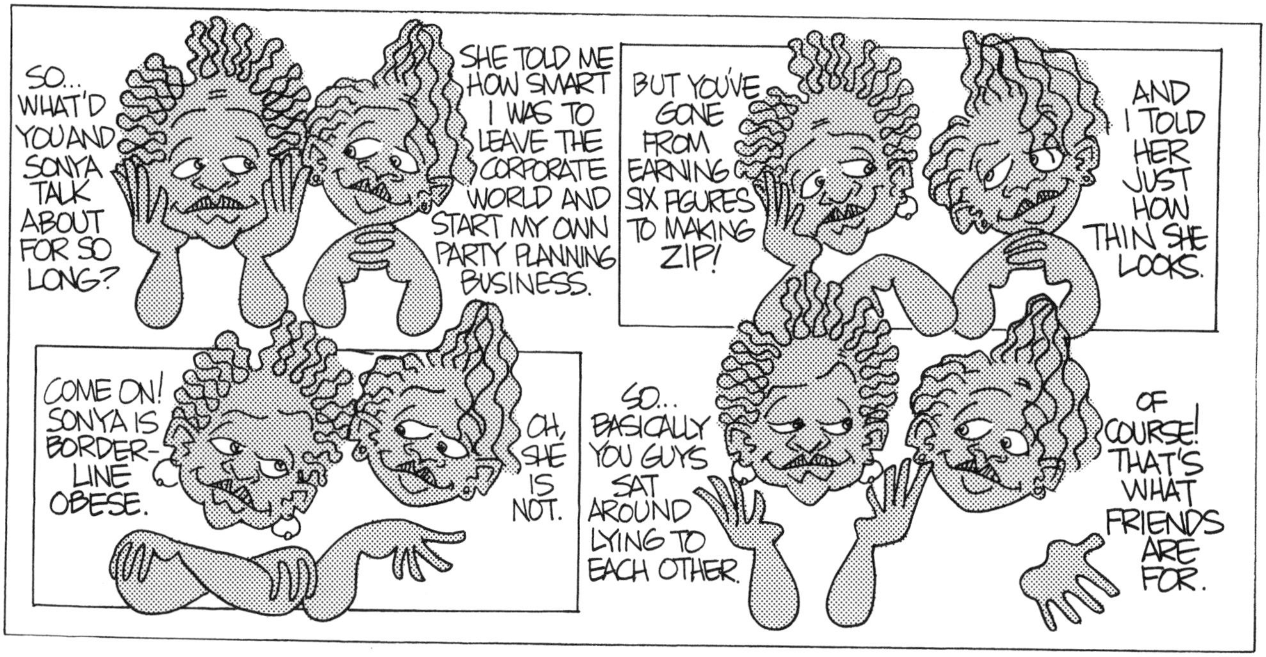
SO... WHAT'D YOU AND SONYA TALK ABOUT FOR SO LONG?
SHE TOLD ME HOW SMART I WAS TO LEAVE THE CORPORATE WORLD AND START MY OWN PARTY PLANNING BUSINESS.
BUT YOU'VE GONE FROM EARNING SIX FIGURES TO MAKING ZIP!
AND I TOLD HER JUST HOW THIN SHE LOOKS.
COME ON! SONYA IS BORDER-LINE OBESE.
OH, SHE IS NOT.
SO... BASICALLY YOU GUYS SAT AROUND LYING TO EACH OTHER.
OF COURSE! THAT'S WHAT FRIENDS ARE FOR.

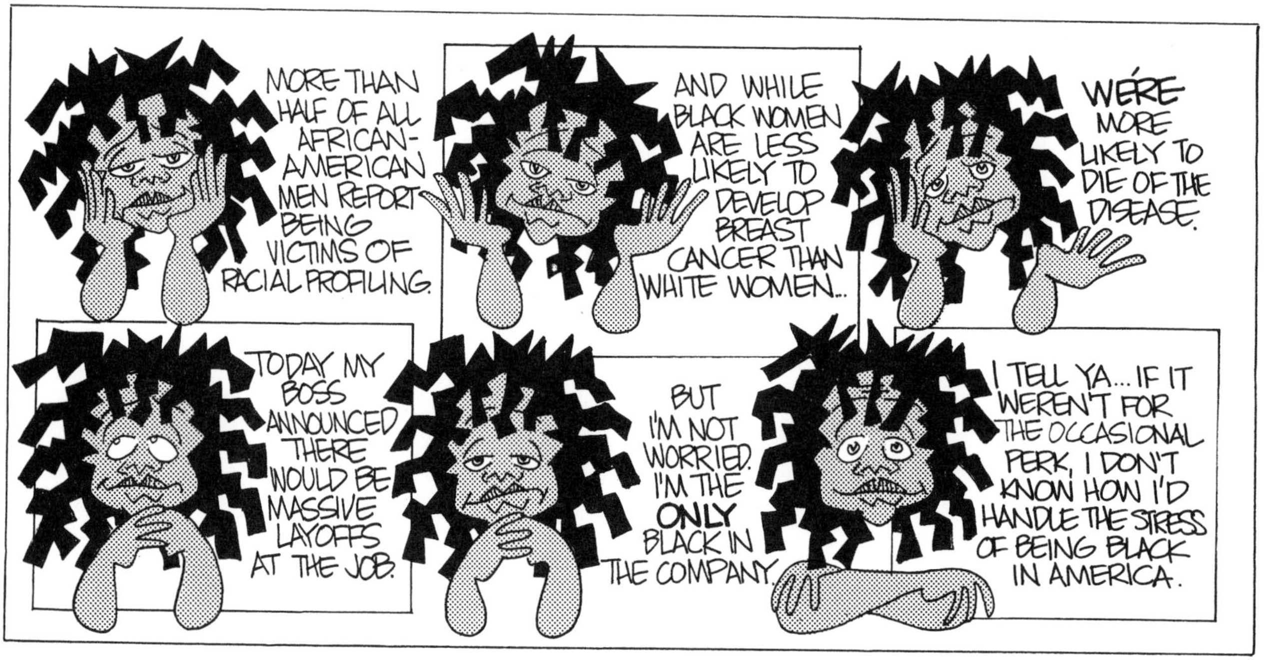
MORE THAN HALF OF ALL AFRICAN-AMERICAN MEN REPORT BEING VICTIMS OF RACIAL PROFILING.
AND WHILE BLACK WOMEN ARE LESS LIKELY TO DEVELOP BREAST CANCER THAN WHITE WOMEN...
WE'RE MORE LIKELY TO DIE OF THE DISEASE.
TODAY MY BOSS ANNOUNCED THERE WOULD BE MASSIVE LAYOFFS AT THE JOB.
BUT I'M NOT WORRIED. I'M THE ONLY BLACK IN THE COMPANY.
I TELL YA... IF IT WEREN'T FOR THE OCCASIONAL PERK, I DON'T KNOW HOW I'D HANDLE THE STRESS OF BEING BLACK IN AMERICA.

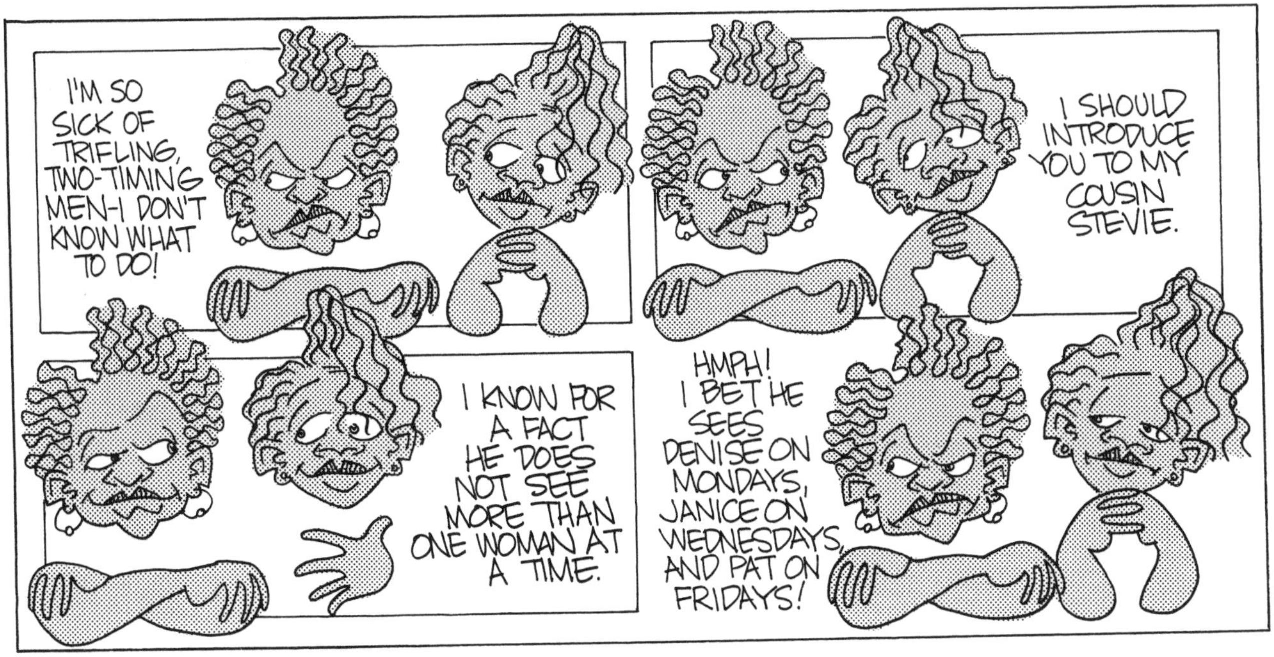
I'M SO SICK OF TRIFLING, TWO-TIMING MEN-I DON'T KNOW WHAT TO DO!
I SHOULD INTRODUCE YOU TO MY COUSIN STEVIE.
I KNOW FOR A FACT HE DOES NOT SEE MORE THAN ONE WOMAN AT A TIME.
HMPH! I BET HE SEES DENISE ON MONDAYS, JANICE ON WEDNESDAYS, AND PAT ON FRIDAYS!

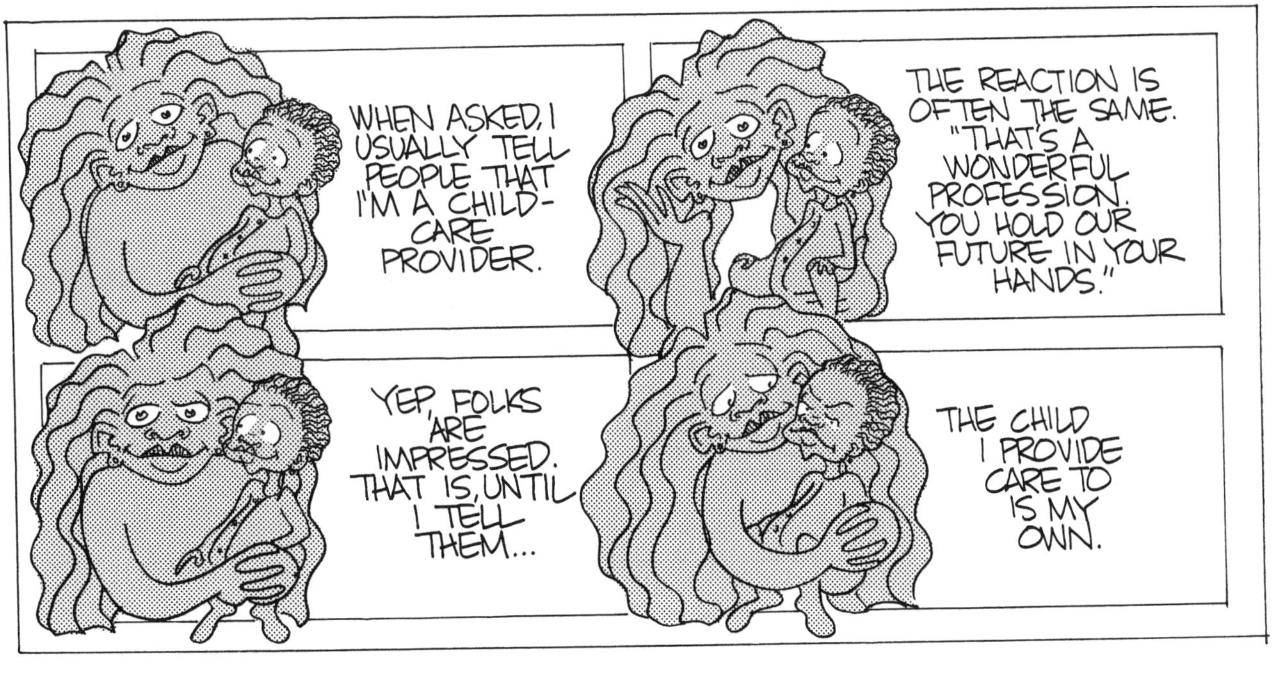
WHEN ASKED, I USUALLY TELL PEOPLE THAT I'M A CHILD-CARE PROVIDER.
THE REACTION IS OFTEN THE SAME. "THAT'S A WONDERFUL PROFESSION. YOU HOLD OUR FUTURE IN YOUR HANDS."
YEP, FOLKS ARE IMPRESSED. THAT IS, UNTIL I TELL THEM...
THE CHILD I PROVIDE CARE TO IS MY OWN.

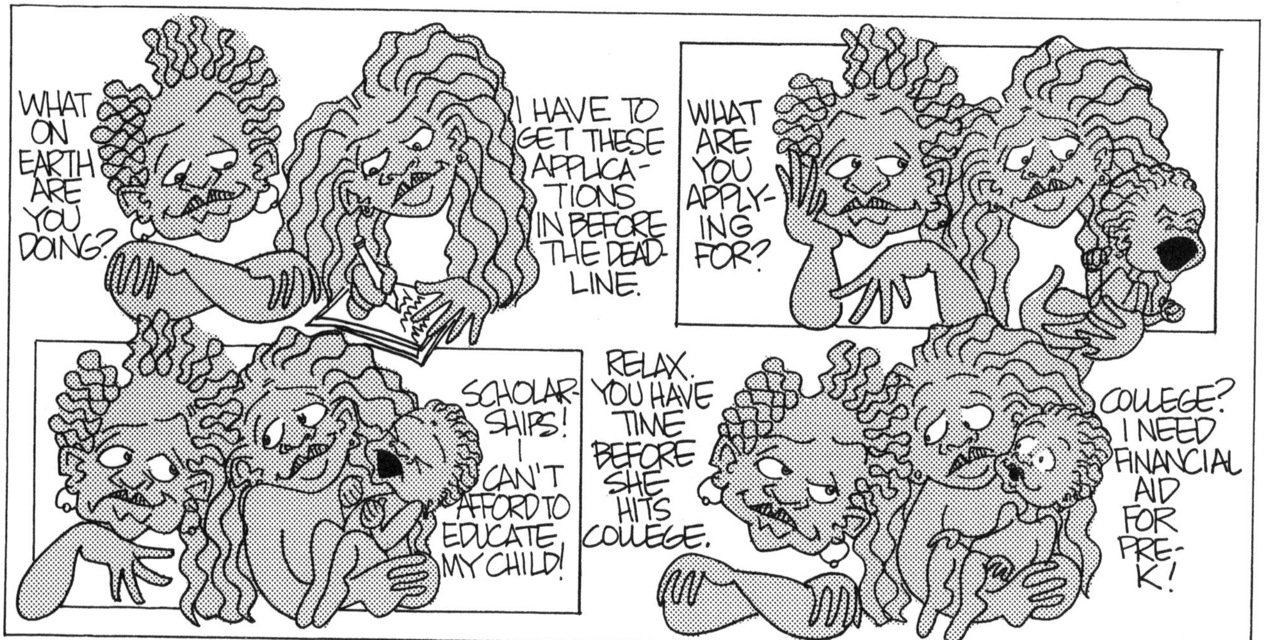
WHAT ON EARTH ARE YOU DOING?
I HAVE TO GET THESE APPLICATIONS IN BEFORE THE DEADLINE.
WHAT ARE YOU APPLYING FOR?
SCHOLARSHIPS! I CAN'T AFFORD TO EDUCATE MY CHILD!
RELAX. YOU HAVE TIME BEFORE SHE HITS COLLEGE.
COLLEGE? I NEED FINANCIAL AID FOR PRE-K!

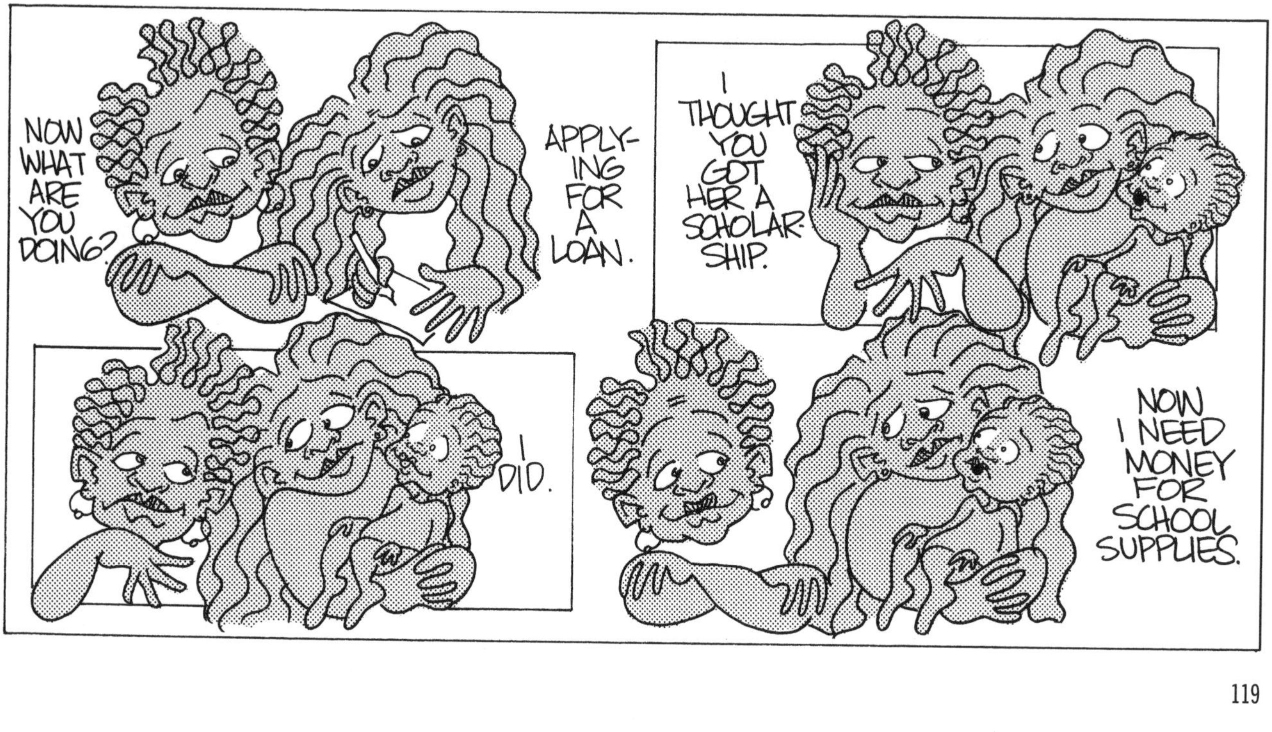
NOW WHAT ARE YOU DOING?
APPLYING FOR A LOAN.
I THOUGHT YOU GOT HER A SCHOLARSHIP.
I DID.
NOW I NEED MONEY FOR SCHOOL SUPPLIES.

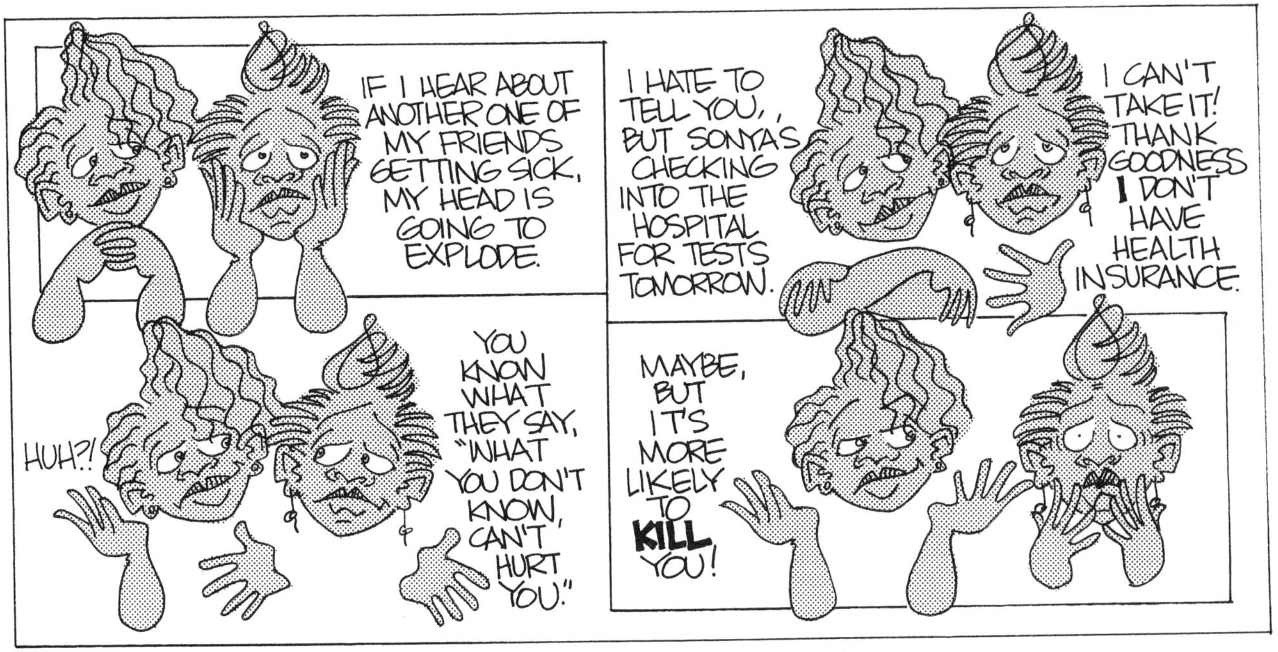
IF I HEAR ABOUT ANOTHER ONE OF MY FRIENDS GETTING SICK, MY HEAD IS GOING TO EXPLODE.
YOU KNOW WHAT THEY SAY, "WHAT YOU DON'T KNOW, CAN'T HURT YOU."
HUH?!
I HATE TO TELL YOU, BUT SONYA'S CHECKING INTO THE HOSPITAL FOR TESTS TOMORROW.
I CAN'T TAKE IT! THANK GOODNESS I DON'T HAVE HEALTH INSURANCE.
MAYBE, BUT IT'S MORE LIKELY TO KILL YOU!

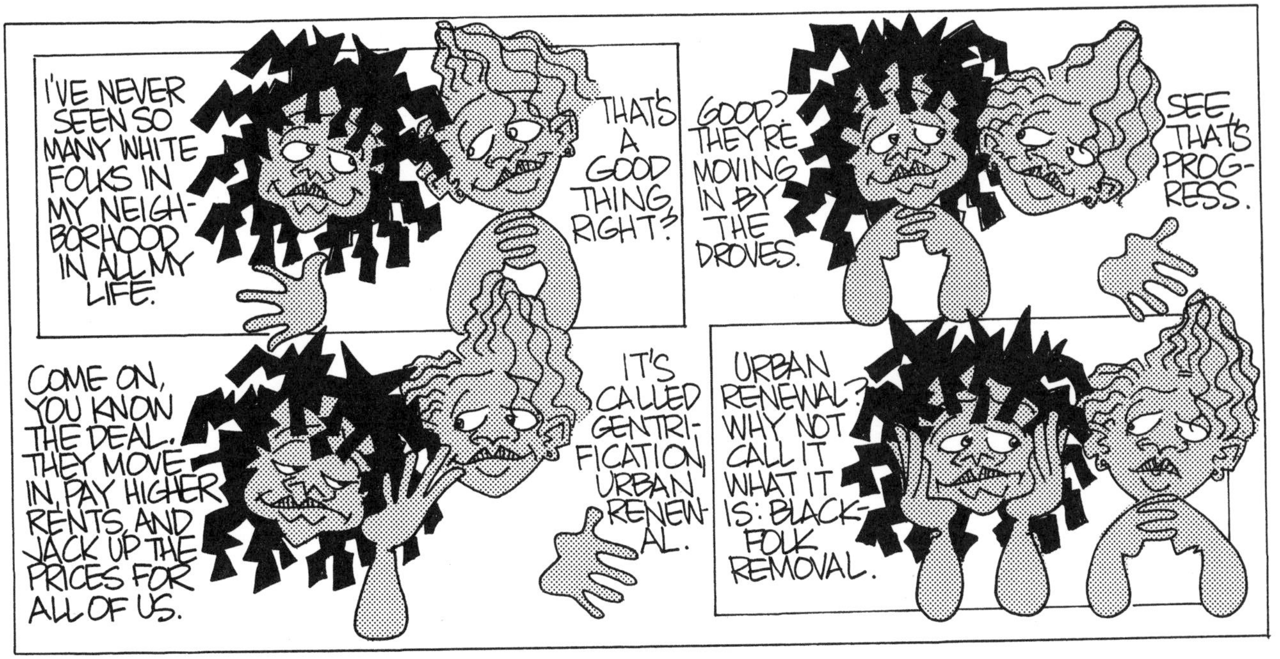
I'VE NEVER SEEN SO MANY WHITE FOLKS IN MY NEIGHBORHOOD IN ALL MY LIFE.
THAT'S A GOOD THING, RIGHT?
COME ON, YOU KNOW THE DEAL. THEY MOVE IN, PAY HIGHER RENTS, AND JACK UP THE PRICES FOR ALL OF US.
IT'S CALLED GENTRIFICATION, URBAN RENEWAL.
GOOD? THEY'RE MOVING IN BY THE DROVES.
SEE, THAT'S PROGRESS.
URBAN RENEWAL? WHY NOT CALL IT WHAT IT IS: BLACK-FOLK REMOVAL.

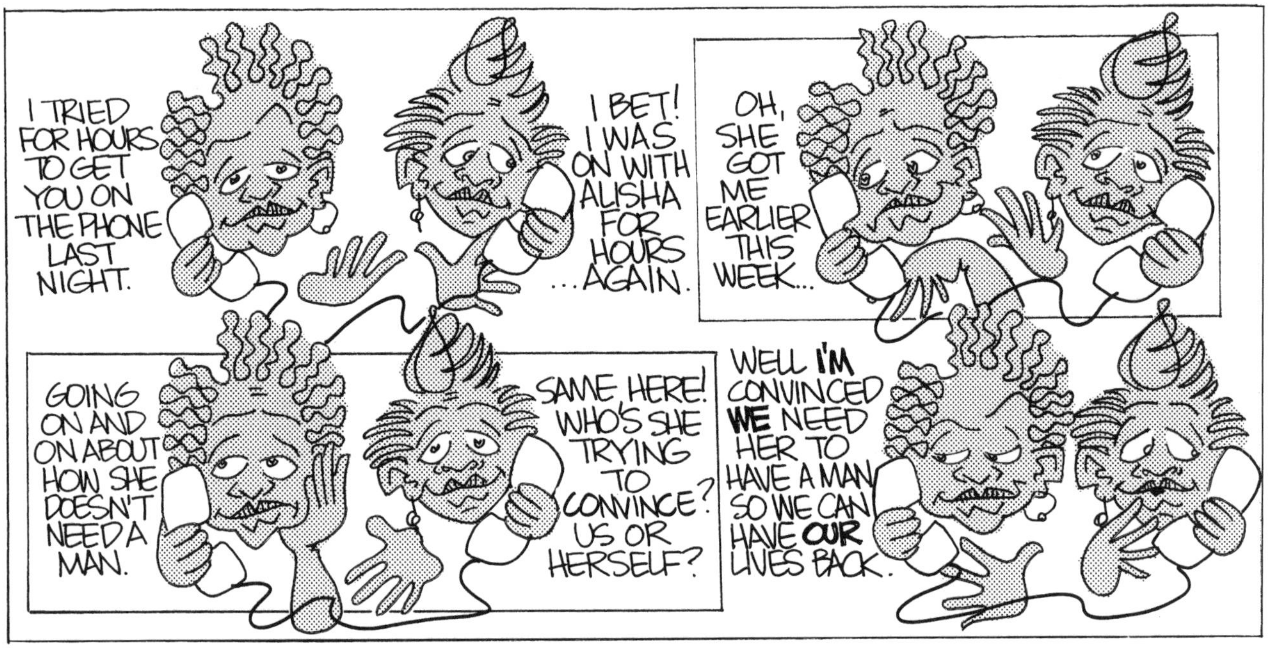

I TRIED FOR HOURS TO GET YOU ON THE PHONE LAST NIGHT.
I BET! I WAS ON WITH ALISHA FOR HOURS ...AGAIN.
OH, SHE GOT ME EARLIER THIS WEEK...
GOING ON AND ON ABOUT HOW SHE DOESN'T NEED A MAN.
SAME HERE! WHO'S SHE TRYING TO CONVINCE? US OR HERSELF?
WELL **I'M** CONVINCED **WE** NEED HER TO HAVE A MAN SO WE CAN HAVE **OUR** LIVES BACK.

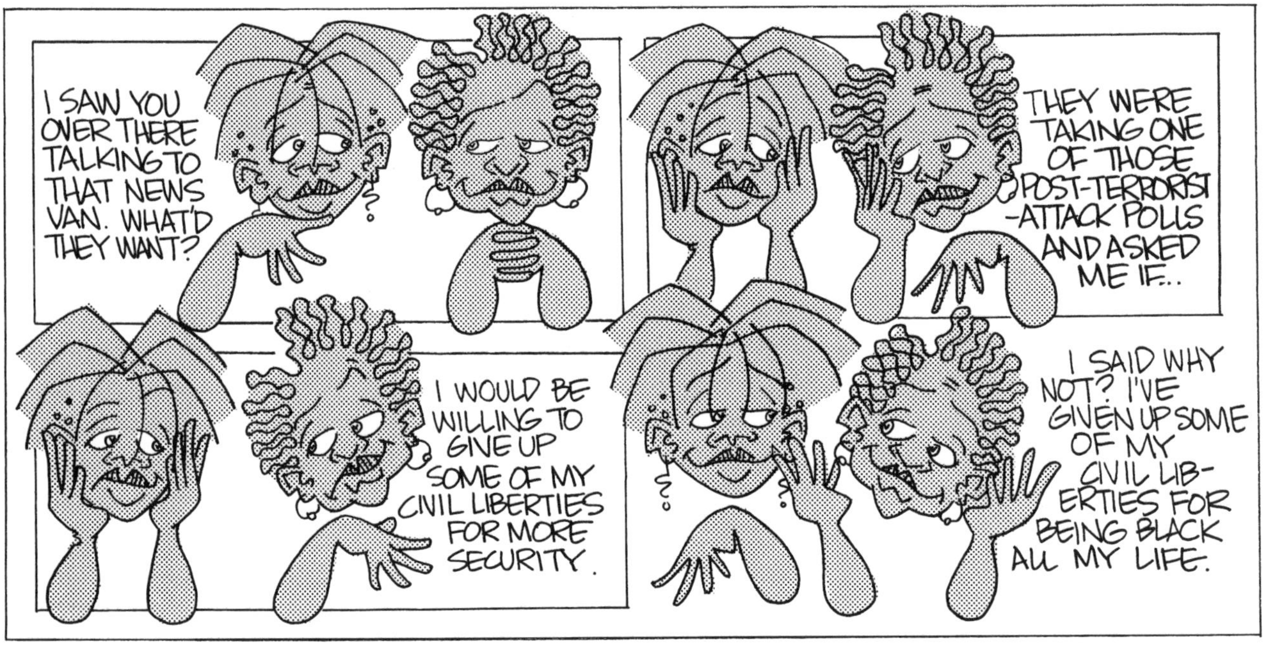

I SAW YOU OVER THERE TALKING TO THAT NEWS VAN. WHAT'D THEY WANT?
THEY WERE TAKING ONE OF THOSE POST-TERRORIST-ATTACK POLLS AND ASKED ME IF...
I WOULD BE WILLING TO GIVE UP SOME OF MY CIVIL LIBERTIES FOR MORE SECURITY.
I SAID WHY NOT? I'VE GIVEN UP SOME OF MY CIVIL LIBERTIES FOR BEING BLACK ALL MY LIFE.

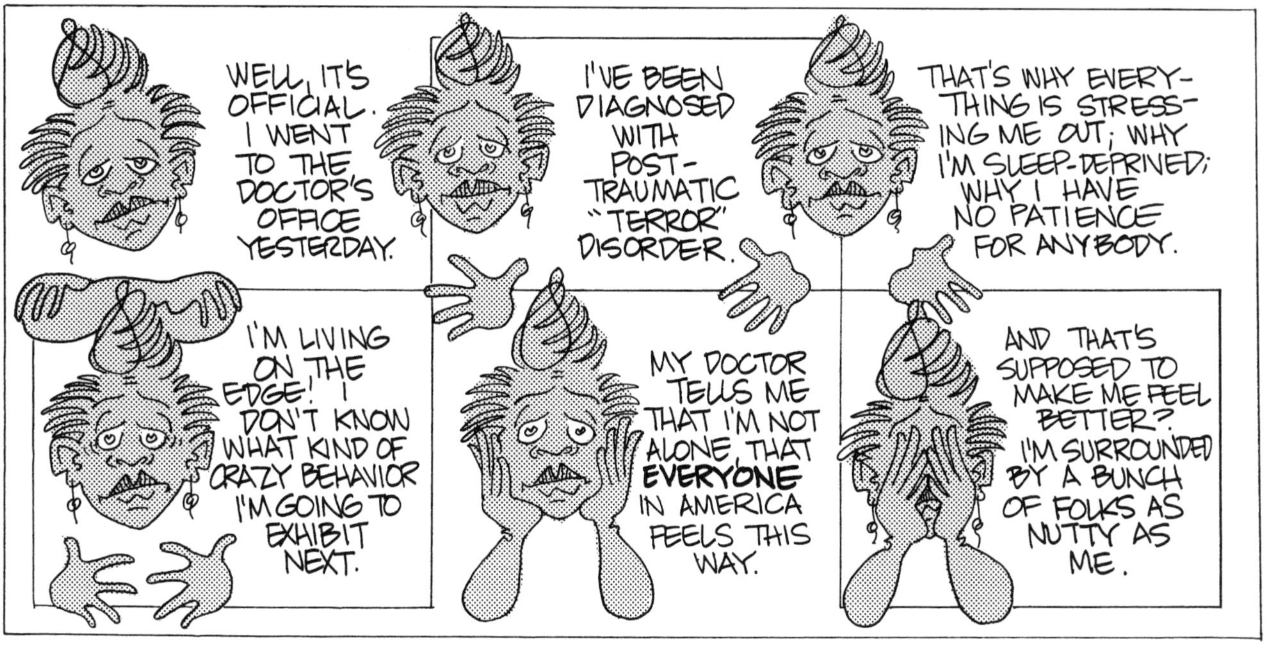
WELL, IT'S OFFICIAL. I WENT TO THE DOCTOR'S OFFICE YESTERDAY.
I'VE BEEN DIAGNOSED WITH POST-TRAUMATIC "TERROR" DISORDER.
THAT'S WHY EVERYTHING IS STRESSING ME OUT; WHY I'M SLEEP-DEPRIVED; WHY I HAVE NO PATIENCE FOR ANYBODY.
I'M LIVING ON THE EDGE! I DON'T KNOW WHAT KIND OF CRAZY BEHAVIOR I'M GOING TO EXHIBIT NEXT.
MY DOCTOR TELLS ME THAT I'M NOT ALONE, THAT **EVERYONE** IN AMERICA FEELS THIS WAY.
AND THAT'S SUPPOSED TO MAKE ME FEEL BETTER? I'M SURROUNDED BY A BUNCH OF FOLKS AS NUTTY AS ME.

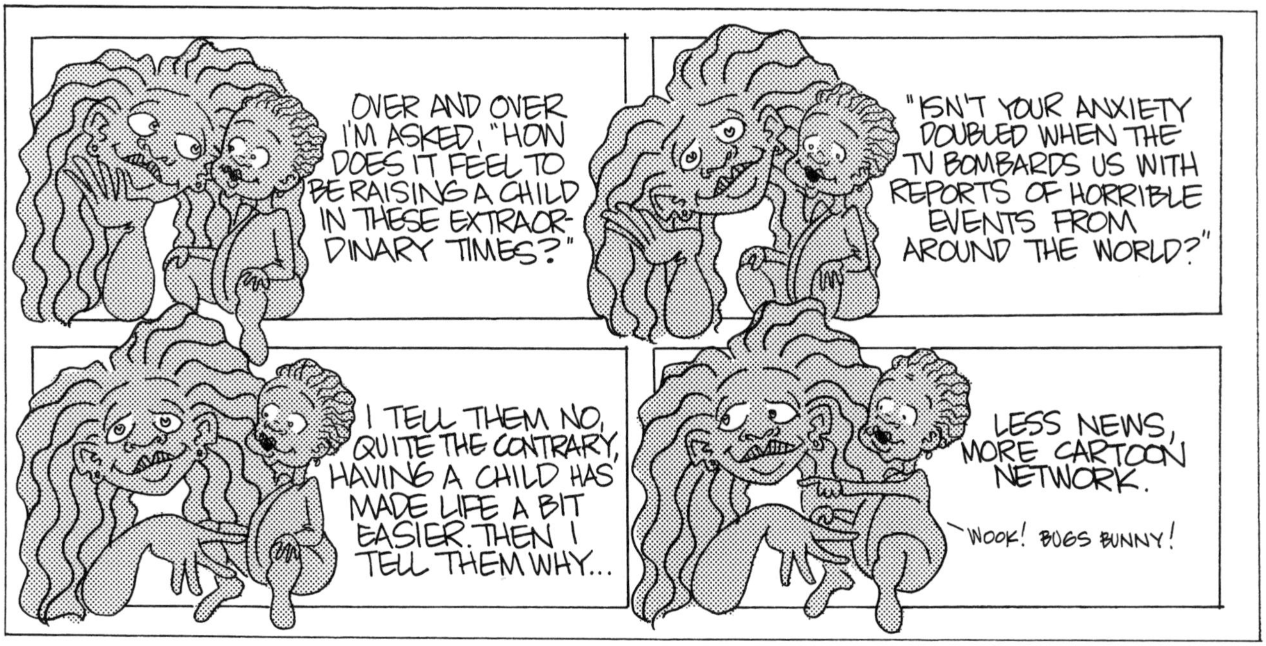
OVER AND OVER I'M ASKED, "HOW DOES IT FEEL TO BE RAISING A CHILD IN THESE EXTRAORDINARY TIMES?"
"ISN'T YOUR ANXIETY DOUBLED WHEN THE TV BOMBARDS US WITH REPORTS OF HORRIBLE EVENTS FROM AROUND THE WORLD?"
I TELL THEM NO, QUITE THE CONTRARY, HAVING A CHILD HAS MADE LIFE A BIT EASIER. THEN I TELL THEM WHY...
LESS NEWS, MORE CARTOON NETWORK.
WOOK! BUGS BUNNY!

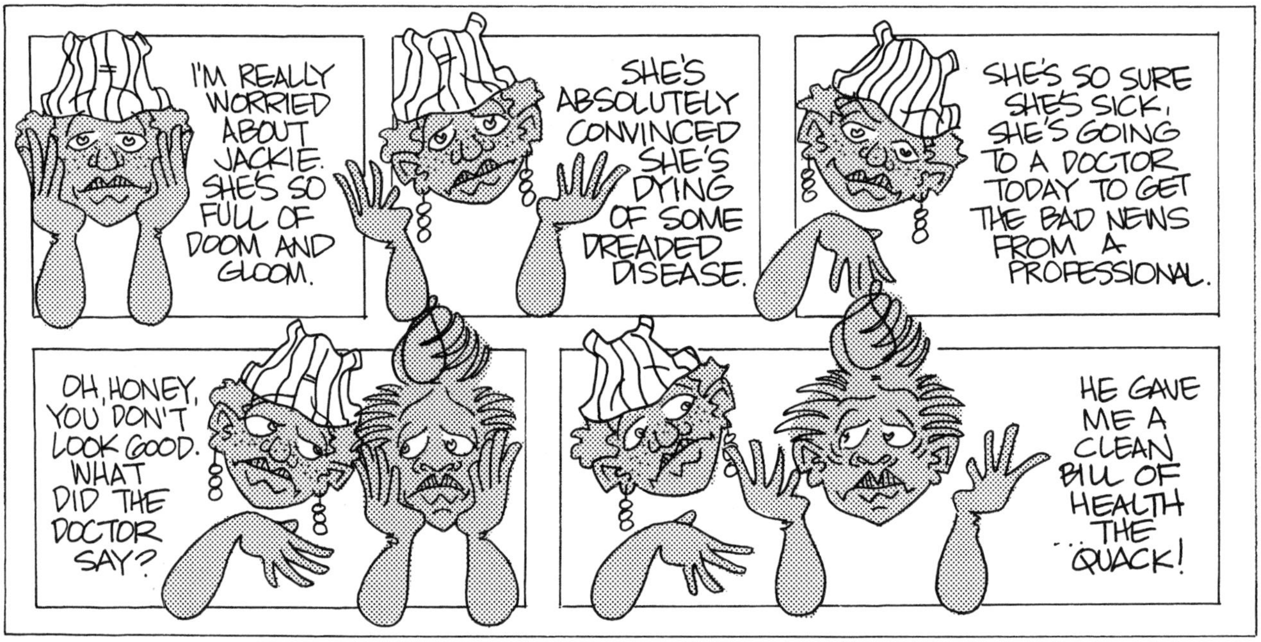
I'M REALLY WORRIED ABOUT JACKIE. SHE'S SO FULL OF DOOM AND GLOOM.
SHE'S ABSOLUTELY CONVINCED SHE'S DYING OF SOME DREADED DISEASE.
SHE'S SO SURE SHE'S SICK, SHE'S GOING TO A DOCTOR TODAY TO GET THE BAD NEWS FROM A PROFESSIONAL.
OH, HONEY, YOU DON'T LOOK GOOD. WHAT DID THE DOCTOR SAY?
HE GAVE ME A CLEAN BILL OF HEALTH ... THE QUACK!

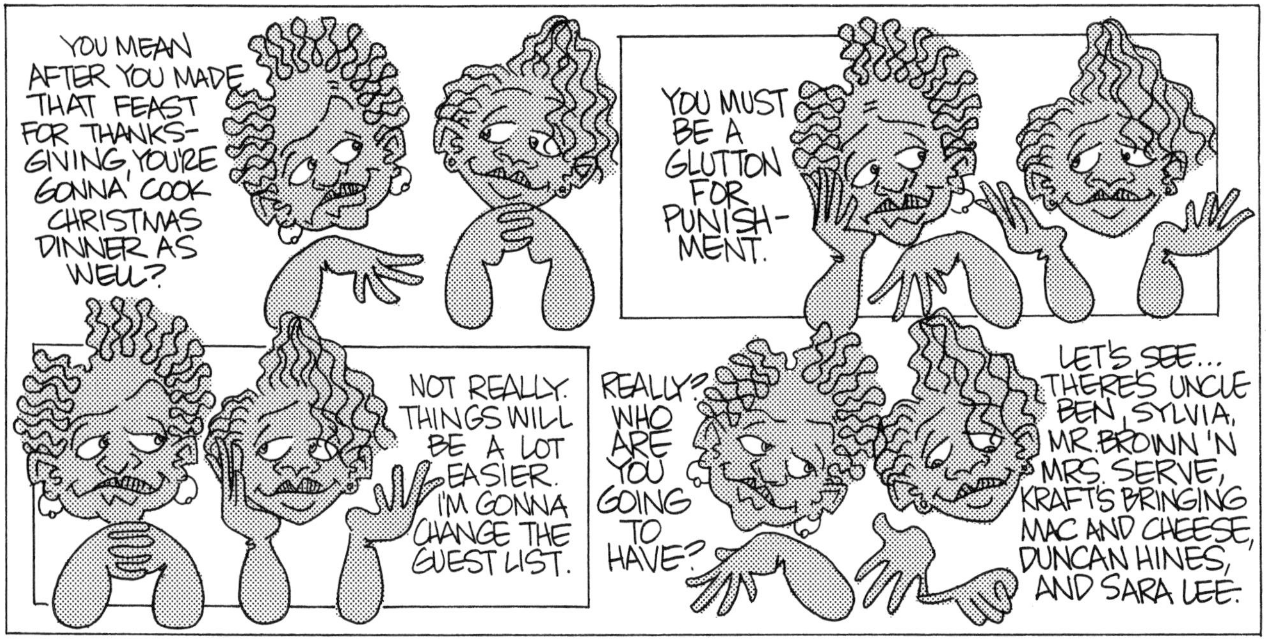
YOU MEAN AFTER YOU MADE THAT FEAST FOR THANKSGIVING, YOU'RE GONNA' COOK CHRISTMAS DINNER AS WELL?
YOU MUST BE A GLUTTON FOR PUNISHMENT.
NOT REALLY. THINGS WILL BE A LOT EASIER. I'M GONNA CHANGE THE GUEST LIST.
REALLY? WHO ARE YOU GOING TO HAVE?
LET'S SEE... THERE'S UNCLE BEN, SYLVIA, MR. BROWN 'N MRS. SERVE, KRAFT'S BRINGING MAC AND CHEESE, DUNCAN HINES, AND SARA LEE.

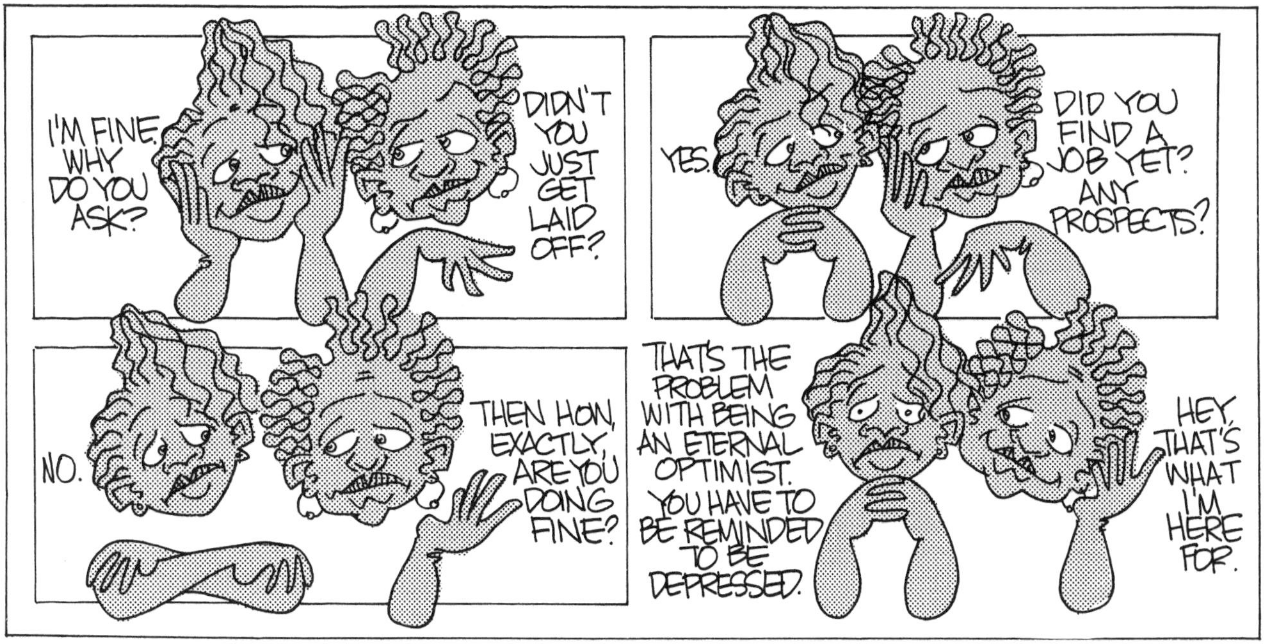
I'M FINE. WHY DO YOU ASK?
DIDN'T YOU JUST GET LAID OFF?
YES.
DID YOU FIND A JOB YET? ANY PROSPECTS?
NO.
THEN HOW, EXACTLY, ARE YOU DOING FINE?
THAT'S THE PROBLEM WITH BEING AN ETERNAL OPTIMIST. YOU HAVE TO BE REMINDED TO BE DEPRESSED.
HEY, THAT'S WHAT I'M HERE FOR.

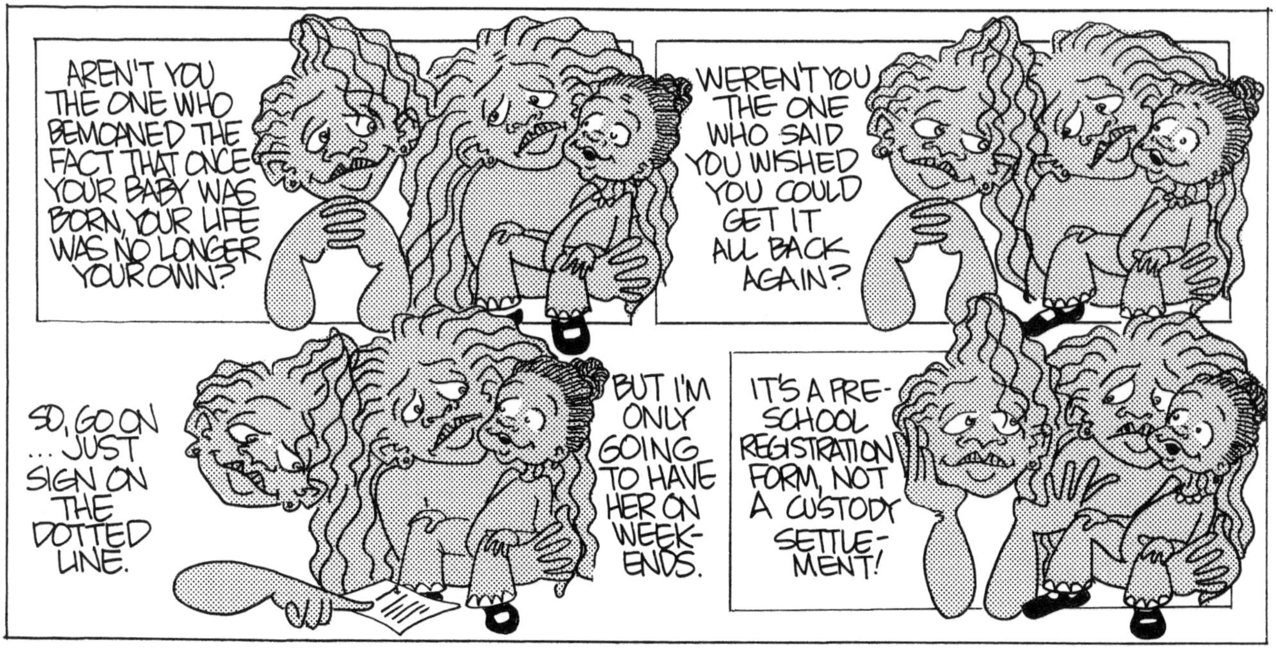
AREN'T YOU THE ONE WHO BEMOANED THE FACT THAT ONCE YOUR BABY WAS BORN, YOUR LIFE WAS NO LONGER YOUR OWN?
WEREN'T YOU THE ONE WHO SAID YOU WISHED YOU COULD GET IT ALL BACK AGAIN?
SO, GO ON ... JUST SIGN ON THE DOTTED LINE.
BUT I'M ONLY GOING TO HAVE HER ON WEEK-ENDS.
IT'S A PRE-SCHOOL REGISTRATION FORM, NOT A CUSTODY SETTLE-MENT!

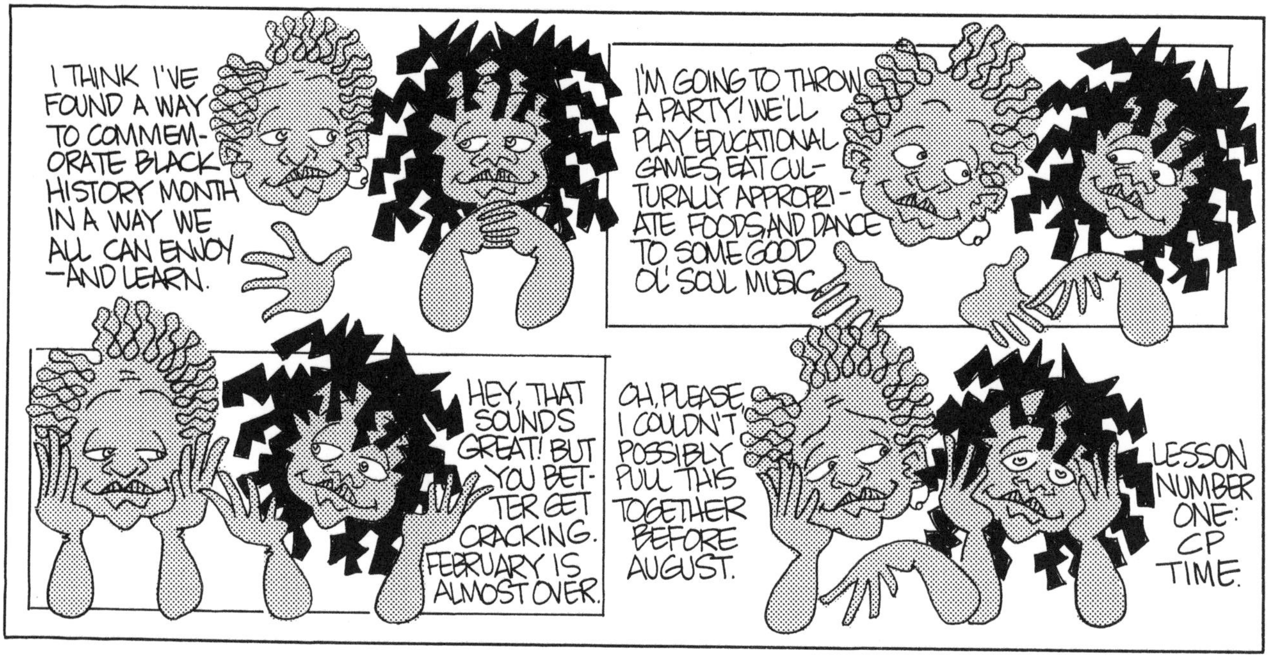
I THINK I'VE FOUND A WAY TO COMMEMORATE BLACK HISTORY MONTH IN A WAY WE ALL CAN ENJOY —AND LEARN.
I'M GOING TO THROW A PARTY! WE'LL PLAY EDUCATIONAL GAMES, EAT CULTURALLY APPROPRIATE FOODS, AND DANCE TO SOME GOOD OL' SOUL MUSIC.
HEY, THAT SOUNDS GREAT! BUT YOU BETTER GET CRACKING. FEBRUARY IS ALMOST OVER.
OH, PLEASE, I COULDN'T POSSIBLY PULL THIS TOGETHER BEFORE AUGUST.
LESSON NUMBER ONE: CP TIME.

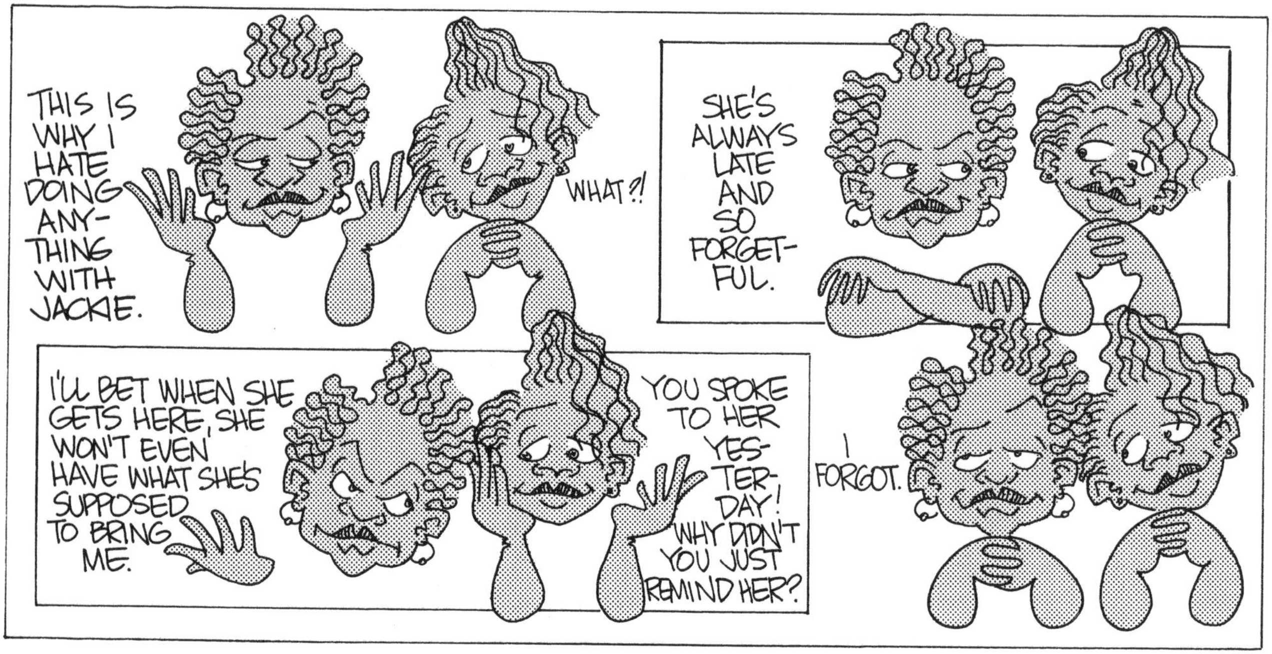
THIS IS WHY I HATE DOING ANYTHING WITH JACKIE.
WHAT?!
SHE'S ALWAYS LATE AND SO FORGETFUL.
I'LL BET WHEN SHE GETS HERE, SHE WON'T EVEN HAVE WHAT SHE'S SUPPOSED TO BRING ME.
YOU SPOKE TO HER YESTERDAY! WHY DIDN'T YOU JUST REMIND HER?
I FORGOT.

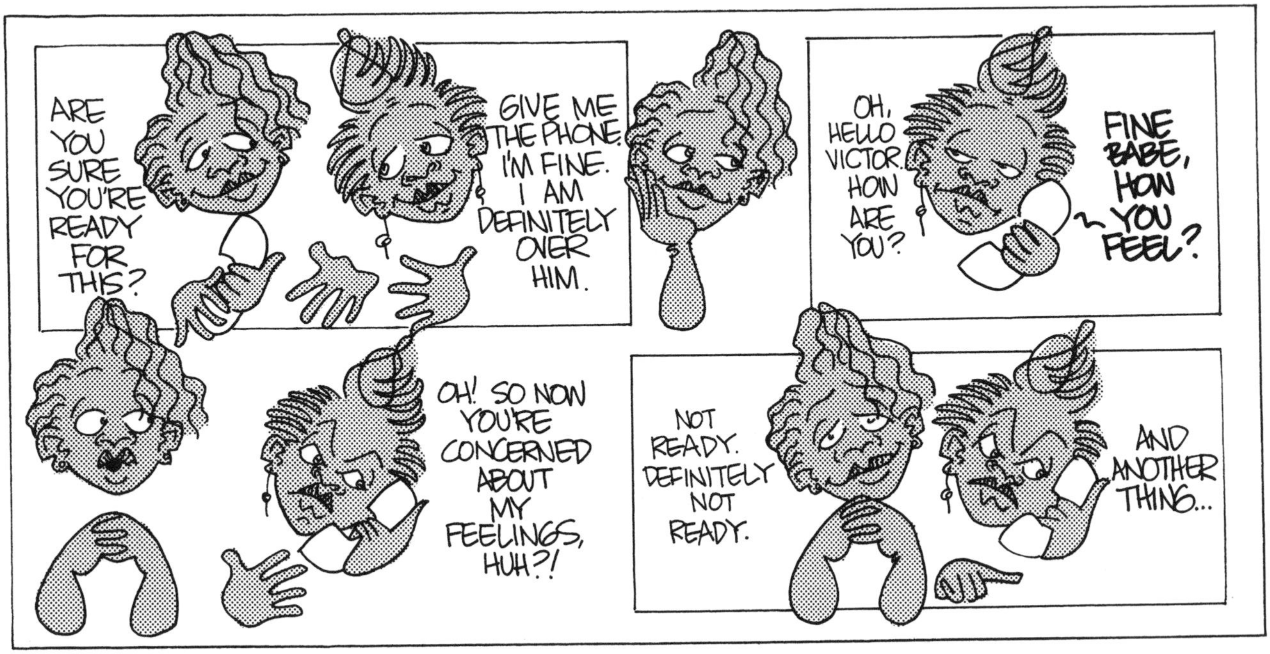
ARE YOU SURE YOU'RE READY FOR THIS?
GIVE ME THE PHONE. I'M FINE. I AM DEFINITELY OVER HIM.
OH, HELLO VICTOR. HOW ARE YOU?
FINE BABE, HOW YOU FEEL?
OH! SO NOW YOU'RE CONCERNED ABOUT MY FEELINGS, HUH?!
NOT READY. DEFINITELY NOT READY.
AND ANOTHER THING...

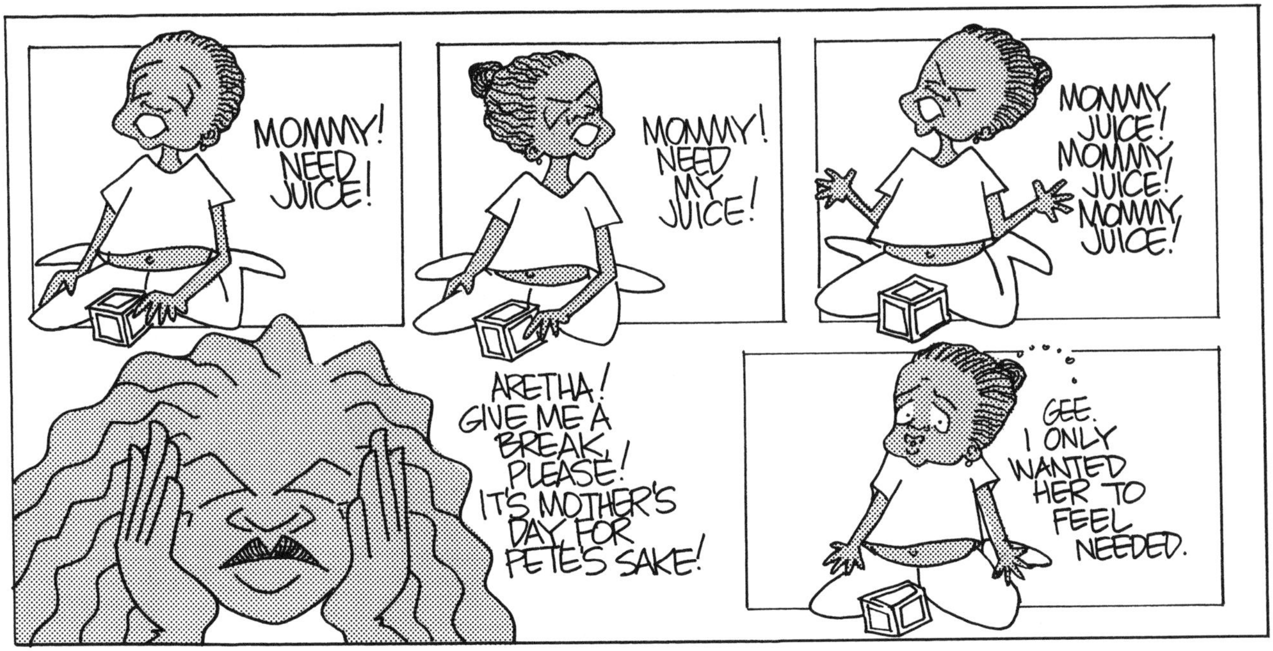
MOMMY! NEED JUICE!
MOMMY! NEED MY JUICE!
MOMMY JUICE! MOMMY JUICE! MOMMY JUICE!
ARETHA! GIVE ME A BREAK, PLEASE! IT'S MOTHER'S DAY FOR PETE'S SAKE!
GEE. I ONLY WANTED HER TO FEEL NEEDED.

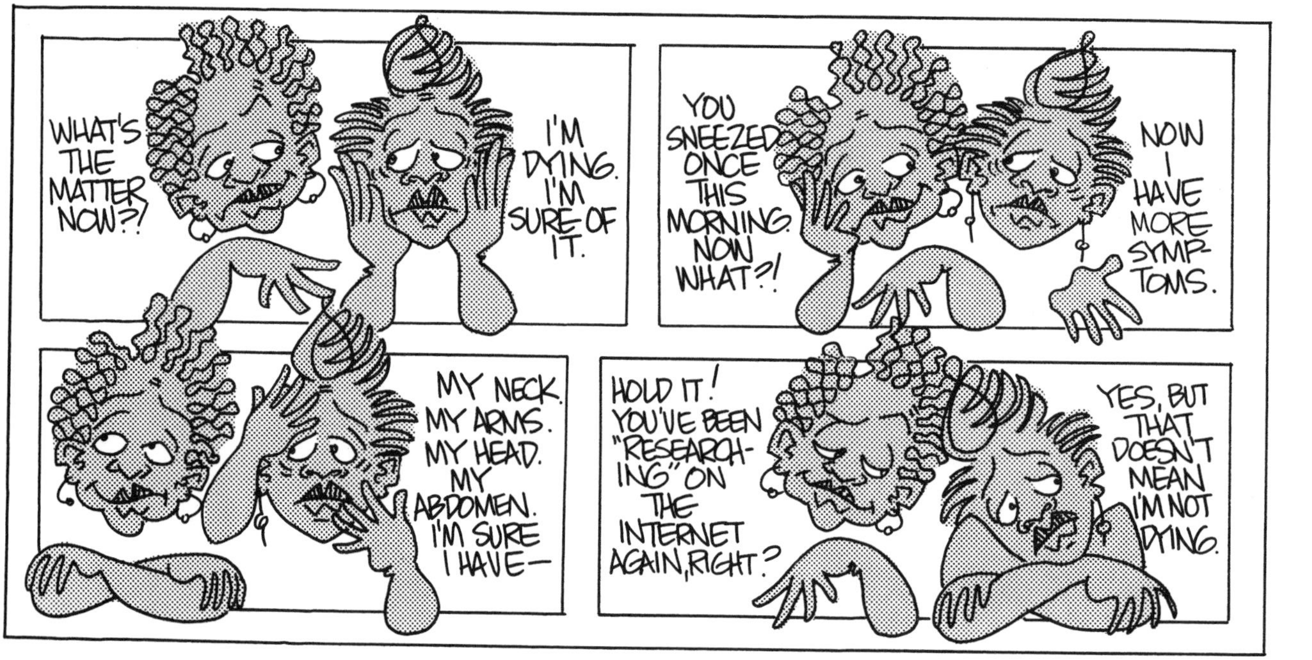
WHAT'S THE MATTER NOW?!
I'M DYING. I'M SURE OF IT.
YOU SNEEZED ONCE THIS MORNING. NOW WHAT?!
NOW I HAVE MORE SYMPTOMS.
MY NECK. MY ARMS. MY HEAD. MY ABDOMEN. I'M SURE I HAVE—
HOLD IT! YOU'VE BEEN "RESEARCHING" ON THE INTERNET AGAIN, RIGHT?
YES, BUT THAT DOESN'T MEAN I'M NOT DYING.

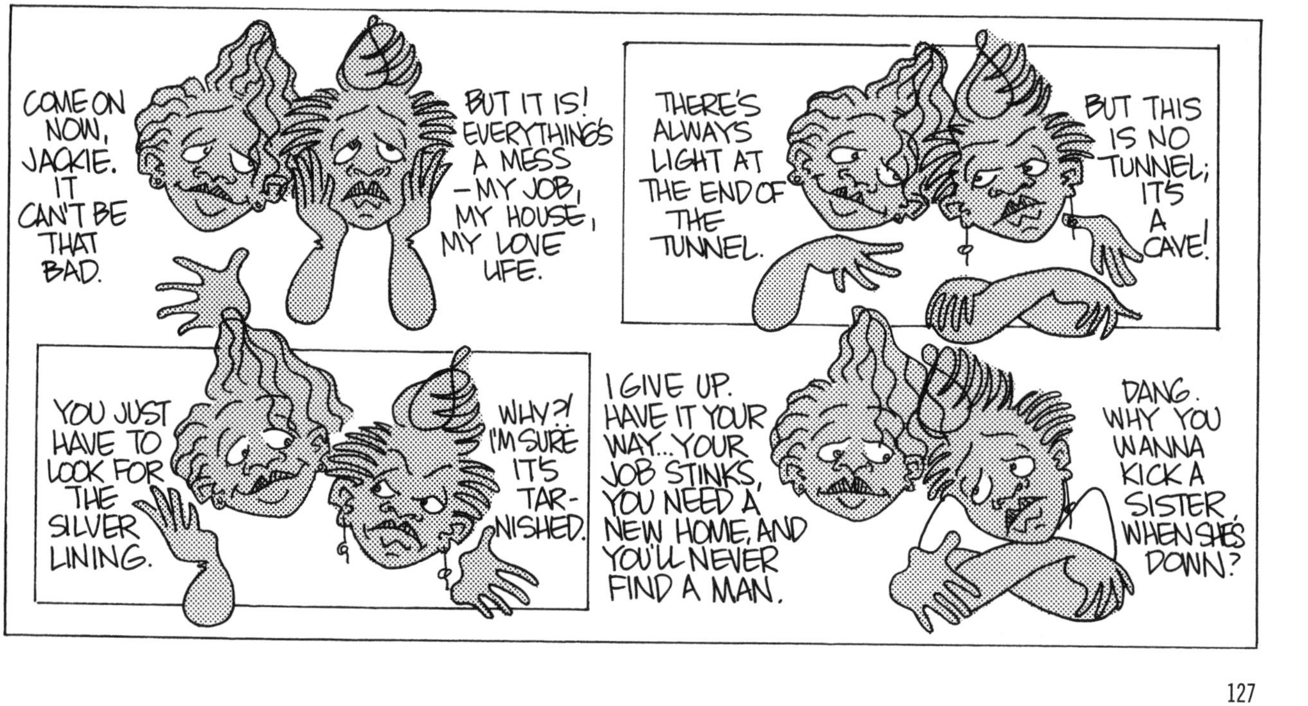
COME ON NOW, JACKIE. IT CAN'T BE THAT BAD.
BUT IT IS! EVERYTHING'S A MESS —MY JOB, MY HOUSE, MY LOVE LIFE.
THERE'S ALWAYS LIGHT AT THE END OF THE TUNNEL.
BUT THIS IS NO TUNNEL; IT'S A CAVE!
YOU JUST HAVE TO LOOK FOR THE SILVER LINING.
WHY?! I'M SURE IT'S TARNISHED.
I GIVE UP. HAVE IT YOUR WAY... YOUR JOB STINKS, YOU NEED A NEW HOME, AND YOU'LL NEVER FIND A MAN.
DANG. WHY YOU WANNA KICK A SISTER WHEN SHE'S DOWN?

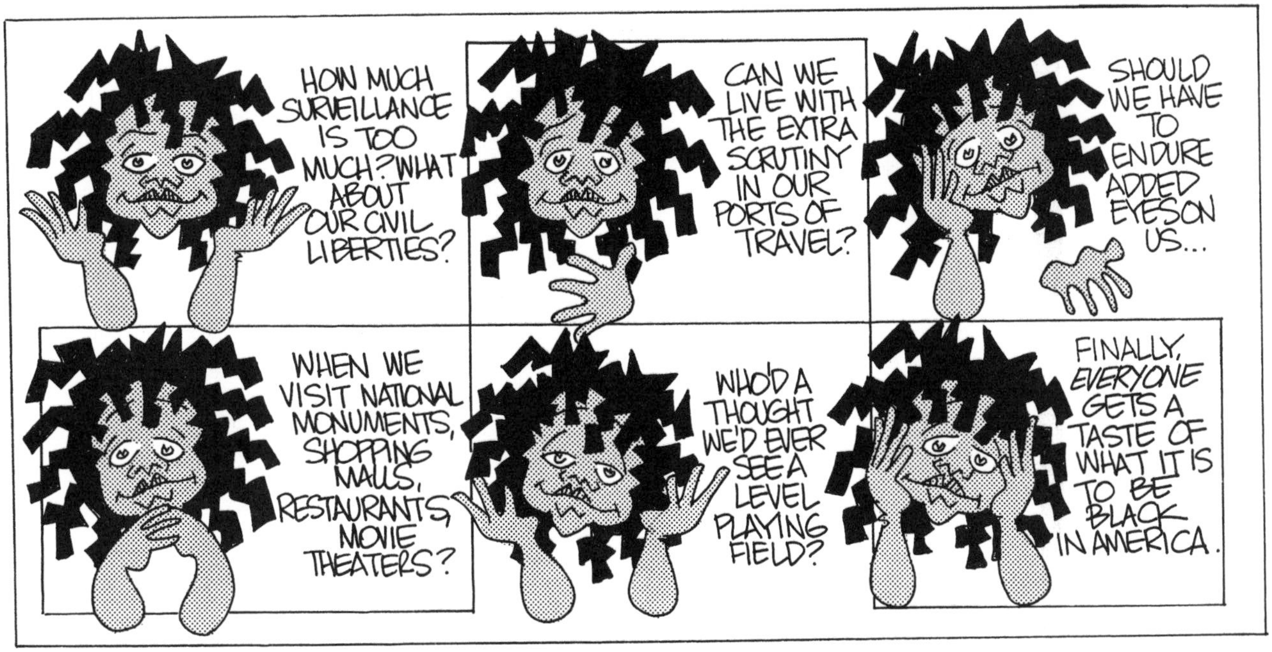
HOW MUCH SURVEILLANCE IS TOO MUCH? WHAT ABOUT OUR CIVIL LIBERTIES?
CAN WE LIVE WITH THE EXTRA SCRUTINY IN OUR PORTS OF TRAVEL?
SHOULD WE HAVE TO ENDURE ADDED EYES ON US...
WHEN WE VISIT NATIONAL MONUMENTS, SHOPPING MALLS, RESTAURANTS, MOVIE THEATERS?
WHO'D A THOUGHT WE'D EVER SEE A LEVEL PLAYING FIELD?
FINALLY, EVERYONE GETS A TASTE OF WHAT IT IS TO BE BLACK IN AMERICA.

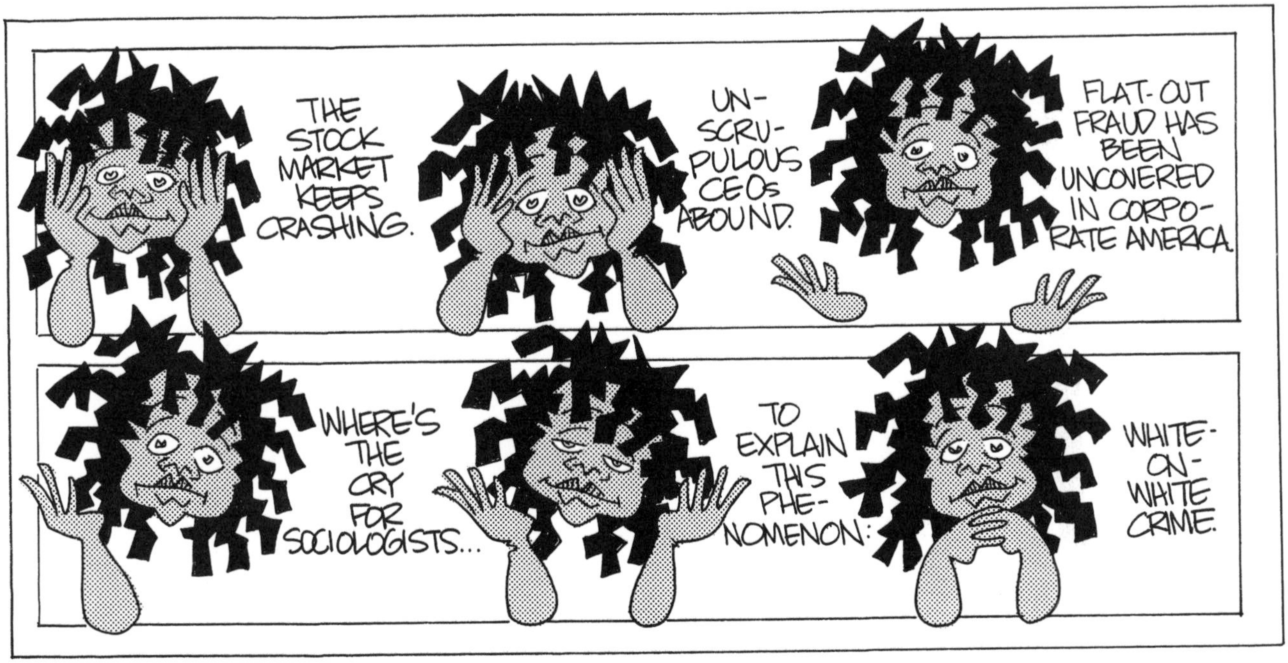
THE STOCK MARKET KEEPS CRASHING.
UN-SCRU-PULOUS CEOs ABOUND.
FLAT-OUT FRAUD HAS BEEN UNCOVERED IN CORPO-RATE AMERICA.
WHERE'S THE CRY FOR SOCIOLOGISTS...
TO EXPLAIN THIS PHE-NOMENON:
WHITE-ON-WHITE CRIME.

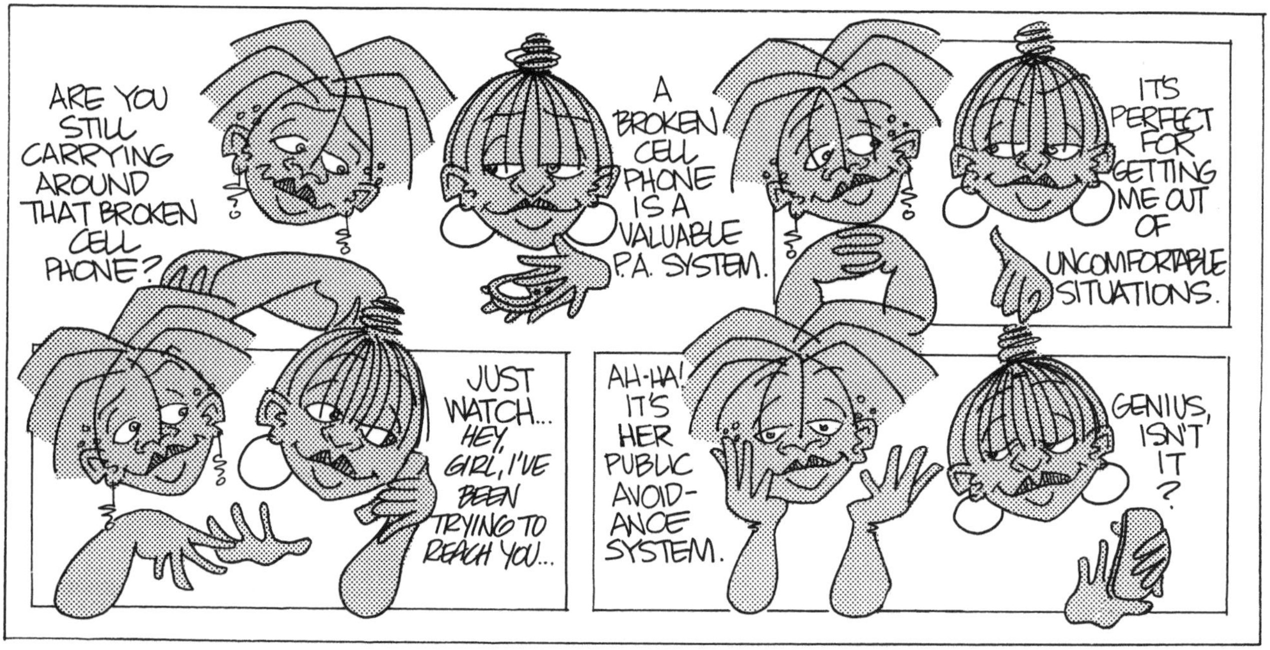
ARE YOU STILL CARRYING AROUND THAT BROKEN CELL PHONE?
A BROKEN CELL PHONE IS A VALUABLE P.A. SYSTEM.
IT'S PERFECT FOR GETTING ME OUT OF UNCOMFORTABLE SITUATIONS.
JUST WATCH... HEY, GIRL, I'VE BEEN TRYING TO REACH YOU...
AH-HA! IT'S HER PUBLIC AVOID-ANCE SYSTEM.
GENIUS, ISN'T IT?

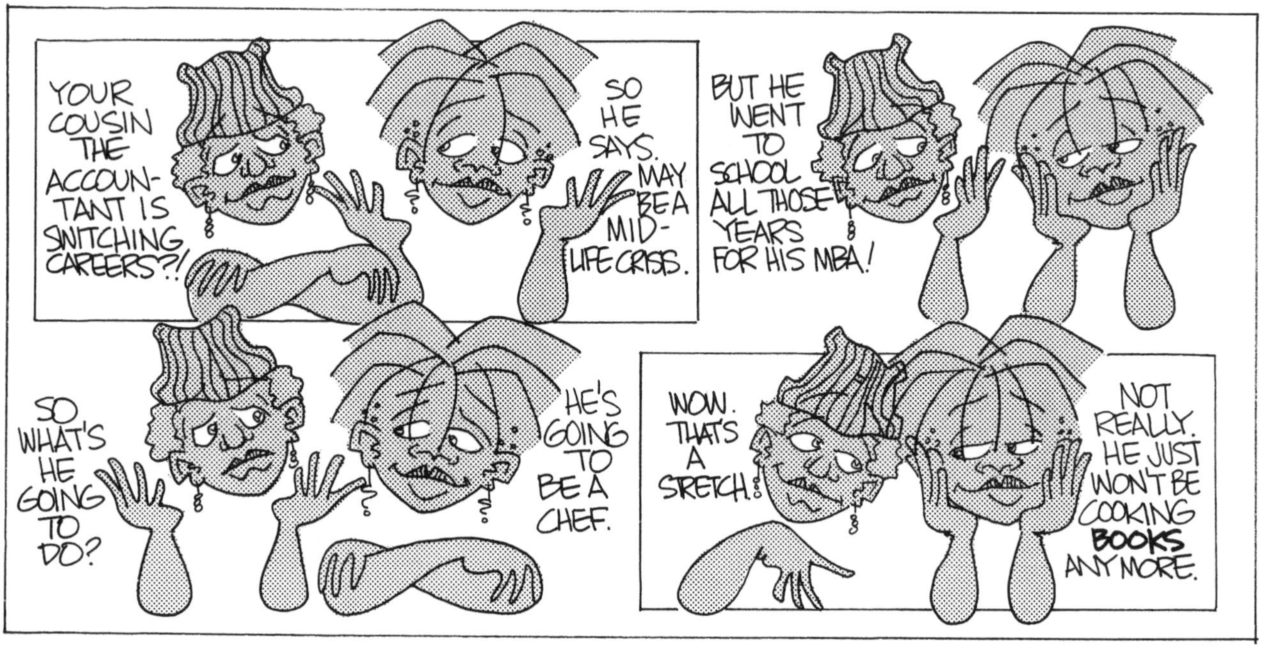
YOUR COUSIN THE ACCOUN-TANT IS SWITCHING CAREERS?!
SO HE SAYS. MAY BE A MID-LIFE CRISIS.
BUT HE WENT TO SCHOOL ALL THOSE YEARS FOR HIS MBA!
SO WHAT'S HE GOING TO DO?
HE'S GOING TO BE A CHEF.
WOW. THAT'S A STRETCH.
NOT REALLY. HE JUST WON'T BE COOKING BOOKS ANY MORE.

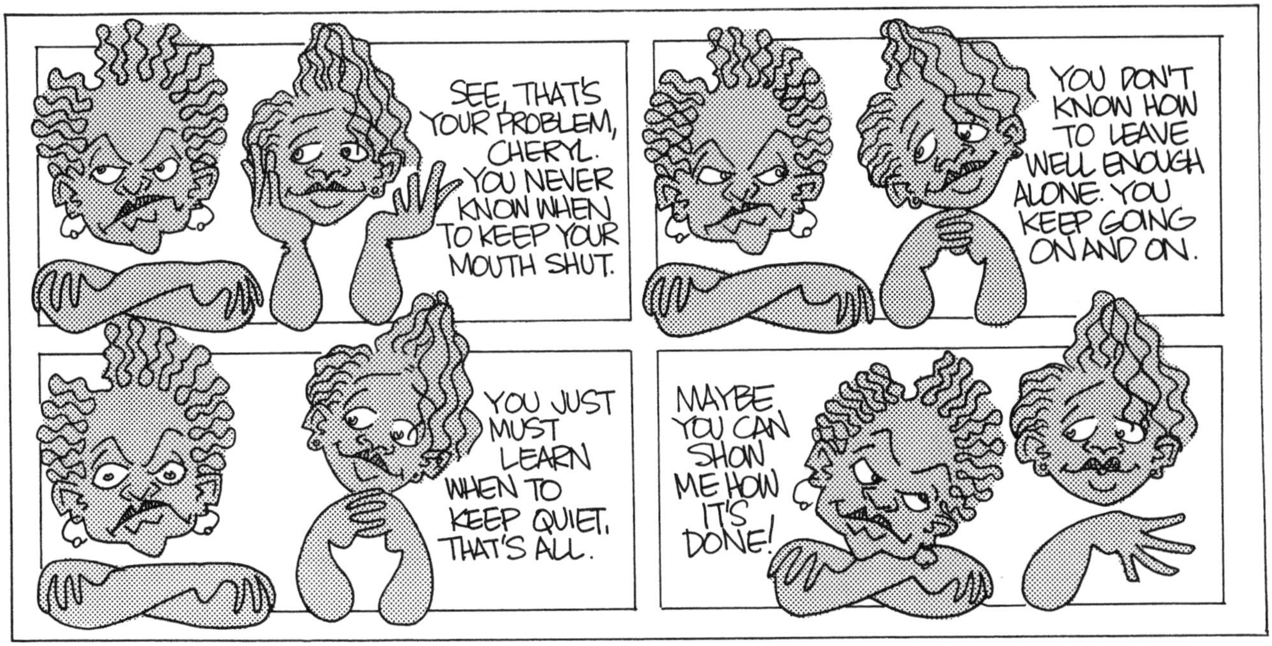
SEE, THAT'S YOUR PROBLEM, CHERYL. YOU NEVER KNOW WHEN TO KEEP YOUR MOUTH SHUT.
YOU DON'T KNOW HOW TO LEAVE WELL ENOUGH ALONE. YOU KEEP GOING ON AND ON.
YOU JUST MUST LEARN WHEN TO KEEP QUIET. THAT'S ALL.
MAYBE YOU CAN SHOW ME HOW IT'S DONE!

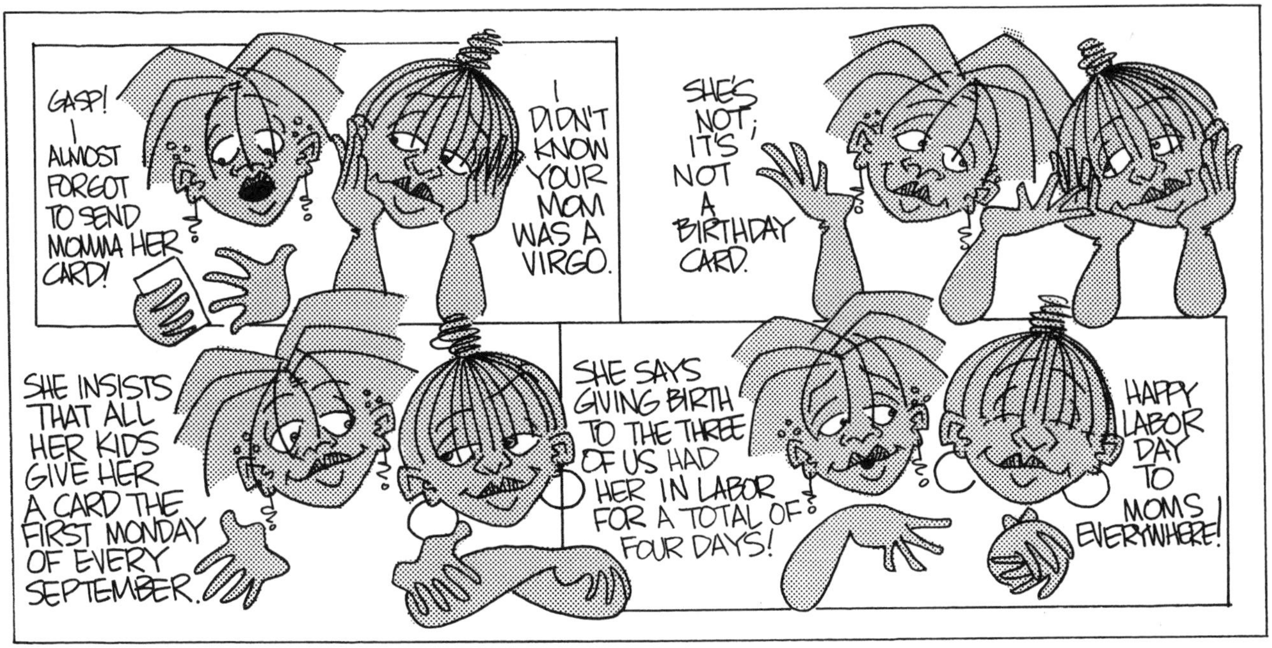
GASP! I ALMOST FORGOT TO SEND MOMMA HER CARD!
I DIDN'T KNOW YOUR MOM WAS A VIRGO.
SHE'S NOT; IT'S NOT A BIRTHDAY CARD.
SHE INSISTS THAT ALL HER KIDS GIVE HER A CARD THE FIRST MONDAY OF EVERY SEPTEMBER.
SHE SAYS GIVING BIRTH TO THE THREE OF US HAD HER IN LABOR FOR A TOTAL OF FOUR DAYS!
HAPPY LABOR DAY TO MOMS EVERYWHERE!

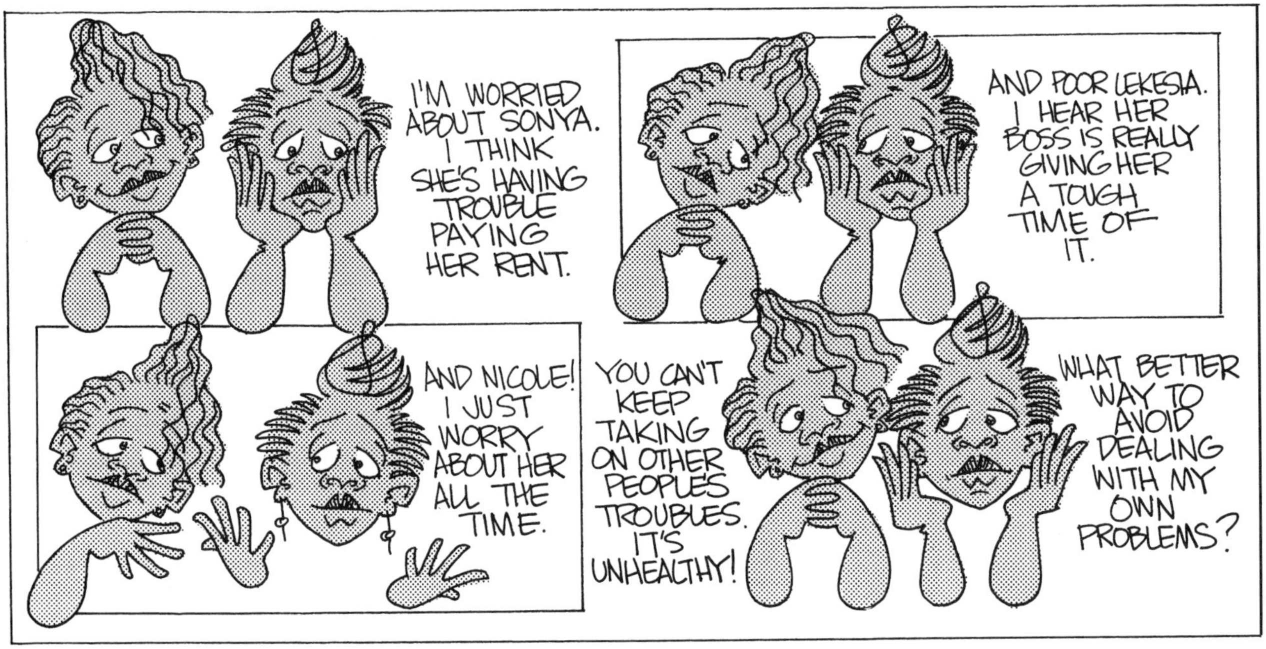
I'M WORRIED ABOUT SONYA. I THINK SHE'S HAVING TROUBLE PAYING HER RENT.
AND POOR LEKESIA. I HEAR HER BOSS IS REALLY GIVING HER A TOUGH TIME OF IT.
AND NICOLE! I JUST WORRY ABOUT HER ALL THE TIME.
YOU CAN'T KEEP TAKING ON OTHER PEOPLE'S TROUBLES. IT'S UNHEALTHY!
WHAT BETTER WAY TO AVOID DEALING WITH MY OWN PROBLEMS?

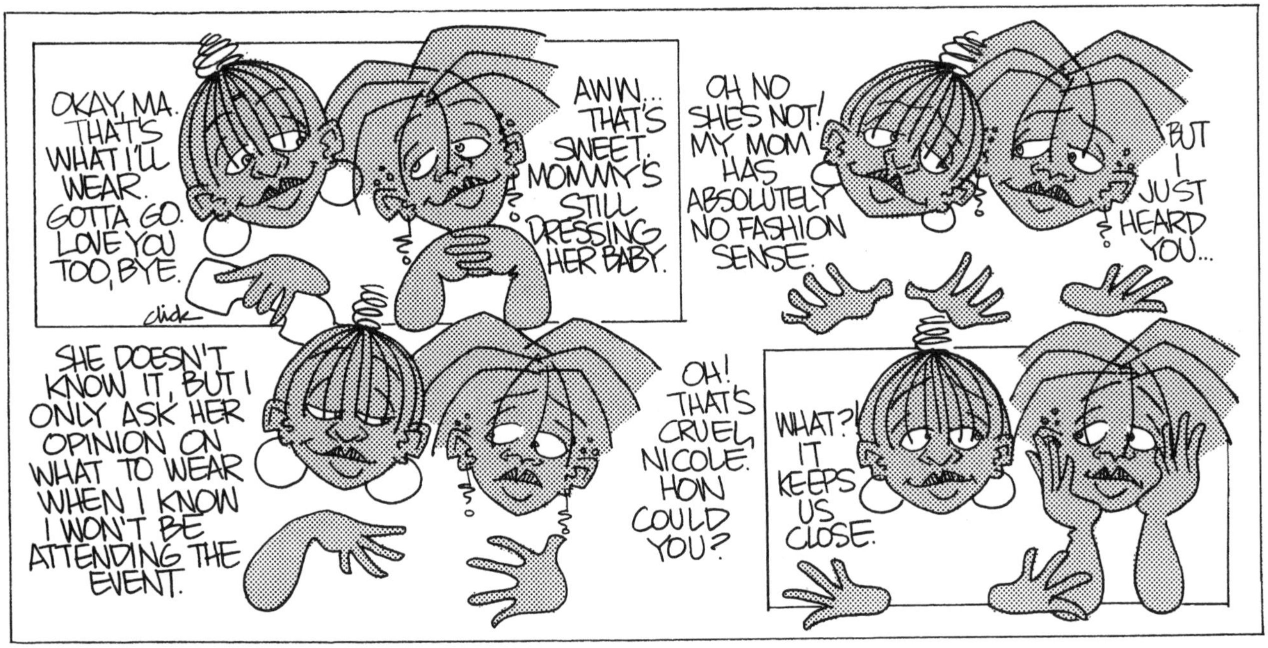
OKAY, MA. THAT'S WHAT I'LL WEAR. GOTTA GO. LOVE YOU TOO, BYE.
click
AWW... THAT'S SWEET. MOMMY'S STILL DRESSING HER BABY.
OH NO SHE'S NOT! MY MOM HAS ABSOLUTELY NO FASHION SENSE.
BUT I JUST HEARD YOU...
SHE DOESN'T KNOW IT, BUT I ONLY ASK HER OPINION ON WHAT TO WEAR WHEN I KNOW I WON'T BE ATTENDING THE EVENT.
OH! THAT'S CRUEL, NICOLE. HOW COULD YOU?
WHAT?! IT KEEPS US CLOSE.

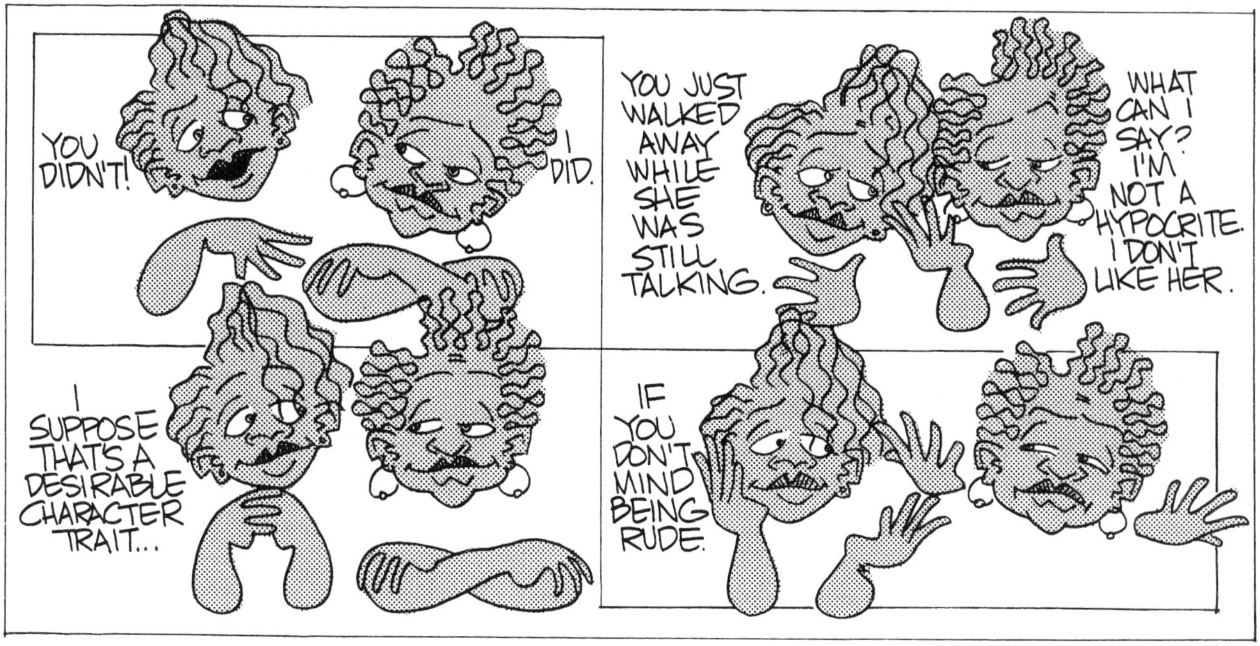
YOU DIDN'T!
I DID.
YOU JUST WALKED AWAY WHILE SHE WAS STILL TALKING.
WHAT CAN I SAY? I'M NOT A HYPOCRITE. I DON'T LIKE HER.
I SUPPOSE THAT'S A DESIRABLE CHARACTER TRAIT...
IF YOU DON'T MIND BEING RUDE.

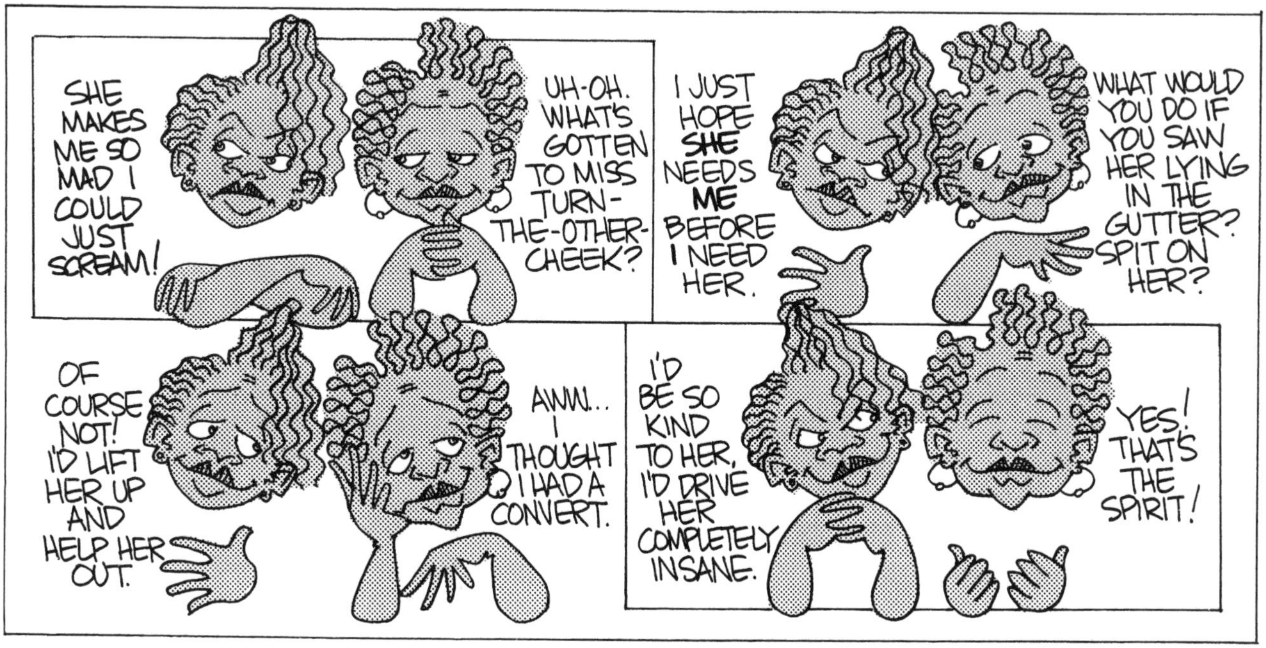
SHE MAKES ME SO MAD I COULD JUST SCREAM!
UH-OH. WHAT'S GOTTEN TO MISS TURN-THE-OTHER-CHEEK?
I JUST HOPE SHE NEEDS ME BEFORE I NEED HER.
WHAT WOULD YOU DO IF YOU SAW HER LYING IN THE GUTTER? SPIT ON HER?
OF COURSE NOT! I'D LIFT HER UP AND HELP HER OUT.
AWW... I THOUGHT I HAD A CONVERT.
I'D BE SO KIND TO HER, I'D DRIVE HER COMPLETELY INSANE.
YES! THAT'S THE SPIRIT!

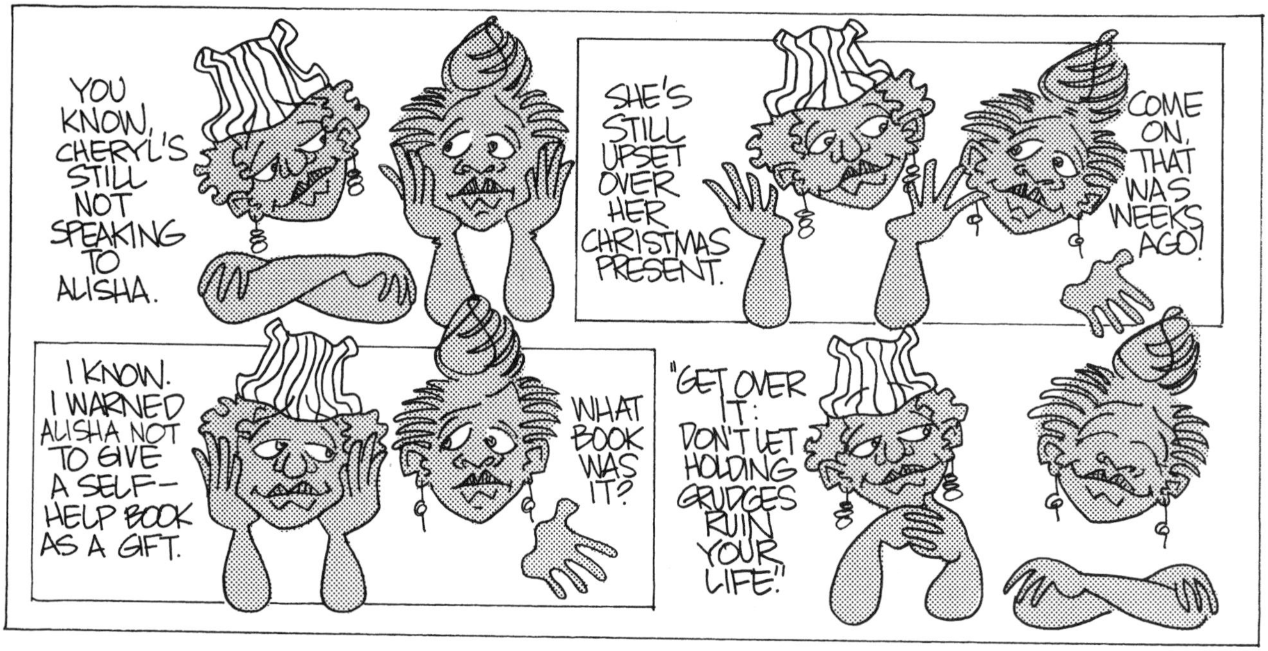
YOU KNOW, CHERYL'S STILL NOT SPEAKING TO ALISHA.
SHE'S STILL UPSET OVER HER CHRISTMAS PRESENT.
COME ON, THAT WAS WEEKS AGO!
I KNOW. I WARNED ALISHA NOT TO GIVE A SELF-HELP BOOK AS A GIFT.
WHAT BOOK WAS IT?
"GET OVER IT: DON'T LET HOLDING GRUDGES RUIN YOUR LIFE."

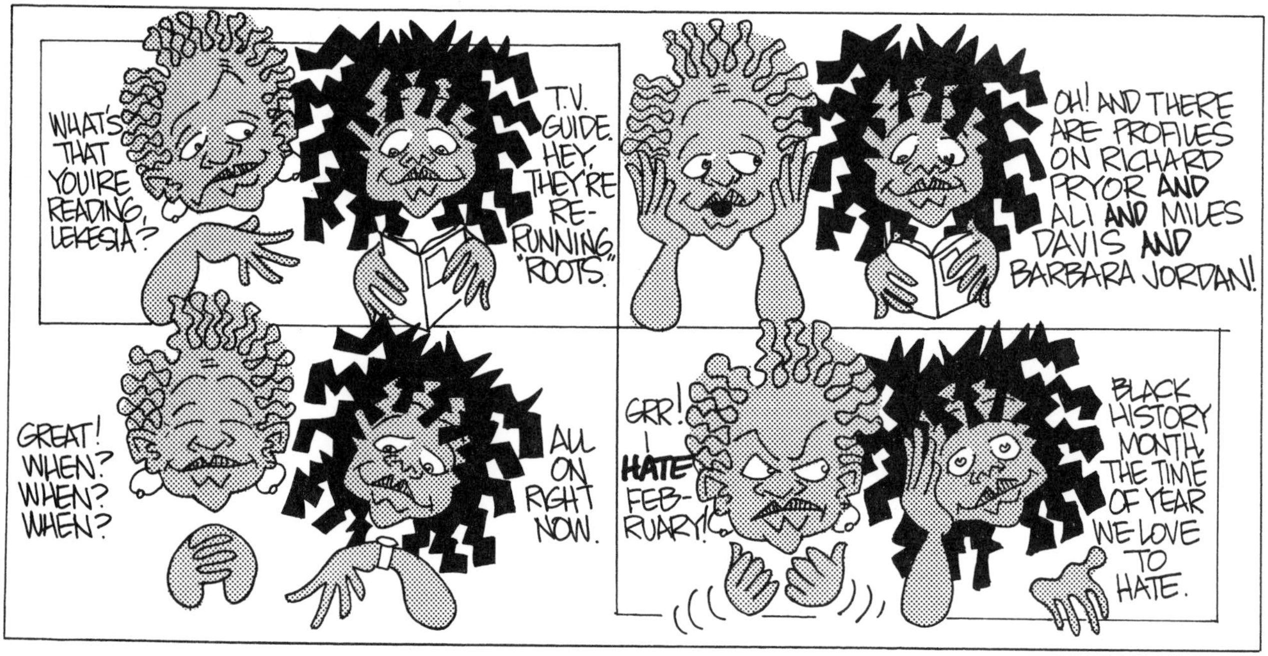
WHAT'S THAT YOU'RE READING, LEKESIA?
T.V. GUIDE. HEY, THEY'RE RE-RUNNING "ROOTS."
OH! AND THERE ARE PROFILES ON RICHARD PRYOR AND ALI AND MILES DAVIS AND BARBARA JORDAN!
GREAT! WHEN? WHEN? WHEN?
ALL ON RIGHT NOW.
GRR! I HATE FEB-RUARY!
BLACK HISTORY MONTH, THE TIME OF YEAR WE LOVE TO HATE.

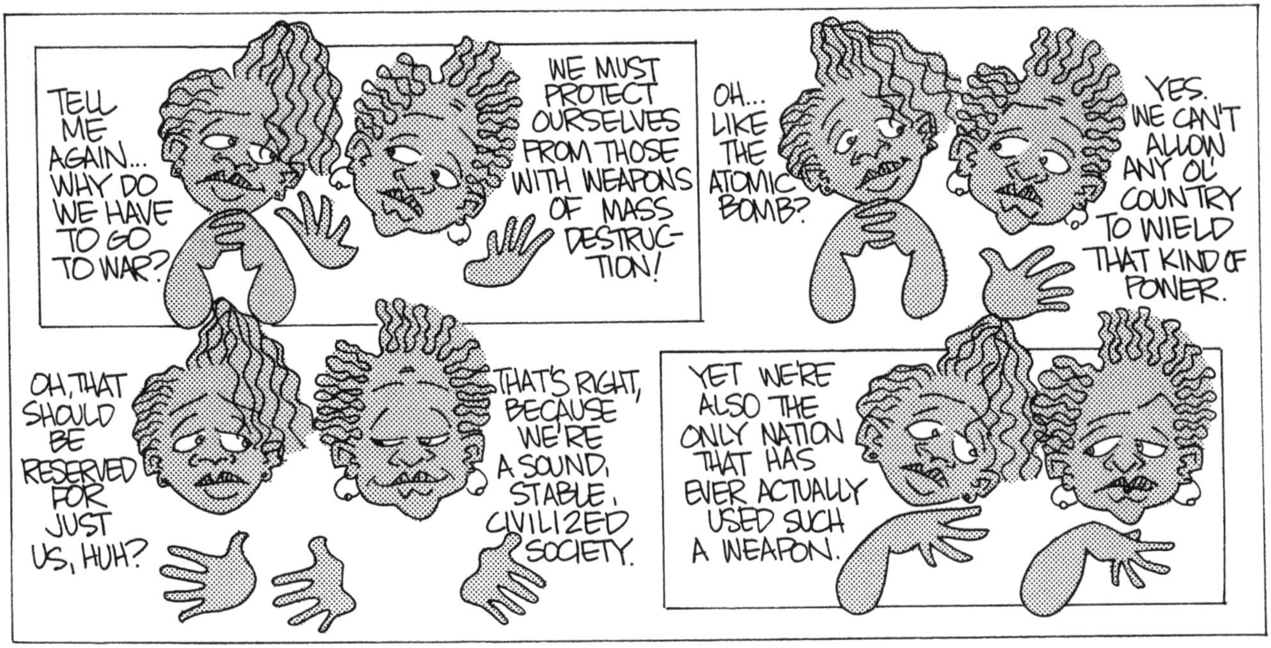
TELL ME AGAIN... WHY DO WE HAVE TO GO TO WAR?
WE MUST PROTECT OURSELVES FROM THOSE WITH WEAPONS OF MASS DESTRUCTION!
OH... LIKE THE ATOMIC BOMB?
YES. WE CAN'T ALLOW ANY OL' COUNTRY TO WIELD THAT KIND OF POWER.
OH, THAT SHOULD BE RESERVED FOR JUST US, HUH?
THAT'S RIGHT, BECAUSE WE'RE A SOUND, STABLE, CIVILIZED SOCIETY.
YET WE'RE ALSO THE ONLY NATION THAT HAS EVER ACTUALLY USED SUCH A WEAPON.

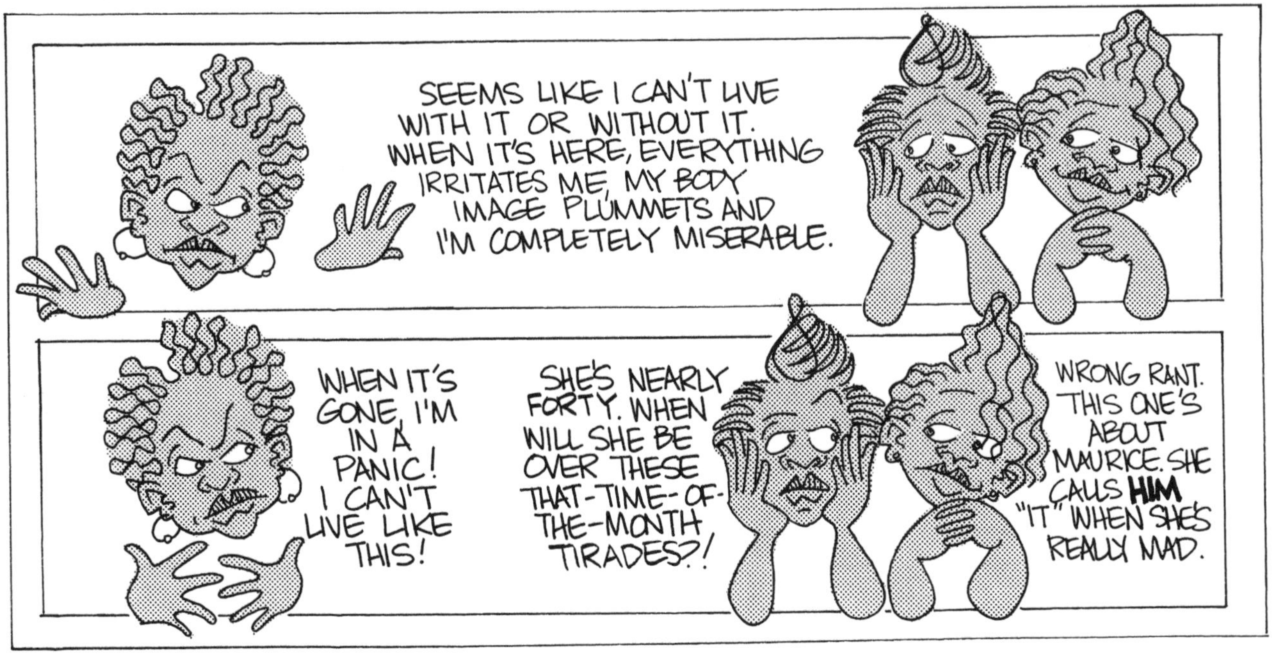
SEEMS LIKE I CAN'T LIVE WITH IT OR WITHOUT IT. WHEN IT'S HERE, EVERYTHING IRRITATES ME, MY BODY IMAGE PLUMMETS AND I'M COMPLETELY MISERABLE.
WHEN IT'S GONE, I'M IN A PANIC! I CAN'T LIVE LIKE THIS!
SHE'S NEARLY FORTY. WHEN WILL SHE BE OVER THESE THAT-TIME-OF-THE-MONTH TIRADES?!
WRONG RANT. THIS ONE'S ABOUT MAURICE. SHE CALLS **HIM** "IT" WHEN SHE'S REALLY MAD.

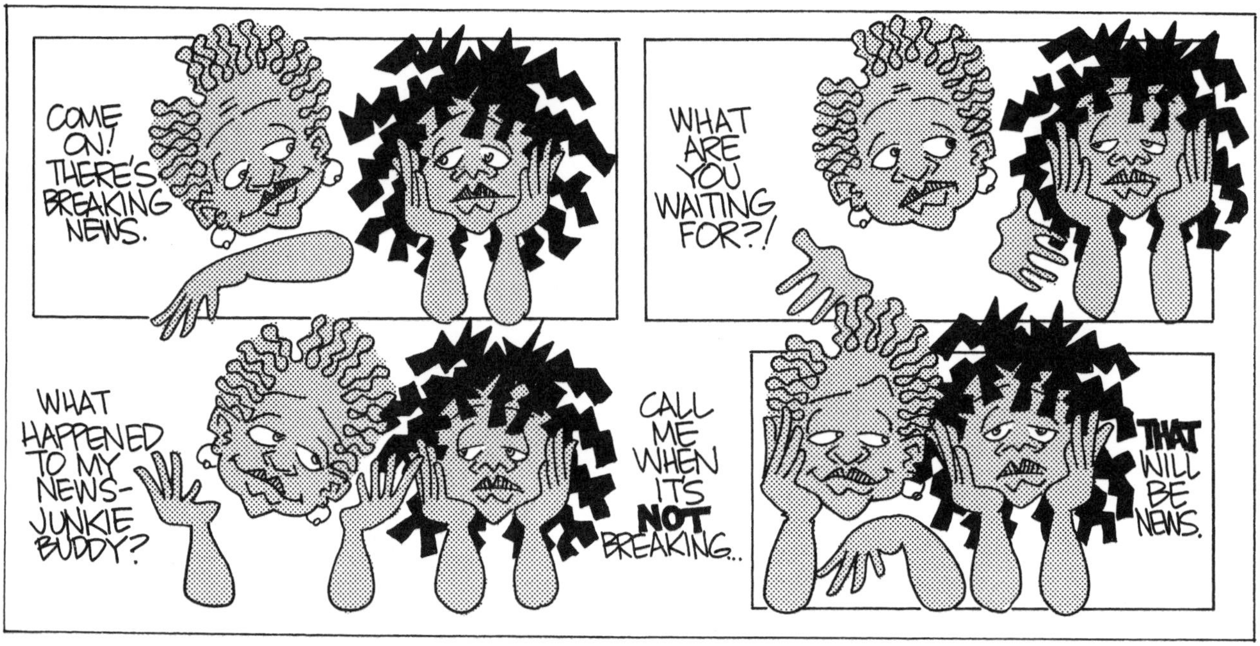
COME ON! THERE'S BREAKING NEWS.
WHAT ARE YOU WAITING FOR?!
WHAT HAPPENED TO MY NEWS-JUNKIE BUDDY?
CALL ME WHEN ITS **NOT** BREAKING...
THAT WILL BE NEWS.

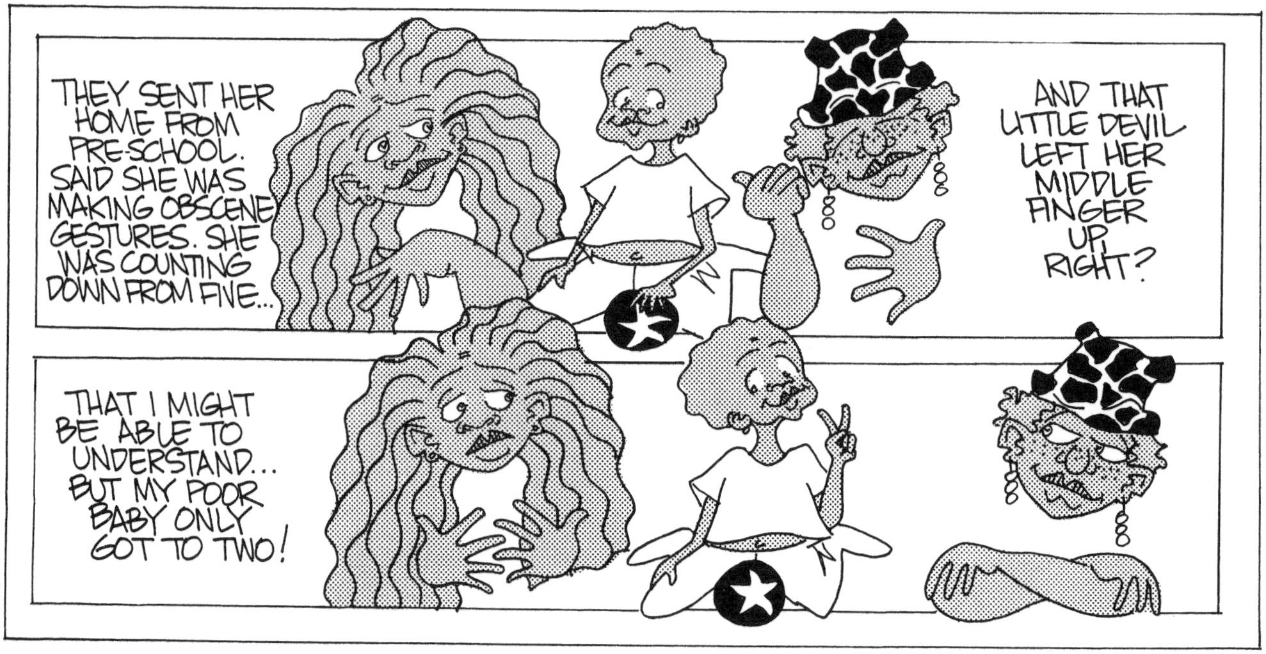
THEY SENT HER HOME FROM PRE-SCHOOL. SAID SHE WAS MAKING OBSCENE GESTURES. SHE WAS COUNTING DOWN FROM FIVE...
AND THAT LITTLE DEVIL LEFT HER MIDDLE FINGER UP, RIGHT?
THAT I MIGHT BE ABLE TO UNDERSTAND... BUT MY POOR BABY ONLY GOT TO TWO!

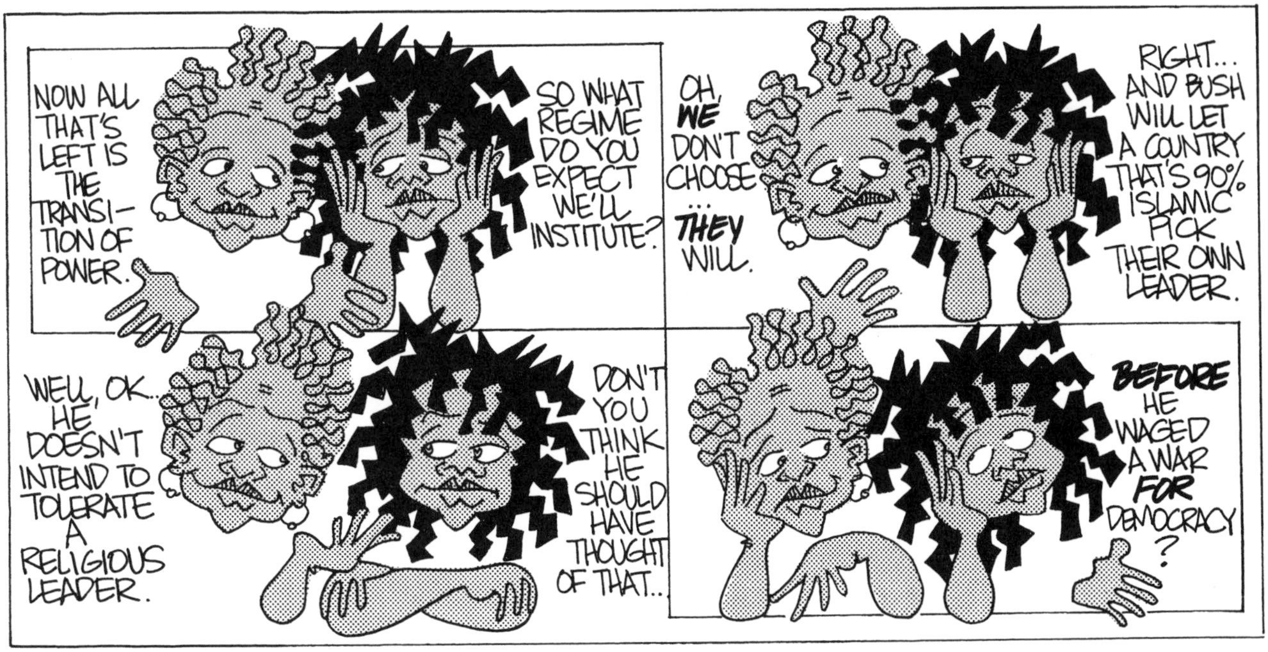
NOW ALL THAT'S LEFT IS THE TRANSI-TION OF POWER.
SO WHAT REGIME DO YOU EXPECT WE'LL INSTITUTE?
OH, WE DON'T CHOOSE ... THEY WILL.
RIGHT... AND BUSH WILL LET A COUNTRY THAT'S 90% ISLAMIC PICK THEIR OWN LEADER.
WELL, OK... HE DOESN'T INTEND TO TOLERATE A RELIGIOUS LEADER.
DON'T YOU THINK HE SHOULD HAVE THOUGHT OF THAT...
BEFORE HE WAGED A WAR FOR DEMOCRACY?

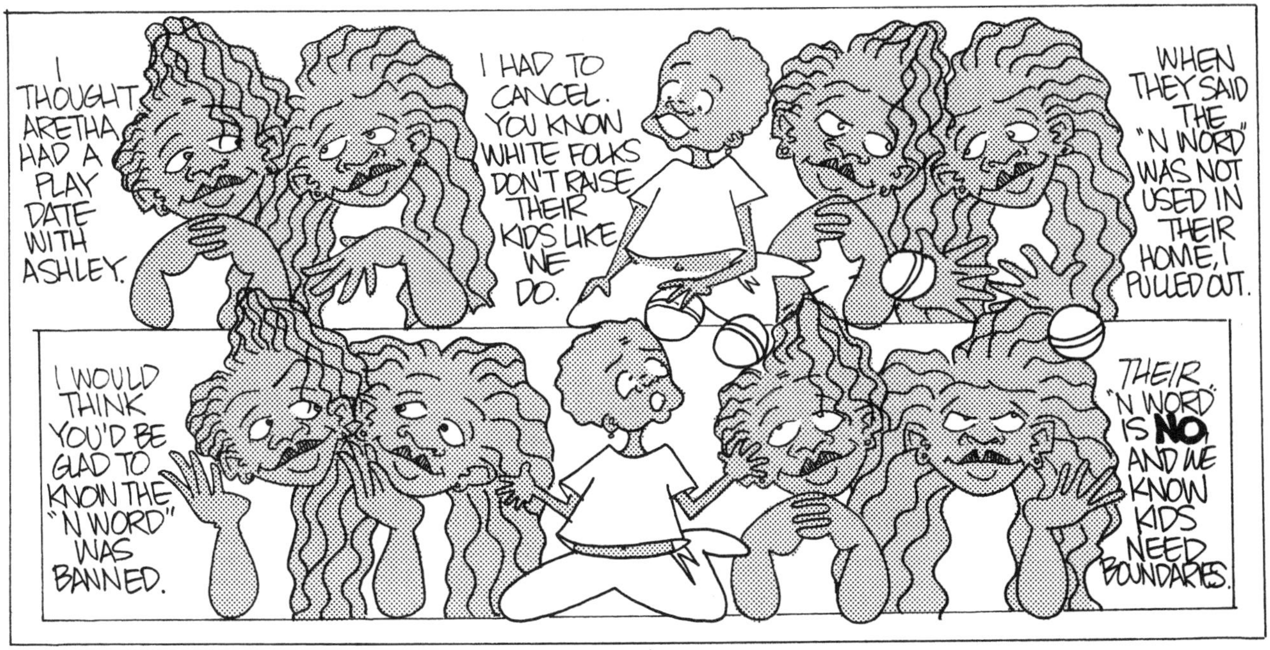
I THOUGHT ARETHA HAD A PLAY DATE WITH ASHLEY.
I HAD TO CANCEL. YOU KNOW WHITE FOLKS DON'T RAISE THEIR KIDS LIKE WE DO.
WHEN THEY SAID THE "N WORD" WAS NOT USED IN THEIR HOME, I PULLED OUT.
I WOULD THINK YOU'D BE GLAD TO KNOW THE "N WORD" WAS BANNED.
THEIR "N WORD" IS NO, AND WE KNOW KIDS NEED BOUNDARIES.

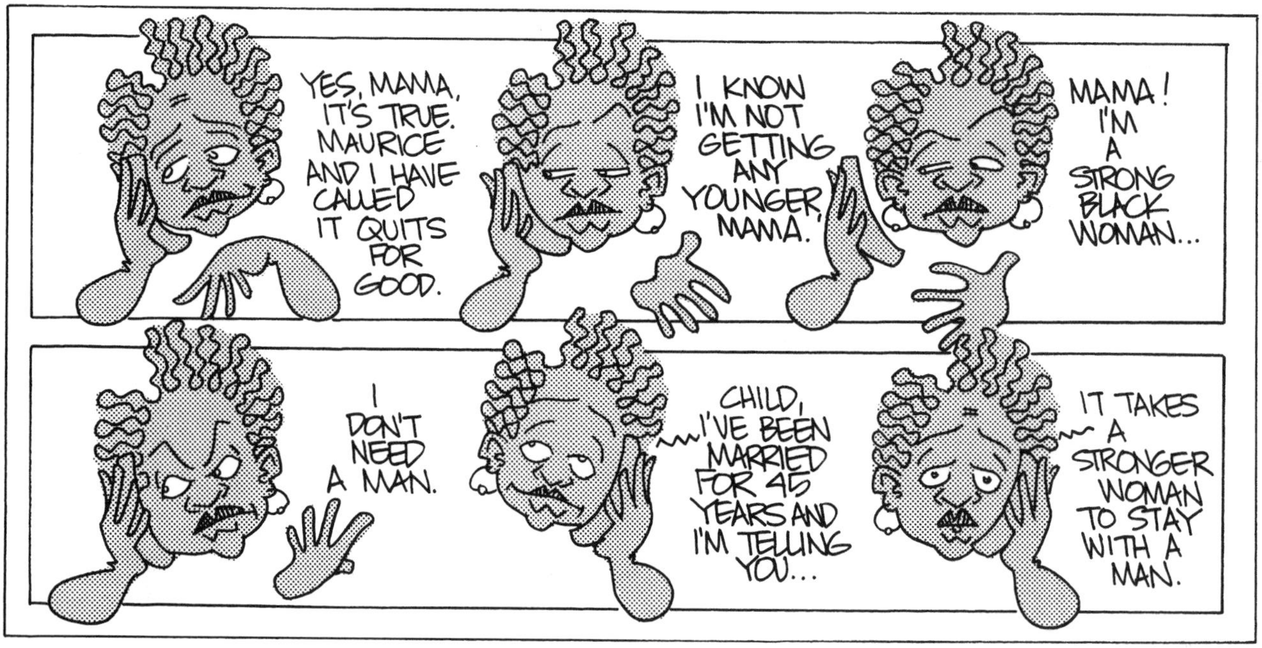
YES, MAMA, IT'S TRUE. MAURICE AND I HAVE CALLED IT QUITS FOR GOOD.
I KNOW I'M NOT GETTING ANY YOUNGER, MAMA.
MAMA! I'M A STRONG BLACK WOMAN...
I DON'T NEED A MAN.
CHILD, I'VE BEEN MARRIED FOR 45 YEARS AND I'M TELLING YOU...
IT TAKES A STRONGER WOMAN TO STAY WITH A MAN.

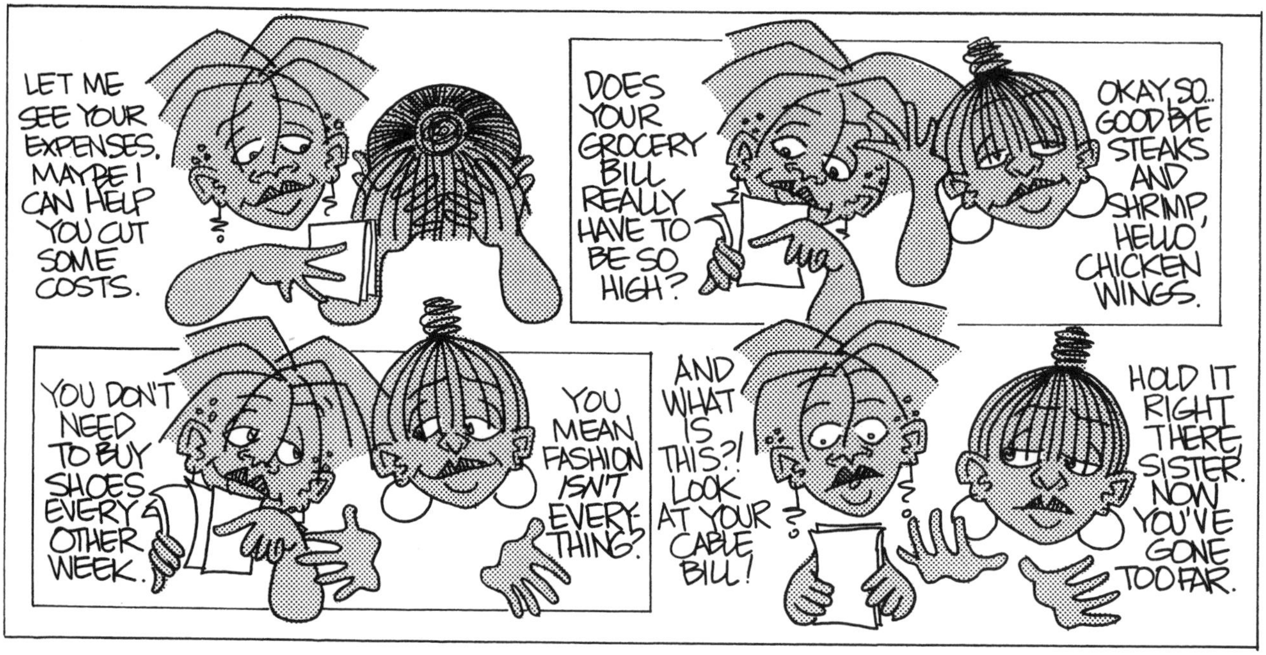
LET ME SEE YOUR EXPENSES. MAYBE I CAN HELP YOU CUT SOME COSTS.
DOES YOUR GROCERY BILL REALLY HAVE TO BE SO HIGH?
OKAY, SO... GOOD BYE STEAKS AND SHRIMP, HELLO CHICKEN WINGS.
YOU DON'T NEED TO BUY SHOES EVERY OTHER WEEK.
YOU MEAN FASHION ISN'T EVERYTHING?
AND WHAT IS THIS?! LOOK AT YOUR CABLE BILL!
HOLD IT RIGHT THERE, SISTER. NOW YOU'VE GONE TOO FAR.

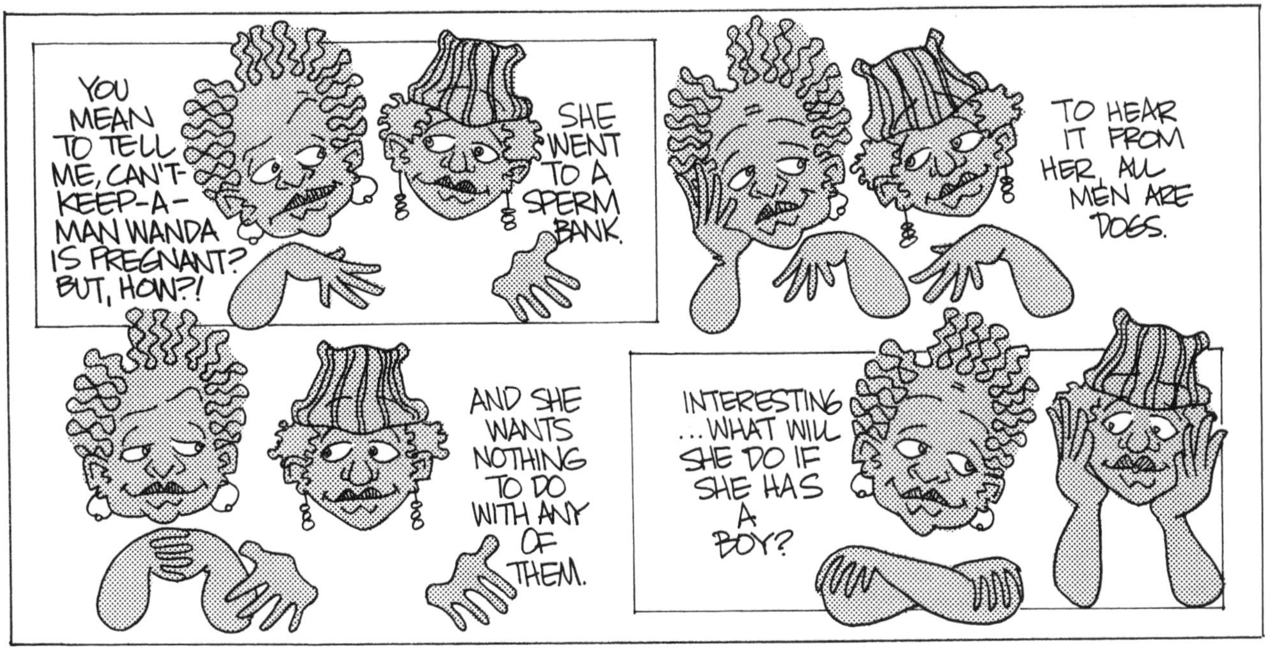
YOU MEAN TO TELL ME, CAN'T-KEEP-A-MAN WANDA IS PREGNANT? BUT, HOW?!
SHE WENT TO A SPERM BANK.
TO HEAR IT FROM HER, ALL MEN ARE DOGS.
AND SHE WANTS NOTHING TO DO WITH ANY OF THEM.
INTERESTING ...WHAT WILL SHE DO IF SHE HAS A BOY?

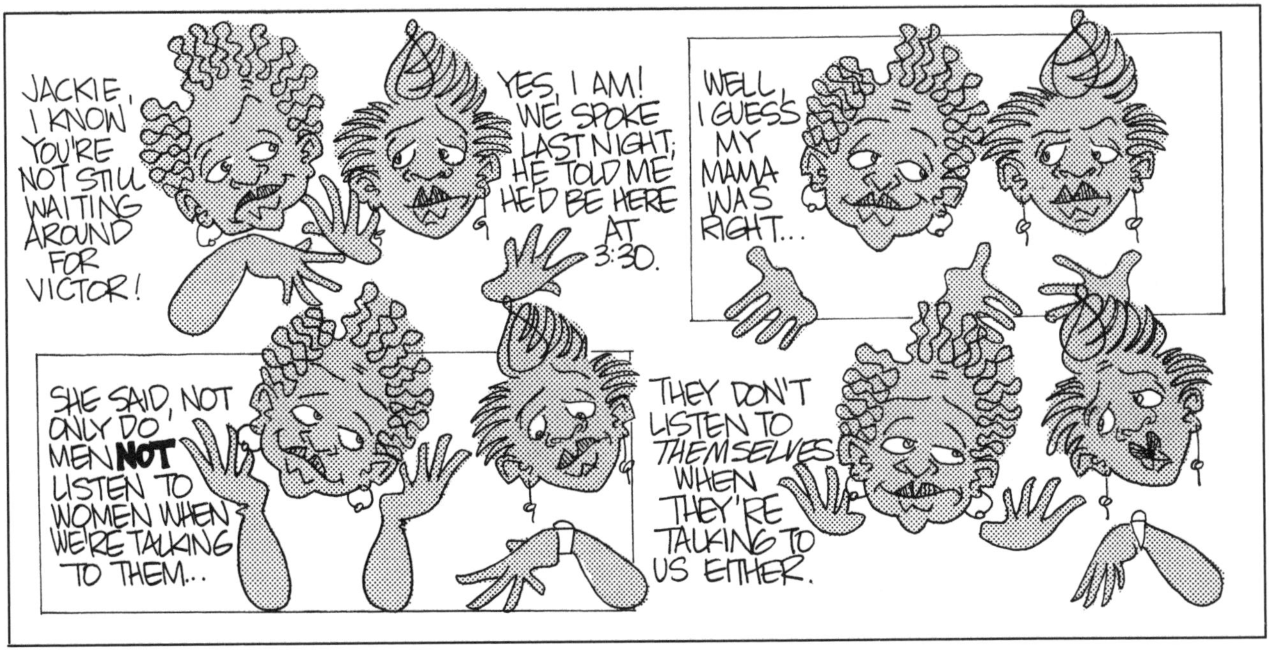
JACKIE, I KNOW YOU'RE NOT STILL WAITING AROUND FOR VICTOR!
YES, I AM! WE SPOKE LAST NIGHT; HE TOLD ME HE'D BE HERE AT 3:30.
WELL, I GUESS MY MAMA WAS RIGHT...
SHE SAID, NOT ONLY DO MEN NOT LISTEN TO WOMEN WHEN WE'RE TALKING TO THEM...
THEY DON'T LISTEN TO THEMSELVES WHEN THEY'RE TALKING TO US EITHER.

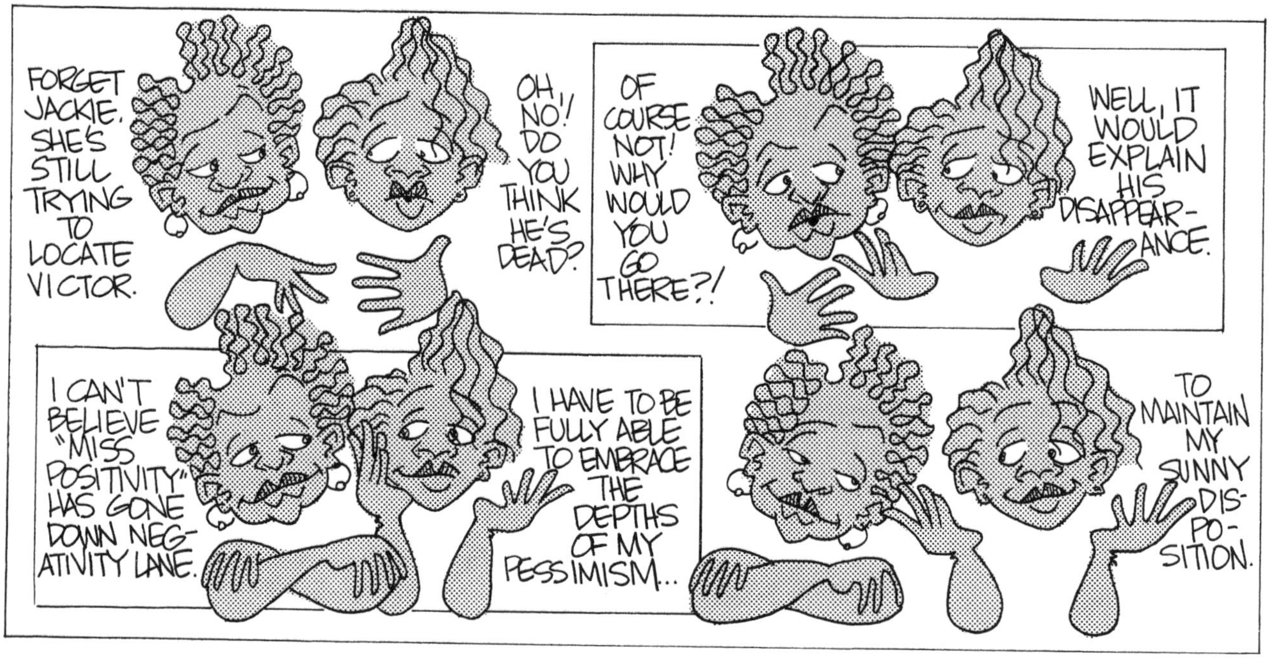
FORGET JACKIE. SHE'S STILL TRYING TO LOCATE VICTOR.
OH, NO!! DO YOU THINK HE'S DEAD?
OF COURSE NOT! WHY WOULD YOU GO THERE?!
WELL, IT WOULD EXPLAIN HIS DISAPPEARANCE.
I CAN'T BELIEVE "MISS POSITIVITY" HAS GONE DOWN NEGATIVITY LANE.
I HAVE TO BE FULLY ABLE TO EMBRACE THE DEPTHS OF MY PESSIMISM...
TO MAINTAIN MY SUNNY DISPOSITION.

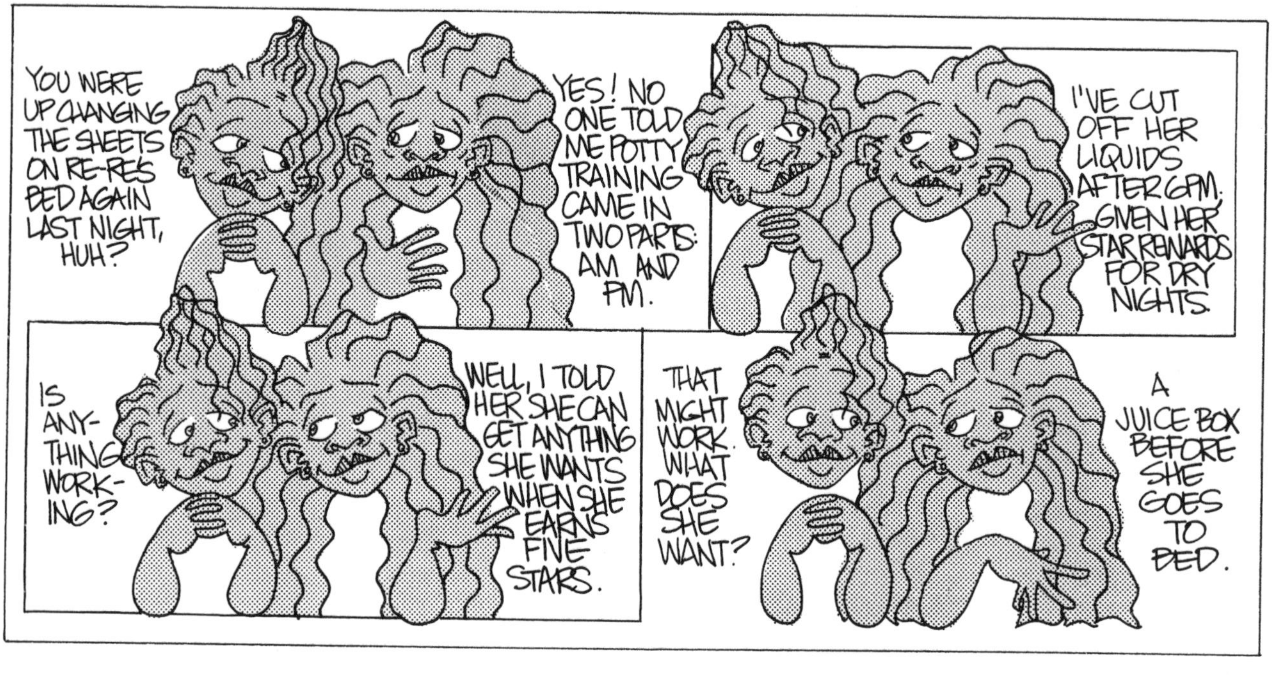
YOU WERE UP CHANGING THE SHEETS ON RE-RE'S BED AGAIN LAST NIGHT, HUH?
YES! NO ONE TOLD ME POTTY TRAINING CAME IN TWO PARTS: AM AND PM.
I'VE CUT OFF HER LIQUIDS AFTER 6PM. GIVEN HER STAR REWARDS FOR DRY NIGHTS.
IS ANYTHING WORKING?
WELL, I TOLD HER SHE CAN GET ANYTHING SHE WANTS WHEN SHE EARNS FIVE STARS.
THAT MIGHT WORK. WHAT DOES SHE WANT?
A JUICE BOX BEFORE SHE GOES TO BED.

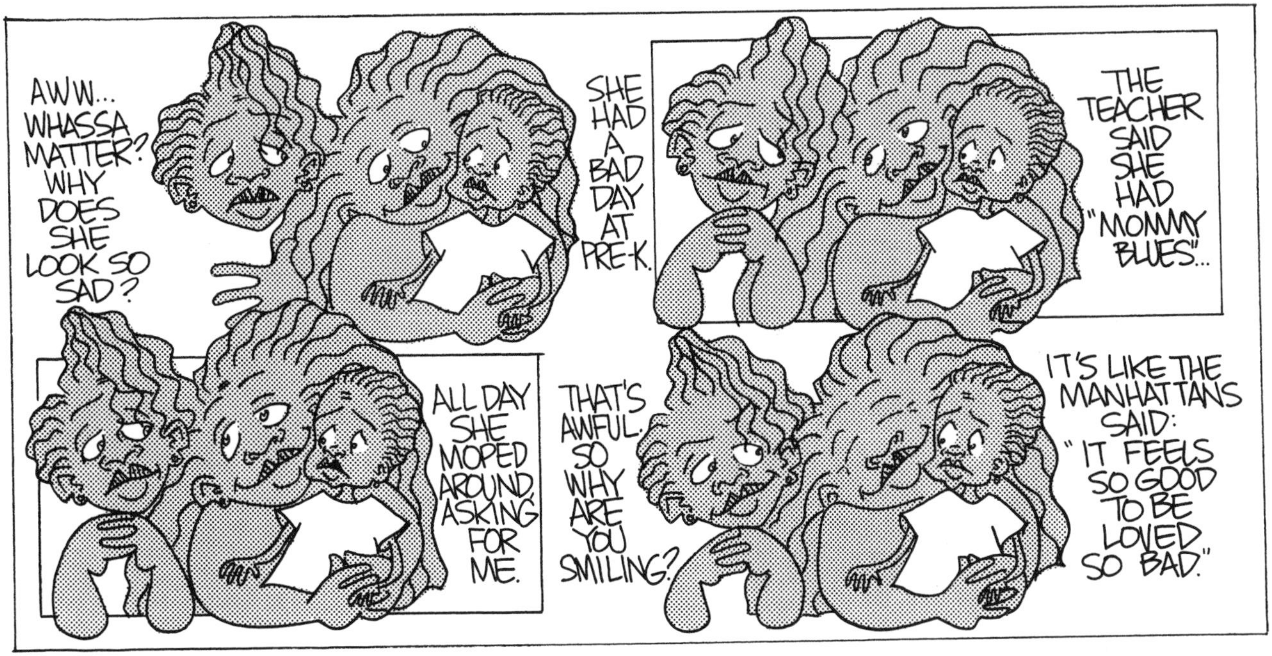
AWW... WHASSA MATTER? WHY DOES SHE LOOK SO SAD?
SHE HAD A BAD DAY AT PRE-K.
THE TEACHER SAID SHE HAD "MOMMY BLUES"...
ALL DAY SHE MOPED AROUND, ASKING FOR ME.
THAT'S AWFUL. SO WHY ARE YOU SMILING?
IT'S LIKE THE MANHATTANS SAID: "IT FEELS SO GOOD TO BE LOVED SO BAD."

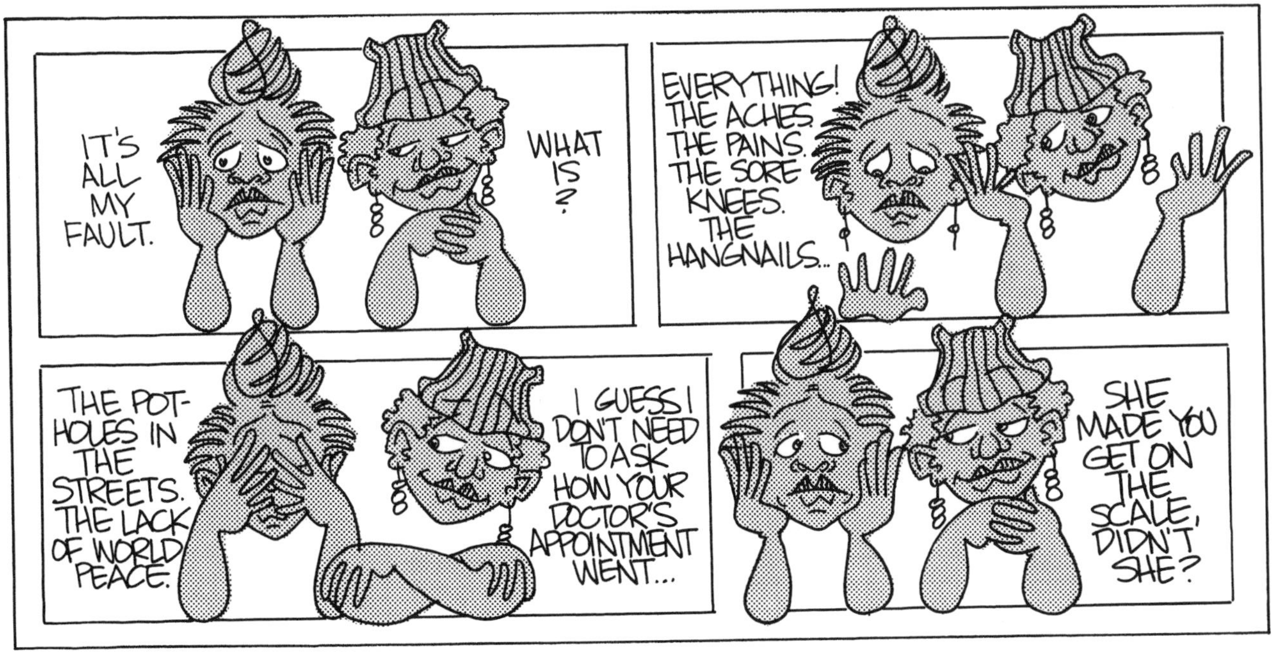
IT'S ALL MY FAULT.
WHAT IS?
EVERYTHING! THE ACHES. THE PAINS. THE SORE KNEES. THE HANGNAILS...
THE POT-HOLES IN THE STREETS. THE LACK OF WORLD PEACE.
I GUESS I DON'T NEED TO ASK HOW YOUR DOCTOR'S APPOINTMENT WENT...
SHE MADE YOU GET ON THE SCALE, DIDN'T SHE?

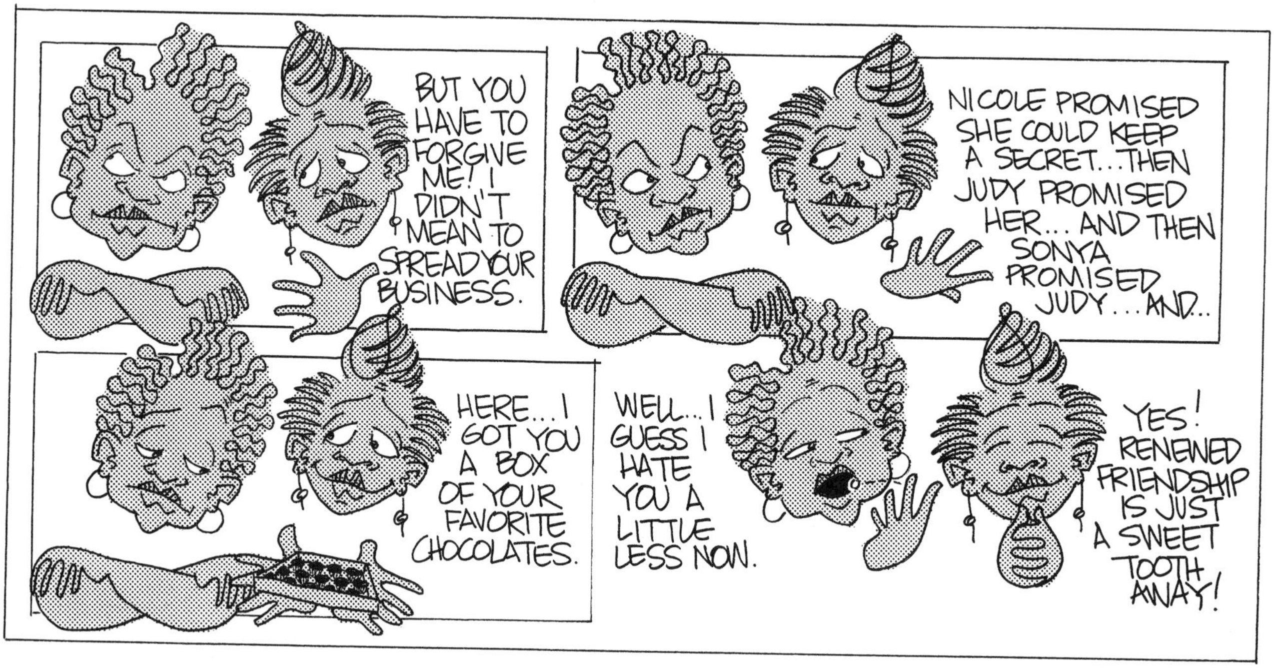
BUT YOU HAVE TO FORGIVE ME! I DIDN'T MEAN TO SPREAD YOUR BUSINESS.
NICOLE PROMISED SHE COULD KEEP A SECRET... THEN JUDY PROMISED HER... AND THEN SONYA PROMISED JUDY... AND...
HERE... I GOT YOU A BOX OF YOUR FAVORITE CHOCOLATES.
WELL... I GUESS I HATE YOU A LITTLE LESS NOW.
YES! RENEWED FRIENDSHIP IS JUST A SWEET TOOTH AWAY!

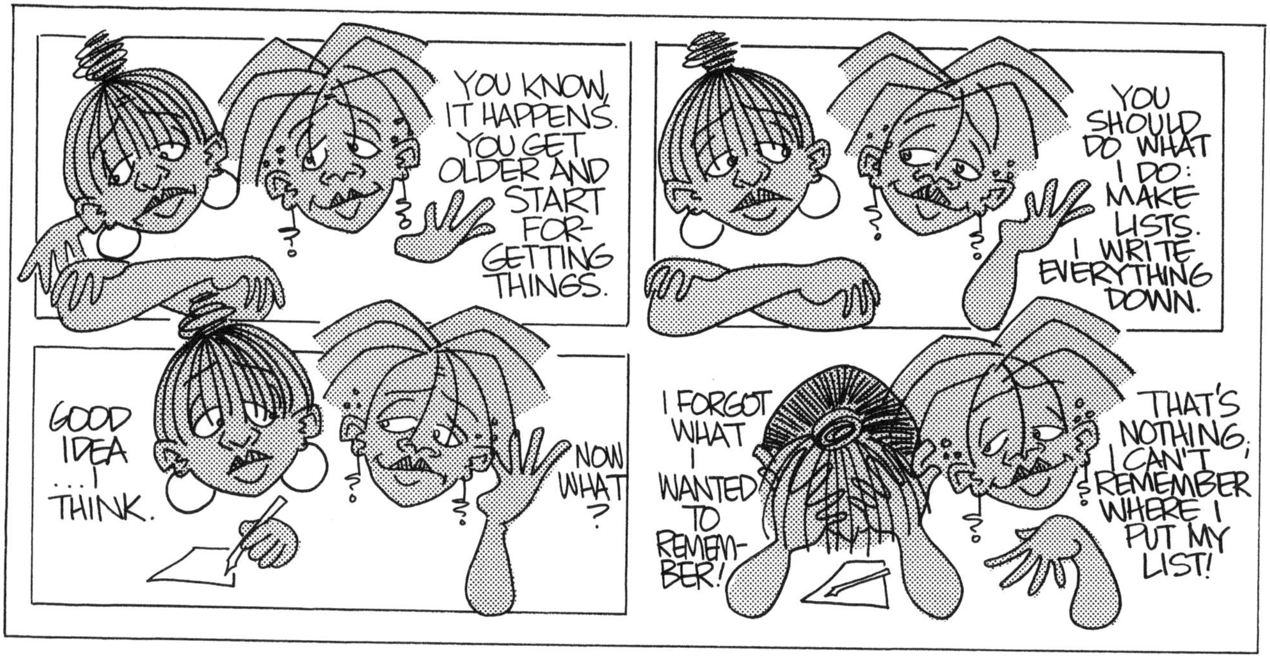
YOU KNOW, IT HAPPENS. YOU GET OLDER AND START FOR-GETTING THINGS.
YOU SHOULD DO WHAT I DO: MAKE LISTS. I WRITE EVERYTHING DOWN.
GOOD IDEA ... I THINK.
NOW WHAT ?
I FORGOT WHAT I WANTED TO REMEM-BER!
THAT'S NOTHING; I CAN'T REMEMBER WHERE I PUT MY LIST!

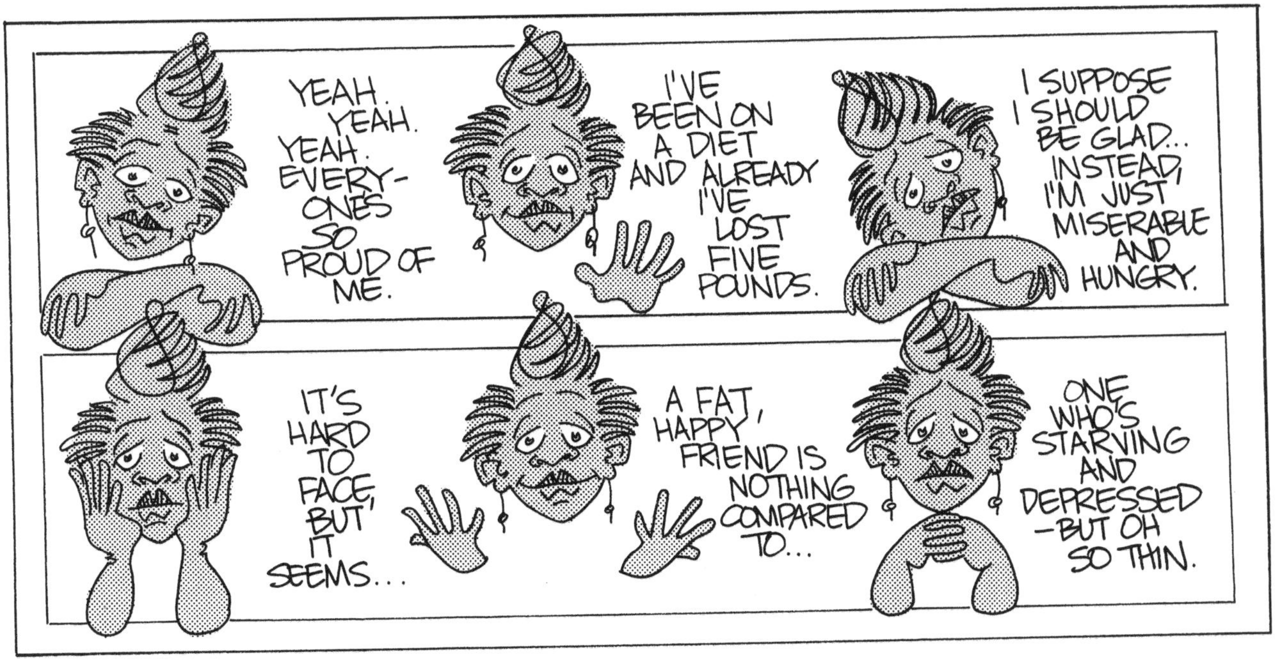
YEAH. YEAH. YEAH. EVERYONE'S SO PROUD OF ME.
I'VE BEEN ON A DIET AND ALREADY I'VE LOST FIVE POUNDS.
I SUPPOSE I SHOULD BE GLAD... INSTEAD, I'M JUST MISERABLE AND HUNGRY.
IT'S HARD TO FACE, BUT IT SEEMS...
A FAT, HAPPY FRIEND IS NOTHING COMPARED TO...
ONE WHO'S STARVING AND DEPRESSED -BUT OH SO THIN.

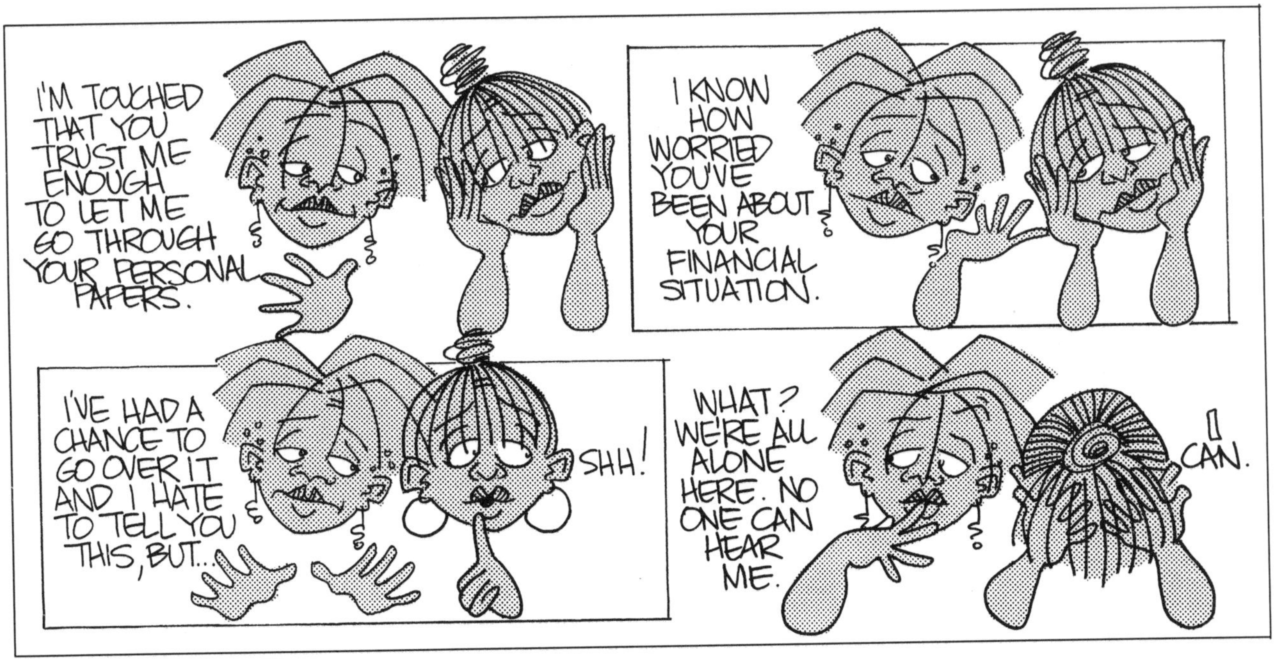
I'M TOUCHED THAT YOU TRUST ME ENOUGH TO LET ME GO THROUGH YOUR PERSONAL PAPERS.
I KNOW HOW WORRIED YOU'VE BEEN ABOUT YOUR FINANCIAL SITUATION.
I'VE HAD A CHANCE TO GO OVER IT AND I HATE TO TELL YOU THIS, BUT...
SHH!
WHAT? WE'RE ALL ALONE HERE. NO ONE CAN HEAR ME.
I CAN.

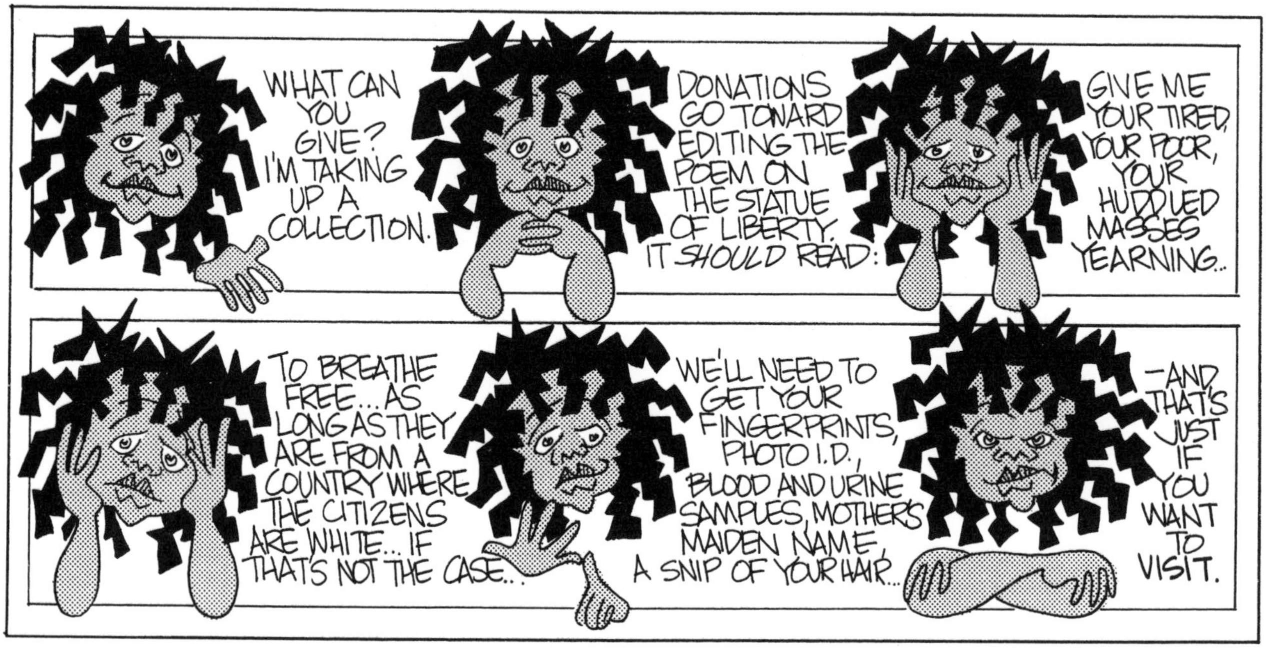
WHAT CAN YOU GIVE? I'M TAKING UP A COLLECTION.
DONATIONS GO TOWARD EDITING THE POEM ON THE STATUE OF LIBERTY. IT SHOULD READ:
GIVE ME YOUR TIRED, YOUR POOR, YOUR HUDDLED MASSES YEARNING...
TO BREATHE FREE... AS LONG AS THEY ARE FROM A COUNTRY WHERE THE CITIZENS ARE WHITE... IF THAT'S NOT THE CASE...
WE'LL NEED TO GET YOUR FINGERPRINTS, PHOTO I.D., BLOOD AND URINE SAMPLES, MOTHER'S MAIDEN NAME, A SNIP OF YOUR HAIR...
-AND THAT'S JUST IF YOU WANT TO VISIT.

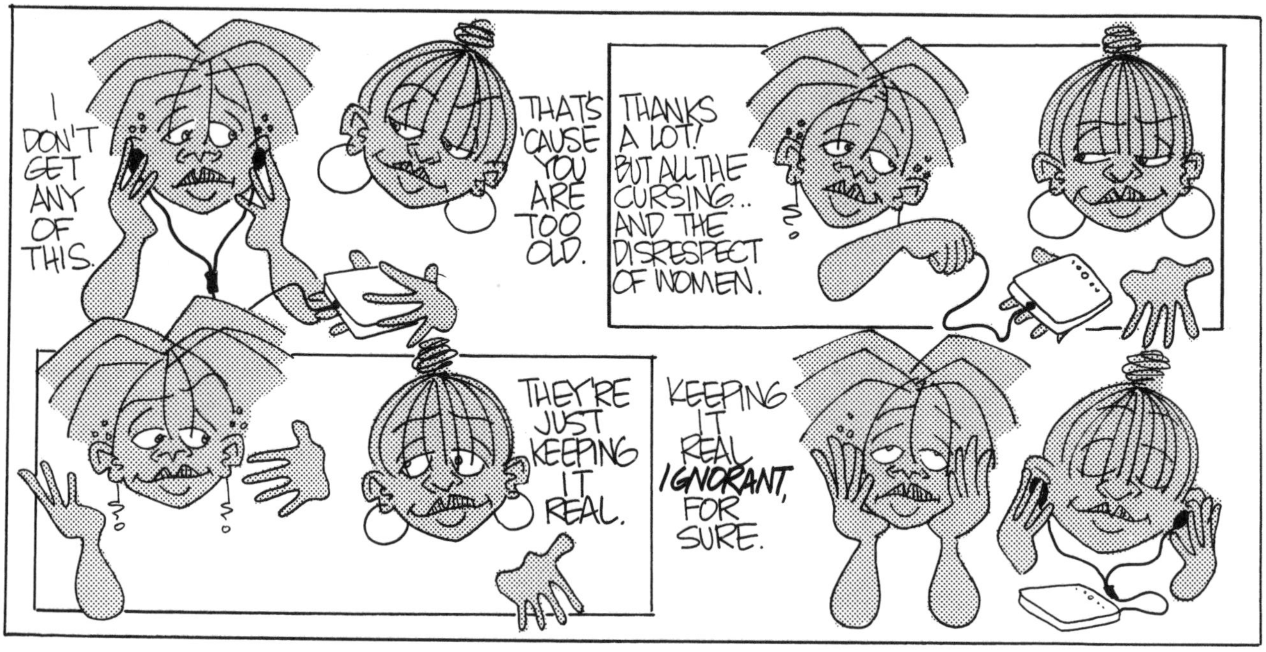
I DON'T GET ANY OF THIS.
THAT'S 'CAUSE YOU ARE TOO OLD.
THANKS A LOT! BUT ALL THE CURSING... AND THE DISRESPECT OF WOMEN.
THEY'RE JUST KEEPING IT REAL.
KEEPING IT REAL IGNORANT, FOR SURE.

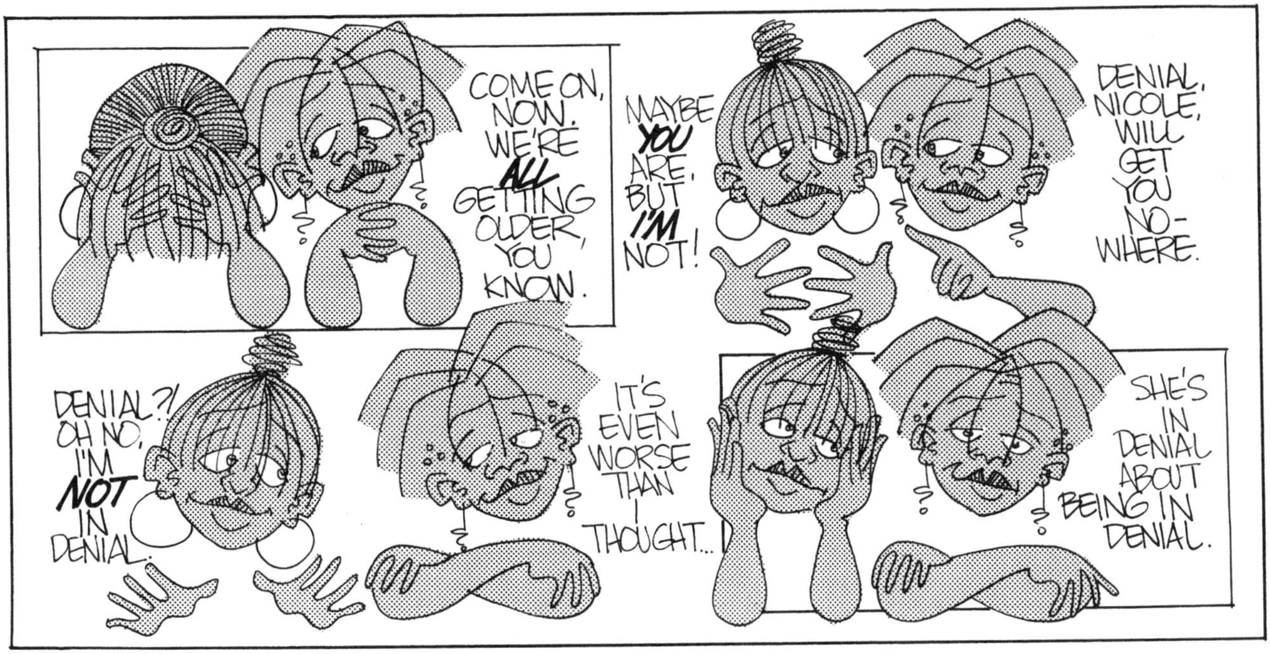
COME ON, NOW. WE'RE ALL GETTING OLDER, YOU KNOW.
MAYBE YOU ARE, BUT I'M NOT!
DENIAL, NICOLE, WILL GET YOU NO-WHERE.
DENIAL?! OH NO, I'M NOT IN DENIAL.
IT'S EVEN WORSE THAN I THOUGHT...
SHE'S IN DENIAL ABOUT BEING IN DENIAL.

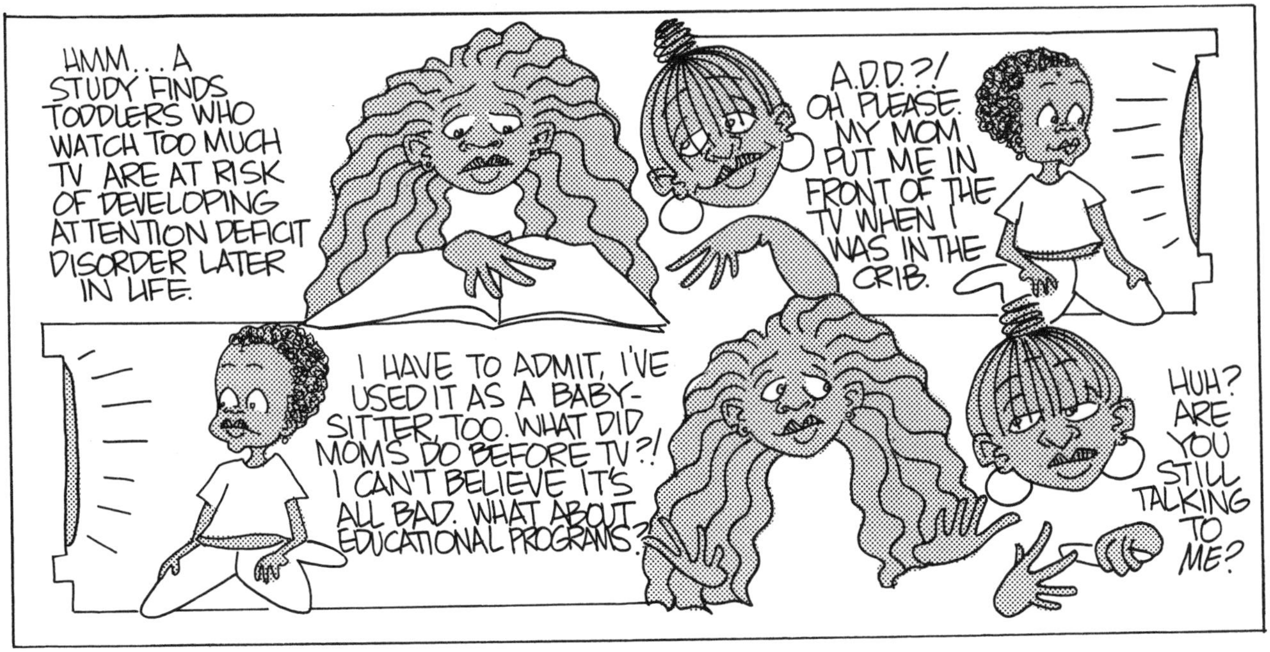
HMM... A STUDY FINDS TODDLERS WHO WATCH TOO MUCH TV ARE AT RISK OF DEVELOPING ATTENTION DEFICIT DISORDER LATER IN LIFE.
A.D.D.?! OH PLEASE. MY MOM PUT ME IN FRONT OF THE TV WHEN I WAS IN THE CRIB.
I HAVE TO ADMIT, I'VE USED IT AS A BABY-SITTER, TOO. WHAT DID MOMS DO BEFORE TV?! I CAN'T BELIEVE IT'S ALL BAD. WHAT ABOUT EDUCATIONAL PROGRAMS?
HUH? ARE YOU STILL TALKING TO ME?

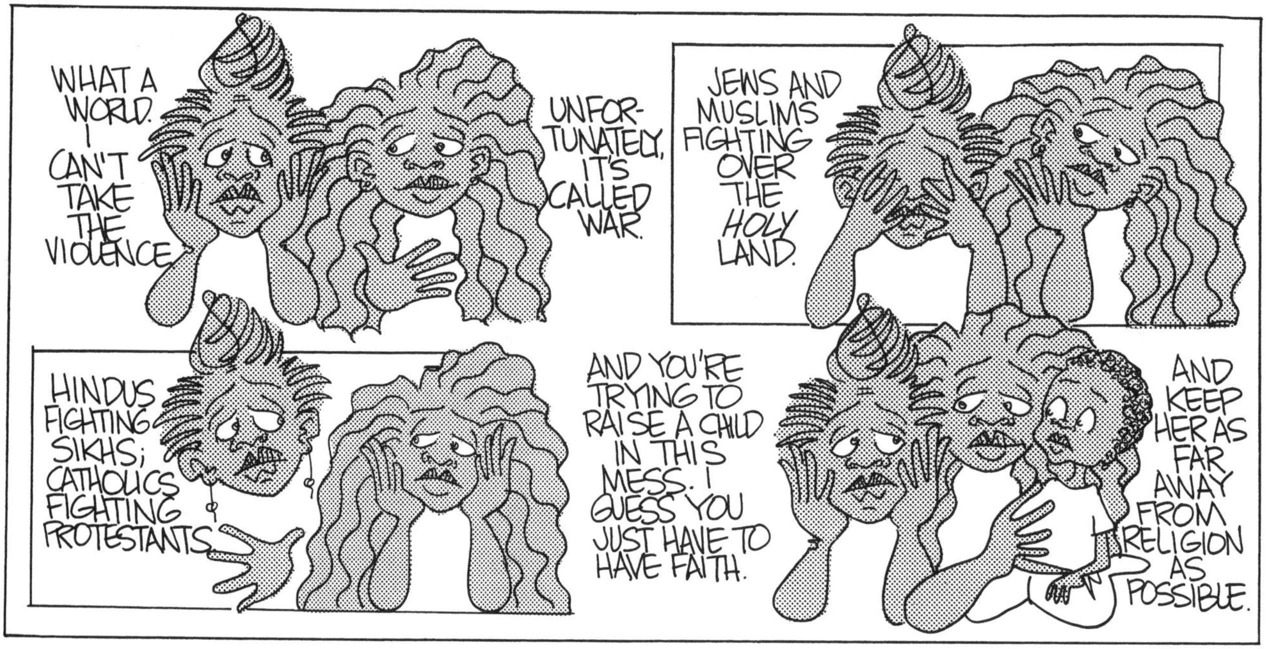
WHAT A WORLD. I CAN'T TAKE THE VIOLENCE.
UNFORTUNATELY, IT'S CALLED WAR.
JEWS AND MUSLIMS FIGHTING OVER THE *HOLY* LAND.
HINDUS FIGHTING SIKHS; CATHOLICS FIGHTING PROTESTANTS.
AND YOU'RE TRYING TO RAISE A CHILD IN THIS MESS. I GUESS YOU JUST HAVE TO HAVE FAITH.
AND KEEP HER AS FAR AWAY FROM RELIGION AS POSSIBLE.

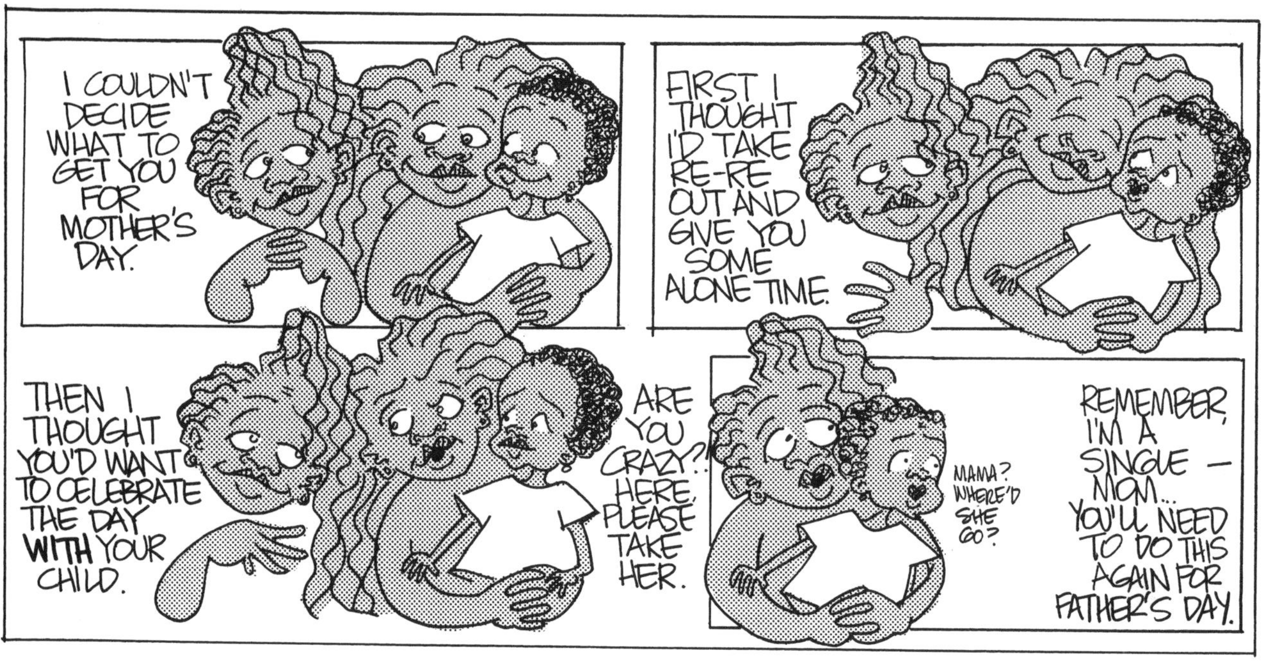
I COULDN'T DECIDE WHAT TO GET YOU FOR MOTHER'S DAY.
FIRST I THOUGHT I'D TAKE RE-RE OUT AND GIVE YOU SOME ALONE TIME.
THEN I THOUGHT YOU'D WANT TO CELEBRATE THE DAY **WITH** YOUR CHILD.
ARE YOU CRAZY?! HERE, PLEASE TAKE HER.
MAMA? WHERE'D SHE GO?
REMEMBER, I'M A SINGLE — MOM... YOU'LL NEED TO DO THIS AGAIN FOR FATHER'S DAY.

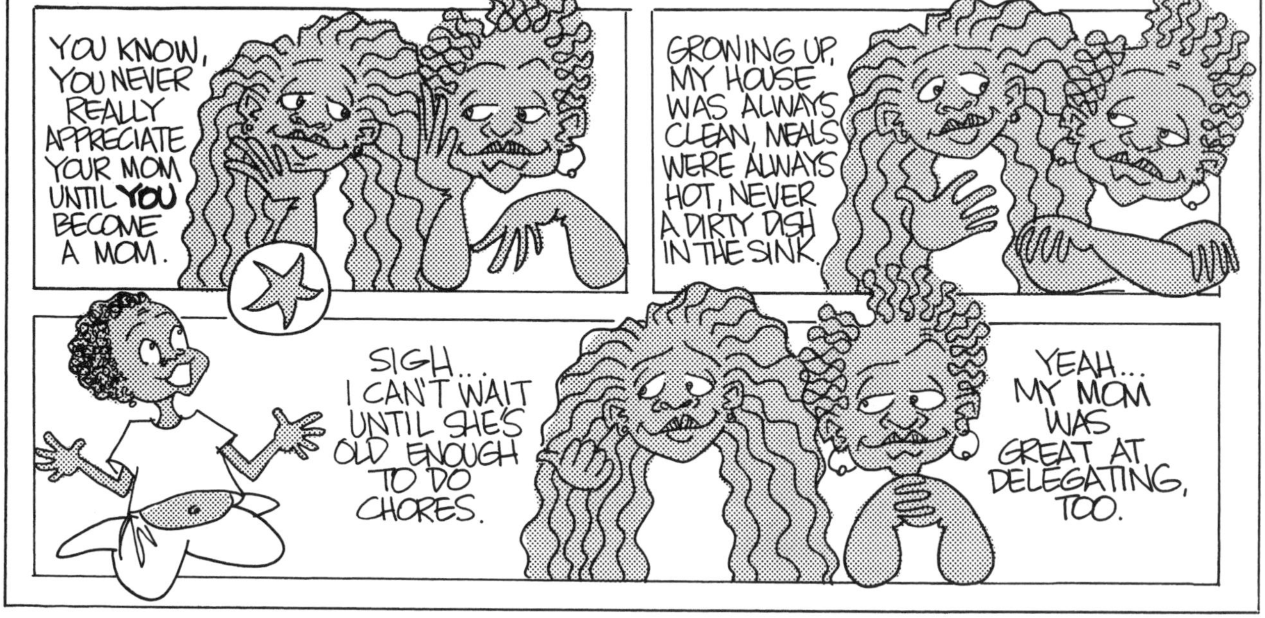
YOU KNOW, YOU NEVER REALLY APPRECIATE YOUR MOM UNTIL **YOU** BECOME A MOM.
GROWING UP, MY HOUSE WAS ALWAYS CLEAN, MEALS WERE ALWAYS HOT, NEVER A DIRTY DISH IN THE SINK.
SIGH... I CAN'T WAIT UNTIL SHE'S OLD ENOUGH TO DO CHORES.
YEAH... MY MOM WAS GREAT AT DELEGATING, TOO.

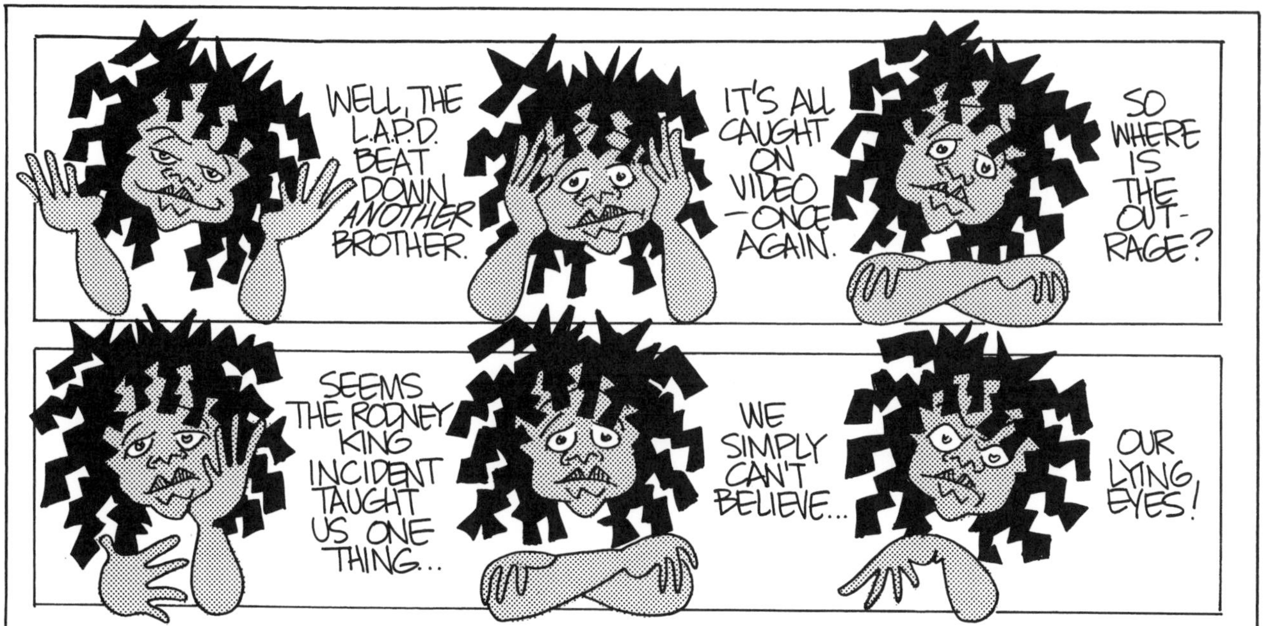
WELL, THE L.A.P.D. BEAT DOWN *ANOTHER* BROTHER.
IT'S ALL CAUGHT ON VIDEO —ONCE AGAIN.
SO WHERE IS THE OUT-RAGE?
SEEMS THE RODNEY KING INCIDENT TAUGHT US ONE THING...
WE SIMPLY CAN'T BELIEVE...
OUR LYING EYES!

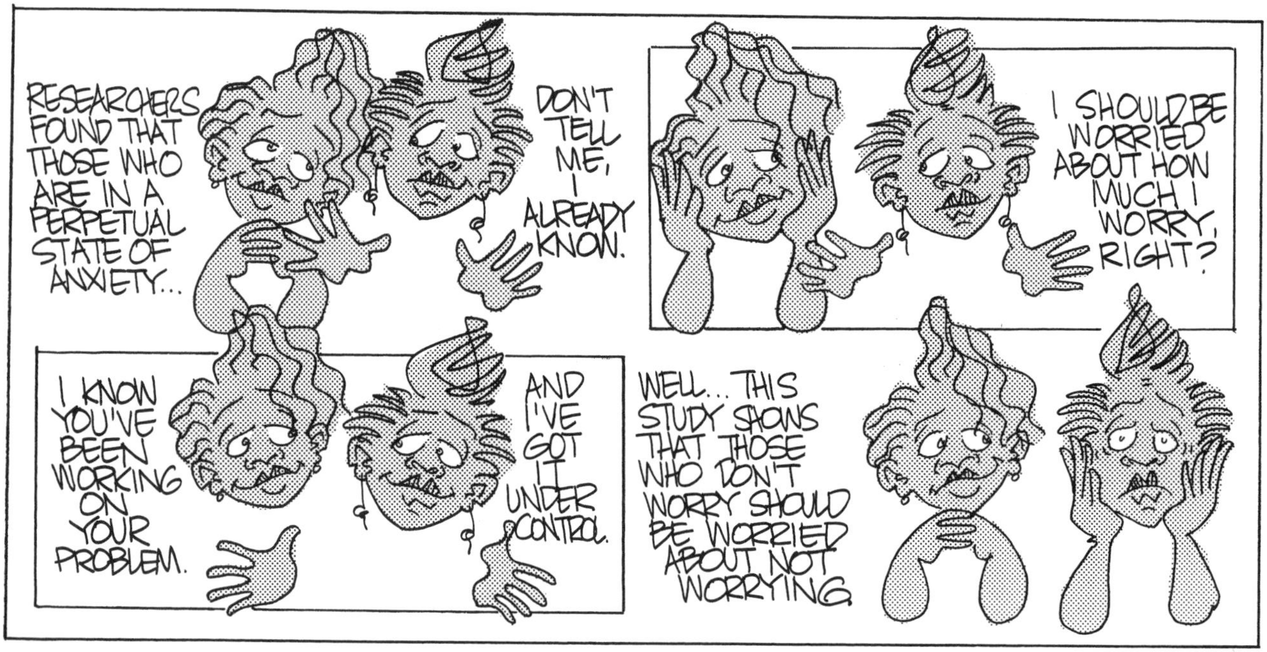

RESEARCHERS FOUND THAT THOSE WHO ARE IN A PERPETUAL STATE OF ANXIETY...
DON'T TELL ME, I ALREADY KNOW.
I SHOULD BE WORRIED ABOUT HOW MUCH I WORRY, RIGHT?
I KNOW YOU'VE BEEN WORKING ON YOUR PROBLEM.
AND I'VE GOT IT UNDER CONTROL.
WELL... THIS STUDY SHOWS THAT THOSE WHO DON'T WORRY SHOULD BE WORRIED ABOUT NOT WORRYING.

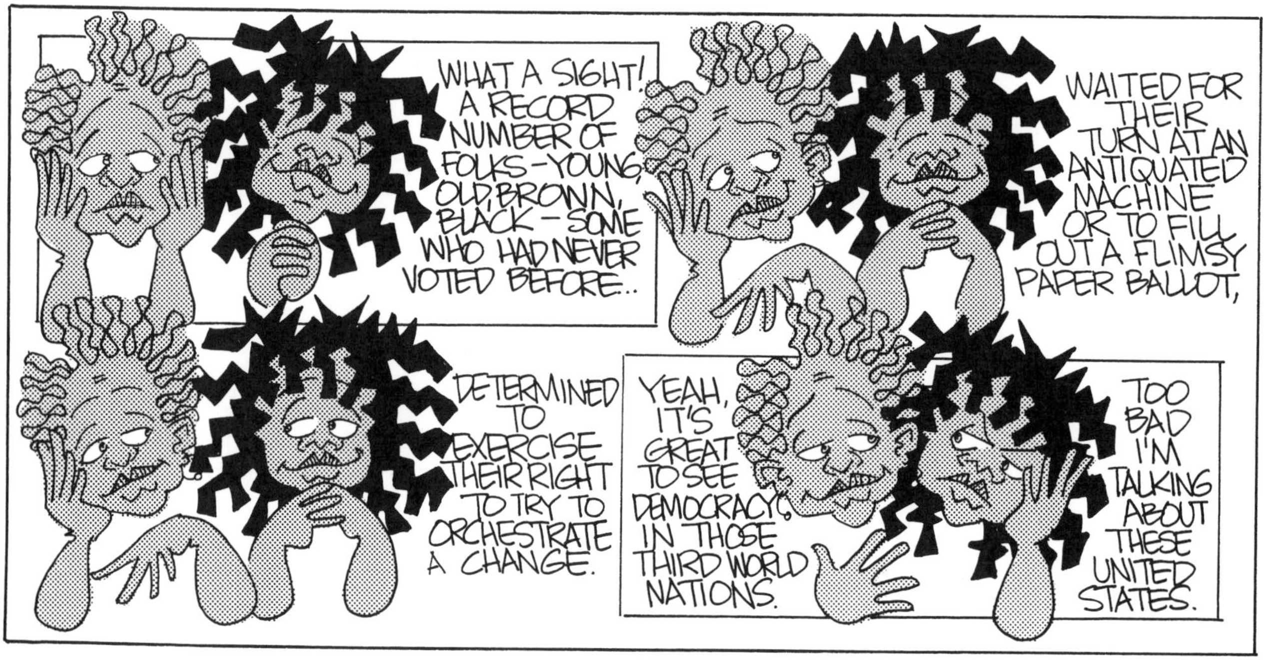

WHAT A SIGHT! A RECORD NUMBER OF FOLKS - YOUNG, OLD, BROWN, BLACK - SOME WHO HAD NEVER VOTED BEFORE...
WAITED FOR THEIR TURN AT AN ANTIQUATED MACHINE OR TO FILL OUT A FLIMSY PAPER BALLOT,
DETERMINED TO EXERCISE THEIR RIGHT TO TRY TO ORCHESTRATE A CHANGE.
YEAH, IT'S GREAT TO SEE DEMOCRACY, IN THOSE THIRD WORLD NATIONS.
TOO BAD I'M TALKING ABOUT THESE UNITED STATES.

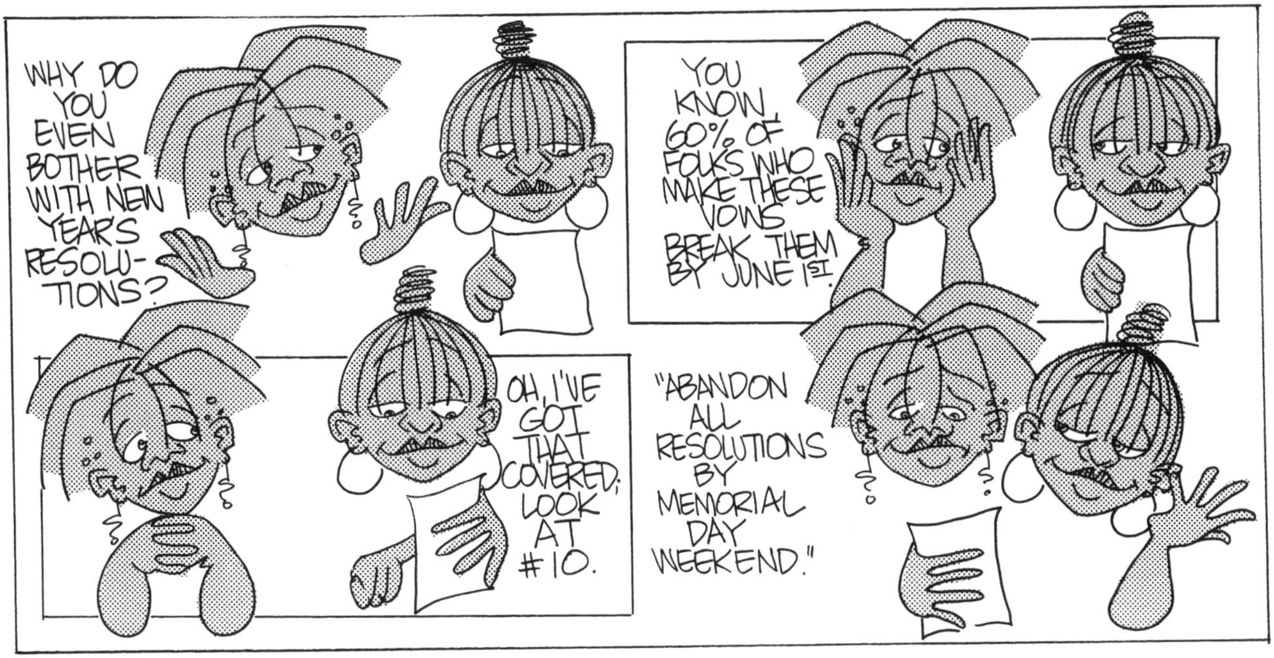
WHY DO YOU EVEN BOTHER WITH NEW YEAR'S RESOLUTIONS?
YOU KNOW, 60% OF FOLKS WHO MAKE THESE VOWS BREAK THEM BY JUNE 1ST.
OH, I'VE GOT THAT COVERED; LOOK AT #10.
"ABANDON ALL RESOLUTIONS BY MEMORIAL DAY WEEKEND."

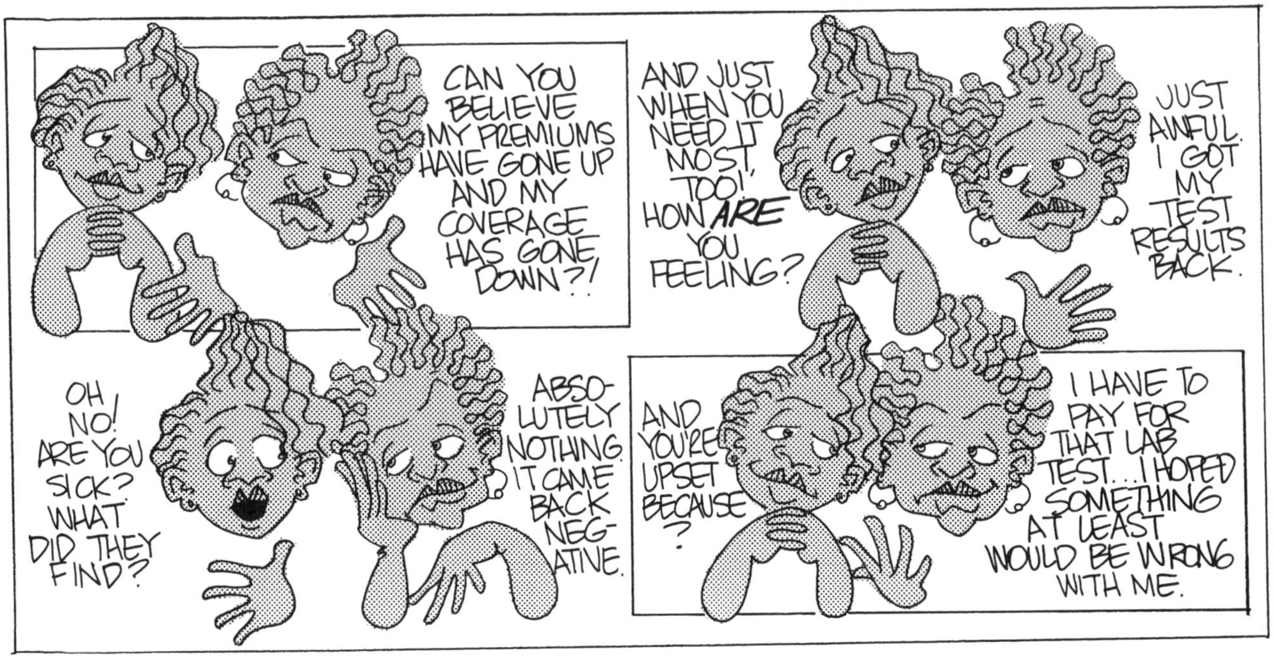
CAN YOU BELIEVE MY PREMIUMS HAVE GONE UP AND MY COVERAGE HAS GONE DOWN?!
AND JUST WHEN YOU NEED IT MOST, TOO! HOW ARE YOU FEELING?
JUST AWFUL. I GOT MY TEST RESULTS BACK.
OH NO! ARE YOU SICK? WHAT DID THEY FIND?
ABSOLUTELY NOTHING. IT CAME BACK NEGATIVE.
AND YOU'RE UPSET BECAUSE ?
I HAVE TO PAY FOR THAT LAB TEST... I HOPED SOMETHING AT LEAST WOULD BE WRONG WITH ME.

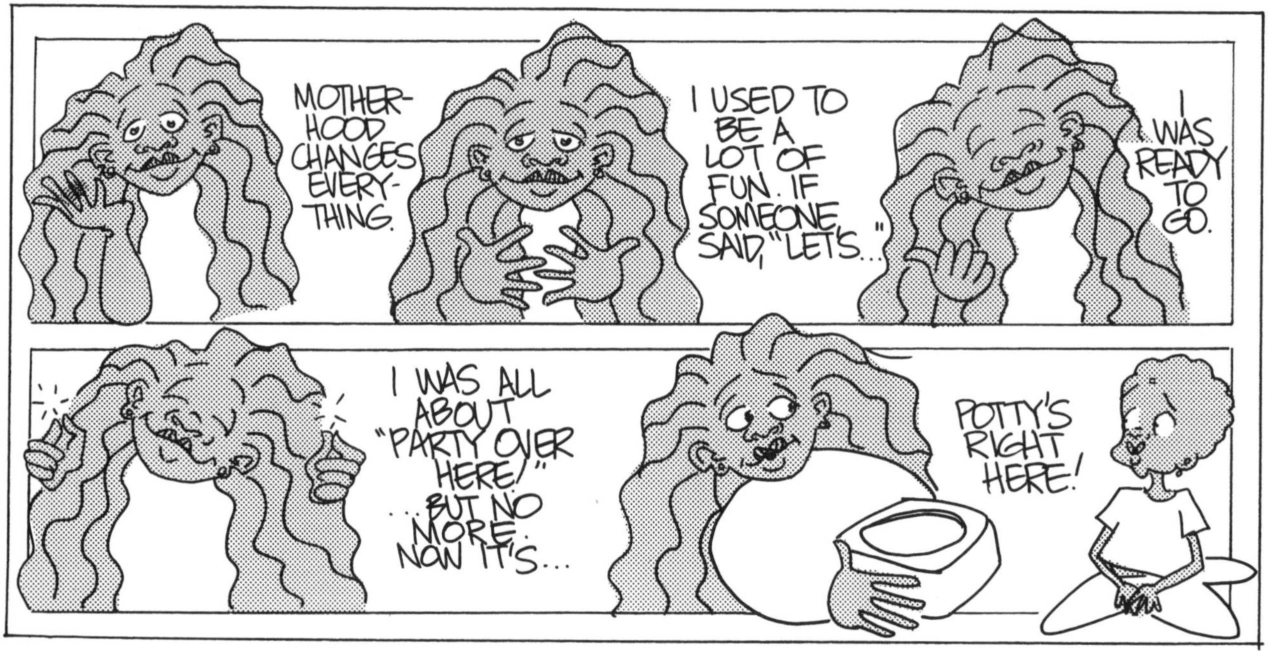

MOTHERHOOD CHANGES EVERYTHING.
I USED TO BE A LOT OF FUN. IF SOMEONE SAID, "LET'S..."
I WAS READY TO GO.
I WAS ALL ABOUT "PARTY OVER HERE!" ...BUT NO MORE. NOW IT'S...
POTTY'S RIGHT HERE!

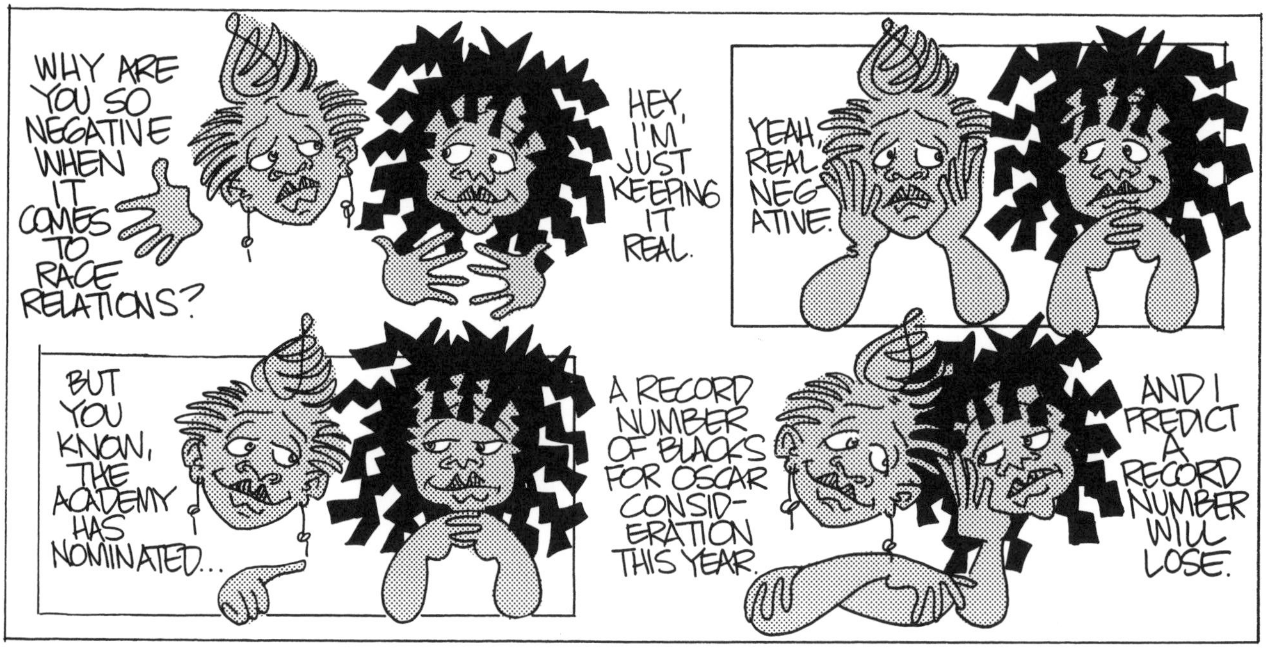

WHY ARE YOU SO NEGATIVE WHEN IT COMES TO RACE RELATIONS?
HEY, I'M JUST KEEPING IT REAL.
YEAH, REAL NEGATIVE.
BUT YOU KNOW, THE ACADEMY HAS NOMINATED...
A RECORD NUMBER OF BLACKS FOR OSCAR CONSIDERATION THIS YEAR.
AND I PREDICT A RECORD NUMBER WILL LOSE.

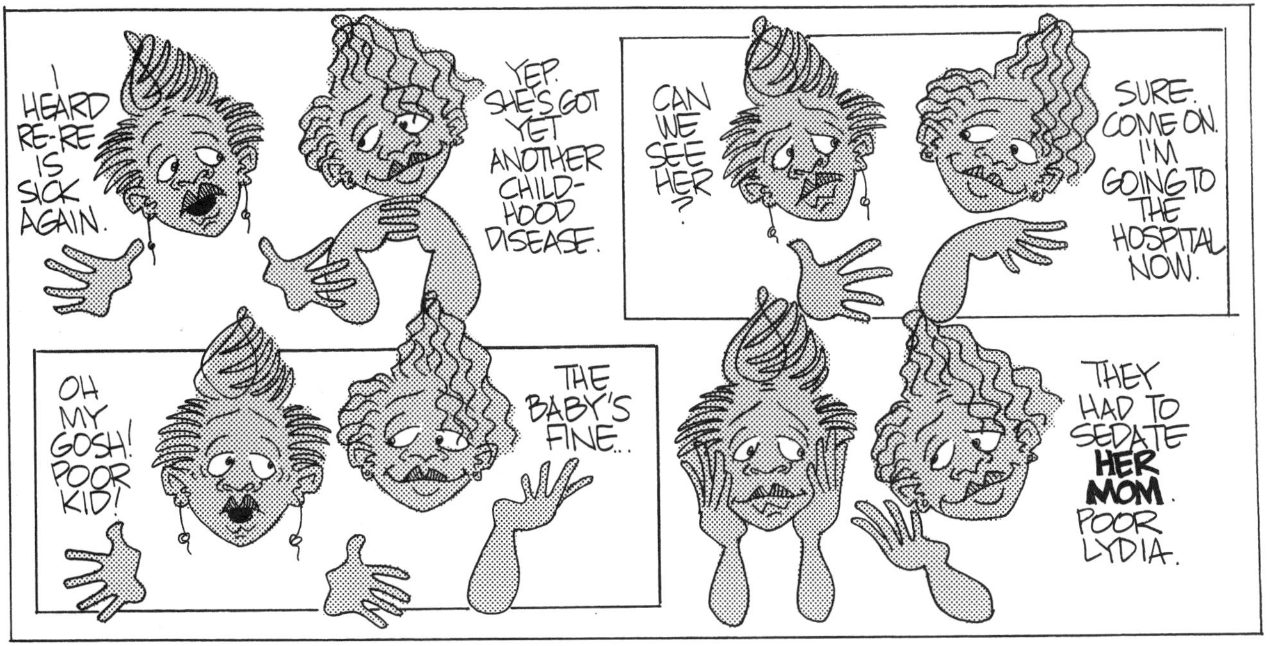
I HEARD RE-RE IS SICK AGAIN.
YEP. SHE'S GOT YET ANOTHER CHILD-HOOD DISEASE.
CAN WE SEE HER?
SURE. COME ON. I'M GOING TO THE HOSPITAL NOW.
OH MY GOSH! POOR KID!
THE BABY'S FINE...
THEY HAD TO SEDATE **HER MOM**. POOR LYDIA.

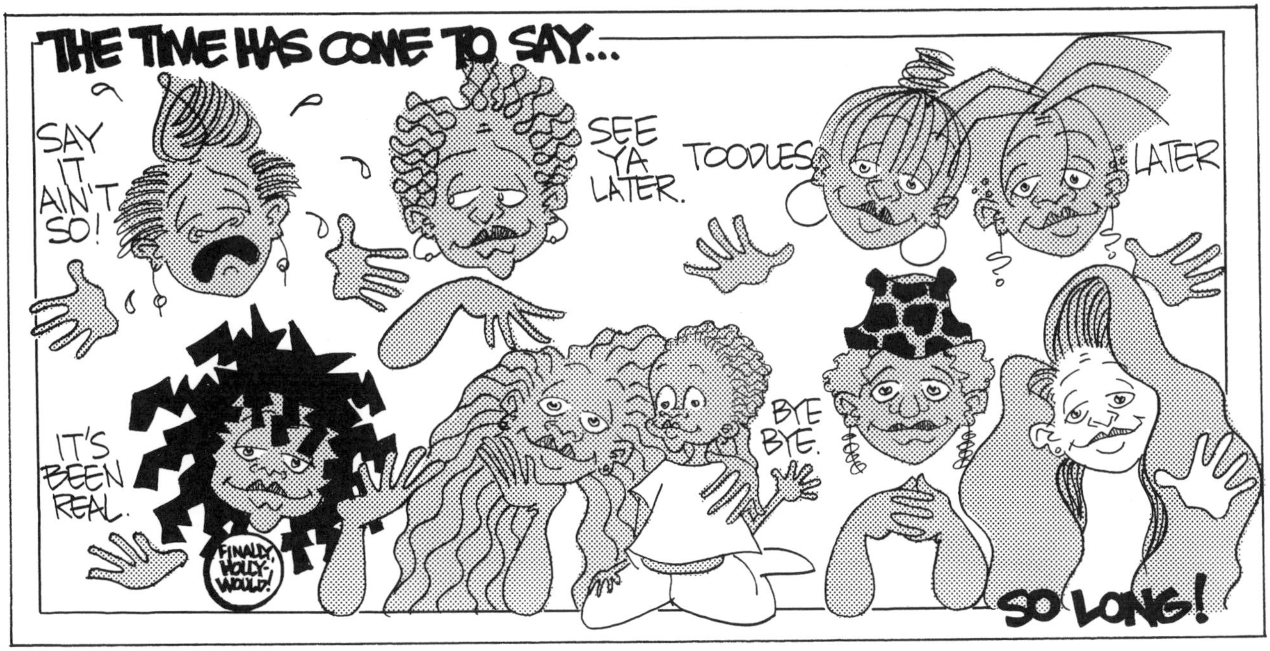
THE TIME HAS COME TO SAY...
SAY IT AIN'T SO!
SEE YA LATER.
TOODLES
LATER
IT'S BEEN REAL.
FINALLY, HOLLY-WOULD!
BYE BYE.
SO LONG!

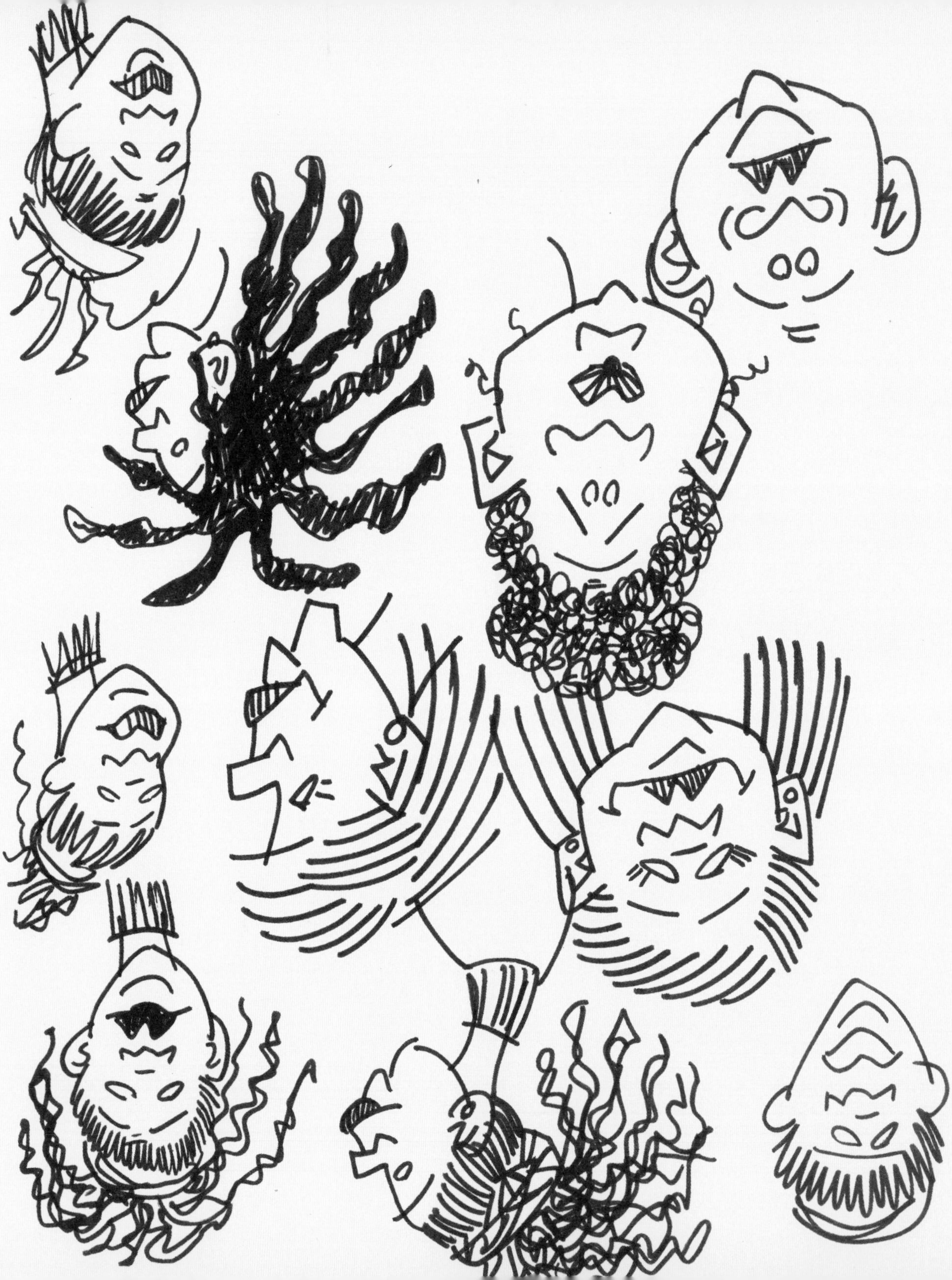

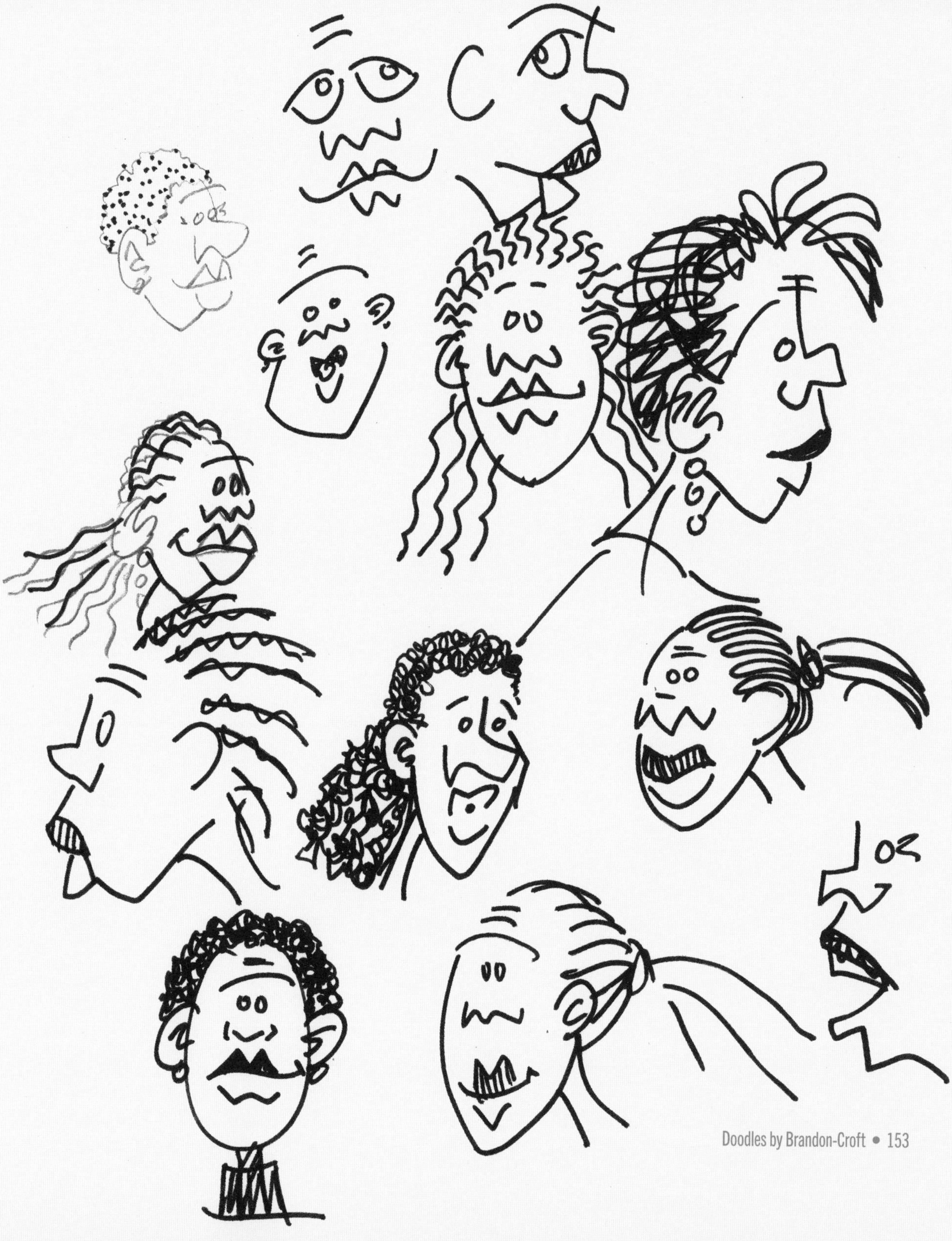

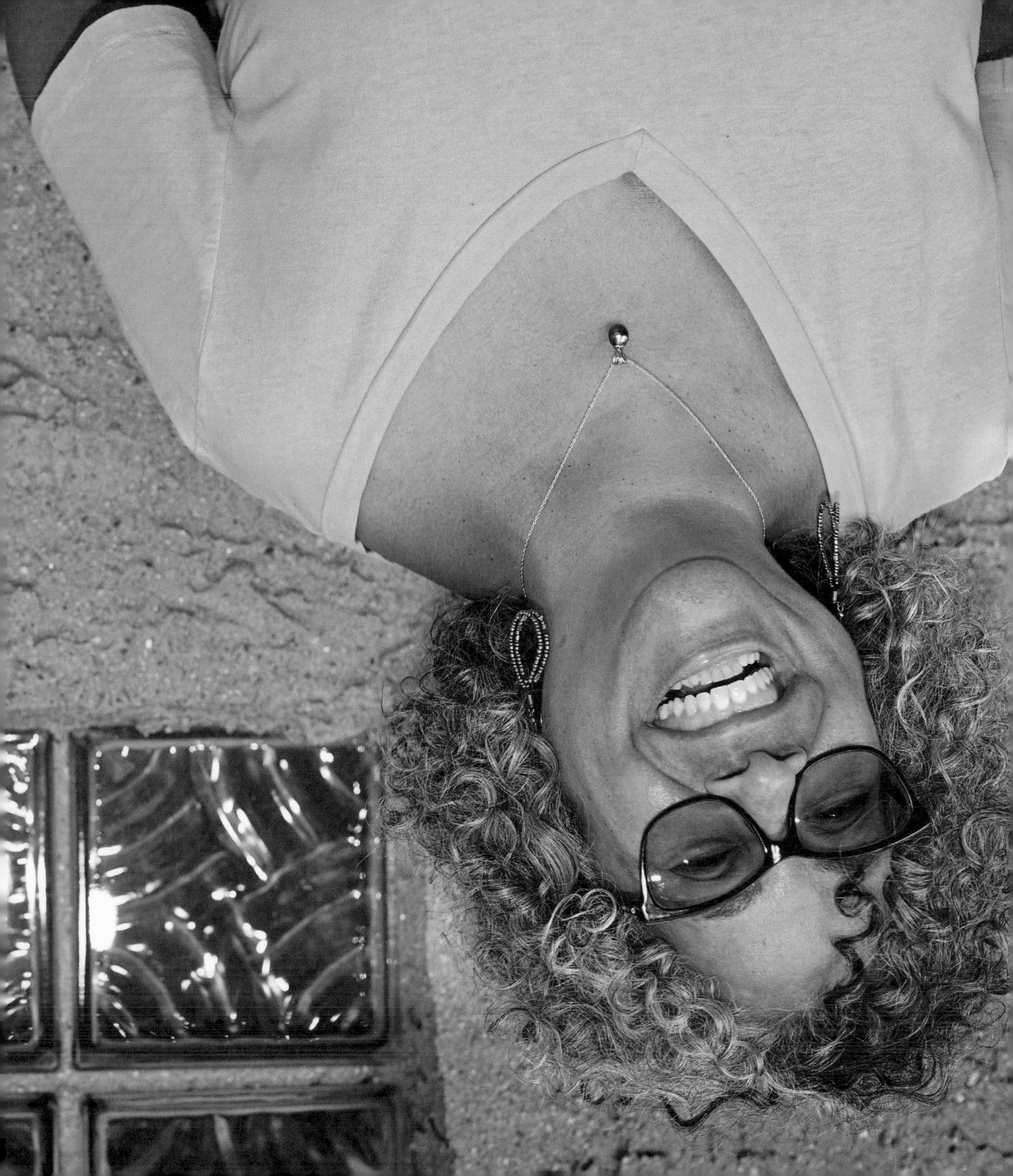

Where I'm Coming From Now
Barbara Brandon-Croft

So these days, when I run into someone who I haven't seen in a while, I might be asked, "Are you still doing that, 'art thing?'" Ha! A question every artist *loves* to hear. They may have a vague recollection of me doing some cartooning *somewhere*. It's actually a fair question. My syndication ended in 2005. All the fanfare I received when I got my first major newspaper then landed a huge syndicate— and made history for being the *first* Black woman in the mainstream press—has long since faded. It's wild to think that when I started pitching my comic, I was a fearless, wide-eyed twenty-something. Today I'm a more pragmatic mom of a college graduate and celebrating my *silver* wedding anniversary. Wow, *Now, that's* a lot of time.

Between then and now, life happened—marriage, baby (for sure), and much gotta-pay-the-bills employment. I worked a bunch of jobs—even while in syndication. You have to have a lot of newspapers (like *hundreds*) to make a living in this field. I had a respectable amount of papers (around sixty-five), and at my peak, I didn't have to hustle for extra work to make ends meet, but that time was short lived.

So I worked other jobs, most often in the fashion industry. Which made sense, since that's what I knew. (My first job while still in Syracuse was at JCPenney, dressing mannequins.) I worked sample sales, runway shows, even as a fashion features editor at *Women's Wear Daily* for a time. A friend from my *Essence* years as the fashion and beauty writer turned me onto fact checking. (Thank you, Ruth Manuel Logan!) Now *that* was a gig that stuck.

I started out a freelancer and ended up as the research director at *Parents* magazine for some eighteen years until it folded. It was during my time at *Parents* when my syndication ended. I knew it was coming. My newspaper count had dropped to under a dozen. For the longest, no one there even knew I was a cartoonist. *When/how exactly does that conversation even come up?* Some folks would comment on how they liked my handwriting and, on occasion, I'd disclose my alter ego. But as the 9-to-5 intensified (being a fact checker is no joke), "my girls" took a back seat. Oh, I still watched the news insatiably and still held strong opinions on life, but only those closest to me were privy to my point of view. I no longer processed my thoughts through my characters with my pen.

While "my girls" played a lesser role in my otherwise busy life, they were never far. After all, I'd based them on my real-life friends and, of course, myself. So how far *could* they go? We all (my friends—real and imagined) reveled in the idea of an Obama presidency back in 2007 when he announced his plan to run, and like in actual life, the "we" was not a monolith. Some of us thought it could never happen, while others (like I imagine, a more grown up Re-Re) held an unyielding hope that it would. Those two camps were absolutely generational. And then during Obama's eight years as president, I knew that for the overwhelming majority, the sentiment among my characters would be that Obama could do no wrong, while a smaller contingency would be wary and worried that he wasn't doing enough. I didn't record these times on paper, but my observations and interpretations remained clear.

In pulling this book together, I was asked to go through *all* the strips I'd done for Universal Press Syndicate. It was a daunting task. I don't know an artist alive who can look over their past work—let alone work they did twenty-plus years ago—and not expect the experience to be a bit wince-worthy. But while editing down those fourteen years of *Where I'm Coming From*, I started thinking, *Hey, I wasn't so bad. I was actually kinda good.* I even chuckled a few times, amazed at how I still feel very much what I felt then.

I have to credit my dad for my comic strip chops. My indoctrination into the language of cartooning was total immersion. My dad lived and breathed comics—*his* comics, in particular. All my life he was constantly working on something. That's all I saw: Dad drawing. Growing up, we were surrounded by his art on the walls of our home. When his strip *Luther* was picked up for national syndication back in the late sixties, it was a dream come true for him. But even before then (and certainly after), he was drawing and writing comics nonstop. I had a sho' 'nuff, living role model *in my house*! That's why when I was asked if I could come up with a cartoon feature, I had the confidence to say yes without hesitation. I didn't really doubt my abilities because I had *seen* it done.

My dad was on a mission. His work deliberately pointed to this nation's inability to reckon with or even recognize the impact of racism. My champion at Universal Press Syndicate, the late Lee Salem, then-editorial director (who I miss beyond measure), encouraged me to amp up my views on racism and sexism as well. I started talking less about romantic relationships and more about women's issues—Black women's issues in particular—and where we fit in this world that continues to marginalize us.

It was about ten years ago when someone, who I didn't know but who knew me (or at least, knew my work), told me that she was one of many who still loved *Where I'm Coming From*. She said she knew women who said that my work had made an impact on their lives. I had no idea I had a "following." *What?* I mean, I knew *Where I'm Coming From* was filling a void. Nowhere on the comics pages did you see Black women speaking their minds. My characters directed their thoughts straight to the reader. It was kind of an in-your-face vibe I was going for. When I had them talking to each other, I hoped to invoke an intimacy with the reader, as if they were eavesdropping on a private conversation. It hadn't occurred to me then that the strip was actually resonating with so many people and even capable of leaving an indelible mark. I did get letters from women thanking me for telling their story (*sweet!*), but I also got some not-so-fan letters from others accusing me of being anti-men and anti-white (*rolling eyes emoji*). So I wasn't sure exactly where my work landed on the "impact scale."

That young woman who knew me but I didn't know? Tara Nakashima Donahue very gingerly and respectfully asked me if I would agree to participate in an exhibit she was putting together of women cartoonists. I was like, *me?* I haven't done anything new since…well, *forever*. Frankly, I wasn't sure I still had it in me. Hadn't my drawing table morphed into a computer stand? Weren't all my pens completely dried out? Where had I stashed my light box anyway? She said, we could show strips you've already done. Hmm. Now I'm thinking, *no need to do anything extra? I can get with that*. So, I agreed. From that point on, Tara became this gentle, encouraging force in my life. And like an archeologist on a dig, she started to unearth and dust off the old cartoonist inside me. My very own Mary Leakey!

It was Tara who suggested that if I didn't have the time to draw new strips (a full-time gig at a magazine leaves you little extra time), she could scan some of my past work and digitally remove the dialogue and I could use those drawings to make new strips. She was delicately peeling back the layers of the dormant cartoonist within. Yet, I remained unconvinced. I was like, *we'll see*. Truth be told, I knew I had something to offer and maybe, just maybe, my voice still *needed* to be heard.

Then it happened—the unimaginable. In 2016, an unmitigated clown was elected the 45th president of the United States, following my precious Obama. All the fear, rage, disbelief was bubbling up inside of me. I had to get it out. *Now* I was ready! Where were those images Tara so carefully doctored for me? I remember being at work trying to figure out how to find the scanned strips on my Google Drive. This was quite an undertaking for me since I am a complete technophobe. I didn't want to ask anyone on the job for help; after all, I wasn't exactly fact-checking a manuscript. But I had to *do* something and I needed to do it *immediately*. Ah ha! There they were. Now, could

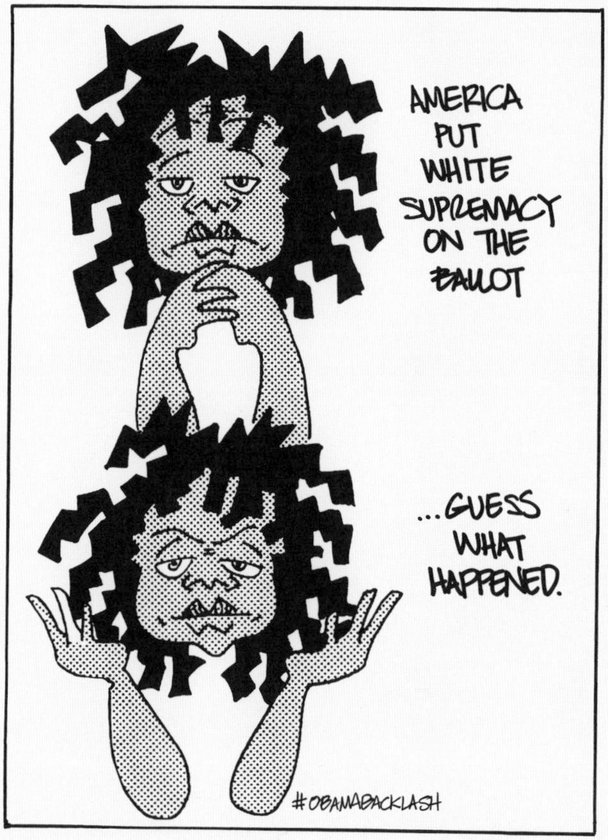
AMERICA PUT WHITE SUPREMACY ON THE BALLOT
…GUESS WHAT HAPPENED.
#OBAMABACKLASH

I find Lekesia? Yes! There *she* was. My very first strip post-syndication was copied and pasted (and I mean that quite literally…I printed out the strips, scissored out the images, and pasted them on a piece of paper). I wrote in my new dialogue and I was hooked—again. I was able to find a forlorn Lekesia who *now* says, "America put white supremacy on the ballot;" then rhetorically asks, "…Guess what happened?" #OBAMABACKLASH

Since then, I'm back to drawing my characters and don't rely on the old scanned images, but it was this confluence of circumstances that was the jump-start this cartoonist needed. And what a relief! It's not healthy keeping so much locked inside.

Here's some of what "my girls" have been up to lately…

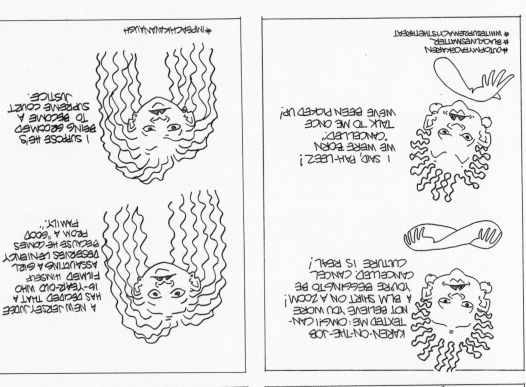

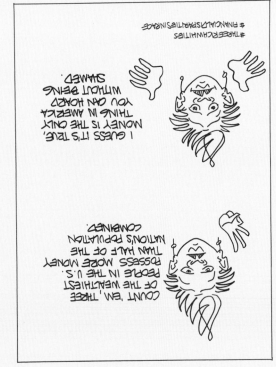

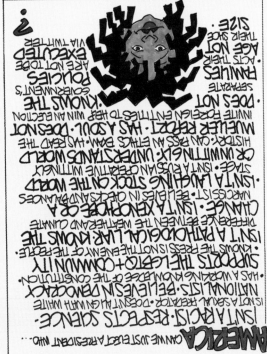

AMERICA CAN WE JUST ELECT A PRESIDENT WHO...
ISN'T A RACIST · RESPECTS SCIENCE · IS NOT A SEXUAL PREDATOR · DOESN'T ALIGN WITH WHITE NATIONALISTS · BELIEVES IN DEMOCRACY · HAS A WORKING KNOWLEDGE OF THE CONSTITUTION · SUPPORTS THE LGBTQ+ COMMUNITY · KNOWS THE PRESS IS NOT THE ENEMY OF THE PEOPLE · ISN'T A PATHOLOGICAL LIAR · KNOWS THE DIFFERENCE BETWEEN THE WEATHER AND CLIMATE CHANGE · ISN'T A XENOPHOBE OR A NARCISSIST · BELIEVES IN CHECKS AND BALANCES · ISN'T A LAUGHING STOCK ON THE WORLD STAGE · ISN'T A RUSSIAN OPERATIVE WITTINGLY OR UNWITTINGLY · UNDERSTANDS WORLD HISTORY · CAN PASS AN ETHICS EXAM · HAS READ THE MUELLER REPORT · HAS A SOUL · DOES NOT INVITE FOREIGN ENTITIES TO HELP WIN AN ELECTION · DOES NOT SEPARATE FAMILIES · ACTS THEIR AGE NOT THEIR SHOE SIZE · KNOWS THE GOVERNMENT'S POLICIES ARE NOT TO BE EXECUTED VIA TWITTER
?
COUNT 'EM, THREE OF THE WEALTHIEST PEOPLE IN THE U.S. POSSESS MORE MONEY THAN HALF OF THE NATION'S POPULATION COMBINED.
I GUESS IT'S TRUE, MONEY IS THE ONLY THING IN AMERICA YOU CAN HOARD WITHOUT BEING SHAMED.
#THREERICHWHITIES
#FINANCIALDISPARITIESINRACE
KAREN-ON-THE-JOB TEXTED ME: OMG! I CAN-NOT BELIEVE YOU WORE A BLM SHIRT ON A ZOOM! YOU'RE BEGGING TO BE CANCELLED. CANCEL CULTURE IS REAL!
I SAID, PAH-LEEZ! WE WERE BORN "CANCELLED." TALK TO ME ONCE WE'VE BEEN PICKED UP!
#OUTOFMYFACEKAREN
#BLACKLIVESMATTER
#WHITESUPREMACYISTHETHREAT
A NEW JERSEY JUDGE HAS DECIDED THAT A 16-YEAR-OLD WHO FILMED HIMSELF ASSAULTING A GIRL DESERVES LENIENCY BECAUSE HE COMES FROM A "GOOD FAMILY."
I SUPPOSE HE'S BEING GROOMED TO BECOME A SUPREME COURT JUSTICE.
#IMPEACHKAVANAUGH

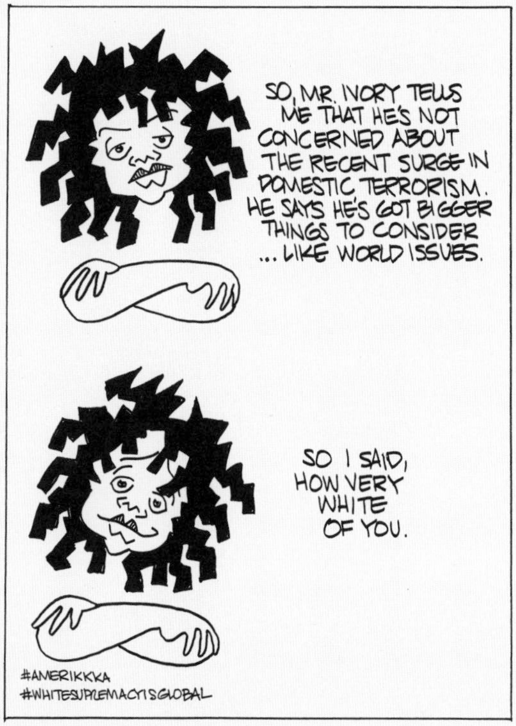
SO, MR. IVORY TELLS ME THAT HE'S NOT CONCERNED ABOUT THE RECENT SURGE IN DOMESTIC TERRORISM. HE SAYS HE'S GOT BIGGER THINGS TO CONSIDER ... LIKE WORLD ISSUES.
SO I SAID, HOW VERY WHITE OF YOU.
#AMERIKKKA
#WHITESUPREMACYISGLOBAL

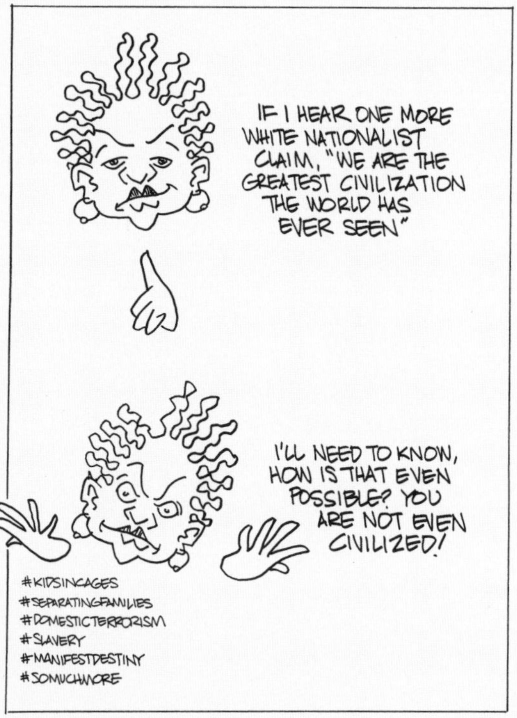
IF I HEAR ONE MORE WHITE NATIONALIST CLAIM, "WE ARE THE GREATEST CIVILIZATION THE WORLD HAS EVER SEEN"
I'LL NEED TO KNOW, HOW IS THAT EVEN POSSIBLE? YOU ARE NOT EVEN CIVILIZED!
#KIDSINCAGES
#SEPARATINGFAMILIES
#DOMESTICTERRORISM
#SLAVERY
#MANIFESTDESTINY
#SOMUCHMORE

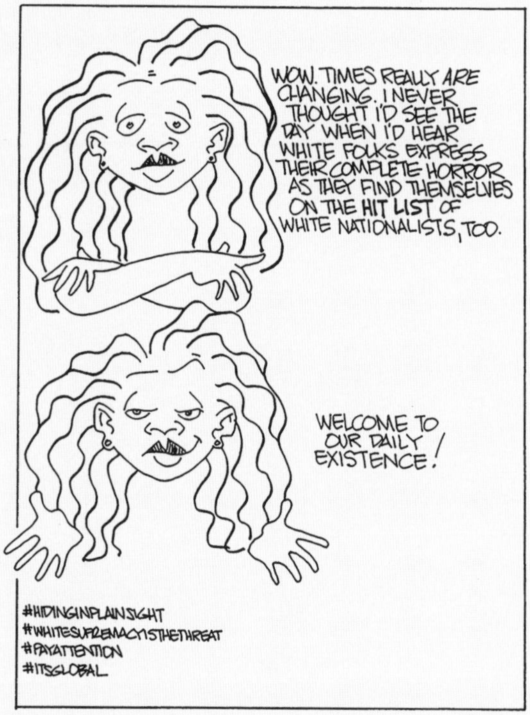
WOW. TIMES REALLY ARE CHANGING. I NEVER THOUGHT I'D SEE THE DAY WHEN I'D HEAR WHITE FOLKS EXPRESS THEIR COMPLETE HORROR AS THEY FIND THEMSELVES ON THE HIT LIST OF WHITE NATIONALISTS, TOO.
WELCOME TO OUR DAILY EXISTENCE!
#HIDINGINPLAINSIGHT
#WHITESUPREMACYISTHETHREAT
#PAYATTENTION
#ITSGLOBAL

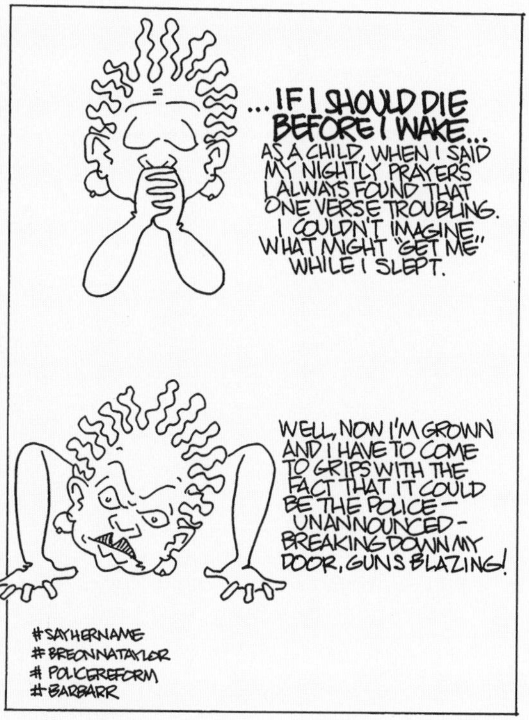
...IF I SHOULD DIE BEFORE I WAKE...
AS A CHILD, WHEN I SAID MY NIGHTLY PRAYERS I ALWAYS FOUND THAT ONE VERSE TROUBLING. I COULDN'T IMAGINE WHAT MIGHT "GET ME" WHILE I SLEPT.
WELL, NOW I'M GROWN AND I HAVE TO COME TO GRIPS WITH THE FACT THAT IT COULD BE THE POLICE — UNANNOUNCED — BREAKING DOWN MY DOOR, GUNS BLAZING!
#SAYHERNAME
#BREONNATAYLOR
#POLICEREFORM
#BARBARR

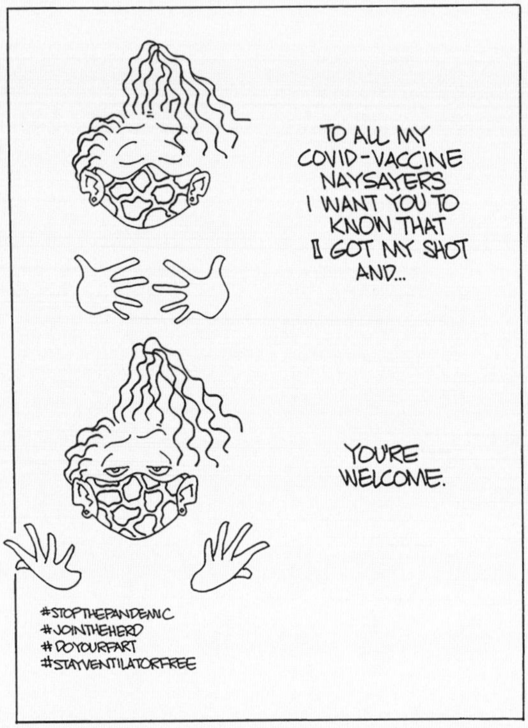
TO ALL MY COVID-VACCINE NAYSAYERS I WANT YOU TO KNOW THAT I GOT MY SHOT AND...
YOU'RE WELCOME.
#STOPTHEPANDEMIC
#JOINTHEHERD
#DOYOURPART
#STAYVENTILATORFREE

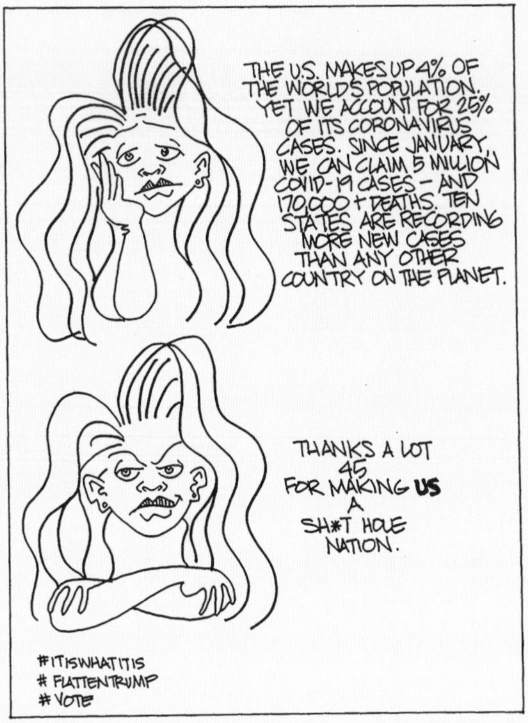
THE U.S. MAKES UP 4% OF THE WORLD'S POPULATION. YET WE ACCOUNT FOR 25% OF ITS CORONAVIRUS CASES. SINCE JANUARY, WE CAN CLAIM 5 MILLION COVID-19 CASES – AND 170,000 + DEATHS. TEN STATES ARE RECORDING MORE NEW CASES THAN ANY OTHER COUNTRY ON THE PLANET.
THANKS A LOT 45 FOR MAKING **US** A SH*T HOLE NATION.
#ITISWHATITIS
FLATTENTRUMP
VOTE

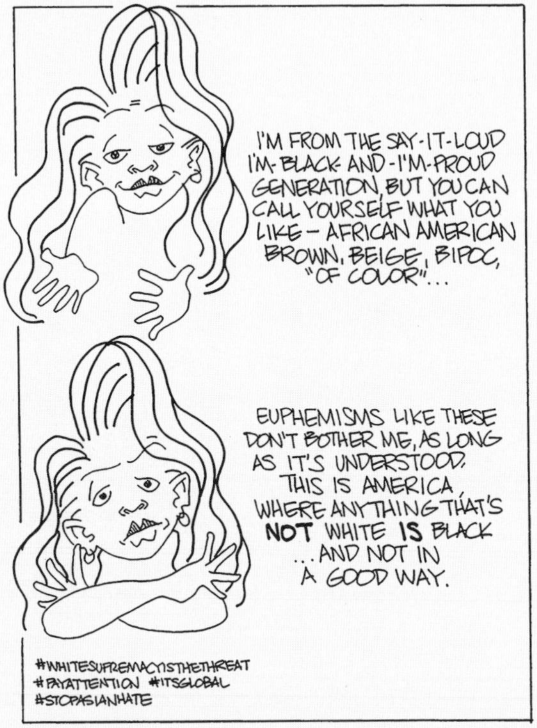
I'M FROM THE SAY-IT-LOUD I'M-BLACK-AND-I'M-PROUD GENERATION, BUT YOU CAN CALL YOURSELF WHAT YOU LIKE – AFRICAN AMERICAN BROWN, BEIGE, BIPOC, "OF COLOR"...
EUPHEMISMS LIKE THESE DON'T BOTHER ME, AS LONG AS IT'S UNDERSTOOD. THIS IS AMERICA, WHERE ANYTHING THAT'S **NOT** WHITE **IS** BLACK ...AND NOT IN A GOOD WAY.
#WHITESUPREMACYISTHETHREAT
#PAYATTENTION #ITSGLOBAL
#STOPASIANHATE

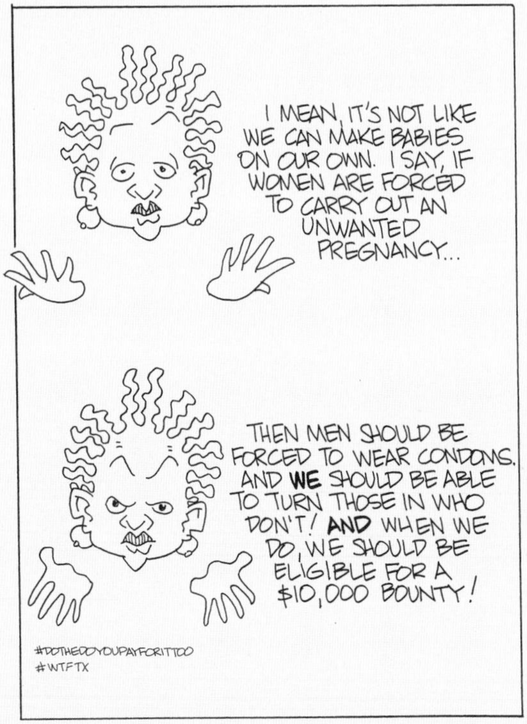
I MEAN, IT'S NOT LIKE WE CAN MAKE BABIES ON OUR OWN. I SAY, IF WOMEN ARE FORCED TO CARRY OUT AN UNWANTED PREGNANCY...
THEN MEN SHOULD BE FORCED TO WEAR CONDOMS. AND **WE** SHOULD BE ABLE TO TURN THOSE IN WHO DON'T! **AND** WHEN WE DO, WE SHOULD BE ELIGIBLE FOR A $10,000 BOUNTY!
#DOTHEDOYOUPAYFORITTOO
#WTFTX

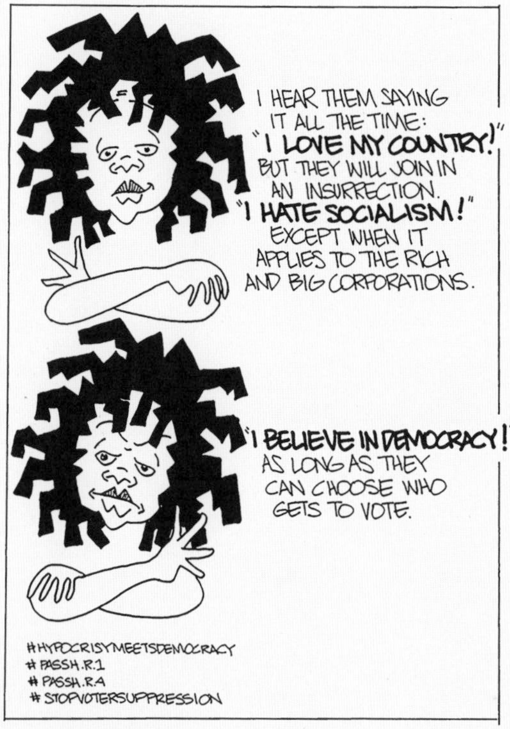
I HEAR THEM SAYING IT ALL THE TIME: "I LOVE MY COUNTRY!" BUT THEY WILL JOIN IN AN INSURRECTION. "I HATE SOCIALISM!" EXCEPT WHEN IT APPLIES TO THE RICH AND BIG CORPORATIONS.
"I BELIEVE IN DEMOCRACY!" AS LONG AS THEY CAN CHOOSE WHO GETS TO VOTE.
#HYPOCRISYMEETSDEMOCRACY
PASSH.R.1
PASSH.R.4
STOPVOTERSUPPRESSION

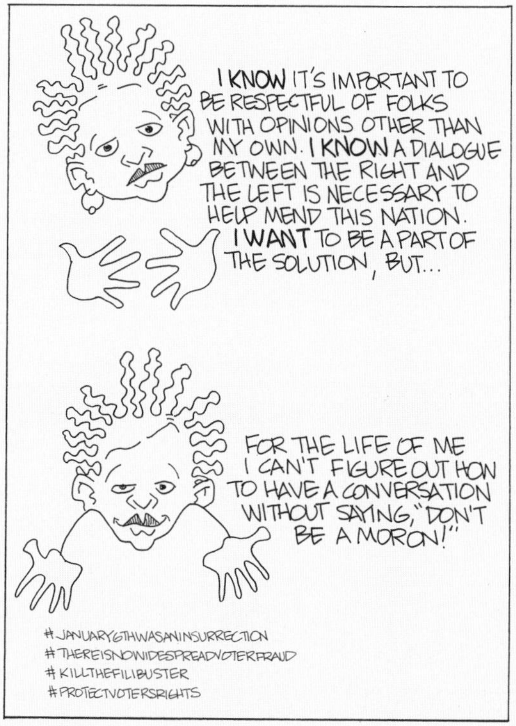
I KNOW IT'S IMPORTANT TO BE RESPECTFUL OF FOLKS WITH OPINIONS OTHER THAN MY OWN. I KNOW A DIALOGUE BETWEEN THE RIGHT AND THE LEFT IS NECESSARY TO HELP MEND THIS NATION. I WANT TO BE A PART OF THE SOLUTION, BUT...
FOR THE LIFE OF ME I CAN'T FIGURE OUT HOW TO HAVE A CONVERSATION WITHOUT SAYING, "DON'T BE A MORON!"
JANUARY6THWASANINSURRECTION
THEREISNOWIDESPREADVOTERFRAUD
KILLTHEFILIBUSTER
PROTECTVOTERSRIGHTS

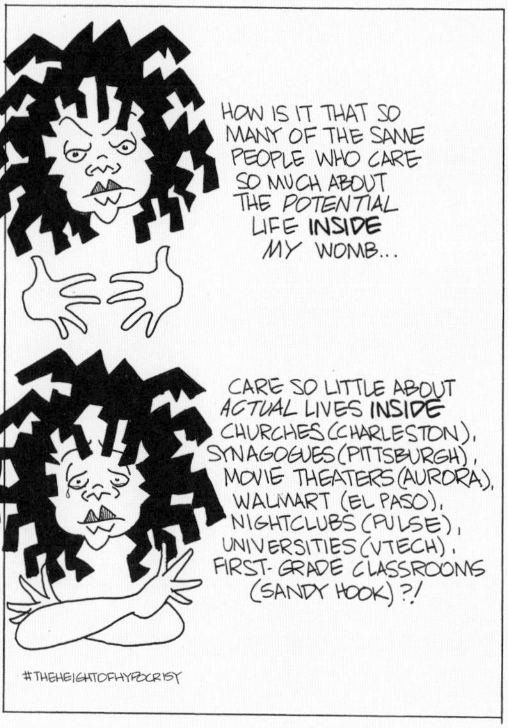
HOW IS IT THAT SO MANY OF THE SAME PEOPLE WHO CARE SO MUCH ABOUT THE POTENTIAL LIFE INSIDE MY WOMB...
CARE SO LITTLE ABOUT ACTUAL LIVES INSIDE CHURCHES (CHARLESTON), SYNAGOGUES (PITTSBURGH), MOVIE THEATERS (AURORA), WALMART (EL PASO), NIGHTCLUBS (PULSE), UNIVERSITIES (VTECH), FIRST-GRADE CLASSROOMS (SANDY HOOK) ?!
#THEHEIGHTOFHYPOCRISY

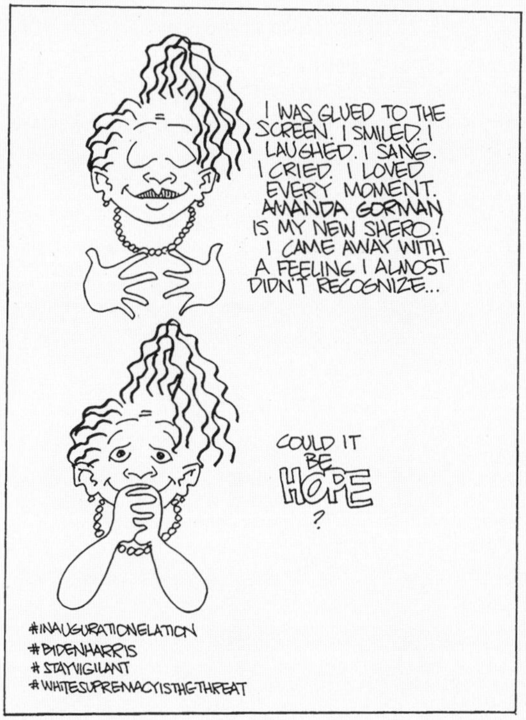
I WAS GLUED TO THE SCREEN. I SMILED. I LAUGHED. I SANG. I CRIED. I LOVED EVERY MOMENT. AMANDA GORMAN IS MY NEW SHERO! I CAME AWAY WITH A FEELING I ALMOST DIDN'T RECOGNIZE...
COULD IT BE HOPE ?
#INAUGURATIONELATION
#BIDENHARRIS
STAYVIGILANT
WHITESUPREMACYISTHETHREAT

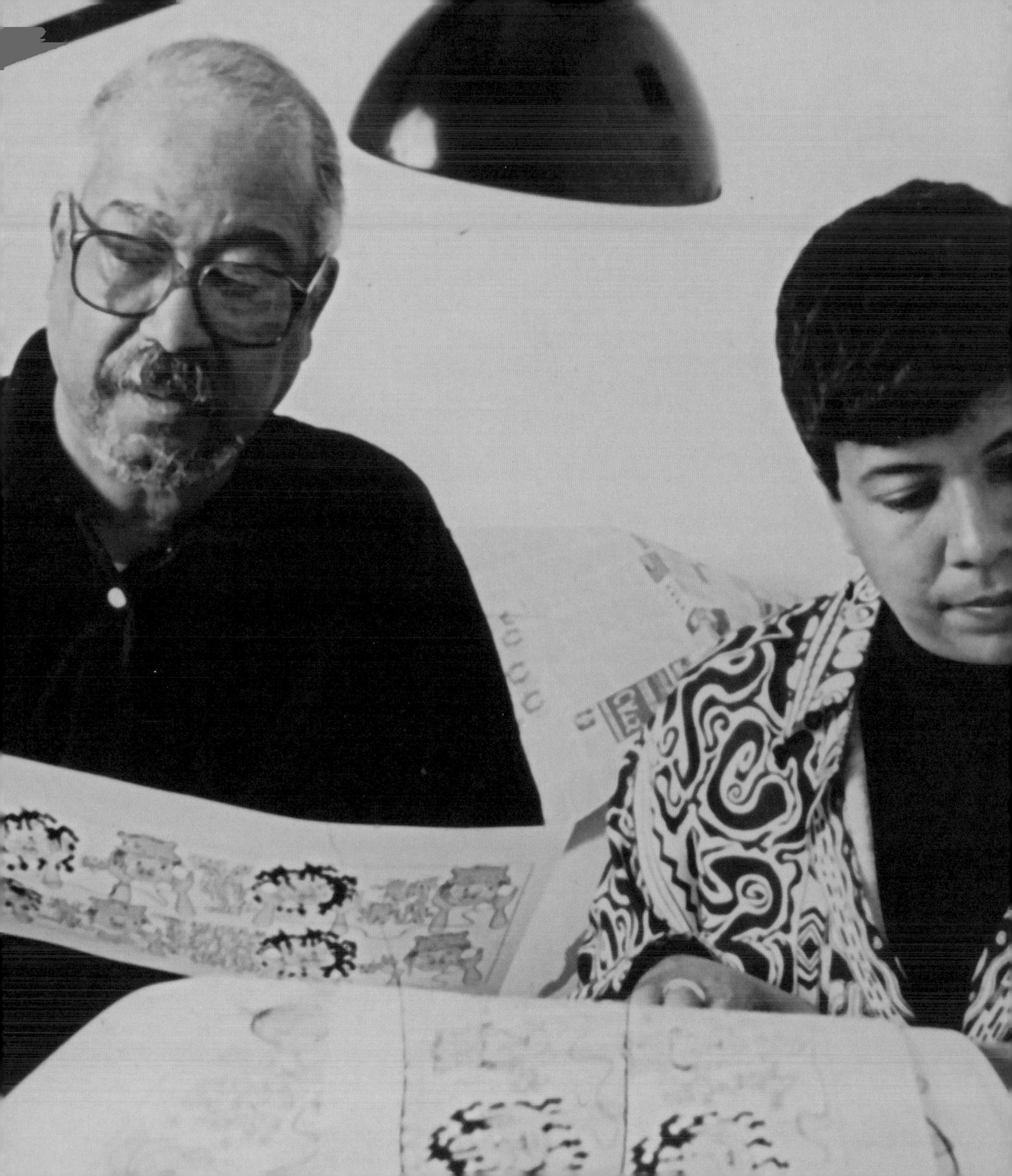

That's Pretty Cool When You Think About It
Sharon Pendana

Barbara Brandon-Croft is refreshingly humble and good-naturedly humorous. To be in her presence is to be enveloped in a subtle radiance, not the scorching heat of the attention seeker, but the soft warmth of her kind heart. Her hands dance to the euphony of her voice, punctuating her points of speech as expressively as they have illustrated her work as the first African American woman to create a nationally syndicated comic strip in the mainstream press. We meet at her favorite "urban oasis," Greenacre Park, a secluded pocket park anchored by a twenty-five-foot waterfall in midtown Manhattan, to chat.

To tell Barbara's story is also to tell her father's. Native Washingtonian Brumsic Brandon, Jr. excelled in art classes at D.C.'s Armstrong High School, as did a young Duke Ellington with the same dedicated teacher, Mr. Dodson, decades earlier. While studying studio art at New York University, he was drafted into the US Army. He attained the rank of Sergeant while serving two years in post-WWII occupied Germany, before returning to the nation's capital, marrying his love, Rita, and beginning a family: daughter Linda, then son Brumsic III. The Brandons would relocate to Brooklyn, New York, where baby Barbara was born. During her infancy, the young family built a home on Rushmore Street in New Cassel, Long Island, near Westbury. "It was a segregated Long Island—that was the only place they'd let us live, by the railroad tracks," she chuckles. "I can remember my mom telling the story of when we first moved into the house. My mom's this very fair-skinned Black woman and the people across the street were like, 'What's this Black man doing with this white woman and these kids? What the hell is all this?' But they all became the closest of friends." Barbara and Leslie, her "friend from the beginning of time," played hard and got dirty. "We were tomboys, two peas in a pod, and wanted to play football with the boys." They would not be relegated to cheerleaders on the sidelines of the fun. "I had a great childhood in a Black neighborhood," she says with her cheery smile.

Brumsic père supported the family with his work at a motion picture animation studio in New York City, Bray Studios. "My dad was an animator there until 1970," Barbara says. "I didn't even know what that was, but we always had paper and pens available." Nevertheless, he submitted editorial cartoons to several papers and in 1963, self-published *Some of My Best Friends*, a twenty-four-page book of social commentary cartoons on "the plight of the Negro," which garnered the praise of Langston Hughes. Rita Brandon was a stay-at-home mom until each of her children reached school age; she then went on to shape countless young Long Island minds as a first-grade teacher, with her creative, youngest child, Barbara, helping her set up her classroom. But Mrs. Brandon always had dinner prepared by 5 p.m. and served in a dining room lined with Mr. Brandon's sardonic illustrations of the seven deadly sins. "Oh yes," Barbara remembers. "I had to be home at five o'clock…always."

Barbara's lifelong love for Muhammad Ali has its roots on Rushmore Street: "I remember Mr. Conway across the street was a boxer—they called him 'Connie'—and Cassius Clay came by. We were peeking through the curtain at them sparring." When Clay shed his "slave name" for Muhammad Ali, the Brandons listened. They subscribed to *Muhammad Speaks*, "probably the only ones on our block" to do so, Barbara laughs. Emerson Brandon, her father's brother, changed his name to Waliakbar Muhammad. "Now that was something! He wasn't Uncle Emerson anymore."

From Mr. Brandon's trenchant observations of Black life in 1960s America, he conceived of a board game akin to Monopoly—"CULLUD: (a phonetic corruption of 'colored') The Game That Tells It Like It Is." He created instructions for gameplay and purchased wittily selected miniatures for use as Monopoly-styled game pieces: a beer stein, wine bottle, switchblade, etc. "It was really brilliant," Barbara says. "This parlor game with the idea that you can't win." To reproduce the game for sale, he enlisted the family: "We were all an assembly line, putting it together," she remembers. It was distributed exclusively through *Freedomways* magazine, where he was a contributor, for $3.95 each. *Jet* magazine mentioned it in their December 28, 1967 issue as "in time for the holidays."

The rioting in the aftermath of the 1968 assassination of Rev. Dr. Martin Luther King, Jr. made its way to New Cassel, and Barbara remembers having a nine-year-old's sense of being part of something meaningful. She and her ace, Leslie, took cover in the basement. "We were on the ground—making something out of nothing—but when it was over, the auto parts [shop] on the corner had burned down, and there was a bullet hole on the side of our house. In some crazy way, we were proud that we were part of this national uproar," she says.

The same year, her father debuted *Luther* (so named for MLK) in the Long Island-based newspaper, *Newsday*. Set in the fictitious, inner-city Alabaster Avenue Elementary school, the comic strip wryly chronicled the experiences of Black third-grader Luther, his schoolmates, and teacher Miss Backlash, underscoring themes of social justice. With the acquisition of *Newsday* in 1970, the Times Mirror company, through its Los Angeles Times Syndicate, placed *Luther* among the first comic strips created by Black cartoonists and centering the lives of African Americans to gain mainstream national syndication. In a 2001 interview, Mr. Brandon said, "My objective, in my comic strip, was to bring to light not only the long-ignored Black perspective, but the many various philosophical postures found therein."

Barbara recalls her introduction to the work of a cartoonist when her dad tested his kids for artistic aptitude. "He gave us all a drawing test, I think I was in junior high by then, and I was a little better at it," she says humbly. "So I was chosen to help him do *Luther*—putting on the Zipatone and filling in silhouettes, and I got paid for it." When most of her peers received an allowance for household chores, Barbara was compensated for her artistic ability, unwittingly auguring her future.

She enjoyed drawing most, but dabbled in painting. "Leslie and I would have art shows in her basement— paintings—and charge people. It was such a rich, supportive community." Leslie's maternal great aunts were Fredi Washington (actress) and her younger sister Isabel Washington Powell (former Cotton Club performer and Adam Clayton Powell, Jr's first wife). Her aunt was a painter, so the girls had access to the materials they needed to create. And Barbara had her dad's affirmation. "I'll see these old neighbors of mine, and they'll say, 'I used to see you and you'd say, *Come over, and give us a nickel, we put on a show!*' We put on shows all the time."

In March 1970, jazz vocalist Joya Sherrill (formerly of the Duke Ellington Orchestra) became the first African American woman to host a kids' television program in New York City. Broadcast on Sunday mornings on WPIX Channel 11, *Time for Joya!* appealed to a multicultural audience. To illustrate the stories Ms. Sherrill would tell, WPIX commissioned Mr. Brandon to contribute drawings. After an appearance on the show for the children to see the person behind the artwork, he, with his natural rapport, was made a member of the cast, known as "Mr. BB." Together, Barbara's parents crafted a puppet called "Seymour the Bookworm" to be voiced and manipulated by Mr. Brandon on the show. Mr. BB and Seymour became beloved characters, still remembered fondly by those who grew up in New York during the seventies. "Everybody loved my dad, he was just that kind of guy," Barbara says. But at the time, she was embarrassed by it. "Oh, your dad's on TV?!" She feigns a grimace, "Oh jeez."

When it came time for college, Barbara chose Syracuse University's College of Visual and Performing Arts. "I thought, *I'll be a fashion illustrator; I'll be a this, I'll be a that. I'll do fine art,* but I didn't like painting. I took classes in what I liked: I liked sociology. I took speech because I hate talking in front of people. Oh, I'll swim, they have a pool. Lifeguard, maybe. I worked at an art gallery and helped curate. I stumbled into everything. I was all over the place."

After returning downstate, Barbara snagged a fashion reporter and illustrator post with *Retail News Bureau* in 1981. Still, when she learned of a forthcoming new magazine for Black women, poised to be the next *Essence*, she sought an interview. Literary legend and editor-in-chief Marie Brown offered Barbara the opportunity to create a comic strip for the magazine, *Elan*, which she delightedly did. But before Barbara's work could be published, the magazine folded, so she kept it moving...to *Essence*. Although they weren't looking for a cartoonist. They were looking for a fashion and beauty writer to fill in for someone on maternity leave, and Barbara, with her fashion reporting experience, fit the bill. She would work at the top magazine for Black women in the country from 1983–1989 when she became a full-time cartoonist. Prompted by her dad, she'd submitted her comic strip to the *Detroit Free Press* for consideration. They debuted her weekly comic strip *Where I'm Coming From* in May 1989, making her the first African American female cartoonist since Jackie Ormes inked *Torchy Brown in "Dixie to Harlem"* in 1937 in the *Pittsburgh Courier* and later another bastion of the "Negro press," the *Chicago Defender*. Having witnessed the benefits of syndication through her father, Barbara diligently pursued several syndicates. In 1991, she became the first Black woman to create a nationally syndicated comic strip in the mainstream press when Universal Press Syndicate (home to *Cathy, Doonesbury, Garfield, The Far Side, Calvin and Hobbes*, and later, *The Boondocks*) signed her.

Barbara and her friends, her "girls" in real life, inspired "the girls" on the page, the nine characters in *Where I'm Coming From*. Giving authentic voice to Black women—noticeably underrepresented in the cartoon world—the strip was in syndication until 2005. "I'm proud of it," she says. "I am, there's no getting around it. And I'm proud that it was in Canada, it was in South Africa, it was in Jamaica, it was in the *Gleaner*, it was in *Drum*. I'm proud I've made a mark in history, and it doesn't matter whatever else happens. That's indelible. I could do nothing else and still be able to say that." She laughs, adding, "One of the seven deadly sins, Pride, be careful!"

"Getting married was not high on my to-do list," Barbara says. She was living in Fort Greene, Brooklyn during a culturally significant time; she'd hit her stride as a cartoonist, and she'd published her first *Where I'm Coming From* book. Life was sweet. Then she met Monte Croft, a talented musician impressed by her collection of 45s and smitten with her. She thought he was "kinda cute" but says it was a slow burn. "We grew closer and closer. My connection to Monte felt right and real. We tied the knot in 1997."

Chase Ian Croft, their son, was born in 1998, and his mama is still in awe that he's here. "We thought we'd try for a family, but didn't plan to go through hoops. Even with me being close to forty with a history of endometriosis and just one ovary, extra medical help to have children was not an option we considered. The following year I was pregnant. Our son is simply amazing. He teaches me more about life and myself than I could ever teach him." What surprised her most about motherhood was "how it takes over. How it alters you ENTIRELY. There's not anything that's the same after—anything!" She loves her son's dry humor and says, "He's been funny forever. He once asked, 'Why do we have the smallest house in Queens?' He was three!" She cracks up. "What does he know about Queens?"

"Monte, Chase, and me. It's a good solid feeling." Family is everything. Monte praises his father-in-law to the rafters; his creativity, wit, and commitment to craft. Barbara says, "I see a lot of my dad in Monte. The idea of working all the time, Dad couldn't stop. It was very frustrating for him to get Parkinson's and not be able to draw." Despite the cruel ravages of Parkinson's disease, Brumsic Brandon, Jr. lived to enjoy sixty-four years of marriage to his beloved Rita and make it to November 27, 2014, the fifty-fourth birthday of their youngest child, Barbara. He joined the ancestors the next day.

Little did Barbara know, back in 1967 when she and her family helped her father package his satirical, no-win board game, "CULLUD," that she'd one day mount an exhibition of the same name displaying her father's works alongside her own. Now chair of the Brumsic Brandon, Jr. Art Trust, Barbara has, with the help of "incredible" curator Tara Nakashima Donahue, exhibited twice at New York's Medialia Gallery. First in 2016, *From Panel to Panel: "CULLUD": Brumsic Brandon, Jr. & Barbara Brandon-Croft In An Exhibition Of Social Commentary Cartoons, Comic Strips And More, Spanning 1963–2008*; and in 2017, *Soul: Cartoons in Context*. Together, Tara and Barbara curated *STILL Racism in America: A Retrospective in Cartoons* at the Billy Ireland Cartoon Art Library & Museum, spotlighting the many issues both father and daughter covered thirty years apart that remain relevant to this day.

As for her accomplishments, Barbara is certain of what she is most proud: "That my dad and I make the only nationally syndicated father/daughter cartoonists, Black or white. I love that it wasn't as if I took over his comic strip (like some father/son cartoonists have done). We made our distinction as Black cartoonists in the mainstream press independently—via different syndicates and creating separate comic strips. That's pretty cool when you think about it."

Sharon Pendana writes about art, culture, and travel. She is author and photographer of *Secret Washington D.C.*, and creator of the online magazine, *THE TROVE*.

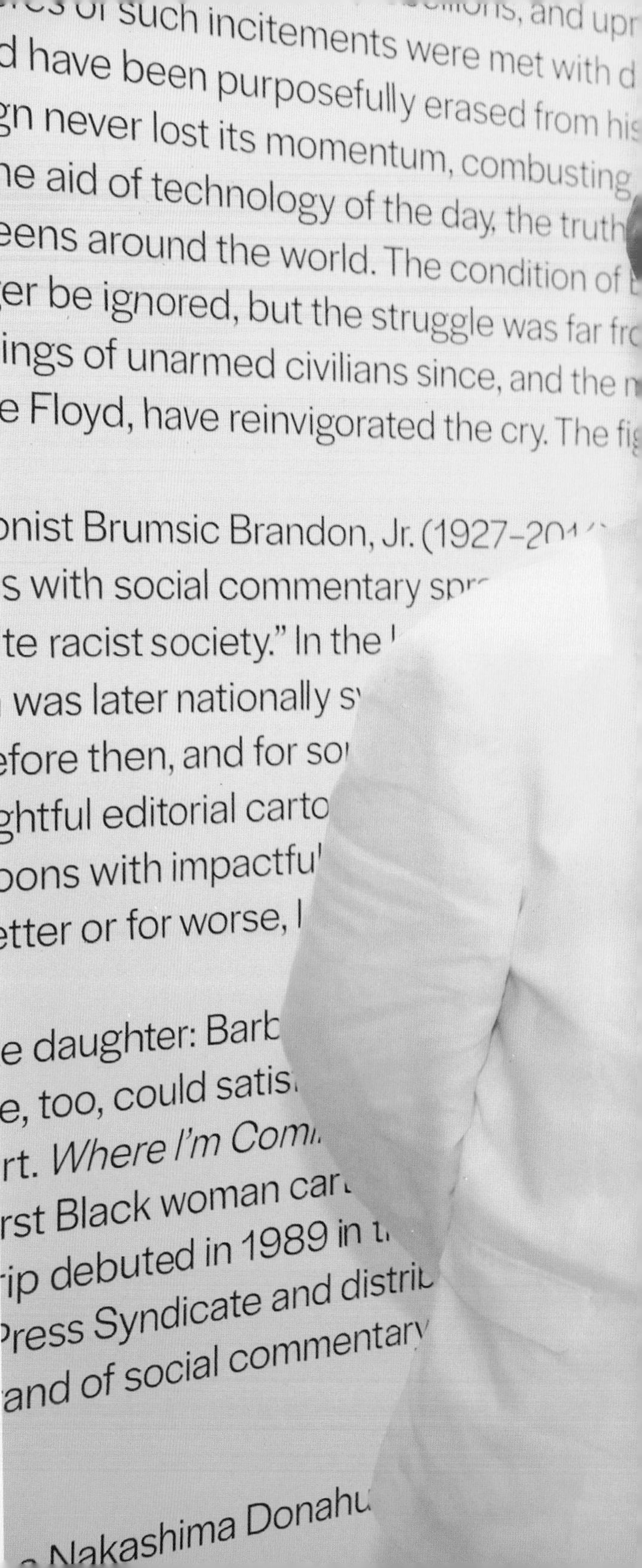
such incitements were met with
have been purposefully erased from
never lost its momentum, combusting
aid of technology of the day, the truth
around the world. The condition of
be ignored, but the struggle was far
of unarmed civilians since, and the
Floyd, have reinvigorated the cry.
Brumsic Brandon, Jr.
with social commentary
racist society." In the
was later nationally
then, and for
editorial
with
or for worse,
daughter:
too, could
Where I'm
Black woman
debuted in 1989 in
Syndicate and
of social
Nakashima

The partially visible text on the poster reads:

100 years —
e organized and
onately violent
the
rld
on
a
one-
to

167

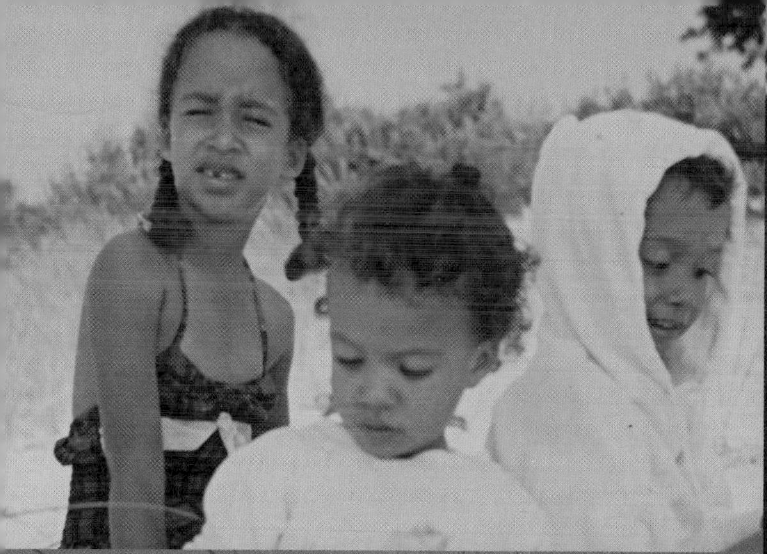

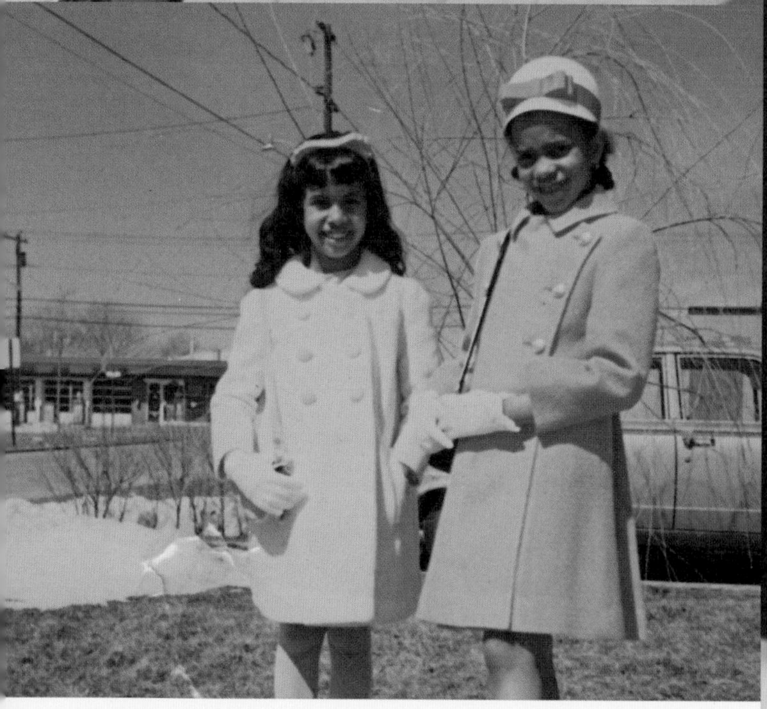

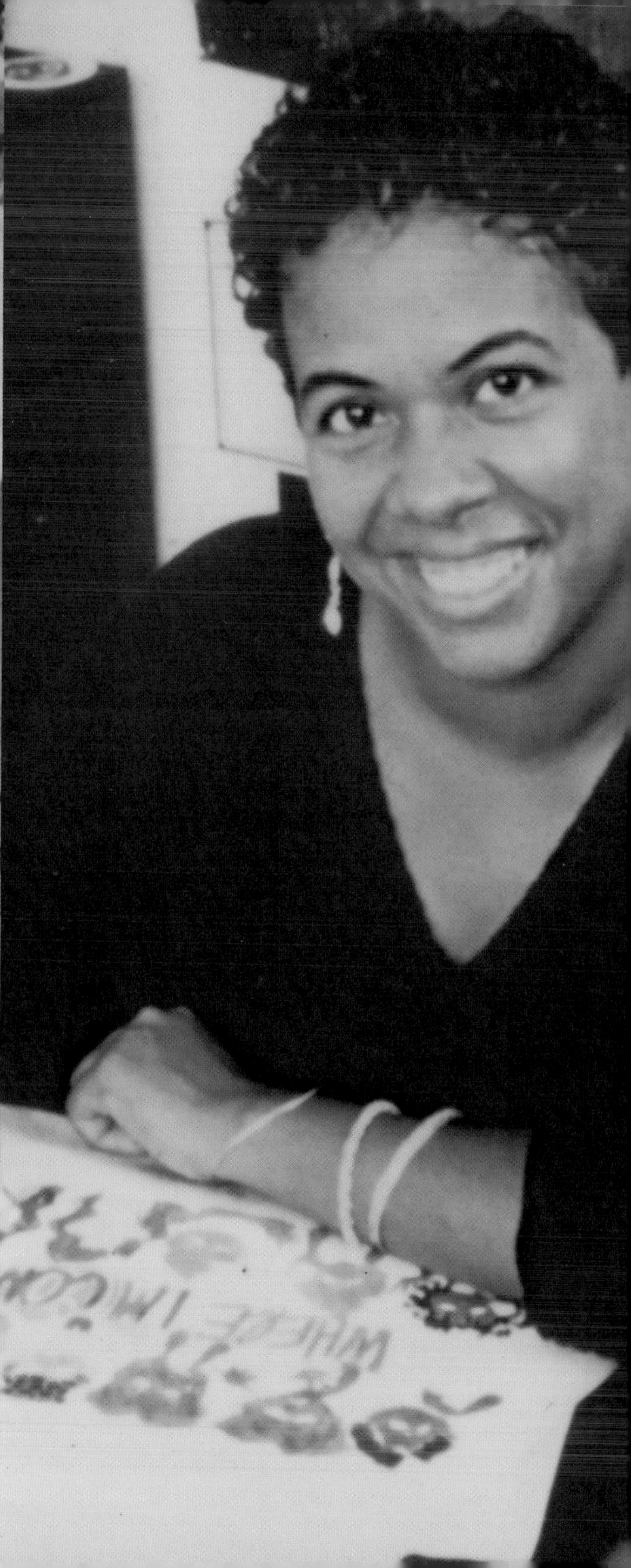

Left: Brandon-Croft with her siblings, Linda and Brumsic III, 1962; Brandon-Croft with her best friend for life, Leslie Codrington, on Easter 1969

Middle: Brandon-Croft in her studio with the cover of the first *Where I'm Coming From* collection, 1993

Right: Kitchen shot from left: Marcelle, Judy, Barbara, and Dari, late 1980s; The Belize Girls Trip from left: Barbara, Sharon, Judy, and Denise (with the owner of the yacht club), 1990

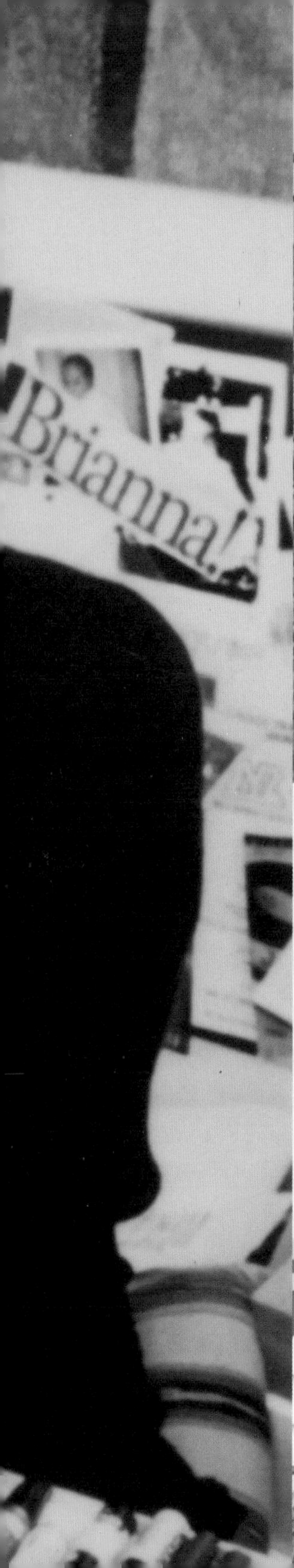
Brianna!
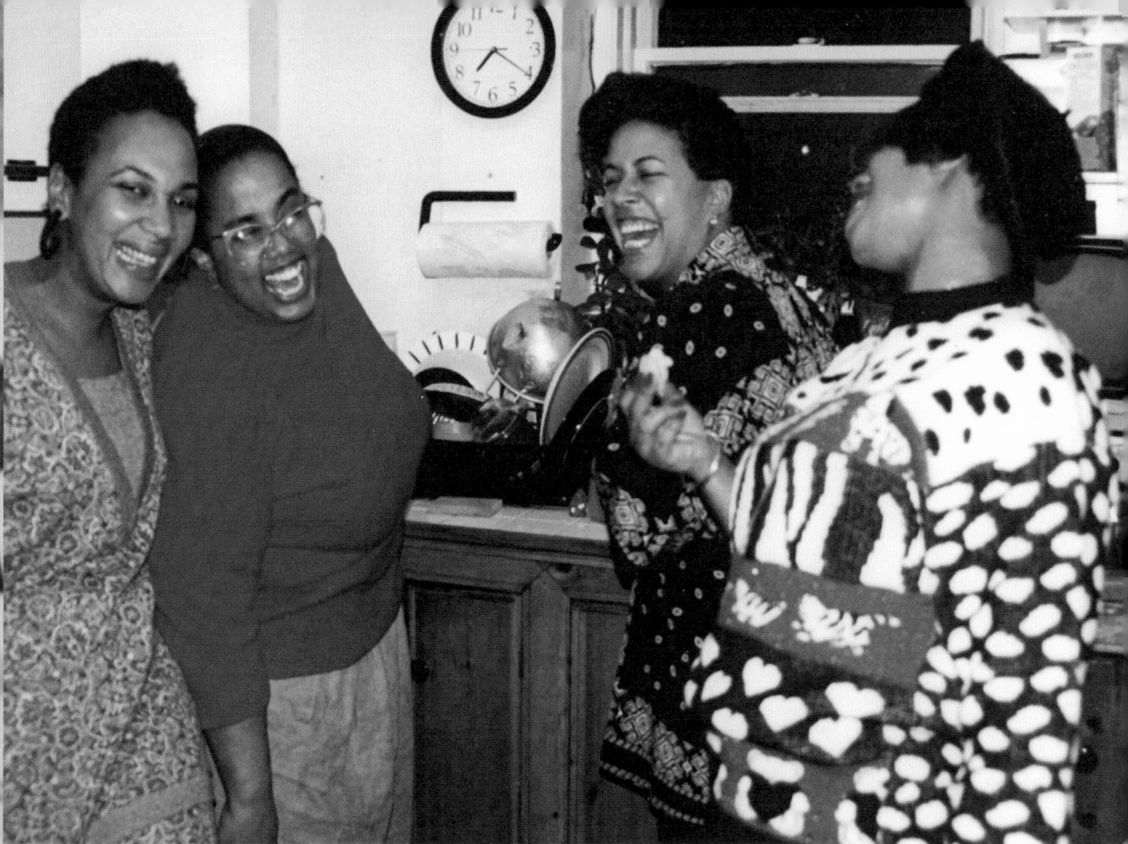
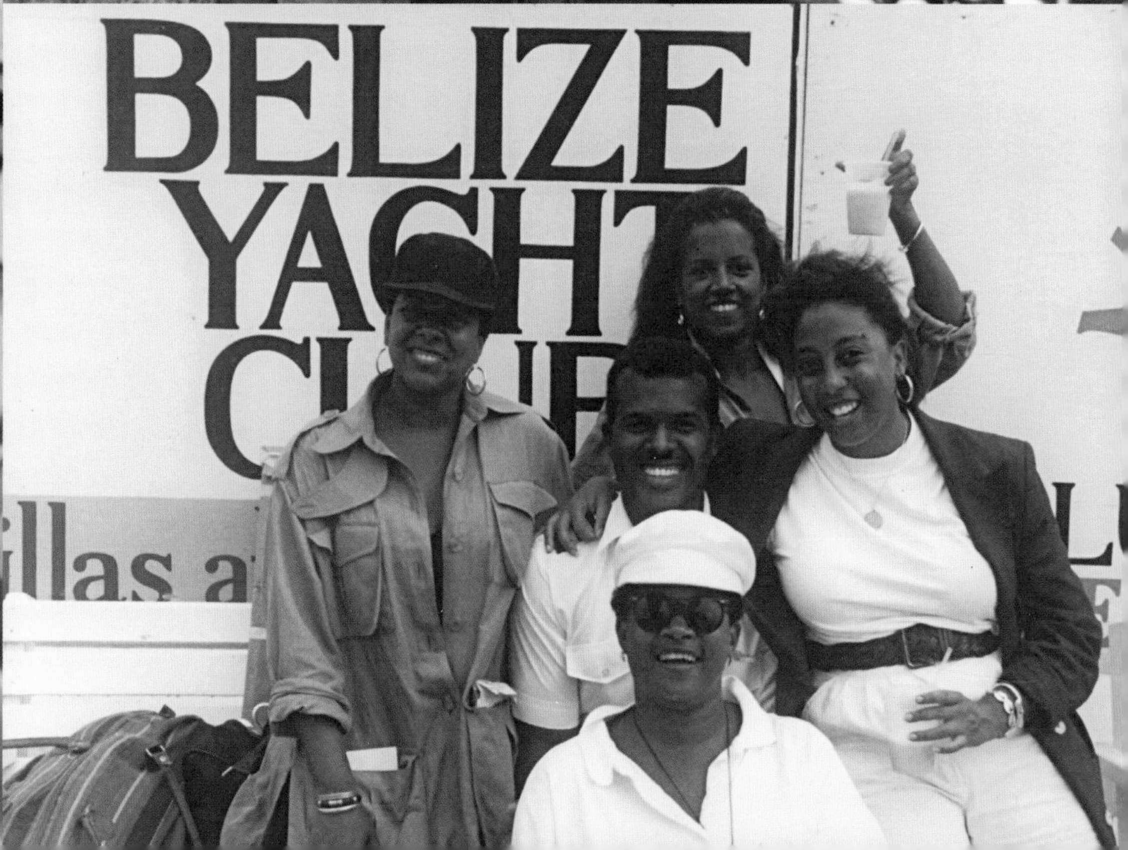
BELIZE
YACHT
CLUB

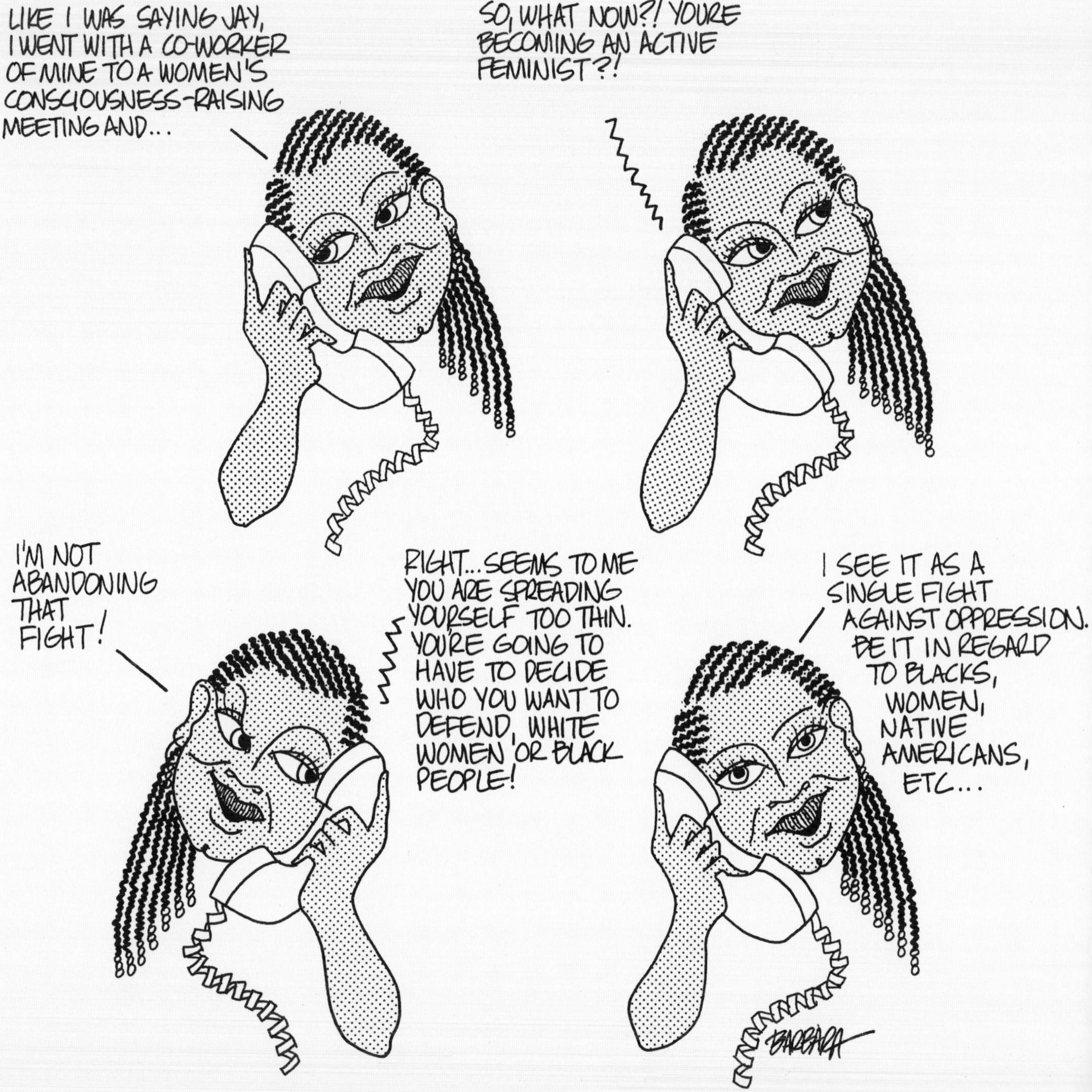
LIKE I WAS SAYING JAY, I WENT WITH A CO-WORKER OF MINE TO A WOMEN'S CONSCIOUSNESS-RAISING MEETING AND...
SO, WHAT NOW?! YOU'RE BECOMING AN ACTIVE FEMINIST?!
I'M NOT ABANDONING THAT FIGHT!
RIGHT... SEEMS TO ME YOU ARE SPREADING YOURSELF TOO THIN. YOU'RE GOING TO HAVE TO DECIDE WHO YOU WANT TO DEFEND, WHITE WOMEN OR BLACK PEOPLE!
I SEE IT AS A SINGLE FIGHT AGAINST OPPRESSION. BE IT IN REGARD TO BLACKS, WOMEN, NATIVE AMERICANS, ETC...
BARBARA

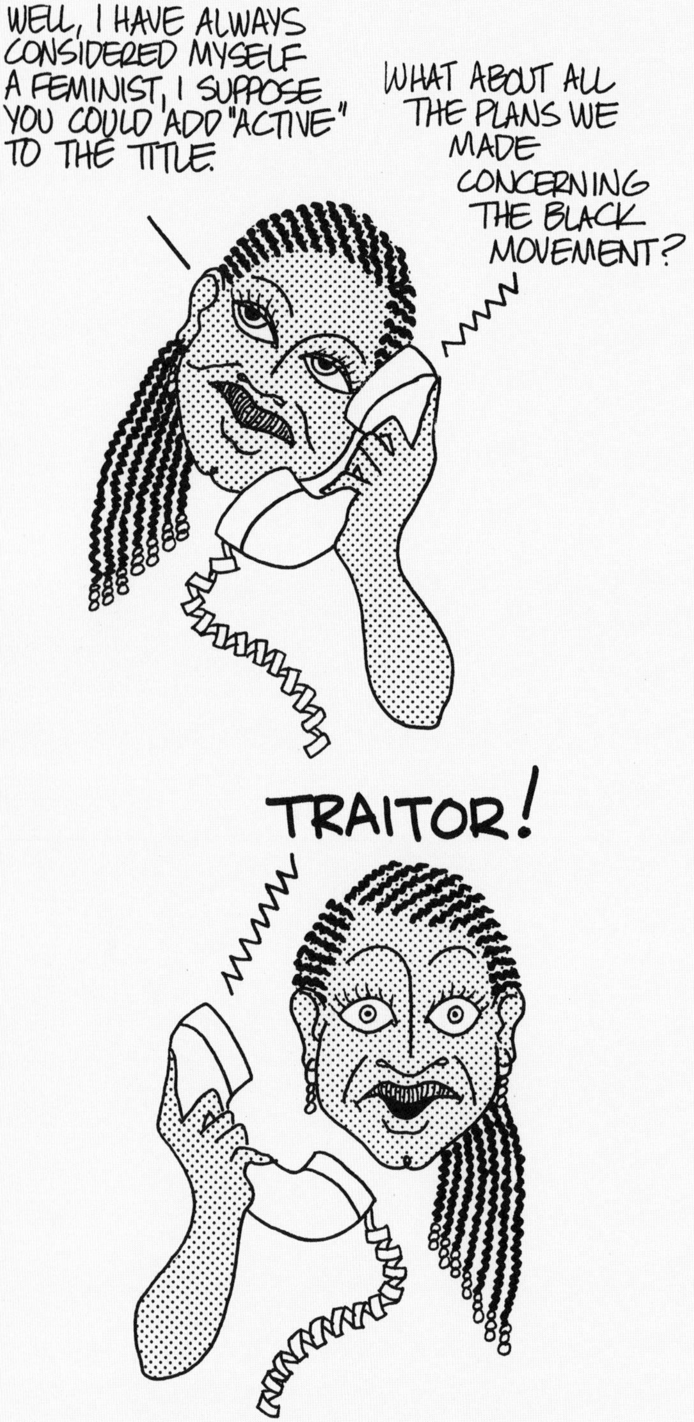
WELL, I HAVE ALWAYS CONSIDERED MYSELF A FEMINIST, I SUPPOSE YOU COULD ADD "ACTIVE" TO THE TITLE.
WHAT ABOUT ALL THE PLANS WE MADE CONCERNING THE BLACK MOVEMENT?
TRAITOR!

Syndicated Sisterhood

Rebecca Wanzo

African American women have a specific way of talking with one other. They are by no means a homogenous group, but their speech is often inflected with an ironic acknowledgment of the "double jeopardy" of Blackness and womanhood, as well as other forms of oppression such as class.[1] In the twenty-first century, people would use Kimberlé Williams Crenshaw's term "intersectionality" to refer to these interlocking systems of oppression that shape African American women's experiences, an idea Crenshaw conceived of and wrote about in the late 1980s and early 1990s—an incredibly generative period for Black feminist thinking and cultural production.[2] Novels, films, television shows, and visual art of the period would call attention to how African American women spoke to each other, with speech often marked by the African American vernacular and what's known as "mother wit." Work in the 1990s was shaped by a post-Civil Rights Movement sensibility—conscious of history, cognizant of ongoing struggles, but with a deep investment in showing the style, laughter, and pleasures shared between Black folks. Barbara Brandon-Croft's comic strip *Where I'm Coming From* (1989–2005) highlighted African American women's way of talking together, revealing the often satirical nexus between pleasure and everyday struggles. And as the first African American woman to have her comic strip syndicated in newspapers outside of the Black press, she brought that tone to a place that had lacked the voices of adult African American women—the white funny pages.

When it initially ran in the *Detroit Free Press*, *Where I'm Coming From* depicted nine Black women with only their heads visible. Later, Brandon-Croft would also include forearms and hands in order to give her characters a fuller range of expression. While providing readers with insight into how these women read the world, Brandon-Croft uses the absence of their bodies to push against how Black women, in turn, are read. These women are "types"—the activist, the single mother, the woman whose life revolves around having a man—but the conversations between them serve both to present these typologies as funny and thoughtful human beings, while also exploring complex issues that Black women were negotiating in the period. In the 1990s, many African American creators were challenging the boundaries of Black representation and proving that everyday stories of Black life were marketable.

Blackness on the Funny Pages

Blackness has been represented in US newspaper comic strips throughout history, often with racist caricature. Early strips such as Winsor McCay's *Little Nemo* (1905–1911) prominently featured a jungle imp. Will Eisner had a sidekick with simian features named Ebony White in his superhero comic *The Spirit*. These stereotypes peppered the funny pages but as Bruce Lenthall explains, the move toward national syndication in the 1920s began taking Black people and "race in general" out of comics, and after World War II the pages rarely represented people of color. He argues that the United States became very conscious that it was representing itself as an upholder of equal rights and democracy after the war (despite widespread legal discrimination). In mass media, "not recognizing the presence of African Americans" became a mechanism for "white America" to "maintain the illusion of a culture that treated everyone equally."[3] The Black press was a response to both the lack of and negative representations. Newspapers such as the *Chicago Defender* and the *Pittsburgh Courier* countered not only stories told in white newspapers but their visual imagery. Ollie Harrington (*Dark Laughter*), Jackie Ormes (*Torchy Brown*, *Patty Jo 'n' Ginger*), Leslie Rogers (*Bungleton Green*), and many other cartoonists produced strips within the same genres as the white press while often putting a Black spin on the content.[4]

Hailed as the first African American woman cartoonist, Jackie Ormes's comic strips modeled a Black feminist sensibility.[5] *Patty Jo 'n' Ginger* was a single-panel comic produced for the *Pittsburgh Courier* in which the preco-cious little Black girl Patty Jo delivered her observations about the world to her fashionable older sister. In the Black colloquial, we would describe Patty Jo as "acting grown." It was not uncommon for Patty Jo to speak about discrimination, and the dissonance created by this very cute and polished-looking girl delivering political realities to her always perfectly-styled older sister challenged common representations of Black girlhood and womanhood in the United States. While Patty Jo would have been a wonderful foil to the conservative observations of Little Orphan Annie if placed on the same page, the strip was never syndicated outside of African American publications.

Barbara Brandon-Croft always explained that she was not the first African American woman cartoonist with a comic strip in a newspaper, acknowledging Ormes's importance and legacy. Like Ormes's *Patty Jo 'n' Ginger*, Brandon-Croft's work was initially destined for a Black publication—the short-lived magazine for Black women, *Elan* (1982). Brandon-Croft conceived of her work as having a Black audience from its inception. After *Elan* folded, she tried to have it published in *Essence*—a well-established magazine for African American women. She would go on to do other work for *Essence*, but unlike Ormes, she got her start in comics outside of the Black newspapers when she was published in the *Detroit Free Press* in 1989 before achieving national syndication in 1991.

In the wake of the Civil Rights Movement, white newspapers in the United States—like many other media industries—realized they needed to diversify. While some might argue that George Herriman integrated the newspapers with *Krazy Kat* (1913–1944) and his other work in the early twentieth century, no one knew of his Black ancestry until after his death, and Black politics were arguably invisible or covert in his strip.[6] It is safe to say that it would be decades before the comics pages really moved toward including Black creators and desegregating content. Morrie Turner's *Wee Pals*, with its multicultural cast of characters; Brumsic Brandon, Jr.'s *Luther*; and Ted Shearer's *Quincy* were syndicated between 1965 and 1970.

Brumsic Brandon, Jr. was Barbara Brandon-Croft's father, and her first comics job was helping him with his work. His influence on her sense of humor is clear—*Luther* was also a strip depicting Black people in conversation, but about inner-city youth reflecting on the world around them. His punchlines in *Luther* were often a biting commentary on the treatment of Black people and Black youth in particular. For example, a running theme is that one character named Pee Wee never had enough to eat. In one strip, a white child tells Pee Wee and titular character Luther that his father says, "The country is rich enough to have both guns and butter!" The last beat of the panel is Pee Wee asking, "What's butter, Luther?"[7] The painful joke—that the Black child knows what guns are but not butter—illustrates Brandon, Jr.'s ability to blend pathos with humor. This would also become a characteristic of his daughter's strip, but she would apply it to the challenges facing young African American women at the end of the twentieth century. And as with her father's work, many of the painful jokes about politics continue to resonate decades later.

Black Comics and the History of Black Art

The role of jokes and politics in comics may contribute to Black cartoonists being left out of many histories of Black visual culture. This is a curious exclusion, since racist representations produced by non-Black artists are often featured in histories that explore the very images Black people contest. When discussing major moments of African American cultures of letters and creativity, people often point to the Harlem Renaissance in the 1920s and the Black Arts Movement in the 1960s and 1970s. In this earlier movement in the twentieth century, artists fought over what Black art should be. African American sociologist, writer, and activist W. E. B. Du Bois argued that Black art must be propaganda to support a project of racial uplift.[8] Cartooning often fits into this category—not only editorial cartooning but strips like Brandon-Croft's, which comment on political issues. The explicitness of such commentary is one of a number of reasons that some people do not characterize comics with an editorial bent as art.

Alain Locke, editor of the important Harlem Renaissance anthology, *The New Negro*, pushed back against

Du Bois, arguing that this approach limited the possibilities for Black aesthetics and Black people by tying them to a limited form of expression.[9] In the 1930s, another version of this argument appeared in what is known as the "Hurston-Wright" debate.[10] Richard Wright (*Black Boy, Native Son*) criticized the focus on romantic love in Zora Neale Hurston's *Their Eyes Were Watching God*, believing that her focus on women and sexuality was not a worthy object for Black literature. He also saw her use of a poetic Black vernacular as a caricature of Black people that would appeal to white readers who enjoy racial stereotypes. Versions of Wright's criticisms would continue to characterize attacks on some Black women's work. Black women creators like Hurston and Brandon-Croft see a focus on Black womanhood and sex as central to Black life *and* the Black liberation struggle. And some forms of Black humor—which often makes use of Black vernacular—can trouble people within the Black community who do not think serious issues confronting Black people should be addressed with humor. Black humor that engages race and sexual topics can also challenge the mores of those who adhere to Black respectability politics—the belief that adhering to normative models of behavior propagated by the predominantly white society will uplift the race.

During the Black Arts Movement, Black creatives foregrounded the relationship between politics and Black aesthetics. Critics such as Larry Neal pushed against the idea of integration within white cultural and art institutions. Debates about what makes Black art and the tension between integrating white institutions and establishing totally Black-owned work continues well into the twentieth century—including cartooning. On the one hand, many Black creators see creating for Black venues as offering the opportunity for people to speak to their own communities and not be constricted by the commercial implications of how non-Black audiences would interpret the work. On the other hand, inclusion in white publications offers not only greater financial rewards and recognition but also brings Black voices to non-Black audiences that otherwise may not encounter them. Of course, many creators often operate on a register that speaks to people who share their background or cultural contexts, while also to a broader audience. *Where I'm Coming From* certainly does.

We should position Black cartoonists like Brandon-Croft within a wider Black art tradition, because they participate in the very same conversations as other Black creatives. But recognition of the Black specificity in the work of Black creatives does not mean that their themes do not resonate across racial boundaries. In the case of Brandon-Croft's work, struggles with relationships clearly speak to many women—although ignoring the cultural specificity can mean missing aesthetic and content differences.

An unfortunate interpretative tendency characteristic of the inclusion of underrepresented creators in the white press is that they can be seen as a "Black version" of a white creator's work. With Brandon-Croft, that comparison was often to Cathy Guisewite's long-running strip, *Cathy* (1976–2010). Like *Where I'm Coming From*, *Cathy* was inspired by the creator's life as a single woman, and focused on dating. Political issues were a much rarer topic in Guisewite's strip. But what such comparisons miss is how much *Where I'm Coming From* is about relationality between Black women and conversations between friends. Readers are either entering these conversations between characters or feel as if the characters are talking directly to them. With *Cathy*, readers rooted for her to get married, and the strip ended with the announcement that she was pregnant with a baby girl. In contrast, Brandon-Croft said that while all of her characters were single and some might one day marry, that was not the direction of the strip. One character, Lydia, had a child outside of marriage. This is a choice that many women increasingly made at the end of the twentieth century—and African American women made this choice in greater numbers. The character is not vilified for this choice, and as much as Brandon-Croft's characters were often striving toward finding long-term relationships, the journey of the strip was the community between women and what their lives looked like in the moment.

Where My Girls At?: Representing Black Women in the "Post"-Civil Rights Era

Brandon-Croft produced *Where I'm Coming From* in the middle of the complex representational politics of the 1980s and 1990s, which had positive representations of Black women that reflected the gains of the Civil Rights Movement and feminism. She was born in 1958, four years after the Supreme Court said segregated schools were unconstitutional in *Brown v. Board of Education*. The following year, 1955, fourteen-year-old Emmett Till was murdered in Mississippi, and Rosa Parks refused to give up her seat in Montgomery. A year before her birth, the Little Rock Nine integrated Little Rock Central High School. When she was a child, the news was filled with valiant young people integrating schools, fighting racist police and other citizens. Her parents would take her to the March on Washington in 1963 when she was four. The formative first ten years of her life would be in what the activist Bayard Ruskin called the classical period of the Civil Rights Movement, beginning with *Brown v. Board* and ending with Martin Luther King's assassination. She explains that when she was growing up "...all kinds of politically aware things were in the house," and that her upbringing was "probably the biggest influence" in her life.[11] The next decade of her childhood would occur in the midst and wake of various cultural revolutions. She was undoubtedly a beneficiary of the legal and cultural gains of the fight for Black and feminist liberation, but would also struggle with the incompleteness of these movements, as well as the backlash.

Even so, Black women were also frequently demonized and devalued in mass media. In 1976 (the year she graduated high school), Ronald Reagan would talk about a "welfare queen" defrauding the government. While never describing her as Black, the idea of the welfare queen would be associated with Black women. *The Cosby Show* would become the number one show in the 1980s with Claire Huxtable modeled as the ideal mother on network television, but the news would also be overrun with stories about the crack cocaine epidemic and accompanying panic about the future of "crack babies" birthed by addicted (Black) mothers. Authors Gloria Naylor and Alice Walker would be celebrated for the stories they told about Black women and Black life, but they would also be condemned by some for representing intimate violence within the Black community and accused of demonizing Black men. Hip-hop would become a major force within the music industry, but it was a music genre that all too often included misogyny in lyrics and female objectification in music videos.

But perhaps no narrative about African American women reflected the push-pull between positive and negative representations of African American women—and has continued to be more prominent—than the discourse around dating challenges for African American women. In the first half of the twentieth century, marriage rates among African American women had been lower than those of white women, but only slightly. By the 1990s, the rates for African American women began to drop precipitously in comparison to women in all other racial groups. In the early 1970s, ten percent of African American women had never been married. By the end of the nineties, it would be thirty percent.[12] In 1987, sociologist William Julius Wilson argued that the marriage rate had begun to drop for African Americans and would continue to do so because the pool of "marriageable men" had declined since African American men in the inner-city were not obtaining education and employment at the same rate as African American women (and exogamy has been less likely for Black women than other groups).[13] Wilson's argument would be controversial, and some people would see it as a continuation of the Moynihan Report's Black matriarchy thesis, which suggested that African American families were still dealing with the disruption to their family formation in slavery, and were thus unable to take normative head of household roles.[14] The discourse around Black marriage will often point to Black women's educational and professional successes as a deficit in the marriage market. Many others would point to the war on drugs and the prison industrial complex as a major cause of removing Black men from communities.

While not explicitly addressed in Brandon-Croft's comics, the discourse about greater challenges for Black women in the dating market was certainly swirling about in the period. The most prominent text in the 1990s that dealt with this theme was undoubtedly Terry McMillan's *Waiting to Exhale*[15] (page 30). Published in 1992, the novel was adapted into a film in 1995 starring Whitney Houston, Angela Bassett, Loretta Devine, and Lela Rochon. The story of four very different Black women struggling with relationships but finding succor and support with each other, the novel, film, and soundtrack were huge successes. Other books, films, and television series would also focus on friendships between Black women, and *Where I'm Coming From* should be thought of within this canon of Black women's texts that deal with friendships and romantic relationships.

Despite such discourse surrounding Black women and marriage only being alluded to in *Where I'm Coming From*, Brandon-Croft did specifically touch on many other issues in the nineties, a number of which still resonate today. While the Supreme Court ruled in 1973 that women had a constitutional right to abortion, abortion clinics constantly had to be on guard from violent anti-abortion activists. In 1993 and 1994, two physicians and a clinic escort were murdered in two separate attacks in Florida. Receptionists were killed in attacks in Massachusetts in 1994. Brandon-Croft called attention to the hypocrisy of anti-choice activists saying that murder is a sin and murdering people who worked in clinics—or sanctioning it (page 51). And although violence at abortion clinics did decline, discussing the conflicts over abortion rights is even more relevant in the twenty-first century, with *Roe* overturned in 2022 and many people pointing to the hypocrisy of some who support the Supreme Court decision by not supporting life in various other contexts.

In 1991, an African American man named Rodney King was brutally beaten by four Los Angeles police officers, and the assault was caught on tape. People in the twenty-first century are all too familiar with videos of police brutality, but evidence of such violence was rarely available before camera phones. The officers were charged with excessive force, and when a jury failed to convict any

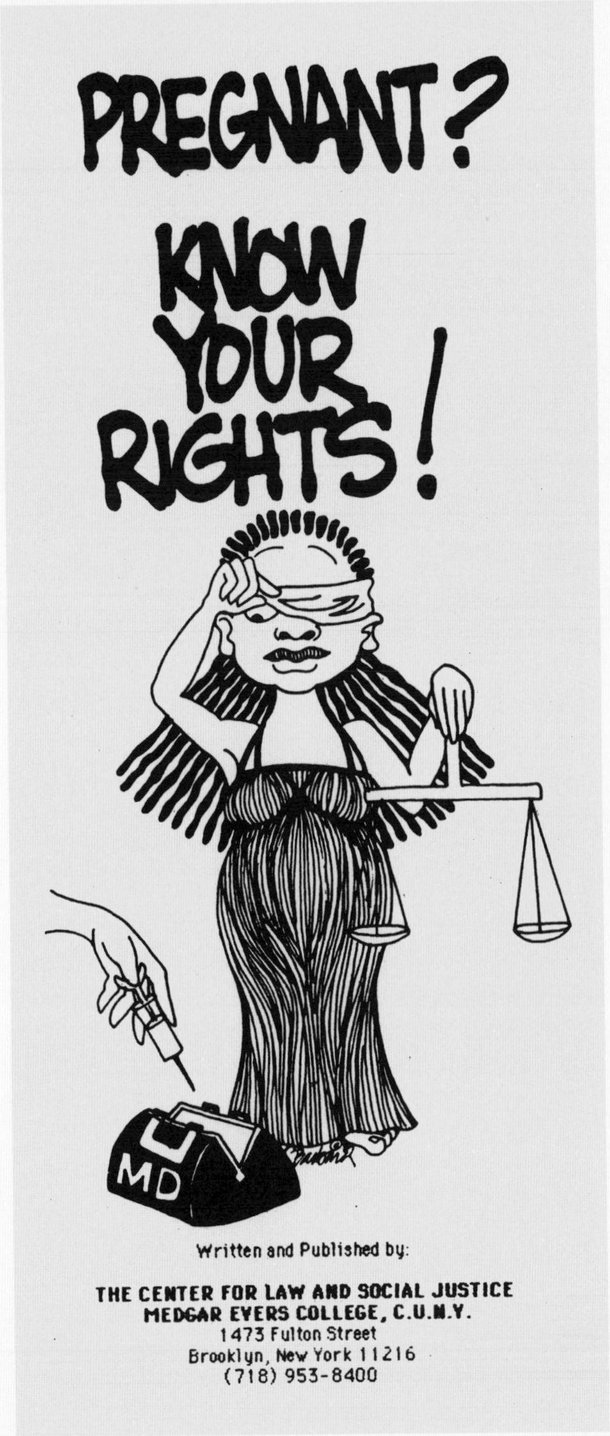
PREGNANT?
KNOW YOUR RIGHTS!
MD
Written and Published by:
THE CENTER FOR LAW AND SOCIAL JUSTICE
MEDGAR EVERS COLLEGE, C.U.N.Y.
1473 Fulton Street
Brooklyn, New York 11216
(718) 953-8400

176 • Reproductive rights pamphlet illustrated by Brandon-Croft, undated

of them, Los Angeles erupted in protests. The "LA Race Riots" or "Los Angeles Uprising" took place between April 29 and May 4 of 1992. During the events, King famously pleaded on television for the civil unrest to end, asking, "Can we all get along?" People had divided reactions to his response, with some celebrating what they saw as a call for non-violent protest. Others took issue with the framing as a Pollyanna-like approach to state violence against Black bodies. Brandon-Croft responded to King's statement with a picture of her activist character, Lekesia, in front of a wall with writing on it that says, "We CAN all get along," holding up a sign that reads, "When there's equal justice." Just as her father created strips about police brutality and other issues that still resonate, Brandon-Croft's resistance to peace without justice is just as resonant in the wake of the Black Lives Matter Movement.

Many issues of the Clinton era, while specific to the period, are time capsules pointing to a long history of conflict still at play in the twenty-first century. In 1993, President Clinton announced his "Don't Ask, Don't Tell" policy. This was supposedly the fulfillment of a campaign pledge that would allow all people to serve in the military, but required all queer people to be closeted. The military would not ask service people about their sexual orientation, but personnel were prohibited from serving if they self-identified as gay or lesbian. During this period, Brandon-Croft introduced a guest character named Dee who was a military hopeful and cousin of the character Cheryl. When Dee comes out as a lesbian, Brandon-Croft illustrates the challenges people can face with their families when they come out, but also demonstrates how free the woman felt when she was honest about her identity. The cartoonist acknowledges the limitations of the policy, noting that, for Dee, speaking her truth wasn't possible in "Clinton's military" (page 49 & 177). While the policy no longer exists, the comic still has relevance in relation to the "Don't Say Gay" policy passed in Florida in 2022, which prohibits schools from using the word "gay."[16]

Brandon-Croft's strips about the difference in how the war in the former Yugoslavia was described in contrast to the conflict in Somalia also continues to resonate in the twenty-first century. Her characters note that these wars

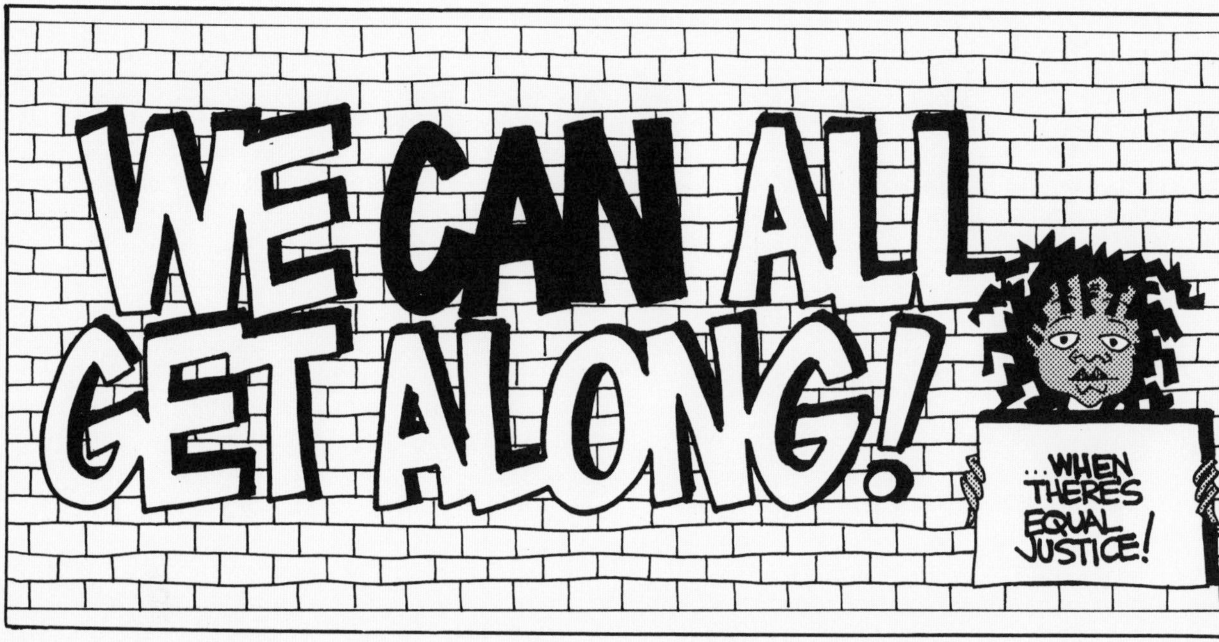
WE CAN ALL GET ALONG!
...WHEN THERE'S EQUAL JUSTICE!

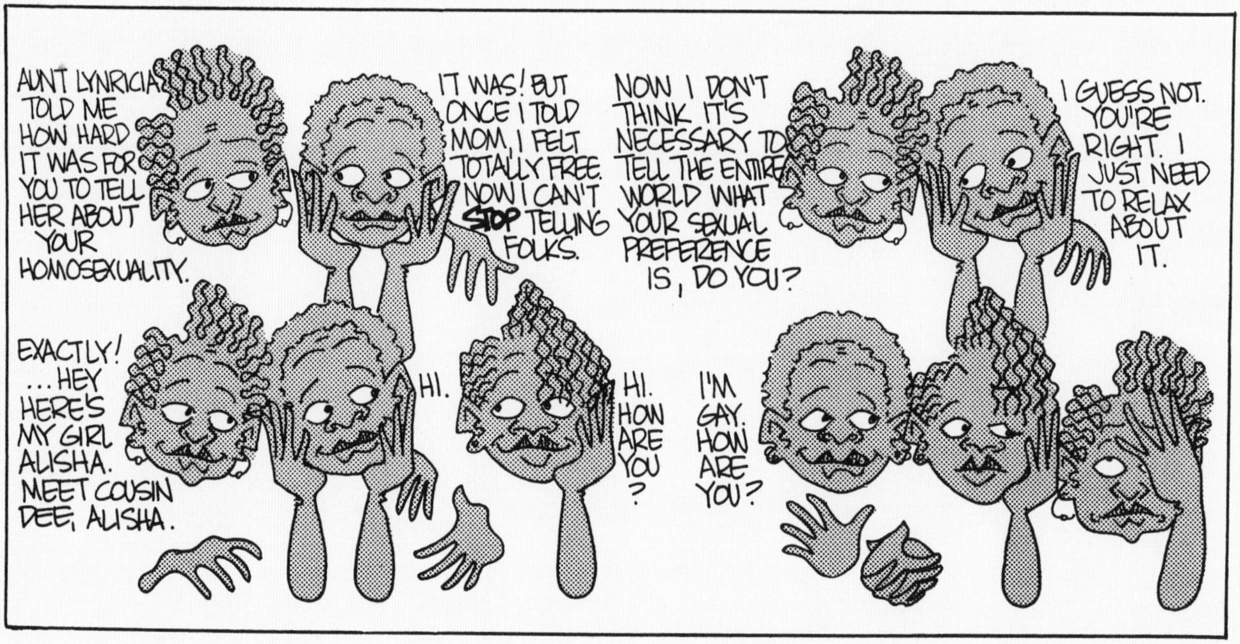
AUNT LYNRICIA TOLD ME HOW HARD IT WAS FOR YOU TO TELL HER ABOUT YOUR HOMOSEXUALITY.
IT WAS! BUT ONCE I TOLD MOM, I FELT TOTALLY FREE. NOW I CAN'T STOP TELLING FOLKS.
NOW I DON'T THINK IT'S NECESSARY TO TELL THE ENTIRE WORLD WHAT YOUR SEXUAL PREFERENCE IS, DO YOU?
I GUESS NOT. YOU'RE RIGHT. I JUST NEED TO RELAX ABOUT IT.
EXACTLY! ...HEY HERE'S MY GIRL ALISHA. MEET COUSIN DEE, ALISHA.
HI.
HI. HOW ARE YOU?
I'M GAY. HOW ARE YOU?

are described as civil wars in eastern Europe but as gangs and warlords running amok in Africa (page 55). The logic she highlights was apparent in 2022 when people would say that the war in Ukraine was particularly disturbing because they were "obviously not refugees" fleeing places "like the Middle East or North Africa." They were "civilized" and "European people with blue eyes and blonde hair being killed."[17] Part of the pleasure of going back to political comics throughout history is that they capture perspectives—and feelings—that are typically absent from Wikipedia entries. Many people who lived through these events may not even know that an anti-racist critique of media coverage of these wars existed. Holding onto this kind of comics archive is no different from holding on to the political essays of important writers.

While some parts of Brandon-Croft's body of work require that people be familiar with the politics of the moment, other parts are completely evergreen. Equal pay for equal work is still an issue in the twenty-first century. In one comic, an employer is "tired" of women complaining about inequality and two characters reply, "We're tired too!" (page 57). Black feminists are often accused by both Black men and other Black women of betraying the race for claiming feminism (page 56 & 170). A specific touchstone in that period was the O. J. case. Some Black women could hold two truths in their heads at the same time—there was racism and misconduct in the investigation and trial, but he also had a history of violence toward his ex-wife, Nicole Brown Simpson. The differences of opinion between the women and men on the other end of the phone line (always off panel) highlights the diversity of the Black community.

Picturing Black Women

Seeing variations in Blackness is one of the real pleasures of *Where I'm Coming From*. In his influential visual treatise about the comics medium, Scott McCloud argues that what makes comics work is abstraction. For McCloud, if it is realistic, it is the image of "another," and readers are more likely to pay attention to an abstract face. He believes such specificity causes readers to be "far too aware of the *messenger* to fully receive the *message*."

With an abstract image, it "would never even *occur* to you to wonder what my *politics* are," and if "who I am matters *less*, maybe what I say will matter *more*."[18] McCloud is more than a bit disingenuous about race. White people are often allowed to function as universal, which has been part of the challenge for people of color attempting to break into any industry in which they must appeal to a general audience.

There is an alternative to McCloud's theory that we see playing out through Brandon-Croft's work. If we acknowledge that who people are matters in how their words are evaluated, we can learn to pay attention to voices that have traditionally been valued less. It matters that Brandon-Croft chose to draw a wide variety of Black women who can be distinguished by the differences in their personalities, features, and hair. Representations of Black women in comics and cartoons often had a mammy representation with blackface minstrel-like features. It is a stereotype that would cross national borders. Representations of Black hair were often the "picaninny" caricature from the nineteenth century to the present, with braids askew on top of a Black child's head. In short, realistic representations of adult Black women in comics was all too infrequent outside of the Black press until after the Civil Rights Movement.

Varied textures of Black hair and the embrace of natural hair styles was rare in comics. While the Afro and braids grew in popularity in the 1970s, there would continue to be a push for Black women to chemically process their hair so that they could present hair textures unlike their own. Just the presence of varied natural Black hair styles is political expression. Legal discrimination against Black girls and women for their hairstyles is so common that state legislatures began passing the *CROWN* Act (Creating a Respectful and Open World for Natural Hair) that would prohibit discrimination on the basis of hairstyles in the twenty-first century, with Democrats in the US House of Representatives passing it in 2022. Brandon-Croft's characters have relaxed hair, dreadlocks, curly natural hair, and haircuts popular with African American women during the period.

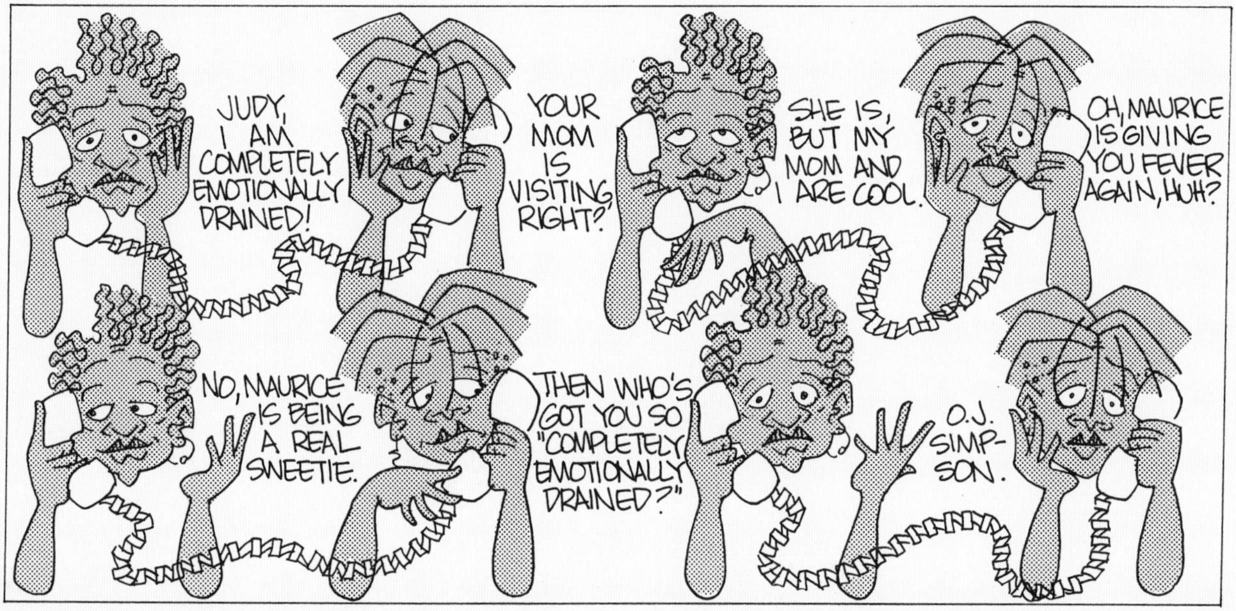
JUDY, I AM COMPLETELY EMOTIONALLY DRAINED!
YOUR MOM IS VISITING RIGHT?
SHE IS, BUT MY MOM AND I ARE COOL.
OH, MAURICE IS GIVING YOU FEVER AGAIN, HUH?
NO, MAURICE IS BEING A REAL SWEETIE.
THEN WHO'S GOT YOU SO "COMPLETELY EMOTIONALLY DRAINED?"
O.J. SIMP-SON.

Brandon-Croft's choice to only represent hands and forearms in addition to the face also plays with conventional representations of African American women. By keeping the hands and forearms, she signals cultural specificity, but she also does not graphically replicate the kinds of gestures that are often presented as stereotypes—like snapped fingers, a palm in the air, or a chastising finger. Caricature has often been used as a weapon against African Americans, but Brandon-Croft, like some other Black cartoonists, makes use of the caricature to create a more expansive representation of Black identity. She embraces rhythms of conversation and gesture in order to show the intimate connections in Black worlds, referencing the familiar but insisting on variation.

In an interview, Brandon-Croft was asked, "What is the most important thing you would like to be remembered for?" She responded, "I was given the opportunity to record our experience. A hundred years from now, if someone can look at *Where I'm Coming From* and say, 'So that's what they were going through,' then, hopefully, they'll be able to identify with their past."[19] This collection is only thirty years into the future instead of a hundred. But it still provides a time capsule of an era while highlighting an emergent moment in mass media during which friendships between Black women were increasingly a focus of Black women creatives.

Part of the legacy of *Where I'm Coming From* is that many of the issues she explores demonstrate—for better or worse—that the past is not totally past. For better, we now have a rich collection of works exploring intimacy and community between Black women. Brandon-Croft's work deserves to be rediscovered and as well-known as that of other Black women that tell stories of Black women's lives with nuance and joy.

Rebecca Wanzo is professor of the Department of Women, Gender, and Sexuality Studies at Washington University in St. Louis. She is the author of *The Suffering Will Not Be Televised: African American Women and Sentimental Political Storytelling* and *The Content of Our Caricature: African American Comic Art and Political Belonging.*

1   Frances M. Beal, "Double Jeopardy: To Be Black and Female." originally published as a pamphlet in 1969.
2   Kimberlé Crenshaw, "Demarginalizing the Intersection of Race and Sex: A Black Feminist Critique of Antidiscrimination Doctrine, Feminist Theory and Antiracist Politics." *University of Chicago Legal Forum* 1, no. 8 (1989): 139–167.
3   Bruce Lenthall, "Outside the Panel—Race in America's Popular Imagination: Comic Strips Before and After World War II." *Journal of American Studies* 32, no. 1 (1998): 47.
4   For biographies of early African American cartoonists, see Tim Jackson, *Pioneering Cartoonists of Color* (Jackson: University Press of Mississippi, 2016).
5   Nancy Goldstein, *Jackie Ormes: The First African American Woman Cartoonist* (Ann Arbor: University of Michigan Press, 2008).
6   For more on George Herriman's life, see Michael Tisserand, *Krazy: George Herriman, a Life in Black and White* (New York: Harper, 2016).
7   See Rebecca Wanzo, *The Content of Our Caricature: African American Comic Art and Political Belonging* (New York: New York University Press, 2020), 153.
8   William Edward Burghardt Du Bois, "Criteria of Negro Art." *The Crisis* 32, no. 6 (1926): 290–297.
9   Alain Locke, "Art or Propaganda?" *Harlem: A Forum of Negro Life* 1, no. 1 (1928): 1–2.
10 Richard Wright, "Review of *Their Eyes Were Watching God.*" *The New Masses* 5 (1937): 16–17.
11 Interview with Barbara Brandon-Croft from *Together We Shall Overcome*, vol. 2, no. 2 (Summer 1991): 4–5.
12 R. Kelly Raley, Megan Sweeney, and Danielle Wondra, "The Growing Racial and Ethnic Divide in US Marriage Patterns." *Future Child* 25, no. 2 (2015): 89–109.
13 William Julius Wilson, *The Truly Disadvantaged: The Inner City, the Underclass, and Public Policy* (Chicago: University of Chicago Press, 1987).
14 Daniel Patrick Moynihan, *The Negro Family: The Case for National Action* (1965).
15 Terry McMillan, *Waiting to Exhale* (New York: Penguin, 1992).
16 Patricia Mazzei, "DeSantis Signs Florida Bill That Opponents Call 'Don't Say Gay.'" *The New York Times.* March 28, 2022.
17 Rashawn Ray, "The Russian invasion of Ukraine shows racism has no boundaries." *How We Rise* (blog). The Brookings Institution. March 3, 2022
18 Scott McCloud, *Understanding Comics: The Invisible Art* (Northampton: Kitchen Sink Press, 1993).
19 Interview with Barbara Brandon-Croft from *Together We Shall Overcome*, vol. 2, no. 2 (Summer 1991): 4–5.

WERE IT NOT FOR...

I have to admit, I've always been pretty lucky. Not win-lots-of-money-in-the-lottery lucky, but the kind of lucky that leaves you rich in so many other ways. Like being able to recognize opportunities when they present themselves. Like being smart—or some might consider dumb—enough to take chances. Like having the right people around me when my insecurities well up, and having the grace to be open to their guidance. That's the kind of luck I've been gifted with. I've had more angels in my life than anyone could ask for. Now I have an opportunity to show my appreciation, yet I worry about unintended omissions (I am 64, after all). But I'm gonna try...

LEE SALEM My goodness, Lee was the best! If he had thrown my work in the rejection pile (as so many other syndicates did), this story would have taken a very different path. He championed my work—and me. An advocate of the first order, he brought me on at Universal Press Syndicate and stood by me the entire ride. I am ever so grateful and I will miss him evermore.

MARTY CLAUS It was her letter to my dad hoping to re-cruit Black cartoonists that prompted me to send her my idea. As oddball as *Where I'm Coming From* was, she immediately liked it and took a chance. I am forever grateful to her and the *Detroit Free Press*.

MARIE BROWN The literary icon who on our first meeting, made a simple observation, then posed a question that changed the trajectory of my life: "You're funny and you can draw. Can you come up with a comic strip?" Yes, Marie, I can!

PEGGY BURNS who reached out to me and convinced me that this book was necessary; REBECCA WANZO who put my work into historical context; and SHARON PENDANA for being my friend and telling my story. Also, thanks to my agent STEVEN MALK and the entire D+Q TEAM. And a special shout out to DIANE DEBROVNER who walked me through this new land of book publishing.

To all the folks who kept me afloat when drawing a comic strip wasn't enuf...

FREDA SOIFFER and RICHARD HASKIN You guys have been so great to me. You made my cartooning career possible by giving me work in the other industry I adore—fashion. Thank you always!

KATHLEEN KREMS When freelancing as a fact checker and jumping from one magazine to the next, you brought me over to *Parents* and that led to my second career. The timing could not have been more perfect. Chase was a toddler and would not have known just how robust Santa could be had it not been for *Parents*.

ALL MY GIRLS What can I say? There would be nothing to write about without you ALL. I appreciate each and every one of you! Named and unnamed, I know you know who you are and where you fit in my life. Like MyPal4Life; my peeps from Rushmore Street; New Cassel; Westbury, my Dragon Ladies; omg SU!!; *Essence*!!; One South Elliott Place!; *Parents*; my Dalton moms, Yvette and Virginia; ALL my Judys! All my Sharons! All my Lindas! All my Jens! Ruthie! Tara! Wendy! Anka! Paula! Claudette! Oh and the list goes on...I appreciate you all!

MY FAMILY My rock, my roll, my everything. Thank you Monte for steadying me when I get wobbly and loving me un-conditionally. Thank you Chase for being your glorious self. I relish in your humor, your intelligence, and your patience. My thanks also to my sister and brother, my sisters-in-law, my niece and nephew, their partners, my aunts and uncles, and my cousins. And the ultimate WERE IT NOT FOR... my Mom and Dad.

I dedicate this book to my
very funny, very supportive, very goofy
cousin

Stevie
aka
William "Weeeyum" Stephenson

1957–2019
I miss you so

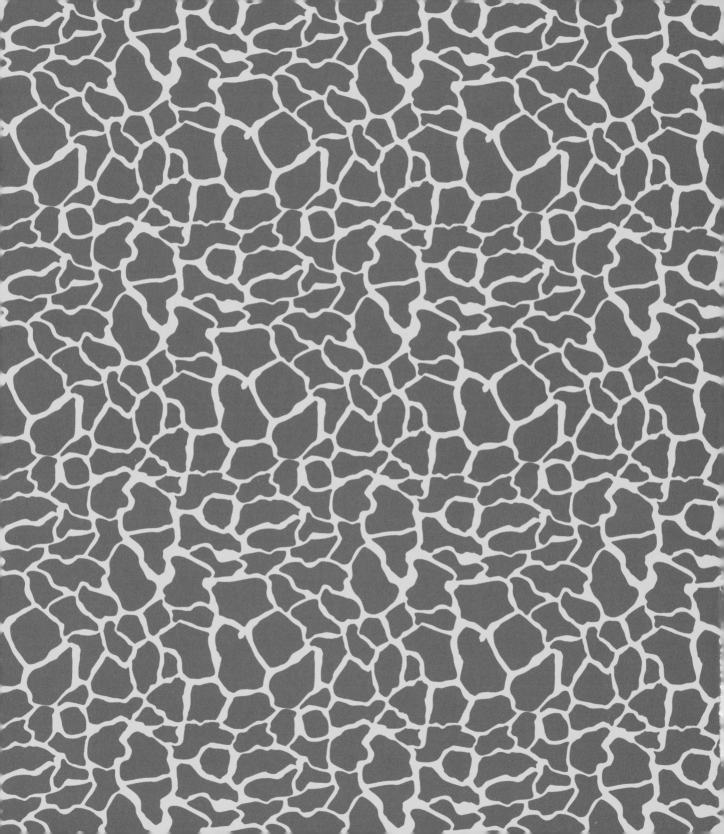

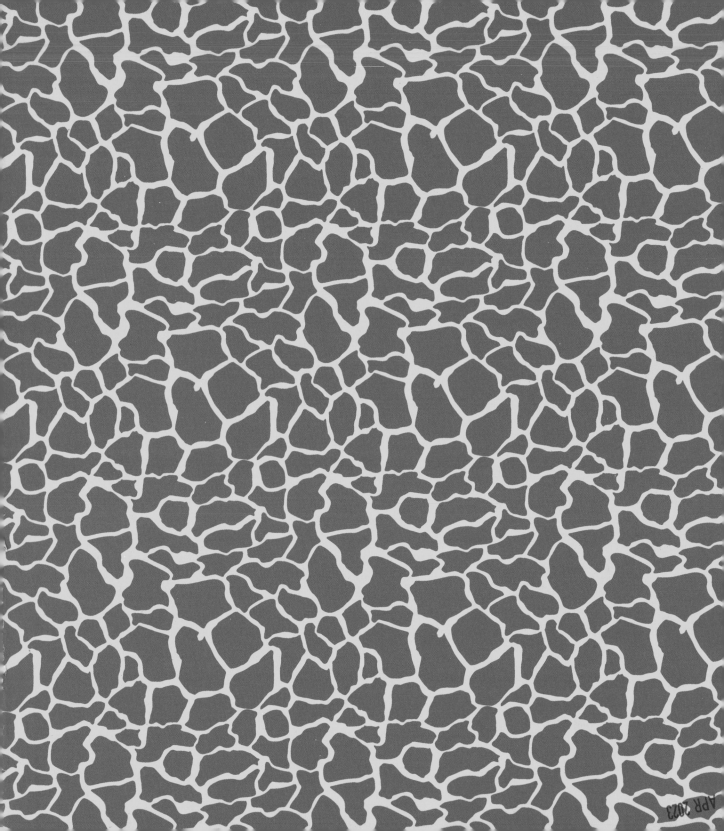